Logistics Management and Optimization through Hybrid Artificial Intelligence Systems

Carlos Alberto Ochoa Ortiz Zezzatti
Juarez City University, México

Camelia Chira
Babes–Bolyai University, Romania

Arturo Hernández-Aguirre
CIMAT, Mexico

Miguel Basurto
UAEM, Mexico

Information Science
REFERENCE

Managing Director:	Lindsay Johnston
Senior Editorial Director:	Heather A. Probst
Book Production Manager:	Sean Woznicki
Development Manager:	Joel Gamon
Development Editor:	Myla Harty
Acquisitions Editor:	Erika Gallagher
Cover Design:	Nick Newcomer, Lisandro Gonzalez

Published in the United States of America by
Information Science Reference (an imprint of IGI Global)
701 E. Chocolate Avenue
Hershey PA 17033
Tel: 717-533-8845
Fax: 717-533-8661
E-mail: cust@igi-global.com
Web site: http://www.igi-global.com

Library of Congress Cataloging-in-Publication Data

Logistics management and optimization through hybrid artificial intelligence systems / Carlos Alberto Ochoa Ortiz Zezzatti ... [et al.].
    p. cm.
  Includes bibliographical references and index.
  Summary: "This book offers the latest research within the field of HAIS, surveying the broad topics and collecting case studies, future directions, and cutting edge analyses, investigating biologically inspired algorithms such as ant colony optimization and particle swarm optimization"-- Provided by publisher.
  ISBN 978-1-4666-0297-7 (hardcover) -- ISBN 978-1-4666-0298-4 (ebook) -- ISBN 978-1-4666-0299-1 (print & perpetual access) 1. Operations research--Data processing. 2. Business logistics--Data processing. 3. Artificial intelligence. I. Ochoa Ortiz Zezzatti, Carlos Alberto, 1974-
  TS155.6.L64 2012
  658.4'034--dc23
                                    2011044977

British Cataloguing in Publication Data
A Cataloguing in Publication record for this book is available from the British Library.

All work contributed to this book is new, previously-unpublished material. The views expressed in this book are those of the authors, but not necessarily of the publisher.

Table of Contents

Section 1
Logistics of Products and Services

Section 4
Technological Application using Intelligent Optimization

Detailed Table of Contents

Section 1
Logistics of Products and Services

Carlos Alberto Ochoa Ortiz Zezzatti, Juarez City University, México
Nemesio Castillo, CIS-UACJ, México
Wilebaldo Martínez, CIS-UACJ, México
Socorro Velázquez, CIS-UACJ, México

The optimization problems have been widely attacked in the area of evolutionary computation, this has been due mainly to the kindness they have shown to solve these problems. This chapter addresses the solution to the problem of optimizing the space within the vehicle to distribute purified water. To solve this problem using a cultural algorithm which helps determine the appropriate charge that provides the best value for the company of this kind of services to the customers of the product. This is done taking into account the space that is available within the vehicle and the different presentations that are distributed. In turn, this study helps us to understand the behavior of (Cultural Algorithms) with respect to the issues raised in the optimization of space vehicle for distributing purified water. In addition prepare a comparative analysis of the results obtained with respect to another method of solving optimization space, and finally describe an extended Partially Dynamic Vehicle Routing which permits determine complicated scenarios and reorganize the stratagems to solute these scenarios.

Julio Cesar Ponce Gallegos, Autonomous University of Aguacalientes, Mexico
Fatima Sayuri Quezada Aguilera, Autonomous University of Aguacalientes, Mexico
José Alberto Hernandez Aguilar, Autonomous University of Morelos, Mexico
Christian José Correa Villalón, Institute of Education of Aguascalientes, Mexico

The contribution of this chapter is to present an approach to explain the Ant Colony System applied on the Waste Collection Problem, because waste management is moving up to the concern over health and environmental impacts. These algorithms are a framework for decision makers in order to analyze and simulate various spatial waste management problems. In the last decade, metaheuristics have become increasingly popular for effectively confronting difficult combinatorial optimization problems. In the present work, an individual metaheuristic Ant Colony System (ACS) algorithm is introduced, implemented and discussed for the identification of optimal routes in the case Solid Waste collection. This algorithm is applied to a waste collection and transport system, obtaining recollection routes with the less total distance with respect to the actual route utilized and to the solution obtained by a previously developed approach.

Marco Antonio Cruz-Chávez, Autonomous University of Morelos State, CIICAp, Mexico
Abelardo Rodríguez-León, Technological Institute of Veracruz, Mexico
Rafael Rivera-López, Technological Institute of Veracruz, Mexico
Fredy Juárez-Pérez, Autonomous University of Morelos State, CIICAp, Mexico
Carmen Peralta-Abarca, Autonomous University of Morelos State, FCQeI, Mexico
Alina Martínez-Oropeza, Autonomous University of Morelos State, CIICAp, Mexico

Around the world there have recently been new and more powerful computing platforms created that can be used to work with computer science problems. Some of these problems that are dealt with are real problems of the industry; most are classified by complexity theory as hard problems. One such problem is the vehicle routing problem with time windows (VRPTW). The computational Grid is a platform which has recently ventured into the treatment of hard problems to find the best solution for these. This chapter presents a genetic algorithm for the vehicle routing problem with time windows. The algorithm iteratively applies a mutation operator, first of the intelligent type and second of the restricting type. The algorithm takes advantage of Grid computing to increase the exploration and exploitation of the solution space of the problem. The Grid performance is analyzed for a genetic algorithm and a measurement of the latencies that affect the algorithm is studied. The convenience of applying this new computing platform to the execution of algorithms specially designed for Grid computing is presented.

Section 2
Improve of Optimization Applied Intelligent Techniques

María Dolores Torres, Autonomous University of Aguascalientes, Mexico
Aurora Torres Soto, Autonomous University of Aguascalientes, Mexico
Carlos Alberto Ochoa Ortiz Zezzatti, Juarez City University, México
Eunice E. Ponce de León Sentí, Autonomous University of Aguascalientes, Mexico
Elva Díaz Díaz, Autonomous University of Aguascalientes, Mexico
Cristina Juárez Landín, Autonomous University of Mexico's State, Mexico
César Eduardo Velázquez Amador, Autonomous University of Aguascalientes, Mexico

This chapter presents the implementation of a Genetic Algorithm into a framework for machine learning that deals with the problem of identifying the factors that impact the health state of newborns in Mexico. Experimental results show a percentage of correct clustering for unsupervised learning of 89%, a real life training matrix of 46 variables, was reduced to only 25 that represent 54% of its original size. Moreover execution time is about one and a half minutes. Each risk factor (of neonatal health) found by the algorithm was validated by medical experts. The contribution to the medical field is invaluable, since the cost of monitoring these features is minimal and it can reduce neonatal mortality in our country.

Chapter 5

In this chapter a hybrid algorithm is constructed, implemented and tested for the optimization of graph drawing employing a multiobjective approach. The multiobjective optimization problem for graph drawing consists of three objective functions: minimizing the number of edge crossing, minimizing the graph area, and minimizing the aspect ratio. The population of feasible solutions is generated using a hybrid algorithm and at each step a Pareto front is calculated. This hybrid algorithm combines a global search algorithm (EDA — Estimation of Distribution Algorithm) with a local search Algorithm (HC — Hill Climbing) in order to maintain a balance between the exploration and exploitation. Experiments were performed employing planar and non-planar graphs. A quality index of the obtained solutions by the hybrid MOEA-HCEDA (Multiobjective Evolutionary Algorithm - Hill Climbing & Univariate Marginal Distribution Algorithm) is constructed based on the Pareto front defined in this chapter. A factorial experiment using the algorithm parameters was performed. The factors are number of generations and population size, and the result is the quality index. The best combination of factors levels is obtained.

This chapter presents the use of multi-objective optimization for on-line automatic verification of handwritten signatures; as discriminating features of each signer are used here some functions of time and space of the position of the pen on the paper; these functions are directly used in a multi-objective optimization task in order to obtain high values of false positives indicators (FAR False Acceptance Rate) and false negatives (FFR, false rejection rate). The genetic algorithms are used to create a signer's model that optimally characterizes him, thus rejecting the skilled forgeries and recognizing genuine signatures with large variation with respect to the training set.

Chapter 7

Rodolfo A. Pazos R. Instituto Tecnológico de Cd. Madero, Mexico

Ernesto Ong C. Instituto Tecnológico de Cd. Madero, Mexico

Héctor Fraire H. Instituto Tecnológico de Cd. Madero, Mexico

Laura Cruz R. Instituto Tecnológico de Cd. Madero, Mexico

José A. Martínez F. Instituto Tecnológico de Cd. Madero

The theory of NP-completeness provides a method for telling whether a decision/optimization problem is "easy" (i.e., it belongs to the P class) or "difficult" (i.e., it belongs to the NP-complete class). Many problems related to logistics have been proven to belong to the NP-complete class such as Bin Packing, job scheduling, timetabling, etc. The theory predicts that for any pair of NP-complete problems A and B there must exist a polynomial time transformation from A to B and also a reverse transformation (from B to A). However, for many pairs of NP-complete problems no reverse transformation has been reported in the literature; thus the following question arises: do reverse transformations exist for any pair of NP-complete problems? This chapter presents results on an ongoing investigation for clarifying this issue.

Chapter 8

Claudia Gómez Santillán, Instituto Tecnológico de Ciudad Madero, México

Laura Cruz Reyes, Instituto Tecnológico de Ciudad Madero, México

María Lucila Morales Rodríguez, Instituto Tecnológico de Ciudad Madero, México

Juan Javier González Barbosa, Instituto Tecnológico de Ciudad Madero, México

Oscar Castillo López, Instituto Tecnológico de Tijuana, México

Gilberto Rivera Zarate, Instituto Tecnológico de Ciudad Madero, México

Paula Hernández, Instituto Tecnológico de Ciudad Madero, México

The Vehicle Routing Problem (VRP) is a key to the efficient transportation management and supply-chain coordination. VRP research has often been too focused on idealized models with non-realistic assumptions for practical applications. Nowadays the evolution of methodologies allows that the classical problems could be used to solve VRP problems of real life. The evolution of methodologies allows the creation of variants of the VRP which were considered too difficult to handle by their variety of possible restrictions. A VRP problem that includes the addition of restrictions, which represent the variants in the problem, is called Rich VRP. This work presents an algorithm to optimize the transportation management. The authors are including a case of study which solves a real routing problem applied to the distribution of bottled products. The proposed algorithm shows a saving in quantity of vehicles and reduces the operation costs of the company.

Chapter 9

Laura Cruz Reyes, Instituto Tecnológico de Cd. Madero, México

Claudia Gómez Santillán, Instituto Tecnológico de Cd. Madero, México

Marcela Quiroz, Instituto Tecnológico de Cd. Madero, México

Adriana Alvim, Federal University of the State of Rio de Janeiro, Brasil

Patricia Melin, Instituto Tecnológico de Tijuana, México

Jorge Ruiz Vanoye, Universidad Autónoma del Estado de Morelos, México

Vanesa Landero Najera, Universidad Politécnica de Nuevo León, México

This chapter approaches the Truck Loading Problem, which is formulated as a rich problem with the classic one dimensional Bin Packing Problem (BPP) and five variants. The literature review reveals that related work deals with three variants at the most. Besides, few efforts have been done to combine the Bin Packing Problem with the Vehicle Routing Problem. For the solution of this new Rich BPP a heuristic-deterministic algorithm, named DiPro, is proposed. It works together with a metaheuristic algorithm to plan routes, schedules and loads. The objective of the integrated problem, called RoSLoP, consists of optimizing the delivery process of bottled products in a real application. The experiments show the performance of three version of the Transportation System. The best version achieves a total demand satisfaction, an average saving of three vehicles and a reduction of the computational time from 3 hrs to two minutes regarding their manual solution. For the large scale the authors have develop a competitive genetic algorithm for BPP. As future work, it is intended integrate the approximation algorithm to the transportation system.

Chapter 10

    Camelia Chira, Babes-Bolyai University, Romania
    Anca Gog, Babes-Bolyai University, Romania

The Travelling Salesman Problem (TSP) is one of the most widely studied optimization problems due to its many applications in domains such as logistics, planning, routing, and scheduling. Approximation algorithms to address this NP-hard problem include genetic algorithms, ant colony systems, and simulated annealing. This chapter concentrates on the evolutionary approaches to TSP based on permutation encoded individuals. A comparative analysis of several recombination operators is presented based on computational experiments for TSP instances and a generalized version of TSP. Numerical results emphasize a good performance of two proposed crossover schemes: best-worst recombination and best order recombination which take into account information from the global best and/or worst individuals besides the genetic material from parents.

Section 3
Social Application on Logistic

Chapter 11

    Carlos Alberto Ochoa Ortiz Zezzatti, Juarez City University, México
    Sandra Bustillos, Juarez City University, Mexico
    Yarira Reyes, Juarez City University, Mexico
    Alessandra Tagliarducci-Tcherassi, Universitá Della Sapienza, Italy
    Rubén Jaramillo, LAPEM/CIATEC, Mexico

Evolve computing is the generic name given to the resolution of computational problems, based in models of an evolutionary process. Most evolutionary algorithms propose biological paradigms, and concepts of natural selection, mutation, and reproduction. Nevertheless other paradigms exist which can be adopted in the creation of evolutionary algorithms. Many problems involve environments not structured which can be solved from the perspective of cultural paradigms, which offer plenty of category models where one does not know the possible solutions of a problem, a common situation in real life. This research analyzed the organization of a project using a Crowdfunding Model, supporting to social networking. Sociological research shows that Crowdfunding tends to reveal a bias toward social similarity. Therefore, in order to model this Project supported with Crowdfunding, the authors developed an Agent-Based Model that already manages the social interaction, together with featuring information of issues in different habitats and evolutionary belief spaces. To introduce these theoretical concepts Cultural Algorithms were used in the approach, explaining the process in detail. In recent decades, in all World supporting Environmental Projects evolved from its traditional form of swapping issues with another friend's and stashing those involving too many people from diverse countries all dedicated to conservation of habitats, Natural Reserve or National Parks.

Chapter 12

Carlos Alberto Ochoa Ortiz Zezzatti, Juarez City University, México

José Martínez, Technological Institute of Ciudad Madero, México

Nemesio Castillo, Juarez City University, Mexico

Saúl González, Juarez City University, Mexico

Paula Hernández, Technological Institute of Ciudad Madero, México

Research examining the role of species bias in the Memory Alpha card market has been an emerging area of inquiry. However, empirical knowledge on the question: "Does the specie of the personage's role on a series affect the value of the card?" remains inconclusive. This chapter analyzes one of the first studies on this topic. Data were derived for 787 Alpha, Beta. Gamma & Delta species from Memory Alpha which were elected by a vote of the users in this Web Community conformed by fans. Data for each species' society, technology performance registers, design card price, and card availability with a range from common to extremely rare were obtained from secondary sources associated with Memory Alpha. Findings indicate that card availability and, to a lesser extent, technology performance is the most important factor affecting the value of a species' card, while importantly, a society's species is not a significant contributor to card value. Suggestions for future research are outlined.

Chapter 13

Carlos Alberto Ochoa Ortiz Zezzatti, Juarez City University, México

Darwin Young, COMIMSA Centro Conacyt, Mexico

Camelia Chira, Babeș-Bolyai University, Romania

Daniel Azpeitia, Juarez City University, México

Alán Calvillo, Aguascalientes University, México

Evolve computing is a generic name given to the resolution of computational problems with base in models of an evolutionary process. Most of the evolutionary algorithms propose biological paradigms, and concepts of natural selection, mutation, and reproduction. Nevertheless other paradigms exist and can be adopted in the creation of evolutionary algorithms. Many problems involve environments not structured which can be solved from the perspective of cultural paradigms, which offer plenty of category models, where one does which do not know the possible solutions at problem, a common situation in the real life. The intention of this research is analyze the Crowdfunding Model, supporting to a social networking to an Indie Pop Band. Sociological research shows that Crowdfunding tends to reveal a bias toward social similarity. Therefore, in order to model this Project supported with Crowdfunding developing an Agent-Based Model that already manages the social interaction, together with featuring information of MySpace Music evolutionary belief spaces. To introduce these theoretical concepts the authors decided use Cultural Algorithms in our approach, explaining the process in detail.

Section 4
Technological Application using Intelligent Optimization

Data mining is a complex process that involves the interaction of the application of human knowledge and skills and technology. This must be supported by clearly defined processes and procedures. This Chapter describes CRISP-DM (Cross-Industry Standard Process for Data Mining), a fully documented, freely available, robust, and non proprietary data mining model. The chapter analyzes the contents of the official Version 1.0 Document, and it is a guide through all the implementation process. The main purpose of data mining is the extraction of hidden and useful knowledge from large volumes of raw data. Data mining brings together different disciplines like software engineering, computer science, business intelligence, human-computer interaction, and analysis techniques. Phases of these disciplines must be combined for data mining project outcomes. CRISP-DM methodology defines its processes hierarchically at four levels of abstraction allowing a project to be structured modularly, being more maintainable, scalable and the most important, to reduce complexity. CRISP-DM describes the life cycle of a data mining project consisting of six phases: business understanding, data understanding, data preparation, modeling, evaluation, and deployment.

This chapter describes the experimental study partial discharges (PD) activities with artificial intelligent tools. The results present different patterns using a hybrid system with Self Organizing Maps (SOM) and Hierarchical clustering, this combination constitutes an excellent tool for exploration analysis of massive data such a partial discharge on underground power cables and electrical equipment. The SOM has been used for nonlinear feature extraction and the hierarchical clustering to visualization. The hybrid system is trained with different dataset using univariate phase-resolved distributions. The results show that the clustering method is fast, robust, and visually efficient.

Advanced Manufacturing Technology (AMT) constitutes one of the most important resources of manufacturing companies to achieve success in an extremely competitive world. Decision making processes for the Evaluation and Selection of AMT in these companies must lead to the best alternative available. Industry is looking for a combination of flexibility and high quality by doing significant investments in AMT. The proliferation of this technology has generated a whole field of knowledge related to the design, evaluation and management of AMT systems which includes a broad variety of methodologies and applications. This chapter presents a theoretical review of the term AMT, its diverse classification and a collection of the most effective multi-attribute models and methodologies available to support these processes. Relevant advantages are found in these models since they can manage complex decision making problems which involve large amount of information and attributes. These attributes frequently can be tangible and intangible when vagueness and uncertainty exist. There are several multi-attribute methodologies which are extensively known and used in literature; nevertheless, a new fuzzy multi-attribute axiomatic design approach is explained for an ergonomic compatibility evaluation of AMT.

Computer science and electronics have a very big incidence in several research areas; optics and photonics are not the exception. The utilization of computers, electronic systems, and devices has allowed the authors to develop several projects to control processes. A description of the computer tool called Laser Micro-Lithography (LML) to characterize materials is realized. The Reasoning Based on Cases (RBC) and its implementation in the software using Java are presented. In order to guarantee the lithography precision, a control system based on a microcontroller was developed and coupled to the mechanical system. An alternative of LML, considering the use of a Personal Digital Assistant (PDA), instead of a Personal Computer (PC) is described. In this case, C language is used for programming. RBC optimizes the materials characterization, recovering information of materials previously characterized. The communication between the PDA and the displacement table is achieved by means of a system based on a micro-controller DSPIC. The developed computers tool permits obtaining lithography with channels narrower than an optical fiber with minimum equipment. The development of irradiance meters based on electronic automation is shown; this section includes the basic theoretical concepts, the experimental device design and the experimental results. Future research trends are presented, and as a consequence of the developed work, perspectives of micro drilling and cutting are also analyzed.

Overall performance of hydraulic submersible pump is strongly linked to its geometry, impeller speed and physical properties of the fluid to be pumped. During the design stage, given a fluid and an impeller speed, the pump blades profiles and the diffuser shape has to be determined in order to achieve maximum power and efficiency. Using Computational Fluid Dynamics (CFD) to calculate pressure and velocity fields, inside the diffuser and impeller of pump, represents a great advantage to find regions where the behavior of fluid dynamics could be adverse to the pump performance. Several trials can be run using CFD with different blade profiles and different shapes and dimensions of diffuser to calculate the effect of them over the pump performance, trying to find an optimum value. However the optimum impeller and diffuser would never be obtained using lonely CFD computations, by this means are necessary the application of Artificial Neural Networks, which was used to find a mathematical relation between these components (diffusers and blades) and the hydraulic head obtained by CFD calculations. In the present chapter artificial neural network algorithms are used in combinations with CFD computations to reach an optimum in the pumps performance.

Foreword

We are highly parallel and connectionist in nature. In short, we are a hybrid of independent methods that integrate together and result in the highest form of intelligence on the planet - Tim Jones 2009, in his book Artificial Intelligence a Systems Approach

This edited collection of papers entitled "Logistics Management and Optimization through Hybrid Artificial Intelligence Systems" presents a set of applications which purpose is to solve a wide variety of modern and real world problems on logistics management and optimization by means of Hybrid Artificial Intelligence Systems.

This book consists of eighteen chapters, grouped in four main areas: Logistics, Optimization, Social, and Technological applications, where are discussed several applications using Hybrid Artificial Intelligence Systems that result of integrating different Artificial Intelligence Techniques on different fields. Chapters describe important relatively new or emerging areas of work in which the authors are personally involved; most of them hot topics of discussion in Scientific and Academic Community.

LOGISTICS

This section consists of three chapters, Chapter 1, "Logistics Applied to Improve Bottling Water Distribution," addresses the solution to the problem of optimizing the space within the vehicle to distribute purified water using a cultural algorithm approach; Chapter 2, "Logistics for the Garbage Collection through use of Ant Colony Algorithms" shows the application of Ant Colony Algorithm for the identification of optimal routes for collecting solid wastes by means of a transportation system and finally the Chapter 3, "Grid Platform Applied to the Vehicle Routing Problem with Time Windows for the Distribution of Products" presents a genetic algorithm implemented over the grid that is applied to solve the Vehicle Routing Problem with Time Windows.

OPTIMIZATION

The second section, the largest on the book, consists of seven chapters: Chapter 4, "Hybrid Algorithm Applied to the Identification of Risk Factors on the Health of Newly Born in Mexico" presents the implementation of a Genetic Algorithm into a framework for machine learning that deals with the problem of identifying the factors that impact the health state of newborns in Mexico; Chapter 5, "An Evolutionary

Algorithm for Graph Drawing with a Multiobjective Approach" shows a hybrid algorithm combines a global search algorithm (EDA — Estimation of Distribution Algorithm) with a local search Algorithm (HC — Hill Climbing) in order to maintain a balance between the exploration and exploitation for non planar graphs; Chapter 6, "Handwritten Signature Verification Using Multi objective Optimization with Genetic Algorithms in a Forensic Architecture" presents the use of multi-objective optimization for on-line automatic verification of handwritten signatures based on genetic algorithms that allows characterize optimally users; Chapter 7, "Looking for Reverse Transformations between NP-Complete Problems" presents results of ongoing research for clarifying the question do reverse transformations exist for any pair of NP-complete problems?; Chapter 8, "Variants of VRP to Optimize Logistics Management Problems" presents an algorithm to optimize the transportation management applied on a Rich Vehicle Transportation Problem (RVTP) that allows saving quantity of vehicles used and reducing operational cost of companies; Chapter 9, "Heuristic Algorithms: An Application to the Truck Loading Problem" is presented a solution for the Rich Bin Packing Problem by means of a heuristic-deterministic algorithm, named DiPro, that works together with a metaheuristic algorithm to plan routes, schedules and loads; and Chapter 10, "Recombination Operators in Permutation-based Evolutionary Algorithms for the Travelling Salesman Problem" performs a comparative analysis of several recombination operators based on computational experiments for TSP (Traveling-Salesman-Problem) instances and a generalized version of it.

SOCIAL APPLICATIONS

The Social Applications section consists of three chapters: Chapter 11, "Crowfunding to Improve Environmental Projects' Logistics" tries to analyze one of the first studies on this topic related to the question does the specie of the personage's role on a series affect the value of the card? and the implications to the collectors; Chapter 12, "Improve Card Collection from Memory Alpha using Sociolinguistics and Japanese Puzzles" analyzes the organization of a project using a Crowdfunding Agent-Based Model supporting to a social networking, which manages social interaction, featuring information of issues in different habitats and evolutionary belief spaces by means of cultural algorithms; and Chapter 13, "Mass Media Strategies: Hybrid Approach using a Bioinspired Algorithm and Social Data Mining" analyzes the Crowdfunding Model, supporting to a social networking for an Indie Pop Band.

TECHNOLOGICAL

This section consists of five chapters: Chapter 14, "Optimization of a Hybrid Methodology (CRISP-DM)" analyzes the contents of the official Version 1.0 of CRISP-DM (Cross-Industry Standard Process for Data Mining), a fully documented, freely available, robust, and non proprietary data mining model; Chapter 15, "Data Mining Applications in the Electrical Industry" outlines work that has been done to achieve optimal use of diagnostic data on underground transmission system by means of data mining; Chapter 16, "Decision Making Approaches for Advanced Manufacturing Technology Evaluation and Selection" presents a theoretical review of the term AMT (Advanced Manufacturing Technology), its diverse classification and a collection of the most effective multi-attribute models and methodologies available to support these processes, likewise a new fuzzy multi-attribute axiomatic design approach is explained for an ergonomic compatibility evaluation of AMT; Chapter 17, "Optical Application Improved with Logistics of Artificial Intelligent and Electronic Systems" presents a computer tool to perform Laser Micro-Lithography (LML) by means of Case Base Reasoning and ad-hoc software developed in Java for personnel computers, and in C for Personal Digital Assistants (PDAs), future research trends, such as hardware optimization are presented, finally, perspectives of micro drilling and cutting are also analyzed; and Chapter 18, "Optimization of the Impeller and Diffuser and Hydraulic Submersible Pump Using Computational Fluid Dynamics and Artificial Neural Networks" discuss an artificial neural network algorithm that is used in combination with CFD (Computational Fluid Dynamics) computations to reach an optimum in the pumps performance.

All these chapters provide an interesting prospective on where this important field is going at the beginning of the second decade of the twenty-first century.

José Alberto Hernández-Aguilar
Autonomous University of Morelos State, Mexico

José Alberto Hernández Aguilar *obtained his Ph.D. degree on Engineering and Applied Sciences in November 2008 at Universidad Autónoma de Morelos (UAEM). Since November 2008, he is working as full time professor at the Sciences Faculty at UAEM. He is candidate to SNI. Areas of interest: Databases, Artificial Intelligence, On-line Assessment Systems, Marketing Research, and e-commerce.*

Preface

Logistics Management and Optimization through Hybrid Artificial Intelligence Systems is an adequate source of information that compiles interdisciplinary perspectives about diverse issues related with Logistics, Optimization, Social applications and Technology applications each one with a different perspective about the correct solution of this kind of methodologies. This book is a collective effort to introduce new ideas from a variety of perspectives using innovative techniques and methodologies.

A book specialized on optimization considers different aspects to realize this "Optimization" tries to improve with innovative techniques and methodologies different daily aspects of our lives, in each one of them is possible understand the necessity of improve time, costs, spaces and a plethora of features associated with the modern life.

We received manuscripts from renowned researchers from all around the world with expertise on improving optimization related with Logistics of products and services, Optimization of different elements in the time and location, Social Applications to enjoy of a visit at the zoo, collect items and obtain recommendation in a specialized Thematic Web Radio, and finally, Technologies Applications of diverse ways to increase our Life Quality.

The book open with a section entitled *Logistics of Products and Services*, featuring three chapters on the improvement of services and products through the use of new paradigms on Logistics are Evolving Compute and Vehicle Route Problem to understand the best way to resolve this kind of problem. The first chapter of this section is "Logistics Applied to Improve Bottling Water Distribution," which aboard the resolution of a small company in the North of Mexico and the improvement of their routes of delay using Data Mining and a Bioinspired Algorithm.

The Chapter "Logistics for the Garbage Collection through use of Ant Colony Algorithms," explains a real problem about the logistics to organize a Waste System in a Society and the best options to organize this service on the time take as important factor the locations and ubiquities of each point in the city.

Finally in this section is presented "Grid Platform Applied to the Vehicle Routing Problem with Time Windows for the Distribution of Products," this chapter proposes new ideas related with the delivery of products and detailed a novel technique to analyze the restriction of Time Windows.

The next section is named *Improve of Optimization Applied Intelligent Techniques*, featuring seven chapters related with different comparatives of Logistics in the search to improve resources in diverse aspects of our lives.

The chapter of "Hybrid Algorithm Applied to the Identification of Risk Factors on the Health of Newly Born in Mexico" discusses a new paradigm related with the health babies on Mexico.

In the next chapter entitled "An Evolutionary Algorithm for Graph Drawing with a Multiobjective Approach," a novel paradigm is explained related with an application to determine a graph in a variety of uses as Social Networking and Topologies.

The chapter "Handwritten Signature Verification Using Multi objective Optimization with Genetic Algorithms in a Forensic Architecture" explains the correct way to determine the authenticity of a signature and the comparative with another in the search to characterize an individual on Forensic applications.

"Looking for Reverse Transformations between NP-Complete Problems" explains many topics related with the diminution on NP-Complete problems and their approach from a more soft perspective.

In the chapter "Variants of VRP to Optimize Logistics Management Problems" is possible understand different variants of Vehicle Routing Problem associated with time, locations and process different.

"Heuristic Algorithms: An Application to the Truck Loading Problem" describes a variety of Bioinspired algorithms to resolve different problems associated with Logistics.

The importance of chapter "Analysis of Recombination Operators in Permutation-Based Evolutionary Algorithms for the Travelling Salesman Problem" is the value of Bioinspired applications on different aspects related with travel on Logistics.

In the section entitled *Social Application on Logistic* grouped three different papers related with solutions derived of specific aspects try to improve daily activities on social topics.

In the chapter "Crowdfunding to Improve Environmental Projects' Logistics" explains the way to obtain funds to conservation parks and natural reserves to protect flora and fauna and improve routes in a Zoo to different kind of people.

"Improve Card Collection from Memory Alpha using Sociolinguistics and Japanese Puzzles" describes the way to collect thematic objects and improve these collections using sociolinguistics and Japanese puzzles related with the Social Networking associated with these collectors group.

The chapter entitled "Mass Media Strategies: Hybrid Approach using a Bioinspired Algorithm and Social Data Mining" explains different strategies to access to Mass Media including Music, Web and Merchandise.

Finally the last section *Technological Application using Intelligent Optimization*, is a group of chapters which involved Technology and their effect on the society.

In the chapter "Optimization of a Hybrid Methodology (CRISP-DM)" is described a novel technique which permits improve data mining processes.

"Data Mining Applications in the Electrical Industry" is an interesting chapter related with novel proposes in the Electrical Industry try to improve processes which implicate many different tasks in diverse locations where is produced the energy and send to another locations where this is used by people.

An Industrial Application is presented in "Decision Making Approaches for Advanced Manufacturing Technology Evaluation and Selection" describing an interesting study related with ergonomics and their applications in diverse aspects of our lives.

The next chapter "Optical Application improved with Logistics of Artificial Intelligent and Electronic Systems" involves an innovative proposal related with the use of Electronics and Artificial Intelligence to improve the use of Optics in the Industry and a new paradigm on the art state of this kind of applications.

Finally the chapter "Optimization of the Impeller and Diffuser and Hydraulic Submersible Pump Using Computational Fluid Dynamics and Artificial Neural Networks" is a novel technique used on Mechanics to improve the feature of a system based on mechanical geometries and propose to adequate the necessities of Industrial sector on Mexico.

The research community must be alert to investigate all these issues in a timely fashion, opening avenues for subsequent edition of this interesting book.

The chapters were selected following a rigorous analysis done by the book editors, and each chapter was double-blind peer-reviewed by at least two experts in the area. This would not have been possible without the valuable help of the Editorial Advisory Board; our sincere appreciation to: Dra. Lourdes Margain, Dra. Dolores Torres, Dra. Sayuri Quezada, Dr. Julio Ponce, Dr. Francisco Ornelas, Dr. Christian Correa, and two Ph.D. students in their last year: Sergio Enriquez and Rubén Jaramillo; finally, at Dr. Alberto Hernández by your dedication to write the Foreword.

We also thank many other anonymous researchers from around the world – Halina Iztebegovic, Montenegro University; Irina Döring, Volgogrado University; Dagmar Zuraevic, Sarajevo University; Chloë Malépart, UQAM Québec; Simonné Suarent, Technical Univesity of Mauritius; Taardemi Suaromi, Technical University of Oulu, Finland; Czongor Sziladzi, Pécs University Hungary; Antonio Padméterakiris, Nicosia University Cyprus; Aliya Tatkedhek, Kalmykya University, Russia Federation; Namri Löntsän, Oslo University, Norway -that helped with the peer-reviewing process. We also wish to sincerely thank Myla Harty for her clerical assistance during the critical final stages in the preparation of this book.

A book that aims to improve our lives without affect to environment would not be complete without giving to this cause. Therefore, from the very beginning of the project, we decided to humbly donate all of our revenue generated by this book to World Wild Foundation.

The content of the chapters included in this book is the sole responsibility of the authors. The views, opinions or positions expressed by the chapter authors are solely those of the authors, and do not necessarily reflect the views, opinions or positions of the editors. All trademarks, trade names, service marks, and logos referenced in the chapters of this book belong to their respective companies.

Carlos Alberto Ochoa Ortiz Zezzatti
Juarez City University, México

Camelia Chira
Babes-Bolyai University, Romania

Arturo Hernández-Aguirre
CIMAT, Mexico

Miguel Basurto
UAEM, Mexico

Acknowledgment

We encountered many challenges and had to make sacrifices in the development of this book. I would like to thank my lovely family and fiancée for their wholehearted and unconditional support, encouragement, and sincere advice not only throughout this project but in each and every aspect of my personal and professional life. I humbly dedicate all the efforts I put into this book to them. Thank you to each member of my family especially to my Grandmother Reyna, my Father Porfirio, my nephew Sebastián and my daughter Mimma and you, Jacqueline to put in me the "Leguízamo-Povedano Syndrome."

Carlos Alberto Ochoa Ortiz Zezzatti
Juarez City University, México

I would like to thank my colleagues and friends from different parts of the world whom have supported me in my academic endeavors, and particularly those who contributed to this book. Their assistance and advice have been very valuable. Finally to my family who support all my dreams.

Camelia Chira
Babes-Bolyai University, Romania

I am thankful to my parents who taught me the value of the education; Special thanks are due to my wife Celia, whose endless understanding and support have been profound throughout the difficult times. Without her love and encouragement I am sure that I would not have been able to achieve so much. I also dedicate this book to my daughters, for filling my life with happiness.

Miguel Basurto
UAEM, Mexico

I would like to thank the many people who have helped me grow professionally. I would also like to acknowledge to my team support in CIMAT Research Center whom are very special to me. However, I would like to especially acknowledge my wife, whom has been so patient with me during the edition of this book.

Arturo Hernández-Aguirre
CIMAT, Mexico

Section 1
Logistics of Products and Services

Chapter 1
Logistics Applied to Improve Bottling Water Distribution

Carlos Alberto Ochoa Ortiz Zezzatti
Juarez City University, México

Nemesio Castillo
CIS-UACJ, México

Wilebaldo Martínez
CIS-UACJ, México

Socorro Velázquez
CIS-UACJ, México

ABSTRACT

The optimization problems have been widely attacked in the area of evolutionary computation, this has been due mainly to the kindness they have shown to solve these problems. This chapter addresses the solution to the problem of optimizing the space within the vehicle to distribute purified water. To solve this problem using a cultural algorithm which helps determine the appropriate charge that provides the best value for the company of this kind of services to the customers of the product. This is done taking into account the space that is available within the vehicle and the different presentations that are distributed. In turn, this study helps us to understand the behavior of (Cultural Algorithms) with respect to the issues raised in the optimization of space vehicle for distributing purified water. In addition prepare a comparative analysis of the results obtained with respect to another method of solving optimization space, and finally describe an extended Partially Dynamic Vehicle Routing which permits determine complicated scenarios and reorganize the stratagems to solute these scenarios.

"For you is an isolated piece of rock, for me is all my World, my home, Argo City"

- Alura In-Zee, Leadership of the Resistance to reubicate in Rokyn Planet

DOI: 10.4018/978-1-4666-0297-7.ch001

INTRODUCTION

The Water Purifier and Distributor "La Noria" is a company located in Fresnillo Zacatecas, which is the greatest municipality in Zacatecas State located in Mexico and with the greater economic activity, it is located 60 km to the northeast of the capital, its population dedicates itself mainly to the mining, commerce and industry.

The heading of the water purification, is competed very, this due to several factors, firstly the great companies that count on a great merchandise power and therefore of sales; also, the fillers, places to which people go to fill his water container of 5 gallons denominate in Spanish "Garrafón" by very low costs without stating the quality of the water finally and the local companies with greater antiquity and then also count on a system of distribution and root within the municipality. Therefore, looking for to position the product implies a greater complexity by already set out.

Another important factor is the lack of awareness of the people to use purified water, since much people prefer to directly take it from the faucet since they do not accept the change towards the purified water or by custom or for want of resource. Therefore in this investigation the problem is attacked of Routing and product Accommodate within a water purifier, looking for therefore the solidification of the same, for which, is used altogether a based methodology Mining of Data with the evolutionary algorithms with which work tools were generated, which they are detached one to one so that in the end the conjunction of the same provides the solution to us of the problem.

Data Mining is a technique that reunites the advantages of several areas like Statistic, Artificial intelligence, Linear Regression, among others, using as raw material the data bases; a traditional definition is the following one: "Joint of techniques or tools applied to the process non-trivial to extract and to present/display the implicit process, previously unknown, potentially useful and humanly comprehensible, from 3 great data sets, with the intention of predicting of automated form tendencies and behaviors previously not known" (Ochoa et al., 2008).

This chapter is divided in 5 sections, which are satisfied of the following way: The problem is described and in this way it is spoken about the state-of-the-art with base in works carried out on the basis of Data Mining and Evolutionary Algorithms that are related to the investigation displayed in this investigation. The basic concepts used are provided to realize our investigation and finally, the tools used for the resolution of our problem are described in detail. The arguments that give sustenance to the accomplishment of this project, the main general objectives as much particular and the hypotheses are mentioned that considered solving the problem. The propose techniques are explained, in first plane, became use of some tools of quality and the value chain is described of which it comprises the water purifier as well as the tools based on Data Mining in combination with the Evolutionary Calculation, in this case the Cultural Algorithms. It is before realized a detailed analysis of the results of the programs for the elaboration of routes and Bin Packing and later. Finally design of experiments is realized on our software of Data Mining and a comparative one of the Bin Packing. The conclusions of the work carried out occur and the possible future work is detailed to realize.

JUSTIFICATION OF THE LOGISTICS RESEARCH

Generally when we spoke to increase the volume and sale of some product or service, express comes to the mind concepts or tools like:

- Logistic, since it is a tool that handles and controls flows of merchandise or information.

- Marketing, that it looks for to satisfy the needs with the clients, and simultaneously to obtain a benefit.

Both they work generally of the hand, nevertheless, in search of managing to satisfy the client; in this work development a tool based on Data Mining, with the aim of finding landlords, tendencies or rules repetitive that explain the behavior of the reported data of sale in the water purifier in which realizes the study.

Of this way the Data Mining within a heading is implemented that had not been applied as is it Logistic on watch to the Client, and thus to contribute with the development of the company. In addition, with the use of Cultural Algorithms, which to the being a tool of the relatively new Artificial intelligence, implement for the first time in problems of space optimization, contributing a new use to the same, and entailing to his it was worth methodological. The previous thing must be previously realized a study of the value chain marks that rules to see us the generating areas of value for this way having a solid sustenance to the implementation of the mining of data and therefore a holistic work.

General Objectives

- To establish a system of distribution of the product that allows optimizing the costs of the company.
- To determine the factors that take part in logistic of distribution and the sale of the water purified in Fresnillo City and the communities surround that it, to contribute to the development of the company.
- To propose a system of optimization of the space used by "garrafones" in the vehicles to cover the demand of the product in the distribution routes.

Particular Objectives

- To show a solid system of distribution of the product that allows offering the service that the market deserves and that simultaneously this endorses the trustworthiness of the same.
- To identify those zones in which it exists majors sale possibilities considering that the incursion and the permanence are feasible within the coverage area of the company.
- To obtain a growth sustained in the sales and so that thus, it is possible to be obtained more economic income in relation to a period of previous time.
- To obtain that the service is in the amounts and suitable conditions, so that of this form, the service gives in the places and precise moments at which they need it to the clients or they wish.

Hypothesis of this Research

When not being realized an appropriate study of logistic distribution and, the acceptance of the product did not occur with the force that was required. When settling a down a solid system of distribution and service, will be obtained the increase and positioning of the market in the region. The sales are improved when finding the hidden landlord between the distribution variables and sale.

Logistics

Practically from the start of the times, the products that people wished, took place agreed to their needs and characteristics. At that time, the food and other products existed in abundance only at certain times of the year. At the outset, the humanity had to choose to consume products in the place where they were or to transport them to a certain place and to store them for later use there. As it did not exist a developed system of transport and storage, the movement of products was limited which a person could carry, and the storage of perishable products was possible only a short period. This system of transport and storage forced the people to live near the production places and to consume a quite small product range or services.

When the logistic systems began to improve, the consumption and the production were separating geographically. The different zones specialized in which they could produce more efficiently. Thus, the excess of production could be sent of profitable form to other regions and the products that did not make in the zone could be concerned.

Often we have listened to speak of the logistics; nevertheless we have a vague idea than it is. Logistic it is defined as: "the art and science to handle and to control the flows of merchandise, energy and information", were used to solve the conflict between the lack of coordination between the sales and the production, being established the nexus between the demand of the market and the activities of production of the company.

This term, arises in the military area, to determine how and when to mobilize resources to the places where they are necessary, with the aim of maintaining the lines of provision own and interrupting those of the enemy (Lund Karsten et al, 1996).

The product explosion and its disorderly commercialization caused that new alternatives looked for; therefore the evolution of the logistic term is demonstrated from the necessity of the military, to own activities of the enterprise world, such as the purchase, production, transport, storage, maintenance, organization and the planning of these activities. The merit corresponds to him to the author Peter Drucker, in the decade of 1960. The guru call of the administration identified the problem and focused its attention in the challenges and opportunities that the field of the logistics offered and the distribution, becoming witness of advances and significant progresses in the field of these concepts (Gendreau, 1998).

Figure 1. Logistics on the services

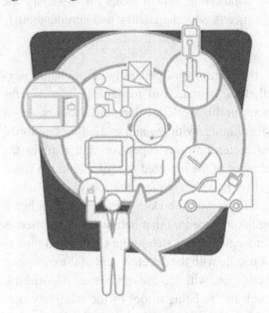

The distribution consists of the union of the aspects related to the transport, storage, packing, load/unloading and distribution and a system of support and information; this is related closely to other activities of the logistics that are identified with the area of obtaining, production and sales, that is to say, with the entrances, processes of transformation of these entrances and the logouts (Figure 1).

Nowadays the subject of the logistics is such an important subject that the companies create specific areas for their treatment, has been developed through time and is at present a basic aspect in the constant fight for being a company of the first world.

Previously the logistic era only, to have the right product, in the right site, the opportune time, to the smaller possible cost, at the moment these apparently simple activities has been redefined and now they are everything a process.

The logistics have many meaning, one of them, are the one in charge of the efficient distribution of products of a certain company with a smaller cost and an excellent service to the client, nevertheless, also determines and coordinates in optimal form the correct product, the correct client, the correct place and the correct time. If we assumed that the roll of the trade is to stimulate the demand, the roll of the logistics will be indeed to satisfy it.

Only through a detailed analysis of the demand in terms of level, lease and time, it is possible to determine the departure point for the profit of the final result of the logistics operations, to take care of this demand in terms of costs and effectiveness.

The supply function is in charge of the management of the physical flows (raw materials, finished products…) and one is interested to his surroundings. These surroundings correspond in this case to:

- resources (human, consumable, electricity)
- necessary goods to the accomplishment of the benefit (own warehouses, own tools, trucks, computer science systems…)
- services (subcontracted transports or warehouse,…)

The supply function manages the physical flows directly and indirectly associate the financial flows and of information. The physical flows generally are divided between those "of purchase" (between a supplier and its client), "of distribution" (between a supplier and the final client), "of return" (logistic inverse).

VEHICLE ROUTING PROBLEM

The Vehicle Routing Problem consists of, given to a set of clients and dispersed deposits geographically and a fleet of vehicles to determine a set of routes of minimum cost that begin and finish in plant visiting to all the clients in an order list.

The Clients

Each client has certain demand that will have to be satisfied by some vehicle. In many cases the demand is a good that occupies place in the vehicles and is usual that the same vehicle cannot satisfy the demand of all the clients with a single route. In other cases the demand is not a good but a service where the client simply must be visited by a vehicle. A vehicle could potentially visit all the clients.

The Deposit

As much the vehicles as the merchandise to distribute usually are in a deposit or plants matrix, usually it is requested that each route initiates and it finishes in the same point to begin with it.

The Vehicles

The capacity of each vehicle could have several dimensions, as for example weight and volume. When in a same problem different products exist to be distributed, the vehicles could have compartments so that the capacity of the vehicle depends on the merchandise that transfers. Some classic techniques of Vehicle Routing Problem are possibly to mention (Sommer, 1997):

- Problem of the travelling agent.
- Problem with time windows.
- Problem with heterogeneous fleet in the delivery .or with Algorithms of savings.

THE SIMULATION OF DATA TO VEHICLE ROUTING PROBLEM

As mentioned in last section randomly generated data rather than real life datasets are often used when analyzing and designing dynamic vehicle routing systems. In this chapter we will discuss some of the important issues that should be addressed when generating random test data. The times of new immediate requests calling in for service, the geographical locations, the on-site service times, and the demands of the customers are all parameters subject to stochastic within a dynamic vehicle routing problem. We discuss these parameters in order to provide some guidelines for dealing with stochastic when simulating DVRP scenarios.

Throughout the chapter an empirical case study will be examined. The data of this study originate from a real-life scenario in a Bottle Water Distributor and to compare with a Delivery Company of a long-distance courier mail and packages service provider. The routing problem faced by such companies is examined in further detail in this chapter.

Request Times of New Customers

Naturally, the arrival process for generating the time when the immediate request customers call in for service is essential when analyzing a dynamic routing system. In this section this arrival process is analyzed. Firstly, we provide a brief study on the commonly used Poisson process. Then, the call times of the long-distance courier mail case study are presented. Finally, we propose a time-dependent Poisson process for generating call times in a constantly changing environment.

The Poisson Process

Traditionally, the main reason for using the Poisson process is that this process is very simple to work with as well as the fact that it possesses some nice statistical characteristics which means that it is possible to derive analytical expressions describing the system in question. The most important statistical properties of the Poisson process could be summarized as follows: The arrival intensity parameter of the Poisson process, usually denoted λ, denotes the number of requests per time unit, i.e., if the time unit is 1 hour, the Poisson process with $\lambda = 2.5$ generates 2.5 requests per hour in average. The expected number of requests during the period of T hours is therefore λT. The time interval between two requests is exponentially dis-

tributed, i.e., the Poisson process has no memory of old events.

Pick-up of Courier Mail - Case Study

In Figure 2 the relation between the numbers of calls received by the call center of a long-distance courier mail service provider is shown as a function of the time of the day. The X-axis has been sampled at 15 minutes' intervals so that all calls received within each 15-minute interval were accumulated before printing. This was done to remove noise from outliers and hereby making the trend in the data more clear. The figure is based on all immediate requests received during a two-week (Monday-Friday) period in four almost adjacent service areas. The number of immediate requests total 283 calls for service during this period. The figure shows extensive variations in the number of calls throughout the day. The call center opens at 8:00 and closes at 18:00. The morning hours are relatively slow, but the number of calls increases towards noon. During lunch breaks (approximately 12:00 - 13:00) the number of calls is relatively low. The number of calls increases during the first part of the afternoon and reach its maximum at approximately 14:30.

THE TIME-DEPENDENT POISSON PROCESS

The previous section clearly indicates that the call intensity varies during the day. Naturally, the actual shape of the distribution depends heavily on the application. In the scenario the majority of the customers call in during the afternoon, because most offices close between 16:00 and 17:00. In other scenarios such as the distribution of oil to private households one would expect the majority of the customers to call in early during the morning hours after a cold night without heating. Obviously, this means that using a distribution with a constant intensity parameter does not give an

Figure 2. The number of calls in a real-life instance of a long-distance courier mail service provider as a function of the time of the day

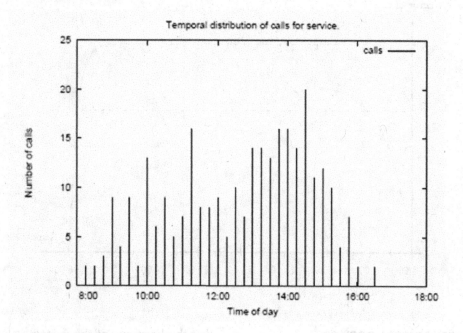

adequate description of the actual real-life situation. Alternatively, other distributions for arrivals could be used. The peak hour phenomenon could for instance be modeled by using a time-dependent Poisson process. In Figure 3 an example of a continuous time-dependent Poisson process is shown. The generation of time-dependent Poisson distributed numbers could for instance be done by using the so-called *rejection method* (Larson & Odon, 1980) which is based on a geometrical interpretation of the probability density function. With reference to the example shown in Figure 3 the rejection method could be explained as follows:

1. Estimate the average arrival intensity rate, $\bar{\lambda}$, over the time period T.

$$\bar{\lambda} = \frac{1}{T} \int_0^T \lambda(t)dt \qquad (1)$$

2. Find the number of requests to be generated, k, by sampling the Poisson process with the arrival intensity of $\bar{\lambda}$ over the time period T.

3. Generate two uniformly distributed random numbers, r_1 and r_2, where $0 \leq r_1 \leq T$ and $r_2 = max_t \lambda(t) = \lambda'$. If $r_2 \leq \lambda(r_1)$, accept r_1 as the i'th time instant $_{Ti}$. Repeat this step until k time instants have been accepted.

4. Sort the time instants $_{Ti}$, $i = 1,2,...,k$ into an ordered set.

We believe that new generation methods should consider using time-dependent arrival processes since the arrival intensities within a dynamic distribution context are often seen to be subject to relatively heavy variations. However, the time-dependent Poisson process will not be considered in the remaining part of this thesis. The reason for not considering this aspect is that including such information would introduce yet more parameters which increase the risk of blurring the general picture.

Figure 3. An example of a time-dependent Poisson distribution

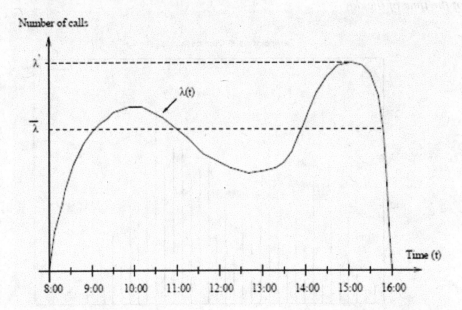

The Geographical Location of Customers

The spatial distribution of the customers' geographical location is one of the most essential parameters in both static and dynamic vehicle routing problems. The major part of the work on static vehicle routing uses Solomon's test dataset (Jensen, 1997) for reference. These datasets are divided into 6 groups, denoted R1, R2, C1, C2, RC1 and RC2. Each group consists of 8 to 12 different instances. The R1 and R2 datasets are randomly generated according to a uniform distribution. The C1 and C2 datasets are clustered, while the RC1 and RC2 datasets are a mixture of being clustered and randomly distributed. All problems consist of 100 customers located in a 100 x 100 square area.

Courier Mail Services - Case Study

Figure 4 shows the geographical distribution of the customers from the long-distance courier mail service application. It can be seen from the figure that the locations of the customers are strongly correlated. Furthermore, it should also be noted that a number of the customers are located outside the most congested areas. The strong tendency towards clustering could be explained by the type of the application. The spatial distribution of the customers in Figure 4 seems natural, because the long-distance courier mail services are mostly used by big corporations which tend to be located in \ industrial neighborhoods" or even in office buildings with a number of different corporations in the same building. The outliers are either company located in a remote area or private household's only receiving/sending long-distance mail once in a while.

Generating Geographical Locations

In order to be able to capture the spatial distribution, the service region can be divided into *n* smaller sub regions, in which the arrival intensity in the customer generation process varies from sub region to sub region. In Figure 5 an example of this method is shown. The customer locations

Figure 4. The geographical distribution of customers of a real-life instance for the long-distance courier mail problem

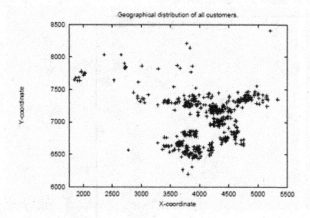
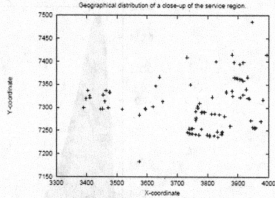

were generated by dividing the 1000 x 1000 sized service regions into 100 sub regions. In each sub region a uniform distribution generated the geographical locations. The number of customers in each sub region was generated by using a Poisson process with intensity parameters which depended on the sub region. The generation of customers could of course also be performed in several other ways; for instance by using more sophisticated probabilistic distributions.

On-Site Service Times

In the major part of the research on time constrained vehicle routing problems (like for instance the VRPTW) constant values are used for describing the on-site service times. However, in real-life and especially within a dynamic setting the on-site service times are subject to stochasticity. In most distribution contexts the on-site service time involves loading/un-loading physical items. In most cases this means that the service requires human interaction of some form. An evident example of this could be the situation that occurs when the mail man delivers a parcel and the receiver must sign a document. The time spent on this situation could of course vary from few seconds to several minutes. These factors suggest that using only

Figure 5. Illustration of the process of generating a combination of clustered and randomly distributed locations of customers using a 10 x 10 grid

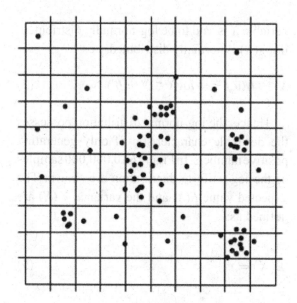

constant service times might not be the most appropriate approach.

The Log-Normal Distribution

The log-normal distribution is a transformation of the well-known normal distribution. A stochastic

Figure 6. Simulation of 10,000,000 randomly generated numbers in the log-normal distribution

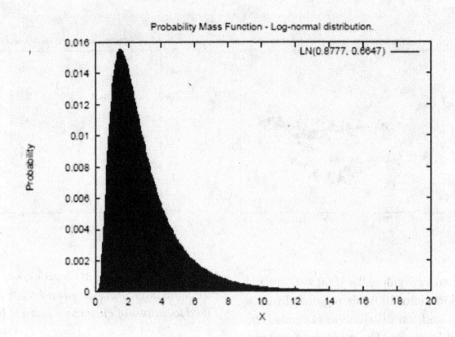

variable X is said to be log-normally distributed, if $log(X)$ is normally distributed, i.e.:

$$X \in LN(\alpha, \beta^2) \Leftrightarrow logX \in N(\alpha, \beta^2) \qquad (2)$$

Hence, the log-normal distribution possesses the desirable characteristic of only generating positive numbers. In Figure 6 10,000,000 samples of the log-uniform distribution are shown. The expected value $E(X)$ and the variance $V(X)$ are defined as:

$$E(X) = e^{\alpha + \frac{1}{2}\beta^2} \qquad (3)$$

$$V(X) = e^{2\alpha + \beta^2}(e^{\beta^2} - 1) \qquad (4)$$

and the parameters α and β are defined as:

$$\alpha = \log_e \mu - \frac{1}{2}\log_e \mu(\frac{\sigma^2}{\mu^2} + 1) \qquad (5)$$

$$\beta^2 = \log_e \mu(\frac{\sigma^2}{\mu^2} + 1) \qquad (6)$$

where $\mu = E(X)$ and $\sigma^2 = V(X)$. This means that the expected value and the variance should be 3.0 and 5.0 respectively. A simple method for generating samples in the log-normal distribution can be found in Ross (1990). In the following we will use the log-normal distribution to generate on-site service times, as we believe that this distribution will give a fair description of the on-site service times within the above sketched distribution contexts. Before using this distribution in a real-life context an empirical analysis should be considered in order to test whether or not the distribution gives a fair description of the real-life data. Also, this analysis should provide the planners with the α and β parameters of the distribution.

Customer Demands

The actual demand of customers - advance request as well as immediate request customers - may also be subject to strong variations. This problem is usually referred to as the vehicle routing problem with stochastic customers and demands. As was the case with the previously mentioned parameters, several different statistical distributions could be used for generating suitable customer demands. The actual application will have to show which distribution is the most realistic one to use. The subject of stochastic customer demands will not be studied in further detail in this chapter.

Travel Times

The final system parameter subject to stochastic to be considered in this chapter is the travel time between the customers. The uncertainty in this parameter is due to for instance reduced travel speed caused by congestion in the traffic network or it could be caused by unforeseen events such as road construction and traffic accidents. The lateness caused by such events often results in considerable delays. Hence, a true dynamic routing system should be able to deal with stochastic travel times and the routing system must be able to deal with these situations. Jørgensen (1984) analyzes the implications of a noise-filled travel time matrix for a static vehicle routing problem with time windows. The noise is determined by using a random generator which multiplies each element in the travel time matrix by a parameter, *pnoise*. Three different scenarios are considered. In the first scenario *pnoise 2* [0.95; 1.05], in the second *pnoise 2* [0.90; 1.10] and in the third *pnoise 2* [0.75; 1.25]. This means that the average level of the noise is 0! The conclusion is that the total distance driven by the vehicle is only subject to very small changes (from less than 1% to approximately 5%) for the first two scenarios, while the total distance driven might be up to 25% longer for the last scenario. However, in real-life

situations the noise would usually only be in the direction of longer travel times so that the average noise level is greater than 0. Therefore, one might expect that the stochasticity in the travel time matrix means that the total distance driven actually increases for increasing values of travel times. The subject of stochastic travel times will not be studied in further detail in this research.

In this chapter a number of parameters potential to be subject to stochastic were discussed. In general, when using simulation as an analytical tool to assess the characteristics of a system the risk of misuse and wrong conclusions are present if the right data are not used. Therefore, it is of paramount importance that the analyst tries to identify which distributions to use for generating the test instances in order to be able to give a consistent and precise description of the system. However, in most real-life dynamic vehicle routing scenarios the use of very simple simulation techniques should be sufficient in order to provide the model with the necessary information.

Design of Experiment (Analysis Experimental of the Algorithms)

Design of Experiments is an organized effort of a scientist to acquire knowledge on a natural or artificial process. The design can need many self-studies, each with specific objectives. Design of Experiments must take a complete sequence of taken steps beforehand to assure that the appropriate data will be obtained so that they allow an objective analysis that leads to valid deductions with respect to the established problem. An experiment must be limited investigations that establish a particular set of circumstances, under a specific protocol to observe and to evaluate the implications of the resulting observations. The investigator determines and controls the protocols of an experiment to evaluate and to prove something that to a large extent does not know until that moment (Andersen, 1995).

Objective of the Design of Experiments

- To reduce the registered data to numerical form.
- To apply suitable techniques of the Mathematical Statistic.
- To provide the maximum amount of information corresponding to the investigated problem.
- The design must be as simple as it is possible.
- The greater efficiency is due to carry out (saving of time, money, personnel and experimental material).

Interpretation and Report of Results

At the time of interpreting the results, it is important to consider all the data observed; others, one is due to limit the conclusions to strict deductions from the obtained evidence.

Also, one is due to try by means of independent experiments, the controversies that provoke the data thus to be able to reach conclusions with respect to the technical result from the results like the statistical significance (Rosholm, 1987). Finally in the elaboration of the report, the work is due to describe clearly giving antecedent, pertinent explanations of the problem and the meaning of the results; also, use is due to do of graphical and tabular methods of such efficient form that the presentation of the data is clear and of such form that the information is sufficient so that the reader can verify the results and of drawing his own conclusions.

Development of the Realized Research

By means of the described tools previously, was realized a Ideas Rain or Brainstorm in order to find the possible causes that the personnel attributed to the problematic one of the distribution

and the sales of the plant and profit obtained the following listing:

Possible Causes of the Water purifier and distributor "La Noria" about the bad distribution.

- Lack of Organization.
- Vehicles in Evil Been.
- Lack of control on the workers.
- Climate.
- Bad Marketing research.
- Distances between clients.
- Rotation states of personnel.
- Ignorance of customer on the part of the landlords.
- Loss of clients.
- Lack of tests of admission for distributors (Test).
- Badly seal of "garrafones".
- Bad Pays.
- Laziness in the workers.
- Competition.
- Bad distribution of routes.
- Bad communication (Used Landlord).
- Ignorance of the implementation of routes.
- "Garrafones" in evil been.
- Broken labels.
- Binnacles do not exist.
- Ignorance of time of route by route.

There is no qualification.

With base to this listing it is necessary to give another format him in such a way that it is of easy understanding for the personnel and who it is possible to be worked on the basis of it, for which made the diagram Cause Effect (Ishikawa).

Development of Diagram Cause Effect (Ishikawa)

It shows us to the Diagram that on the basis of the perception of the employees external in the rain of ideas, the problematic one mainly concentrates in the methods used for the distribution and sale

Figure 7. Determination of the Chain of value in which it comprises the purifier and the part concerning the distribution

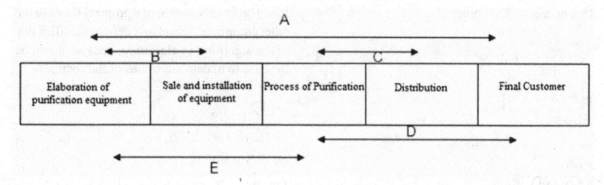

that transforms into the service the client who is finally the objective of any chain of value.

Application of the Chain of Value

By the previous thing, it was come to the determination from the Chain of Value of the Purifier, and therefore the activities that general value and consequently gain and thus of defining if the Evolutionary application of the Mining and Algorithms are viable for the development of the thesis.

Literature mentions the classic us that Primary Activities exist and Activities You would second, as can be observed in Figure 7 the part corresponding to the distribution on the basis of this, corresponds to a primary activity.

Application of Data Mining

As first step were obtained a map of Fresnillo City in order to locate to each client who had itself registered in the data base to determine the areas in which had major number of sale. Once realized this, the map of the city in 4 four quadrants was divided and therefore 4 zones, stop from this, to assign co-ordinate to each client whereupon it counted as well as the new ones. Once they were grouped in zones by coordinates, it was come to the clustering (to group) to be able to apply the Mining of Data with the method of k-means.

Well it is known that different techniques exist that allow to apply mining of data, nevertheless, the algorithm of "k-means" is referring the main one between the diverse methods to select representative groups between the data unlike which they are used for the clustering process. The algorithm generates group of data, without having predefined classes, being based on a function of similarity of the values that own their different attributes, being realized of form non supervised (that is to say, they discover landlords or tendencies in the data). K-means is a partition method of clustering (it begins absolutely to the individual), where the partition process of a data base of n is realized objects in a set of k groups, looking for to optimize the chosen criterion of partition process. In K-means each grouping of data is represented by a centroid, to others, tries to form k groups, with k predetermined before the beginning of the process. The objective is to diminish the intra-group total variance. A series exists first that constitutes the foundation for the implementation of this type of algorithm, their different variants are based essentially on the form to measure distances between the data and the groups, the criterion to define the property of the data to each group and the form to update these groups. Next we will mention the matrices used for the implementation of the algorithm:

Matrix of Data

This matrix of RxN order,

$$
\begin{array}{c}
\quad C1\ C2\ \ldots\ Cn \\
\begin{array}{c} x \\ y \end{array}
\begin{bmatrix} 1 & 2 & \ldots & n \\ 2 & 3 & & n \end{bmatrix}
\end{array}
\tag{1}
$$

Where:

N= Not of Clients

R= Characteristics to identify and to group each client.

For each client the characteristics consist of their location in the coordinate axis proposed based on their position x and y.

Matrix of Centroids

It is of NxC order, the centroids that are generated during the evolution of the algorithm of clustering go being stored in the matrix.

$$
\begin{array}{c}
\quad c1\ c2\ \ldots\ cn \\
\begin{array}{c} x \\ y \end{array}
\begin{bmatrix} 1 & 2 & \ldots & n \\ 2 & 3 & & n \end{bmatrix}
\end{array}
\tag{2}
$$

Where:

N= number of characteristics that characterize to each cluster

C= Number of Centroids that is desired to have.

For this case in particular 3 centroids were used, because it was desired to determine 3 routes different from distribution.

Matrix of Distances

It is of order cxN, defines the property to one or the other group here. This matrix defines the efficiency of the algorithm of clustering, because it will be the base to update the values of the centroids.

$$
\begin{array}{c}
\quad\quad C1\ \ \ C2\ \ \ldots\ \ \ Cn \\
\begin{array}{c} c1 \\ c2 \\ cn \end{array}
\begin{bmatrix} 1.5 & 1.8 & \ldots & n \\ 2.3 & 2.4 & \ldots & n \\ n & n & & n \end{bmatrix}
\end{array}
\tag{3}
$$

Where:

N= number of characteristics that characterize to each cluster

C= Number of Centroids that is desired to have. In this matrix the distances of each one of the clients will be stored to each one of the centroids, which will become by means of the euclideana formula of distances, it is possible to mention that there are other methods, but for this case east type was used since it offers to good results and ease of use.

Matrix of Properties

It is of CxN order, it is determined on the basis of the matrix of distances, is the first base for the iteration of the algorithm since from its values the update of the matrix of centroids was determined until getting to converge.

$$
\begin{array}{c}
\quad\quad C1\ C2\ \ldots\ Cn \\
\begin{array}{c} c1 \\ c2 \\ cn \end{array}
\begin{bmatrix} 0 & 0 & \ldots & 1 \\ 1 & 0 & \ldots & 0 \\ 0 & 1 & & 0 \end{bmatrix}
\end{array}
\tag{4}
$$

Where:

C: He is equal to the number of centroids.

N: He is equal to the number of clients.

Application of the Cultural Algorithm

The previous things the conditions for the application of Data Mining by means of k-means are fulfilled, nevertheless, lack the complement that allows the tool to be able to make decisions to determine the distribution routes. The following part was realized by means of a Cultural Algorithm, which handles different entrances, unique that he controls directly the user is the size of the population or number of agents, to the respect hopes itself that to that is increased, major will be the knowledge and influences cultural that is had better obtaining therefore one and faster optimization. The Cultural Algorithm generates a population of n agents (an agent, is the computer simulation of a person), who conform a society based on cultural algorithms, which will be in charge to determine, to the passage of the times, the optimal route. At time zero (she is when the program is initialized, and the agents own an empty space of beliefs), all the agents obtain the generated data of each colony, each of them will propose a route, it will give rise to the negotiation between the agents to select which the best route is proposed at certain time. The space of beliefs will be updated only when the proposed route is better than previously stored previously, initiating a cycle of improvements that will be interrupted when amount of times (iterations in the behavior of the agents) without improvements to the routes happens m or when a condition of unemployment is realized.

PROPOSED CULTURAL ALGORITHM

Once the location was determined, the construction of Data Warehouse, organized in the following fields was undertaken:

- Cultural algorithm.

- Client.
- Visit.
- Update of the Percentage.
- Product.
- Sales.
- Salesman.

Each of these fields conforms the part of the menu of the Intelligent System, their operation would be explained in detail in the following section.

Presentation of the Interface

Function of the Cultural Algorithm is the main screen shows the menu on which it counts Figure 17, the option Cultural Algorithm, allows the execution of the program and thus to obtain the routes suggested on the basis of the reported sales. Since at the moment it is counted on 3 vehicles of distribution, at the time of executing itself software throws 3 proposed routes (One by each vehicle), the propose routes are those that count on the best route and the smaller time. It is possible to indicate that the routes modified on the basis of the reported sales and the clients who are registered.

Icon of Salesman

The High option of Salesman, allows like its name the East Indian, to enter the data base to a salesman, for which it is necessary to assign to a idvendedor (key) Software registers to others, the name, including last names and password which select the salesman, and thus, at the time of access to the system is registered its sale. In the same way in this option they handle another Selling Low option; this option allows eliminating a salesman of software but it's not thus historical ones of sale since of being thus it would harm in the generation of the routes. The following option that comprises of the menu is referring to the clients, shows the form in which this option unfolds:

Icon of the Client

First that is mentioned is High Client, this option allows to register to a new client when thus it is necessary, the requirements that software requests are: You go Client who assigns the same software to it on the basis of the consecutive one which she handles, Street, Colony and Coordinates in which she is located on the basis of the map which I am used for the allocation of coordinates, once we give him to accept, the client is registered and ready for when he realizes a purchase, the sales-man can discharge from the hospital his sale. In the same way Loss of Client is handled, who is used when a client remains certain time without purchase or no longer can lives in his address, this client be eliminated of the data base by means of this option. Finally it must Publish Client, this is used when some client change of address but continues acquiring our product, is necessary to update his new direction so that software deter-mines if it is continued with his route of visit or if is changed of route.

Icon of the Product

Concerning the product 4 presentations are han-dled, to which to assigned idProducto to him, to be able to register to the product we were located in the option Product, Discharge of Product, as-signed solely there you go as well as its cost, in this way at the time of registering the sale will request idproducto to us to register the sale. Like in the previous options we can drop from rolls some product by means of the option Low Product

Icon of Visits

When the routes are generated, it is important to indicate that software as I explain myself in the process of cultural algorithm, works on the basis of a cultural influence, in this case it deduces who are the potential clients, in this way it does not mean that all the clients generated in the route

are going to buy, but is a greater possibility of sale, therefore when he is visited and some sale was not obtained, the distributor reports the visit but not it sale, this does in the menu by means of the option of Discharge of Visit, in which it gives the idcliente and the idvendedor to report that I visit myself but sale was not obtained, shows the previous thing

Icon of Sales

Shows to the option of Discharge of Sales, this option is used, since the daily sales of each sales-man are registered here, the unique thing who is needed is to register the product, the idcliente, date and the hour to which the sale is registered, in this way is updated the historical one of sales, to put it another way, is the mouth of the tool, since if the sales do not register, the generated routes do not be real, therefore the sales are the food of the system.

Icon to Update Percentage

Finally, software is programmed with certain elitism, according to establishes the Literature of cultural algorithms, which we delimited with a percentage of purchase, so that the client leaves drawn for in the routes, is necessary that he has a percentage of purchase, for our case, we have chosen a percentage of 50%, thus, at the time of generating new routes Update Percentage and in this way they choose the best clients, this is realized monthly to determine the routes on the basis of the update of sales and therefore of the data base.

Space to Optimization

The problem to explain formally because an al-gorithm follows certain behavior when solving a set instance of a problem can describe of the following way.

Dices:

1. A metaheuristic algorithm *A* solving a problem *P*,
2. A set of instances I = {$i_1, i_2, \ldots i_n$} of problem *P*,
3. A set of metric that characterizes factors of the problem and of the algorithm which they hit in the performance F = {$f_1, f_2 \ldots f_m$}.

One looks for:

1. A joint one R = {r1, r2... r,}, for $1 \leq p \leq m$, like each r_i establishes a causal relation between the elements of G_i, where G_i F,
2. to apply the acquired knowledge, through R, in the redesign of algorithm A. In such a way that what one looks for, he is to identify relations between the factors critics for the algorithmic performance who allow to explain because the algorithm study object follows certain behavior when solving a set of cases of test and of applying to the knowledge acquired in the improvement of performance of the algorithm (Papastavrou, 1996).

Problem of (Bin Packing), that in the following thing we will call BPP, is a variant of the problem of the knapsack; a set of objects consists of dice which have a weight and a benefit or utility, it is desired to find a subgroup of objects that maximizes the benefit either total utility of the objects selected without exceeding the capacity of the containers or deposits, see Figure 8, the problem objective can imagine formally through the equation 7 that is next:

$$\max \sum_{j=1}^{n} p_j x_j \text{ sujeto a} \sum_{j=1}^{n} r i_j x_j \leq c \qquad (7)$$

Where:
pj is the Benedit to select the object *j*,
xj is worth 1 or if element j exists in the solution,

rij is the space that ocupéis the object,

The summatory of the weight of the selected objects must be $\leq$ to the capacity of container C.

The BPP can also be treated like a multiobjectic problem because on the one hand the utility of the objects is due to maximize and on the other to diminish the weight of the objects not to exceed the capacity of the containers of fixed size (Dial, 1995).

The complexity of the problem of distribution of objects in containers practically makes the use impossible of exact algorithms for its solution. These procedures include heuristic simple that are different by the way in which the objects are treated before being rich and by the form in which the container is chosen that will store each object. The main determinist strategies for BPP are described next (Malandraki, 1989):

- *First Adjustment* (First Fit, FF): Each considered object is placed in the first container that has sufficient capacity available. If no partially full container can store it, the object is placed in a new container (empty). A variation to this method settles down when the objects are taken according to the decreasing order of their weights (the objects are ordered from largest to smallest weight before being rich), variant happiness is well-known as First Decreasing Adjustment (First Fit Decreasing, FFD).
- *Better Adjustment* (Best Fit, BF): Each object is rich in the container fuller it can store than it, adding containers when it is necessary. Of equal way that with FF, exists a variation, call Better Decreasing Adjustment (Best Fit Decreasing, BFD), that in sequence considers the objects decreasing of its weights.
- *Worse Adjustment* (Worst Fit, WF): In opposition to the previous strategy (Best Fit, BF), each object in consideration is stored in the less full container with residual ca-

Figure 8. Description of bin packing problem

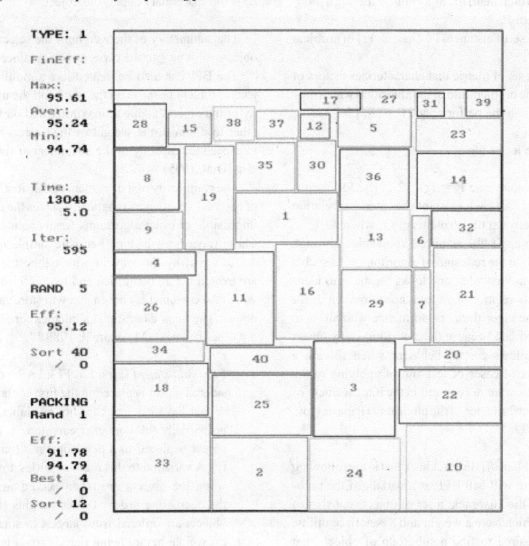

pacity sufficient to contain it. The variant that takes the objects according to the decreasing order from its weights is denominated Worse Decreasing Adjustment (Worst Fit Decreasing, WFD).

• Best 3-Fit Decreasing (B3FD) (Powell, 1995): Initially limit of containers is abre to a number. If an empty container exists, it is selected and the present object is placed, otherwise, it is tried to exactly fill each container with objects that have not been selected and by pairs they add the residual capacity of the container. For the rest of the objects, the present element is inserted in the fullest container in the one than it fits (like in BF). If a new container does not exist container with sufficient capacity it is added to the solution.

Bin Packing Problem Application

With regard to the space optimization, was constructed a software with capacity to choose the best arrangement, this based on the concept of Bin Packing but using cultural algorithms, in complexity simpler, but for that reason less notable. The

Table 1. Description of the product

PRODUCT	CAPACITY	% DEMAND	VOLUME	UTILITY
1	20 lt	45	36500cm3	$ 10.00
2	1.5 lt	15	26731cm3	$ 26.50
3	1 lt	15	18435cm3	$ 21.60
4	.500lt	25	18177cm3	$ 38.50

main difference consists of which not take into account the weight of the objects for our case, the presentations of the product (Water Purified), but the volume of the same stops on the basis of them to determine its better arrangement within the distribution vehicles. As first step were realized the taking of measures of the distribution vehicle on which was realized the study to determine the space with which it get ready in m^3, as well as the measurement of the different presentations and its respective volume, for this way being able to pose the problem and its respective restrictions. Also take into account the demand of the different presentations, for this way, more accurately to determine the utility of the product, which be observed in Table 1, with respect to Table 2 is possible observe the behavior of Cultural Algorithm (with a population of 850 agents) with a specific number of iterations (850), this is the step condition when is to reach is shown the results and determine the best optimization in the routes and the capacity of product.

PARTIALLY DYNAMIC VEHICLE ROUTING

In this section we further explore the degree of dynamism measure by introducing the Partially Dynamic Traveling Repairman Problem (PDTRP). A number of simple online dynamic policies to minimize the routing costs and the waiting time experienced by the customers are described. The results of the computational study indicate that an increase in the dynamic level results in a linear increase in route length for all policies studied. Furthermore, for relatively congested systems, a Nearest Neighbor policy performed uniformly better than the other dispatching rules studied.

We examine the impact of the degree of dynamism measure on solution methodology and quality. To give practical meaning to this concept, we introduce the Partially Dynamic Traveling Repairman Problem (PDTRP). And discuss how to simulate the PDTRP. The results of the simulation are discussed too. Finally, we discuss how the PDTRP could be extended and then we offer finally our conclusions. The work presented in this chapter is also described in Larsen et al. (1999).

The Partially Dynamic Traveling Repairman Problem (PDTRP)

In the Dynamic Traveling Repairman Problem introduced by Bertsimas and Van Ryzin (1991) all demands are dynamic, i.e., all customers are immediate request customers. The Partially Dynamic Traveling Repairman Problem (PDTRP) is a variant of this problem involving both advance and immediate request customers. We will define the PDTRP as follows:

- A repairman (or a vehicle/server) travels at constant velocity in a bounded region A of area A.
- A subset of demands are dynamic. These arrive in time according to a Poisson process with intensity parameter λ. The locations of the demands are independently and uniformly distributed in A.

Table 2. Results with iterations of our Intelligent Tool developed using Data Mining and Cultural Algorithms with a population of 850 agents and 850 iterations

No. 1	Rutas	Mayor	Menor	Optimizacion	Epocas	Rutas	Mayor	Menor	Optimizacion	Epocas	Rutas	Mayor	Menor	Optimizacion	Epocas
1	1	35	30	5	14	2	81	76	5	9	3	31	31	0	8
2	1	36	31	5	10	2	80	78	2	11	3	36	36	0	8
3	1	34	30	4	17	2	81	75	6	11	3	41	41	0	8
4	1	34	29	5	18	2	79	76	3	8	3	37	37	0	8
5	1	33	29	4	13	2	84	74	10	10	3	32	32	0	8
6	1	33	33	0	13	2	75	72	3	12	3	36	36	0	8
7	1	34	32	2	12	2	81	74	7	16	3	37	37	0	8
8	1	35	30	5	9	2	86	78	8	12	3	39	39	0	8
9	1	34	31	3	10	2	83	73	10	18	3	37	37	0	8
10	1	32	32	0	8	2	79	79	0	14	3	37	37	0	8
11	1	35	29	6	12	2	85	75	10	12	3	32	32	0	8
12	1	34	32	2	14	2	79	72	7	9	3	32	32	0	8
13	1	35	33	2	10	2	81	71	10	20	3	33	33	0	8
14	1	36	31	5	11	2	80	72	8	17	3	37	37	0	8
15	1	32	30	2	18	2	78	76	2	9	3	31	31	0	8
16	1	33	32	1	9	2	81	73	8	12	3	34	34	0	8
17	1	32	32	0	8	2	83	72	11	11	3	36	36	0	8
18	1	33	32	1	13	2	87	73	14	9	3	35	35	0	8
19	1	30	30	0	8	2	81	75	6	16	3	40	40	0	8
20	1	36	28	8	18	2	83	76	7	16	3	31	31	0	8
21	1	35	34	1	9	2	78	78	0	8	3	35	35	0	8
22	1	34	28	6	14	2	78	72	6	14	3	33	33	0	8
23	1	32	32	0	8	2	81	72	9	13	3	41	41	0	8
24	1	34	32	2	9	2	82	74	8	22	3	34	34	0	8
25	1	33	31	2	13	2	81	75	6	15	3	33	33	0	8
26	1	36	30	6	12	2	81	69	12	13	3	35	35	0	8
27	1	34	29	5	10	2	83	72	11	14	3	36	36	0	8
28	1	31	28	3	15	2	75	72	3	10	3	36	36	0	8
29	1	37	31	6	10	2	84	71	13	12	3	35	35	0	8
30	1	36	31	5	15	2	75	74	1	14	3	36	36	0	8

- Each demand requires an independently and identically distributed amount of on-site service time that becomes known once the service is completed.
- The route is updated only at customer locations. That is, a vehicle cannot change its destination while traveling.
- The objective is to minimize the repairman routing cost.

The PDTRP differs from the DTRP in two major aspects. First, the geographical locations of a subset of the customers to be serviced are already known by the dispatcher before the server leaves the depot. Note also that the service times of advance as well as immediate requests are not known to the dispatcher, until the service at the respective customers is completed. Second, the problems seek to optimize different objective functions. In a pure dynamic model it makes good sense to seek to minimize the overall system time. This has been defined as the sum of the waiting time and the on-site service time of the demands. However, in a partially dynamic setting the dispatcher may be more interested in minimizing the distance traveled by the repairman. Nevertheless, the immediate request customers should be served in some prioritized order - so that customers calling in late would not be serviced before customers that have been waiting for a relatively long period of time. Such scenarios include residential appliance repair services and courier mail pick up where customers are not offered a specific time window for service. For example, the advance request customers could have their appliances fixed in the morning and the immediate request customers in the afternoon.

Routing Policies

We consider several heuristics originally analyzed by Bertsimas and Van Ryzinm (1991) for the DTRP. We give below a brief description of these policies:

- First Come First Serve (FCFS).

The demands are served in the order in which they are received by the dispatcher.

- Stochastic Queue Median (SQM).

This is a modification of the FCFS rule where the server travels directly from the median of the service region to the next demand location. After the service has been completed, the server returns to the median and waits for the next demand.

- Nearest Neighbor (NN). ·

After completing service at one location the server travels to the nearest neighboring demand.

- Partitioning policy (PART).

The service region is partitioned into a number of smaller subregions, n_{subreg}, in which the demands are served using an FCFS policy.

We chose these policies because they include routing cost based policies - NN, waiting time based policies - FCFS, FCFS-SQM, and a mixture of these - PART.

The FCFS policy schedules the advance requests first without considering the locations of the requests. The immediate requests are added to the schedule as they are received by the dispatcher. In scenarios with more than one advance request a more elegant version of the FCFS would take the locations of the advance requests into consider-

ation. A natural way of including this information into the policy is to construct a tour through the advance requests for instance by using the nearest neighbor method.

This gives another version of the FCFS policy which we will refer to as the Nearest Neighbor - FCFS (NN-FCFS) policy. Similarly one could argue that for the PART policy advance requests should be visited according to an NN rule rather than at random within each subregion. Hence, the PART policy examined in the remaining part of this chapter will visit all requests which were received by the dispatcher at the same time according to an NN rule. However, to customer whose requests for service are received at unique points in time the FCFS rule still applies. The FCFS-SQMrule has been shown to give asymptotically optimal system time in light traffic. However, from a routing perspective, in environments where the triangle inequality holds, this policy will always produce longer distances than FCFS. It should be noted that the number of subregions used in the PART policy parameterizes this - i.e., the number of subregions should be found by optimization. We next consider the behavior of the above policies under conditions where the number of dynamic requests varies relatively to the number of static requests.

Simulation of the PDTRP

We have simulated the PDTRP to examine the empirical behavior of certain system parameters and solution methodologies. Specifically, we have focused on the impact of the degree of dynamism on the distance traveled and the relative performance of the heuristics described above. To explore these issues, we have selected the geographic locations of the customers to be uniformly distributed in the square [0,10000] x [0,10000], with the depot located at the median, i.e., at (5000,5000). The vehicle speed was set at 40 km/h. Note that we used a scaling factor of 100 units per km, i.e., the service region is equivalent to 10 km x 10 km.

The service times were generated according to the log-normal distribution $LN(0.8777; 0.6647)$. This means that the average service time was 3 minutes, while the variance was 5. These values were chosen to resemble the service times of pick-ups and deliveries in long-distance courier mail services.

Generation of Datasets

In order to be able to examine scenarios with varying degrees of dynamism comprehensive data material was generated. In the following the process for generating the datasets will be described. Prior to the actual data generation process the expected number of customers, $E\{n_{tot}\}$, was chosen. This parameter should be seen as the number of customers we expect to generate on average over the entire dataset. The generation process of each single instance could be seen as a four step process:

1. The number of advance request customers, n_{adv}, is randomly generated in the interval $[0; E\{n_{tot}\}]$.
2. The geographic locations and the service times of n_{adv} advanced request customers are generated.

A stochastic number of immediate request customers, n_{imm}, is created using a conventional Poisson process with the length of the time horizon, T, equal to eight hours. The intensity parameter of the Poisson process, λ, is calculated from the following expression:

$$\lambda = \frac{E\{n_{tot}\} - n_{adv}}{T} \qquad (6)$$

4. The geographic locations and the service times of n_{imm} immediate request customers are generated.

In order to ensure that scenarios with the same degree of dynamism are represented in the dataset by the same number of instances we continue to generate new instances, until we have exactly n_{rep} instances with $dod = \{0,5,10,\ldots,95,100\}\%$. All other instances will be rejected. The process of generating datasets could be summarized as shown in the algorithm 1 shown in Figure 9. The data generation algorithm was implemented in the Java Builder programming language. Three different settings were considered. In Scenario A $E\{n_{tot}\}$ was set at 20. In Scenario B we let $E\{n_{tot}\} = 30$ and in Scenario C $E\{n_{tot}\} = 40$. Given these values, all three scenarios resulted in medium to heavy.

Traffic situations are calculated - with only little idle time for the repairman. For all three scenarios, we used $n_{rep} = 50$, i.e., 50 different instances were generated for $dod = \{0,5,10,\ldots,95,100\}\%$. This means that each scenario consisted of 21 x 50 = 1050 instances in total.

Computational Results

Our computational experiments are summarized in Figures 10 through 14. Figures 10 through 12 depict the average total traveled distance by the repairman as a function of the number of immediate requests for Scenarios A, B and C, respectively. In the log files and the actual routes of a single instance of the Scenario B dataset produced by the NN-FCFS and the PART policies are shown. Immediate requests begin to be generated at 8:00 and new customers are generated according to equation 6 at rate $\lambda = 1.125$ requests/hour until the clock turns 16:00. In this case a total of 30 customers were generated, 21 of these were advance requests and the remaining 9 were immediate requests (please note that customer number 22 is an immediate customer calling in at 8:00:02 - two seconds after the calling center opens).

Using the terminology mentioned above we have $n_{tot} = 30$, $n_{adv} = 21$ and $n_{imm} = 9$. The degree of dynamism then is $dod = n_{imm}/n_{tot} = 0.3$. This

Figure 9. Algorithm to generation of datasets

Algorithm 1 Generation of datasets

Choose n_{rep}
Choose $E\{n_{tot}\}$
repeat
   Find n_{adv} by sampling $U(0, E\{n_{tot}\})$
   Generate customer data for n_{adv} advance request customers.
   Find λ according to equation 5.1.
   repeat
      Find the request time for the i'th immediate customer by sampling
      $P(\lambda)$.
      Generate customer data for the i'th immediate request customer.
   until $(time = T)$
   Calculate the *dod*.
   if $(dod\ MOD\ 5 = 0)$ & $(|D(dod)| < n_{rep})$ **then**
      Accept instance and increment $|D(dod)|$ by 1.
   end if
until $(|D(dod)| = n_{rep} \forall i)$

Figure 10. Scenario A: The distance traveled as a function of the degree of dynamism in the system

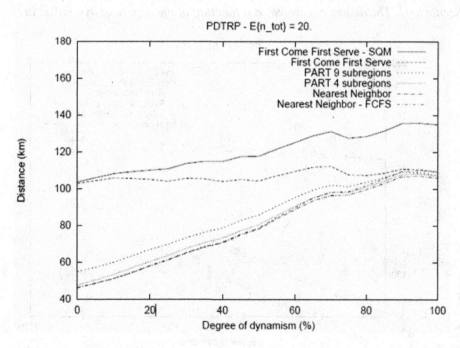

Figure 11. Scenario B: The distance traveled as a function of the degree of dynamism in the system

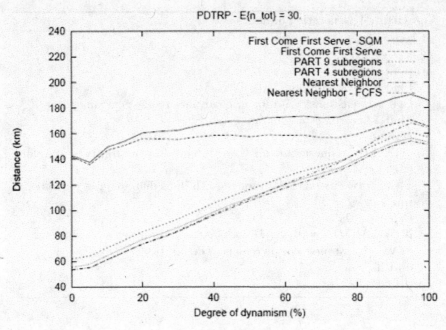

Figure 12. Scenario C: The distance traveled as a function of the degree of dynamism in the system

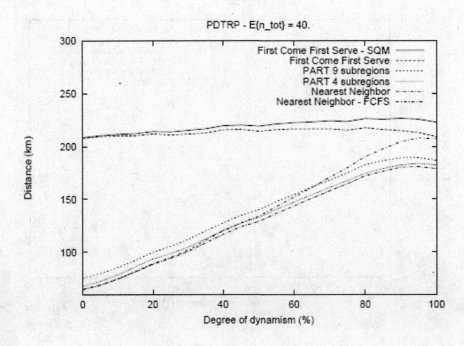

Figure 13. The busy time of the repairman for scenarios A, B and C as a function of the degree of dynamism in the system

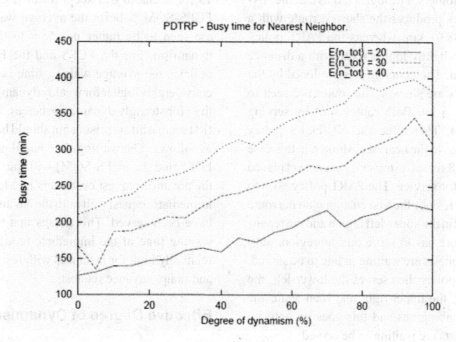

Figure 14. Scenario C: The distance as a function of the degree of dynamism for the different versions of the PART policy

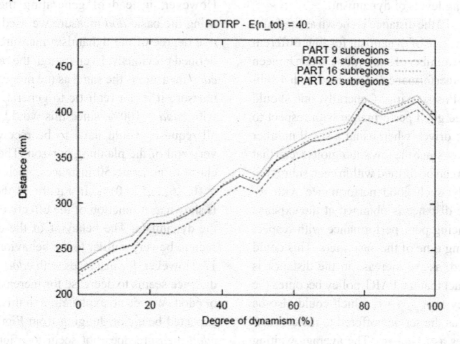

means that 30% of the customers are immediate request customers. The logies tell us that the NN-FCFS policy produces the shortest route with a length of 88.91 km, whereas the PART policy produces a slightly longer route with a distance of 89.61 km. The actual routes produced by the two policies are shown. The routes are seen to differ quite a lot. Both routes start by serving Customer 4. Thereafter, the NN-FCFS policy chooses to go to the nearest customer, in this case Customer 18 since Customer 25 has not yet placed its request for service. The PART policy goes to Customer 11, since the first customer on the route was located in the upper-left region and the repairman therefore has to serve this subregion, until no more requests are waiting in line to be served. The PART policy then serves the lower-left, the lower-right, the upper-right and then again the upper-left subregions and this goes on until no more requests are waiting to be served.

Figure 11 shows the average number of minutes the repairman is busy serving or traveling to customers as a function of the degree of dynamism. The busy time is seen to increase considerably for increasing levels of dynamism.

In Figure 12 the distance is shown as the function of the degree of dynamism for four different values of the number of subregions. It can be seen that the best performance is obtained with 4 subregions for this scenario. Generally, one should expect to see good performance with respect to the distance driven when using a small number of subregions, since the few subregions mean that good routes can be formed within each subregion

Naturally, such good performance with respect to the distance is obtained at the expense of experiencing poor performance with respect to the waiting time of the customers. This could be explained, as the increase in the distance is due to the fact that the PART policy becomes the FCFS policy as $n_{subreg} \rightarrow \infty$, which could also be formulated as the service offered to the customers increases as $n_{subreg} \rightarrow \infty$. The average waiting time of the immediate requests are shown as a

function of the degree of dynamism in Figure 13 for Scenario C. Except for the FCFS and the FCFS-SQM policies the average waiting times are seen to be rather invariant to the level of dynamism. For the FCFS and the FCFS-SQM policies the average waiting time is seen to be considerably higher for weakly dynamic instances than for strongly dynamic instances. This may at first seem a bit surprising but should be explained as follows: The waiting time based policies (the FCFS and the FCFS-SQM) will start by serving the advance request customers and let the (few) immediate request wait until the advance requests have been served. This means that the average waiting time of the immediate requests will be relatively high for instances with few immediate and many advance requests.

Effective Degree of Dynamism

In addition to the three scenarios we also considered a special instance of Scenario C. We will refer to this scenario as Scenario C*. As for the other scenarios we generated 50 different instances. However, instead of generating the instance using the basic *dod* measure we used the effective degree of the dynamism measure, *edod,* as defined previously. Even though the range of the *edod* measure is the same as the range of the *dod* measure it is not realistic to generate instances with *edod* = 100%, since this would mean that all requests would have to be received at the very end of the planning horizon. Therefore we chose to generate 50 instances, each with *edod* = {0,3,6,...,57,60}%. In Figure 14 the distance is shown as a function of the effective degree of the dynamism. The behavior of the distance is seen to be very similar to the behavior of Figure 12. However, for instances with *edod* > 50% the distance seems to decrease for increasing values of edod. We see no explanation to this rather unexpected behavior. Judging from Figure 15, the *edod* measure does not seem to offer anything special not already captured by the more simple

Figure 15. Scenario C: The average waiting time of the immediate requests as a function of the degree of the dynamism

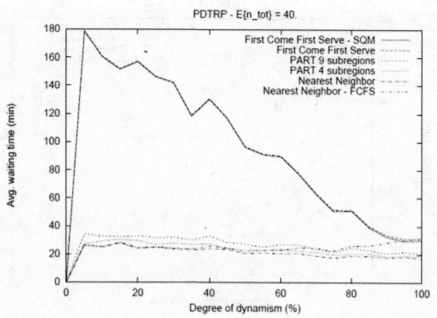

dod measure. During the tests we tried to generate 50 instances each with *edod* = {0,4,8,...,76,80}%. However, after more than 3000 minutes of computation time on an HP/9000-785 computer only instances with *edod* ≤ 68% were complete and only 7 instances with *edod* = 72 and none with *edod* > 76% were generated.

General Observations

For all three scenarios one also notes that as the level of dynamism becomes stronger, the behavior of NN increasingly resembles that of FCFS. This is because the presence of larger numbers of immediate request customers spreads their scheduling over time, implicitly decreasing the set of neighbors each customer has at any given point in time. At the higher end of dynamism the customer currently being serviced may only have one neighbor - the next immediate request customer. Hence, as the level of dynamism increases, we observe an expected transition from a geographical to a temporal emphasis. Furthermore, the figures

illustrate that the average total distances for the FCFS and the FCFS-SQM policies were almost independent of the degree of dynamism. The difference was larger in Scenario A than in B and C (Figure 16) since the repairman had slightly more idle time with only 20 expected customers to serve (ref. to Figure 12. Finally, the PART policy, based on a mixture of routing costs and waiting time, produced intermediate route lengths.

EXTENSIONS

In this section future research issues for refining the proposed PDTRP will be discussed. The use of a-priori information on future requests seems to be an interesting issue for further research. However, such information may not be known for the length of the operational horizon or for the whole region. Nevertheless, information may be known for a shorter time period and clustered geographically. A simple algorithm would divide the service region into smaller subregions and the

Figure 16. Scenario C: The distance as a function of the effective degree of dynamism

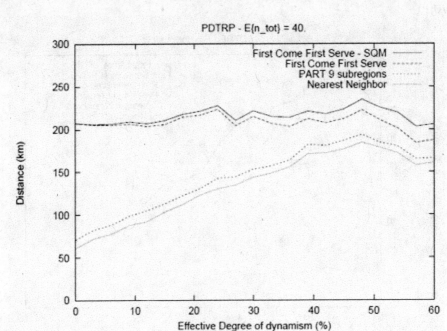

Figure 17. Algorithm to determine a busiest subregion

Algorithm 2 "Go to the busiest" subregion

Choose Δt
Estimate λ_i
Initialize *time*
repeat
    for $i = 1$ to n_{subreg} **do**
        $E\{n_{tot_i}\} = \Delta t \cdot \lambda_i + n_{adv_i}$
    end for
    $sub\_region = \max_i E\{n_{tot_i}\}$
    Serve sub_region
    Update *time*
until ($time \geq T$) and (all requests are served)

where

λ_i	denotes the arrival rate of the Poisson process generating the immediate request customers in subregion i.
n_{adv_i}	denotes the number of advance requests in subregion i.
n_{tot_i}	denotes the number of total (advance + immediate) requests in subregion i.
Δt	denotes the time interval to look forward.

Figure 18. Urban Dyoram Map with locations to each sport using Intelligent Logistics

day of operation into time periods. The a-priori information on the arrival intensity of immediate requests could then be used to find and serve the subregion with the highest number of expected requests in the next time period. The basic idea of such an algorithm is outlined in algorithm 2, see in Figure 17.

Each time a new set of demands has been collected in a region, a policy minimizing the route length could be used. If updates have to be done frequently, a simple policy like the Nearest Neighbor should be used, while in cases with few updates a more computational requiring method like the Traveling Salesman Policy should be used. Another interesting issue for further research would be to examine other criteria such as the total schedule time. For example, the FCFS-SQM policy forces the repairman to return to a central position, when he is idle with the expectation of decreased waiting times of future requests. This aspect can only be captured by time-oriented objectives.

CONCLUSION AND FUTURE RESEARCH

In this chapter, was describe a real Logistics Resolution from Fresnillo in Mexico using diverse Artificial Intelligence Techniques and Partially Dynamic Traveling Repairman Problem which was proposed to resolve this situation and was introduced with a number of different routing policies to minimize routing costs which were examined. The empirical study conducted illustrated a linear relationship between the degree of dynamism and the route cost in fairly busy systems. The simulation test runs also suggested the use of a Nearest Neighbor policy over the other policies examined. Finally, an extension of the degree of dynamism measure was briefly examined. However, the computational study did not show any benefits obtained by using the extended measure over the basic one.

In a new project using Cultural Algorithms and Intelligent Logistics was possible built an Urban Dyoram (Figure 18) to establish the best locations to practice different sports in a largest City (Ochoa et al., 2011), this research will be supported by CIS Research at Juarez City University in Mexico.

This research will be intend to reduce the high incidence of violence and social isolation in Juarez City in Mexico considered as the most violent city on the World.

REFERENCES

Andersen, A. T. (1995). *Modelling of packet traffic with matrix analytic methods* (Doctoral dissertation). Lyngby, Denmark: IMM, The Technical University of Denmark.

Bertsimas, D., & Van Ryzin, G. (1991). A stochastic and dynamic vehicle routing problem in the Euclidean Plane. *Operations Research, 39,* 601–615. doi:10.1287/opre.39.4.601

Dial, R. B. (1995). Autonomous dial a ride transit – Introductory overview. *Transportation Research Part C, Emerging Technologies, 3,* 261–275. doi:10.1016/0968-090X(95)00010-G

Gendreau, M., & Potvin, J.-Y. (1998). Dynamic vehicle routing and dispatching . In Crainic, T. G., & Laporte, G. (Eds.), *Fleet management and logistics* (pp. 115–126). Boston, MA: Kluwer Academic. doi:10.1007/978-1-4615-5755-5_5

Jensen, C. N. (1997). *Nonlinear systems with discrete and continuous elements* (Doctoral dissertation). Lyngby, Denmark: IMM, The Technical University of Denmark.

Jørgensen, M. (1984). *Distribution of everyday necessities - Minimization of the fleet size* (Master's thesis). Lyngby, Denmark: IMM, The Technical University of Denmark.

Larsen, A., Madsen Oli, B. G., & Solomon, M. M. (1999). *Partially dynamic vehicle routing - Models and algorithms (Tech. Rep.).* Lyngby, Denmark: The Department of Mathematical Modelling, The Technical University of Denmark.

Larson, R. C., & Odoni, A. R. (1980). *Urban operations research.* Upper Saddle River, NJ: Prentice Hall.

Lund, K., Madsen Oli, B. G., & Rygaard, J. M. (1996). *Vehicle routing problems with varying degrees of dynamism (Tech. Rep.).* Lyngby, Denmark: IMM, The Department of Mathematical Modelling, The Technical University of Denmark.

Malandraki, C. (1989). *Time dependent vehicle routing problems: Formulations, solution algorithms and computational experiments* (Unpublished doctoral dissertation). Northwestern University, New York, NY.

Ochoa, A., et al. (2011). Decision support system based on cultural algorithms to organize sportive promotion in a largest city. In *Proceedings of the First Bioinspired Algorithms Workshop*, Morelia, México.

Ochoa, A., Hernández, A., González, S., Castro, A., Gelbukh, A., Hernández, A., & Iztebegovič, H. (2008). Social data mining to improve bioinspired intelligent systems . In Giannopoullou, E. G. (Ed.), *Data mining in medical and biological research.* Vienna, Austria: I-Tech.

Papastavrou, J. D. (1996). A stochatic and dynamic routing policy using branching processes with state dependent immigration. *European Journal of Operational Research, 95*(1), 167–177. doi:10.1016/0377-2217(95)00189-1

Powell, W. B., Jaillet, P., & Odonim, A. (1995). Stochastic and dynamic networks and routing . In Ball, M. O., Magnanti, T. L., Monma, C. L., & Nemhauser, G. L. (Eds.), *Network routing* (pp. 141–295). Amsterdam, The Netherlands: Elsevier Science. doi:10.1016/S0927-0507(05)80107-0

Rosholm, A. (1987). *Statistical methods for segmentation and classification of images* (Doctoral dissertation). Lyngby, Denmark: IMM, The Technical University of Denmark.

Ross, S. M. (1990). *A course in simulation*. New York, NY: Maxwell Macmillan International.

Sommer, H. M. (1997). *Variability in microbiological degradation experiments - Analysis and case study* (Doctoral dissertation). Lyngby, Denmark: IMM, The Technical University of Denmark.

ADDITIONAL READING

Beniaminy, I., Yellin, D., Zahavi, U., & Zerdin, M. (2009). When the rubber meets the road: Bio-inspired field service scheduling in the real world. In Pereira, F. B., & Tavares, J. (Eds.), *Bio-inspired algorithms for the vehicle routing problem: Studies in computational intelligence* (*Vol. 161*). New York, NY: Springer. doi:10.1007/978-3-540-85152-3_9

Cheong, C. Y., & Tan, K. C. (2009). Hybridizing problem-specific operators with meta-heuristics for solving the multi-objective vehicle routing problem with stochastic demand. In Pereira, F. B., & Tavares, J. (Eds.), *Bio-inspired algorithms for the vehicle routing problem: Studies in computational intelligence* (*Vol. 161*). New York, NY: Springer. doi:10.1007/978-3-540-85152-3_5

Esparcia-Alcázar, A., Cardós, M., Merelo Guervós, J. J., Martínez-García, A., García-Sánchez, P., Alfaro-Cid, E., & Sharman, K. (2009). EVITA: An integral evolutionary methodology for the inventory and transportation problem. In Pereira, F. B., & Tavares, J. (Eds.), *Bio-inspired algorithms for the vehicle routing problem: Studies in computational intelligence* (*Vol. 161*). New York, NY: Springer. doi:10.1007/978-3-540-85152-3_7

Ombuki-Berman, B. M., & Hanshar, F. (2009). Using genetic algorithms for multi-depot vehicle routing. In Pereira, F. B., & Tavares, J. (Eds.), *Bio-inspired algorithms for the vehicle routing problem: Studies in computational intelligence* (*Vol. 161*). New York, NY: Springer. doi:10.1007/978-3-540-85152-3_4

Pereira, F. B., & Tavares, J. (Eds.). (2009). *Bio-inspired algorithms for the vehicle routing problem: Studies in computational intelligence* (*Vol. 161*). New York, NY: Springer. doi:10.1007/978-3-540-85152-3

Prins, C. (2009). A GRASP × Evolutionary local search hybrid for the vehicle routing problem. In Pereira, F. B., & Tavares, J. (Eds.), *Bio-inspired algorithms for the vehicle routing problem: Studies in computational intelligence* (*Vol. 161*). New York, NY: Springer. doi:10.1007/978-3-540-85152-3_2

Repoussis, P. P., Tarantilis, C. D., & Ioannou, G. (2009). An evolutionary algorithm for the open vehicle routing problem with time windows. In Pereira, F. B., & Tavares, J. (Eds.), *Bio-inspired algorithms for the vehicle routing problem: Studies in computational intelligence* (*Vol. 161*). New York, NY: Springer. doi:10.1007/978-3-540-85152-3_3

Van Hemert, J. I., & La Poutré, J. A. (2009). Exploiting fruitful regions in dynamic routing using evolutionary computation. In Pereira, F. B., & Tavares, J. (Eds.), *Bio-inspired algorithms for the vehicle routing problem: Studies in computational intelligence* (*Vol. 161*). New York, NY: Springer. doi:10.1007/978-3-540-85152-3_6

KEY TERMS AND DEFINITIONS

Bin Packing: Intelligent algorithm used by the accommodation of object with the intention of improve the space.

Cultural Algorithm: Bioinspired algorithm based on an artificial society and related with a population, their belief space and a time horizon measured in époques.

Logistics: Group of techniques to improve services and products related with a variety of economical activities and their commercialization in different locations.

Vehicle Routing Problem: Technique used on Logistics to resolve the problem of delivery products and services and affected by time and resources with the intention to reduce them to obtain more benefits.

Chapter 2
Logistics for the Garbage Collection through the use of Ant Colony Algorithms

Julio Cesar Ponce Gallegos
Autonomous University of Aguacalientes, Mexico

Fatima Sayuri Quezada Aguilera
Autonomous University of Aguacalientes, Mexico

José Alberto Hernandez Aguilar
Autonomous University of Morelos, Mexico

Christian José Correa Villalón
Institute of Education of Aguascalientes, Mexico

ABSTRACT

The contribution of this chapter is to present an approach to explain the Ant Colony System applied on the Waste Collection Problem, because waste management is moving up to the concern over health and environmental impacts. These algorithms are a framework for decision makers in order to analyze and simulate various spatial waste management problems. In the last decade, metaheuristics have become increasingly popular for effectively confronting difficult combinatorial optimization problems. In the present work, an individual metaheuristic Ant Colony System (ACS) algorithm is introduced, implemented and discussed for the identification of optimal routes in the case Solid Waste collection. This algorithm is applied to a waste collection and transport system, obtaining recollection routes with the less total distance with respect to the actual route utilized and to the solution obtained by a previously developed approach.

DOI: 10.4018/978-1-4666-0297-7.ch002

Figure 1. Life-cycle of waste generation

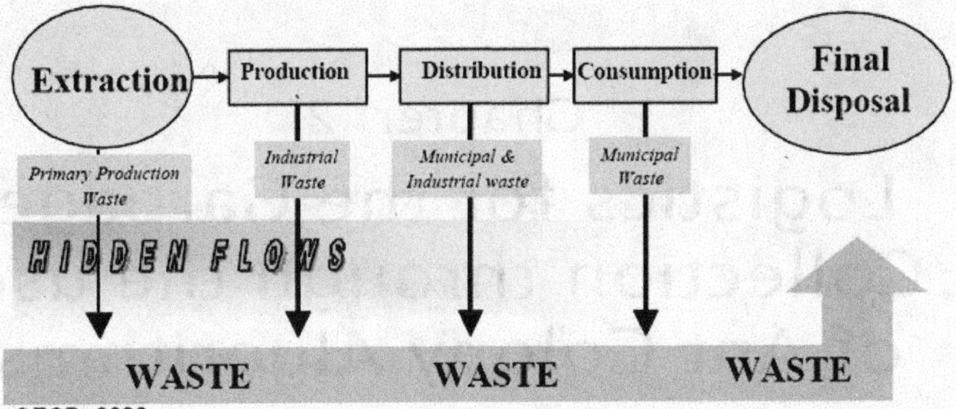

Source: OECD, 2000.

1. INTRODUCTION

Solid waste management is undoubtedly an increasingly important element in terms of efficiency and profitability for any municipality, particularly in industrialized nations. Its especially complex dimension is a result not only of the direct relationship with a number of factors that originate the living standard of a society, but also of our continuously rising consuming lifestyle which analogically enhances the existing operational difficulties.

Sustainable waste management is moving up to the concern over health and environmental impacts. Special emphasis, particularly in industrial-ized nations, is placed on concrete, comprehensive analysis of the waste management situation. To the extent possible, is necessary to highlight the areas in which an efficient improvement is feasible and how these goals derived from the objectives and principles of the waste management act can be achieved, while making available an appropriate basis of information (Figure 1 and Table 1).

Some critical areas for solid waste collection are:

- Solid Waste Collection Vehicle Routing
- Waste Characterization Studies
- Sustainable Development

Table 1. Global dimensions of solid waste problem

Factor	Observation
Population	By 2050 the global population is projected to be 50% larger than today (i.e., 9 billion people), and 95% of that growth is expected to occur in developing countries.
Consumption	Consumers in certain rapidly expanding non-OECD economies are emulating the ecologically challenging consumption patterns of consumers in OECD countries.
Affluence	Some of the highest GDP growth rates in the world is taking place in countries outside the developed world, such as China, India, Brazil, and Indonesia.
Technology	The World Bank reports that "massive levels" of industrial investment will occur in developing countries (Hanrahan 1995). In principle, "leap-frogging" the dirty technologies of the past may be possible because many developing countries have fewer sunken costs in older "eco-unfriendly" technologies.
Impact	A five -fold increase in global waste generation is possible by 2025.

Source: OECD, 2000.

- Expert Witness Services – environmental, solid waste management and transportation industry sectors
- Operational Performance Assessments (OPAs) for Collection Companies, Material Recovery Facilities (MRFs), and Transfer Stations
- Solid Waste Collection Rate Studies, Analysis and Recommendations
- Fleet Management – maintenance cost analysis and payload logistics
- Disposal Site Optimization Studies / Analysis
- Waste-by-Rail – track layout, intermodal facility layout, railroad negotiations, feasibility studies
- Transfer Trucking Operations – equipment optimization, payload maximization analysis, carrier contract management and negotiations
- Solid Waste Collection Cost of Service Analysis
- Solid Waste Efficiency Studies
- Transportation and Disposal Feasibility Studies
- Logistical Analysis for Facility Sitings
- Waste Diversion
- Solid Waste Strategic Management Plans
- Landfill Alternative Technologies

Actually, there have been numerous technological advances, new developments, mergers and acquisitions in the waste industry. The result is that both private and municipal haulers are giving serious consideration to new technologies such as computerized vehicle routing solutions (Nuortioa, 2005). It has been estimated that, of the total amount of money spent for the collection, transportation, and the disposal of solid waste, approximately 60–80% is spent on the collection phase (Municipality of Athens, 2003). Therefore, it can be proved extremely beneficial planning waste recovery in an environmentally friendly and economically viable way.

The routing optimization problem in waste management has been already explored with a number of evolutionary algorithms. The complexity of the problem is high due to many alternatives that have to be considered. Cost reduction strategies in solid waste routing may include minimizing the number of truck trips to disposal site, or optimizing the collection routing, thus minimizing the traveled distance and traveling time.

Fortunately, many algorithms have been developed and discussed in order to find an optimized solution, leading to various different results. The reason for this diversity is that the majority of routing algorithms include the use of heuristic algorithms. Heuristic algorithms are ad hoc trial-and-error methods which do not guarantee to find the optimal solution but are designed to find near-optimal solutions in a fraction of the time required by optimal methods.

In the last years, much effort has been made in Urban Solid Waste Collection and Transport Management. The problem can be classified as either a Vehicle Routing Problem. For this particular problem, several solutions and models have been proposed (Karadimas, 2005).

Both residential and commercial collection problems can be classified as a variation of vehicle routing problems with time windows (VRPTW), but with additional constraints. In the literature, a typical vehicle routing problem (VRP) is comprised of a set of vehicles, stops, and a depot. Each vehicle starts from the depot, visits a number of stops, and ends at the depot. Depending on the nature of each application, VRP may possess different characteristics, including types of vehicles (homogeneous or heterogeneous) and number of depots (single or multiple). VRPTW is defined as VRP extended by additional time constraints associated with each stop. Similarly, the depot also has a time window. Each vehicle has a single capacity constraint, such as maximum volume or maximum travel time. The objective function(s) generally minimizes total costs – total travel time. The VRPTW is NP-hard and makes possible finding a feasible solution with a fixed fleet size is an NP-complete problem (Cordeau et al., 2002).

Other characteristic that can be use in the simulation of this problem is the deferent types of garbage truck. A garbage truck, known as a dustcart or dustbin wagon, is a truck specially designed to haul waste to landfills and other recycling / disposal facilities. They are a common sight in most urban areas. There are two basic models of garbage truck:

- Front Loaders generally service commercial and industrial sites using dumpsters. They have large prongs on the front which are carefully aligned with arms on the dumpster. The dumpster is then lifted over the truck, until it is upside-down and the trash will then fall out into the receptacle.
- Rear Loaders commonly service residential areas. They have an opening at the rear that a trash collector can throw garbage bags or empty the contents of trash cans into. Often (particularly in Europe) they have a lifting mechanism to automatically empty wheeled bins (from both residential and commercial premises) without the operator having to lift the waste by hand. They are usually equipped with some type of compactor that will compress the garbage, and move it towards the front of the vehicle.

Side loaders are versions of either front or rear loaders that lift small trash containers or have openings on either side to deposit trash. Some side loaders are equipped with a mechanical remote-control arm that grasps a trash container such as a wheeled bin and empties it into the truck in the same manner as front loaders. This type of garbage truck requires only one arm-operator/driver but residents must position their wheeled bins carefully near the kerb and at least two meters away from nearby objects.

There are also larger trucks that carry trash over long distances, usually modified dump trucks.

Garbage trucks empty their trash in landfills. Most rear loaders lift the rear section so that the garbage will spill out. Front loaders more commonly have a moving wall that pushes the garbage out. Some larger landfills will have large contraptions that tip the entire truck, thus allowing the trucks to do not have to carry their own method of emptying the garbage.

Is important considered the type of truck garbage in the solution of this problem.

2. THE VEHICLE ROUTING PROBLEM

The classic VRP can be stated as follows: design least-cost routes from a central depot to a set of geographically dispersed points (customers, stores, schools, cities, warehouses, etc.) with various demands. Each customer is to be serviced exactly once by only one vehicle, and each vehicle has a limited capacity. The problem can be further characterized by type of fleets, number of depots, and types of operations (pick-ups, deliveries, and mixed).

The Vehicle Routing Problem (VRP) is a combinatorial hard problem, which is related with the use of some mode of transport, with different characteristics and capacities, to deal products to locations with certain demands and constraints. The objective is to find the shortest route or the use of minimum vehicles (Vehicle Routing Problem), taking in account, that exist one or more depots and a number of locations (costumers) to visit with the available transport which have to return to depots.

The interest in VRP is the application to a great number of real problems in diverse private and public institutions with different activities; for example, mail delivery, school bus routing, solid waste collection, heating oil distribution and many others (Rizzoli, 2004), and also for the cost that implies to the companies.

2.1. VRP Description

The relevance of this problem is because is an important part of transportation and logistics which are crucial in a traditional business model. The elements of this model are: production, distribution and sales (Rizzoli, 2004). The cost of the transportation is added to the final price of any product but in some cases this cost is high. For these reason, many research have been done to improve this situation.

Disciplines like Supply Chain Management try to integrate the data and management procedures, but this was not easy because there was no integration between Enterprise Resource Planning (ERP) and the Enterprise Data Processing (EDP) system (Sodhi, 2001).

In the 90's began to integrate ERP and DRP implementing logistic system which saw the supply chain like a unique process from the start to the end, where the improvement of the transportation cost was the key of this chain.

The use of these systems allows significant savings from 5% to 20% (Toth, 2001). This is possible, even though the minimization cost is tiny, because the distribution process is carried out daily.

2.2. VRP Formulation

The VRP was defined 40 years ago (VRP, 2007) and some example is the paper published en 1959 (Dantzig, 1959). The VRP is related with two problems: Traveling Salesman Problem (TSP) and the Bin Packing Problem (BPP).

The Traveling Salesman Problem is a NP-Hard routing problem in the optimization version (Garey, 1979). This problem is about a salesman that has to visit n cities, each of them exactly once, and he/she should start and finish the tour in the same city. In this problem is considered that the transport have unlimited capacity.

Other variant of this problem is the m-TSP, where the m-salesman has to cover the n cities and each city has to be visited by only one salesman. Every salesman goes out from the same city (depot), and must return to this city again (Vehicle Routing and Traveling Salesman Problems). Until this point the VRP is like the m-TSP but, in addition, the number of vehicles is considered like minimization criterion.

The Bin Packing Problem is other NP-Hard problem (Garey, 1979) which is about to pack object of different volume in a finite number of bins with a capacity C so that the number of bin used is minimum.

In general terms, VRP try to find the optimum route to attend all customers using a fleet of vehicles (Rizzoli, 2004). The constraints that should be considered are: the vehicle capacity and the driver's maximum working time, to finally minimize the total transportation cost (including the use of minimum number of vehicles).

The VRP is a problem of Nonlinear Programming but its combinatorial nature and characteristics can be represented by a graph and on that basis describe the objective function and restrictions.

Given a graph G(V, E) where V is the vertexes set and E is the edges set, the VRP is formulated as follows (VRP, 2007):

$V = \{v_0, v_1, ..., v_n\}$ is a vertexes set, where:
v_0 is considered as a depot.
And $V' = V \setminus \{v_0\}$ be used as the set of n costumers.
$A = \{(v_i, v_j) \mid v_i, v_j \in V; i \neq j\}$ is an arc set
C is a matrix of costs (positives) or distances c_{ij} between customers v_i and v_j.
d is a vector of the customer demands.
R_i is the route for vehicle i
m is the number or vehicles with the same characteristics. One route is assigned to each vehicle.

When the problem is symmetric, it means, $c_{ij}=c_{ji}$ for all $(v_i, v_j) \in A$, then $E= \{(v_i, v_j)| v_i, v_j \in V; i<j\}$

With each vertex v_i in V' is associated a quantity q_i of some goods to be delivered by a vehicle. The VRP thus consists of determining a set of **m** vehicle routes of minimal total cost, starting and ending at a depot, such that every vertex in V' is visited exactly once by one vehicle. For easy computation, it can be defined $b(V)=[(\Sigma_{vi \in v} d_i)/C]$, an obvious lower bound on the number of trucks needed to service the customers in set V.

If is considered a service time ∂_i (time needed to unload all goods), required by a vehicle to unload the quantity q_i at **vi**. It is required that the total duration of any vehicle route (travel plus service times) may not surpass a given bound **D**, so, in this context the cost **cij** is taken to be the travel time between the cities. The VRP defined above is NP-hard (Lenstra, 1981).

The feasible solution of it can be represented as follows:

a partition $R_1,...,R_m$ of V; and
a permutation σ_i of $R_i \cup 0$ specifying the order of the customers on route **i**.

The cost of a given route (Ri=$\{ v_0, v_1, ..., v_{m+1} \}$), where $v_i \in V$ and $v_0=v_{m+1}=0$ (0 denotes the depot), is given by:

$$C(Ri\}) = \sum_{i=0}^{m} C_{i,i+1} + \sum_{i=1}^{m} \partial_i \qquad (1)$$

A route R_i is feasible if the vehicle stop exactly once in each customer and the total duration of the route does not exceed a pre-specified bound D: $C(R_i) \leq D$.

Finally, the cost of the problem solution S is:

$$F_{VRP}(S) = \sum_{i=0}^{m} C(R_i) \qquad (2)$$

2.2.1. Variants

There exist few variants of VRP (Table 2) depending on the constraints of the particular problem. Then, is presented a brief description each one of them (The VRP Web).

3. ANT COLONY OPTIMIZATION

This section describes the Ant Colony System (ACS), is a meta heuristic inspired in the behavior of natural ant colonies to solve combinatorial optimization problems, based on simple agents that work cooperatively communicating by artificial pheromone trails. The description starts with the ant metaphor, which is a model of real ants of how they look for food sources. Then, it follows a discussion of how Ant System has evolved. Ant Colony System Algorithm is the base of the logistic application for the waste collection.

3.1. Behavior of Ant Colony

The Ant System was inspired by collective behavior of real ants. While they search of food, they deposit a chemical substance on in the crossed way. This substance is called pheromone. The Pheromone communication is an effective way of coordinating the activities in the colony. For this reason, pheromone rapidly influences the behavior of the ants: they will tend to take those paths where there is a larger amount of pheromone.

This behavior followed by real ants is modeled as a probabilistic process with artificial ants. In the beginning do not exist an amount of pheromone, and the ants explore the neighboring area in a totally random way. In presence of an amount of pheromone, the ants follow a path in a controlled random way.

With crossed paths, the ant will follow the trail with the largest amount of pheromone with a higher probability. During the traveling all ants deposit additional pheromone in his path, then

Table 2. Variants of Vehicle Routing Problem

Variant	Description	Objective	Principal constraint
Capacitated VRP – CVRP	CVRP is a Vehicle Routing Problem (VRP) in which a fixed fleet of delivery vehicles of uniform capacity must service known customer demands for a single commodity from a common depot at minimum transit cost. That is, CVRP is like VRP with the additional constraint that every vehicle must have uniform capacity of a single commodity.	The objective is to minimize the vehicle fleet and the sum of travel time, and the total demand of commodities for each route may not exceed the capacity of the vehicle which serves that route.	Every vehicle has a limited capacitate
VRP with time windows – VRPTW	The VRPTW is the same problem that VRP with the additional restriction that in VRPTW a time window is associated with each customer, defining an interval wherein the customer has to be supplied. The interval at the depot is called the scheduling horizon.	The objective is to minimize the vehicle fleet and the sum of travel time and waiting time needed to supply all customers in their required hours.	Every customer has to be supplied within a certain time window
Multiple Depot VRP – MDVRP	A company may have several depots from which it can serve its customers. If the customers are clustered around depots, then the distribution problem should be modeled as a set of independent VRPs. However, if the customers and the depots are intermingled then a Multi-Depot Vehicle Routing Problem should be solved. A MDVRP requires the assignment of customers to depots. A fleet of vehicles is based at each depot. Each vehicle originates from one depot, service the customers assigned to that depot, and return to the same depot.	The objective is to minimize the vehicle fleet and the sum of travel time, and the total demand of commodities must be served from several depots.	The vendor uses many depots to supply the customers
VRP with Pick-Up and Delivering - VRPPD	The Vehicle Routing Problem with Pick-up and Delivering (VRPPD) is a VRP in which the possibility that customers return some commodities is contemplated. So in VRPPD it's needed to take into account that the goods that customers return to the delivery vehicle must fit into it. This restriction makes the planning problem more difficult and can lead to bad utilization of the vehicles capacities, increased travel distances or a need for more vehicles. Hence, it is usually to consider restricted situations where all delivery demands start from the depot and all pick-up demands shall be brought back to the depot, so there are no interchanges of goods between the customers. Another alternative is relaxing the restriction that all customers have to be visited exactly once. Another usual simplification is to consider that every vehicle must deliver all the commodities before picking up any goods.	The objective is to minimize the vehicle fleet and the sum of travel time, with the restriction that the vehicle must have enough capacity for transporting the commodities to be delivered and those ones picked-up at customers for returning them to the depot.	Customers may return some goods to the depot

Continued on following page

the food-search process evolves with positive feedback. Since the pheromone evaporates, the non-used trails tend to disappear slowly, increasing the positive feedback effect. In this stochastic process, the best ant receives reward with the highest amount of pheromone, while the worst ant is punished with the lowest amount of pheromone (Ochoa, 2011).

Table 2. Variants

Variant	Description	Objective	Principal constraint
Split Delivery VRP - SDVRP	SDVRP is a relaxation of the VRP wherein it is allowed that the same customer can be served by different vehicles if it reduces overall costs. This relaxation is very important if the sizes of the customer orders are as big as the capacity of a vehicle. It is more difficult to obtain the optimal solution in the SDVRP that in the VRP.	The objective is to minimize the vehicle fleet and the sum of travel time needed to supply all customers.	The customers may be served by different vehicles
Stochastic VRP - SVRP	Stochastic VRP (SVRP) are VRPs where one or several components of the problem are random. Three different kinds of SVRP are the next examples:	The objective is to minimize the vehicle fleet and the sum of travel time needed to supply all customers with random values on each execution for the customers to be served, their demands and/or the service and travel times.	Some values (like number of customers, theirs demands, serve time or travel time) are random
Periodic VRP – PVRP	In classical VRPs, typically the planning period is a single day. In the case of the Period Vehicle Routing Problem (PVRP), the classical VRP is generalized by extending the planning period to M days.	The objective is to minimize the vehicle fleet and the sum of travel time needed to supply all customers.	The deliveries may be done in some days
VRP with Satellite Facilities	An important aspect of the vehicle routing problem (VRP) that has been largely overlooked is the use of satellite facilities to replenish vehicles during a route. When possible, satellite replenishment allows the drivers to continue making deliveries until the close of their shift without necessarily returning to the central depot. This situation arises primarily in the distribution of fuels and certain retail items.		

3.2. Artificial Ants

The Ant System was inspired in the natural optimization process followed by real ants, this algorithm was developed by Dorigo (1991). The algorithm is a general frame than can be applied to the solution of many combinatorial optimization problems. The artificial society, formed by ants, repeats the food-search process. Each ant builds one path that represents a solution to the optimization problem. The ants share a pheromone structure, which is a common memory (global information) that is used to guide the search process; this can be accessed and updated simultaneously.

The Ant System is considered a multi-agent system where low level interactions between single ant-agent (artificial ant) result in a complex behavior of the whole ant colony. Each ant-agent has incomplete information or insufficient skill to solve a problem. They need the whole colony to get the final objective (food source).

The simulation of this kind of collaboration, there is not global control, data is decentralized, and the computation is asynchronous. Besides, the ant colonies exhibit an emergent behavior. This emergent conduct happens because they build their result in an incremental manner, thus algorithms are considered constructive. The ant colonies are considered adaptive, complex and distributed multi-agent systems.

The Ant Colony Optimization algorithms are based on the following idea (Karadimas et al., 2008):

- Each path followed by an ant on a graph is associated with a candidate solution for a given problem. Ants perform stochastic walks in the graph, consisting of a series of stochastic steps until the termination criterion is reached.

- When an ant follows a path, the amount of pheromone deposited on that path is proportional to the quality of the corresponding candidate solution for the target problem. Moreover, artificial pheromone evaporation is often used to avoid premature convergence on a suboptimal solution (stagnation).

- When an ant has to choose between two or more paths, the path(s) with a higher amount of pheromone has a greater probability of being chosen by the ant. What is relevant to realize is that a stochastic choice is made based on the probability distribution. The possibility of an ant choosing a path with low probability is often decisive because it enables the discovery of new solutions. The stochastic state transition rule is responsible for defining the relevance of different local variables, like the emphasis on pheromone values or other local heuristics.

The Ant System Algorithms was originally proposed to solve only two problems: the Traveling Salesman Problem (TSP), and the Quadratic Assignment Problem (QAP). Nowadays exist several variants of Ant System designed to solve specific problems or to extend the characteristics of the basic algorithm. Now is possible to solve a lot of problems like scheduling, machine learning, data mining (Ponce et al., 2009), among others. Next the most important variants of this algorithm are described in order of appearance: Ant Colony

Optimization (ACO) was introduced initially by Dorigo (1991). The Ant Colony Optimization algorithms use two main characteristics: ηij *(heuristic information)* and τij *(pheromone concentration)*. The heuristic information ηij is used to measure the predilection to travel between a pair of nodes (i,j). The trails of artificial pheromone τrs is used to compute the learned reference of traveling in a determined arc (i,j). It is formed by three algorithms: Ant-density, Ant-quantity and Ant-Cycle. Ant-density and Ant-quantity use the update of pheromone trails in every step of the ants, while Ant-Cycle makes updates after a complete cycle of the ant. A study realized by Dorigo of the correct configuration of Ant System for solving Traveling Salesman Problem concludes that the main parameter is β, the relative importance of the heuristic information. The study establishes that the optimal number of ants is equivalent to the number of nodes of the problem (Ochoa, 2010).

The Ant-Q was development by Gambardela and Dorigo in 1995, the Ant-Q algorithm is an algorithm with learning, which is based on the principles of Q-learning. It was applied for solving the Traveling Salesman Problem and Asymmetric Traveling Salesman Problem (ATSP). Ant-Q uses a table of values Q to indicate how good a determined movement from node r to s is. It applies a rule to choose the next node to be visited and uses reinforcement learning to update Q with the best tour of the ants (Gambardela, 1995).

Max-Min Ant System algorithm (MMAS) was developed by Stützle and Hoose (1996). It uses the elements of AS. However, it modifies three aspects: updating rule, pheromone values, and the next movement. The updating rule was modified to choose the best tour in every cycle, increasing the probability of early stagnation, Maximum and minimum limits for the pheromone trails were established. These limits avoid repeated movements: bounding the influence of the trail intensity, and leading to a higher degree of exploration.

Other variant of Ant System, named ASrank, was developed by Bullnheimer et al. (1997). All solutions are ranked according to their fitness. The amount of deposited pheromone is weighted for each solution, such that the best result deposits more pheromone than bad solutions. This algorithm was tested with Traveling Salesman Problem and VRP instances. The developed technique is based on the Distributed Q-Leaning algorithm (DQL).

3.3. Ant Colony System (ACS)

Dorigo and Gambardela (1996) improved Ant System with an algorithm named Ant Colony System (ACS). It presents three main differences with regard to Ant System:

- New Achievements in Evolutionary Computation transition rule, global updating and local updating.
- The transition-state rule is modified to establish a balance between the exploration of new arcs and the priority exploitation of a problem.
- The global updating rule is applied only to the arcs of the best ant tour. A local updating of the pheromone is done while ants build a solution.

The Ant Colony System was applied to Traveling Salesman Problem and Asymmetric Traveling Salesman Problem with the addition of a local search based on a 3-opt scheme.

The Ant Colony System is a well known algorithm is one of the best ant algorithms. Ant Colony System has the best performances and the majority of references (Asmar, 2005).

4. ANT COLONY OPTIMIZATION ALGORITHM TO SOLVE THE WASTE COLLECTION ROUTE PROBLEM

4.1. Ant Colony to the Simple Waste Collection Route in a Specific Area

In the state of the art exist several works with Ant Colony Optimization algorithm focused on the route problem, and only one of this works is tested on the solid waste collection and transport problem. Karadimas use an Ant Colony System simple to solve the route problem in a specific suburb in Athens. In the algorithm a garbage truck must travel among a set of loading spots, passing from each bin only once. The artificial colony is created and at first it randomly travels the complete circuits that contain every loading spot for the given set. During the first step, local travel closer to the loading spots is favored. After a complete circuit is determined, "pheromone" is deposited on each of link (Edge). The amount of pheromone is inversely proportional to the length of the circuit; shorter distances receive more pheromone. The colony is then released to travel circuits again, but this time ants favor links with higher concentrations of pheromone in addition to the links that are shorter. The pheromone evaporates at a constant rate, and links that are not part of efficient overall circuits eventually fall out of favor. The ant approach to this problem also provides the advantage of backup routes. Since the ants are continuously exploring different paths, alternative routes already exist if the link between two loading spots becomes unusable (Karadimas, 2005).

The development algorithm for the solution of waste collection problem was based on the Ant algorithm proposed by Dorigo (Dorigo & Maniezzo, 1996; Dorigo & Caro 1999), where each ant is a simple agent with the following characteristics:

Figure 2. The ACS algorithm

```
Ant_Colony_System ( )

Initialize Data Structures
Do
   For each ant: initialize its solution
   Do
      For each ant:
         Pseudo-random-rule(ηij, τij)is applied to build a solution
         Local-update(τij)
      Until all ants have completed their solutions
   Global-update(τij)
Until stop criteria is reached
```

- Initially an ant is placed in every loading spot. The number of ants is equal to the number of loading spots.
- Every ant chooses the bin to go to with a probability that is a function of the movement cost between two loading spots and of the amount of trail pheromone.
- Movements to already visited loading spots are disallowed until a tour is completed.
- When a tour is completed, ants update pheromone on each edge (i, j) they visited.

Figure 2 shows the pseudo code of the ACS algorithm.

As mentioned, the optimization quantity is the collecting time and not necessarily the distance of the route. Thus, the truck movement cost between loading spot i and j, is a function of all separate costs for each factor which affects the track route:

$$d_{ij} = \propto da_{ij} + \beta db_{ij} + \gamma dc_{ij} + ... \qquad (3)$$

Let $t_{ij}(t)$ be the *intensity of trail* on edge (i,j) at time t.

Each ant at time t chooses the next loading spot, where it will be at time t+1. Therefore, if we call an *iteration* of the ACO algorithm the n moves carried out by the n ants in the interval (t,

t+1), then for every n iterations of the algorithm (which we call a cycle) each ant has completed a tour. At this point the trail intensity is updated according to the following formula:

$$\tau_{ij}(t + n)\rho.\tau_{ij}(t) + \Delta\tau_{ij} \qquad (4)$$

Where ρ is a coefficient such that $(1 - \rho)$ represents the *evaporation* of trail between time t and t+n,

$$\Delta\tau_{ij} = \sum_{k=1}^{m} \Delta\tau_{ij}^{k} \qquad (5)$$

Where $\Delta\tau_{ij}$ k is the quantity per unit of length of trail substance (pheromone in real ants) laid on edge (i,j) by the k-th ant between time t and t+n; it is given by:

$$\Delta\tau_{ij}^{k} = \begin{cases} \dfrac{Q}{L_k} & \text{if k ant uses edge (i,j) in its tour} \\ 0 & \text{Otherwise} \end{cases}$$

$$\qquad (6)$$

where Q is a constant and Lk is the tour length of the k-th ant.

Table 3. Example of the 50-costumer problem in Eilon et al. (1971)

I	x-coor.	y-coor.	ρ_i
0	5.00	4.00	-
1	1.89	0.77	4-7
2	9.27	1.49	2-9
3	9.46	9.36	3-5
4	9.20	8.69	0-4

The coefficient ρ must be set to a value <1 to avoid unlimited accumulation of trail (note 1). In our experiments, we set the intensity of trail at time 0, tij(0), to a small positive constant c.

In order to satisfy the constraint that an ant visits all the n different loading spots, we associate with each ant a data structure called the *hlist*, that saves loading spots already visited up to time t and forbids the ant to visit them again before n iterations (a tour) have been completed. When a tour is completed, the *hlist* is used to compute the ant's current solution (i.e., the movement cost of the path followed by the ant). The *hlist* is then emptied and the ant is free to choose again.

$$\eta_{ij} = \frac{1}{d_{ij}} \qquad (7)$$

We call *visibility* hij the quantity 1/dij. This quantity is not modified during the run of the AS, as opposed to the trail which instead changes according to the previous formula (7). We define the transition probability from loading spot i to loading spot j for the k-th ant as

$$p_{ij}^k = \frac{\left[\tau_{ij}(t)\right]^\alpha \cdot \left[\eta_{ij}\right]^\beta}{\sum_{k \in allowed_k} \left[\tau_{ik}(t)\right]^\alpha \cdot \left[\eta_{ik}\right]^\beta} \qquad (8)$$

where allowedk = {N - *hlist*} and where a and b are parameters that control the relative importance of trail versus visibility. Therefore the transition probability is a trade-off between visibility (which states that close loading spots should be chosen with high probability, thus implementing a greedy constructive heuristic) and trail intensity at time t (which states that if there is a lot of traffic on edge (i,j) then this edge is highly desirable, thus implementing the auto catalytic process).

4.2. Ant Colony to Waste Collection Problem by Means of ACO Algorithm

The researchers Ismail and Loh propose an algorithm based on an Ant System (2009) to solve solid waste collection problem which is formulated like VRPSD model where a street or some nearby streets which had been group together as one unit is represented by the nodes (customers' locations). The customers' locations are in form of Cartesian coordinate where each point appears uniquely in a plane through two numbers, called x-coordinate and y-coordinate while demands of customers which are stochastic are recorded in a range form.

There is no open source data for VRPSD problem, they used a set of data modified from the well known 50-customer problem in Eilon et al. (1971) (Table 3).

The problem described can be modeled as a Vehicle Routing Problem with Stochastic Demand (VRPSD) as the amount of solid waste is stochastic and may be presented in a complete graph (Ismail & Irhamah, 2008) like Secomandi (2000, 2001). Let the set of nodes be {0, 1,…,n}.

Node 0 denoting the depot node and V = {1,…,n} is a set of customer locations. Distances between nodes are assumed to be symmetric and it satisfies the triangle inequality. Customers' demands are stochastic variables, ξ_i = 1, 2,…,n independently distributed with known distribution. It follows a discrete probability distribution with v possible values, $\xi_1, \xi_2,…,\xi_v$ denoted by $p_{i,k}$ = Prob ($\xi_I = \xi_k$). Actual demand is only known when the vehicle arrives at the customer location.

After the vehicle completed service at customer w, suppose the vehicle has remaining load q and let fw(q) denotes the expected cost from node w onward until the n customer and the way back to depot. With this notation, the expected cost of the a priori tour is $f_0(Q)$. The dynamic programming recursion is shown as follows (Yang et al., 2000):

$$f_w(q) = \min\{f_w^p(q), f_w^r(q)\} \qquad (9)$$

Where:

$$f_w^p(q) = c_{w,w+1} + \sum_{k:\xi^k \leq q} f_{w+1}(q - \xi^k) +$$
$$\sum_{k:\xi^k > q} \left[b + 2c_{w+1,0} + f_{w+1}(q + Q - \xi^k) \right] P_{w+1,k}$$

$$(10)$$

and

$$f_w^r(q) = c_{w,0} + c_{0,w+1} + \sum_{k=1} f_{w+1}(Q - \xi^k) P_{w+1,k}$$

$$(11)$$

with the boundary condition:

$$f_n(q) = c_{n,0} \cdot q \in S_n \qquad (12)$$

Equation 9 and 10 represents the cost of proceeding directly to the next customer and the cost of the restocking action respectively. Assume that one single vehicle with fixed capacity Q departs from the depot node to deliver goods at different customer locations according to their demands and at the same time, it has to minimize the total expected distance traveled. After all the demands have been served, the vehicle returns to the depot. The vehicle visits the customers according to the sequence in the given a priori tour. It has to choose depending on the customer's demand either proceed directly to the next customer or

return to depot for restocking. Thus, the goal of this study is find a vehicle route and a routing policy (threshold) at each node in order to minimize the total expected cost (Bianchi, 2006).

Ant Colony System is different from Ant System in three main aspects. Firstly, state transition rule gives a direct way to balance between exploration of new edges and exploitation of a priori and accumulated information about the problem. Secondly, global updating rule is applied only to those edges which belong to the best ant tour and lastly, while ants construct the tour, a local pheromone updating rule is applied.

Basically, Ant Colony System (ACS) works as follows: m ants are initially positioned on n nodes chosen according to some initialization rule such as choosing by randomly, with at most one ant in each customer point. Each ant builds a tour incrementally by applying a state transition rule. While constructing the solution, ants also updating the pheromone on the visited edges by local updating rule. Once the ants complete their tour, the pheromone on edges will be updated again by applying global updating rule. During construction of tours, ants are guided by both heuristic information and pheromone information. Heuristic information refers to the distances of the edges where ants prefer short edges. An edge with higher amount of pheromone is a desirable choice for ants. The pheromone updating rule is designed so that ants tend to leave more pheromone on the edges which should be visited by ants. The Ant Colony System algorithm is given as in Figure 2 (Dorigo & Gambardella, 1997a, 1997b). There are 3 main components which led to the definition of Ant colony System; they are state transition rule, global updating rule and local updating rule. Each of these components will be shown in detail as follow: In the ant ACS, an artificial ant k after serves customer r chooses the customer s to move to from set of Jk (r) that remain to be served by ant k by applying the following state transition rule which is also known as pseudo-random-proportional-rule:

$$s = \begin{cases} \arg\max\limits_{u \in J_k} \left\{ \dfrac{[\tau(r,u)] \cdot}{[\cdot (r,u)]^\beta} \right\} & \text{if } a \leq a_0 \text{ (exploitation)} \\ S & \text{otherwise (biased exploration)} \end{cases}$$

(13)

where:

β=The control parameter of the relative importance of the visibility

$\tau(r,u)$=The pheromone trail on edge (r,u)

$n(r,u)$=Function which was chosen to be the inverse distance between r and u

A= A random number uniformly distributed in [0,1]

$a_0 (0 \leq a_0 \leq 1)$ = A parameter

S = A random variable selected according to the probability distribution which favors edges which is shorter and higher amount of pheromone.

It is same as in Ant system and also known as random-proportional-rule given as follow

$$p_k(r,s) = \begin{cases} \dfrac{[\tau(r,s)] \cdot [\cdot (r,s)]^\beta}{\sum\limits_{u \in J_k(r)} [\tau(r,u)] \cdot [\cdot (r,u)]^\beta} & \text{if } s \in J_k(r) \\ 0 & \text{otherwise} \end{cases}$$

(14)

where, pk(r,s) is the probability of ant k after serves customer r chooses customer s to move to. The parameter of a0 determines the relative importance of exploitation versus exploration. When an ant after serves customer r has to choose the customer s to move to, a random number a $(0 \leq a \leq 1)$ is generated, if a $\leq$ a0, the best edge according to Eq. 13 is chosen, otherwise an edge is chosen according to Eq. 14 (Dorigo & Gambardella, 1997a). While building a tour, ants visits edges and change their pheromone level by applying local updating rule as follows:

$$\tau(r,s) = (1-\rho).\tau(r,s) + \rho.\Delta\tau(r,s), \; 0 < \rho < 1$$

(15)

where:

ρ = A pheromone decay parameter

$\Delta\tau(r,s) = \tau 0$ (initial pheromone level)

Local updating makes the desirability of edges change dramatically since every time an ant uses an edge will make its pheromone diminish and the edge becomes less desirable due to the loss of some of the pheromone. In other word, local updating drives the ants search not only in a neighborhood of the best previous tour.

Global updating is performed after all the ants have completed their tours. Among the tours, only the best ant which produced the best tour is allowed to deposit pheromone. This choice is intended to make the search more directed. The pheromone level is updated by a global updating rule as follow:

$$\tau(r,s) = (1-\alpha).\tau(r,s) + \alpha.\Delta\tau(r,s), \; 0 < \alpha < 1$$

(16)

Where:

$$\Delta\tau(r,s) = \begin{cases} 1/L_{gb} & \text{if } (r,s) \in \text{global - best - tour} \\ 0 & \text{otherwise} \end{cases}$$

(17)

Lgb is the length of the global best tour from the beginning of the trial. (global-best) and a is pheromone decay parameter. Global updating is intended to provide greater amount of pheromone to shorter tours. Eq. 16 dictates that only those edges belonging to globally best tour will receive reinforcement. From the experiments done by previous researchers, the numerical parameters are set as following values:

β=2, a_0=0.9, α=ρ=0.1, τ_0=(n. L_{nn})$^{-1}$

Where:

Lnn = The tour length produced by the nearest neighbor heuristic
n = The number of customers

The number of ants used is m = 10. These values were obtained by a preliminary optimization phase in which it was found that the experimental optimal values of the parameters were largely independent of the problem except for τ_0 (Dorigo & Gambardella, 1997b).

5. CONCLUSION AND FUTURE RESEARCH

In solid waste management system, collection of solid waste is the most important process for total disposal costs. In order to decrease total solid waste disposal costs, is necessary to design optimal routes for each truck to minimize the time and costs. Waste collection is a difficult problem to solve due to complex interactions between conflicting requirements and the restrictions. When a requirement is improved another one is worse, because is necessary taking in account the capacity of the trucks and the capacity of the containers. In order to solve the waste collection problem, this is modeled like VRP.

In order to solve the waste collection problem, this is modeled like VRP which is an intractable problem. Two different Ant colony algorithms for the collection and transport of the solid waste were shown. Each one uses a different way to solve the problem. The first use the algorithm proposed by Marco Dorigo and they calculate the minimum tour for the garbage truck. In this case they consider only one truck and it have to visit n loading spots. The disadvantage of this approach is that they do not model the problem using n trucks with different capacity and they do not consider the capacity of the containers and naturally the problem is not modeled like a

VRP. The second approach is more complex, and the problem is modeled like VRPSD, a variant of VRP, using the algorithm created by Marco Dorigo with a local search algorithm (descent method) which produces good solutions. In this case the algorithm can be used to solve VRPTW (Vehicle Routing Problem with Time Windows), measure the efficiency and observe which modeling for the problem is better. We improved the understanding substantially to obtain the "best routs" to solve the waste collection problem in any community; we show in this work the implementation of ant colony algorithm, logistics for the garbage collection through the use of ACS.

There is a very interesting research area because in every city the people and the industry produces solid waste and is very cheap collect that garbage and it has environmental consequences too.

As future work we propose the implementation of more complex and efficient algorithms that solve real problems emphasizing in the model of VRP and its variants. These types of algorithms to route management delivered reduce operational costs by 1) organizing routes to minimize overlap and thereby reduce the number of vehicles required to service customers; and 2) sequencing the stops along a route to make the best use of fuel, driver schedules, and disposal trips. In this chapter, is possible to see the Ant Colony algorithms produce good results to the VRP problem, nevertheless many characteristics are not taken into account, and they are associated with the waste collection problem, because making it will complicate the modeling, and is necessary to use multi-objective optimization, multicriterion or restrictions.

The future research or study must consider all of the possibilities in order for the waste collection problem to be an effective solution in spite of the uncertainties with these algorithms, and solve problems of waste generation, prediction and optimal allocation of waste stream for recycling, incineration, landfill and composting. The model should also include direct interaction with data and analysis of data, and also overcome the problems associated with the previous algorithms and models explained before.

REFERENCES

Asmar, D. C., Elshamli, A., & Areibi, S. (2005). A comparative assessment of ACO algorithms within a TSP environment. *Dynamics of Continuous Discrete and Impulsive Systems-Series B-Applications & Algorithms, 1*, 462–467.

Bianchi, L., Birattari, M., Chiarandini, M., Manfrin, M., Mastrolilli, M., & Schiavinotto, T. (2006). Hybrid metaheuristics for the vehicle routing problem with stochastic demands. *Journal of Mathematical Modelling and Algorithms, 5*, 91–110. doi:10.1007/s10852-005-9033-y

Bullnheimer, B., Hartl, R., & Strauss, C. (1997). *A new rank based version of the ant system: a computational study (Tech. Rep.)*. Vienna, Austria: Institute of Management Science, University of Vienna.

Chalkias, C., & Lasaridi, K. (2009). A GIS based model for the optimisation of municipal solid waste collection: the case study of Nikea, Athens, Greece. *WSEAS Transactions on Computers, 5*(10).

Cordeau, J., Desaulniers, G., Desrosiers, J., Solomon, M., & Soumis, F. (2002). The VRP with time windows. In Murphy, S. (Ed.), *Monographs on discrete mathematics and applications* (pp. 157–193). Philadelphia, PA: SIAM.

Dantzig, G. B., & Ramser, R. H. (1959). The truck dispatching problem. *Management Science, 6*, 80–91. doi:10.1287/mnsc.6.1.80

Dorigo, M. (1991). *Positive feedback as a search strategy* (Tech. Rep. No. 91-016). Milano, Italy: Politecnico.

Dorigo, M., & Di Caro, G. (1999). Ant algorithms optimization. *Artificial Life, 5*(3), 137–172. doi:10.1162/106454699568728

Dorigo, M., & Gambardella, L. M. (1996). *Ant colony system: A cooperative learning approach to the traveling salesman problem* (Tech. Rep. No. TR/IRIDIA/1996-5). Brussels, Belgium: IRIDIA, Université Libre de Bruxelles.

Dorigo, M., & Gambardella, L. M. (1997a). Ant colonies for the traveling salesman problem. *Biosystem, 43*, 73–81. doi:10.1016/S0303-2647(97)01708-5

Dorigo, M., & Gambardella, L. M. (1997b). Ant colony system: A cooperative learning approach to the traveling salesman problem. *IEEE Transactions on Evolutionary Computation, 1*, 53–66. doi:10.1109/4235.585892

Dorigo, M., & Maniezzo, V. (1996). The ant system: optimization by a colony of cooperating agents. *IEEE Transactions on Systems, Man, and Cybernetics, 26*(1), 1–13.

Eilon, S., Watson-Gandy, C. D. T., & Christofides, N. (1971). *Distribution management: Mathematical modeling and practical analysis*. UK: Compton Printing.

Gambardella, L. M., & Dorigo, M. (1995). Ant-Q: A reinforcement learning approach to the traveling salesman problem. In *Proceedings of the Twelfth International Conference on Machine Learning*, Tahoe City, CA (pp. 252-260).

Garey, M. R., & Johnson, D. S. (1979). *Computer and intractability: a guide to the theory of NP-completeness* (pp. 1-76, 74, 214-226). Paris, France: Bell Telephone Laboratories.

Ismail, Z., & Irhamah. (2008). Solving the vehicle routing problem with stochastic demands via hybrid genetic algorithm-tabu search. *Journal of Mathematics and Statistics, 4*(3), 161–167. doi:10.3844/jmssp.2008.161.167

Ismail, Z., & Loh, S. L. (2009). Ant colony optimization for solving solid waste collection scheduling problems. *Journal of Mathematics and Statistics*, *5*(3), 199–205. doi:10.3844/jmssp.2009.199.205

Karadimas, N., Doukas, N., Kolokathi, M., & Defteraiou, G. (2008). Routing optimization heuristics algorithms for urban solid waste transportation management. *WSEAS Transactions on Computers*, *7*(12), 2022–2031.

Karadimas, N., Kouzas, G., Anagnostopoulos, I., Loumos, V., & Kayafas, E. (2005). Ant colony route optimization for municipal services. In *Proceedings of the 19th European Conference on Modelling and Simulation*.

Lenstra, J. K., & Rinnooy Kan, A. H. G. (1981). Complexity of vehicle routing and scheduling problems. *Networks*, *11*, 221–227. doi:10.1002/net.3230110211

Municipality of Athens. (2003). *Estimation, evaluation and planning of actions for municipal solid waste services during Olympic Games 2004*. Athens, Greece: Author.

Nuortioa, T., Kytöjokib, J., Niskaa, H., & Bräysy, O. (2005). Improved route planning and scheduling of waste collection and transport. *Expert Systems with Applications*, *30*(2), 223–232. doi:10.1016/j.eswa.2005.07.009

Ochoa, A., Hernández, A., Cruz, L., Ponce, J., Montes, F., Li, L., & Janacek, L. (2010). Artificial societies and social simulation using ant colony, particle swarm optimization and cultural algorithms . In Korosec, P. (Ed.), *New achievements in evolutionary computation*. Rijeka, Croatia: InTech.

Ombuki, B. M., Runka, A., & Hanshar, F. T. (2007). Waste collection vehicle routing problem with time windows using multi-objetive genetic algorithms. In *Proceedings of the Third IASTED International Conference on Computational Intelligence* (pp. 91-97).

Parker, M. (2007). *Planning land information technology research project: Efficient Recycling Collection Routing in Pictou County, 2001*. Retrieved from http://www.cogs.ns.ca/planning/projects/plt20014/images/research.pdf

Ponce, J., Hernández, A., Ochoa, A., Padilla, F., Padilla, A., Álvarez, F., & Ponce de León, E. (2009a). Data mining in Web applications . In Ponce, J., & Karahoca, A. (Eds.), *Data mining and knowledge discovery in real life applications*. Rijeka, Croatia: InTech.

Rizzoli, A. E., Oliverio, F., Montemanni, R., & Gambardella, L. M. (2004). *Ant colony optimisation for vehicle routing problems: from theory to applications*. Retrieved from http://www.idsia.ch/idsiareport/IDSIA-15-04.pdf

Secomandi, N. (2000). Comparing neuro-dynamic programming algorithms for the vehicle routing problem with stochastic demands. *Computers & Operations Research*, *27*, 1171–1200. doi:10.1016/S0305-0548(99)00146-X

Secomandi, N. (2001). A rollout policy for the vehicle routing problem with stochastic demands. *Operations Research*, *49*, 796–802. doi:10.1287/opre.49.5.796.10608

Sodhi, M. S. (2001). Applications and opportunities for operations research in internet-enabled supply chains and electronic marketplaces. *Interfaces*, *31*(2), 56–69. doi:10.1287/inte.31.2.56.10633

Stützle, T., & Hoos, H. H. (1996). *Improving the ant system: A detailed report on the MAXMIN ant system* (Tech. Rep. No. AIDA-96-12). Darmstadt, Germany: FG Intellektik, FB Informatik, TU Darmstadt.

Toth, P., & Vigo, D. (2001). The vehicle routing problem . In Murphy, S. (Ed.), *Monographs on discrete mathematics and applications*. Philadelphia, PA: SIAM.

VRP. (2007). *The VRP Web*. Retrieved from http://neo.lcc.uma.es/radi-aeb/WebVRP/

Yang, W. H., Kamlesh, M., & Ronald, H. B. (2000). Stochastic vehicle routing problem with restocking. *Transportation Science*, *34*, 99–112. doi:10.1287/trsc.34.1.99.12278

ADDITIONAL READING

Apaydin, O., & Gonullu, M. T. (2007). Route optimization for solid waste collection: Trabzon (Turkey) case study. *Global NEST Journal*, *9*(1), 6–11.

Bani, M. S., Rashid, Z. A., Hamid, K. H. K., Harbawi, M. E., Alias, A. B., & Aris, M. J. (2009). The development of decision support system for waste management, a review. *World Academy of Science . Engineering and Technology*, *49*, 161–168.

Cheng, S., Chan, C. W., & Huang, G. H. (2003). An integrated multi-criteria decision analysis and inexact mixed integer linear programming approach for solid waste management. *Engineering Applications of Artificial Intelligence*, *16*, 543–554. doi:10.1016/S0952-1976(03)00069-1

Cruz Reyes, L., Nieto-Yáñez, D. M., Rangel-Valdez, N., Herrera Ortiz, J. A., González, J. B., Valdez, G. C., & Delgado-Orta, J. (2007). DiPro: An algorithm for the packing in product transportation problems with multiple loading and routing variants. In A. Gelbukh & Á. F. K. Morales (Eds.), *Proceedings of the 6th Mexican International Conference on Advances in Artificial Intelligence* (LNCS 4827, pp. 1078-1088).

Cruz Reyes, L., Orta, J. F. D., Barbosa, J. J. G., Jimenez, J. T., Huacuja, H. J. F., & Cruz, B. A. A. (2008). DiPro: An ant colony system algorithm to solve routing problems applied to the delivery of bottled product. In A. An, S. Matwin, Z. W. Ras, & D. Slezak (Eds.), *Proceedings of the 17th International Symposium on Foundations of Intelligent Systems* (LNCS 4994, pp. 329-338).

Florios, K., Kiranoudis, C., & Mavrotas, G. (2005). Heuristics for urban solid waste collection. In *Proceedings of the International Conference HELCO* (pp. 1-11).

Lin, L. Y., & Malasri, S. (1998). The use of a genetic algorithm in solid waste collection analysis. *Journal of Solid Waste Technology and Management*, *25*(1), 27–32.

Oliveira, E., & Borenstein, D. (2007). A decision support system for the operational planning of solid waste collection. *Waste Management (New York, N.Y.)*, *27*, 1286–1297. doi:10.1016/j.wasman.2006.06.012

Ombuki, B., Ross, B., & Hanshar, F. (2006). Multi-objective genetic algorithms for vehicle routing problem with time windows. *Applied Intelligence*, *24*(1), 17–30. doi:10.1007/s10489-006-6926-z

Salazar, E., & Ruiz, N. (2009). ACO model applied to the waste collection by containers. Ingeniare. *Revista chilena de ingeniería*, *17*(2), 236-243.

KEY TERMS AND DEFINITIONS

Ant Colony Optimization: Meta-heuristic based on the natural ants. The algorithm can be applied to the solution of many combinatorial optimization problems. The artificial society, formed by ants, repeats the food-search process. Each ant builds one path that represents a solution to the optimization problem.

Garbage Truck: A dustcart or dustbin wagon, is a truck specially designed to haul waste to landfills and other recycling / disposal facilities. They are a common sight in most urban areas.

Metaheuristic: Computational method that optimizes a problem by iteratively trying to improve a candidate solution with regard to a given measure of quality. Metaheuristics make few or no assumptions about the problem being optimized and can search very large spaces of candidate solutions. However, metaheuristics do not guarantee an optimal solution is ever found. Many metaheuristics implement some form of stochastic optimization.

Traveling Salesman Problem: (TSP), Also known as the traveling salesperson problem, is a problem in discrete or combinatorial optimization. Given a number of cities and the costs of traveling from any city to any other city, what is the cheapest round-trip route that visits each city once and then returns to the starting city.

Vehicle Routing Problem: Combinatorial hard problem, which is related with the use of some mode of transport, with different characteristics and capacities, to deal products to locations with certain demands and constraints. The objective is to find the shortest route or the use of minimum vehicles.

Vehicle Routing Problem Time Windows: Same problem that Vehicle Routing Problem with the additional restriction that in Vehicle Routing Problem Time Windows, a time window is associated with each customer, defining an interval wherein the customer has to be supplied. The interval at the depot is called the scheduling horizon. The objective is to minimize the vehicle fleet and the sum of travel time and waiting time needed to supply all customers in their required hours.

Waste: Produced as part of everyday life. Many cities generate a waste stream of great complexity, toxicity, and volume. It includes municipal solid waste, industrial solid waste, hazardous waste, and other specialty wastes, such as medical, nuclear, mining, agricultural waste, construction and demolition waste, household waste, etc.

Waste Collection Problem: Each vehicle must travel in the study area and visit all the waste bins, in a way that minimizes the total travel cost: most often distance or time but also fuel consumption.

Waste Container: Container for temporarily storing waste, and is usually made out of metal or plastic. Common terms are dustbin, rubbish bin, refuse bin, litter bin, garbage can, trash can, trash barrel, trash bin, skip, dumpster, waste basket, waste paper basket, waste receptacle, litter receptacle, container bin, wheelie bin, bin, and kitchen bin. The words "garbage", "trash", "can", and "basket" are more common in American English usage.

Chapter 3
Grid Platform Applied to the Vehicle Routing Problem with Time Windows for the Distribution of Products

Marco Antonio Cruz-Chávez
*Autonomous University of Morelos State,
CIICAp, Mexico*

Fredy Juárez-Pérez
*Autonomous University of Morelos State,
CIICAp, Mexico*

Abelardo Rodríguez-León
Technological Institute of Veracruz, Mexico

Carmen Peralta-Abarca
*Autonomous University of Morelos State, FCQeI,
Mexico*

Rafael Rivera-López
Technological Institute of Veracruz, Mexico

Alina Martínez-Oropeza
*Autonomous University of Morelos State,
CIICAp, Mexico*

ABSTRACT

Around the world there have recently been new and more powerful computing platforms created that can be used to work with computer science problems. Some of these problems that are dealt with are real problems of the industry; most are classified by complexity theory as hard problems. One such problem is the vehicle routing problem with time windows (VRPTW). The computational Grid is a platform which has recently ventured into the treatment of hard problems to find the best solution for these. This chapter presents a genetic algorithm for the vehicle routing problem with time windows. The algorithm iteratively applies a mutation operator, first of the intelligent type and second of the restricting type. The algorithm takes advantage of Grid computing to increase the exploration and exploitation of the solution space of the problem. The Grid performance is analyzed for a genetic algorithm and a measurement of the latencies that affect the algorithm is studied. The convenience of applying this new computing platform to the execution of algorithms specially designed for Grid computing is presented.

DOI: 10.4018/978-1-4666-0297-7.ch003

INTRODUCTION

The problems of resource assignment based on scheduling are well-known combinatorial problems in the computer science research community. Complexity theory classifies them as a very difficult set of problems to solve; they are the NP-complete problems (Garey & Johnson, 1979). This complexity is due to the combinatorial feature of these problems to handle only discrete variables in their formulation, and because the number of solutions to the problem grows exponentially with increasing size of the instance to solve. At times, the instance of a problem containing a small number of variables is an unknown solution; we have only knowledge of an upper or lower bound close to the solution. This behavior occurs in scheduling problems, for example, in transportation problems with time windows for 1000 clients, as proposed by Homberger and Gehring (1999), there is currently no known solution due to the hardness of this problem (NP-complete), as mentioned by Toth and Vigo (2001). For this type of symmetrical transport problems, the solution space size is bound as $((1+n/r)!)^r$, much like a multiple traveling salesman problem as presented by Mitrovic-Minic and Krishnamurti (2006), where n is the number of customers that need attention and r indicates the number of paths that must be traveled, the symmetry indicates that there are the same number of customers per path.

Due to the hardness of solving problems of resource assignment, it is necessary use nondeterministic Meta heuristics to bind in polynomial time the search for the best possible solution with good performance in both efficacy and efficiency for the algorithm. For this reason, the scientific community has worked to improve the performance of Meta heuristics in several ways. For example, one way is the hybridization of two or more methods, one of which is an exact method, thereby taking advantage of the best features of each. Another way to improve the performance of the Meta heuristic is to improve the neighbor-

hood structure for local search, because several of these methods work with iterated local search, as suggested in Hansen and Mladenovic (2001) and Cruz-Chavez et al. (2010). Another way is the partial or total parallelization of the algorithm. All these alternatives have been successful, resulting in the improvement of the upper/lower bounds of solutions for unsolved instances. The main Meta heuristics that have been applied to VRPTW are genetic algorithms, used to solve constraint satisfaction models, ant colony and simulated annealing.

The industry needs a transport to distribute their products and the savings achieved through the efficient scheduling of distribution paths. This in turn could lead to a decrease in transportation costs, resulting in a substantial savings for the company, making it more competitive nationally and/or internationally, due to decreased price for the same product quality. Good resource assignment will result in savings in several ways: less gasoline, fewer transport units and therefore savings in depreciation of the units, fewer expenses in payment to drivers who have a smaller number of paths to meet (every driver completes their daily work in a single path). In this type of resource assignment, good use of the storage capacity of the units is also involved. Better use of the transport units' space and a better selection of merchandise to be transported lead to the transportation optimum.

The type of infrastructure used to solve the VRPTW has been varied over the years; PCs, workstations, supercomputers and clusters have been used. Considering that this is a hard problem, and attempts are made to find the global optimum solution, a new type of infrastructure is currently being used in the world for application in various areas. It is beginning to be used in the area of combinatorial optimization to minimize the runtime of Meta heuristics as applied to NP-complete problems. Cruz-Chavez et al. (2010b) use the new infrastructure, called grid computing, in their work with the Job Shop Scheduling Problem to reduce communication between nodes on a Grid. Grid computing is simply the union of several clusters of computers that are geographically distant, using an operating system to work with the cluster of computers as a single supercomputer. The Grid has been used in Fujisawa et al. (2004) to work with optimization problems. The Meta heuristic that has been used in the Grid, due to ease of programming in a distributed environment, is the genetic algorithm, as presented in Chang et al. (2006), Lim et al. (2007), and Moon et al. (2008).

The approach generated in the use of Grid computing to work with NP-complete hard problems in computational science involves the availability of all the processing cores of the Grid, in order to implement a computer program that can launch a number of processes. This allows the tasks of the algorithm to be divided, in this case a Meta heuristics, in order to obtain good solutions to the problem in a very short execution time or to significantly increase the search of the solution space to improve or find the global optimum, while requiring a reasonable execution time.

Working with the VRPTW, or any NP-complete type problem in a Grid environment, requires the development of two important elements. The first element is the generation of a computational Grid infrastructure that will allow running a computer program which can make use of all available processing cores on the Grid. At present, most of the Grids in the world allow the use of a single computing cluster for the execution of a computer program. The second element is the design of a computer program that allows the use of total processing cores in parallel/distributed, and also helps reduce the total latency in the execution of computer program. Latency is the time required to bring and take a data packet between a pair of clusters that belong to the Grid.

This infrastructure was developed as an experimental MiniGrid between two educational institutions; the MiniGrid consists of two computer clusters, a cluster located at the Autonomous University of Morelos State in Cuernavaca, Morelos and the other cluster located in the Technological

Institute of Veracruz, in Veracruz, Veracruz. The link to the MiniGrid is Internet 2 which offers a bandwidth of 5 Gbs.

To use all of the MiniGrid cores easily, a genetic algorithm computer program was chosen because the parallelization and distribution of the algorithm in the MiniGrid becomes very simple in relation to the division of the population of the genetic design in the number of cores available. The genetic design includes reducing the total latency generated during the execution of the computer program.

The Grid architecture provides an alternative to the use of computers with parallel processing supercomputing, which is still extremely expensive and therefore available in very few institutions. The use of Grid computing enables the sharing of computing resources among academic and private institutions. This represents an area of opportunity both in research and in industry application. An example of using a Grid for optimization problems is shown, it is a genetic algorithm of the VRPTW, which is of interest to researchers but also has wide application in industry.

BACKGROUND

This chapter presents a model of the vehicle routing problem with time windows and the development of a genetic algorithm for this problem which works in a Grid environment. A description of the characteristics of the Experimental MiniGrid developed to study the VRPTW follows. Next, the tests run using the MiniGrid with a genetic algorithm for the VRPTW are shown. Finally the conclusions of this chapter are presented.

VRPTW MODEL

The vehicle routing problem with time windows, VRPTW, is a model that applies to the supply chain and school transport. The following is the mathematical model of Integer Linear Programming representing the problem and as presented by Toth and Vigo (2001):

VRPTW Mathematical Model

$$\min f = \sum_{k \in K} \sum_{(i,j) \in A} C_{ij} x_{ijk} \qquad (1)$$

s.t.

$$\sum_{k \in K} \sum_{j \in \Delta^+(i)} x_{ijk} = 1 \qquad (2)$$

$$\sum_{j \in \Delta^+(0)} x_{0jk} = 1 \qquad (3)$$

$$\sum_{i \in \Delta^-(j)} x_{ijk} - \sum_{i \in \Delta^+(j)} x_{ijk} = 0 \qquad (4)$$

$$\sum_{i \in \Delta^-(n+1)} x_{i,n+1,k} = 1 \qquad (5)$$

$$w_{ik} + s_i + t_{ij} + w_{jk} \leq \left(1 - x_{ijk}\right) M_{ij} \qquad (6)$$

$$a_i \sum_{j \in \Delta^+(i)} x_{ijk} \leq w_{ik} \leq b_i \sum_{j \in \Delta^+(i)} x_{ijk} \qquad (7)$$

$$E \leq w_{ik} \leq L \qquad (8)$$

$$\sum_{i \in N} d_i \sum_{j \in \Delta^+(i)} x_{ijk} \leq C \qquad (9)$$

$$x_{ijk} \geq 0 \qquad (10)$$

$$x_{ijk} \in \{0,1\} \qquad (11)$$

The objective function presented in (1) represents the total cost, which can be interpreted as the travel time, distance traveled or the total cost generated in monetary units. It is required to obtain the minimum cost of the total travel using the smallest number of vehicles. The x_{ijk} variable takes a value of 1, when the k vehicle serves the route from client i to client j. The depot is represented as $i = 0$ or $i = 1 + n$.

The constraints that must be met are presented in (2) through (11). Constraint (2) restricts the assignment of each customer to a single vehicle route, i.e., customers who belong to the same route are served by the same vehicle. Constraints (3) to (5), stipulate the characteristics of the route to be followed by each vehicle k. Constraint (3) defines, for each vehicle k, the number of customers j that can be reached directly without going through another customer from the depot 0, i.e., for each vehicle k, only one client j can be reached if it comes from the depot. Constraint (4) indicates that for each vehicle unit, the number of vehicles arriving to a client is the same number of vehicles that exit.

Constraint (5), defines, for each vehicle k, the number of customers i that can directly reach the deposit $n + 1$. That is, for each vehicle k, there is only one client that connects to the depot. Restriction (6) through (8) and (9) guarantee the feasibility of a solution with respect to time conditions and aspects of capacity respectively. Restriction (6) indicates that a service to client j cannot start if client i has not been served and if the vehicle has not reached customer j. Here, M is a constant which allows constraint (6) to be satisfied in the special case that vehicle k does not address the route from client i to client j. Constraint (7) indicates that for each vehicle unit and each customer i, the initial service time w_{ik} must be started within the time window $[a_i, b_i]$, where a_i is the lower bound time and b_i is the upper bound time for initiation of service of vehicle unit k to client i. Constraint (8) indicates that for each vehicle unit k in the depot 0, the start time of service w_{ik} must begin

Figure 1. Instance of the VRPTW with 8 customers

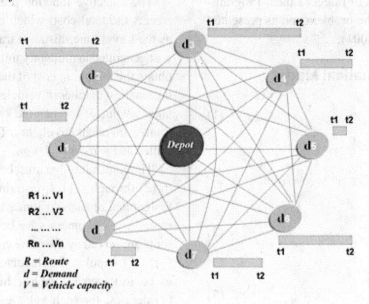

within the time window $[E, L]$, i.e., there is a time window in which vehicle k is allowed out of the depot to serve customers. Constraint (9) indicates that for every vehicle k, the sum of the demands of all customers served should not exceed the vehicle capacity. Constraint (10) forbids negative values for the variables x. Constraint (11) defines the linear model as a binary integer linear model.

VRPTW Representation by a Disjunctive Graph

An instance of the VRPTW can be represented by a disjunctive graph which forms a clique. Figure 1 shows an instance for the problem of 8 clients. The graph represents, in a general form, the planning of the problem, each vertex representing a client. Each client has a time window $[t_p\ t_j]$ in which it can receive the goods. At the beginning, each client has the ability to connect with any customer and the depot.

One solution to this instance of 8 clients is to define the number of routes to be used (one route per vehicle), so as to comply with the restrictions (2) through (11). A solution is presented in the

digraph in Figure 2. The solution graph shows each time window in red, the time of service w_{ik} to the customer. The solution presented defines three routes, thus three vehicles used for delivery. It also shows the order in which each vehicle serves its customers. The restrictions presented explicitly in the solution graph in Figure 2 are (2), (3), (4), (5), (6) and (7). Naturally, some of the restrictions seen in the mathematical model are treated implicitly; these are (8), (9), (10) and (11).

GENETIC ALGORITHM IN THE GRID ENVIRONMENT FOR THE VRPTW

For the genetic design of distributed parallel processing in the MiniGrid, the computer program of the genetic algorithm was structured to reduce the total latency time that is generated in the use of the MiniGrid. In the genetic design, the weakness of this kind of Meta heuristics was addressed. The algorithm applied population genetics work efficiently in exploring the solution space to find the best solution, but they have a deficiency. The exploitation they do in the solu-

Figure 2. Solution for the VRPTW instance with 8 clients

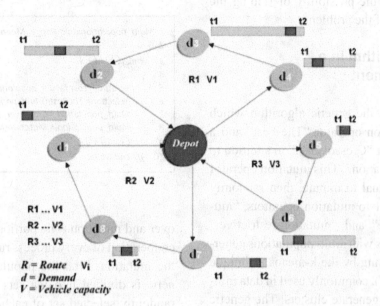

tion space in search of local optima is very weak because they do not worry about finding the best solution in the neighborhoods that would generate each individual in population genetics. That is, they do not find the local optimum in a solution neighborhood as defined by each individual in the population. This is important because a local optimal solution can also be the global optimal solution. To improve the search operation, genetic hybridization is performed in the mutation phase by applying two types of iterative mutations, using a local search such as that defined by Papadimitriou and Steiglitz (1982). The first type of mutation is a restrictive one, as presented by Cruz-Chavez et al. (2007), which is a mutation iteratively solving the constraint satisfaction model of the VRPTW that is presented in equations (2) through (11) of the mathematical model. The second type of mutation is an intelligent mutation, as presented by Díaz-Parra and Cruz-Chavez (2008), which develops an iterative intelligent mutation for each individual to be mutated. The type of mutation used in genetic execution is random. This type of genetic mutation applied in an iterative genetic procedure, known as iterated local search, is usually referred to as

a memetic algorithm. Moscato and Cotta (2010) give a comprehensive explanation of the features of a memetic algorithm.

With the advantages provided by the MiniGrid that can use all the cores, the parallelization of the computer program is structured so that the execution of the mutation is sent iteratively to the MiniGrid nodes as a cooperative process for each individual in the population to be mutated. Individuals are distributed in all MiniGrid nodes through a communication scheme presented in Rodriguez-Leon et al. (2010). This is done in each generation of the genetic. The mutation process is the most time consuming portion of the algorithm. The efficiency of the algorithm depends on the number of nodes used in the MiniGrid and total latency of the algorithm. With more nodes and greater communication between MiniGrid nodes, the total latency is higher, so it is necessary to minimize communication between nodes. On the other hand, with a larger number of nodes, the population that can withstand the algorithm will be larger. This provides a better solution to the problem with greater efficacy, because it is possible to explore and exploit a larger solution space, increasing the possibility of finding the global optimum of the problem.

Genetic Algorithm in a Grid Environment

Figure 3 presents the genetic algorithm which contains a selection operator "The best" and a crossover operator "Crossover-k," in addition to the operator "Mutation." This mutation operator selects an individual to mutate, then randomly chooses between two mutation operators, "mutation-intelligence" and "mutation-restrictive." The Genetic works with multi populations generated at the beginning by the k-means technique (MacQueen, 1967), commonly used in data mining techniques to generate clusters. The genetic algorithm creates populations through k-means clustering where the individuals are feasible according to their geographical distribution. The operator "the best," selects the best individuals from each population according to their fitness percentage, and performs a crossover of these individuals. With the crossover-k, the size of each population is maintained, and exploration of the solution space is allowed. The iterative mutation operator improves the fitness function but also allows individuals to choose mutations that do not improve the fitness function; the mutation operator performs a local search to find a local optimum. The above procedure is repeated for each multipopulation generation. The stop criterion for the algorithm is defined by the maximum number of generations G_n. The population size Pz is defined by the number of nodes present in the MiniGrid. $Pz = Pz_1 + Pz_2 + Pz_3 + ... + Pz_n$. It is Pz_i, where Pz_i is the population size present in each MiniGrid node and n is the number of nodes present in the MiniGrid.

The distributed processing applied to the algorithm is presented by a flowchart in Figure 4. It is noted that each MiniGrid node executes a genetic with a feasible population of size Pz_i. Each node independently performs the selection, cross-

Figure 3. Multi population genetic algorithm

```
1  Multi_population=Init_Pop_k_MeansClustering (Pz);
2  G=0;
3  while(G != Gn)
4  {
5      aptitude_cost (Multi_population);
6      selection= TheBest (Multi_population);
7      Multi_population = Crossover_K(selection);
8      Multi_population = Mutation(Multi_population);
9      G=G+1;
10 }// end while
```

over and mutation. The portion that requires the cooperation of every process running a genetic is the mutation. First the population of each genetic is divided into nm sets of individuals, a randomly selected set of each population Pz_i is taken, and the mutation is applied to this set. The processes in each MiniGrid node communicate to exchange part of their population. The set nm of mutated individuals migrate to another population Pz_i. This is a representation of the reality that happens to immigrant groups, in this case there is migration from one population to another. In the communicative processes between MiniGrid nodes, a large latency is generated, which is higher when nodes are farther apart geographically. This can affect the efficiency of the genetic algorithm, so it is important to study this latency. The experimental results section presents an analysis of the latency generated by the genetic algorithm. Figure 4 is a description of the two mutation operators used in the genetic algorithm.

The process of selection and crossover of the genetic algorithm is very fast; it does not depend on the processes running on other MiniGrid nodes and thus requires a very short time. It defines an algorithm structure where mutations take place in the CPUs of the MiniGrid, which makes the algorithm work efficiently because it does not require communication between nodes in order to execute mutations, i.e., it does not affect the

Figure 4. Execution of a genetic algorithm for VRPTW using the MiniGrid UAEM-ITVER via Internet 2

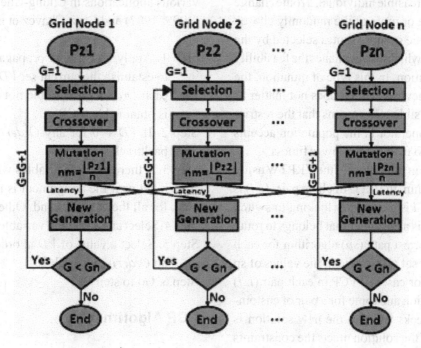

latency in the process or later in the algorithm. The algorithm only requires communication once the mutation has taken place in MiniGrid nodes; this prevents latency from negatively influencing the execution of the algorithm. The genetic algorithm in Figure 4 can use all the resources of the MiniGrid independent of its size. If the MiniGrid has more high performance CPU resources it may lead to greater exploration and exploitation for the VRPTW with growth in polynomial time of the algorithm. This is because the population size *Pz* is directly proportional to the number of nodes used in the MiniGrid.

Restrictive Mutation Operator as a Model of Constraint Satisfaction

An adaptation of the Precedence Constraint Posting (PCP) method to the vehicle routing problem with time windows as a constraint satisfaction problem (CSP) using the VRPTW model can be made without taking into account the objective function. PCP was proposed by Cheng-Chung and Smith (1995, 1997). In Cruz-Chavez et al. (2007), the PCP method is proposed for the relaxed VRPTW model of constraint satisfaction where the size of each time window is infinite. The PCP method has been applied in a genetic algorithm for the VRPTW in Cruz-Chávez and Díaz-Parra (2010), only to build the initial population, but has not been implemented as part of an iterative mutation.

The restrictive mutation is a local search that involves the use of the shortest path that begins and ends in the depot and passes by all customers. It also requires finding the shortest path between pairs of nodes and the evaluation of each one of the cases that form the PCP procedure. To work with restrictive mutations, it is necessary to use an incidence matrix that represents the graph model of each individual of the VRPTW, as presented in Figure 2. The application of these techniques allows the evaluation of a solution that result in the constraint satisfaction VRPTW model. If this is the case, the individual (solution) is a feasible individual of the genetic population. To generate a mutation in the feasible individual, a route change is made for one or more of the randomly chosen customers, to one or more routes selected by the PCP procedure which also evaluates the feasibility of the new solution. In this type of mutation, the quality of the new individual does not matter as long as it is feasible. This means that the restrictive mutation operator in the population accepts individuals who may have a lower fitness.

To evaluate an individual of the VRPTW using the PCP algorithm, the set Ω of client pairs (i, j) is defined, where i is a customer looking to switch to route k and j is a customer that belongs to route k. Then the shortest path (sp) algorithm for each pair (i, j) of the set Ω is applied. The values of sp are evaluated for cases of PCP in each pair (i, j) to set the direction and route for a pair of customers (i, j). It checks whether the new solution is feasible, i.e., if the solution meets the constraints in the mathematical model. If it is not a feasible solution, backtracking is performed, (Cormen et al., 2001), returning to the previous nodes and the PCP procedure is repeated.

To apply the mutation process to CSP as presented in Chung-Cheng and Smith (1997) and Christodoulou et al. (1994), the restrictive mutation is based on the PCP algorithm. To find a feasible solution to the VRPTW model, it is necessary to identify the tuple $\{V, D, C\}$. The set V is formed by *Ordering$_{ij}$* variables; each pair of customers (i, j) defines one of these variables. The set D is the set of values for the variables in V, each *Ordering$_{ij}$* can take two possible values, or. That is, customer i is visited followed by j, or customer j is visited followed by i (a precedence is defined among customers i and j). The set C of constraints on V is given for each pair (i, j) representing a variable *Ordering$_{ij}$*. This restricts the feasible values for the distance between a pair (i, j). PCP defines the set of restrictions based on four cases which are explained in the PCP algorithm. The basic search procedure for the VRPTW as a CSP is composed of six steps which are presented for

various applications in Chung-Cheng and Smith (1995, 1997) and Cruz-Chavez et al. (2007).

Step 1. Apply constraints propagation in order to establish the current set *VD* of values for each *Ordering$_{ij}$* variable not assigned. *VD* is obtained by PCP.

Step 2. If $VD = 0$ for any *Ordering$_{ij}$* variable, backtrack.

Step 3. If there are not variables without assignment or if the assignment is not consistent for all the variables end. Otherwise,

Step 4. Select an *Ordering$_{ij}$* variable not assigned.

Step 5. Select a value of *VD* in order to assign it an *Ordering$_{ij}$* variable.

Step 6. Go to step 1.

PCP Algorithm

Within the search procedure, PCP builds the solution through Depth First using partial assignments of Ω. The PCP algorithm carries out a pruning of the search space early on and provides a heuristic for the value assignment of the *Ordering$_{ij}$* variables.

PCP consists of a series of cases in which it is necessary to prove whether the shortest path sp between a pair of nodes (i, j) that represents the *Ordering$_{ij}$* variable has a value that fulfills some of the PCP cases. According to the result obtained upon evaluating the shortest path, the value of *Ordering$_{ij}$* is designated. The evaluation of sp is calculated from i to j (sp_{ij}) and from j to i (sp_{ji}).

For the Restrictive mutation, the PCP algorithm is applied to a partial solution of the VRPTW. PCP obtains a new feasible solution by assigning one or more clients to the same routes in a different sequence, or to other routes. The PCP algorithm applied to the VRPTW for the CSP consists of the four steps that are presented below:

Step 1.- Find the shortest path for each unordered pair of nodes sp_{ij} and sp_{ji}.

Step 2.- Classify the decision of ordination of the pairs unordered with four cases

Figure 5. Partial solution with customer d7 without route assignment

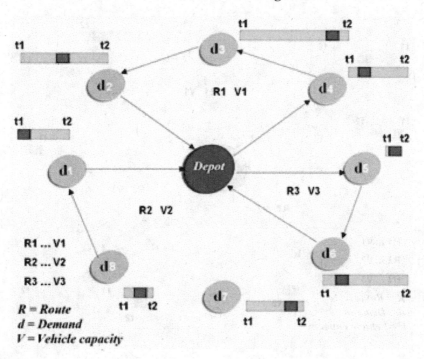

Case 1. If $sp_{ij} >= 0$ and $sp_{ji} < 0$ then $O_i \prec O_j$ should be selected.

Case 2. If $sp_{ji} >= 0$ and $sp_{ij} < 0$, then $O_j \prec O_i$ should be selected.

Case 3. If $sp_{ji} < 0$ and $sp_{ij} < 0$, then the partial solution is inconsistent.

Case 4. If $sp_{ji} >= 0$ and $sp_{ij} >= 0$, then no relationship of order is possible

Step 3.- Existence of cases Does either case 1 or case 2 exist?

If one exists, go to step 4. If neither exists, go to step 1

Step 4.- Fix new precedence for unordered pairs.

To better understand the PCP algorithm, an example of the 8 clients instance is presented in Figure 1. From the solution presented in Figure 2, the customer d7 is randomly selected to change course or sequence. It is removed from the path to which it belongs (Figure 5). The PCP algorithm

is applied to find a route, and a feasible solution is generated. The new solution is presented in Figure 6. In this figure, we see that the client d7 becomes part of the route R3.

Intelligent Mutation Operator

The intelligent mutation operator proposed in Díaz-Parra and Cruz-Chavez (2008), takes a mutation customer candidate (gene-candidate) from the individual that minimizes the objective function presented in (1). Unlike the restrictive mutation that does not pay attention to the quality of the individual, the intelligent mutation operator always tries to improve the quality of the individual.

The procedure starts when the intelligent mutation operator searches for the gene (client) with the greatest distance from another gene, called the gene-candidate, and finds the gene that produces this distance, called gene-mutation-1. The gene-mutation-2 should be the one with the lowest

Figure 6. New solution with restrictive mutation

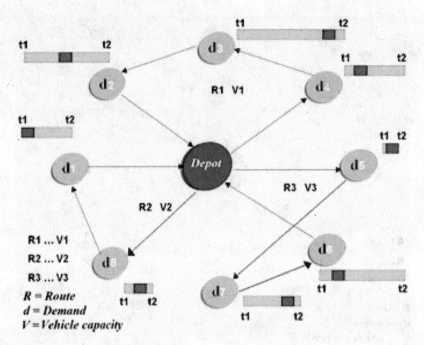

distance from the gene-candidate. Once they are identified, the pair of genes is swapped; the change is made only if the change does not violate time window and capacity constraints in the vehicle. In case of violation of any restriction, the process starts again. With these iterative gene mutations in an individual, the intelligent mutation operator minimizes the objective function of the VRPTW.

Figure 7 shows an example of a case in which the intelligent mutation operator is applied for an individual made up of 10 genes. The value of the objective function of the individual is 65.3. In the beginning of the procedure, the matrix of Euclidean distances from the gene is used to find the greatest distance. In this case gene-mutation-1 = 6 and gene-candidate = 2 are farthest apart; the distance from gene 2 to gene 6 is 11.1. In this case, the two genes are present in route V3. Next, the Euclidean distance matrix for the entire individual is searched to find the genes with a distance of less than 11.1 from the gene-candidate. The gene that has the shortest distance from the gene-candidate is the gene-mutation-2 = 10 which has a distance

of 5 from the gene-candidate. In this case the gene is present in route V2. Because this distance of 5 is less than 11.1, a permutation between gene-mutation-1 and gene-mutation-2 is performed. Figure 2 presents the new mutated individual. It verifies that demand does not exceed the vehicle capacity, which is 12. It also verifies that the ready time of service of each gene (customer) is within the time window for each client. Finally, the value of the objective function of the individual mutation is 55, which improves the value of the objective function of the individual before mutation.

EXPERIMENTAL MINIGRID INFRASTRUCTURE

The experimental technique used to connect computing infrastructure performance through a virtual private network is based on software; this is the way to create the MiniGrid.

Distributed systems provide mechanisms to help make it easier to manage databases,

Figure 7. Intelligent mutation operator. Taken from Díaz-Parra and Cruz-Chávez (2008)

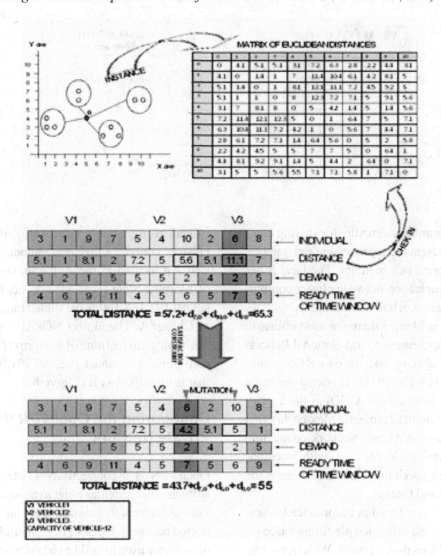

Web systems, email, and phones, among other services. These distributed systems have been developed under the client-server scheme. Over many decades, great progress has been made with respect to the integration of resources, but with an approach based on local networks where they reach the lowest latencies, leaving only the Internet to consult their data, which does not require large bandwidths. Distributed systems are defined as a coordinated, transparent and secure way to share information resources across geographically distributed sites. Recently, distributed computing has given way to Grid computing, more specifically to the Computational Grid. Foster and Kesselman (2004) present everything related to the Grid phenomenon, mainly due to an increase in connection capacity of the Internet and private networks of wide coverage. The Grid takes these clusters and super computers to the next level by making a connection between localized clusters in different geographical areas, thus achieving collaborative resource sharing between institutions, companies and others.

Figure 8. Two geographically separated clusters on two different subnets A and B

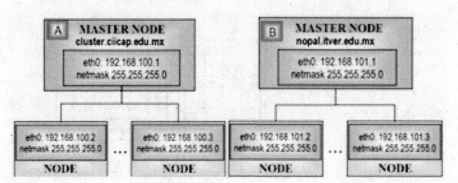

The Grid is an infrastructure for sharing computing resources (numeric processing and storage), using the Internet as a medium. The Grid is not simply communication between cluster computers; its goals are much more ambitious.

Currently in Mexico there are joint efforts to develop and implement a Grid National Laboratory. Corporación Universitaria para el Desarrollo de Internet 2 (CUDI, 2011), is one of the main promoters of these efforts. CUDI is the agency managing the Internet 2 project in Mexico. Internet 2 is a high-speed academic network connecting several universities in Mexico, with interconnection to high-speed university networks in the United States and Canada.

The Grid is developed in accordance to standard protocols and reference platforms based on open source for its development. Widely used by researchers and research centers, grid computing is rapidly emerging as the means used by corporate companies to collaborate, share data and software, store more information than in existing networks, and access large amounts of processing power without investing significant sums on expensive computers.

The experimental MiniGrid developed for the implementation of genetic algorithms to study the VRPTW consists of two high-performance clusters, which are geographically distant but are united through a Virtual Private Network network-to-network using OpenVPN (software)

instead using routers (hardware). In principle, clusters contain a different subnet. The cluster CIICAp located at the Autonomous University of Morelos State (UAEM) was configured as a subnet 192.168.100.0, the subnet that is identified as Cluster A. The cluster NOPAL located at the Technological Institute of Veracruz (ITVER) was configured as a subnet 192.168.101.0, the subnet that is identified as B (Figure 8).

Configuring the OpenVPN Virtual Private Network

OpenVPN is a connectivity solution based on software that provides point to point connectivity via the Internet to validate users and hosts connected remotely. OpenVPN is an implementation of software used to build a virtual private network via routers without hardware; it supports various authentication means such as certificates, usernames and passwords. OpenVPN configuration can be summarized in three types:

- **Machine to Machine.** It is the simplest method for encrypting communications between two computers which can send packets directly to each other either because they are connected to the same local network or because both are connected to the Internet and are accessible to each other.

Figure 9. Two geographically separated clusters in different sub networks A and B linked via VPN

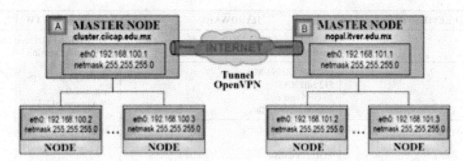

- **Road Warrior.** This is one of the most used and requested ways to connect to a network. It allows a machine outside the local network to communicate with the OpenVPN server and once authenticated, to access local network resources.

- **Network to Network.** Through this type of configuration, two separate and geographically distant networks can come together and share each other's resources. Communication between the two networks is encrypted outside the OpenVPN servers until it reaches the other end (destination).

The idea for these configurations is based on being able to use a single channel of communication, called tunnel (Figure 9), to send all communications back and forth from one extreme to another, which allows one to see all the machines connected, as if they were physically attached via cables. It follows that, to join two clusters, it is necessary to join two OpenVPN configuring networks, using Internet 2 as the media.

To configure a network to network connection it is necessary to define who will be the server and who will be the client. Here the cluster ciicap. edu.mx is the server and nopal.itver.edu.mx is the client. The only two machines that are connected are the master nodes from each cluster. The implementation of routing packets is required to achieve the master nodes that are at the ends of the VPN.

The infrastructure deployed in the high-performance clusters of the ITVER and UAEM that comprise the MiniGrid is made with the same software, but not with the same hardware. The result is two high-performance heterogeneous clusters, due to differences in processors, memory and communication equipment, both in the Master nodes and in the processing nodes. Thus, the first overview of this infrastructure is that each entity has its own HPC Cluster. The computer hardware and software that integrate MiniGrid are specified in Tables 1 and 2. Table 1 presents the hardware and software used by the CIICAp cluster at UAEM. Table 2 presents the hardware and software used by the NOPAL cluster at ITVER.

EXPERIMENTAL TESTS

The results of the genetic algorithm with message passing (MPI) in the VRPTW model are presented, as implemented using the experimental MiniGrid. Evidence of latency and bandwidth between clusters of the MiniGrid with Internet 2 communication is also reported.

A Measure of Bandwidth on the Grid

The bandwidth in the MiniGrid was calculated, this covers only the master nodes between the points cluster.ciicap.edu.mx and nopal.itver. edu.mx. Because traffic on the network directly

Table 1. Hardware and software infrastructure of the CIICAp cluster at UAEM

ELEMENT	HARDWARE	SOFTWARE
Communication	Switch Cisco C2960 24/10/100 Internal Cable level 5	S.O. Red Hat Enterprise Linux 4 gcc compiler version 3.4.3
Master node	Pentium 4, 2793 MHz 512 MB RAM 80 GB Hard disk 2 cards 10/100 Mb/s	OpenMPI 1.2.8 MPICH2-1.0.8 Ganglia 3.0.6 NIS ypserv-2.13-5 NFS nfs-utils-1.0.6-46
Processing node 01	Pentium 2, 266 Mhz 256 MB RAM 4 GB Hard disk 1 card 10/100 Mb/s	OpenVPN
Processing node 02	Pentium 2, 133 Mhz 128 MB RAM 4 GB Hard disk 1 card 10/100 Mb/s	
Processing node 03 Processing node 04 Processing node 05	Intel® Pentium® Dual Core, 2800 MHz, 1GB RAM, 160GB Hard disk, 1 card 10/100 Mb/s	
Processing node 06 Processing node 07 Processing node 08	Intel® Celeron® Dual Core, 2000MHz, 2 GB RAM, 160GB Hard disk, 1 card 10/100 Mb/s	

Table 2. Hardware and software infrastructure of the NOPAL cluster at ITVER

ELEMENT	HARDWARE	SOFTWARE
Communication	Switch 3com 8/10/100 Internal Cable level 5	S.O. Red Hat Enterprise Linux 4 Compilador gcc versión 3.4.3
Master node	Pentium 4, 2394 Mhz 512 GB RAM 60 GB Hard disk 2 cards 10/100 Mb/s	OpenMPI 1.2.8 MPICH2-1.0.8 Ganglia 3.0.6 NIS ypserv-2.13-5 NFS nfs-utils-1.0.6-46
Processing node 01	Pentium 4 Dual Core, 3200 Mhz 1 GB RAM 80 GB Hard disk 1 card 10/100 Mb/s	OpenVPN
Processing node 02	Pentium 4 Dual Core, 3201 Mhz 1 GB RAM 80 GB Hard disk 1 card 10/100 Mb/s	

affects communications, several measurements were made per day, and these tests were repeated for three days.

Figure 10 shows the experimental measurement of the bandwidth between the CIICAp and NOPAL clusters. Specifically, the measurement is made between various pairs of nodes, one corresponding to the CIICAp cluster and the other corresponding to NOPAL cluster, as shown in Figure 10. It can be seen that the bandwidth taken at different times on the first day of testing varies between 0.1 and 1 Mbps, with reference to several pairs of nodes in the experimental MiniGrid. Most measurements are between 0.1 and 0.5 Mbps. Figure 10 shows a peak between 4 and 4.5 Mbps at 18 hours. One can see that the bandwidth for

Figure 10. Bandwidth on March 23 (Mbps), monitored on Day 1

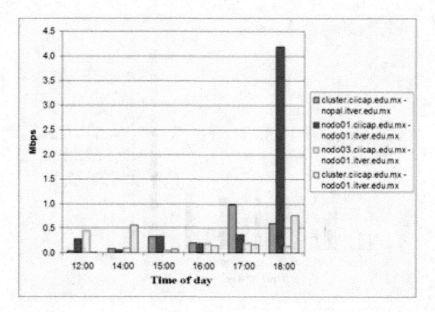

any pair of nodes is never stable, and is well below the reported maximum bandwidth of 16 Mbps of Internet 2 for connection of the MiniGrid. An increase in the bandwidth can be observed as the day progresses, this may be because there is less use of Internet 2 in the two institutions (UAEM-ITVER) in the afternoon.

Figure 11 shows the experimental measurement of the bandwidth between the CIICAp and NOPAL clusters with Internet 2 connection. The measurement is made between various pairs of nodes, one for the CIICAp cluster and another for the NOPAL cluster, as shown in Figure 11. It can be seen that the bandwidth taken at different times during the second day of testing varies between 0.1 and 0.4 Mbps, with reference to several pairs of nodes in the experimental MiniGrid. The figure shows a peak between 1.2 and 1.4 Mbps at 18 hours. It can also be seen that the bandwidth in any pair of nodes is never stable, and is well below the reported maximum bandwidth of 16 Mbps of Internet 2 for connection of the MiniGrid. A decrease in bandwidth can be observed from 12 to 14 hours, and an increase observed between 14 and 18 hrs. This may be due to the use of Internet

2, which may have had more traffic that day from 13 to 15 hours.

Figure 12 shows the experimental measurement of the bandwidth between the NOPAL and CIICAp clusters with an Internet 2 connection. Specifically, the measurement is made between various pairs of nodes, one corresponding to the CIICAp cluster and the other corresponding to the NOPAL cluster, as shown in Figure 12. It can be seen that the bandwidth taken at different times on the third day of testing varies between 0.1 and 0.5 Mbps, with reference to several pairs of nodes in the experimental MiniGrid. The figure shows a peak between 3 and 3.5 Mbps at 14 hrs. It can also be seen that the bandwidth in any pair of nodes never is stable, and is well below the reported maximum bandwidth of 16 Mbps of Internet 2 for connection of the MiniGrid. It can be observed that the width of the band has a tendency to increase as the day passes. This may be because of less network traffic on Internet 2 in the two institutions (UAEM-ITVER) in the afternoon.

Comparing the three measured days shown in Figures 10, 11, and 12, it can be seen that the

Figure 11. Bandwidth (Mbps), monitored on Day 2

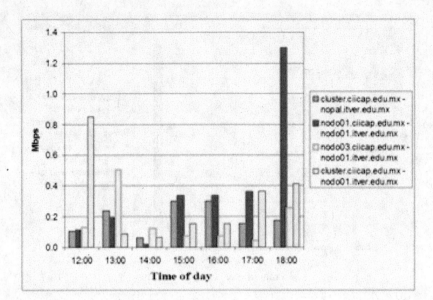

Figure 12. Bandwidth (Mbps), monitored on Day 3

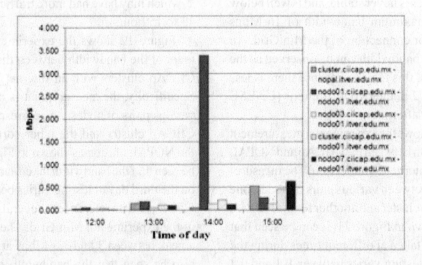

major peaks of bandwidth occur during the afternoon, starting around 14 hrs. It can also be seen that the measures of bandwidth are smaller in the morning, before 14 hrs.

Figure 13 presents the average bandwidth on the first day of testing between pairs of nodes. One can see that the pair of nodes that has the lowest average bandwidth is the pair nodo03.ciicap.edu. mx - nodo01.itver.edu.mx, and the pair of nodes

that has the highest average bandwidth is the pair nodo01.ciicap.edu.mx - nodo01.itver.edu.mx. The bandwidth ranges from 0.2 to 0.9 Mbps.

Figure 14 presents the average bandwidth on the second day of testing between pairs of nodes. One can see that the pair of nodes that has the lowest average bandwidth is the pair of master nodes cluster.ciicap.edu.mx - nopal.itver.edu.mx and the pair of nodes that has the highest average

Figure 13. Average bandwidth (Mbps), monitored on Day 1

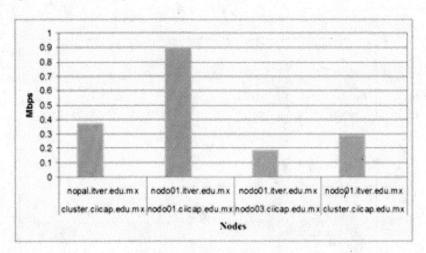

Figure 14. Average bandwidth (Mbps), monitored on Day 2

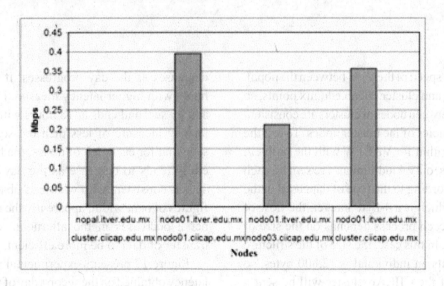

bandwidth is the pair nodo01.ciicap.edu.mx - nodo01.itver.edu.mx. The bandwidth ranges from 0.15 to 0.4 Mbps.

Figure 15 presents the average bandwidth on the third day of testing between pairs of nodes. One can see that the pair of nodes that has the lowest average bandwidth is the pair of nodes nodo03.ciicap.edu.mx - nodo01.itver.edu.mx and the pair of nodes that has the highest average bandwidth is nodo01.ciicap.edu.mx torque -

nodo01.itver.edu.mx. The bandwidth ranges from 0.05 to 0.98 Mbps.

It can be observed in Figures 13, 14, and 15 that the pair of nodes nodo01.ciicap.edu.mx - nodo01.itver.edu.mx throughout the three days, consistently had a higher bandwidth and the pair nodo03.ciicap.edu.mx - nodo01.itver.edu.mx had the lowest bandwidth in two of the three days of testing.

Latency measurement in the Grid. The calculation of latency is based on transfer rates, which

Figure 15. Average bandwidth (Mbps), monitored on Day 3

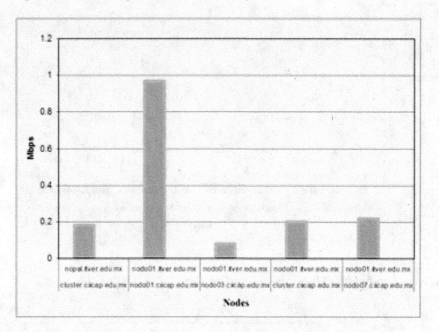

adjusts to the speed of the VPN between the nopal. itver.edu.mx and cluster.ciicap.edu.mx points, so the latency between nodes of clusters are consistent with the latencies of the master nodes. To test the genetic algorithm for VRPTW with the problem of 100 clients, only 4 individuals are sent by each process. According to the type of data used in the algorithm, which is a 4-byte integer, the flow of data sent in each process depends on the size of the structure. In this case, the size of the structure that represents an individual is 12,800 bytes, so each CPU of the CIICAp cluster will be sent a flow of 51.200 bytes. The calculation of latency in the experimental MiniGrid involved launching the algorithm from the CIICAp cluster, and required the transmission via Internet 2 of a stream of data to the NOPAL cluster of 204,800 bytes (200kb), during each iteration of the genetic algorithm. According to this data stream, the latency is calculated in the MiniGrid and is presented in Figures 16 through 19.

Figure 16 presents experimental proofs of the latency obtained on the first day of testing from 12 to 18 hours. It is observed that the latency

decreases as the day progresses. It starts at 12 hours with higher latency measured between 40 and 45 sec, and ends at 18 hours with the lowest latency measure of less than 0.4 sec. It can be seen that for each pair of nodes, the latency generally tends to decrease as the day progresses. This is consistent with what was observed in the figures of bandwidth, apparently the use of Internet 2 decreases in the afternoon, causing the transfer of data to be more efficient.

Figure 17 presents experimental proof of the latency obtained on the second day of testing from 12 to 18 hours. It is observed that the latency behavior neither increases nor decreases as the day progresses, not at 14 hours or at 16 hours, which is when most latency exists in all pairs of nodes on average. The increased latency is measured at 16 hours for most pairs of nodes, this being between 60 and 70 sec. It has the lowest latency at 18 hours for all pairs of nodes. As in Figure 16, the lowest latency occurs at 18 hours.

Figure 18 presents the experimental proof of latency obtained on the third day of testing from 12 to 18 hours. It is observed that the latency

Figure 16. Latency monitored on the first day of testing

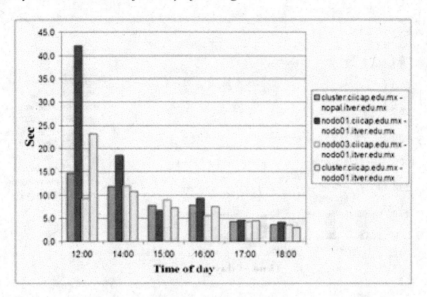

Figure 17. Latency monitored on the second day of testing

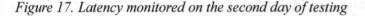

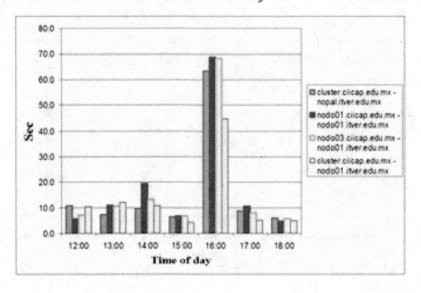

decreases as the day progresses. It starts at 12 hours with higher latency measuring between 70 and 75 sec and ends at 18 hours with the lowest latency measuring less than 0.8 sec. It can be seen that in each pair of nodes, latency generally tends to decrease as the day progresses. This is consistent with what was observed in the figures of bandwidth, apparently the use of Internet 2 de-creases in the afternoon, causing the transfer of data to be more efficient.

Figure 19 presents the average latency of the first day of testing between pairs of nodes. One can see that the pair of nodes that has the lowest average latency is the pair nodo03.ciicap.edu.mx - nodo01.itver.edu.mx and the pair of nodes that has the highest average latency is the pair nodo01.

Figure 18. Latency monitored on the third day of testing

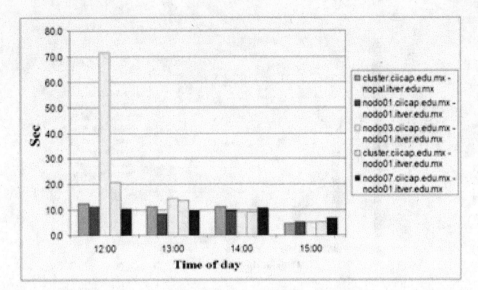

Figure 19. Average Latency (sec), monitored on the first day of testing

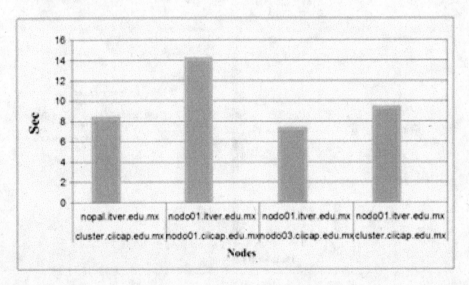

ciicap.edu.mx - nodo01.itver.edu.mx. The latency on the first day is between 6 and 14 sec.

Figure 20 presents the average latency of the second day of testing between pairs of nodes. It can be seen that the pair of nodes that has the lowest average latency is the pair cluster.ciicap.edu.mx - nodo01.itver.edu.mx and the pair of nodes that has the highest average latency is the

pair nodo01.ciicap.edu.mx - nodo01.itver.edu.mx. The latency on the second day is between 12 and 18 sec.

Figure 21 presents the average latency of the third day of testing between pairs of nodes. It can be see that the pair of nodes that has the lowest average latency is the pair (nodo01.ciicap.edu.mx - nodo01.itver.edu.mx) and the pair of nodes

Figure 20. Average Latency (sec), monitored on the second day of testing

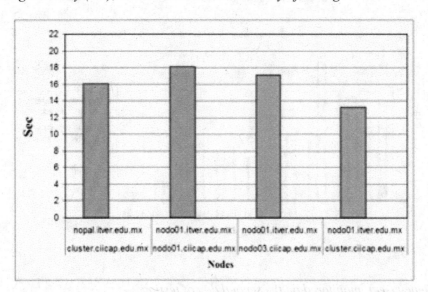

Figure 21. Average Latency (sec), monitored on the third day of testing

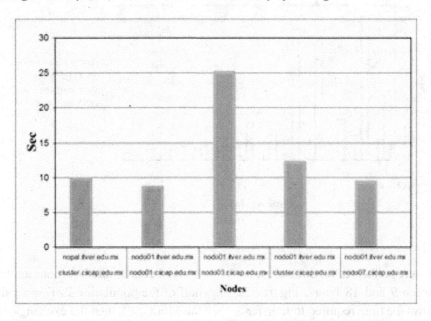

that has the highest average latency is the pair nodo03.ciicap.edu.mx - nodo01.itver.edu.mx. The latency of the third day is between 8 and 25 sec.

It can be seen in Figures 19, 20 and 21, that the pair of nodes nodo01.ciicap.edu.mx - nodo01. itver.edu.mx, during two of the three days, had

the highest latency. With respect to lower latency, there were no distinctive pairs of nodes.

There was also a measurement recorded of the time required to answer when sending a file of 200kb from node to master node CIICAp and NOPAL (frontends), and back. The completion time for writing the file was also recorded. These

Figure 22. Latency (sec), monitored on the first day of testing

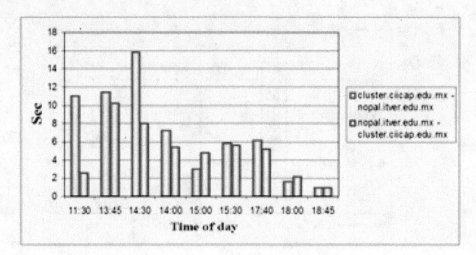

Figure 23. Latency (sec), monitored on the second day of testing

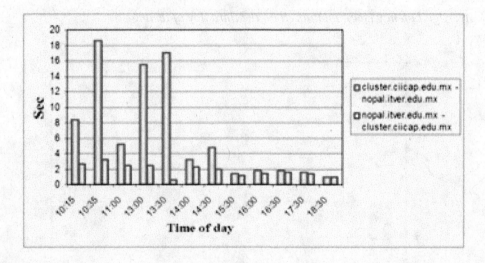

measurements were performed for three consecutive days between 9 and 18 hours. Figures 22 through 24 shows the time required to transfer a file of 200kb. The same behavior can be observed in all the figures. Latency is the largest from the CIICAp cluster to the NOPAL cluster. Latency is more perceptible in the morning and decreases in the afternoon.

To take advantage of the resources of the experimental MiniGrid and accelerate the multi-population evolutionary algorithm, reducing la-

tency was attempted. A mutation was applied to half of the population Pz (for a pair of nodes in the MiniGrid), then the exchange of the mutated population was performed with an additional node. The exchange took place by sending the information via a temporary file with the half of the population missing from the Grid node. Once the population was complete, the fitness evaluation process of each individual was performed and a new generation was started.

Figure 24. Latency (sec), monitored on the third day of testing

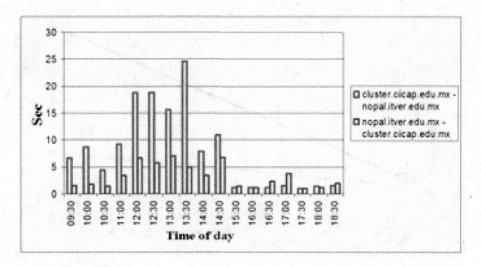

The parallel genetic algorithm tests were performed as follows:

- Between nopal.itver.edu.mx cluster nodes (10 Mbs Ethernet communication).
- Between cluster.ciicap.edu.mx cluster nodes (100 Mbs Ethernet communication).
- Between the frontend of the clusters cluster.ciicap.edu.mx and nopal.itver.edu.mx (Internet 2 communication).

The two instances used to measure the efficiency of the parallelized algorithm were of 100 customers, C102-100 and C103-100, taken from the set of 56 test problems proposed by Solomon. These problems can be found in Gehring and Homberger (1999). These problems have a common number of customers and demands. Each customer always makes a demand and the maximum number of vehicles that can be used is 25. In addition to the topological distribution, the differences are given by the demand quantities and different time windows. To test the genetic algorithm, a population of 1000 individuals and 20 generations was used.

Different numbers of nodes were used, as they were available on each platform:

Figure 25 presents the speedup measurement obtained for the two benchmarks used. The ITVER cluster is very limited, mainly because there are few processors and the internal interconnection network of the cluster is 10 Mbps.

In the CIICAp cluster, tests were performed with 8 processors. As shown in Figure 26, the scalability is good and the behavior is very close to ideal. This is because the machines have a great amount of RAM (2 GB per node) and there is a 1 Gbs network, resulting in better use.

In the MiniGrid, tests were performed with the benchmark C102 for 2, 4, and 8 processors. These runs sought the same number of processor cores in both clusters so that the system was balanced.

In Figure 27 it can be seen that the behavior is similar to that observed in the CIICAp cluster presented in Figure 26, which means that good results using the MiniGrid are obtained when data traffic is not too intense.

Figure 28 shows the average efficiencies obtained in all test configurations used in relation to Speedup for the two problems C102 and C103 of VRPTW. This figure shows that the efficiency of the MiniGrid is above 70% when using 8 processors. This efficiency is higher than that of the

Figure 25. Speedup of testing C102 and C103 in the NOPAL cluster

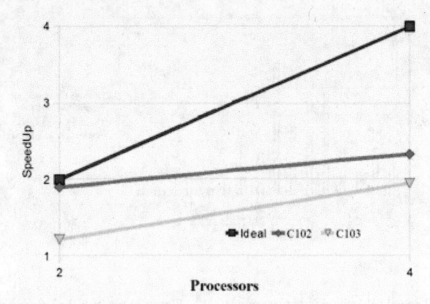

Figure 26. Speedup of testing C101 and C106 in the CIICAP cluster

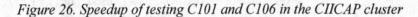

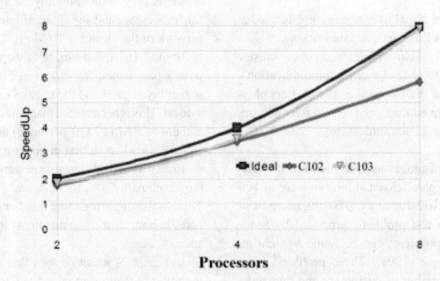

cluster CIICAp. When using 2 and 4 processors in the MiniGrid, efficiency is very similar to that obtained in the CIICAp cluster and better than that obtained in the NOPAL cluster. When using the MiniGrid, an increase in the efficiency of the algorithm is noted by increasing the number of processors from four to eight. When using each cluster separately, a decrease in efficiency is suffered.

With regard to the algorithm efficacy, the optimum of the two problems reported by Solomon for C102-100 and C103-100 was obtained in all executions by the genetic algorithm.

The efficacy of the algorithms can be increased by increasing the exploration and exploitation of

Figure 27. Speedup of testing C102 in the MiniGrid

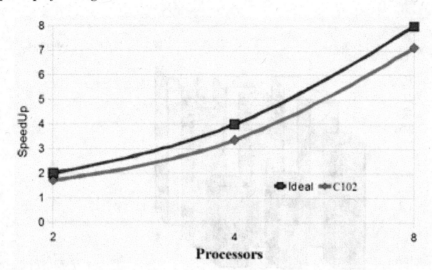

the solution space. This is possible if the number of CPUs available increases in the MiniGrid, which in turn is possible due to the design of the genetic algorithm. The genetic algorithm suffers an increase in population size Pz if the number of CPUs increases (Figure 4), while the execution time remains relatively constant.

FUTURE WORK

Future work will attempt to improve the infrastructure MiniGrid. The infrastructure used as a test scenario works, but for a production infrastructure, its performance is poor because the computer equipment and communications are not suitable. Because of this, the number of nodes in each cluster and the number of participating institutions will be increased, in order to increase the number of clusters in the MiniGrid. Future work will also attempt to make each cluster independent of local network traffic on Internet 2 in each of the participating institutions, to increase bandwidth and decrease the latency existing in the MiniGrid. When the MiniGrid is conditioned for production, real applications related to the logistics of product transport to companies will be sought. The

theoretical study of the VRPTW for instances of 1000 customers will also be continued.

CONCLUSION

This chapter presents preliminary results of the execution of an iterative genetic algorithm, using an experimental MiniGrid. It involves mutation combined with two types of local search for solving the VRPTW model, which is NP-complete.

It can be concluded that the use of a grid platform for such problems is highly recommendable when searching for a better solution bound for problems of large instances in much shorter times. The reduction in time for finding better bounds is presented in terms of the number of CPUs available in the MiniGrid. The efficacy of the algorithms becomes larger because the exploration and exploitation in the solution space increases as the number of CPUs available in the MiniGrid increases, while the algorithm execution time remains relatively constant. When using the MiniGrid, an increase in the efficiency of the algorithm is observed when the number of processors is increased from four to eight. When using

Figure 28. Average efficiencies

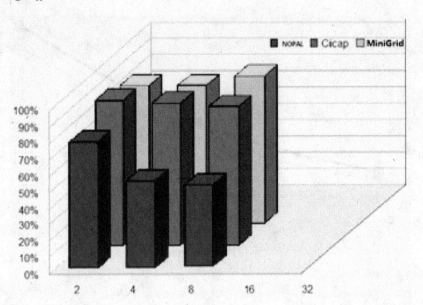

each cluster separately, a decrease in efficiency is suffered.

The bandwidth is constantly changing and tends to improve in the afternoon, so it is recommended that the execution of algorithms that require extended communication time be performed in the evenings.

It is always advisable to keep communication between processes minimal when using a Grid platform for the execution of genetic algorithms. A structure of the algorithm should be defined that allows a reduction in the communication time between processes during its implementation. This paper presents a structure in which the mutation process is effective and independent of other processes and requires a great deal of CPU time. The process of selection and crossing is very fast, and does not depend on other processes running in the MiniGrid. It is important to define an algorithm structure where the iterative mutation takes place in the CPUs of the MiniGrid. This enables the algorithm to work efficiently because it does not require communication between nodes while performing the mutation, i.e., it does not affect the algorithm. The algorithm requires

communication only once the mutation has taken place in MiniGrid nodes. This prevents latency from negatively influencing the implementation of the algorithm.

The genetic algorithm presented in this chapter can use all the resources of the MiniGrid, independent of the size of its platform. The more CPU resources the MiniGrid has, the greater exploration and exploitation it can perform for NP-complete problems in polynomial time. Thus, the Grid generally benefits the field of study of the models classified by complexity theory as the most difficult models in the world to solve. One of these models that benefits from study using this type of platform is the VRPTW model.

ACKNOWLEDGMENT

This work was supported by project FOMIX MOR-2009-C02-120102 and project I0101/131/07 C-229-07, CUDI-CONACYT, 2008-2009.

REFERENCES

Chang, Y., Cheng, W., Liu, X., & Xie, X. (2006). Application of grid technology in multi-objective aircraft optimization system. In *Proceedings of the 10ᵗʰ International Conference on Computer Supported Cooperative Work in Design* (pp. 1-5).

Cheng-Chung, C., & Smith, S. F. (1995). *A constraint satisfaction approach to makespan scheduling*. Pittsburgh, PA: Carnegie Mellon University.

Cheng-Chung, C., & Smith, S. F. (1997). *Applying constraint satisfaction techniques to job shop scheduling*. Pittsburgh, PA: Carnegie Mellon University.

Christodoulou, N., Wallace, M., & Kuchenhoff, V. (1994). Constraint logic programming and its application to fleet scheduling. *Information and Decision Technologies, 19*(3), 135–144.

Cormen, T. H., Leiserson, C. E., Rivest, R. L., & Stein, C. (2001). *Introduction to algorithms*. Cambridge, MA: MIT Press.

Corporación Universitaria para el Desarrollo de Internet (CUDI). (2011). *A. C. Internet 2, México*. Retrieved July 17, 2011, from http://www.cudi.mx/index.html

Cruz-Chávez, M. A., & Díaz-Parra, O. (2010). Evolutionary algorithm for the vehicles routing problem with time windows based on a constraint satisfaction technique. *Computación y Sistemas, IPN, 13*(3), 257–272.

Cruz-Chávez, M. A., Díaz-Parra, O., Hernández, J. A., Zavala-Díaz, J. C., & Martínez-Rangel, M. G. (2007, September 25-28). Search algorithm for the constraint satisfaction problem of VRPTW. In *Proceedings of the Electronics, Robotics and Automotive Mechanics Conference*, México (pp 746-751).

Cruz-Chávez, M. A., Martínez-Oropeza, A., & Serna Barquera, S. A. (2010, September 28-October 1). Neighborhood hybrid structure for discrete optimization problems. In *Proceedings of the Electronics, Robotics and Automotive Mechanics Conference*, México (pp. 108-113).

Cruz-Chávez, M. A., Rodríguez-León, A., Ávila-Melgar, E. Y., Juárez-Pérez, F., Cruz-Rosales, M. H., & Rivera-López, R. (2010). Gridification of genetic algorithm with reduced communication for the job shop scheduling problem. *International Journal of Grid and Distributed Computing, 3*(3), 13–28.

Díaz-Parra, O., & Cruz-Chávez, M. A. (2008). Evolutionary algorithm with intelligent mutation operator that solves the vehicle routing problem of clustered classification with Time Windows. *Polish Journal of Environmental Studies, 17*(4), 91–95.

Foster, I., & Kesselman, C. (Eds.). (2004). *The Grid 2, Second Edition: Blueprint for a new computing infrastructure* (The Elsevier Series in Grid Computing). San Francisco, CA: Morgan Kaufmann.

Fujisawa, K., Kojima, M., Takeda, A., & Yamashita, M. (2004). Solving large scale optimization problems via grid and cluster computing. *Journal of the Operations Research Society of Japan, 47*(4), 265–274.

Garey, M. R., & Jonson, D. S. (1979). *Computers and intractability a guide to the theory of NP-completeness*. New York, NY: W. H. Freeman.

Gehring, H., & Homberger, J. (1999). *A parallel hybrid evolutionary metaheuristic for the vehicle routing problem with Time Windows* (pp. 57-64). Jyvaskyla, Finland: University of Jyvaskyla. Retrieved from http://www.sintef.no/Projectweb/TOP/Problems/VRPTW/Homberger-benchmark/

Hansen, P., & Mladenovic, N. (2001). Variable neighborhood search: Principles and applications. *European Journal of Operational Research, 130,* 449–467. doi:10.1016/S0377-2217(00)00100-4

Lim, D., Ong, Y.-S., Jin, Y., Sendhoff, B., & Lee, B.-S. (2007). Efficient hierarchical parallel genetic algorithms using grid computing. *Future Generation Computer Systems, 23*(4), 658–670. doi:10.1016/j.future.2006.10.008

Luna, F., Nebro, A., Alba, E., & Durillo, J. (2008). Solving large-scale real-world telecommunication problems using a grid-based genetic algorithm. *Engineering Optimization, 40*(11), 1067–1084. doi:10.1080/03052150802294581

MacQueen, J. B. (1967). Some methods for classification and analysis of multivariate observations. In *Proceedings of the 5th Berkeley Symposium on Mathematical Statistics and Probability,* Berkeley, CA (Vol. 1, pp. 281-297).

Mitrovic-Minic, S., & Krishnamurti, R. (2006). The multiple TSP with Time Windows: Vehicle bounds based on precedence graphs. *Operations Research Letters, 34*(1), 111–120. doi:10.1016/j.orl.2005.01.009

Moscato, P., & Cotta, C. (2010). A modern introduction to memetic algorithms. In Gendreau, M., & Potvin, J.-Y. (Eds.), *Handbook of metaheuristics, international series in operations research & management science* (*Vol. 146,* pp. 141–183). New York, NY: Springer.

Papadimitriou, C. H., & Steiglitz, K. (1982). *Combinatorial optimization: Algorithms and complexity.* Upper Saddle River, NJ: Prentice Hall.

Rodriguez-León, A., Cruz-Chávez, M. A., Rivera-López, R., Ávila-Melgar, E. Y., Juárez-Pérez, F., & Díaz-Parra, O. (2010, September 28-October 1). A communication scheme for an experimental grid in the resolution of VRPTW using an evolutionary algorithm. In *Proceedings of the Electronics, Robotics and Automotive Mechanics Conference,* México (pp. 108-113).

Toth, P., & Vigo, D. (2001). *The vehicle routing problem.* Philadelphia, PA: Society of Industrial and Applied Mathematics.

ADDITIONAL READING

Baptista-Pereira, F., & Tavares, J. (Eds.). (2010). *Bio-inspired algorithms for the vehicle routing problem, studies in computational intelligence.* Berlin, Germany: Springer-Verlag.

Cruz-Chávez, M. A., Díaz-Parra, O., Juárez-Romero, D., Barreto Sedeño, E., Zavala Díaz, C., & Martínez Rancel, M. G. (2008). Un Mecanismo de Vecindad con Búsqueda Local y Algoritmo Genético para Problemas de Transporte con Ventanas de Tiempo. In *CICos 2008 6to Congreso Internacional de Cómputo en Optimización y Software, ACD,* Junio, México (pp. 23-32, 25-27).

Cruz-Chávez, M. A., Díaz-Parra, O., Juárez-Romero, D., & Martínez-Rangel, M. G. (2008). Memetic algorithm based on a constraint satisfaction technique for VRPTW. In L. Rutkowski, R. Tadeusiewicz, L. A. Zadeh, & J. M. Zurada (Eds.), *Proceedings of the 9th International Conference on Artificial Intelligence and Soft Computing* (LNCS 5097, pp. 376-387).

Díaz-Parra, O., & Cruz-Chávez, M. A. (2008). General methodology for converting sequential evolutionary algorithms into parallel algorithms with OpenMP as applied to combinatorial optimization problems. *Polish Journal of Environmental Studies, 17*(4), 240–245.

Golden, B., Raghavan, S., & Wasil, E. (Eds.). (2010). *The vehicle routing problem, latest advances and new challenges.* New York, NY: Springer.

KEY TERMS AND DEFINITIONS

Genetic Algorithm: Search type Meta heuristic that works in a non-deterministic manner, which mimics the natural process of evolution using techniques such as inheritance, mutation, selection and crossover. It is applied to find solutions to optimization problems.

Grid Computing: Set of geographically dispersed computing clusters, united by a virtual private network and considered to be a super virtual computer.

Latency: Measured time delay experienced by a Grid. The latency between two computing clusters, geographically distant but belonging to a common computational Grid, is the time the round trip takes, of sending a data packet from one cluster to another and back again.

Local Search: Heuristic method that seeks to improve the starting solution in a problem's solution space, through neighborhoods defined by a neighborhood structure. This generates a small perturbation in the starting solution, resulting in a neighboring solution with similar characteristics to the starting solution, which may be a better or worse solution.

Speedup: Relates to parallel computing and refers to a comparison of speed (faster) between the parallel form and the sequential form of the same algorithm.

Section 2
Improve of Optimization Applied Intelligent Techniques

Chapter 4
Hybrid Algorithm Applied to the Identification of Risk Factors on the Health of Newly Born in Mexico

María Dolores Torres
Autonomous University of Aguascalientes, Mexico

Eunice E. Ponce de León Sentí
Autonomous University of Aguascalientes, Mexico

Aurora Torres Soto
Autonomous University of Aguascalientes, Mexico

Elva Díaz Díaz
Autonomous University of Aguascalientes, Mexico

Carlos Alberto Ochoa Ortiz Zezzatti
Juarez City University, México

Cristina Juárez Landín
Autonomous University of Mexico State, Mexico

César Eduardo Velázquez Amador
Autonomous University of Aguascalientes, Mexico

ABSTRACT

This chapter presents the implementation of a Genetic Algorithm into a framework for machine learning that deals with the problem of identifying the factors that impact the health state of newborns in Mexico. Experimental results show a percentage of correct clustering for unsupervised learning of 89%, a real life training matrix of 46 variables, was reduced to only 25 that represent 54% of its original size. Moreover execution time is about one and a half minutes. Each risk factor (of neonatal health) found by the algorithm was validated by medical experts. The contribution to the medical field is invaluable, since the cost of monitoring these features is minimal and it can reduce neonatal mortality in our country.

DOI: 10.4018/978-1-4666-0297-7.ch004

INTRODUCTION

There are several factors that can be used as health indicators of societies, but infantile mortality is the one that better describes life conditions (Blum & Langley, 1997) since it depends of nutrition, general care, educational level, quality of medical services, etc.

This work is center on the application of artificial intelligence to the neonatal risk factor determination, because this problem is not only of social relevance, but also corresponds to a field called feature subset selection that has been widely studied since the last sixty years.

Some researches show that this problem has been addressed by different approaches. For example, Torres, Torres, Ponce, and Díaz (2004) used a combination of logistic regression and correlation and then in 2005 the same researchers approached the problem by graphical modeling (Torres, Torres, Ponce, & Torres, 2005).

The determination of risk factors during pregnancy is very important to prevent neonatal mortality because it allows medical staff to act on time. "Approximately two thirds of neonatal deaths correspond to precocious ones, reflecting mainly problems of quality on attention during childbirth, asphyxia and malformations; the remaining of deaths is caused mainly by infectious problems, premature birth, and low weight on born" (Solis, Mardones, Castillo, & Romer, 1993). However, most of these deaths can be prevented by means of simple and cheap interventions according to Dawudo in his study "Neonatal mortality: Effects of selective pediatric interventions" (Dawudo & Effiong, 1985).

Because of the importance of such researches, results are usually validated by experts of the medical area. In this study results were evaluated by pediatricians from "Instituto Mexicano del Seguro Social" (IMSS).

The feature subset selection problem consists on choosing a subset from all variables who describes a phenomenon, by the elimination of features with low discriminative and predictable information (Pelikan, Sastry, & Cantu-Paz, 2006). An appropriate feature selection is important on removing irrelevant data, increasing learning accuracy, and improving comprehension of results (Blum & Langley, 1997).

On the case of the risk factors during pregnancy and childbirth, to know the variables that rebound on the health of children could not only to reduce risk of childbirth but also to prevent baby from death.

The approach proposed in this work, combines two different techniques; one taken from the world of evolutionary computation and the other taken from the wonderful world of mathematics. The techniques are the genetic algorithm and the logic-combinatorial approach called testor analysis. The objective is to combine both tools to find the subset of variables that impact the most on the health state of the newly born. To prove the effectiveness of this approach, results were validated by medical experts. Physicians verified each resulted variable and agreed with the importance degree assigned by the system.

IDENTIFICATION OF RISK FACTORS DURING PREGNANCY

Nowadays in medicine like in any other science, the use of computational tools to make a better use of data gathered about a specific phenomenon results essential. Pediatrician from all over the world have always had the need to be well informed about maternal antecedents and previous and actual obstetric record, when acquire the responsibility of a new patient (Hobel, Hyvarinen, Okada, & Oh. 1973); therefore, many researchers have focused on the identification of risk factors of neonatal mortality, stillbirth and morbidity, in order to improve prognosis and to prevent complications.

This work has the goal of identify the features that impact the most on the health state of the

Table 1. General condition of the sample (Torres, Torres, Ponce, & Torres, 2005)

Feature	Risk factor	
	Present (%)	Absent (%)
Mother´s age	156 (22.3)	545 (77.7)
Mother's BMI[1]	258 (36.8)	443 (63.2)
Mother's schooling	309 (44.1)	392 (55.9)
Gestational age	201 (28.7)	500 (71.3)
Birth weight	145 (20.7)	556 (79.3)
Morbidity	481 (68.6)	220 (31.4)
Stillbirth	19 (2.7)	682 (97.3)
Mortality	24+19 (6.1)	658 (93.9)

newly born, identify the features that are less important and the ones that can be ignore; giving to medical staff a decision support tool to intervene opportunely during pregnancy.

Manipulated data is the result of a transverse study with a sample of 701 pregnancy cases assisted on the zone no.1 with familiar medicine of the Mexican Institute of Social Security and hospitals 1, 2, 5, 7, 45 and 49 in the city of San Luis Potosí, México on 1999 (Torres, 1999).

Initially data base was discretized according to medical literature. Table 1 shows the general conditions of the sample mentioned before.

Original data base consisted on 46 features that can be classified chronologically according to the next groups (Torres, Torres, Ponce, & Torres, 2005). Maternal antecedents:

This group contains the features that describe maternal backgrounds like age, body mass index, schooling, obstetric history, interpregnancy period, parity, etc.

Pregnancy Information

This category group together the features that describe the whole pregnancy process like the presence of toxemia, polyhydramnios, not toxemic hypertension, etc.

Childbirth and Newly Born Information

Here are included the features that describes the birth and the health state of the newly born. Features of this group are type of birth, presentation, forceps, weight, stature, body mass index, gestational age, minute Apgar, five minutes Apgar, etc.

Result Features

The features that describe the results of the birth are morbidity, stillbirth and mortality. The first represents all the babies who present any kind of disease; the second refers to babies who already were died at the birth moment, and the third, is the total amount of dead babies; whether were dead at the birth time or have died after.

Once the data base was prepared, the hybrid system for the subset selection took place. The mentioned system had the goal of reduce the number of important features as much as possible and to label them in percentage terms as very important (100%) or less important (50%).

Due to the system use specialized techniques and concepts, next sections are focus on the general description of them.

Figure 1. Filter

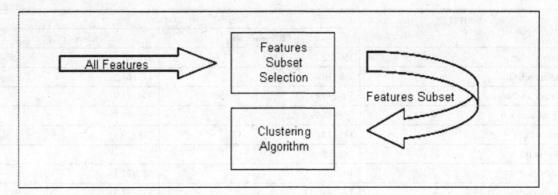

FEATURE SUBSET SELECTION

Regularly, feature subset selection is used to reduce dimensionality. This task can be done taking out irrelevant or redundant features. This is an important task because reducing the number of features may help to decrease the cost of acquiring data and also make the classification models easier to understand (Boz, 2002). Also, the number of features could affect the accuracy of classification (Torres, Ponce, Torres, & Díaz, 2008). Some authors have also studied the bias feature subset selection for classification learning (Torres, Ponce, Torres, & Díaz, 2008). This justifies the importance of a good feature subset selection for learning.

Can been seen two groups of authors: who consider that reduced subsets have to conserve features that are relevant and no redundant (Dash & Liu, 1997) and who consider the importance of the difference between optimal and relevant features that reduced subset have kept (Kohavi & Jhon, 1997).

The two most frequently used feature selection methods, are filter and wrapper (Kohavi & Jhon, 1997; Pelikan, Sastry, & Cantu-Paz, 2006; Liu, Zhu, Liu, Li, & Zhang, 2005). Filter methodology selects features based on the general characteristics of the training data, while wrapper methodology uses a learning algorithm to evaluate the accuracy of the potential subsets in predicting a target.

Filter methods are independent of the classifier and select features based on properties that a good feature sets are presumed to have, such as class separability or high correlation with the target while wrapper treats the induction algorithm as a black box that is used by the search algorithm to evaluate each candidate (Pelikan, Sastry, & Cantu-Paz, 2006).

While wrappers methodologies give good results in terms of accuracy of the final classifier are computationally expensive and may be impractical for large datasets (Pelikan, Sastry, & Cantu-Paz, 2006). That is why we tried to rescue the better of both methods creating a new framework that is based on the Liu et al. (2005); but ours is more flexible, because it fits to both: supervised and unsupervised learning.

On Figure 1, we can see the main components of filter methodology while Figure 2 presents the methodology known as wrapper.

Even though wrapper methodology has higher computational costs than filter (Liu et al., 2005), it has received considerable attention (Blum & Langley, 1997; Kohavi & Jhon, 1997). Nevertheless, filter methodologies are faster and also adequate for large dataset (Pelikan, Sastry, & Cantu-Paz, 2006; Liu et al., 2005). Filter methods can be further categorized into two groups: attribute evaluation algorithms and subset evaluation algorithms, which refer to whether they rate the relevance of individual features or feature subsets.

Figure 2. Wrapper

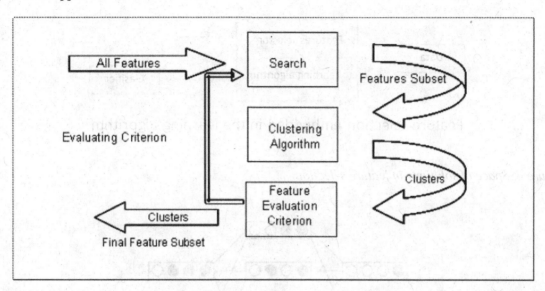

Attribute evaluation algorithms study the features individually, and ponder each one according to each feature's degree of relevance to the target feature. In this research, we focus on feature subset selection (FSS) for both supervised and unsupervised learning.

Feature subset selection methodologies in machine learning can be grouped as: Filter, Wrapper, Embedded and hybrid considering its application mode (Blum & Langley, 1997; Araúzo, 2006; Saeys, Inza, & Larrañaga, 2007).

The two new methodologies that this classification includes are: embedded and hybrid.

Embedded Methodology

In this category, the search of a good subset is obtained in the construction of the classifier, and this could be seen like a search in the combined set of features and hypothesis (Saeys, Inza, & Larrañaga, 2007). So, "embedded" methodologies are very specific for an algorithm of given learning.

The "embedded" methods have the advantage that they include the interaction with the classification pattern, being at the same time, far from being computationally intensive as wrapper methods.

In this methodology, the subset selection is included in the learning algorithm like a non detachable part. In this case, the advantage is that the selection of characteristics is designed in a specific way for that learning. This is expected that enhances its performance.

The "embedded" algorithms (Figure 3) indicate the characteristics they have selected, and the classifiers they generate will only need that subset. However, the tolerance to irrelevant features it doesn't reduce the used features.

When indicating the selected features, these can be used by another learning algorithm and, this way, to use the method "embedded" like filter in another learning system. For example, C4.5 includes a selection method, that let to know the features used by the generated tree, and this way to use them as selection for another method (Last, Kandel, & Maimon, 2001).

Hybrid

The last type of methodologies for selection of characteristics is the one that corresponds to a combination of the previous ones (filter, wrappers, embedded) to take out the biggest profit in

Figure 3. Embedded

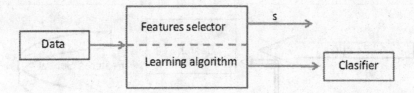

Feature selection embedded in the learning algorithm

Figure 4. Space of solutions in feature selection

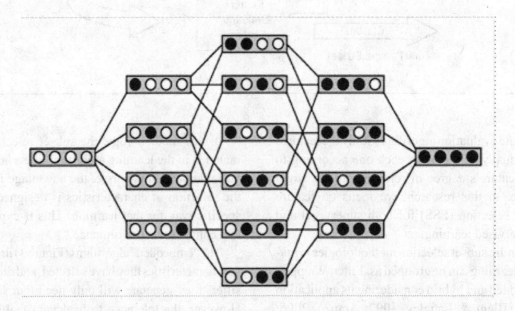

each one. An interesting possibility is to carry out a quick search type filter and, later on, to use wrapper strategy to tune the selection (Boz, 2002; Uncu & Türksen, 2007).

Space of Solutions

When one speaks about feature selection, one can see in Figure 2 that if the total group of initial characteristics is N, then the total number of subsets of the search space is 2^N. This implies that even with sizes of medium N, this is a big number, if this number grows; the problem turns to a very complicated one.

Figure 4 originally proposed by Pat Langley in 1994 in their article: "Selection of Relevant Features in Machine Learning" can be appreciated that for a small number of 4 variables, the space of subsets of variables is of $2^4 = 16$ possible combinations. Although usually the group without variables is not feasible, equally it is part of the possible combinations to be obtained. Here it is assumed that white circle is equal to consider the variable, while black circle implies the absence of the variable.

Figure 5. Pseudocode of the SGA

Simple Genetic Algorithm
1. Let be t=0 (generation counter)
2. Initialize P(t)
3. Evaluate P(t)
4. While (stop criterion do not be reached) do
a) For i=1,...,N/2 do
i. Select 2 fathers from P(t)
ii. Apply crossover to selected parents with probability p_c
iii. Mutate offspring with probability p_m
iv. Insert 2 new individuals in P(t+1)
End for
End while

GENETIC ALGORITHM

Genetic algorithm initially called genetic plans by Holland (1992), is a search heuristic that mimics the process of natural evolution. This technique belongs to the larger class of evolutionary algorithms, and has been used mainly on optimization and search problems. Repeatedly the genetic algorithm has proved its effectiveness in the solution of complex optimization problems. In 1989, when Goldberg published his book, already cited more than 70 successful applications.

According to Koza (1992) this heuristic can be defined as a mathematical any highly parallel algorithm, which transforms a group of individual objects with an associated fitness value in a new populations by means of the Darwinian principle of reproduction and survival of the most capable.

The general process of the genetic algorithm can be summarized as follows: The first step consists on the random generation of a population (consisted of n possible solutions to the proposed problem). Then, this population has to be transformed into a new one by the application of three operators; classic operators of any genetic algorithm are selection, crossover and mutation. And finally, once generational cycle has been finished, the result has to be evaluated to stop the algorithm or to repeat the process.

The pseudocode in Figure 5 illustrates the simplest version of the genetic algorithm, known as SGA (Simple Genetic Algorithm).

Even though, the general mechanism of the SGA is very simple, it has been demonstrated by Markov's chains that it will converge when elitist selection mechanisms are used (Rudolph, 1996).

Representation

In order to implement this algorithm in a practical problem, some issues have to be solved. The first step is to find a genetic representation of the solution domain (individual). The standard representation uses strings of bits to code a solution. Although binary representation is very natural and efficient for certain kind of problems, its use depends on the problem. Other kinds of representations use strings of integers, graphs, arrays, etc.

The representation used in this work is a string of bits. When a bit is 1, it means that the variable it represents is important and has to be considered; when the bit is 0, it means that the variable it represents is not relevant. The whole string represents a testor. This concept is going to be discussed in the next section.

Figure 6. Crossover

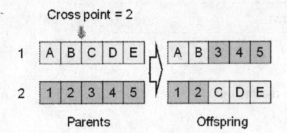

Figure 7. Mutation

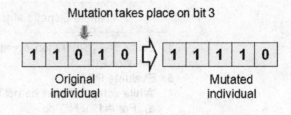

Fitness Function

Once representation has been established, a fitness function to evaluate the quality of the solution has to be designed. The fitness function depends on the problem since has to reflect the "adaptation ability of an individual". If the solution is very good, the fitness function must have a good valuation; and if the solution is bad, the fitness function valuation has to be poor.

The genetic algorithm used, is programmed to evaluate pretty good solutions that correspond to a typical testor, and to be kind with solutions that represents testors (see next section).

Genetic Operators

Finally, the implementation of a genetic algorithm also implies to establish the way a solution is going to be transformed into another. This transformation process is performed by means of the genetic operators. The three basic operators are: selection, crossover and mutation.

Selection, frequently pointed out like one of the most important parts of the genetic algorithm, is the step in which solutions of the actual generation are chosen to be spread to next generation (Jones, 2005).

The simplest and most frequently used form of crossover is performed over one cross point. In this crossover, each bit of the offspring is created copying it from one of the parents until the cross point; after this, offspring will inherit its

bits from the other parent. Figure 6 illustrates the operation principle of this genetic mechanism with a representation based on strings.

While crossover is an operator that builds new solutions from a couple of parents, mutation does it from a simple individual (Mitsuo & Runwei, 2000). Mutation guarantees the introduction of new genetic material and so, a better search.

Mutation begins with the random selection of an individual, followed by the selection of the part that is going to be changed. In the case of a binary representation, mutation implies to complement a bit. If the bit is 0 after mutation is performed, the bit will be 1; and if the original bit is 1, after mutation it will be 0. Figure 7 illustrates mutation on a string of bits.

TESTORS AND TYPICAL TESTORS

The concept of testor appeared around the fifties used mostly on electrical circuit fault detection by Cheguis and Yablonskii (1955); and later it was used in supervised classification and feature subset selection in geology (Alba, Santana, Ochoa, & Lazo, 2000). One of the pioneer works of feature subset selection with this technique is the performed by Dmitriev, Zhuravlev, and Krendeleiev (1966).

A testor is a set of features capable to distinguish elements from different classes. A typical testor is the smallest testor (regarding the number of features); if a feature is eliminated from a typical testor, it will be not more a testor (Santiesteban & Pons, 2003). Testors usually applied to pattern recognition, belong to the logic combinatorial focus; and there are several exhausted algorithms created to find subfamilies of them, like the case of typical testors.

Some Important Concepts

Let's suppose U is a collection of objects, and these objects are described by a set of n features and these objects belong to k classes.

The difference matrix is made starting from the comparison of each feature of the objects from the same class against objects from different classes. Different matrix (DM) is the matrix whose content let us distinguish objects from different classes.

Once the DM has been made, the basic matrix (BM) has to be created. This basic matrix is constituted by all the basic rows from DM.

Lets ip and iq be two rows from MD: *ip* is a basic row from MD, if there is not any row lesser than *ip* in MD. We say that ip<iq if $\forall$i $ip_i \leq iq_i$ and $\exists$j such as $ip_j \neq iq_j$.

The subset of features T of a certain BM is a testor, if when eliminate from BM all features except those who belong to T, there is not any zero row. The set T is typical, if by eliminating a feature j$\in$T, T is no more testor.

The set of all typical testors of MD is equal to the set of all typical testors of MB (Lazo & Shulcloper, 1995).

The determination of all typical testos of a certain BM is a very complex problem, so different algorithms have been developed. Some of them are: BT (Shulcloper, Aguila, & Bravo, 1985), TB (Shulcloper, Aguila, & Bravo, 1985), REC (Shulcloper, Alba, & Lazo, 1995), and LEX (Santiesteban & Pons, 2003). Sánchez and Lazo (2008) have established that this problem has an exponential complexity and it depends on the size of the BM. The determination of all typical testors constitute by itself a work line on the testors theory according to Lazo (2003).

In order to apply the testor and typical testor concepts is important to establish how compari-

sons are going to be made. One of the most common comparison criterions is known as strict equality because is applicable to any kind of domain. The way this kind of comparison is performed is described below.

Let be $\Omega=\{O_1, O_2,...,O_m\}$ a set of m objects and $I(O_1), I(O_2),...,I(O_m)$ their descriptions on terms of their features, $R=\{x_1, x_2, ..., x_n)$, where each feature x_j, has associated a set of acceptable values M_j i.e., $I(O_i)=(x_1(O_i), x_2(O_i), ..., x_n(O_i)$, and $x_j(O_i)\in M_j$, j=1, 2, ..., n and i=1, 2, ..., m (Santiesteban & Pons, 2003).

Each type of variable depends of the nature of its set of acceptable values; a set M_j could be $\{0,1\}$, the set of real numbers, the set integer numbers, etc.

The strict comparison criterion is the next function:

$$\begin{cases} C_k\left[x_k\left(O_i\right), x_k\left(O_j\right)\right] = & 0 \quad if \quad x_k\left(O_i\right) = x_k\left(O_j\right) \\ & 1 \; other\,wise \end{cases}$$

HYBRIDIZATION

The increasing complexity of problems that people has to deal with, has promoted the combination of conventional metaheuristics with either mechanisms from other metaheuristics or mechanisms outside their scope; this kind of product are referenced as hybrid metaheuristics (Raidl, 2006).

Motivation behind algorithmic hybridization is to obtain better performance, through the exploitation of the strength of certain mechanisms working together. According to the "no free lunch" theorem (Wolpert, 1996) no one metaheurística works well with any problem; therefore, is not surprising that researchers began to combine them long time ago.

The present work proposes the hybridization of the genetic algorithm with the testor concept, with the objective to determine the risk factors on the

Figure 8. EH_FSSL Framework

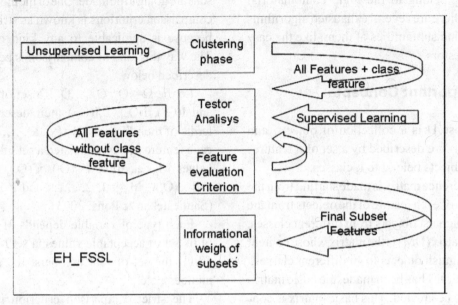

health of newly born in México. The description of the developed algorithm and the special designed operators are presented on the next section.

THE FRAMEWORK

The global model is presented in Figure 8. This is the result of several successive refinements. The framework is robust and flexible because it allows giving solution to problems of supervised, semi-supervised and unsupervised learning beside of that, it can exchange the algorithms that complete the modules. The name assigned to this framework is: EH-FSSL since it was presented in their complete form in an English-speaking article (Torres, Ponce, Torres, Ochoa, & Díaz, 2009) and these are the initials in English of "Evolutionary Hybridized Mechanisms for Feature Subset Selection both: supervised and unsupervised learning."

The first block, has the "Clustering Algorithm." Here, you can set the clustering technique that must use, in this work, the algorithm was used is K-means; however, the framework is open and another technique can be used in its place.

The clusters analysis divides the data in groups (clusters) that are much related, then, the clusters can capture the natural structure of the data. In some cases, the clusters analysis is only an initial point for other purposes as summarization of data. However, the clusters analysis has played an important paper in a wide variety of fields like psychology and other social sciences, biology, statistical, patterns recognition, recovery of information, automatic learning and data mining (Tan, Steinbach, & Kumar, 2006).

In this first block, it is added to the group of features, other more that it will contain the solution proposed by the cluster algorithm as a part of the features of the original problem. The intention of creating a virtual variable in this stage, responds to the possibility of to convert the unsupervised learning problem in a supervised one.

In the second stage, a typical testors's analysis is made with the purpose of identifying the most important features in the problem. When the original problem corresponds to supervised learning, then it is incorporated in the second block. This second stage have vital importance for this group of problems, since instead of accepting the data-

Table 2. Hypothetical basic matrix

Basic Matrix
1110
0001

Table 3. On projected on the basic

O_n Projected on BM
0
1

base like "it comes", the algorithm, first makes an inconsistencies search in it, so even when the problem is from a supervised learning one, the data are purified taking out the inconsistent and unreliable information.

Table 2 is one of the characteristics that offer potentiality and flexibility to this work, due to data rarely are refined in the real applications. Also, it is proven that usually the databases for feature subset selection in supervised learning contain important problems of consistency (Araúzo, 2006) and if data were considered such as they be received, the results would have important biases.

The block 3 "Features Evaluation Criterion" it is another important contribution from (Torres, 2010). And it refers to the way each subset is evaluated to determine if it is a promising solution or not for this problem. This block is executed in an interactive way with the block 2, until reaching a stop criterion.

The block 4 "Informational weigh of subsets" it is the part of the methodology that makes a final valuation of each component of the solution. Having the information generated during the interactive process, it is assigned a weight or informational valuation to each feature with the purpose of being able to emit a criterion with regard to groups or single feature.

Evaluation Function

The evaluation function used in the framework presented, let us use a technique called logical combinatory focus with an artificial intelligence technique: a genetic algorithm for the feature subsets selection in learning.

The evaluation function is intimately related with the status of a solution in terms of if the solution is a testor, a typical testor or if the solution is not a testor.

No Testor Condition

For explaining the way the evaluation function works, here we have a little example:

If we have the next basic matrix (BM):

Generated from a Learning Matrix of four variables, let us consider that an individual that must be evaluated is: $On=0001$, this individual should be compared against all the elements of the previously shown basic matrix, the evaluation function makes a projection on the basic matrix in the columns in those that the individual to evaluate, has value of 1. In Table 3, the projection of O_n is presented in the basic matrix.

On this projection, lines of zeros are looked for, when finding a line of zeros (row 1), then this individual is pondered as a no-testor, the lowest valuation that an individual can receive.

Typical Testor Condition

If instead of the individual $O_n=0001$, the individual to analyze were: $O_{n+1}=1001$, then the projection of the basic matrix would be like the one shown in Table 4.

We can see that in the projection of the basic matrix there are not lines of zeros, then the individual O_{n+1} is a testor and also is a candidate to be a typical testor. So, you can opt to eliminate anyone of the features presented in On+1. If we make it, either, the line one or the line two in the projected basic matrix results, will become line of zeros. This is the case of a typical testor. A typical testor is a testor to which none of their features can be eliminated without it loses its condition of testor.

To generalize the condition of a typical testor, we will analyze the following example:

If in certain moment, it is found that the basic matrix of a problem (a bigger than the examples shown up to now) is like the one in Table 5.

Table 4. O_{n+1} projected on the Basic Matrix

Basic Matrix	
X_1	X_4
1	0
0	1

Table 5. Basic matrix

Basic Matrix			
X_1	X_2	X_3	X_4
1	1	0	0
1	0	1	1
0	1	1	0
0	1	0	1
1	0	0	1

Then, the search of testors could be done in the search space that is presented in Table 6.

With the purpose of knowing if one of the chains in the power set (or group of all the solutions in the space of solutions) is a typical testor, the projection mask should be generated in the basic matrix, as in Table 10.

Starting from a previous knowledge of the problem, it is known that the following groups of elements belonging to the power set are the ones shown in Tables 7, 8, and 9.

Considering each one of the individuals and knowing their condition (if it is a no-testor, testor or typical testor) the following projections of the individuals are obtained on the basic matrix in Table 10.

Table 6. Projections of the Individuals 1, 2, and 3 in the basic matrix

Table 7. Power Set

Basic Matrix			
X_1	X_2	X_3	X_4
0	0	0	1
0	0	1	0
0	0	1	1
0	1	0	0
0	1	0	1
0	1	1	0
0	1	1	1
1	0	0	0
1	0	0	1
1	0	1	0
1	0	1	1
1	1	0	0
1	1	0	1
1	1	1	0
1	1	1	1

Table 8. No testors

No testers (NT)			
X_1	X_2	X_3	X_4
0	0	0	1
0	0	1	0
0	0	1	1
0	1	0	0
0	1	1	0
1	0	0	0
1	0	0	1
1	0	1	0

Table 9. Testors

Testors (T)			
X_1	X_2	X_3	X_4
0	1	1	1
1	1	0	1
1	1	1	0
1	1	1	1

Table 10. Typical testers

Typical Testors (TT)			
X_1	X_2	X_3	X_4
0	1	0	1
1	0	1	1
1	1	0	0

As can be seen in Table 6, the individuals are shown in color blue, while the columns in yellow are those that correspond to the projection of "1's" of that individual on the basic matrix. The reader will notice that framed lines are those who cause that the individual be a non testor and appear like (NT) – marking the found lines of zeros.

In a same way, the individuals 4, 5 and 6 are presented in Table 11.

As the reader can appreciate in the previous table, the projection of the individual "5" doesn't cause lines of zeros, because this individual is at least a testor and probably a typical testor. In Table 12 (power set) is shown individual "5" as typical testor, however, the condition to guarantee that indeed it is a typical testor and not of only a testor will presented after.

Continuing with the analysis, in Table 12, the projections of the individuals 7, 8, and 9 are presented.

In the previous table, there is a testor and two non testores, in the case of the non testores, one can see that the individual's projections on the

basic matrix generate at least a line of zeros; but the lector can see that this does not happens with the individual "7." This individual is a testor.

Tables 13 and 14 present the rest of the projections of the individuals on the basic matrix.

In the previous table, there are 2 typical testors and 1 non testor, it is very clear in the projection, the condition of a non testor.

Finally, the last individuals of the power set are shown for the example problem in Table 14.

Table 11. Projections of the Individuals 4,5 and 6 in the basic matrix

Table 12. Projections of the Individuals 7,8 and 9 in the basic matrix

Table 13. Projections of the Individuals 10,11 and 12 in the basic matrix

Table 14. Projections of the Individuals 13, 14, and 15 in the basic matrix

individual 13	individual 14	individual 15
1 1 0 1	1 1 1 0	1 1 1 1
BM	BM	BM
1 1 0 0	1 1 0 0	1 1 0 0
1 0 1 1	1 0 1 1	1 0 1 1
0 1 1 0	0 1 1 0	0 1 1 0
0 1 0 1	0 1 0 1	0 1 0 1
1 0 0 1	1 0 0 1	1 0 0 1
T	T	T

Typical Testor Condition

The reader will see that none of the individuals "13, 15 or 15" generate lines of zeros, so, we assume the condition of testors. However, the distinction between a testor and a typical testor could be reduced to the fact that if anyone of the features of a typical testor is eliminated, then it will lose its testor condition; or said in another way: when carrying out its projection in the basic matrix, it will generate at least one line of zeros. The above-mentioned, doesn't happen with a testor that is not typical, because if we select any of the redundant features, then the testor won't get lost its testor condition.

The aforementioned will only happen, if we try to eliminate a feature that is indispensable and not in the case of anyone of the features that constitute the testor.

After the previous differentiation between a testor and a typical testor, we will present the automated way to distinguish them in the evaluation function used in the genetic Algorithm (GA).

When a testor is typical this means that to eliminate anyone of its components this will cause that it will not be anymore a testor, and consequently this implies that it generates at least a line of zeros in the basic matrix, implicitly can be said that L conditions exists in the basic matrix that accomplish.

$$L - \left[\sum_{i=1}^{L} \left(x_i \mid x_i = 0 \right) \right] = 1$$

Equation 1. Typical testor conditions

Where **L** is the number of "different chains" that they fulfill the equation 1 and L is also the longitude of the chain projected on the basic matrix. Said in another way; **L** is the number of present features in an individual that is a testor (or the number of features with value ="1").

To make evident the conditions that allow the clear differentiation between a testor and a typical testor, the analysis of these conditions is presented immediately.

The first testor, is also identified as typical testor in Table 11. Its analysis and the generalization presented in equation 1 is presented in Table 15.

In the previous table, we can see that the generated projection by the two present features, two "different chains" was generated in those chains where equation 1 is completed. The chains of the projection that have been marked in a square, are

Table 15. Analysis of Individual "5"

those that are considered, because the line three and the line 5 of the projection are no longer different to the chains of the line one and the line two.

When finding these marked chains with a square in the previous table, this can guarantee himself that if anyone of the $L = 2$ features that compose this testor is eliminated, then at least, a line of zeros will be generated, and then this testor loses its condition. Therefore, we meet with a testor that is also a typical testor.

If the two lines that fulfill the condition of the equation 1 are considered, one will be able to see that the lines form an identity matrix of size = L.

Remember that an identity matrix or unit matrix of size n is the n×n square matrix with ones on the main diagonal and zeros elsewhere. It is denoted by I_n, or simply by I if the size is immaterial or can

be trivially determined by the context. (In some fields, such as quantum mechanics, the identity matrix is denoted by a boldface one, **1**; otherwise it is identical to I.)

It is possible that this identity matrix (Table 16) is not formed in an immediate way in all the cases, but if we reorder the **L** obtained lines, one will be able to appreciate it in those cases the order doesn't coincide exactly.

Therefore, the analysis of the other cases is presented next for the typical testors (individuals "11" and "12") and later on, the cases of the simple testores (individuals "7", "13", "14" and "15").

In Table 17, we can see that the identity matrix of size 3 is formed after the "11" individual's analysis. The above-mentioned means that none of the 3 characteristics used in the testor is dispensable.

In Table 18, the situation of the 5th individual analysis is repeated, there are some chains, but two different chains that complete the equation 1 and that they constitute the identity matrix, so we know that individual 12 is a typical testor.

Table 19 is representative of what happens when one has a testor that is not typical.

Note that the individual's projection that are considered here, are only those who completed equation 1. (The same case occurs in following tables.)

As you can see, it is not completed that the **L** different chains that fulfill the equation 1 exist. When not completing the identity matrix, it means that the individual analyzed is a non typical testor.

Table 16. Identity matrix

$$I_1 = [1], \quad I_2 = \begin{bmatrix} 1 & 0 \\ 0 & 1 \end{bmatrix}, \quad I_3 = \begin{bmatrix} 1 & 0 & 0 \\ 0 & 1 & 0 \\ 0 & 0 & 1 \end{bmatrix}, \quad \cdots, \quad I_n = \begin{bmatrix} 1 & 0 & \cdots & 0 \\ 0 & 1 & \cdots & 0 \\ \vdots & \vdots & \ddots & \vdots \\ 0 & 0 & \cdots & 1 \end{bmatrix}$$

The same thing can be observed in the analyses of the individuals "13", "14" and "15".

In the case that is shown in Table 20, the projection (that accomplishes equation 1) only contains one of three chains that constitute the identity matrix of size 3; so 13th individual is a testor (Table 21).

Finally, in Table 22, the case of the most redundant testor is presented (the one that contains all the features).

After presenting the case of all the testores that are not typical (or minimum), one can notice that while more redundant is the testor, then less lines of the identity matrix will be in the projection on the basic matrix.

If all the lines are found in the projection, then it is not doubt that the individual that is analyzed is a typical testor.

When identifying the condition of an individual is "typical testor", this is pondered with

Table 17. Analysis of individual 11

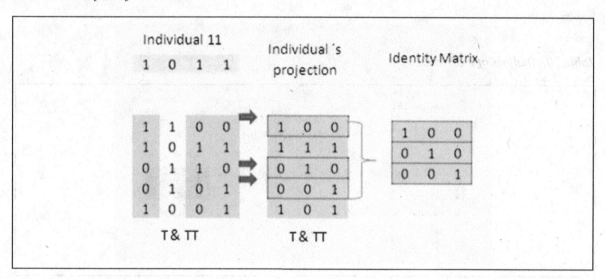

Table 18. Analysis of individual 12

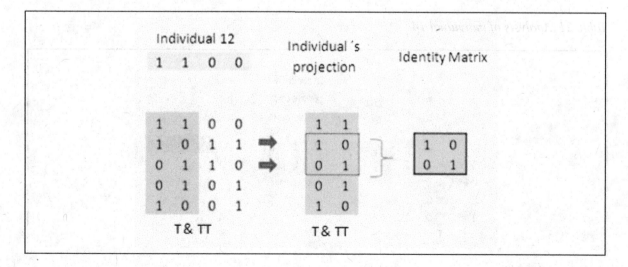

Table 19. Analysis of individual 7

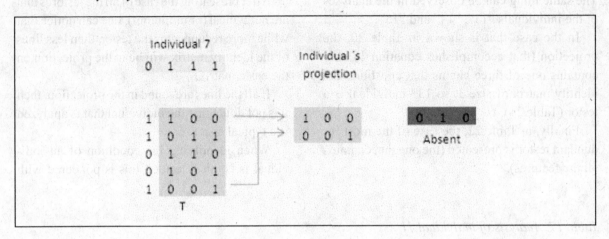

Table 20. Analysis of individual 13

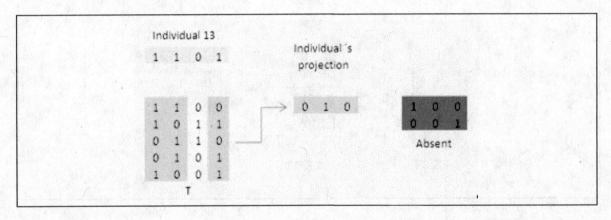

Table 21. Analysis of individual 14

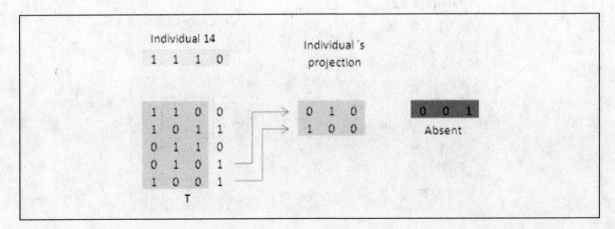

Table 22. Analysis of individual 15

Table 23. Projection of 1101 on the Basic Matrix

Basic Matrix
110
001

the highest value in its function of adaptability (also well-known as fitness).

In other case, if the individual to be analyzed were: $O_{n+2}=1101$, then the projection on the basic matrix would be that shown in Table 23.

In this third case, there are not lines of zeros in the projection of the basic matrix, because the individual is a testor. However, if we decide either to remove X_1 or X_2, it will continue being a testor that is why the individual's current condition is of a testor and not of a typical testor. To this type of individuals, we assigned a half ponder, since they have enough information to distinguish the classes, but this information contains even certain redundancies.

Operator of Acceleration

The operator of acceleration provides to the metaheuristic a very important mechanism that allows the identification of promising areas in the solution space.

Although metaheuristics of artificial intelligence are good to explore very wide spaces of solutions, it is also right that they cannot explore the specific area in which the best solution is located by default.

Before incorporating this operator to the metaheuristic, the results were enough bad, since in a random way, in a space of solutions that it grows exponentially, it is very probable that the "blind" exploration mechanism doesn't achieve any good result. We could experience this frustration when we let that an algorithm carried out blind searches of typical testores in a "big" basic matrix of 29 X 65549.

For sizing this problem, we calculated the space of solutions (the number of possible subsets of features is of 536 870 911 subsets) so, an exhaustive algorithm with a basic matrix of 65549 lines should analyze 536 870 911 times.

The reference above-mentioned is made because when the problem begins to grow, it does in a disproportionate way, that is the reason this is recognized as a problem of exponential complexity, well-known as intractable.

So, the operator of acceleration is very important in its operation, the small example that will be presented has been considering academic one.

Consider that one has the basic matrix for the operator of acceleration or accelerating operator (OA) that is shown in Table 24.

Table 24. Basic matrix

Basic Matrix			
X_1	X_2	X_3	X_4
1	1	1	0
0	0	0	1

Table 25. Basic Matrix "1" (AO)

Basic Matrix			
X_1	X_2	X_3	X_4
1	1	0	0
0	0	0	1
0	0	1	0

If we do a superficial analysis of the basic matrix before looking for cases that we have denominated atypical (Torres, Ponce, Torres, & Díaz, 2008) then we will be able to identify quickly that the line two of that basic matrix contain an atypical case.

An atypical case is present when a line with only 1 one is accompanied by pure zeros. We know that this line, it will cause "problems" because this kind of atypical situations, are those that cause lines of zeros when the projection of the characteristics doesn't contemplate this variable (the only one with value of 1).

If the basic matrix was the one that is presented in this case, then when identifying this atypical line, it provides us enough information "to know" that any typical testor associated to that basic matrix "obligatorily" has to have the variable X_4, because without it, the line two of the basic matrix will produce a line of zeros in the projection. So, anyone of the other variables (X_1, X_2, X_3) they won't be able to avoid that this line of zeros be generated. That is why is impossible to generate a single typical testor without variable X_4.

The reader will notice that this simple procedure, in a problem with a space of solutions of $2^N-1 = 15$ possible different subsets, when fixing the position of X_4, the solution space will reduce in the exponent. The search space is now $2^{N-1}-1=7$ (approximately the half).

If the basic matrix of the problem had been the one shown next (only with academic purposes) (Table 25).

It would be known that a typical testor would contain the variable X_3 and X_4 to avoid that the

lines 2 or 3 of the basic matrix 1 (AO) produced a line of zeros.

With this simple analysis, the search space decreased to $2^{N-2}-1=3$ possible subsets, and in general terms this reduction can be generalize to:

$$2^{N-L} - 1 \text{ (Torres et at., 2009)}$$

Equation 2. Reduction's generalization

Where **N** is the number of features in the original problem and **L** is the number of atypical cases inside the basic matrix associated to a specific training matrix.

The acceleration operator is a tool that allows jump spaces of the searching space that are not promising, this way we take advantage of resources in the evaluation of only those spaces that are promissory.

The operator was denominated "accelerating operator" because generates a considerable improvement diminishing the searching space in its exponent.

Once the atypical cases are identified, we create a chain "chain of ownership" (Torres, Ponce, Torres, & Díaz, 2008). This chain of ownership is a bits sequence that works as a "mask" allowing that the space of solutions has previously identified areas as "potentials" or "tabu" (that should be avoided).

This can be expressed graphically as that shown in Figure 9.

The previous figure represents the effect of the accelerating operator in the space of solutions. It is important to mention that although the reduction in the space of solutions is geometric, Figure

Figure 9. Space of solutions

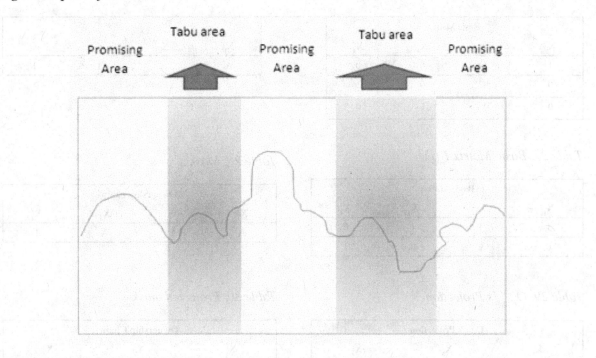

1 shows that it could be discontinuities of different sizes depending on the bits that can be obviated in the search.

The "chain of ownership", once it is made, it works as a mask: in the previous example, the mask could be interpreted as shown in Table 26.

The information shown in the chain of ownership, indicates to the evolutionary algorithm that the position corresponding to X_1 and to X_2, can be any value (A=any 1 or 0), while the values of the variable X_3 and X_4 should be 1 in order to find a typical testor.

Mechanism of Improvement

The mechanism of improvement was developed inspired by the mechanism of improvement that uses scatter search.

Scatter search appears in the decade of the seventies. Although the first publication related with this technique was reported in 1977 (Glover, 1977; Martí & Laguna, 2003). Glover consolidates it in its publication of 1998. This metaheuristic

has an improvement mechanism that tries to recompose or transform a potential solution that is not feasible in the way it is.

The improvement mechanism (IM) can be described as an exploitation mechanism that potentializes the finding of typical testors by the "knowledge" in the way that testors behave.

Once a promissory area is identified this operator, makes a local search to improve the current solution. This search is applied in the sense of reduction of the chain; it is feasible to change a bit 1 for 0 (if the individual is a no-typical testor) or in opposed sense (if we do not have a testor). To be clearer, we will present an academic example again (Table 27).

If we have the basic matrix shown in previous table, for the operator of acceleration, it is known that X_4 is indispensable for the conformation of a testor. Said in another way, the behavior mask will be the one shown in Table 28.

Let us think that the following individual is presented for its analysis: $O_{n+m} = 1011$.

Table 26. Chain of ownership and Basic Matrix "1" (AO)

Basic Matrix			
X_1	X_2	X_3	X_4
1	1	0	0
0	0	0	1
0	0	1	0

X_1	X_2	X_3	X_4
A	A	1	1

Table 27. Basic Matrix 1 (IM)

Basic Matrix			
X_1	X_2	X_3	X_4
1	1	1	0
0	0	0	1

Table 28. Mask

Ownership chain			
X_1	X_2	X_3	X_4
A	A	A	1

Table 29. O_{n+m}'s Projection

O_{n+m}'s Projection		
X_1	X_3	X_4
1	1	0
0	0	1

Table 30. Projected mask

Ownership Chain		
X_1	X_3	X_4
A	A	1

First of all, we can say that this is an individual that is located in a promissory area because it has the feature X4.

In second place, and after making the projection in the basic matrix, we can say that we have a testor in the hands (Table 29).

Inside each testor there is minimum a typical testor. This asseveration could be proven analyzing individual O_{n+m} because its projection induces that we could omit the variable X_1 or X_3, but not both of them and on the other hand, variable X_4 is indispensable.

Our improvement mechanism acts like a "intelligent" mutation because it leaves the good part of an individual while examines the other parts.

1. As we know the ownership chain, we projected it in the basic matrix (Table 30).
2. We can see that there are 2 variables that can be modified (X_1 and X_3), randomly we

choose one of them and then mutate it to obtain:

a) 1 0 0 1 or
b) 0 0 1 1

This is a fortunate case of the intelligent mutation or mechanism of improvement, because it does not matter which bit was selected, the result of this operation will produce a typical testor.

Obviously, this is not the general case of all the applications of the operator, but it is a fact that when making an intelligent mutation, the probabilities to find a hidden testor there, are increased positively.

The most important premise that gave place to this operator was the unequivocal knowledge that in any testor, it exists at least one typical testor "hidden."

Figure 10. HGAFSSL algorithm

```
Algorithm 1 - HEGAFSSL
Begin /* Hybridized Evolutionary GA for FSS in
Learning*/
    Initial pre-processing for taking out some
        features
    If supervised learning then goto 0
    else Training clustering mechanism.
    Cluster phase.
0 Generating DM phase.
    Generating BM phase.
    Generate initial population (randomly).
    Apply accelerating operator.
    Apply improvement mechanism.
    Compute fitness
    population <- new initial population
    Repeat
        Begin /* New Generation */
        Repeat
            Begin /* reproductive cycle for pairs of
                individuals */
                Apply selection operator.
                Apply crossover operator.
                Apply accelerating operator.
                Apply improvement mechanism.
                Compute fitness.
                Count- Count+1;
            End.
            Until Count - (generation size/ 2).
            Order of population by fitness.
            Apply elitism.
            Population <- new population
        End.
        Until (stopping criterion is reached)
        Final set of typical testors analysis.
        Compute informational weight for each feature
        Get final features subset selection.
End /* Hybridized Evolutionary AG for FSS in Learning*
```

The Proposed Genetic Algorithm

The Hybridized Evolutionary Genetic Algorithm for Feature Subset Selection in Learning is shown in Figure 10. We can see that the metaheuristic hybridized with a local mechanism that improves a particular solution looking for a typical testor from a single testor. Besides that, elitism was used for accelerating the typical testors search and also, a global search operator was incorporated. This global operator (accelerating operator), was obtained from a simple analysis of the BM. This way, we rescued the best of the interior and exterior scale algorithms, used for finding typical testors. Finally the logical combinatory focus was integrated to our methodology.

EXPERIMENTATION AND RESULTS

The database used in this research corresponds to the problem of neonatal mortality in the central cities of the Mexican Republic. The problem attacked, is related with the risk factors in the health condition of newly born in Mexico. The cost of the care of these critical factors is insignificant and the benefits are invaluable. That is why, many researchers in the health care, consider that this is a topic of vital importance.

Through the application of the framework was possible to identify the variables of more importance in pregnant women along their pregnancy and childbirth. We could identify that these variables are 24, however 20 were 100% indispensable,

Table 31. Features of the neonatal database

Dataset features	Multivariate	Number of Instances	711
Attributes features	Real, integer and categorical	Number of features	46
Associated Tasks	Clustering and classifying	Null values	No

Table 32. Experiments with dataset "neonatal"

Method	HEGA-FSSL	Exhausted
Dataset	Neonatal	Neonatal
Features	46	46
Instances	711	711
% Typical Testors found	100%	100%
Average time (running) mseconds	131,989.30	259.2×10^6

while 4 obtained 50% of importance in terms of their informational weight.

In fact, we could decrease the group of features from 46 to 29 after the preprocessing and finally, we find 24 features after the complete process.

The experimental results show that although the Genetic Algorithm (GA) is known as quick-convergence algorithm, thanks to the acceleration operator and the improvement mechanism, our GA maintained a search that conserved the diversity required in the solutions space of the problem.

The database of the problem of real application is shown in Table 31.

We could observe, that as the size of the problem grows, the efficiency of using the algorithm HEGA-FSSL increases too, this is very evident for the database "Neonatal" because the space of solutions for this problem is huge: 536, 870, 911 combinations.

Experimental results can be reviewed in Table 32.

After the preprocessing, 29 of the 46 original variables were conserved and was identified that 24 are indispensable while the remaining 5, can be eliminated (simultaneously 22 variables can be conserved and they constitutes a typical testor).

The proportion of those results could be seen in Figure 11.

In the previous figure, we can observe that the quantity of variables that we must consider in the problem of risk factors of neonatal morbidity is 52.17% of those considered initially, this means that a reduction of 47.83% was achieved. Each variable was validated by expert medical personnel that coincided with their incidence in the problem of neonatal health.

Data were associated with the next three classes:

1. Healthy
2. The ones who born live and got sick in the first 28 days of life
3. The ones who born dead.

It is feasible to predict the class to which belongs a new case with only 22 of the 24 identified variables; what represents 47.82% of those considered initially. This represents a level of reduction of 53.78%.

The parameters used in the experimentation phase are shown in Table 33.

The results show that there are features that impact strongly the health conditions of the

Figure 11. Subsets of variables identified

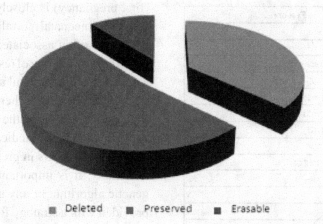

■ Deleted   ■ Preserved   ■ Erasable

newly born babies (these features are marked with "black 1's" in the next chromosome while blue ones, are important, but not in the same proportion, they are marked with "blue 1´s" in Figure 12. Finally, the features market with 0's are the ones who can be eliminated without losing vital information.

The chromosome used corresponds to those shown in Figure 13.

Table 33. Parameters used

Population size	20
Number of features	29
Number of generations	40
Crossover likelihood	60%
Mutation likelihood	3.33%

Figure 12. Informational chromosome

CONCLUSION AND FUTURE RESEARCH

The real problem handled in this work, is a major issue in the field of neonatal health in Mexico, so it has to be said that the use of such tools in the medical field is a success for the computer sciences.

All features present in the typical testors found by the algorithm, have been recognized by experts and literature as risk factors for pregnancy. For example, the body mass index, which is a crude measure of the nutritional status of a person (BMI) that correspond to the ratio of weight by the square of the height, is considered a risk factor for pregnancy because according to Jimenez and Gay in 1997, mother's malnutrition before or during pregnancy contributes to the born of low weight or underweight children. By the other side, the World Health Organization (WHO) and other expert organizations establish the boundaries of this indicator for an adult are from 18.5 to 25.

Figure 13. Chromosome correspondences

Bit	Feature
1	Mother age
2	Mother weight
3	Index of the mother's corporal mass
4	Mother height
5	Number of pregnancies
6	Number of childbirths
7	Number of abortions
8	Number of caesarean
9	Last time among pregnancies
10	Toxemia
11	Polyhydramnios
12	Bleeding
13	Not toxaemic hypertension
14	Urinal via infection
15	Antecedents of malformations
16	Smoking
17	Alcoholism
18	Newly born gender
19	Newly born weight
20	Index of corporal mass of the newly born
21	Newly born height
22	Gestation age
23	Type from birth
24	Presentation
25	Childbirth type
26	1 minute Apgar
27	5 minutes Apgar
28	Forces
29	Malformations

Above this range is considered overweight and below it, low weight.

Quesada Chaviano also found in his study "Edad materna, riesgo nutricional preconcepcional y peso al nacer", that in the case of mothers with BMI less than 19.8 kg/m², the rates of low weight and underweight at birth, are twice in relation to mothers with a BMI greater than or equal to 19.8 kg/m² (Chaviano & López, 2000).

According to several researchers, primiparity (first pregnancy) is closely related to low-birth-weight and neonatal mortality. However, multiparity is also often associated with adverse results according to a number of researchers on risk factors associated with perinatal and neonatal mortality.

Just like these, the other features present on the typical testors found by the genetic algorithm have a justification in the medical field that recognizes them as risk factors in pregnancy.

Finally, it is important to note that when a genetic algorithm or any other metaheurística is provided with a strategy for exploring the search space of a higher level, its efficiency is greatly increased.

A well known weakness of the genetic algorithm is its fast convergence to local optima; this aspect was overcome by the guidance of the solution generation through the concepts of testor and typical testor in combination with built-in mechanisms.

Analyzing the results obtained by the genetic algorithm, it can be concluded that the hybrid evolutionary mechanisms are efficient for the identification of factors that affect the health status of infants in Mexico; and that the researcher is not forced to have a deep knowledge of a particular medical area to find relevant information, when artificial intelligence is been used.

Some future research lines that are been explored by the authors of this work are: the generalization of the presented tool, to be implemented with other metaheuristics. The use of mechanisms from other approaches could exploit their strengths, and reduce their weaknesses.

Authors are also working on the multiobjective optimization field with the intention of undertake the risk factors of pregnancy problem with Pareto´s mechanisms; in order to find the relationship between the Pareto´s front and the typical testors.

REFERENCES

Alba, C. E., Santana, R., Ochoa, R. A., & Lazo, C. M. (2000). Finding typical testors by using an evolutionary strategy. In *Proceedings of the 5th Iberoamerican Workshop on Pattern Recognition*, Lisbon, Portugal (pp. 267-278).

Araúzo, A. (2006). *Un Sistema Inteligente para Selección de Características en Clasificación* (Unpublished doctoral dissertation). Universidad de Granada, Granada, Spain.

Blum, A., & Langley, P. (1997). Selection of relevant features and examples in machine learning. *Artificial Intelligence, 97*(1-2), 245–271. doi:10.1016/S0004-3702(97)00063-5

Bobadill, J. L., & Langer, A. (1990). La mortalidad infantil en México: un fenómeno en transición. *Revista Mexicana de Sociologia, 52*(1), 111–131. Retrieved from http://www.jstor.org/stable/3540648 doi:10.2307/3540648

Boz, O. (2002). Feature subset selection by using sorted feature relevance. In *Proceedings of the International Conference on Machine Learning and Applications* (pp. 147-153).

Chaviano, Q., & López, S. (2000). *Edad materna, riesgo nutricional preconcepcional y peso al nacer*. Matanzas, Cuba: Centro Provincial de Higiene y Epidemiología.

Cheguis, I. A., & Yablonskii, S. V. (1955). About testors for electrical outlines. *Uspieji Matematicheskij Nauk, 4*(66), 182–184.

Dash, M., & Liu, H. (1997). Feature selection for classification. *Intelligent Data Analysis, 1*, 131–156. doi:10.1016/S1088-467X(97)00008-5

Dawudo, A. H., & Effiong, C. E. (1985). Neonatal mortality: Effects of selective pediatric interventions. *Pediatrics, 75*(1), 51–57.

Dmitriev, A. N., Zhuravlev, Y. I., & Krendeleiev, F. P. (1966). On the mathematical principles of patterns and phenomena classification. *Diskretnyi Analiz, 7*, 3–15.

Glover, F. (1977). Heuristics for integer programming using surrogate constrains. *Decision Sciences, 8*, 156–166. doi:10.1111/j.1540-5915.1977.tb01074.x

Glover, F. (1998). A template for scatter search and path relinking. In J.-K. Hao, E. Lutton, E. M. A. Ronald, M. Schoenauer, & D. Snyers (Eds.), In *Proceedings of Selected Papers from the Third European Conference on Artificial Evolution* (LNCS 1363, pp. 3-54).

Goldberg, D. E. (1989). *Genetic algorithms in search optimization & machine learning*. Reading, MA: Addison-Wesley.

Hobel, C. J., Hyvarinen, M. A., Okada, D. M., & Oh, W. (1973). Prenatal and intrapartum high-risk screening. I. Prediction of the high-rish neonate. *American Journal of Obstetrics and Gynecology, 117*(1), 1–9.

Holland, J. (1992). *Adaptation in natural and artificial systems*. Ann Arbor, MI: University of Michigan Press.

Jiménez, S., & Gay, J. (1997). *Vigilancia nutricional materno infantil. Guías para la atención primaria de salud*. La Habana, Cuba: Editorial Caguayo.

Jones, T. M. (2005). *AI application programming* (2nd ed.). Hingham, MA: Charles River Media.

Kohavi, R., & Jhon, G. H. (1997). Wrappers for feature subset selection. *Artificial Intelligence, 97*(1-2), 273–324. doi:10.1016/S0004-3702(97)00043-X

Koza, J. R. (1992). *Genetic programming: On the programming of computers by means of natural selection*. Cambridge, MA: MIT Press.

Last, M., Kandel, A., & Maimon, O. (2001). Information theoretic algorithm for feature selection. *Pattern Recognition Letters*, *22*(6-7), 799–811. doi:10.1016/S0167-8655(01)00019-8

Lazo, C. M. (2003). *Reconocimiento Lógico Combinatorio de Patrones*. Havana, Cuba: Instituto de Cibernética, Matemática y Física.

Lazo, C. M., & Shulcloper, R. J. (1995). Determining the feature relevance for non classically described objects and a new algorithm to compute typical fuzzy testors. *Pattern Recognition Letters*, *16*, 1259–1265. doi:10.1016/0167-8655(95)00077-8

Liu, P., Zhu, J., Liu, L., Li, Y., & Zhang, X. (2005, June 13-15). Data mining application in prosecution committee for unsupervised learning. In *Proceedings of the International Conference on Services Systems and Services Management* (Vol. 2, pp 1061-1064).

Martí, R., & Laguna, M. (2003). Scatter Search: Diseño básico y estrategias avanzadas. Inteligencia Artificial. *Revista Iberoamericana de Inteligencia Artificial, 19*.

Mitsuo, G., & Runwei, C. (2000). *Genetic algorithms & engineering optimization*. New York, NY: John Wiley & Sons.

Pelikan, M., Sastry, K., & Cantu-Paz, E. (2006). *Scalable optimization via probabilistic modeling: From algorithms to applications*. New York, NY: Springer.

Raidl, G. R. (2006). A unified view on hybrid metaheuristics. In F. Almeida, M. J. B. Aguilera, C. Blum, J. M. M. Vega, M. Pérez Pérez, A. Roli, & M. Sampels (Eds.), *Proceedings of the Third International Conference on Hybrid Metaheuristics* (LNCS 4030, pp. 1-12).

Rudolph, G. (1996). Convergence of evolutionary algorithms in general search spaces. In *Proceedings of the Third IEEE Conference on Evolutionary Computation*.

Saeys, Y., Inza, I., & Larrañaga, P. (2007). A review of feature selection techniques in bioinformatics. *Bioinformatics (Oxford, England)*, *23*(19), 2507–2517. doi:10.1093/bioinformatics/btm344

Sánchez, D. G., & Lazo, C. M. (2008). CT-EXT: An algorithm for computing typical testor set. In L. Rueda, D. Mery, & J. Kittler (Eds.), *Proceedings of the 12th Iberoamericann Congress on Progress in Pattern Recognition, Image Analysis and Applications* (LNCS 4756, pp. 506-514).

Santiesteban, A., & Pons, P. A. (2003). Lex: Un Nuevo Algoritmo para el Cálculo de los Testores Típicos. *Revista Ciencias Matemáticas*, *21*(1), 85–95.

Shulcloper, J. R., Aguila, F. I., & Bravo, M. A. (1985). Algoritmos BT y TB para el cálculo de todos los tests típicos. *Revista Ciencias Matemáticas*, *6*(2), 11–18.

Shulcloper, J. R., Alba, C., & Lazo, C. (1995). *Introducción al reconocimiento de Patrones: Enfoque Lógico Combinatorio (Serie Verde No. 51)*. México: Cinvestav-IPN.

Solis, F., Mardones, G., Castillo, B., & Romer, M. I. (1993). Mortalidad por Inmadurez e hipoxia como causas de atención obstétrica y neonatal. *Revista Chilena de Pediatría*.

Tan, P. N., Steinbach, M., & Kumar, V. (2006). *Introduction to data mining*. Reading, MA: Addison-Wesley.

Torres, M. D. (2010). *Metaheurísticas Híbridas en Selección de Subconjuntos de Características para Aprendizaje no Supervisado* (Unpublished doctoral dissertation). Universidad Autónoma de Aguascalientes, Aguascalientes, México.

Torres, M. D., Ponce, L. E., Torres, A., & Díaz, E. (2008). Selección de Características Basada en el Peso Informacional de las Variables en Aprendizaje no Supervisado mediante Algoritmos Genéticos. In *Cuarto Congreso Internacional de Computación Evolutiva, Centro de Investigaciones en Matemáticas*, Guanajuato, México.

Torres, M. D., Ponce, L. E., Torres, A., & Díaz, E. (2008). Selección de Características Basada en el Peso Informacional de las Variables en Aprendizaje no Supervisado mediante Algoritmos Genéticos. In *Cuarto Congreso Internacional de Computación Evolutiva, Centro de Investigaciones en Matemáticas*, Guanajuato, México.

Torres, M. D., Ponce, L. E., Torres, A., Ochoa, A., & Díaz, E. (2009). Hybridization of evolutionary mechanisms for feature subset selection in unsupervised learning. In A. H. Aguirre, R. M. Borja, & C. A. R. Garciá (Eds.), *Proceedings of the 8th Mexican International Conference on Advances in Artificial Intelligence* (LNCS 5845, pp. 610-621).

Torres, R. A. (1999). *Factores de Riesgo para Morbimortalidad Neonatal*. San Luis Potosí, Mexico: Instituto Mexicano del Seguro Social.

Torres, S. A., Torres, S. M. D., Ponce, L. E., & Díaz, D. E. (2004). Representacion De Los Factores de Riesgo Directos e Indirectos De Los Resultados Del Parto Utilizando Un Modelo Grafico. In *IX Foro Regional De Investigacion En Salud del IMSS*.

Torres, S. A., Torres, S. M. D., Ponce, L. E., & Torres, R. A. B. (2005). *Modelo Grafico de Los Factores de Riesgo Durante el Embarazo y su Impacto en el Parto*. Revista Cubana De Informática Médica.

Uncu, O., & Türksen, I. B. (2007). A novel feature selection approach: Combining feature wrappers and filters. *Information Sciences, 177*(2), 449–466. doi:10.1016/j.ins.2006.03.022

Wolpert, D. (1996). The lack of a priori distinctions between learning algorithms. *Neural Computation,* 1341–1390. doi:10.1162/neco.1996.8.7.1341

ADDITIONAL READING

Dréo, J., Siarry, P., Pétrowski, A., & Taillard, E. (2006). *Metaheuristics for hard optimization. Methods and case studies*. Berlin, Germany: Springer-Verlag.

Glover, F., & Kochenberger, G. (2003). *Handbook of metaheuristics*. Boston, MA: Kluwer Academic.

Larrañaga, P., & Lozano, J. A. (2002). *Estimation of distribution algorithms: A new tool for evolutionary computation*. Boston, MA: Kluwer Academic.

MacQueen, J. B. (1967). Some methods for classification and analysis of multivariate observations. In *Proceedings of the 5th Berkeley Symposium on Mathematical Statistics and Probability*, Berkeley, CA (Vol. 1, pp. 281-297).

Narendra, P. M., & Fukunaga, K. (1977). A branch and bound algorithm for feature subset selection. *IEEE Transactions on Computers, 26*(9), 917–922. doi:10.1109/TC.1977.1674939

Sánchez, D. G., & Lazo, C. M. (2002). Modificaciones al algoritmo BT para mejorar sus tiempos de ejecución. *Revista Ciencias Matemáticas, 20*(2), 129–136.

Schaffer, J. D., Caruna, R. A., Eshelman, L. J., & Das, R. (1989). A study of control parameters affecting online performance of genetic algorithms for function optimization. In *Proceedings of the Third International Conference on Genetic Algorithms* (pp. 51-60).

Shulcloper, J. R., Guzmán, A. A., & Martínez, T. F. (1999). Enfoque Lógico Combinatorio al Reconocimiento de Patrones . In *Selección de Variables y Clasificación Supervisada. Serie Avance en Reconocimiento de Patrones. Ciudad de México*. Distrito Federal, Mexico: Editorial IPN.

Torres, A., Torres, M. D., Díaz, E., & Ponce de León, E. (2004). Representación gráfica de regresión logística por etapas para las variables del embarazo. In *XI Simposio de Investigación y desarrollo tecnológico*, Aguascalientes, México.

Torres, A., Torres, M. D., Ponce de León, E., & Pinales, F. J. (2005). Algoritmo Genético para la Selección de Variables de Morbimortalidad Neonatal. In *Segundo Congreso de Computación Evolutiva COMCEV*, Aguascalientes, México (pp. 79-83).

Torres, M. D., Ponce, E. E., Ochoa, C. A., Torres, A., & Díaz, E. (2009, July). *Mecanismos de Aceleración en Selección de Subconjuntos de Características Basada en el Peso Informacional de las Variables para Aprendizaje no Supervisado. In 6*. Orlando, FL: Conferencia Iberoamericana en Sistemas, Cibernética e Informática.

Torres, M. D., Torres, A., Ponce, E. E., & Ochoa, C. A. (2007). Typical testors on the subset selection problem: A real application. In *Memories of ENC*, Morelia, Mexico.

Yu, L., & Liu, H. (2003). Feature selection for high-dimensional data: A fast correlation-based filter solution. In *Proceedings of the Twentieth International Conference on Machine Learning*, Washington, DC.

KEY TERMS AND DEFINITIONS

Genetic Algorithm (GA): A search heuristic that mimics the process of natural evolution. This heuristic is routinely used to generate useful solutions to optimization and search problems. Genetic algorithms belong to the larger class of evolutionary algorithms (EA), which generate solutions to optimization problems using techniques inspired by natural evolution, such as inheritance, mutation, selection, and crossover.

Hybrid Metaheuristic: Consists on combining simple strategies for obtaining better results. The main motivation for the hybridization of different algorithmic concepts has been to obtain better performing systems that exploit and combine advantages of the individual pure strategies, that is, hybrids are believed to benefit from synergy.

Matrix: (plural matrices, or less commonly matrixes) Is a rectangular array of numbers, symbols, or expressions. The individual items in a matrix are called its elements or entries. Is the way the information is arranged.

Morbidity: Of the nature or indicative or disease. Origin middle 17th century From Latin morbidus, from morbus 'disease.'

Mortality Rate: The number of deaths in a given area or period, or from a particular cause. Origin late middle English via old French from Latin mortalitas, from mosrtalis.

Risk Factors: In epidemiology, a risk factor is a variable associated with an increased risk of presenting certain disease or infection.

Stillbirth: A baby that is born dead.

Testor: T is a testor from a Learning Matrix (LM) if no zero's rows exist in M after eliminating all columns that do not belong to the set T. Said in other words a testor is the set of features that let us know the class an object belongs to.

Typical Testor: The set T is typical if by eliminating any feature j |j∈T, T loses its condition of testor. Said in other way, a typical testor is the testor without redundancies.

ENDNOTE

[1] BMI: Bodi Mass Index

Chapter 5
An Evolutionary Algorithm for Graph Drawing with a Multiobjective Approach

Sergio Enríquez Aranda
Autonomous University of Aguascalientes,
Mexico

Alejandro Padilla Díaz
Autonomous University of Aguascalientes,
Mexico

Eunice E. Ponce de León Sentí
Autonomous University of Aguascalientes,
Mexico

María Dolores Torres Soto
Autonomous University of Aguascalientes,
Mexico

Elva Díaz Díaz
Autonomous University of Aguascalientes,
Mexico

Aurora Torres Soto
Autonomous University of Aguascalientes,
Mexico

Carlos Alberto Ochoa Ortiz Zezzatti
Juarez City University, México

ABSTRACT

In this chapter a hybrid algorithm is constructed, implemented and tested for the optimization of graph drawing employing a multiobjective approach. The multiobjective optimization problem for graph drawing consists of three objective functions: minimizing the number of edge crossing, minimizing the graph area, and minimizing the aspect ratio. The population of feasible solutions is generated using a hybrid algorithm and at each step a Pareto front is calculated. This hybrid algorithm combines a global search algorithm (EDA — Estimation of Distribution Algorithm) with a local search Algorithm (HC — Hill Climbing) in order to maintain a balance between the exploration and exploitation. Experiments were performed employing planar and non-planar graphs. A quality index of the obtained solutions by the hybrid MOEA-HCEDA (Multiobjective Evolutionary Algorithm - Hill Climbing & Univariate Marginal Distribution Algorithm) is constructed based on the Pareto front defined in this chapter. A factorial experiment using the algorithm parameters was performed. The factors are number of generations and population size, and the result is the quality index. The best combination of factors levels is obtained.

DOI: 10.4018/978-1-4666-0297-7.ch005

INTRODUCTION

Graph drawing problems are a particular class of combinatorial optimization problems whose goal is to find plane layout of an input graph in such a way that certain objective functions are optimized. A large number of relevant problems in different domains can be formulated as graph layout problems. Among these problems are optimization of networks for parallel computer architectures, VLSI circuit design, information retrieval, numerical analysis, computational biology, graph theory, scheduling and archaeology. Most interesting graph drawing problems are NP-hard and their decisional versions are NP-complete (Garey & Johnson, 1983), but, for most of their applications, feasible solutions with an almost optimal cost are sufficient. As a consequence, approximation algorithms and effective heuristics are welcome in practice (Díaz et al., 2002).

Visualization of complex conceptual structures is a support tool used on several engineering and scientific applications. A graph is an abstract structure used to model information. Graphs are USD to represent information that can be modeled as connections between variables, and so, to draw graphs to put information in an understandable way.

The usefulness of graphs visualization systems depends on how easy is to catch its meaning, and how fast and clear is to interpret it. This characteristic can be expressed through of aesthetic criterions (Sugiyama, 2002; Di Battista et al., 1999) as the edges' crossing minimization, the reduction of drawing area and the minimization of aspect ratio deployment, among others. When a graph is drawn, several aesthetic criterions have to be taken into account in order to make the graph easily readable. Planarity of a graph (graph without crosses), reduction of the drawing area, and the draw aspect ratio minimization are frequently very desirable characteristics (Di Battista et al., 1999) on graph visualization applications (Tamassia et al., 1988; Huang et al., 2000).

In order to enhance the legibility of the graph drawing is important to keep as low as possible the number of crosses as well as to keep a good aspect ratio in the draw. Another point is to maintain symmetric the drawing region (same drawing height and width). Also it is very desirable, to keep the drawing area small. This last requirement avoids the waste of screen space.

These objectives are in conflict with each other. Different objectives can produce conflict of interests (Deb, 2001). These kinds of problems are becoming very common nowadays because they are present in a wide variety of disciplines. This kind of problems has been named "multiobjective problems" and can be solved by mathematical programming (Miettinen, 1999) or by metaheuristics (Coello et al., 2009).

In order to make a graph legible (easily readable), several in conflict objectives have to be considered in the drawing, therefore the graph drawing problem can be formalized as a multiobjective problem (for example the graph drawing on a minimum area, the graph drawing with a minimum number of crossing edges and a good aspect ratio), so that, is important to establish a commitment among objectives in order to solve the different graph drawing problems. This perspective let us see that the graph drawing problem is inherently multiobjective (Enríquez, 2009).

In this chapter the following in conflict objectives have been considered:

Minimization of the number of crossing edges in the graph: The total number of crossing edges of the graph has to be minimized.

Minimization of the graph area: to minimize the total space used by the graph.

Minimization of the graph aspect ratio: the graph has to be visualized in a perfect square area.

To reach the minimum crossing edges in the graph drawing is frequently to need a bigger area. At the same time, for minimizing the aspect ratio of the graph is needed to draw the nodes in a symmetrically delimited region.

The reduction of the used area increases the number of crosses because as closer the edges are, there is less space to do the crossing edges minimization. Besides, area reduction of the sketching also affects the symmetrical delimitation of the region used by the graph.

The aspect ratio minimization is affected by the crossing edges minimization due that just to get a node outside the defined area contributes to the imbalance of the symmetry reached until that moment. So, the reduction of the drawing area affects directly the aspect ratio of the graph because generally this kind of reduction is not symmetric.

These three mentioned objectives are in conflict when the graph drawing is performed automatically. Those aesthetic criterions (Sugiyama, 2002; Di Battista et al., 1999) are naturally associated to hard optimization problems. In this chapter, a hybrid algorithm is presented for the solution of automatic graph drawing. This algorithm is constituted by a global search mechanism (UMDA Univariate Marginal Estimation Algorithm) and a local search mechanism (HC—Hill Climbing). The algorithm was designed, implemented and proved by means of a multiobjective approach and was termed "MOEA-HCEDA" (Multiobjective Evolutionary Algorithm - Hill Climbing & Univariate Marginal Distribution Algorithm). The Pareto front is based on three objective functions: minimizing the number of crossing edges, minimizing the graph area, and to minimizing the aspect ratio of the graph sketch.

Chapter Contents

The organization of the present chapter is as follows: In introductory section, we present an outline of the automatic graph drawing, its definition, the problems existing at the time to draw a graph, and the proposal to solve this problem. The optimization problem, solution representation and evaluation functions section, gives an explanation of the optimization problems evolved in the graph drawing, its solution representation, and its evaluation functions. The description of the algorithm components section, gives an explanation of the basic algorithms used to create the proposed algorithm to solve problems in the graph drawing. The multiobjective optimization section explains the methodology used during the process of optimizing a given problem, as well as evolutionary algorithms used in conjunction with the multi-objective optimization. The proposed hybrid MOEA-HCEDA algorithm section, defines how carried out the implementation of the algorithm MOEA-HCEDA and its pseudocode. The experiment design, results and discussion section explains the experimental design used to assess the quality of the proposed algorithm, and define the best combination of algorithm parameters. In the discussion we compare results among three algorithms, HUx algorithm (Enríquez et al., 2010), GA (Vrajitoru, 2009), and MOEA-HCEDA algorithm, and some conclusions with regard to main research's contributions are outlined.

OPTIMIZATION PROBLEM, SOLUTION REPRESENTATION AND EVALUATION FUNCTIONS

In this section we present the graph drawing as an optimization problem in which some different objective functions can be considered. An explanation is given to each of the objective functions forming part of the graph drawing problem. A very important part in order to solve a problem is how the solution representation is. In this case we use a very simple representation of the graph drawing. The objective functions are used as evaluation functions for the quality of a graph drawing.

The Solution Representation

Let $G = (V, E)$ be a graph, let V be a set of vertexes and E be a set of edges. MG is the adjacency matrix and P the Cartesian plane. The problem involves finding a pair $(x, y) \in P$ for each $v \in V$ such that the some aesthetic criteria are fulfilled. Each pair (x, y) represents a position of the vertex v in the Cartesian Plane P. For any two vertexes $v = (x, y)$ $v\,' = (x', y\,')$, $x \neq x'$ and $y \neq y'$. In this chapter, the graph's edges are considered straight lines.

Let N be the number of vertexes of the graph. The solution representation S (i.e., a graph drawing, or graph layout) is as follows:

$$S = (x_1, y_1, x_2, y_2, \ldots, x_i, y_i, \ldots, x_N, y_N)$$

Each pair xi, yi represents the position of the i-th vertex in the Cartesian Plane P.

Optimization Problem

The goal in this work is draw graphs in the plane automatically by a hybrid algorithm using a multiobjective approach. The graph drawing problem can be seen as a multiobjective problem. We have selected three objective functions to optimize: f1, f2, f3. These are functions of 2k quantitative variables, which represent the coordinates of the vertexes of a graph in the plane supported by the computer screen.

Minimization of the Edge Crossing Number (f1)

The graph edges crossing number optimization problem can be described as follows (Enríquez et al., 2008):

The problem involves finding a pair $(x, y) \in$ P for each $v \in V$ such that the number of crossings between the edges of the graph is minimum.

A graph drawing S is evaluated by the number of crossings edges in this graph draw S. The number of crossings is obtained by solving an equation system for all pair of edges of the graph. The following cases are analyzed: crossing edges, overlapping edges, and overlapping vertexes.

Minimization of the Area of the Drawing (f2)

This aesthetic criterion is defined as the area of the smallest rectangle with horizontal and vertical sides covering the drawing (Di Battista et al., 1999).

Minimization of the Aspect Ratio of the Drawing (f3)

The minimization of the aspect ratio of the drawing is defined as the ratio of the length of the longest side to the length of shortest side of the smallest rectangle with horizontal and vertical sides covering the drawing (Di Battista et al., 1999).

DESCRIPTION OF THE ALGORITHMIC COMPONENTS OF MOEA-HCEDA ALGORITHM

This section gives a description of the components of this algorithm, which is built of two main components. One of them used for exploration (UMDA) and the other for the exploitation (RMHC), this algorithm is a hybrid.

Hill Climbing Algorithm (HC)

The hill climbing algorithm (Mitchell, Holland, & Forrest, 1994) is an optimization technique which belongs to the local search family. This algorithm uses a series of iterations where it is constantly shifting towards the direction with a better value. When the algorithm reaches a point where its result cannot be further improved, it needs to start all over at another point where it can direct its search. This is achieved by a random restart of the algorithm. The best result obtained thus far, is saved as the algorithm's iterations progress, and it stops when no significant progress has been accomplished. The algorithm's stop condition may be set by a fixed number of iterations or when the

Algorithm 1. Pseudocode HC

```
function HILL_CLIMBING(problem) returns a solution state
    inputs: problem, a problem
    static: current, a node
            next, a node
    current ← MAKE-NODE(INITIAL-STATE[problem])
    loop do
            next ← a highest-valued successor of current
            if VALUE[next] < VALUE[current] then return
            current ← next
    end
```

best result has not improved over the course of a number of iterations.

Hill climbing provides a close to optimum solution, but it does not guarantee to find the best. This algorithm finds a solution very fast but can be trapped on some states like:

Local maximum: Is the better state of a neighborhood, but is not the absolute best.

Plateau: Is a space where several neighbor solutions have the same value.

Ridges: Are challenging problems for HC algorithm, because HC only changes a variable in each step. If the target function creates a narrow alley that descend in non-aligned direction. The HC can only ascend the ridge by zig-zagging. If the sides of the ridge are very steep, then the hill climbing may be forced to take very tiny steps and the initial time could be unreasonable length to ascend the ridge (or descend the alley).

To avoid local maximums, the algorithm can go back to previous state and explore on a different direction. In the case of plateaus, a big jump to another direction could be an appropriate solution. For cliffs, two or more rules can be applied before of proving the new state; this is like several directions movements. In Algorithm 1,

pseudocode describes the general Hill Climbing Algorithm (Mitchell, Holland, & Forrest, 1994).

Random Mutation Hill Climbing (RMHC)

In Random Mutation Hill Climbing (Mitchell, Holland, & Forrest, 1994), a string is chosen at random and its fitness is evaluated. The string is mutated at a randomly chosen single locus, and the new fitness is evaluated. If mutation leads to an equal or higher fitness, the new string replaces the old string. This procedure is iterated until the optimum has been found or a maximum number of function evaluations have been performed.

The algorithm RMHC (Skalak, 1994) works as follows: repeat until the optimum is found (or a maximum number of function evaluations have been performed):

Pseudocode RMHC

Choose a binary string at random. Call this string best-evaluated.

1. Mutate a bit chosen a random in best-evaluated.
2. Compute the fitness of the mutated string. If the fitness is greater than the fitness of the best best-evaluated, then set the best-evaluated to the mutated string.

3. If the maximum number of function evaluations has been performed return the best evaluated, otherwise, go to step 2.

The RMHC algorithm was implemented in the MOEA-HCEDA algorithm for carried out the exploitation during evaluation of population process.

Estimation of Distribution Algorithms (EDAs)

Estimation of distribution algorithms (Larrañaga et al., 2003, Neil, 2003), are a set of methods that belong to the evolutionary computation. This methods substitute crossover and mutation by the estimation and sample of the probability distribution, learned by means of selected individuals. These kinds of algorithms are becoming very important in the solution of combinatorial optimization problems. EDAs were proposed by Mühlenbein and Paaß (1996), and are used on the evolutionary computation area.

Contrary to genetic algorithms, EDAs do not need crossover and mutation operators. Individuals of new generation are obtained by the probability distribution estimated from a set of data. The mentioned data contain the selected individuals from the previous generation. Interrelations among variables are expressed by joint probability distribution in each generation (Larrañaga et al., 2003, Larrañaga & Lozano, 2002).

$$p_l(x) = p(x \mid Dl_{l-1}^{Se}) = \prod_{i=1}^{n} p_l(x_i) = \leftarrow$$

Pseudocode: Algorithm begins with the random generation of M individuals. This generation could be made from a uniform distribution for each variable. The first population D0 is constituted by the M individuals generated and then each individual is evaluated. In the next step the better N (N ≤ M) individuals according to the fitness function are selected. Using this group, the n-dimensional probabilistic model that better reflects the interrelations among variables is inducted. In the third step M new individuals are obtained by means of the simulation of the probability distribution learned on the previous step. These three steps are repeated until a stop criterion is reached; an example of common stop criterion is certain generations' number.

The general pseudocode of EDA algorithm is presented (Larrañaga et al., 2003).

Pseudocode EDA

$D_0 \leftarrow$ Generate M individuals at random (initial population)

Repeat for l = 1, 2, . . . until stop criterion is verified.

$D_{l-1}^{Se} \leftarrow$ Select $N \leq M$ individuals from D_{l-1} according to selection method

Estimate the distribution probability of the selected individuals

D_l Sample M individuals (new population) from $p_l(x)$.

Univariate Marginal Estimation Algorithm (UMDA)

Introduced by Mühlenbein (Mühlenbein et al., 1998; Mahnig & Mühlenbein, 2001; Neil, 2003), this is a particular case of EDAs which is considered as having no dependencies; its distribution of n-dimensional joint probability factorizes as a product of n univariate and independent probability distributions (Larrañaga et al., 2003).

Example:

$$p_l\left(x\right) = \prod_{i=1}^{n} p_l(x_i) \tag{1}$$

The joint probability distribution of each generation was estimated from individuals $p_l(x)$

selected. The joint probability distribution factorizes as the product of independent univariate distributions.

Example:

$$p_l(x) = p(x \mid D_{l-1}^{Se}) = \prod_{i=1}^{n} p_l(x_i) \qquad (2)$$

Every univariate probability distribution is estimated by marginal frequencies:

$$p_l(x) = \frac{\sum_{j=1}^{N} \delta_j(X_i = x_i \mid D_{l-1}^{Se})}{N} \qquad (3)$$

where:

$$\delta_j(X_i = x_i D_{l-1}^{Se}) = \begin{cases} 1 & if\,on\,the\,j-th\,case\,of \\ & D_{l-1}^{Se}, X_i = x_i \\ 0 & in\,another\,case \end{cases}$$

The general pseudocode of UMDA algorithm is presented (Larrañaga et al., 2003).

Pseudocode UMDA

D_0 Generate M individuals at random (initial population)

Repeat for l = 1, 2,... until stop criterion is verified.

$D_{l-1}^{Se} \leftarrow$ Select $N \le M$ individuals from D_{l-1} according to selection method.

$$p_l(x) = p(x \mid D_{l-1}^{Se}) = \prod_{i=1}^{n} pl(x_i) = \prod_{i=1}^{n} \frac{\sum_{j=1}^{N} \delta_j(X_i = x_i \mid D_{l-1}^{Se})}{N} \leftarrow$$

Obtain estimate of combined probability distribution

$D_{l-1} \leftarrow$ Sample M individuals (new population) from $p_l(x)$.

MULTIOBJECTIVE OPTIMIZATION

Optimization processes have as objective to find the best possible solution of a problem. Solutions can be evaluated as good or bad solutions according to one objective function; for example: to minimize the production cost of a product, to maximize the efficiency of a process, etc. Nevertheless one-objective optimization is very common in productive processes and research; most of real problems involve more than one objective, for example: to minimize production cost and simultaneously to maximize its quality. Multiobjective optimization exhibits in conflict objectives (Deb, 2001).

Evolutionary algorithms (EAs) have become a very popular tool among researchers due to its easy implementation and good performance. EAs are based on natural selection (Goldberg, 1989). These algorithms apply evolution to a population of individuals through random actions and selection according to a given criterion; so better individuals (those more able to became adapted) can be identified. Those well adapted individuals are the ones that will survive, while those with a poor adaptation will be discarded (Enríquez, 2009). The ability to deal with sets of solutions of EAs, makes them pretty good to the solution of multiobjective problems; besides EAs are well known because of its ability to deal with different kind of problems without specific knowledge about a problem (Coello et al., 2009).

First multiobjective evolutionary algorithms (MOEAs) were introduced on the eighties (Schaffer, 1985), but become more popular by the middle of nineties. Nowadays MOEAs begin to extend to any discipline; for example on mapping and simultaneous location (Li, 2006), on chemical engineering (Coello, Coello, & Lamont, 2004), on bioinformatics (Herman et al., 2000), among others.

First implementation of a MOEA is attributed to David Schaffer. He developed Vector Evaluated Genetic Algorithm (VEGA) in the middle of the eighties (Schaffer, 1985). VEGA was developed to solve machine learning problems.

Between 1980 and 1990, few MOEAs were developed because those algorithms were strongly influenced by mathematical programming techniques.

In 1989 Goldberg made an analysis of the algorithm VEGA, and he suggested a classification based on the Pareto optimality (no dominance), that became a standard for the creation of modern MOEAs. This technique termed Pareto's ranking, is mainly based on finding the group of individuals from population that are not dominated by the remaining individuals. The classification assigned to these individuals is the highest and then they are withdrawn from the competition. Remaining individuals that were dominated by the previous classification, are then analyzed to determine how many of them are not dominated and will be labeled with the next highest classification. This process continues until all individuals have been classified according to their non dominancy. Goldberg suggested a mechanism based on niches (Goldberg & Richardson, 1987), so the evolutionary algorithm converges to a single solution of Pareto (1986). From these works, were born the three main MOEAs.

Multiobjective Genetic Algorithm (MOGA). In the algorithm MOGA (Fonseca & Fleming, 1993), classification of an individual corresponds to the number of solutions of the actual population that dominates it. This algorithm became very popular because of its effectiveness and easy use.

Non-Dominated Sorting Genetic Algorithm (NSGA). This algorithm is based on different layers of individuals (Srinvas & Deb, 1994). Before the population is classified, a selection based on the non dominance is performed; afterwards all non dominated individuals are classified in a category according to a fitness function that is proportional to the population's size. Once this individuals have been classified will be ignored, and another layer of non dominated individuals

is created. This process will continue until all individuals have been classified.

Niche-Pareto Genetic Algorithm (NPGA). This algorithm uses a tournament based selection based on Pareto's dominance (Horn et al., 1994). The NPGA consists on selecting and comparing two individuals randomly against a subset of the populations (about 10% of the population). So there are two possible results: (1) one of them is dominated by the randomly selected subset but not the other; (2) anyone of the two selected individuals are dominated or are not; in this case the tournament result is determined by fitness sharing (Goldberg & Richardson, 1987). Due to NPGA does not classify the whole population; it is more efficient algorithmically than MOGA and NSGA. By the end of the nineties few comparative studies were carried out and they indicate MOGA is the most efficient and effective approach, followed by NPGA and the last is NSGA (Van Veldhuizen, 1999).

Basic Concepts

A Multi-Objective Optimization Problem (MOOP) has a number of objective functions that can be maximized or minimized, as well as a number of constraints which should be satisfied. The general form of a MOOP is the following (Deb, 2001):

A solution x is a vector of n decision variables: $x = (x_1, x_2, ..., x_n)^T$. The last set of constraints corresponds to the limits of variables; because it establishes the lower $x_i^{(l)}$ and upper $x_i^{(u)}$ value for each decision variable. These limits constitute the decision variable space D.

Associated to the problem are the inequality constraints J and the equality constraints K. Terms $g_j(x)$ and $h_k(x)$ are termed constraints functions. And finally is important to point out that there are M objective functions $f(x) = (f_1(x), f_2(x), ..., f_M(x))^T$.

Dominance Concept

In most multi-objective optimization problems is used the concept of dominance (Deb, 2001). Two solutions are compared on the basis of whether a solution dominates another or not. Assuming there are M objective functions could be said that a solution $x^{(1)}$ dominates other solution $x^{(2)}$, if the following conditions are satisfied:

- Solution $x^{(1)}$ is not worse than $x^{(2)}$ for all objectives.
- Solution $x^{(1)}$ is strictly better than $x^{(2)}$ in at least one objective.

Minimize/Maximize subject to:

$$
\begin{aligned}
f_m(x_i), & \qquad m = 1, 2, ..., M \\
g_j(x) \geq 0, & \qquad j = 1, 2, ..., J \\
h_k(x) = 0, & \qquad k = 1, 2, ..., K \\
x_i^{(l)} \leq x_i \leq x_i^{(u)}, & \quad i = 1, 2, ..., n
\end{aligned}
\tag{4}
$$

Relative Evaluation of the Pareto Front Performance

Given two Pareto fronts, a relative evaluation of the first front with respect to the second can be given as follows:

Let $x_i^{(1)}$ be one solution of the first Pareto front and let $n_i = n(x_i^{(1)})$ be the number of times $x_i^{(1)}$ is not dominated by the elements of the second Pareto front. To normalize this quantity it is divided by the number of solutions of the second front. The quantity obtained is a quality index to evaluate the solution $x_i^{(1)}$. Let now $\sum n_i$ be the sum of the number of times all the solutions of the first Pareto front are not dominated by the solutions of the second front. To normalize this

quantity, it is divided by the number of solutions in both fronts. This last quantity can be considered a relative quality index of the first Pareto front with respect to the second.

PROPOSED HYBRID MOEA-HCEDA ALGORITHM

This section defines the implementation of the hybrid MOEA-HCEDA algorithm and its pseudocode.

General Design

The overall design of the MOEA-HCEDA algorithm was constructed in six general stages. A flow chart of the general design is shown in Figure 1.

Stages:

1. Output file Initialization: the algorithm initialize a file used to store the final results.
2. Initial population: all individuals (graphs) of the initial population are created randomly by the RMHC (Skalak, 1994) algorithm.
3. Initial Pareto front: all individuals created in the 2 step, are evaluated using the dominance criterion and then it is determinate how many solutions (individuals) of the population are non-dominated solutions. In this step is created the initial Pareto front.
4. Evolution of the population: the initial Pareto front is processed by the hybrid MOEA-HCEDA algorithm; this process is based on generations (parameter given by the user). At each generation all individuals (non-dominates solutions) are subject to an evolutionary process carried out by the hybrid MOEA-HCEDA algorithm (UMDA is used to the exploration process and RMHC is used to the exploitation process). A new population of individuals is obtained and evaluated by Multi-Objective optimization determining how many individuals

Figure 1. General design

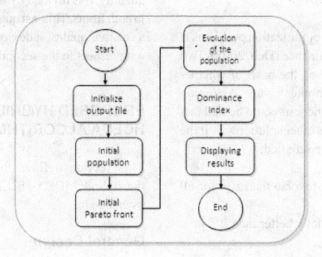

are non-dominates, this way is obtained an approximated Pareto front. This process is repeated until reaching the total of generations. At the end, an approximated Pareto front is obtained.

5. Dominance index: The Pareto front is stored in the output file. A dominance index is

6. Displaying results: The final results are shown in a table results and any solution (graph) can be drawn on the screen.

7. Output file Initialization

The first step undertaken by the hybrid algorithm MOEA-HCEDA for automatic generation of graphs is to read the input file and to create the output file that will contain the found solutions at the end of the process. These solutions found by the algorithm represent the Pareto front. The first step in this process is described.

Input File

The algorithm begins reading the input file that is in simple text format. All input files used as benchmarks have the same kind of information. The stored information has the next format:

*   The first line in the file represents the total number of vertex and the total number of edges in the graph.
*   Next lines (from line 2 to the last one), represent the relationship between each pair of vertex of the graph; so each line represents an edge of the graph.

Output File

After reading the input file, the algorithm creates an output file, which is used to store the set of solution generated by the hybrid algorithm MOEA-HCEDA. These solutions represent the Pareto front. The output file format is stored in a table in MySQL database (Sun Microsystems, 2008b). Figure 2 shows an example with the results generated by the algorithm.

The format of the table and its fields is described.

*   Graph: This field represents a sequential number generated for each graph (solution).
*   Crosses: This field represents the total number of crossings found in each graph (solution).

Figure 2. View of output file

GRAPH	CROSS	AREA	ASPECT	REPEAT	FRONT	GENERATION	POPULAT	DOMINANCE	X1	Y1	X2	Y2	X3	Y3	X4
1	13	164025	1	1	1	500	150	0.990521327014218	467	147	483	145	703	200	509
2	13	159570	1.02791878172589	1	1	500	150	0.919431279620853	467	143	483	145	703	200	509
3	13	163215	1.00496277915633	1	1	500	150	0.964454976303318	467	147	483	145	703	200	509
4	16	163620	1.0024752475247	1	1	500	150	0.981042654028436	510	147	483	145	703	200	574
5	16	162812	1.00248138957816	1	1	500	150	0.981042654028436	510	147	483	145	703	200	574
6	16	154448	1.00510204081633	1	1	500	150	0.9739306492891	510	143	483	145	703	200	574
7	42	162409	1	1	1	500	150	0.779620853080569	467	147	483	145	703	200	574
8	49	153660	1.01025641025641	1	1	500	150	0.687203791469194	510	147	483	145	703	200	574
9	45	162006	1.0024875621890S	1	1	500	150	0.720379146919431	510	147	483	145	703	200	574
10	15	126736	1	1	2	500	100	0.997601918465228	474	250	476	318	459	385	370
11	25	111890	1.00299401197605	1	2	500	100	0.973621103117506	474	250	476	318	459	385	370

- Area: This field refers to the occupied area by each graph (solution).
- Aspect: This field represents the aspect ratio of each graph (solution).
- Repetition: This field represents the graph (solution) generated in each repetition; that is going to be used to calibrate the algorithm.
- Front: Field used as a parameter of the algorithm.
- Generation: Field used as a parameter of the algorithm.
- Population: Field used as a parameter of the algorithm.
- Dominance: This field is used to determine the degree of dominance among different repetitions.
- X1, Y1, X2, Y2, ..., Xn, Yn.: These fields show the coordinates of each vertex generated by the algorithm.

Initial Population

Initial population has the objective to generate randomly a population of size 2n, which will be the basis for the creation of the initial Pareto front. The steps performed by the algorithm in this part are described.

Steps to generate the initial population:

1. Vertex from a graph are generated randomly (this will be the "old solution").
2. The evaluation function is performed on the graph and the values of each objective function (total crossings in the graph, graph area and aspect ratio of the graph) are obtained.
3. A copy of the graph termed "new solution" is made.
4. New solution is altered by the random selection of a vertex and its subsequent substitution by a randomly generated new vertex.
5. Evaluation function is applied to the new solution and values of the objective functions (total crossings in the graph, graph area and aspect ratio of the graph) are obtained.
6. Using the approach of multiobjective optimization (Deb, 2001), algorithm determines which of the two solutions (old and new) dominates the other. Dominated solution is updated with the solution that dominates it. If none of the solutions is dominated by the other, then new solution information is updated with old solution information.
7. This process is repeated five times (go back to step 4) in order to improve the quality of individuals that will be part of the initial population.
8. New solution is stored in the initial population and the whole process is repeated (go back to step 1) until the population has

reached a size of 2n individuals. Note that initial population is stored in RAM (random access memory)

Implemented pseudocode of this part of the process is shown in Algorithm 2.

Initial Pareto Front

After creating the initial population, it will be used to create the initial Pareto front. This first front will be used in the population evolution process. The evolution process of population is the next step the MOEA-HCEDA will perform.

Steps to generate the initial Pareto front:

1. The first step of this process is to check which solutions (graphs) from the initial population are not dominated by others. Non-dominated solutions are marked to separate them from the ones that were dominated by others.
2. Then, a file is created in memory to keep the initial Pareto front.
3. The solutions marked like non-dominated are selected from initial population to be sent to the initial Pareto front file. Thus, solutions that were not selected in the initial population will be automatically deleted.
4. Finally, a Pareto front that contains only non-dominated solutions is obtained.
5. The next step is to create a file in memory that represents a population of individuals termed "oldpop", whose size is equal to the initial Pareto front.
6. Solutions on the initial Pareto front are stored in oldpop. By means of the hybrid algorithm MOEA-HCEDA, this population will evolve with each generation, improving the quality of solutions provided by the initial Pareto front.

The algorithm implemented to create the initial Pareto front is described in Algorithm 3.

Evolution of the Population

All solutions of the initial Pareto front obtained in the previous step were copied into the population termed oldpop. This population will be evolved by the hybrid algorithm MOEA-HCEDA, based on a number of generations (parameter given by the user to start the program). At the end of each generation, new solutions created by the evolutionary process are stored in a new population named "newpop", obtaining a new population of individuals better than the previous one. Next step is to copy into a new file, solutions contained in newpop, as well as solutions stored in the initial Pareto front. The new obtained file is evaluated by means of multiobjective optimization to find out what solutions are not dominated by others, and stored them in a new file that will become the new Pareto front. This process is repeated a number of generations, and eventually the final Pareto front is obtained. The steps carried out by the hybrid MOEA-HCEDA algorithm are described below:

1. A file in memory is created. It represents a population of individuals termed newpop of size n (n is a parameter supplied by the user at the beginning of the program), which will be used to generate the new population from oldpop.
2. The hybridization process of the algorithm MOEA-HCEDA starts using 20 cycles of hill climbing algorithm (Russell, 1995) to a randomly selected individual from oldpop.
3. A copy of the selected individual is made.
4. A vertex from the selected individual is selected randomly.
5. A new vertex is generated randomly and is replaced the vertex selected on the previous step.
6. The evaluation function is applied on the selected individual and values of each objective function (total crossings in the graph, graph area and aspect ratio of the graph) are obtained.

Algorithm 2. Pseudocode Initial_Population

```
int n = 0;
int index = 0;
// create initial population object (file)
nondominatesfileinitialization = new PopMOO(this.sizefileini);
while (n < this.sizefileini) // repeat while n less than double
{
newSolutions();// free and create objects solutions
initpop();// create graph's vertex (solution)
                        size population parameter
for (int i = 0; i < 5; i++) // loop for perturb best solution
{
solutionDisturb();//perturb one vertex of the best solution
valueMOO();        // objective function evaluation
// initialize array for multiobjective optimization
nondominatesfileinitialization.clsMOO();

// verify who solution is better on cross minimization
nondominatesfileinitialization.chkMOO(this.newsolution.x,this.oldsolution.x,0);

// verify who solution is better on area minimization
nondominatesfileinitialization.chkMOO(this.newsolution.gs,this.oldsolution.
gs,1);

// verify who solution is better on aspect ratio
nondominatesfileinitialization.chkMOO(this.newsolution.ra,this.oldsolution.
ra,2);

// select who solution is the best
nondominatesfileinitialization.chooseMOO(this.newsolution, this.oldsolution,
this.lchrom);
}
// save the best solution
nondominatesfileinitialization.saveIndividual(this.newsolution);
n++;
}
```

Algorithm 3. Pseudocode Initial_Pareto_Front

```
{
Initial_Population; // create Initial Population
n = 0;
// select and mark non-dominated individuals on initial population
nondominatesfileinitialization.whoIsNonDominated();
// create initial Pareto front object (file)
nondominatesparetofile = new PopMOO(n);
// save selected solutions from initial population to initial Pareto front
nondominatesfileinitialization.copyNonDominates(
nondominatesparetofile);
// create UMDA population object (file oldpop)
this.oldpop = new Poblacion(nondominatesparetofile.popmooLength());
// initialize vertex on UMDA population oldpop
initializePopulation(this.oldpop, "oldpop", nondominatesparetofile.popmooL-
ength());
// save initial Preto Front individuals to UMDA population
UMDAFileInitialization();
}
```

7. By means of multi-objective optimization (Deb, 2001) the dominated and the non-dominated individuals are identified. The information of the individual who is dominated by the other, is updated with the information of the non-dominated individual. If there is not a dominated individual, then the new individual information will be updated with the original individual information.

8. This process is repeated twenty times (go back to step 4); its purpose is to improve diversity of the population.

9. At the end, a better individual will be obtained (in most of the cases). Sometimes obtained individual is not changed, because there was not any improvement during hybridization process.

10. After the hybridization of the UMDA (Larrañaga et al., 2003) was performed on oldpop, the probability distribution of population is estimated. This task is made by means of the probabilities vector. This vec-

tor will produce the most viable coordinates for the construction of the new population (newpop).

11. Next step consists on the generation of n new individuals that will form the new population (newpop). This new population is generated on the basis of the coordinates provided by the probabilities vector.

12. Then, the evaluation function is applied to all individuals stored on newpop and values of each objective function (total crossings in the graph, graph area and aspect ratio of the graph) are obtained.

13. A new file is then created on memory and solutions from Pareto front are copied on it; as well as solutions stored on newpop created during the evolution of each generation.

14. Based on this new file, non-dominated solutions are marked for further processing; while dominated solutions are automatically eliminated from this new file.

15. At the end of each generation, a new approximated Pareto front is obtained. This new front will only contain non-dominated solutions.

16. The next step is to create a file in memory. This file will represent a population of individuals (oldpop), with a size equals to the Pareto front created in the previous step.

17. Then, solutions from the approximated Pareto front are copied into new population (newpop).

18. The whole process is repeated (go back to step 1) until a number of generations have been performed. At the end of this process the actual Pareto front is obtained.

The implemented pseudocode for the evolution of populations is shown in Algorithm 4.

This algorithm has a complexity that can be expressed as follows:

The initial population has a complexity of $O(n^2)$, the initial Pareto front has a complexity of $O(n^2)$. The dominance test has a complexity of $O(n^2)$. Another important aspect is the method that evaluates the three objectives and the most complex of these is the total crossings in a drawing. Considering that this assessment is carried out to the entire population the resulting complexity is $O(n^3)$. Finally, taking into account the outer loop that is the number of generations, the MOEA-HCEDA algorithm complexity is $O(n^4)$.

Dominance Index

The results so far have been stored in RAM. This section describes the steps for the storage of the solutions generated during evolution of the population. These solutions that are contained in the Pareto front are sent to a MySQL database (Sun Microsystems, 2008b) for their permanent storage for later processing and exploitation of results.

The next step is to apply a measure of quality (dominance index) for each solution stored in the Pareto front, in order to know the Pareto optimum.

The creation of the dominance index used on the Pareto front, implicates the next steps:

1. Two tables are created in MySQL database (resultsgraph2 and resultsgraph3).

2. All solutions stored on the Pareto front are copied into the two tables created in the previous step (resultsgraph2 and resultsgraph3).

3. Variables k and m are initialized to zero.

4. Variables i, j are initialized to one.

5. resultsgraph2 table is selected to update and the first record of the table is read (r_i).

6. resultsgraph3 table is selected to read only and the first record is read from the table (r_j).

7. Through the multi-objective optimization technique (Deb, 2001) determines if solution r_i dominates solution rj.

8. If solution r_i dominates solution r_j, the dominance counter is incremented in one unit (k).

9. Then, the counter of read records is incremented in one unit (m).

10. The next record from table resultsgraph3 is read $r_j = r_{j+1}$.

11. This process is repeated until the end of the file resultsgraph3 is reached (return to step 7).

12. The field of dominance of the solution r_i is updated by dividing the dominance counter (k) by the counter of read records (m). DOMINANCE$(r_i) = k / m$

13. The next record from table resultsgraph2 is read $r_i = r_{i+1}$.

14. Variable j is initialized in 1.

15. This process is repeated until the end of the file resultsgraph2 is reached (return to step 7).

Steps described above, make possible to update solutions contained in the Pareto front based on a dominance index. The pseudocode used in the creation of the dominance index is shown in Algorithm 5.

Algorithm 4. Pseudocode Generations()

```
{
HILL hill;  // use for object for Hill Climbing
if (oldpop.poblacion.length > 0) // there are any solutions?
{
Do // evolution population loop
{
this.gen++; // generation n+1
nondominatesfileinitialization = null;

/* initialize vertex on UMDA
  population newpop (size = popsize parameter) */
initializePopulation(this.newpop, "newpop", 0);

// create object for Hill Climbing process
hill = new HILL(this.lchrom, this.edges, this.E, this.rnd, 20, 2);
while (i <= 0)  // select one individual from oldpop
i = (int) (this.rnd.nextDouble() * nondominatesparetofile.popmooLength());

// hybrid process carried out by Hill Climbing
this.oldpop.poblacion[i] = hill.hillClimbingUMDA(this.oldpop.poblacion[i]);
calculaVectorP();  // estimated probability vector
valueMooUmda();  // objective function evaluation
// save solutions from initial Pareto front and newpop population to new Pa-
reto front
joinParetoFileUmdaFile();
// select who solutions are non-dominates and create new approximate Pareto
front
paretoFileInitialization();
}while (this.gen < this.maxgen); // repeat until reach max number generations
}
}//end of evolution of population process
```

Displaying Results

In this section the visual interface of the MOEA-HCEDA to show results is presented. It also includes the explanation of the elements involved in the system that aid the visualization of the automatic drawn of graphs. At the end the importance of visualization in this research is commented.

A graphical user interface (GUI) is a program that allows people to interact with electronic devices (computers, gaming devices, etc.), by means of images and graphic objects that represent information; unlike text-based commands that were used in computer equipment during previous decades (Jansen, 1998).

The visual system of MOEA-HCEDA is a GUI, whose purpose is to supply a view of automatic

Algorithm 5. Pseudocode dominanceIndex(String tableName, String tableName2,Statement stmt, Statement stmt2) throws SQLException

```
{
// create object for evaluate dominance
chkdominates = new PopMOO(1);
double domination = 0.00;   // dominance index
double dominancia = 0.00;   // no. dominates
double nrecords = 0.00;     // records read
// string to select records from resultadosgrafo2
String query = "SELECT GRAPH, CROSS, AREA, ASPECT, FRONT, DOMINANCE FROM " +
tableName + " ORDER BY FRONT, GRAFO";
ResultSet rs = stmt.executeQuery(query);
ResultSetMetaData rsmd = rs.getMetaData();
int columnCount = rsmd.getColumnCount();
double front1 = 0.00, graph1 = 0.00, dominate1 = 0.00, cross1 = 0.00, area1 =
0.00, aspect1 = 0.00;
double front2 = 0.00, graph2 = 0.00, dominate2 = 0.00, cross2 = 0.00, area2 =
0.00, aspect2 = 0.00;
String query2;
ResultSet rs2;
ResultSetMetaData rsmd2;
int columnCount2;
while (rs.next())  // repeat while records in file
 {
  // get values from resultsgrafo2
  graph1 = rs.getDouble(1);
  cross1 = rs.getDouble(2);
  area1 = rs.getDouble(3);
  aspect1 = rs.getDouble(4);
  front1 = rs.getDouble(5);
  dominate1 = rs.getDouble(6);
  dominancia = 0.00;
  // string to select records from resultadosgrafo3 and exclude solutions from
actual front
  String query2 = "SELECT GRAPH, CROSS, AREA, ASPECT, FRONT, DOMINANCE FROM "
+ tableName2 + " WHERE FRONT != " + front1 + " ORDER BY FRENTE";
  ResultSet rs2 = stmt2.executeQuery(query2);
  ResultSetMetaData rsmd2 = rs2.getMetaData();
  int columnCount2 = rsmd2.getColumnCount();
  nrecords = 0.00;
  domination = 0.00;
  while (rs2.next())  // repeat while records in file
  {
```

Continued on following page

Algorithm 5. Continued

```
    // get values from resultsgrafo3
    graph2 = rs2.getDouble(1);
    cross2 = rs2.getDouble(2);
    area2 = rs2.getDouble(3);
    aspect2 = rs2.getDouble(4);
    front2 = rs2.getDouble(5);
    dominate2 = rs2.getDouble(6);
    // initialize array for multiobjective optimization
    chkdominates.clsMOO();
    // verify if solution r_i dominates solution r_j on minimization cross
    chkdominates.chkMOO(cross1, cross2,0);
    // verify if solution r_i dominates solution r_j on minimization area
    chkdominates.chkMOO(area1, area2,1);
    // verify if solution r_i dominates solution r_j on minimization aspect ratio
    chkdominates.chkMOO(aspect1, aspect2,2);
// if solution r_i is better than solution r_j add 1 to domination
    if (chkdominates.chooseMOO())
     domination++;
     nrecords++;    // add 1 to records read
  }
  // update DOMINANCIA field on solution r_i
  if (domination > 0)
  {
    dominancia = domination/nrecords;
    rs.updateDouble(6, dominancia);
    rs.updateRow();
  }
  else
  {
    dominancia = 0
    rs.updateDouble(6, dominancia);
    rs.updateRow();
  }
  rs2.close();// close resultsgrafo3 file
}
rs.close();  // close resultsgrafo2 file
} //end of dominance index process
```

drawn graphs. This system is very friendly and therefore easy to use. Through this system, user can get a visual output of one or more automatic drawn graphs (solutions of the Pareto front) generated by MOEA-HCEDA.

Both, MOEA-HCEDA and the visual system use object-oriented programming (OOP). The whole system was implemented in the programming language JAVA (jdk1.9.0_07) (Sun Microsystems, 2008a; Horstmann, 2006; Ceballos, 2008). For output and exploitation of information the MySQL Server MySQL Server 5.0 data base is used (Sun Microsystems, 2008b; Maslakowoski, 2001). The data base connector used for communication between the program and the database is J/JDBC (mysql-connector-java-5.1.6) (Sun Microsystems, 2008c; Melton & Eisenberg, 2002).

Two objects used to display results obtained by MOEA-HCEDA are described.

PanelTable: This object is used to display the graphs generated by MOEA-HCEDA in a window. In this window different fields of the table can be sorted ascending or descending by double clicking on the header of each field. This feature is useful for the independent analysis of a field. In addition, any graph contained in this window can be selected by clicking the drop-dawn list.

Figure 3 shows the output system window with the results the MOEA-HCEDA algorithm produce sorted by the graph number (No. of Graph).

PanelGraph: This object is used by the *PanelTable* object to show the final design of a particular graph. In this window, the user can see how the algorithm solved the problem of automatic drawn of graphs, because it shows the final topology of a graph. Each graph contains visual information about the minimization of the number of crossings, the minimization of area and the minimization of the aspect ratio of the graphs.

Figure 4 shows the system window with the automatic drawn of the graph number 10. This figure shows the graphic results of the multiobjective optimization MOEA-HCEDA algorithm.

EXPERIMENT DESIGN, RESULTS AND DISCUSSION

The design of experiment consists of a factorial experiment with two factor generations: 300, 400, and 500, population size: 50, 100, and 150, with a total of ten runs for each combination of factors (ninety runs): 3 x 3 x10 = 90, each has an output that is a Pareto Front. Each Pareto front is used to evaluate each solution. The evaluation was performed with a dominance index. This index is defined in the section "Dominance Index."

Results

The analysis of variance table shows that simple effects as combination are statistically significant. So, the results showed by the descriptive statistics are statistically significant. Table 1 of the dominance index shows that the best combinatio of factors is generations = 500, population = 150, for mean of 0.756.

Table 2 shows statistical analysis the Analysis of Variance.

The confidence interval in Table 3 obtains the same result as was seen in the Descriptive Statistics table. The best combination is generations = 500, population = 150, dominance index=0.756.

The results are:

a.   The factors levels are statistical significant.
b.   The best combination is generations=500, population=150, dominance index=0.756.

This result is obtained by both types of statistical analysis: analysis of variance and confidence intervals see the Table 1 and Table 3.

Discussion

In this section we compare results among GA (Vrajitoru, 2009) algorithm, HUx (Enríquez et al., 2010) algorithm and MOEA-HCEDA algorithm. Comparing the results of the MOEA-HCEDA

Figure 3. Table results

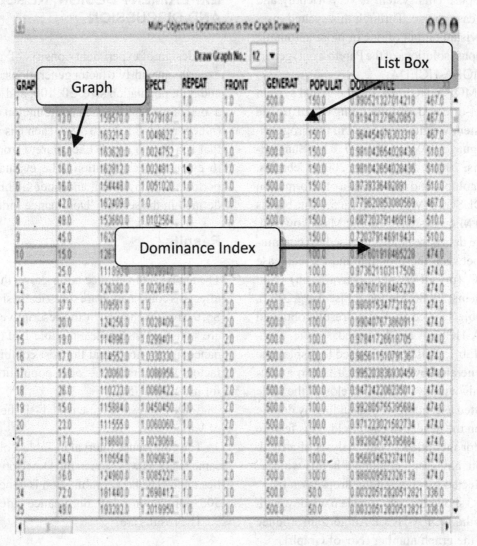

algorithm with HUx algorithm, it is interesting to see that the HUx obtains better results in the objective: number of edges crossing, but the appearance of the graph drawing is not so easy to interpret as the MOEA-HCEDA graph drawing. This is because the drawing area is better in the aspect ratio, and size. See Figure 4 and Figure 5.

The goal of the GA (Vrajitoru, 2009) algorithm is building consistent graph layouts for weighted graphs, in particular following a specified geometric shape using an approach aggregation

function as multiobjective optimization. The focus of this chapter, however, is on that the MOEA-HCEDA algorithm can create a compromise among the problem's objectives using the multi-objective optimization based on the Pareto front and don't taking into account the geometric shape of the graph. The GA algorithm using a population of 50 and 100 individuals, depending on the size of the graph, also used a total of 2000 iterations of the GA, followed by 2000 iterations of the tension vector algorithm. To make a comparison,

Figure 4. Automatic graph drawing for the graph No. 10 (vertex=40, edges=69)

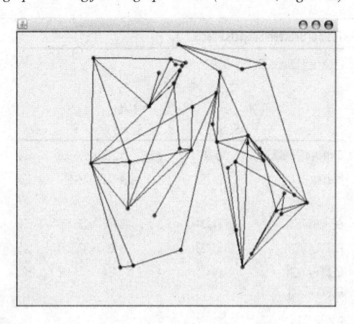

Table 1. Descriptive statistics

Descriptive Statistics

Dependent Variable: DOMINANCE

Generation	Population	Mean	Std. Deviation	N
300	50	0.348	0.223	319
	100	0.419	0.279	521
	150	0.534	0.192	541
	Total	0.448	0.247	1381
400	50	0.221	0.193	710
	100	0.465	0.247	560
	150	0.559	0.238	484
	Total	0.392	0.267	1754
500	50	0.445	0.227	394
	100	0.611	0.319	594
	150	0.756	0.146	466
	Total	0.612	0.277	1454
Total	50	0.311	0.231	1423
	100	0.503	0.296	1675
	150	0.611	0.219	1491
	Total	0.479	0.280	4589

Table 2. Analysis of variance

Tests of Between-Subjects Effects

Dependent Variable: DOMINANCE

Source	Type III Sum of Squares	df	Mean Square	F	Sig
Corrected Model	105.944[a]	8	13.243	238.009	.000
Intercept	1024.773	1	1024.773	18417.751	.000
GENERATION	31.734	2	15.867	285.169	.000
POPULATION	53.109	2	26.555	477.253	.000
GENERATION POPULATION	4.495	4	1.124	20.196	.000
Error	254.834	4580	.056		
Total	1412.149	4589			
Corrected Total	360.777	4588			

a. R Squared = .294 (Adjusted R Squared = .292)

Table 3. Confidence interval

GENERACTION * POPULATION

Dependent Variable: DOMINANCE

Generation	Population	Mean	Std. Error	95% Confidence Interval Lower Bound	Upper Bound
300	50	.348	.013	.322	.374
	100	.419	.010	.399	.440
	150	.534	.010	.514	.553
400	50	.221	.009	.204	.238
	100	.465	.010	.446	.485
	150	.559	.011	.538	.580
500	50	.445	.012	.421	.468
	100	.611	.010	.592	.630
	150	.756	.011	.734	.777

Figure 5. Automatic graph drawing for the best graph (Enriquez et al., 2010), (vertex=40, edges=69)

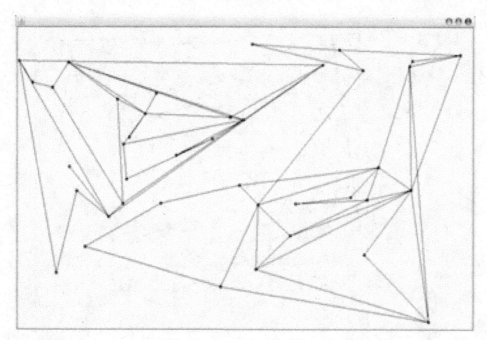

Figure 6. Decagon GA (Vrajitoru, 2009), (vertex=100, edges=180)

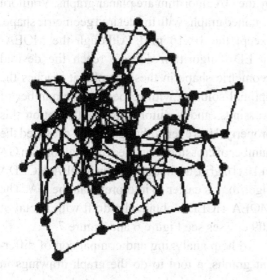

we used the same size population and 2000 iterations of the MOEA-HCEDA algorithm. The GA algorithm used the following sets of test problems: regular rectangular grids, regular polygons of variable number of vertices, the set of Platonic solids, and a particular 3D projection of the 4D hypercube. The following constraints are used by the GA algorithm: surface, volume, angle and overlap. The last one constraint is closely related to the popular criterion of minimizing the edges crossing. This constraint is used as a one of the three optimized objective by the MOEA-HCEDA algorithm. In this experiment were tested the graphs 4x4 grid, tetrahedron, decagon, icosagon, and 10x10 grid. This last one is the most difficult of all graphs, the next figures show the outputs obtained for both the GA algorithm (Figure 6) and the MOEA-HCEDA algorithm (Figure 7). These solutions are hardly recognizable; however, the solution obtained by the MOEA-HCEDA algorithm seems clearer.

GENERAL CONCLUSION

The principal contributions of this chapter are: the construction of the MOEA-HCEDA, consisting in a hybrid algorithm to the graph drawing task. The

Figure 7. Decagon MOEA-HCEDA, (vertex=100, edges=180)

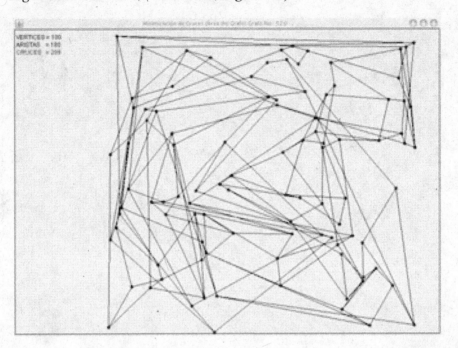

two components of the algorithm are the UMDA global optimization heuristic, and the local heuristic random mutation hill climbing RMHC. The UMDA is used to the exploration of the solution space, and the RMHC is used to exploitation of the solution space.

This algorithm employs three optimization functions and so it is a multiobjective one. The objective functions are: minimization of the crossing edges number, drawing area reduction and the drawing aspect proportion. The performed experiment obtains the best combination of algorithm parameters.

The MOEA-HCEDA is more efficient than the HUXs (Enríquez et al., 2010) because the run time performance, size area, and aspect ratio are better.

The MOEA-HCEDA algorithm has the following advantages over the GA (Vrajitoru, 2009) algorithm: The GA algorithm uses multiobjective optimization based on aggregation functions. However, the MOEA-HCEDA algorithm uses multiobjective optimization, in this approach a dominance index is created with the solutions stored on the Pareto front. All graphs obtained by the GA algorithm are planar graphs. Vrajitoru obtained graphs with the desired geometric shape, except the 10x10 grid. Although the MOEA-HCEDA algorithm doesn't reach the desired geometric shape in these graphs, it reaches the optimal solution with respect to the number of crossings, and Vrajitoru does not mention this property. However, although it isn't provided the number of crossings obtained by the algorithm GA in 10x10 grid, at first glance the MOEA-HCEDA algorithm is easier to interpret than the GA. The MOEA-HCEDA obtained a draft with a total of 209 crosses see Figure 6 and Figure 7.

To help analyzing and comparison of different graphs, a tool to do the graph drawings in independents windows is presented.

FUTURE RESEARCH

To continue this research, the hybridization MOEA-HCEDA with others algorithms, for example using other types of EDAs is a next objective. The testing of the algorithms using others more complex benchmarks and, the comparison of the results between different variants is a very challenging and interesting task for future work. The graphical presentation can be friendlier and dispose other facilities as, for example, the printing of the results.

ACKNOWLEDGMENT

We would like to acknowledge support for this project from the Autonomous University of Aguascalientes, Aguascalientes, Mexico (PII10-2).

REFERENCES

Bandyopadhyay, S., Saha, S., Maulik, U., & Deb, K. (2008). A simulated annealing based multi-objective optimization algorithm: AMOSA. *IEEE Transactions on Evolutionary Computation, 12*(3), 269–283. doi:10.1109/TEVC.2007.900837

Ceballos, F. J. (2008). *Java 2 Interfaces gráficas y aplicaciones para Internet* (3rd ed.). Benito Juárez, Mexico: Alfaomega Ra-Ma.

Coello, C. A., & López, A. (2009). Multi-objective evolutionary algorithms: A review of the state-of-the-art and some of their applications in chemical engineering. In Pandu, R. G. (Ed.), *Multi-objective optimization techniques and applications in chemical engineering* (pp. 61–90). Singapore: World Scientific.

Deb, K. (2001). *Multi-objective optimization using evolutionary algorithms*. Chichester, UK: John Wiley & Sons.

Di Battista, G., Eades, G., Tamassia, R., Ioannis, G., & Tollis, I. (1999). *Graph drawing: Algorithms for the visualization of graphs*. Upper Saddle River, NJ: Prentice Hall.

Díaz, J., Petit, J., & Serna, M. (2002). A survey of graph layout problems. *ACM Computing Surveys, 34*(3), 313–356. doi:10.1145/568522.568523

Enríquez, S. (2009). *Metaheurística Evolutiva Híbrida para la Minimización de Cruces de las Aristas en el Dibujado de Grafos*. Aguascalientes, Mexico: Universidad Autónoma de Aguascalientes, Centro de Ciencias Básicas, Tesis y Disertaciones Académicas.

Enríquez, S., Ponce de León, E., & Díaz, E. (2008). Calibración de un Algoritmo Genético para el Problema de la Minimización de Cruces en las Aristas de un Grafo. In *Avances en Computación Evolutiva, Memorias del IV Congreso Mexicano de Computación Evolutiva, Centro de Investigación en Matemáticas* (pp. 61-66).

Enríquez, S., Ponce de León, E., Díaz, E., & Padilla, A. (2010). A hybrid evolutionary algorithm for graph drawing: Edges crossing minimization problem. *Research in Computing Science, 45*.

Fonseca, C. M., & Fleming, P. J. (1993). Genetic algorithms for multiobjective optimization: Formulation, discussion and generalization. In *Proceedings of the Fifth International Conference on Genetic Algorithms* (pp. 416-423).

Garey, M. R., & Johnson, D. S. (1983). Crossing number is NP-complete. *SIAM Journal on Algebraic and Discrete Methods, 4*, 312–316. doi:10.1137/0604033

Goldberg, D. E. (1989). *Genetic algorithms in search, optimization and machine learning*. Reading, MA: Addison-Wesley.

Goldberg, D. E., & Richardson, J. (1987). Genetic algorithm with sharing for multimodal function optimization. In *Proceedings of the Second International Conference on Genetic Algorithms and their Applications* (pp. 41-49).

Herman, I., Melancon, G., & Marshall, S. (2000). Graph visualization and navigation in information visualization: A survey. *IEEE Transactions on Visualization and Computer Graphics, 6*(1), 24–43. doi:10.1109/2945.841119

Horstmann, C. S., & Cornell, G. (2006). *Core Java – Advanced features* (*Vol. 2*). Santa Clara, CA: Sun Microsystems.

Horstmann, C. S., & Cornell, G. (2006). *Core Java – Fundamentals* (*Vol. 1*). Santa Clara, CA: Sun Microsystems.

Huang, J. W., Kang, L. S., & Chen, Y. P. (2000). A new graph drawing algorithm for undirected graphs. *Software Journal, 11*(1), 138–142.

Jansen, B. J. (1998). The graphical user interface: An introduction. *SIGCHI Bulletin, 30*(2), 22–26. doi:10.1145/279044.279051

Larrañaga, P., & Lozano, J. A. (2002). *Estimation of distribution algorithms: a new tool for evolutionary computation*. Boston, MA: Kluwer Academic.

Larrañaga, P., Lozano, J. A., & Mühlenbein, H. (2003). Estimation of distribution algorithms applied to combinatorial optimization problems. *Inteligencia Artificial, Revista Iberoamericana de Inteligencia Artificial,* (19), 149-168.

Li, M. (2006). Multiobjective evolutionary algorithms with immunity for SLAM. *Advances in Artificial Intelligence, 26,* 27–36.

Mahnig, T., & Mühlenbein, H. (2001). Wright's equation and evolutionary computation. In *Proceedings of the Conference on Advances in Fuzzy Systems and Evolutionary Computation.*

Maslakowoski, M. (2001), *Aprendiendo MySQL en 21 Días* (pp. 10-65, 78-88, 107-154). Upper Saddle River, NJ: Prentice Hall.

Melton, J., & Eisenberg, A. (2002). *SQL y Java, Guía para SQLJ, JDBC y tecnologías relacionadas* (pp. 1-51, 97-325). Benito Juárez, Mexico: Alfaomega RA-MA.

Miettinen, K. M. (1999). *Nonlinear multiobjective optimization*. Boston, MA: Kluwer Academic.

Mitchell, M., Holland, J. H., & Forrest, S. (1994). When will a genetic algorithm outperform hill climbing? *Advances in Neural Information Processing Systems, 6,* 51–58.

Mühlenbein, H., Mahnig, T., & Ochoa, A. (1998). Schemata distributions and graphical models in evolutionary optimization. *Journal of Heuristics, 5*(2), 215–247. doi:10.1023/A:1009689913453

Mühlenbein, H., & Paaß, G. (1996). From recombination of genes to the estimation of distributions I. Binary parameters. In H.-M. Voigt, W. Ebeling, I. Rechenberger, & H.-P. Schwefel (Eds.), *Proceedings of the 4th International Conference on Parallel Problem Solving from Nature* (LNCS 411, pp. 178-187).

Neil, J. (2003). *A mathematical model of fixed-graph estimation of distribution algorithms* (Unpublished doctoral dissertation). Department of Computer Science, University of Birmingham, Birmingham, UK.

Pareto, V. (1986). Cours D'Economie Politique, Vol I and II (F. Rouge, Laussane).

Russell, S., & Norving, P. (1995). *Artificial intelligence: A modern approach* (pp. 111–114). Upper Saddle River, NJ: Prentice Hall.

Schafer, J. D. (1985). Multiple objective optimization with vector evaluated genetic algorithms. In *Proceedings of the First International Conference on Genetic Algorithms and theirs Applications* (pp. 93-100).

Skalak, D. B. (1994). Prototype and feature selection by sampling and random mutation hill climbing algorithms. In *Proceedings of the Eleventh International Conference on Machine Learning* (pp. 293-301).

Srinvas, N., & Deb, K. (1994). Multiobjective optimization using nondominated sorting in genetic algorithms. *Evolutionary Computation, 2*(3), 221–248. doi:10.1162/evco.1994.2.3.221

Sugiyama, K. (2002). Graph drawing and applications for software and knowledge engineers. *Japan Advanced Institute of Science and Technology, 11*, 218.

Sun Microsystems. (2008a). *JavaTM 2 platform standard edition 5.0 API specification*. Retrieved from http://java.sun.com/j2se/1.5.0/docs/api/

Sun Microsystems. (2008b). *MySQL 6.0 reference manual*. Retrieved from http://dev.mysql.com/doc/refman/6.0/en/news-6-0-x.html

Sun Microsystems. (2008c). *MySQL Connector/J manual*. Retrieved from http://dev.mysql.com/downloads/connector/j/5.1.html

Tamassia, R., Di Battista, G., & Batini, C. (1988). Automatic graph drawing and readability of diagrams. *IEEE Transactions on Systems, Man, and Cybernetics, 18*(1), 61–79. doi:10.1109/21.87055

Van VeldHuizen. D. A. (1999). *Multiobjective evolutionary algorithms: Classifications, analyses, and new innovations* (Unpublished doctoral dissertation). Department of Electrical and Computer Engineering, Graduated School of Engineering, Air Force Institute Technology, Wright-Patterson AFB, OH.

Vrajitoru, D. (2009, April 18-19). Multiobjective genetic algorithm for a graph drawing problem. In *Proceedings of the Midwest Artificial Intelligence and Cognitive Science Conference*, Fort Wayne, IN (pp. 28-43).

ADDITIONAL READING

Barbosa, H., & Barreto, A. (2001). An interactive genetic algorithm with co-evolution of weights for multiobjective problems. In *Proceedings of the Genetic and Evolutionary Computation Conference* (pp. 203-210).

Chan, T. M., Goodrich, M. T., Kosarajub, S. R., & Tamassia, R. (2002). Optimizing area and aspect ratio in straight-line orthogonal tree drawings. *Computational Geometry, 23*, 153–162. doi:10.1016/S0925-7721(01)00066-9

Kuntz, P., Lehn, R., & Briand, H. (2000). Dynamic rule graph drawing by genetic search. In *Proceedings of the IEEE International Conference on Systems, Man and Cybernetics* (Vol. 4, pp. 2481-2486).

Zitzler, E., & Thiele, L. (1999). Multiobjective evolutionary algorithms: A comparative case study and the strength Pareto approach. *IEEE Transactions on Evolutionary Computation, 3*(4), 257–271. doi:10.1109/4235.797969

Zitzler, E., Thiele, L., Laumanns, M., Fonseca, C., & Grunert, V. (2003). Performance assessment of multiobjective optimizers: An analysis and review. *IEEE Transactions on Evolutionary Computation, 7*(2), 117–132. doi:10.1109/TEVC.2003.810758

KEY TERMS AND DEFINITIONS

Area Minimization: The area of the smallest rectangle with horizontal and vertical sides covering the drawing.

Aspect Ratio Minimization: The ratio of the length of the longest side to the length of shortest side of the smallest rectangle with horizontal and vertical sides covering the drawing.

Crossing Minimization: The minimization of the total number of crossing between edges.

Dominance Concept: Two solutions are compared on the basis of whether a solution dominates another or not. Assuming there are M objective functions could be said that a solution $x^{(1)}$ dominates other solution $x^{(2)}$, if the following conditions are satisfied: a) Solution $x^{(1)}$ is not worse than $x^{(2)}$ for all objectives; b) Solution x (1) is strictly better than x (2) in at least one objective.

Dominance Index: To apply a measure of quality (dominance index) for each solution stored in the Pareto front, in order to know the Pareto optimum.

Estimation of Distribution Algorithms: A set of methods that belong to the evolutionary computation. This methods substitute crossover and mutation by the estimation and sample of the probability distribution, learned by means of selected individuals.

Graph Drawing: Addresses the problem of constructing geometric representations of graphs, networks, and related combinatorial structures.

Hill Climbing: An optimization technique which belongs to the local search family. This algorithm uses a series of iterations where it is constantly shifting towards the direction with a better value.

Multiobjective Optimization: When an optimization problem involves more than one objective function, the task of finding one or more optimum solutions is known as *multi-objective optimization*.

Pareto Front: A concept that formalizes the trade-off between a given set of mutually contradicting objectives. A solution is Pareto optimal when it is not possible to improve one objective without deteriorating at least one of the other. A set of Pareto optimal solutions constitute the Pareto front.

Chapter 6
Handwritten Signature Verification Using Multi-Objective Optimization with Genetic Algorithms in a Forensic Architecture

Francisco Luna
Insituto Tecnológico de Aguascalientes, Mexico

Julio César Martínez Romo
Insituto Tecnológico de Aguascalientes, Mexico

Miguel Mora-González
Universidad de Guadalajara, Mexico

Evelia Martínez-Cano
Universidad de Guadalajara, Mexico

Valentín López Rivas
Insituto Tecnológico de Aguascalientes, Mexico

ABSTRACT

This chapter presents the use of multi-objective optimization for on-line automatic verification of handwritten signatures; as discriminating features of each signer are used here some functions of time and space of the position of the pen on the paper; these functions are directly used in a multi-objective optimization task in order to obtain high values of false positives indicators (FAR False Acceptance Rate) and false negatives (FFR, false rejection rate). The genetic algorithms are used to create a signer's model that optimally characterizes him, thus rejecting the skilled forgeries and recognizing genuine signatures with large variation with respect to the training set.

DOI: 10.4018/978-1-4666-0297-7.ch006

OBJECTIVE AND OUTLINE OF THIS CHAPTER

The automated signature verification techniques can be broadly classified in on-line and off-line techniques, depending upon the way used to acquire the signature. This chapter presents the use of an optimization multi-objective technique under the hypothesis that the optimal representation of the features will produce a features space with a more clear and tidy class separation, thus promoting a higher performance of an automatic signature verification system; we decided to use a genetic algorithm with elitism cross-fertilized with a gradient method for the multi-objective optimization formulation.

An introduction to the automatic verification of handwritten signatures and their variables, features and prototype functions in signatures can be observed at the beginning of the chapter, next we describe the multi-objective optimization with emphasis in the optimal modeling of features; then we describe and implemented the architecture of the forensic verification approach. The architecture evaluation, results and conclusions can be observed at the end of the chapter.

INTRODUCTION

The task of verifying signatures is essentially to recognize genuine signatures, rejecting imitations. The handwritten signature has many advantages for personal identification. This is the most widespread technique of identity verification for all enlightened communities (Plamondon & Lorette, 1989). It is used to give value to written trade obligations, such as promissory notes, checks, credit card vouchers, treaties, etc. Financial transactions also require the signature to be authenticated (Peerapong & Monthippa, 2010).

The handwritten signature verification is based on the assumption that the signature is the result of ballistic movements and as such, its dynamic

characteristics are largely specific for a person, which are stable and repeatable. To carry the verification out is required to generate a standard reference, based on local or global features, in a direct or averaged way (Wirtz, 1997).

In the last thirty years, several research groups have worked on the design of a computer based system for automatic verification (Plamondon & Lorette, 1989). Verification techniques are classified primarily on on-line and off-line techniques. In the second case, the printed signature on a piece of paper is scanned or digitized, missing thus the information concerning to the sequence of the signature points, which is known as the dynamic of the signature. Verification off-line techniques have some advantages: only a scanner is required to obtain a digital representation of the signature, we can work with signatures on documents previously prepared and they do not need to be in digital format (Gries, 2000). Among its disadvantages is that the processing is complicated, because it requires that the signature is separated from the bottom of the document.

In the *on-line* verification system is used as an input device a graphic tablet (Hangai, Yamanaka, & Hamamoto, 2000) or an instrumented pen (Baron & Plamondon, 1989; Plamondon & Baron, 1989). Figure 1 shows the *SmartPen* pen and a digitizer tablet. The dynamic information related to the process of signing is captured. Both, dynamics data and the shape of the signature, are used for verification, which makes inherently more accurate an on-line system compared with the off-line system. A potential forger must be concerned not just on the shape (or design), but also of how the sequence and timing of certain strokes of the signature should be executed.

The handwritten signature verification is based on the assumption that the signature is the result of ballistic movements and as such, its dynamic characteristics are largely specific for a person, which are stable and repeatable. To carry the verification out is required to generate a standard

Figure 1. On-line signature capture Equipment: a) Instrumented Pen SmartPen, and b) digitalized tablet

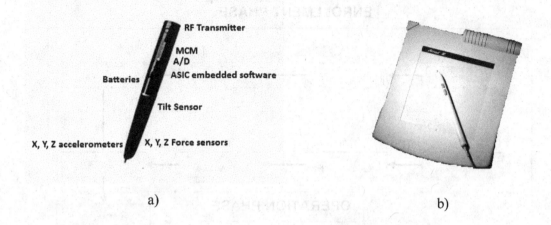

a)   b)

reference, based on local or global features, in a direct or averaged way (Wirtz, 1997).

AUTOMATIC VERIFICATION OF HANDWRITTEN SIGNATURES

Operation of the Signature Verification System

An analysis of existing bibliography about the subject (Nalwa, 1997; Plamondon & Lorette, 1989; Ji, Lee, Cho, & Kim, 2009; Wan-Suck, Mohankrishman, & Paulik, 1998; Wijesoma, Mingming, & Sung, 2000; Azlinah, Rohayu, Sofianita, & Shulina, 2009; Vahid, Reza, & Hamid, 2009; Muhammad, Matthew, Aurangzeb, Khurram, & Ling, 2009; Kumiko, Daigo, Satoshi, & Takashi, 2010; Guru & Prakash, 2009) reveals that the systems of automatic handwritten signature verification are based on an architecture as that shown in Figure 2. Automatic signature verification systems (ASVS) operate in two phases: enrollment and operation.

Enrollment Phase

In the enrollment phase, a volunteer donates a number of instances of his signature, which are

captured on-line or off-line. A processing stage is immediately executed in order to remove noise and standardize the signature in size or temporal duration. After processing, the signature data are subjected to the extraction of distinctive and discriminating features. As a result, the *variable space* is manipulated and a *features space* is generated. Among the common variables are the position, pressure, force, velocity, acceleration, all about time (Plamondon & Shihari, 2000) and the set of the instantaneous pen inclinations with respect to a coordinate axis superposed on the surface of signed, also as function of time (Plamondon & Shihari, 2000; Ohishi, Komiya, Morita, & Matsumoto, 2001).

For the extraction or generation of the features are used mathematical and exploration methods of space representations, time or frequency, among which are wavelets, frequency analysis, mathematical transforms of several types, processing of digital images, etc. As in the case of the variables, the characteristic and distinctive features are also represented by functions, generally of time or space, or by parameters, which can be local or global. The features are grouped together into vectors, known as *features vectors*, which are used to create a reference or template for each feature; it should be insensitive to natural variations in the signer drawing and be able to detect the inher-

Figure 2. Generic architecture of automatic handwritten signature verification systems

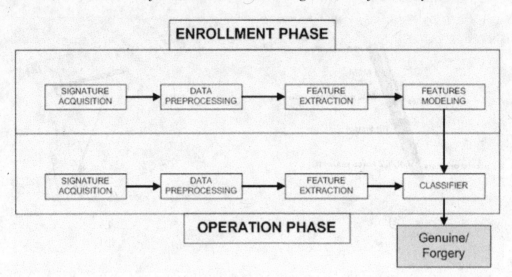

ent variations induced by a forger. One or more feature vectors constitute a model, as shown in Figure 2. To form a model, multiple instances of the same signature should be processed to capture the average behavior and the limit of the writing habits of the signer.

Operation Phase

In the operation phase, a signature to be verified is captured and preprocessed. Once its distinctive features have been computed they are compared against the respective model. Neural networks have been used as comparators or classifiers (Hesketh, 1977; Pender, 1991) neuro-fuzzy architectures (Murshed, Bortolozi, & Sabourin, 1995; Martínez & Alcántara, 2004) vector quantization (learning vector quantization, LVQ) (Bai-Ling, Min-Yue, & Hong, 1998), dynamic time warping (Martens & Claesen, 1996, 1997; Munich & Perona, 1999), regional correlation and tree matching (Plamondon & Parizeau, 1990), Hidden Markov Models (Dolfing, 1998), and Support Vector Machines (Fauziyah & Zahariah, 2009), among others. Sometimes the signature model is built intrinsic or implicitly in the weights of a

neural network or in the membership functions of fuzzy systems (Plamondon & Shihari, 2000) or by other means; they have the disadvantage that it is difficult or there is no way to improve the performance of the signature verification systems that use them.

Performance Indexes

Performance is measured as the percentage of errors incurred by the system to perform a certain number of verification attempts. There are two ways the system can make mistakes (errors). One way is to consider that a genuine signature is a forgery. This is a false rejection, leading to a performance index is known as the FRR, the *false rejection rate*. It is classified as a Type I error. Another possible way of error is to declare a forgery of a signature as genuine; the percentage of the false acceptances is known as *false acceptance rate*, or FAR. This kind of error is called Type II error. Invariably, an improvement in FAR causes a worsening in FRR, and vice versa. Figure 3, taken from Nalwa (1997), shows a graph of the compromise or tradeoff between the two types of errors. Additionally, there is also the combina-

Figure 3. Curves to measure the performance of an automatic signature verification system: a) one parameter vs. FAR and FRR, and b) FAR vs. FRR

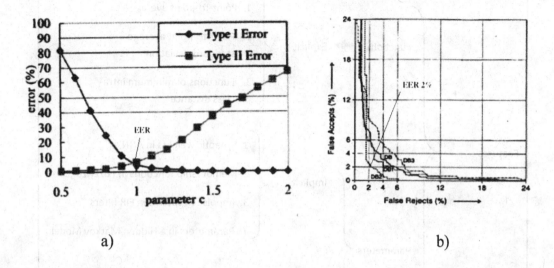

a)   b)

tion of Type I and type II errors in a measure of overall performance, known as the Equal Error Rate (Equal Error Rate, EER), which is the error measured when the Type I error is equal to Type II (Allgrove & Fairhurst, 1998) (Figure 3).

Figure 3a shows one of the ways in which the relation between FAR and FRR can be represented. Here, the x-axis represents a parameter that is varied over a certain range and the values of FRR and FAR are computed for each value of such parameter, then the FRR and FAR are plotted. The point where FAR and FRR intersect is the point of EER, which is an optimal point of operation. In Figure 3b, it is plotted FRR vs. FAR. It's a different view with respect to Figure 3a. In this case, it is not clear which parameter is varied to obtain the different curves of FRR and FAR. Both styles are used in the literature. You can see that FRR and FAR values that tend to zero simultaneously are considered optimal.

The free parameters or classification thresholds of the classifiers used in verification systems are adjusted so that the error rates (FAR, FRR) vary according to different types of applications. For example, in the case of a designed system for credit cards in which the cardholder presents his card to make a purchase and signs on an electronic device that automatically verifies the signature, the FRR must remain conservative, so that the genuine buyer is not bothered by unnecessary rejections. In addition, verification should be fast. On the other hand, in a high security environment, to control the access to facilities or resources it would require a high security grade against intruders and therefore a zero or near zero FAR.

Additionally, as a performance measure of an automatic signature verification system also we find the percentage of successful verification, which should approach to 100% as much as possible. It refers to the successes of the system to genuine signatures and forgeries, simultaneously.

VARIABLES, FEATURES AND PROTOTYPE FUNCTIONS IN SIGNATURES

As mentioned previously, the digitizer tablets provide the position $[x(t), y(t)]$, pressure $p(t)$, and 3-axis tilt of the pen during the signing process. These signals, in its raw form, are the variables of the process (Theodoridis & Koutroumbas,

Figure 4. Classification of the modeling methods of prototypes of features in signature verification

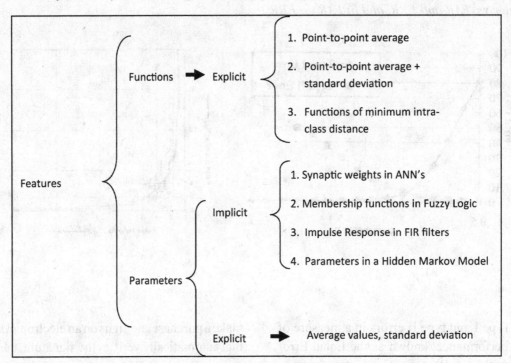

1999); because they form a sequence of values over time they are also considered as *functions*. Any transformation that takes place on these key functions for classification purposes will result in a *feature*, so, a *feature* is derived from a variable when this gets a transformation, but sometimes also the variables act as features. Later we will mention the topic of the transformations used here.

Approaches in Representing Features

According to the publications about automatic signature verification, the method for modeling the prototype function of any feature may be classified as one of those listed in Figure 4. In summary table in Figure 4, in the second level, we can see that a feature may be represented by parameters or by functions. The parameters represent behavior of the features with a few values, such as RMS value, average, minimum, maximum, etc., computed from the sequence of

data that conform the feature. Usually, it is put at the disposal of the verification system a number N of signatures to form the basis of knowledge of a signature, so the system has N sets of parameters that represent to the distinctive and discriminating features of a user.

The information from the N sets of parameters should be used to generate a single representative that summarizes the behavior of all the others for comparison purposes. The representative set should be generated carefully, because, using some vectors distance metric, it will be the reference against which the derived parameters from a questioned signature will be compared.

To form the model of the parameters implicit or explicit constructions are used. In explicit constructions, the parameters keep their identity and thus the average value of each parameter and its standard deviation as well are used as the model. Another tendency in modeling features is the implicit construction. In this case, the distance measure does not apply directly to the parameters, which serve as training data for neural networks, fuzzy systems, design parameters of digital filters, coefficients of autoregressive models, hidden Markov models, etc.., and the model is constituted by the synaptic weights in neural networks, the membership functions or the fuzzy systems rules, impulse response filters, etc. In some cases, functions are processed and parameters are generated, as in Lejtman and George (2001). On where wavelets were used (Daubechis-6), or Fourier descriptors (Berrin & Alisher, 2010).

When parameters are used to represent the signature features, the verification systems tend to have lower performance than when using functions, but it has the advantage to be calculated and compared faster. In some cases, as in Mingming and Wijesoma (2000) both representation methods have been used simultaneously.

Creating Prototypes in the Functions Approach

Returning to the second level of Figure 4, it shows that, in addition to parameters, the features can be represented by functions. This tendency is used more often in the literature because the handwritten signature verification sys terms based on this representation have shown better performance than those based on parameters (Plamondon & Shihari, 2000).

Because the dimensionality of the functions is around one hundred elements or more, the implicit representation techniques are used less frequently than explicit, so that this tendency is not mentioned in the summary table in Figure 4. The explicit representations are more used, which are available directly to model though averaging point to point the N available functions in order to form the knowledge basis of one signature. Typically, the statistical variance of the points of the N observations of a feature is used to weigh their respective average values. Examples of this tendency are Sakamoto, Morita, Ohishi, Komiya, and Matsumoto (2001), Ho, Schroder, and Leedharn

(2001), Fasquel, Stolz, and Bruynooghe (2001), and Allgrove and Fairhurst (2001).

To highlight the existence of techniques not based on the average and standard deviations for the creation of the prototype function of a feature, in the summary table in Figure 4 there is listed another trend, in which as the prototype function is selected one or more functions out of their own set of training functions, as in Komiya and Matsumoto (1999), Ohishi, Komiya, Morita, and Matsumoto (2001), and Die Lecce, Dimauro, Guerreiro, Impedovo, Pirlo, Salzo, and Sarcinella (1999).

MULTI-OBJECTIVE OPTIMIZATION FOR AUTOMATIC VERIFICATION OF SIGNATURES

The optimal modeling of the features can be described as the problem of finding the form -or point values- that should have the function prototype or class representative of a feature, such that the classification errors are minimized in the training data set and in features from "new" signatures not previously seen in these data. In order to get this, the prototype function is formed in a point to point basis while looking directly in the problem solutions space for a final form of the function that maximizes the separation between classes of genuine signatures (ω_0) and forgeries (ω_1) with a low intra-class dispersion for a bi-class problem in which tends to exist overlap of classes in the feature space, as mainly happened with the *form* or *design* features of a signature when a skilled forger reproduces a signature.

Multi-Objective Modeling of the Features

In the sequel, it is defined here the concept of optimal modeling of features in terms of the specific problem of handwritten signatures verification, in the sense that it is described with the variables

Figure 5. The multi-objective optimization strategy

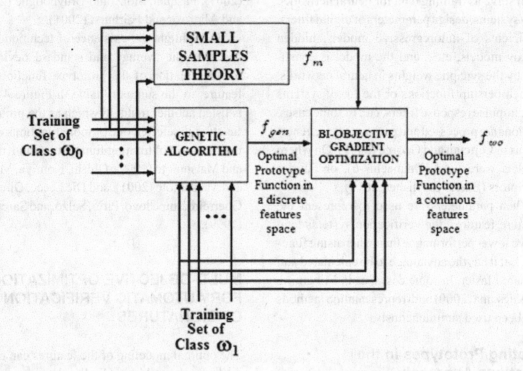

and features of the this field, but all that we be said can be extrapolated to the solution of other bi-class problems of pattern recognition. The *class prototype function* f_x, models and summarizes the behavior of a set of instances of a feature. For verification of handwritten signatures, the problem is centered in finding a representation of each feature of rhythms and form from the instances that are available and, based on them, solve the following optimization problem:

Minimize $[FAR(f_0, f_1, f_2, ..., f_n), FRR(f_0, f_1, f_2, ..., f_n)]$, (1)

that is, minimize FAR and FRR rates as a function of the *prototype function* or *model* of each feature. Note that $f_0, f_1, f_2, ..., f_n$, are the general features, which make that the verifier architecture that is described below is adaptable to any number of other features. The two equations goals of eq. (1) must be achieved simultaneously, pushing the EER point further back in the the FAR and

FRR graph (Figure 3a). Note that it is a case of a two goals multi-objective optimization problem. Figure 5 shows the multi-objective optimization method applied here, and whose demonstration can be found in Martínez (2004).

In particular, the genetic algorithm here is used for their ability to avoid local maxima and local minima, and to allow a discrete approximation to the solution; immediately, having secured a sub-optimal solution, a bi-objective gradient version is used to refine the genetic prototype function f_{gen} such that, simultaneously, their point values are closer to those of a probabilistic version of the feature given by f_m -obtained according to the theory of the small samples- that minimizes the FRR and yet "moves" the function away (in the sense of the Mahalanobis distance) from the closest specimens of the Class ω_1.

Modeling the Features Optimally

When a skilled forger cleverly imitates a hand-written signature, he reproduces the functions or parameters that define the signature to have very similar values to those of the genuine signatures, resulting in an increment of false acceptance (FAR). In an effort to mitigate this effect, the recognition threshold of the classifier can be set to a high value. However, when the threshold is high, there is a risk that genuine signatures are rejected, increasing the false rejection rate (FRR). This is shown in Figure 3a. One way to give a treatment to this problem is TO REPRESENT the prototype functions or parameters so that the two involved classes (genuine class ω_0 – forgery class ω_1) are separated according to a distance measure and the probability of misclassification of genuine signatures is "minimal." This concept should not be confused with the selection and/or optimal generation of features, which can be seen in Theodoridis and Koutroumbas (1999).

The optimal modeling will be derived based on a bi-class problem, where the features will discriminate between the genuine class (ω_0) and the forgery class (ω_1). Consider that there are N exemplars of the class ω_0 and K exemplars in class ω_1. For now, assume a single feature function f of length L. Be $[f_{\omega 0}\ \sigma_{\omega 0}]$ and $[f_{\omega 1}\ \sigma_{\omega 1}]$ the *prototype* and *consistency* functions of classes ω_0 and ω_1, respectively, of length L; $\sigma_{\omega x}$ is the point-to-point standard deviation of the exemplars of the char-acteristic function of the training set. The class distribution of the N + K samples of f is known *a priori*. As a measure of dissimilarity between an instance of the descriptive function of each feature and its prototype function in ω_0 is adopted as:

$$d^2(f, f_{\omega_0}) = (f - f_{\omega_0})\Sigma^{-1}(f - f_{\omega_0})^T, \qquad (2)$$

with

$$\Sigma^{-1} \equiv \begin{bmatrix} 1/\sigma_{\omega_{00}}^{\ 2} & 0 & \cdots & 0 \\ 0 & 1/\sigma_{\omega_{01}}^{\ 2} & 0 & 0 \\ 0 & 0 & \ddots & 0 \\ 0 & 0 & 0 & 1/\sigma_{\omega_{0L}}^{\ 2} \end{bmatrix}, \qquad (3)$$

where Σ^{-1} is the matrix of the inverse of the squares of the standard deviations over the set of the N training samples. We define the vector of distances between each of the instances of the *genuine* class and the prototype function $[f_{\omega 0}\ \sigma_{\omega 0}]$ as $\mathbf{D}_{ia}$ –intra-class distance-, to be:

$$D_{ia} = \begin{bmatrix} d_0 & d_1 & \cdots & d_N \end{bmatrix}. \qquad (4)$$

We define the vector of distances between each of the copies of the *false* class and the prototype function of the genuine class $[f_{\omega 0}\ \sigma_{\omega 0}]$ and $\mathbf{D}_{ie}$ intra class distance as:

$$D_{ie} = \begin{bmatrix} d_0 & d_1 & \cdots & d_K \end{bmatrix}, \qquad (5)$$

in eqs. (4) and (5), the i-*th* distance d_i is computed using eq. (2).

Multi-Objective Optimization for Handwritten Signature Verification

Training Dataset

Given the specimens of a feature (taken from several signers) contained in a database, the training sets for genetic algorithm are selected as follows:

a. Class ω_0: 16 functions derived from genuine signatures.
b. Class ω_1: 200 functions derived from random forgeries from twenty other users (to discriminate the generality of the writing styles) plus 10 synthetically forged functions (to discriminate the skilled forgery.)

Figure 6. Class separation of prototype functions: a) before, and b) after the optimization

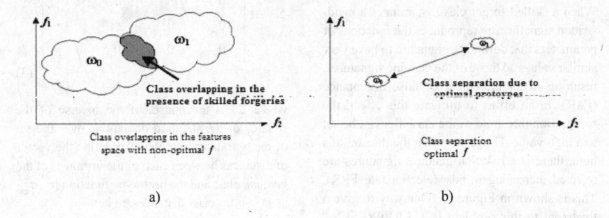

a)   b)

The Multi-Objective Optimization Strategy

The optimization is a research area with decades of results to its credit. Gradient-based methods and gradient-free, have spent years solving problems in various fields of science and engineering (Beveridge & Schechter, 1970). Here, the objective of optimizing the prototype function $[f_{\omega 0} \ \sigma_{\omega 0}]$ of the genuine class, is to build a prototype function such that the dissimilarity measure –eq. (2)- between this and the N examples of genuine class is *small* while the same measure with respect to the *closest* K examples of the forgery class is *large* or at least larger than the largest registered distance measured between the functions of the genuine class and its prototype function, so that the feature is sufficiently discriminant in presence of skilled forgeries. Figure 6a shows the natural overlap that occurs between *genuine class* ω_0 and the *forgery class* ω_1 in the presence of skilled forgeries, considering two discriminating feature functions f_1 and f_2, respectively. Figure 6b shows the expected class separation due to the fact that the representation $[f_{\omega 0} \ \sigma_{\omega 0}]$ of the feature was optimized for the class ω_0, under the same set of training data. To achieve the result shown in Figure 6b, the optimization is performed in two phases.

In a first phase, a genetic algorithm is used to explore the discrete space of solutions; in the second phase, a continuous search method is used by the gradient in two directions: in one direction we look for keep maximizing the distance between classes ω_0 and ω_1, while in the other one the goal is to close the prototype function to another function that tries to minimize the probability of misclassification of genuine signatures P_e. This is a multi-objective optimization problem, multidimensional.

Genetic algorithms are optimization techniques of recent apparition, inspired on mechanisms of natural selection (Goldberg, 1989; Tsoukalas & Uhrig, 1997). The genetic algorithms has been selected to join the first stage of optimization due to its feature of searching multiple points in the surface of the problem solution (each chromosome is an explored point in the solutions space), unlike other methods that perform a search with a single point. This ability of the algorithm allows us to find points that can be a maximum global with more probability (Tsoukalas & Uhrig, 1997) but on the other hand, does not exist a guarantee for this.

Table 1. Examples of encoding of many instances of a feature in a chromosome

Number	Chromosome	Group of signatures to be averaged
1	'0001|1001|0110|1111|1101|1100|0010| . . . 0111'	{1, 9, 6, 15, 13, 12, 2 ... 7}
2	'0011|1101|1101|1111|0010|1001|0101| . . . 0110'	{3, 13, 13, 15, 2, 9, 5, ... 6}
3	'1110|0101|0100|1010|1010|0101|1001| . . . 0000'	{14, 5, 4, 10, 10, 5, 9, ... 0}
4	'0110|0111|1000|1001|1110|0001|0011| . . . 1010'	{6, 7, 8, 9, 14, 1, 3, . . . 10}
5	'1000|0101|0011|0001|1001|0110|1100| . . . 0010'	{8, 5, 3, 1, 9, 6, 12, . . . 2}

Optimization using Genetic Algorithm: Minimizing FAR

Given a feature function of length L and N examples of it as positive examples of a genuine signature and K negative examples of the same feature function -derived from simple and skilled forgeries-, the goal is to find some combination of the N genuine functions such that their average value and standard deviation maximize the min$\{D_{ie}\}$, given the dissimilarity measure $d^2=(f-f_{\omega0})\Sigma^{-1}(f-f_{\omega0})^T$, with Σ^{-1} defined by eq. (3). It is allowed to repeat data from the same example more than once to form the optimized representation of the feature. By selecting averaging it is reasonable to expect values **of D_{ia}** (eq. 4) moderated during the verification phase. Assuming that we have N genuine signatures, the prototype function will be represented by:

$$f_{\omega_0}(i) = \frac{1}{N}\sum_{j=1}^{N} f_j(i), \quad i = 0, 1, 2, ..., L.$$

$$(6)$$

In the chromosome, each feature function is identified by a binary index. The number of bits per index is given by:

$$b = \log_2(N), \qquad (7)$$

while the total number of bits in the chromosome is bc=bXN. The recommended number of chromosomes (Tsoukalas & Uhrig, 1997) is nc:

$$nc \geq bc. \qquad (8)$$

The cost function or *fitness* is related to the eq. (3) and the expressions 4 and 5 is

$$J = \frac{\min(D_{ie})-\max(D_{ia})}{\max(D_{ie})}. \qquad (9)$$

The Table 1 shows some encoding examples of chromosomes. In row 1, a chromosome is encoded with different signatures. 4 bits are used per signature, implying that 16 signatures are used to generate the optimized prototype of the discriminant feature. We introduce the symbol "|" to separate the different instances of the signature from which the characteristic was derived.

The genetic algorithm parameters are shown in Table 2. The optimized prototype function is calculated by averaging the signatures features represented in the chromosome and the corresponding standard deviation.

The final representation of the prototype function obtained by the genetic algorithm for the feature has evolved from random forgeries, -taken from the same feature functions derived from other 20 people's signatures, and skilled forgeries. The purpose of including random forgeries is that the system learns to discriminate some general writing styles and when it is given a ran-

Table 2. Parameters of the genetic algorithm

Element	Type	Comments
Population	First: Random, Constant	The initial population is generated randomly and it stays constant in each evolutionary cycle
Selection	Elitism	Solutions which are then selected to form new solutions (offspring) are selected according to their fitness - the more suitable they are the more chances they have to reproduce
Crossing method	Crossover point	The elements selected is given in a single point
Probability of mutation	PM>0.14%	To take out the evolutionary process to compute the local least
Stop criterion	mean(J) = max(J) or 60 gen	When the fitness average is similar to the fitness of the population or (|) when the number of iterations reaches 60.

dom forgery this one can be discovered easily by the classifier. The skilled forgeries are available in the field by preparing potential forgers about the original signer's style of writing. In a real application environment, however, skilled forgers are not available for training purposes. In our case, to overcome this difficulty we borrowed from Martínez and Alcántara (2004) a technique to generate skilled forgeries.

Gradient Multi-Objective Optimization: Minimizing FRR and FAR

Let the prototype function of length L obtained by the genetic algorithm to be represented by

$$X_{gen} = \begin{bmatrix} \overline{x}_0 & \overline{x}_1 & \overline{x}_2 & \cdots & \overline{x}_L \end{bmatrix}, \qquad (9b)$$

where x_i is any element of it. From here to ahead, a prototype function will be called either function, feature vector or simply a vector.

The motivation for modifying and improving the prototype function resulting from the evolutionary process is that the cost function –eq. (9)- is aimed to reduce false acceptances while false rejections are "controlled" by selecting the average values of each feature point. In theory, since each point of the feature function along several instances behaves as a random variable,

it is natural that the expected value of the next sample is given by

$$E\{x\} = \overline{x}, (10)$$

and then the problem of minimizing false rejections becomes a probabilistic problem, which can be defined as "what is the value of each point x_i of the prototype function that minimizes the probability of a genuine feature vector is erroneously considered as extracted from a forgery?". Using a probabilistic approach it is possible to establish, within a confidence interval 95%, the upper (L_s) and lower (L_i) limits of each point x_i of the function of a feature (Martínez, 2004). In vector form, the characteristic values that make the likelihood of misclassification of genuine signatures theoretically be minimized is

$$\overline{X} = \begin{bmatrix} L_0^i + \left((\hat{x}_0 - \min(x_0)) \big/ (\max(x_0) - \min(x_0)) \right) \cdot (L_0^s - L_0^i) \\ L_1^i + \left((\hat{x}_1 - \min(x_1)) \big/ (\max(x_1) - \min(x_1)) \right) \cdot (L_1^s - L_1^i) \\ \vdots \\ L_L^i + \left((\hat{x}_L - \min(x_L)) \big/ (\max(x_L) - \min(x_L)) \right) \cdot (L_L^s - L_L^i) \end{bmatrix}^T,$$

$$(11)$$

on statistical inference arguments presented in Martínez (2004). The resulting vector will be called *minimizing vector of error probability*, denoted by the subscript *m*. Thus, any of the defined features used here later can be calculated using eq. (11) to arrive, for example, to $Cx_m(l)$, $Cy_m(l)$, $p_m(t)$, etc.

After calculating the averaged feature function X_m of expression 11, it should be make the corresponding point values of the function obtained through genetic optimization to tend to the respective values of the corresponding points of X_m, this is

$$X_{gen} \rightarrow \bar{X} = X_m, \Rightarrow \begin{bmatrix} x_{0gen} \rightarrow \bar{\hat{x}}_{0m} \\ x_{1gen} \rightarrow \bar{\hat{x}}_{1m} \\ \vdots \\ x_{Lgen} \rightarrow \bar{\hat{x}}_{Lm} \end{bmatrix}, \qquad (12)$$

while it seeks to maintain or increase the distance from the instances of the closest function to X_{gen} that is in the class ω_1, providing a bigger discrimination of classes at the expense of exploring *continuous space of solutions* from the surface solution problem. This is a multi-objective optimization problem, similar to the "global criteria." To make X_{gen} to approach to X_m (in order to reduce FRR) and simultaneously getting away from the nearest representative of the class ω_1 identified from here to ahead as $X_{\omega1}$ -(in order to reduce FAR) in the continuous space of solutions, it tackles the problem as simultaneously minimize a cost function J from respective punctual values of X_{gen} and X_m, and maximize between points X_{gen} and $X_{\omega1}$. The function cost selected is the *sum of squared errors:*

$$J(X) = \sum_{i=1}^{L} (Y - X)^2 = \sum_{i=1}^{L} e^2 \text{ and for any point } J(x) = (y-x)^2 = e^2.$$
$$(13)$$

The value of x that minimizes $J(x)$ is iteratively found by:

$$x^k = x^{k-1} - \alpha \frac{\partial e^2}{\partial x}, \qquad (14)$$

where

$$\frac{\partial e^2}{\partial x} = -2(y - x), \qquad (15)$$

so that eq. (14) is like:

$$x^k = x^{k-1} + 2\alpha(y - x), \qquad (16)$$

where α is the factor that controls the speed and accuracy of convergence; let us do $\alpha_0 = 2\alpha$. Each x_i element of X can be updated at a different speed, to adjust more quickly, it is appropriate that the elements that have a lower variance, and therefore lower standard deviation, contribute less to the total error and converge more quickly; that is why it adds a factor to the second term of eq. (16) to eq. (17), in which it has passed from one point to all contained points in the feature vector as follows

$$X^k = X^{k-1} + \alpha_0(Y - X^{k-1})(I - S), \qquad (17)$$

where I is the identity matrix and S is a diagonal matrix whose elements $s_{i,i}$ are the corresponding standard deviations of the elements x_i normalized to the unit. As a result, the convergence factor α_0 is weighted by $(1-s_{i,i})$, in the range of 0 to 1. As higher as the standard deviation is the factor $(1-s_{i,i})$, tends to zero, and as smaller as the standard deviation is $(1-s_{i,i})$, tends to one, the accuracy of the approximation is given by α_0.

On the other hand, the expression that removes or maximizes the cost function $J(x)$ between X and Y' is defined by:

$$X^k = X^{k-1} - \alpha_1(Y' - X), \qquad (18)$$

and each element x_i diverges as fast as the corresponding y_i. In eqs. (17) and (18) terms α_0 and α_1 control the speed with which X distances from Y' and approaches to Y. The values α_0 and α_1 must maintain a relationship such that $\alpha_0 > \alpha_1$ and $3 < \alpha_0/\alpha_1 < 10$, to promote convergence in both directions. As the gradient is double, in fact you cannot

Table 3. Algorithm for the application of dual gradient to minimize FAR and FRR simultaneously

Step	Process
1	To load examples of the class $\omega 1$. To put in a vector of negative examples (gne, group of negative examples) some examples of falsifications random and synthetic skilled of the characteristic Cx.
2	To load examples of the class $\omega 0$. To put in a vector of positive examples (*gpe,* group of negative examples*)* 16 genuine examples of the characteristic Cx.
3	To obtain the vectors Cxgne y Cxm. The characteristic generated genetically is assigned to Cx. To put in Cx_m the vector that minimizes the probability of error of classification of genuine signatures theoretically
4	To find the nearest example of $\omega 1$. To calculate the distance between Cx and each one of the examples of *cen* according to the eq. (8). To make $Cx_{\omega 1}$ similar to the nearest example of cen.
5	Approach Cx a Cxm. To apply the eq. (19a).
6	Move away Cx de Cx$\omega 1$ To apply the eq. (19b).
7	To look convergence. To repeat the steps 4 to 6 until arrives to a limit of iterations *it*. Actually, *it*=2000 gives good results.

always expect a static convergence in the sense that the values of X are stable when the number of iterations tends to infinity, because it has two object features to adjust, but this procedure does increase the movement that seeks to minimize the probability of error. Some appropriate values of α_0 and α_1 can be, for example, 0.0001 and 0.0008, respectively, according to empirical findings. The values of α_0 and α_1 also could be set individually for each feature and for each signer. To illustrate how to calculate an *optimal prototype function*, eqs. (17) and (18) become to the particular case of the features $C_x(l)$ -whose meaning will be discussed below-, and table 3 lists their algorithmic implementation.

$$a) \quad Cx^k = Cx^{k-1} + \alpha_0(Cx_m - Cx^{k-1})(I - S)$$

$$b) \quad Cx^k = Cx^{k-1} - \alpha_1(Cx_{\varpi 1} - Cx^{k-1})$$

$$(19)$$

FORENSIC ARCHITECTURE OF SIGNATURE VERIFICATION

Conforming the prototype function of the features is just a part of any signature verification system; the rest of the system can be represented in a processing architecture. The architecture where we embed the optimal prototype functions is called *forensic architecture*, because it involves processes and capabilities of human checkers experts in handwritten signatures. Here we describe the methodology and implemented algorithms in the signature verifier.

Forensic Verification of Handwritten Signatures

The technique of forensic verification of handwritten signatures is the technique used by experts in the field to determine whether, given a set of genuine copies of a signature, a new signature is genuine or forgery (Slyter, 1995). Some important elements of the methodology verification of a human expert that can be adopted in an automatic verification system of signatures are:

1. The signature is the result of the signer's writing habits, either in rhythms or dynamic as in form or firm design.
2. No writer can generate two identical signatures because the signature performances vary within *natural* limits, which may change over time, so the signature exhibits an *average* behavior in rhythms and form.
3. To know the limits of the variations in the signature and, in general terms, the spatial and dynamic behavior of the signature, the

verifier must have a set of signatures for reference. The forensic verifier *learns* to discriminate and recognize forgeries from genuine signatures of the exhibited traits because of the set of reference signatures.

4. The *hierarchical set of reference* features includes form and rhythm characteristics, as shown in Figure 7, and is fully described in Slyter (1995).

5. The final authenticity decision (authentic/ forgery) comes from a complex balance of rhythms and form elements, and not only of the separately valuation of each of them. The final consists in the certainty degree that a signature is genuine (where 0% means forgery and 100% genuine, with intermediate percentages and certainty intermediate levels).

ELEMENTS OF COMPARISON

Interrelationships of Handwriting Variables

Among the salient features of this approach to verify signatures is:

1. We separately evaluate the individual characteristics of rhythms and form, so it is easy to detect what are the most stable features by signer. Some elements are stable for some signers, not all the features are stable for all signers.

2. You can precisely identify which features of a questioned signature vary beyond a person's normal intrapersonal variations. This enables to elaborate verbal explanations about why a signature should be considered a forgery.

3. The information can be explicitly done, and not intangible, as in the case of the parameters of a hidden Markov model AR model, the weights of a neural network, etc.

4. The system based on human reasoning is inherently easy to interpret and to implement with existing tools of fuzzy logic and neural networks.

The requirements that must contain a system based on a forensic approach are:

1. The input variables should be such that they can derive the *basic elements* of Figure 7, which will be used as *features* for the verification system,

2. To provide adequate means for: a) combining the *basic elements* and generate *secondary elements*, b) to combine *secondary elements* and generate the *primary elements*, and

3. Provide a way to calculate the *critical element* or final, which is the balance *rhythm/ form*, of the genuineness of a questioned signature.

Forensic Verifier Architecture

The automatic verifier architecture is here proposed in Figure 8. We distinguish two phases of operation: training and testing, which are described.

Training Phase

In this phase is assumed that we have previously acquired genuine signatures, forming a database (BD in Figure 8). The *basic elements* are extracted to each signature from de database, Figure 7. It is important to mention that since the capture is dynamic, the secondary speed elements in x,y (V_x, V_y) and *pressure* $p(t)$ are provided directly by the capture device as discrete functions of time. From Figure 8, the first step, *modeling*, is a crucial step in the design of the classifier in any pattern recognition system. In this case, the distinctive features have been selected in function of time and space representing elementary and secondary elements. These time functions

Figure 8. Architecture of our forensic verifier

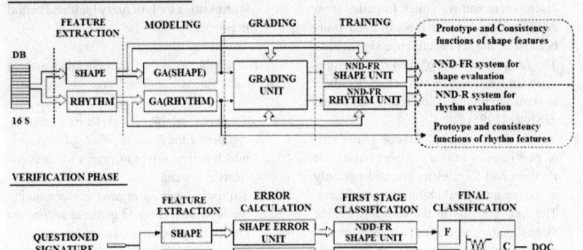

are derived from averages and standard deviation along the training set that will generate the class separation between the *genuine* class ω_0 and the forgery class (random forgeries plus skilled forgeries) ω_1. The signature distinctive features or characteristics are not equally stable for all signatories, so that the *graduation unit* is responsible to assign per signatory a weight to each feature based on how this feature could be discriminant for verification purposes. The *training* block has as an objective to combine the errors or differences in the *secondary elements* of rhythms and form with regard to their reference functions, separately, to generate rhythms and form rating. This combiner is a Takagi-Hayasi fuzzy *reasoning* system implemented by back propagation neural networks, known as *neural network-driven Fuzzy Reasoning* (NND-FR).

The input patterns to each NND-FR system are formed by the measure of dissimilarity or error between the features of genuine signatures and "false signatures" and their respective reference functions. Output patterns are one and zero (1.0) for the *genuine and false* classes, respec-

tively. The combined system not only combines the secondary elements to generate the primary ones, but learns the typical manner that errors have or, in other words, the genuine signer variations with respect to its reference model. These errors are also characteristic and not easily reproducible by a potential forger. For each signatory enrolled in the system, the final products of the training stage are the following, as shown in Figure 8.

1. Optimized prototype functions of the rhythm and form features.
2. Optimized feature functions consistent of rhythm and form.
3. Indices or weight factors, by feature, which define the relevance of each feature for verification.
4. Two systems NND-FR, one of rhythm and other of form (or design) to characterize the signatures on the dynamic and form.

Figure 7. Elements of rhythms and form to verify signatures according to the forensic signature verification theory

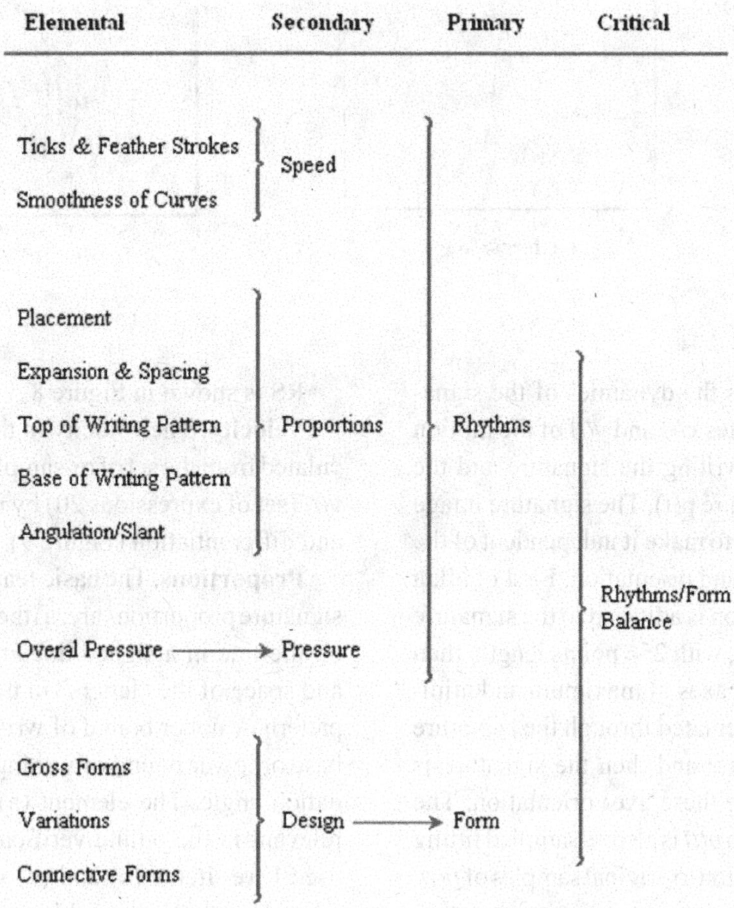

Elemental	Secondary	Primary	Critical
Ticks & Feather Strokes	Speed		
Smoothness of Curves			
Placement			
Expansion & Spacing			
Top of Writing Pattern	Proportions	Rhythms	
Base of Writing Pattern			
Angulation/Slant			Rhythms/Form Balance
Overal Pressure	Pressure		
Gross Forms			
Variations	Design	Form	
Connective Forms			

Verification Phase

Please, refer to the bottom of Figure 8. The first stage of the *verification phase* is the extraction of discriminant features or elements, both dynamic and form. Once extracted, are compared against their respective prototypes, obtaining individual dissimilarity measures. The set of dissimilarity measures of rhythm and form are fed to corresponding NND-FR systems, which deliver a numeric value ranging from 0 to 1, which are the rhythm and form random qualifications of the signature to be verified. This is a first step of verification. In this first step the random forgeries can be easily rejected. The final step of the

automatic verifier is a fuzzy system Mamdani type, with two inputs and one output. The input variables are the rhythm and form rating, and the output is the GDC (degree of certainty) that a firm must be considered genuine.

The following sections describe the stages of automatic verifier previously commented.

Acquisition and Signature Preprocessing

The signature acquisition was on-line and was performed with a digitizer Acecat 302 *Pen and Graphics Tablet,* ACECAD®, shown in Figure 1b. This tablet samples the pen movement at

Figure 9. Positions x(t) and y(t) and velocity of profiles of one signature are shown

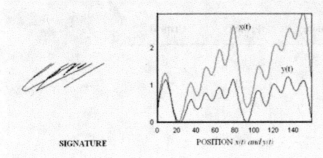

SIGNATURE   POSITION *x(t) and y(t)*

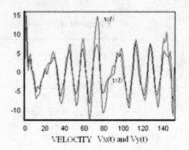

VELOCITY Vx(t) and Vy(t)

200Hz, which gives the dynamics of the signature as the coordinates *x(t)* and *y(t)* of the motion of the hand when writing the signature and the instantaneous pressure p(t). The signature image must be normalized to make it independent of the reason aspect, size and orientation. First of all, a second-order polygon is adjusted to the signature ordered set samples, with 256 points length, then the signature global axes of maximum and minimum inertia are calculated through the signature global center of mass and then the signature is rotated to normalize these axes orientation. The pressure information *p(t)* is also re-sampled fitting a second-order polygon to original samples of *p(t)*. With these operations we obtain a representation in space of the variables as indicated by the set of expressions 20:

$$x\left(t\right)=\left[x_0x_1x_2x_3\cdots x_{255}\right]\ =\mathbf{X}$$
$$y\left(t\right)=\left[y_0y_1y_2y_3\cdots y_{255}\right]\ =\mathbf{Y} \qquad (20)$$
$$p\left(t\right)=\left[p_0p_1p_2p_3\cdots p_{255}\right]\ =\mathbf{P}$$

Calculation of the Discriminating Characteristics of Rhythm

Now we will indicate how to extract secondary features *RS*

RS=[velocity proportions pressure design (form)], $\qquad (21)$

RS is shown in Figure 8.

Velocity. The velocity in the signature is calculated from the set of re-sampled vectors *x(t)* and *y(t)* (set of expressions 20) by numerical filtering and differentiation (Figure 9).

Proportions. The basic features that make the signature proportions are: a) the signature position on the line in a signed document, b) expansion and space of the "letters" in the signature, c) top pattern or upper bound of writing, d) top pattern base or lower bound of writing, and e) and inclination angle. The element (a) of this list is not relevant in the online verification, so do not be used here. Items (b) and (e) will be considered when you touch the subject of design features. The (c) and (d) elements can be calculated from the signature image. Figure 10 shows these features interpretation.

In addition to the form or design of the signature, here it is used a timed version of these. First we detect the appropriate upper and lower points belonging to the external envelope (wrapper) of the normalized image, and then we order them according to the order in which they were drawn during the signing process. These features will be symbolically called as TOW(t) (top of writing) and BOW(t) (base of writing), both as functions of time (Figure 11).

The symbolic representation is shown in the set of expressions 22.

Figure 10. Top and bottom of writing

UPPER ENVELOPE TOP
OF WRITING (TOW)

LOWER ENVELOPE BUTTON
OF WRITING (BOW)

$$TOW(t) = [T_0\ T_1 T_2 T_3 \cdots T_{83}] = \mathbf{T},$$
$$BOW(t) = [B_0\ B_1 B_2 B_3 \cdots B_{83}] = \mathbf{B}.$$

(22)

To obtain the vectors **T** and **B**, every existing point in the envelope (wrapper) are taken and re-sampled by adjusting to them a second order polynomial of 84 points length.

Pressure. Group pressure, changes in pressure and the soft or gradual pressure changes are important. The pressure elements that are interesting for automatic verification are composted of vectors as indicates the set of expressions 23:

$$p(t) = [p_0\ p_1\ p_2\ p_3 \cdots p_{255}] = \mathbf{P},$$
$$dp(t)/dt = [dp_0\ dp_1\ dp_2\ dp_3 \cdots dp_{255}] = \mathbf{dP}.$$

(23)

For the sake of resampling and to maintain constant length vector patterns, an adjustment of p(t) to a second degree polynomial, with length 256 is made.

Calculating the Discriminant Features of the Design Elements of a Signature

The general aspect of the signature, the letters that are picked out from a person's name to make his/her signature, how they connect these "letters" and its variants in the thick and thin, compose the signature design. The design and form term can be used interchangeably, and are also dictated by the signer's writing habits. To represent computationally the design of a signature, it will be used here the approach presented by Nalwa (1997), which is a geometric representation immune to changes in scale and orientation, and is sensitive to changes in the signature design, for example, local variations in the inclination of the signature, variations in the way or sequence that signature is drawn, thick forms or signature "letters", the links between them, etc. These functions will be onward called *form functions*.

Figure 11. The top functions calculation of and base of writing, before the polynomial adjustment

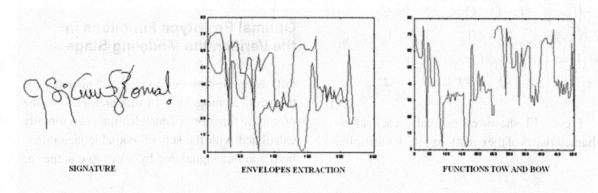

SIGNATURE   ENVELOPES EXTRACTION   FUNCTIONS TOW AND BOW

Figure 12. Elementary features and pseudo-static functions "equivalence"

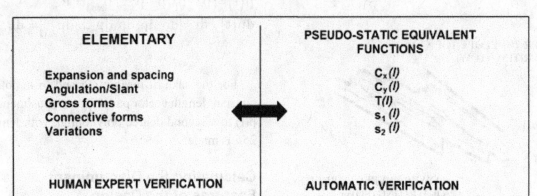

The proportions basic elements (expansion and space between "characters", angle and tilt), will be considered here form function makers. In this way we can establish certain *equivalence* between the form and basic elementary functions, as shown in Figure 12. Note that the relation shown is not one-one and is rather qualitative. The functions have retained the original names, which were published in Nalwa (1997).

The form functions depend on the parameter *l*, which is the length of the samples. The ordered values of *x(t)* and *y(t)* are re-sampled by adjusting a polynomial of second degree of 256 points in length; given its calculation method, the form functions have a cardinality of 82, so the set of relations 24 will describe, -for our purposes- the form factors of the signature:

$$C_x\left(l\right)=\left[C_{x0}\,C_{x1}\,C_{x2}\,C_{x3}\ldots C_{x81}\right]=\mathbf{C_x},$$
$$C_y\left(l\right)=\left[C_{y0}\,C_{y1}\,C_{y2}\,C_{y3}\ldots C_{y81}\right]=\mathbf{C_y},$$
$$T\left(l\right)=\left[T_0\quad T_1 T_2\,T_3\ldots\quad T_{81}\right]=\mathbf{T},$$
$$s1\left(l\right)=\left[\,s1_0\quad s1_1\,s1_2\,s1_3\ldots s1_{81}\right]=\mathbf{s1},$$
$$s2\left(l\right)=\left[\,s2_0\quad s2_1\,s2_2\,s2_3\ldots s2_{81}\right]=\mathbf{s2}.$$

(24)

Figure 13 shows conceptually each of the characteristics of the equations set 24; implemen-

tation details can be found in Nalwa (1997) and Martínez (2004).

Characterizing the Signature: Balance Rhythms/Shape

The total representation of a signature will be composed with the functions of rhythm features and shape. These functions are contained in the expressions 21, 22, 23 and 24. The rhythm functions are summarized below:

$$V\left(t\right)=\left[v_0 v_1 v_2 v_3\ldots v_{255}\right]=\mathbf{V},$$
$$\text{TOW}\left(t\right)=\left[T_0\,T_1 T_2\,T_3\ldots T_{83}\right]=\mathbf{T},$$
$$\text{BOW}\left(t\right)=\left[B_0\,B_1 B_2 B_3\ldots B_{83}\right]=\mathbf{B},$$
$$p\left(t\right)=\left[p_0\,p_1\,p_2 p_3\ldots p_{255}\right]=\mathbf{P},$$
$$\text{dp}\left(t\right)/\text{dt}=\left[\text{dp}_0\,\text{dp}_1\,\text{dp}_2\,\text{dp}_3\ldots \text{dp}_{255}\right]=\mathbf{dP}.$$

(25)

Optimal Prototype Functions in the Verifier, the Modeling Stage

Following the flow of Figure 8, the next stage is the features modeling. In this architecture, the prototype functions of each feature are optimally calculated with the sets of available signatures, both genuine signatures by a genuine signer as

Figure 13. Geometric features that represent the specific signature shape or design

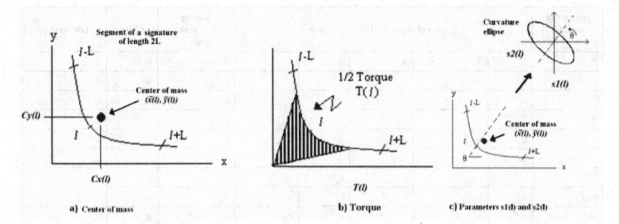

well as general and synthetic skilled forgeries, as described in section *multi-objective optimization for automatic verification of signatures*. For each feature, training sets for the classes ω_0 and ω_1 are generated, and their optimal prototypes functions are determined by the procedures outlined earlier.

Grading Unit and the Discriminant Capability of the Features

The *grading unit* of Figure 8, determines the extent at which an optimized feature is discriminating to a particular user. A feature is usable for verification if

$$\min(D_{ie}) \leq \bar{x}_{error} + 2\sigma_{error}, \tag{26}$$

because probabilistically, it is expected that more than 95% of genuine signatories error measurements will fall into that range; we define its *absolute discriminant power* as:

$$pda_f = (min\{D_{ie}\} - max\{D_{ia}\})/max\{D_{ie}\}, \tag{27}$$

which is the strip ratio or separation band (gap) between intra and inter-class distances with respect to the greatest dissimilarity found in all examples

of class ω_1. The weighting factor w_f of the feature is given by

$$w_f = pda_f \Big/ \sum_i pda_{f_i}, \tag{28}$$

thus it forms a weight vector W by signatory; for features related to the statics and dynamics, separately, it has

$$W_s = [\, w_{Cx} w_{Cy} w_T w_{s1} w_{s2}] \tag{29}$$

and

$$W_d = [\, w_v w_{tow} w_{bow} w_p w_{dp/dt}]. \tag{30}$$

The weighting factor is a common element that applies globally, this means, is a factor that applies to all instances of the same feature derived from a signatures set. In general, it applies the following criteria for rating a feature:

$$C = \begin{cases} 1, & \text{if } 0 \leq \varepsilon \leq \bar{x}_{error} \\ 1 - \dfrac{0.15}{a + 0.3b - \bar{x}_{error}}(\varepsilon - \bar{x}_{error}), & \text{if } \bar{x}_{error} \leq \mu \leq \bar{x}_{error} + 0.3b, \\ 0.85 - \dfrac{0.85}{c - a - 0.3b}(\varepsilon - \bar{x}_{error}), & \text{if } \bar{x}_{error} + 0.3b \leq \mu \leq c \end{cases} \tag{31}$$

Table 4. Rhythm Errors, ratings (grade) and class ownership of all features, per signature

Signature number	Errors of rhythm of the signature					Rating (numeric grade)	Class	Ownership
	2	3	4	5	6	7	8	9
1	ε_v^1	ε_{TOW}^1	ε_{BOW}^1	ε_p^1	$\varepsilon_{dp/dt}^1$	C_d^1	ω_0	1
2	ε_v^2	ε_{TOW}^2	ε_{BOW}^2	ε_p^2	$\varepsilon_{dp/dt}^2$	C_d^2	ω_0	1
3	ε_v^3	ε_{TOW}^3	ε_{BOW}^3	ε_p^3	$\varepsilon_{dp/dt}^3$	C_d^3	ω_0	1
4	ε_v^4	ε_{TOW}^4	ε_{BOW}^4	ε_p^4	$\varepsilon_{dp/dt}^4$	C_d^4	ω_0	1
...	...	...	...	...	...	...	...	...
N-2	ε_v^{N-2}	ε_{TOW}^{N-2}	ε_{BOW}^{N-2}	ε_p^{N-2}	$\varepsilon_{dp/dt}^{N-2}$	C_d^{N-2}	ω_1	0
N-1	ε_v^{N-1}	ε_{TOW}^{N-1}	ε_{BOW}^{N-1}	ε_p^{N-1}	$\varepsilon_{dp/dt}^{N-1}$	C_d^{N-1}	ω_1	0
N	ε_v^N	ε_{TOW}^N	ε_{BOW}^N	ε_p^N	$\varepsilon_{dp/dt}^N$	C_d^N	ω_1	0

where $a=máx(D_{ia})$, $b=|mín(D_{ie})-máx(D_{ia})|$, $c=mín(D_{ie})$. A vector comprised of the ratings of all static features and one of all the dynamics can be expressed as:

$$C_s = [\, C_{Cx} C_{Cy} C_T C_{s1} C_{s2}] \tag{32}$$

and

$$C_d = [\, C_v C_{tow} C_{bow} C_p C_{dp/dt}], \tag{33}$$

and a grade of the *statics* or design (or form) (c_s) and the dynamics or rhythms (c_d) of a signature is calculated using

$$c_s = C_s * W_s^T \tag{34}$$

and

$$c_d = C_d * W_d^T. \tag{35}$$

Thus, any signature can be described. If the rating tends to 1, then the signature tends to be genuine, if the score goes to zero, the firm tends to be a forgery. For training sets of classes ω_0 and ω_1 Table 3 shows some values of interest. Table 4 contains the corresponding information for the primary feature of rhythm.

CLASSIFICATION BASED ON NND-FR SYSTEMS

Neural Networks and Fuzzy Logic

Before describing the neural-network driven fuzzy reasoning systems (NND-FR), a brief commentary on neural networks and fuzzy logic is pertinent here. Since *Neural Networks* (McCulloch & Pitts, 1943), seminal paper (Tsoukalas, & Uhrig, 1997; Kasabov, 1998; Kumiko, Daigo, Satoshi, & Takashi, 2010; Jang, Sun, & Mizutani, 1997; Nuñez, 2010; Sporns, 2011), and *Fuzzy Logic* (Zadeh, 1965) (seminal paper) (McNeill & Freiberger, 1994; Tsoukalas & Uhrig, 1997; Yen & Langari, 1999; Kasabov, 1998; Glover & Kochenberger 2003; Jang, Sun, & Mizutani, 1997; Ross, 2010; Lilly, 2010; Du & Swamy, 2010) are widely explained in several books and articles on literature, this work focuses on providing a comprehensive explanation of the building blocks of the architecture of our digital forensic verification approach. It is up to the interested reader to make a review of those concepts to gain a better understanding of our model.

The classifier architecture is of the multi-classifier type and was shown in Figure 14; it has the advantage that each primary element is

Table 3. Design Errors, ratings (grade) and class ownership of all the features, per signature

Signature number	Errors of design of the signature					Rating (numeric grade)	Class	Ownership
	2	3	4	5	6	7	8	9
1	ε_{Cx}^{1}	ε_{Cy}^{1}	ε_{T}^{1}	ε_{s1}^{1}	ε_{s2}^{1}	C_{s}^{1}	ω_0	1
2	ε_{Cx}^{2}	ε_{Cy}^{2}	ε_{T}^{2}	ε_{s1}^{2}	ε_{s2}^{2}	C_{s}^{2}	ω_0	1
3	ε_{Cx}^{3}	ε_{Cy}^{3}	ε_{T}^{3}	ε_{s1}^{3}	ε_{s2}^{3}	C_{s}^{3}	ω_0	1
4	ε_{Cx}^{4}	ε_{Cy}^{4}	ε_{T}^{4}	ε_{s1}^{4}	ε_{s2}^{4}	C_{s}^{4}	ω_0	1
...	...	...	...	...	...	...	...	...
N-2	ε_{Cx}^{N-2}	ε_{Cy}^{N-2}	ε_{T}^{N-2}	ε_{s1}^{N-2}	ε_{s2}^{N-2}	C_{s}^{N-2}	ω_1	0
N-1	ε_{Cx}^{N-1}	ε_{Cy}^{N-1}	ε_{T}^{N-1}	ε_{s1}^{N-1}	ε_{s2}^{N-1}	C_{s}^{N-1}	ω_1	0
N	ε_{Cx}^{N}	ε_{Cy}^{N}	ε_{T}^{N}	ε_{s1}^{N}	ε_{s2}^{N}	C_{s}^{N}	ω_1	0

evaluated by an expert system and the balance is generated by a third one, using a total of 3 co-operative classifiers; two of them appear in the training section of the training phase of Figure 8, and are described below in that context.

Description NND-FR System

NND-FR comes from "neural-network-driven fuzzy reasoning" (Tsoukalas & Uhrig, 1997) which can be translated as "fuzzy reasoning based on neural networks", and belongs to a family of techniques in which fuzzy reasoning is based on neural networks. The method used here is the one proposed by Takagi and Hayashi, and is described by Tsoukalas and Urigh (1997), here the fuzzy systems is

if $(x_1, x_2, ..., x_n)$ is A^s then $y^s = NN_s(x_1, x_2, ..., x_n)$, (35b)

which is a Sugeno type, in which each rule has the form

If x_1 is A_1 AND x_2 is A_2 AND ... then $y = f(x_1, x_2, ..., x_n)$, (36)

but the function $f(x_1, x_2, ..., x_n)$ is replaced by an artificial neural network, producing the expression 36 where $(x_1, x_2, ..., x_n)$ is the input vector and $y^s = NN_s(x_1, x_2, ..., x_n)$ is a neural network that determines the output y^s of the s-*th* rule and A^s is the antecedent membership function of the s-*th* rule. The procedure of this method is explained in Tsoukalas and Urigh (1997). The block diagram of the T-H technique is shown in Figure 15a, in Figure 15b is shown the adaptation of the T-H method to the signature verifier presented here. Two NND-FR systems are used, one for the rhythm and another one for the form. For the NND-FR system of shape of the signature, the neural network NN_{mem} is trained using as input set all the rows of Table 3 in columns 2 to 6, and as output the corresponding lines in column 9. Thus the degree of membership of the patterns to the classes ω_0 (genuine) and ω_1 (forgery) is calculated according to the following equation:

$$w_i^s = \begin{cases} 1, & \text{si } x_i \in R^s \\ 0, & \text{si } x_i \notin R^s \end{cases} \quad i = 1, ..., r, \quad (36b)$$

the neural network NN_1 will be trained using as input set all the rows of columns 2 to 6, and as output set the corresponding rows of the column

Figure 14. Multi-classifier based on two NND-FR systems and one fuzzy

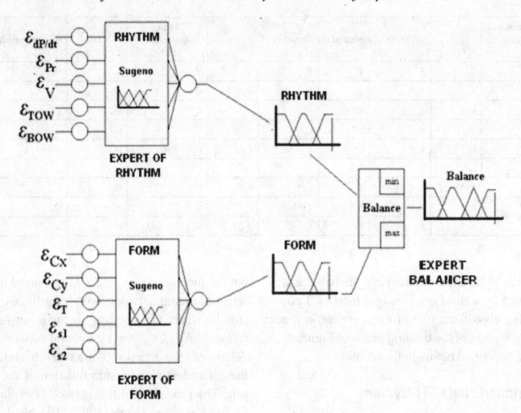

7, so that the consequents are calculated from eq. 36. In the same way input/output patterns are conformed for the neural networks NN_{mem} and NN_1 of the rhythm NND-FR system, referred in Table 4.

Fuzzy Balancer

The last element in the multi-classifier is the fuzzy system balancer. The number of entries are two, one for Cs and Cd, each entry has 5 membership functions related to the grading value, called {*very-bad, bad, low, average, high*}, with the universe of discourse between 0 and 1. The output is called DOC (*Degree of Certainty*) and it is the certainty degree in which a signature should be considered genuine. The membership functions of this linguistic variable are {*false-2, false-1, regular, genuinely low, genuine*}. The block diagram, the

membership functions and set rules are shown in Figure 16, which is self-descriptive and only would be good to mention that the membership functions of inputs "Cs" (rating of form) and "Cd" (rating of the dynamics) are equal, so it is not favored an element over the other. The membership functions are shown in the same part of the figure, denoted "Cs (or Cd)" on the x-axis.

Verification Phase

The verification of a questioned signature takes place after the signature model has been constructed. For verification follow the next steps:

1. Acquisition of the questioned signature.
2. To calculate the discriminating features of the shape.

Figure 15. a) Block diagram of the T-H method. b) T-H method adapted to ASV

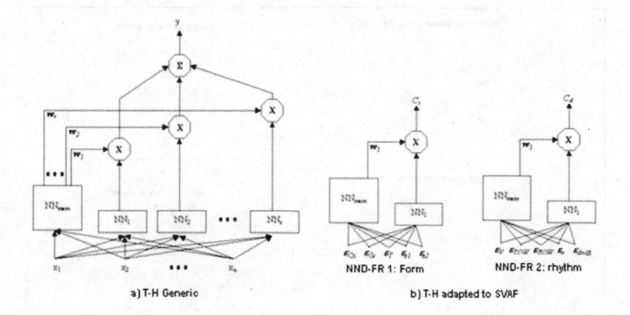

a) T-H Generic

b) T-H adapted to SVRF

3. To calculate the discriminating features of the dynamics.
4. To calculate the dissimilarity of each feature with respect to the respective model.
5. To feed the classifier with the "errors" computed in step 4.
6. To classify the questioned signature according to the DOC established in Table 5.

EXPERIMENTAL EVALUATION AND RESULTS

Methodology

In this section are presented the experiments carried out to demonstrate the accuracy of this approach to on-line signature verification, as well as the results obtained. The goal here is to demonstrate that the verifier is highly successful in the presence of skilled forgeries; to do so, intentional forgeries with training were included in this experiment: the database consisted of genuine signatures, casual forgeries and skilled forgeries.

The database was partitioned into training and testing sets (Table 7), in order to avoid biasing the experimental outcome. The procedures described in this chapter were shown in the architecture of Figure 8.

a) Enrollment phase: the stages of normalization, features extraction, features modeling with multi-objective optimization, grading unit calibration and training, were carried over the training set, thus finally obtaining the optimal prototypes and the NND-FR for rhythms and shape.

b) Verification phase: each signature in the testing set was subject to normalization and feature extraction. Then, to find a numeric indicator of the similarity between the extracted features and the actual optimal prototypes, the respective Mahalanobis distance was calculated, arriving to the error in design (or shape) and the error in dynamics (rhythms), equivalent to the errors in Tables 3 and 4. Once the errors were calculated, the NND-FR systems computed separately the similarity of rhythms and shape. Finally, the fuzzy system in Figure 16 was used to provide

Figure 16. Definition of output fuzzy system: block diagram, membership functions and set of rules

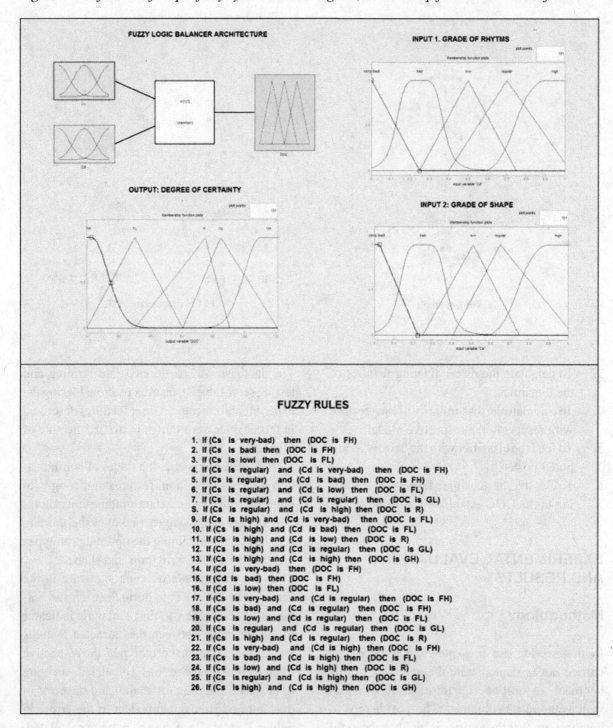

the degree of certainty in which each signature should be considered to be a genuine one.

In the following sections some aspects of the intermediate results are presented.

Database of Signatures Acquisition

The signatures were drawn in a period of a month by a group of 38 volunteers; each one donated 27 genuine signatures. In addition, each signatory was asked to make forgeries from other signatories, allowing them an increasing knowledge of how to get the target signature, including thus skilled forgeries to be used to test our forensic verifier. Table 6 shows the characteristics of the database obtained. As usual, the acquisition stage was not free of capturing errors; the signatures with errors induced during the acquisition process are made known in the last four columns, and were discarded in the experimentation.

Training and Testing Sets

As explained earlier in this section, the 1762 signatures obtained from the acquisition process were divided into two groups: the training set and the testing set. For each set, there are representative signatures of the classes ω_0 and ω_1. Table 7 summarizes the training and testing sets; in this table, the subsets *a, b* and *c* in the training set, and subsets *d, e* and *f* in the testing set, can be identified. The idea behind this particular partitioning is:

Training set: this set is intended to provide the verifier with, at most, 16 exemplars of genuine signatures (subset *a*), so it can learn the habits of signing of each person; subset *b* is intended to let the verifier to know some examples of general signing habits to be rejected; finally, the knowledge about skilled forgeries is embedded in the dataset by including 10 synthetic skilled forgeries, derived from the genuine signatures by digitally filtering the features of 10 genuine signatures.

Testing set: The objective of this set is to determine the false rejection rate (FRR) and false

acceptance rate (FAR); to calculate the FRR, that is, the percentage of misclassified genuine signatures, the subset *d* is comprised of the remaining genuine signatures. The false acceptance rate is tested in two ways: against random forgeries, included in subset *e*, and against real intentional and skilled forgeries included in subset *f*.

Forgeries Quality: Examples of the Signatures

Some exemplars of the signatures are shown in Figure 17, where it can be seen three types of forgery, each one made with a greater degree of training. Note the visual similarity of the skilled forgeries. Figure 18 shows some pre-processed, scaled and rotated signatures.

Normalization: Scaling and Rotation

Figure 18 shows some examples of the normalization process. Before going into the feature extraction process, the signatures were subject to scaling and rotation, in order to produce functions of time normalized with respect to space $(x(t), y(t))$.

Getting Prototype Functions and its Optimal Representation

Figure 19 shows the features of design (or shape) and dynamics extracted from one normalized signature of AAMR. It can be seen here that each feature is represented by more than single point, so the representation of the signature is of the functional type. Each signature was transformed to a set of 10 vectors, and each vector corresponds to one single feature.

The results of the multi-objective optimization of the features of shape of AAMR can be seen in Figure 20, sub-figures 1 to 5. The plot labeled $f_{genCx(l)}$ is the function obtained directly by the genetic algorithm; the plot labeled $f_{\omega 0}$ is the final optimal function, which is capable of rejecting skilled forgeries. There exist a very subtle varia-

Table 6. Identifiers and amount of signatures by type

Num.	Signatory	Total amount of signatures per signatory				Errors in files (x(t), y(t))			
		Genuine	Forgery Type I	Forgery Type II	Forgery Type III	Genuine	Forgery Type I	Forgery Type II	Forgery Type III
1	JMTM	27	11	11	11	0	0	0	0
2	CAVM	25	11	0	11	2	0	0	0
3	JGHV	27	11	11	11	2	0	0	0
4	JARL	27	11	11	11	0	0	0	0
5	MEDG	27	11	11	11	1	0	0	0
6	LOAR	27	11	11	11	0	0	0	0
7	JODG	27	11	11	11	0	0	1	0
8	MAZE	27	11	11	11	3	0	0	0
9	PPMP	11	0	0	0	1	0	0	0
10	DARD	27	11	11	16	0	0	0	0
11	MABM	27	11	11	0	0	1	0	0
12	ERPC	27	11	11	0	1	0	0	0
13	JJCL	27	0	0	0	0	0	0	0
14	ROMS	27	11	11	11	0	1	0	0
15	SEDE	27	11	11	11	1	0	0	0
16	LURM	27	11	11	11	0	0	0	0
17	JBSJ	11	11	11	0	0	0	0	0
18	RAME	27	11	11	11	0	0	1	0
19	JAFP	27	11	11	0	0	1	0	0
20	RMCG	11	11	11	11	0	0	0	0
21	LEAT	27	11	11	0	0	0	0	0
22	MAAM	16	11	11	11	11	0	0	0
23	CMCG	27	11	11	11	0	0	0	0
24	ALFR	27	11	11	0	0	2	0	0
25	EACG	11	11	11	11	1	0	0	0
26	CADO	27	11	11	11	1	0	0	0
27	AAHG	27	11	0	11	11	0	0	0
28	AAMR	27	0	0	11	0	0	0	0
29	NVPM	27	11	11	11	11	0	0	0
30	HUMM	27	0	0	11	3	0	0	0
31	JIOR	27	11	0	11	0	1	0	0
32	ALDV	27	11	11	11	0	0	0	0
33	RURL	27	11	11	11	0	0	0	0
34	VUMS	27	11	11	11	0	0	0	0
35	ALRO	27	0	0	11	5	0	0	0
36	SASB	6	0	0	0	0	0	0	0
37	CLDA	11	0	0	0	0	0	0	0
38	ARCH	10	0	0	0	0	0	0	0

Continued on following page

Table 6. Continued

Num.	Signatory	Total amount of signatures per signatory				Errors in files (x(t), y(t))			
		Genuine	Forgery Type I	Forgery Type II	Forgery Type III	Genuine	Forgery Type I	Forgery Type II	Forgery Type III
	Sum	895	330	297	302	54	6	2	0
	TOTAL	1824							
	Errors	62							
	Final	1762							

Figure 17. Signature exemplars. The level of forgery I, II and III, refers to forgery increasingly executed with a greater training

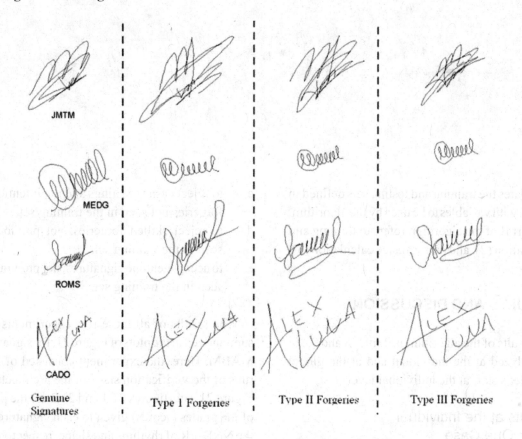

| Genuine Signatures | Type 1 Forgeries | Type II Forgeries | Type III Forgeries |

tion from $f_{genCx(l)}$ to $f_{\omega 0}$, but enough to achieve high performance, as will be seen later.

Finally in Figure 20, sub-figure 6, some other optimal features from RMCG, LOAR, VUMS, MAZE are shown.

Algorithm to Evaluate the Architecture

To evaluate the architecture shown in Figure 8 it was used the extensive algorithm of Tables 8 and 9, in which all the stages of the operation of the architecture can be clearly seen. The first

Figure 18. Normalization of some signatures, scaling and rotation

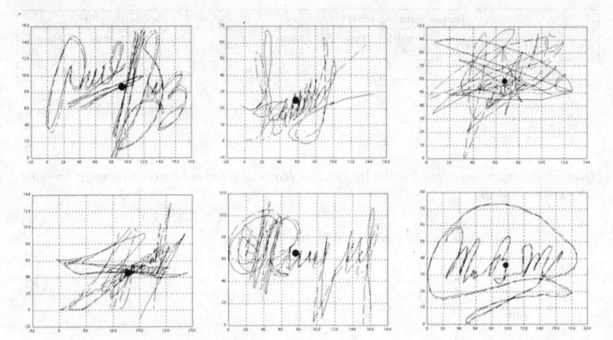

part relates the training and testing sets defined in Table 7 with variables to be used by the algorithm. The part II of the algorithm refers to training and verification (2), and performance calculation (3).

RESULTS AND DISCUSSION

The results of the algorithm in Tables 8 and 9 can be analyzed at the individual and at the global level; let's start at the individual level.

Results at the Individual Level: One Case

For each person enrolled in the system, we define the following five experiments:

a. to accept the genuine signatures seen in the training set,
b. to reject casual writings and not intentional forgeries seen in the training set,

c. to reject casual writings and not intentional forgeries not seen in the training set,
d. to reject skilled forgeries, not previously seen in the training set,
e. to accept genuine signatures, not previously seen in the training set.

The results of all these five experiments are summarized in the plots of Figure 21, for signatory MABM. Here, the experiment consisted of 380 runs of the verification stage of the architecture. Figure 21, sub-figures 21.1 and 21.2 are the plots of the grades (scores) given to each signature by the NND-FR of rhythms and shape, respectively; each value of the x-axis represent one signature, and the y-axis is the respective score. The experiments are related to the x-axis coordinate value in each plot in the following way:

a. test on kwon genuine signatures: from position 1 to 16,

Figure 19. Extraction of the discriminating function features from AAMR signatures

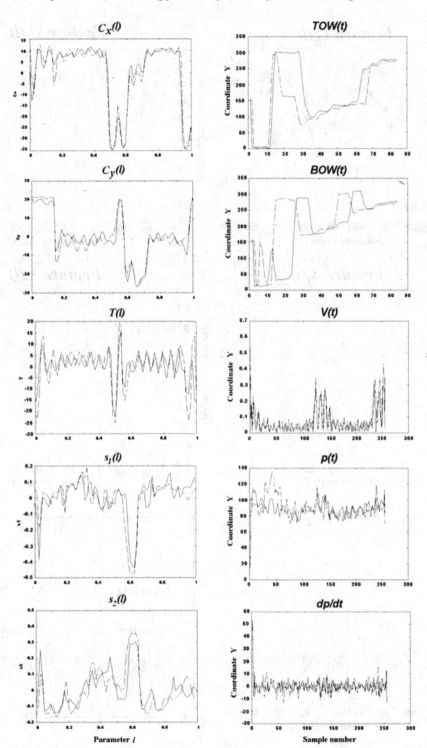

Figure 20. In blue, the prototype function obtained by the GA and, in black, the minimizing function of FRR

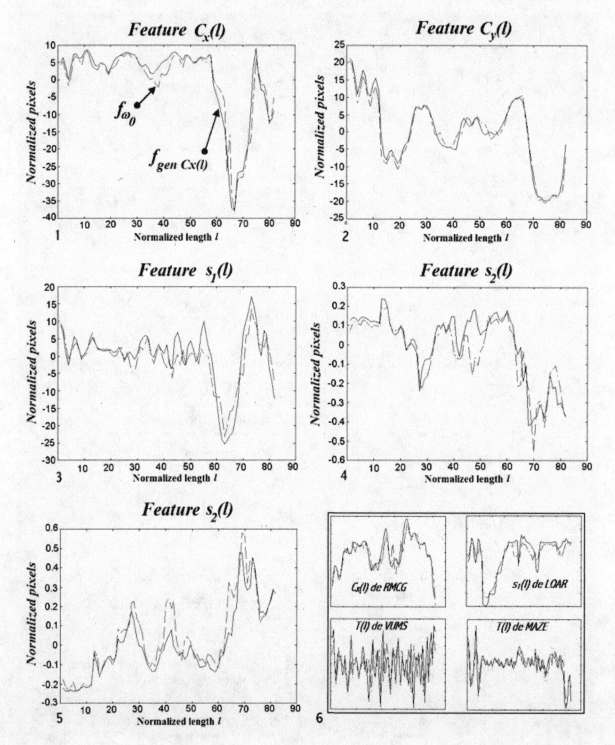

Table 8. Algorithm to evaluate the architecture. Part I

EVALUATION OF THE PERFORMANCE OF THE ARCHITECTURE		
1.- Definition and initialization of variables		
Num.	Name	Meaning
1	$Seen_{\omega 0}$	Genuine signatures "seen" by the ASVS in the training set.
2	$Not\_seen_{\omega 0}$	Genuine signatures not seen by the ASVS in the training set.
3	$Seen_{\omega 1}$	Forgeries seen by the ASVS in the training set
4	$Not\_seen_{\omega 1}$	Forgeries not seen by the ASVS in the training set
5	$FAR_{seen\omega 1}$	Rate of false acceptances on signatures seen in the training set
6	$FAR_{not\_seen\,\omega 1}$	Rate of false acceptances on signatures not seen in the training set
7	$FRR_{seen\omega 0}$	Rate of false rejections on signatures seen in the training set
8	$FRR_{not\_seen\,\omega 0}$	Rate of false rejections on signatures not seen in the training set
9	$E_{seen\,\omega 1}$	Accountant of errors of classification of false signatures seen in the training set, considered by the system like genuine.
10	$E_{not\_seen\,\omega 1}$	Accountant of errors of classification of false signatures not seen in the training set, considered by the system like genuine.
11	$E_{seen\,\omega 0}$	Accountant of errors of classification of genuine signatures seen in the training set, considered by the system like false.
12	$E_{not\_seen\omega 0}$	Accountant of errors of classification of genuine signatures not seen in the training set, considered by the system like false.

Table 9. Algorithm to evaluate the architecture. Part II

	2.- For each signatory of the database, do	
TRAINING	(Training phase)	
	a) To obtain the group of training of the class ω_0, first part of the Table 7.	
	b) To obtain the group of training of the class ω_1, first part of the Table 7.	
	c) To form optimal prototype functions,	
	d) To train the ASVS with discriminating functions of rhythms and shape.	
VERIFICATION	(Verification phase)	
	a) To enlarge the set of specimens of the class ω_0 to generate testing set of the class "genuine"	
	b) To enlarge the set of specimens of the class ω_1 to generate the testing class of the class "forgery"	
	c) To extract the functions of rhythms and shape of the signatures of the classes ω_0 y ω_1	
	d) To calculate the rhythms errors and the shape errors, with regard to the optimized prototype functions of each one of the signatures of the testing set of the class ω_0. To classify the signatures. For each signature seen in the training set and not correctly classified, to make $E_{seen\,\omega 0} = E_{seen\,\omega 0} + 1$; For each signature not seen in the training set and not correctly classified, to make $E_{not\_seen\,\omega 0} = E_{not\_seen\omega 0} + 1$.	
	e) To calculate the rhythms errors and the shape errors, with regard to the optimized prototype functions of each one of the signatures of the testing set of the class ω_1. To classify the signatures. For each signature seen in the training set and not correctly classified, to make $E_{seen\,\omega 1} = E_{seen\,\omega 1} + 1$; For each signature not seen in the training set and not correctly classified, to make $E_{not\_seen\,\omega 1} = E_{not\_seen\,\omega 1} + 1$.	
	3.- To calculate FAR and FRR of the system with *seen* and *not seen* exemplars in the training set	
FAR	$FAR_{seen\omega 1} = E_{seen\omega 1}$ / cardinality(ω_1)	
	$FAR_{not\_seen\omega 1} = E_{not\_seen\omega 1}$ / cardinality(ω_1)	
FRR	$FRR_{seen\,\omega 0} = E_{seen\,\omega 0}$ / cardinality(ω_0)	
	$FRR_{not\_seen\,\omega 0} = E_{not\_seen\,\omega 0}$ / cardinality(ω_0)	

Figure 21. Results of verification for 380 experiments with the signatory MABM

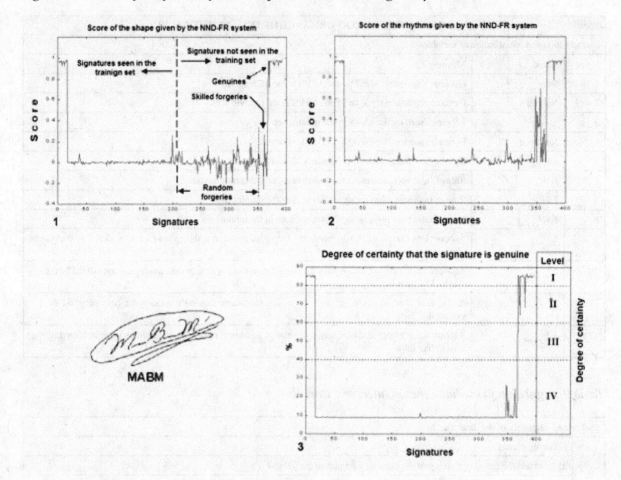

b.   test on known casual writings and non intentional forgeries: from position 17 to 216,

c.   test on new casual writings and non intentional forgeries: from position 217 to 346,

d.   test on new skilled forgeries (type I and II): from position 347 to 368,

e.   test on new genuine signatures: from position 369 to 380.

Sub-figures 21.1 and 21.2 show the grades (or scores) of the rhythms and shape or design, where it can be noted that skilled forgeries (in this case, type I and II) obtain high scores, though not as high as the genuine signatures. This is a confirmation that the dynamic features are really the most difficult ones to forge. Sub-figure 21.3 shows the

outcome of the fuzzy balancer or the final classifier, which indicates that even the skilled forgeries have a degree of certainty of IV that the signature is genuine, which, in an human forensic expert terms it would obtain "*it is demonstrable that the signature is a forgery*," according to Table 5.

Results at the Global Level

When dealing with experiments with all the signatories in the database, the results shown in Figure 21 were mostly repeated, with just a few errors, leading to a very high performance. At the global level, the experiment consisted of 508 genuine signatures from 38 signatories were used for verifier training, as well as 7400 random

Table 5. Certainty level of the genuineness of a questioned Signature

LEVEL	Range of Cs=Cd	Range of GDC (%)	Remarks
I	> 0.95	> 90	The signature is genuine beyond any reasonable doubt
II	0.7 – 0.95	72.90 – 90	It's highly probable that the signature is genuine
III	0.43 – 0.7	38.42 – 72.89	It's very probable that the signature is a very skilled falsification
IV	< 0.43	< 38.42	It's demonstrable that the signature is a falsification

forgeries and 380 synthetic forgeries; to test the verifier 380 genuine signatures were used, 16064 random forgeries and 923 skilled forgeries.

The total amount of false acceptances was 5 and the false rejections were only 1, so it builds evidence in the sense that the system has very high performance. In general:

FAR random forgeries= 0%
FAR skilled forgeries=5/(923)*100=0.54%
FRR =1/380*100=0.26%
On average, the error is: 0.26% at 17,367 verifications

It is important to remark that given the stochastic nature of the genetic algorithms and neural networks, the solution presented here is by no means unique. Better as well as worse results could be obtained in successive runs of the algorithm.

CONCLUSION AND FUTURE WORK

The concept presented of a forensic architecture for signature verification with features obtained using multi-objective optimization, has allowed us to assess the effectiveness of the genetic algorithms as optimization tools; moreover, it was demonstrated here that the combination of genetic algorithms serially with other optimization techniques can still improve the optimization results. It is important to remark that the technique presented to built the optimal prototype functions goes beyond the traditional methods of pattern recognition that deal with feature selection and optimal feature generation, thus challenging traditional feature representations; in the field of signature verification, the whole architecture is also innovative, since there is no antecedent in this field of such a holistic approach to this problem.

It is worth to mention that the features upper and lower envelope in combination with the instant of occurrence of the respective strokes is also novel, since the temporal information is specifically combined with shape information, creating a feature difficult to forge. It was also relevant the introduction of synthetic skilled forgeries, not present in the state of the art of this topic; the relevance is noticeable when the verifier rejects drastically the general handwritings, including non intentional forgeries which, in practice, represents high percentage of forgery attempts (Kiran, 2011). The use of a forensic architecture was also significant because allowed the verifier to separately judge the features of rhythms and shape and to combine them in a final decision; in most of the approaches of the state of the art, all the features are mixed together a given the same weighting.

The discriminant power of the features was enhanced in comparison with other methods for modeling the features.

The use of the NND-FR systems showed a double benefit: to automate the process of learning to achieve a human perspective of this solution and, to help us in avoiding the use of hand-crafted fuzzy systems, two per each signer, which is impractical.

In the future work we are aiming at the use of a number of other intelligent techniques for the decision stage; the NND-FR was successfully used to forecast the chemical demand of oxygen in the Osaka Bay, in Japan. As it could be seen here, this artificial intelligence technique was a good option, with excellent results; however, other fuzzy paradigms with learning can be used here, such as adaptive network fuzzy inference systems (ANFIS) (Jang, Sun, & Mizutani, 1997). Also, it is a matter of the future work to assess the performance of other features in our architecture, since the computational time could be –hopefully– considerably reduced in the training stage, which actually takes about 2 hours for the whole database.

In the horizon of the future work the following actions are visible:

1. To modify the cost function of the genetic algorithm and of the continuous search gradient, perhaps adding one or more objectives to the multi-objective search,
2. To find a way to reduce the time consumed in each stage of the architecture,
3. To customize the fuzzy balancer to each signatory,
4. To modify the architecture in order give to the fuzzy balancer knowledge about the relevance of each feature to a particular signatory,
5. To spread the optimal representation of feature to the realm of off-line signature verification.

It could be important to export this multi-objective technique of feature representation to other problems in pattern recognition, such as the analysis of hearth or epileptic signals, for instance, since this technique improves the accuracy of a system given that the variable and feature selection have already been carried out.

REFERENCES

Allgrove, C. C., & Fairhurst, M. C. (1998). Optimisation issues in dynamic and static signature verification. In *Proceedings of the Third European Workshop on Handwriting Analysis and Recognition* (pp. 1-6).

Allgrove, C. C., & Fairhurst, M. C. (2001). Majority voting for improved signature verification. In *Proceedings of the IEEE Colloquium on Visual Biometrics*, London, UK.

Azlinah, M., Rohayu, Y., Sofianita, M., & Shulina, A. R. (2009). Online slant signature algorithm analysis. *WEAS Transactions on Computers*, 8(5), 864–873.

Bai-Ling, Z., Min-Yue, F., & Hong, Y. (1998). Handwritten signature verification based on neural 'gas' based vector quantization. In *Proceedings of the Fourteenth International Conference on Pattern Recognition* (pp. 1862-1864).

Baron, R., & Plamondon, R. (1989). Acceleration measurement with an instrumented pen for signature verification and handwriting analysis. *IEEE Transactions on Instrumentation and Measurement*, 38(6), 1132–1138. doi:10.1109/19.46414

Berrin, Y., & Alisher, K. (2010). Online signature verification using fourier descriptors. *EURASIP Journal on Advances in Signal Processing*, 1–13.

Beveridge, G. S. G., & Schechter, R. S. (1970). *Optimization: Theory and practice* (Prime ed.). Auckland, New Zealand: McGraw-Hill.

Die Lecce, V., Dimauro, G., Guerreiro, A., Impedovo, S., Pirlo, G., Salzo, A., & Sarcinella, L. (1999). Selection of reference signatures for automatic signature verification. In *Proceedings of the Fifth International Conference on Document Analysis and Recognition* (pp. 597-600).

Dolfing, J. G. A. (1998). *Handwriting recognition and verification. A hidden Markov approach* (Unpublished doctoral dissertation). Eindhoven University of Technology, Centrum, The Netherlands.

Du, K.-L., & Swamy, M. N. S. (2010). *Neural networks in a softcomputing framework* (1st ed.). New York, NY: Springer.

Fasquel, J.-B., Stolz, C., & Bruynooghe, M. (2001). Real-time verification of handwritten signatures using a hybrid opto-electronical method. In *Proceedings of the 2nd International Symposium on Image and Signal Processing and Analysis*, Pula, Croatia (pp. 552-557).

Fauziyah, S. M., & Zahariah, M. H. (2009). Signature verification system using support vector machine. *Journal of Basic and Applied Sciences, 1*(2), 291–294.

Glover, F., & Kochenberger, G. (2003). *Handbook of metaheuristics*. Boston, MA: Kluwer Academic.

Goldberg, D. E. (1989). *Genetic algorithms in search, optimization and machine learning* (1st ed.). Reading, MA: Addison-Wesley.

Gries, F. D. (2000). *On-line signature verification* (Unpublished master's thesis). Michigan State University, Ann Arbor, MI.

Guru, D. S., & Prakash, H. N. (2009). Online signature verification and recognition: an approach based on symbolic representation. *IEEE Transactions on Pattern Analysis and Machine Intelligence, 31*(6), 1059–1073. doi:10.1109/TPAMI.2008.302

Hangai, S., Yamanaka, S., & Hamamoto, T. (2000). On-line signature verification based on altitude and direction of pen movement. In *Proceedings of the IEEE International Conference on Multimedia and Expo* (pp. 489-492).

Hesketh, G. B. (1997). COUNTERMATCH: a neural network approach to automatic signature verification. In *Proceedings of the IEEE Colloquium on Neural Networks for Industrial Applications*, London, UK (pp. 1-2).

Ho, K. K., Schroder, H., & Leedharn, G. (2001). Codebooks for signature verification and handwriting recognition. In *Proceedings of the Seventh International Conference on Intelligent Information Systems*.

Jang, J. S., Sun, C. T., & Mizutani, E. (1997). *Neuro-Fuzzy and soft computing: A computational approach to learning and machine intelligence*. Upper Saddle River, NJ: Prentice Hall.

Ji, H. M., Lee, S. G., Cho, S. Y., & Kim, Y.-S. (2009). A hybrid on-line signature verification system supporting multi-confidential levels defined by data mining techniques. *International Journal of Intelligent Systems Technologies and Applications, 9*(3-4), 262–273.

Kasabov, N. K. (1998). *Foundations of neural networks, fuzzy systems, and knowledge engineering*. Cambridge, MA: MIT Press.

Kiran, K. G. (2011). *Online signature verification techniques* (Unpublished master's thesis). National Institute of Technology Rourkela, Orissa, India.

Komiya, Y., & Matsumoto, T. (1999). On-line pen input signature verification PPI (pen-Position/pen-Pressure/pen-Inclination). In *Proceedings of the IEEE International Conference on Systems, Man and Cybernetics*.

Kröse, B., & Van der Smagt, P. (1996). *An introduction to neural networks* (8th ed.). Amsterdam, The Netherlands: University of Amsterdam. Retrieved from http://www.fwi.uva.nl/research/neuro/

Kumiko, Y., Daigo, M., Satoshi, S., & Takashi, M. (2010). Visual-based online signature verification using features extracted from video. *Journal of Network and Computer Applications, 33*(3), 333–341. doi:10.1016/j.jnca.2009.12.010

Lejtman, D. Z., & George, S. E. (2001). On-line handwritten signature verification using wavelets and back-propagation neural networks. In *Proceedings of the Sixth International Conference on Document Analysis and Recognition*, Seattle, WA.

Lilly, J. H. (2010). *Fuzzy control and identification* (1st ed.). New York, NY: John Wiley & Sons. doi:10.1002/9780470874240

Martens, R., & Claesen, L. (1996). On-line signature verification by dynamic time-warping. In *Proceedings of the 13th International Conference on Pattern Recognition* (pp. 38-42).

Martens, R., & Claesen, L. (1997). Dynamic programming optimisation for on-line signature verification. In *Proceedings of the Fourth International Conference on Document Analysis and Recognition* (pp. 653-656).

Martínez, R. J. C. (2004). *Verificación de Firmas Manuscritas en Línea con Modelado Óptimo de Características y Aproximación Digital Forense* (Unpublished doctoral dissertation). Facultad de Ingeniería, Universidad Nacional Autónoma de México, Ciudad de México, México.

Martínez, R. J. C., & Alcántara, S. R. (2004). Optimal prototype functions of features for on-line signature verification. *International Journal of Pattern Recognition and Artificial Intelligence, 18*(7), 1189–1206. doi:10.1142/S021800140400371X

McCulloch, W., & Pitts, W. (1943). A logical calculus of the ideas immanent in neurons activity. *The Bulletin of Mathematical Biophysics, 5*, 115–133. doi:10.1007/BF02478259

McNeill, D., & Freiberger, P. (1994). *Fuzzy Logic: The revolutionary computer technology that is changing our world*. New York, NY: Simon and Schuster.

Mingming, M., & Wijesoma, W. S. (2000). Automatic on-line signature verification based on Multiple Models. In *Proceedings of the IEEE/IAFE/INFORMS Conference on Computational Intelligence for Financial Engineering* (pp. 30-33).

Muhammad, T. I., Matthew, K. M., Aurangzeb, K., Khurram, S. A., & Ling, G. (2009). On-line signature verification: Directional analysis of a signature using weighted relative angle partitions for exploitation of inter-feature dependencies. In *Proceedings of the 10th International Conference on Document Analysis and Recognition*, Barcelona, Spain (pp. 41-45).

Munich, M. E., & Perona, P. (1999). Continuous dynamic time warping for translational-invariant curve alignment with applications to signature verification. In *Proceedings of the Seventh IEEE International Conference on Computer Vision* (pp. 108-115).

Murshed, N. A., Bortolozi, F., & Sabourin, R. (1995). Off-line signature verification using fuzzy ARTMAP neural network. In *Proceedings of the Third International Conference on Document Analysis and Recognition* (pp. 2179-2184).

Nalwa, V. S. (1997). Automatic on-line signature verification. *Proceedings of the IEEE*, 213-239.

Nuñez, P. L. (2010). *Brain, mind, and the structure of reality*. Oxford, UK: Oxford University Press. doi:10.1093/acprof:oso/9780195340716.001.0001

Ohishi, T., Komiya, Y., Morita, H., & Matsumoto, T. (2001). Pen-input on-line signature verification with position, pressure, inclination trajectories. In *Proceedings of the 15th International Symposium on Parallel and Distributed Processing*, San Francisco, CA (pp. 1757-1763).

Peerapong, U., & Monthippa, U. (2010). Online signature verification using angular transformation for e-commerce services. *International Journal of Information and Communication Engineering, 6*(1), 33–38.

Pender, D. A. (1991). *Neural networks and handwritten signature verification* (Unpublished doctoral dissertation). Stanford University, Stanford, CA.

Plamondon, R., & Baron, R. (1989). Acceleration measurement with an instrumented pen for signature verification and handwriting analysis. *IEEE Transactions on Instrumentation and Measurement, 38*(6), 1132–1138. doi:10.1109/19.46414

Plamondon, R., & Lorette, G. (1989). On-line signature verification: how many countries are in the race? In *Proceedings of the International Carnahan Conference on Security Technology* (pp. 183-191).

Plamondon, R., & Parizeau, M. (1990). A comparative analysis of regional correlation, dynamic time warping, and skeletal tree matching for signature verification. *IEEE Transactions on Pattern Analysis and Machine Intelligence, 12*(7), 710–717. doi:10.1109/34.56215

Plamondon, R., & Shihari, S. N. (2000). Online and off-line handwritting recognition: a comprehensive survey. *IEEE Transactions on Pattern Analysis and Machine Intelligence, 22*(1), 63–84. doi:10.1109/34.824821

Roger, J. S. (1997). *Neuro-fuzzy and soft computing*. Upper Saddle River, NJ: Prentice Hall.

Ross, T. J. (2010). *Fuzzy logic with engineering applications* (3rd ed.). New York, NY: John Wiley & Sons. doi:10.1002/9781119994374

Sakamoto, D., Morita, H., Ohishi, T., Komiya, Y., & Matsumoto, T. (2001). On-line signature verification algorithm incorporating pen position, pen pressure and pen inclination trajectories. In *Proceedings of the IEEE International Conference on Acoustics, Speech, and Signal Processing*, Salt Lake City, UT (pp. 993-996).

Slyter, S. A. (1995). *Forensic signature examination* (1 ed., pp. 1-117). Springfield, IL: Charles C. Thomas.

Sporns, O. (2011). *Networks of the brain*. Cambridge, MA: MIT.

Theodoridis, S., & Koutroumbas, K. (1999). *Pattern recognition* (1st ed.). San Diego, CA: Academic Press.

Tsoukalas, L. H., & Uhrig, R. E. (1997). *Fuzzy and neural approaches in engineering* (1st ed.). New York, NY: John Wiley & Sons.

Vahid, K., Reza, P., & Hamid, R. P. (2009). Offline signature verification using local radon transform and support vector machines. *International Journal of Image Processing, 3*(6), 184–194.

Wan-Suck, L., Mohankrishman, N., & Paulik, M. J. (1998). Improved segmentation through dynamic time warping for signature verification using a neural network classifier. In *Proceedings of the IEEE International Conference on Image Processing* (pp. 929-933).

Wijesoma, W. S., Mingming, M., & Sung, E. (2000). Selecting optimal personalized features for on-line signature verification using GA. In *Proceedings of the IEEE International Conference on Systems, Man and Cybernetics* (pp. 2740-2745).

Wirtz, B. (1997). Average prototypes for stroke-based signature verification. In *Proceedings of the Fourth International Conference on Document Analysis and Recognition* (pp. 268-272).

Yen, J., & Langari, R. (1999). *Fuzzy logic, intelligence, control and information*. Upper Saddle River, NJ: Prentice Hall.

Zadeh, L. A. (1965). Fuzzy sets. *Information and Control*, 8.

ADDITIONAL READING

Castillo, O., & Melin, P. (2010). *Type-2 fuzzy logic: Theory and applications (Studies in fuzziness and soft computing)*. New York, NY: Springer.

Marsland, S. (2009). *Machine learning: An algorithmic perspective*. Boca Raton, FL: Chapman & Hall/CRC.

Revett, K. (2008). *Signature verification, in behavioral biometrics: A remote access approach*. Chichester, UK: John Wiley & Sons.

Theodoridis, S., & Koutroumbas, K. (2008). *Pattern recognition* (4th ed.). Amsterdam, The Netherlands: Elsevier.

Theodoridis, S., Pikrakis, A., & Koutroumbas, K. (2010). *Introduction to pattern recognition: A matlab approach*. Amsterdam, The Netherlands: Elsevier.

KEY TERMS AND DEFINITIONS

Forensic Architecture: A block diagram that represents the computational steps for the solution of a problem with a scientific human approach.

Genetic Algorithms: Algorithms inspired in the theory of evolution of the species aiming at finding the best solution to optimization problems. Some bio-inspired concepts used in genetic algorithms are population, mating, offspring, mutation, and selection of the fittest.

Multi-Objective Optimization: A process in which two or more conflicting optimization objectives with constraints must be simultaneously satisfied.

Optimal Prototypes: In pattern recognition: a prototype is class representative of the discriminant features in a classification problem; in this chapter, an optimal prototype is the prototype that best represents a feature in terms of its capability to discriminate forged signatures.

Signature Verification: Science of the determination of whether a signature presented to a verification process is genuine or is not. It uses a multi-evidential approach to reach a verdict about the questioned signature.

Chapter 7
Looking for Reverse Transformations between NP–Complete Problems

Rodolfo A. Pazos R.
Instituto Tecnológico de Cd. Madero, Mexico

Ernesto Ong C.
Instituto Tecnológico de Cd. Madero, Mexico

Héctor Fraire H.
Instituto Tecnológico de Cd. Madero, Mexico

Laura Cruz R.
Instituto Tecnológico de Cd. Madero, Mexico

José A. Martínez F.
Instituto Tecnológico de Cd. Madero, Mexico

ABSTRACT

The theory of NP-completeness provides a method for telling whether a decision/optimization problem is "easy" (i.e., it belongs to the P class) or "difficult" (i.e., it belongs to the NP-complete class). Many problems related to logistics have been proven to belong to the NP-complete class such as Bin Packing, job scheduling, timetabling, etc. The theory predicts that for any pair of NP-complete problems A and B there must exist a polynomial time transformation from A to B and also a reverse transformation (from B to A). However, for many pairs of NP-complete problems no reverse transformation has been reported in the literature; thus the following question arises: do reverse transformations exist for any pair of NP-complete problems? This chapter presents results on an ongoing investigation for clarifying this issue.

DOI: 10.4018/978-1-4666-0297-7.ch007

1. INTRODUCTION

Nowadays, logistics is an important issue within modern-day organizations so much so that departments are devoted exclusively to it. The logistic process involves packaging and another tasks to manage the flow of goods and services required to satisfy the requirements of customers. The Bin Packing problem (BPP) is a classical problem related with the space minimization of bins or boxes. BPP is widely used to develop applications in logistics, mainly in production and distribution tasks.

Some applications are naturally packing problems. Others are not, but are modeled artificially as such. Examples of the first class are: loading of bottle products into vehicles (Gonzalez-Barbosa et al., 2010), allocating a stack in a block for storage yards of container terminals (Murty, 2007). Among the applications of the second class are the following: selecting the providers of logistics services and the type and quantities required (Crainic et al., 2010), automobile sheet metal forming processes (Sathe et al., 2009), positioning of a set of circuit modules on a VLSI chip or on an FPGA for executing real-time software (Natale & Bini, 2007).

The theory of NP-completeness is a branch of the theory of computation that aims at determining how complex an algorithm has to be depending on the decision/ optimization problem to be solved by the algorithm; in simple words, the theory of NP-completeness provides a method for telling whether a problem is "easy" (i.e., it belongs to the P class) or "difficult" (i.e., it belongs to the NP-complete class).

Many problems related to logistics have been proven to belong to the NP-complete class such as the Bin Packing problem, the Knapsack problem, job scheduling, time-tabling, etc. Examples of problems that belong to the P class are Minimum Spanning Tree, Shortest Path, Minimum Cut, Sequencing with Deadlines, etc. (Karp, 1972). The procedure for classifying problems into the P or NP-complete classes is rather complex and it is briefly described in Section "Background."

The classification of a problem as NP-complete (difficult) or P (easy) has a practical implication: for NP-complete problems no algorithm has been found (and there is little hope to find one) that can solve them in polynomial time. This means (in simple terms) that the time needed to obtain an exact solution for large instances of a problem (which arise in many practical applications) can take an extremely long time, way too much more than users are willing to wait for a solution. For large instances of NP-complete problems, it is advisable to use heuristic algorithms, which can produce fairly good solutions in a reasonable time.

The most widespread use of transformations between decision problems has been for proving that some given problem Π_1 is NP-complete (i.e., difficult) based on the known NP-completeness property of some other problem Π_2. However, transformations are also useful for: adapting an algorithm that solves problem Π_1 so it can be used for solving a similar problem Π_2, and extrapolating some knowledge on problem Π_1 to a similar problem Π_2.

More specifically, the practical usefulness of transformations between optimization problems, resides in the fact that if there exists an efficient solution algorithm for one of the problems, the instances of another problem can be solved using a transformation from this problem to the first one.

In Mahajan et al. (2005) the authors remark that "The emergence of efficient SAT solvers which can handle large structured SAT instances has enabled the use of SAT solvers in diverse domains such as verification, planning, routing, etc." For example, many problems related to logistics, such as planning (Kautz & Selman, 1999; Xing et al., 2006), packing (Grandcolas & Pinto, 2010) and job scheduling (Ohrimenko et al., 2009) problems are transformed to the SATISFIABILITY problem for taking advantage of SAT solvers. In the domain of timetabling problems, a transformation to the graph coloring problem is often carried out followed by a transformation to SAT (Erben, 2001).

Like other problems, the Bin Packing problem and its variants have been approached with general purpose solvers based on the classical SAT and constraint satisfaction (CSP) problems (Piñol, 2009). In this way the efficiencies of these solvers can be exploited and the development of specialized methods can be avoided.

Two common encoding schemes exist: BPP is encoded and solved as a SAT or CSP problem (Cruz-Reyes et al., 2008), BPP is encoded as CSP and then the resulting CSP is encoded and solved as a SAT problem (Soh, 2010). In the opposite direction, an incipient automatic reformulation of a problem into sub-problems, like BPP, is based on the discovery of patterns within the structure of a domain encoding. This way, multiple specialized sub-solvers can be used for probably outperforming a generic solver (Long, 2002).

The theory of NP-completeness predicts that for any pair of NP-complete problems Π_1 and Π_2, there must exist a polynomial transformation from Π_1 to Π_2 and also a reverse transformation (from Π_2 to Π_1). This property has an important practical implication: at least in theory, one can adapt an efficient algorithm that solves an NP-complete problem for solving any other NP-complete problem.

Unfortunately, our survey of the literature on NP-completeness has revealed that, for many transformations between NP-complete problems, there exists a transformation in one direction, but no reverse transformation has been reported. This situation considerably reduces the possibility of adapting an algorithm for solving many different problems as the theory suggests. Therefore, the importance of trying to find reverse transformations, is the purpose of this investigation.

The purpose of this chapter is 1) to explore the possible causes for explaining why there do not exist reverse transformations for most pairs of NP-complete problems, and 2) to suggest some future work for explaining this question.

To this end, in Section "Background" the most important notions from the theory of NP-completeness are presented; then in Section "Anomaly in the Transformation between the Partition and the Bin Packing Problems", the difficulty for devising a reverse transformation from Bin Packing to Partition is described; next in Section "Checking the NP-completeness of the Partition Problem", the possibility that Partition might not be NP-complete (as a possible hypothesis for explaining the anomaly) is studied; afterwards, in Section "Three-hop Reverse Transformation from Partition to SAT", an attempt is made to devise a three-hop reverse transformation from Partition to SAT in order to find out if it can be done as the theory predicts; and finally, derived from the results of this attempt, in Section "Future Research Directions", a possible explanation for the presumed anomaly is presented, which leads to some questions that deserve further study.

2. BACKGROUND

The purpose of this section is to present the most important definitions and fundamental concepts in the theory of NP-completeness that are the most relevant for understanding the rest of this chapter for those readers who are not expert in the theory of NP-completeness. The material does not intend to be neither comprehensive nor detailed, since it is very extensive and complex; however, readers interested in NP-completeness can find more details in Garey and Johnson (1979) and Dasgupta, Papadimitriou, and Vazirani (2006).

2.1. Decision and Optimization Problems

The theory of NP-completeness is designed for being applied only to decision problems, which are defined as problems that have two possible solutions: yes and no. Then the set of instances of a decision problem gets divided into a subset Y of *yes-instances*, which are defined as those instances for which the answer is yes, and a subset of *no-instances*, which are defined as those instances for which the answer is no.

An example of a decision problem is the following: consider a graph $G = (V, A)$, where V and A represent respectively a set of vertices and a set of edges (pair of vertices) of the graph; then, a decision problem consists of determining if there exists a Hamiltonian circuit in G. As it is evident, this problem has only two possible answers: yes and no.

The limitation of considering only decision problems arises from the use of Turing machines in the theory of NP-completeness. Turing machines only generate two possible answers to a chain of symbols which encode a decision problem: accepted (corresponding to a yes answer) and not accepted (corresponding to a no answer).

Though the theory of NP-completeness applies only to decision problems, it is important to point out that its results can be extended to optimization problems (which are problems of more interest in real-life applications), since any optimization problem has an associated decision problem, which can be derived from the optimization problem. Informally speaking, this association is such that if we find out that a decision problem is "easy" then the associated optimization problem is also "easy," and conversely, if we determine that a decision problem is "difficult" then the associated optimization problem is also "difficult."

For example, an optimization problem such as the traveling salesman problem has an associated decision problem, which can be expressed as follows: consider a graph G with distances d (where $C = \{c_1, c_2, ..., c_m\}$ represents a set of cities, $d(c_i, c_j) \in Z^+$ for each pair of cities $c_i, c_j \in C$) and a bound $B \in Z^+$; then, the associated decision problem consists of determining if there exists a Hamiltonian circuit in G, whose length is less than or equal to B.

2.2. Encoding of a Decision Problem

For being able to solve a decision problem using a Turing machine, it is necessary to encode it first. Therefore, it is convenient to introduce the concept of problem encoding.

Let Σ denote a set of symbols and Σ^* be the set of all the strings constituted by sequences of symbols in Σ, thus the encoding of a problem Π into a language under the encoding scheme e is defined as follows (Garey & Johnson, 1979):

$$L[\Pi, e] = \left[\begin{array}{c} \Sigma \text{ is the alphabet used by } e, \text{ and} \\ x \in \Sigma^* : \ x \text{ is the encoding under } e \text{ of an} \\ \text{instance } / \in Y_\Pi \end{array} \right]$$

2.3. The Class P of Decision Problems

A deterministic Turing machine (DTM) consists of the following elements (Figure 1):

1. A bidirectional infinite tape, where the symbols of an encoded instance of a decision problem are written.
2. A read-write head that: reads symbols from the tape for transferring them to the finite state control, writes symbols on the tape by command of the finite state control, and can move to the right or the left.
3. A finite state control, which is implemented as a deterministic finite automaton.

A program for a DTM is defined by the following information (Garey & Johnson, 1979):

1. A finite set Σ of input symbols and a set $\Gamma = \Sigma \cup \{b\}$, where b denotes the blank symbol.
2. A finite set Q of states that includes an initial state q_0 and three halt states q_Y, q_N, q_I

Figure 1. Schematic representation of a DTM (adapted from Garey & Johnson, 1979)

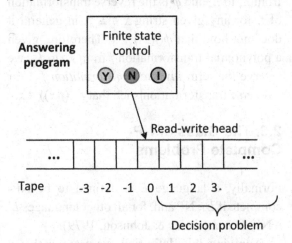

Figure 2. Schematic representation of a NDTM (adapted from Garey & Johnson, 1979)

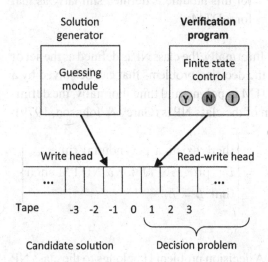

(which correspond to the states where the DTM halts when the input string encodes a yes-instance, a no-instance or an invalid instance of a decision problem).

3. A transition function δ: $(Q - [q_Y, q_N, q_I]) \times \Gamma \rightarrow$: $Q \times \Gamma \times [-1, +1]$.

The transition function receives a state from set Q different from the halt states and an input symbol (read by the head from the tape) and generates a triple that consists of a state (the new state of the DTM), a symbol which is written on the tape, and a movement of the head (where -1 and $+1$ indicate a movement to the left and right symbols on the tape).

Informally, the class P is defined as the set of all the decision problems that can be solved by a DTM in polynomial time. Formally, the definition of the class P is (Garey & Johnson, 1979):

$$P = \left\{ L: \begin{array}{l} \text{there exists a polynomial time} \\ \text{program } M \text{ for a DTM such that} \\ L = L_M \end{array} \right\}$$

A decision problem Π belongs to the class P under an encoding scheme e if $L[\Pi, e] \in$ P; i.e.,

if there exists a polynomial time DTM program that solves Π under encoding scheme e.

2.4. The Class NP of Decision Problems

The model of a nondeterministic Turing machine (NDTM) is very similar to that of a DTM, except for the incorporation of a "guessing" module that has its own write head (Figure 2). A NDTM consists of the following elements:

1. A bidirectional infinite tape, similar to that for a DTM.
2. A write head that writes symbols on the tape by command of the guessing module, and can move to the right or the left.
3. A guessing module, which is implemented as a non-deterministic finite automaton. This module randomly generates a candidate solution for the decision problem and commands the write head to write on the tape the symbols of the candidate solution.
4. A read-write head, similar to that for a DTM.
5. A finite state control, which verifies whether or not the candidate solution is in fact a solu-

tion for the decision problem. The program for this module is defined similarly as that for a DTM.

Informally, the class NP is defined as the set of all the decision problems that can be solved by a NDTM in polynomial time. Formally, the definition of the class NP is (Garey & Johnson, 1979):

$$NP = \left\{ L : \begin{array}{l} \text{there exists a polynomial time} \\ \text{program } M \text{ for a NDTM such} \\ \text{that } L = L_M \end{array} \right\}$$

A decision problem Π belongs to the class NP under an encoding scheme e if $L[\Pi, e] \in$ NP; i.e., if there exists a polynomial time NDTM program that solves Π under encoding scheme e.

2.5. Transformation of Languages

A polynomial transformation from a language $L_1 \subseteq \Sigma_1^*$ to a language $L_2 \subseteq \Sigma_2^*$ is a function $f: \Sigma_1^* \to \Sigma_2^*$ that satisfies the following two conditions (Garey & Johnson, 1979):

A. There is a polynomial time DTM program that computes f.
B. For all $x \in \Sigma_1^*$, $x \in L_1$ if and only if $f(x) \in L_2$.

(Notes: The polynomial transformation from L_1 to L_2 is usually denoted by $L_1 \propto L_2$. Transformations are usually called *reductions*.)

For the purposes of this work, let us consider a polynomial transformation f from L_1 to L_2, then the *reverse transformation* of f is defined as a function $\phi: \Sigma_2^* \to \Sigma_1^*$ that satisfies the following two conditions:

• There is a polynomial time DTM program that computes ϕ.
• For all $y \in \Sigma_2^*$, $y \in L_2$ if and only if $\phi(y) \in L_1$.

Notice that if f is a polynomial transformation from L_1 to L_2 and ϕ is the reverse transformation of f, for any given string $x \in \Sigma_1^*$, in general it does not hold that $\phi(f(x)) = x$. Therefore, given a polynomial transformation f from L_1 to L_2, we reserve the term *inverse transformation* f^{-1} for a reverse transformation such that $f^{-1}(f(x)) = x$.

2.6. The Class of NP-Complete Problems

Formally, a language L is defined to be NP-complete if $L \in$ NP and, for all other languages $L' \in$ NP, $L' \propto L$ (Garey & Johnson, 1979).

Applying this definition for proving that a problem Π_1 is NP-complete is rather cumbersome. The practical approach for proving that Π_1 is NP-complete consists of carrying out the following steps:

1. Show that $\Pi_1 \in$ NP.
2. Select a known NP-complete problem Π_2 (preferably similar to Π_1).
3. Design a polynomial transformation f from Π_2 to Π_1.

3. ANOMALY IN THE TRANSFORMATION BETWEEN THE PARTITION AND THE BIN PACKING PROBLEMS

The class of NP-complete problems has a usually overlooked property: the bi-directionality of the transformation between pairs of NP-complete problems. This property states that for any two NP-complete problems A and B, it must be possible to transform A to B in polynomial time and vice versa.

However, for most pairs of NP-complete problems only the transformation in one direction has been reported in research works but not the transformation in the inverse direction, which hints at a possible anomaly in the bi-directionality of the transformation between NP-complete problems. In particular, this anomaly was detected in the Partition and Bin Packing problems. In order to study this issue, it is necessary to introduce first the formal definitions of these two problems.

Partition problem: Consider a finite set A of items and a size $s(a) \in Z^+$ for each element $a \in A$ (where Z^+ denotes the positive integers), then the Partition problem consists of determining if there exists a subset $A' \subset A$ such that $\sum_{a \in A'} s(a) = \sum_{a \in A-A'} s(a)$.

Bin Packing problem: Consider a finite set U of items, a size $s(u) \in Z^+$ for each $u \in U$, a positive integer bin capacity B, and a positive integer K, then the Bin Packing problem consists of determining if there exists a partition of U into disjoint subsets $U_1, U_2, ..., U_K$ such that the sum of the sizes of the items in each U_i is less than or equal to B.

The first hint of an anomaly in the transformation between two NP-complete problems appeared in a PhD project (Ruiz, 2008). In that project we aimed at finding indicators for characterizing Partition problem instances in order to predict the performance of several algorithms when solving some given instance and choosing the best algorithm for solving the instance.

Since some indicators for a similar problem (Bin Packing) had been previously obtained, a transformation algorithm from Bin Packing to Partition was devised in order to transform the Bin Packing indicators to Partition indicators. When transforming Bin Packing instances to Partition instances for testing the effectiveness of the Partition indicators, it was observed that some yes-instances of Bin Packing were transformed to no-instances of Partition, which indicated that the transformation algorithm had some flaw. Unfortunately, we could not find an easy fix for the transformation algorithm, and thus, the following question arose: is it possible to devise a flawless transformation algorithm from Bin Packing to Partition as the theory of NP-completeness predicts?

In order to formally study this anomaly, it is necessary to understand all the details of trans-

formations between NP-complete problems, in particular all the conditions that transformations must satisfy for being correct.

3.1. Explicit Conditions

The explicit conditions A and B of transformations were presented in the definition of polynomial transformation (Subsection "Transformation of Languages"). Since condition B is somewhat cryptic, it is convenient to expand it as follows:

B. For all $x \in \Sigma_1{}^*$,
1. if $f(x) \in L_2$ then $x \in L_1$ (or equivalently **if $x \notin L_1$ then $f(x) \notin L_2$**) and
2. **if $x \in L_1$ then $f(x) \in L_2$** (or equivalently if $f(x) \notin L_2$ then $x \notin L_1$).

Consequently, for the purposes of this study, the following equivalent expression of condition B will be used:

B. For all $x \in \Sigma_1{}^*$,
1. if $x \in L_1$ then $f(x) \in L_2$ and
2. if $x \notin L_1$ then $f(x) \notin L_2$.

And occasionally, the following alternate expression will be used:

B. For all $x \in \Sigma_1{}^*$,
1'. if $f(x) \in L_2$ then $x \in L_1$ and
2'. if $f(x) \notin L_2$ then $x \notin L_1$.

3.2. Implicit Conditions

In the polynomial transformation between two NP-complete problems Π_1 and Π_2 the following implicit conditions must be satisfied, besides of those explicitly indicated in the definition of polynomial transformation:

C1. *All the instances* of problem Π_1 should be able to be transformed to instances of problem Π_2. (More specifically, all the yes-instances of problem Π_1 must be transformed to yes-instances of problem Π_2, and all the no-instances and invalid instances of Π_1 must be transformed to no-instances and invalid instances of Π_2.)

C2. Each instance of problem Π_1 must be transformed to an *equivalent instance* of problem Π_2.

C3. The transformation should be able to be carried out in *both ways*, i.e., from Π_1 to Π_2 and from Π_2 to Π_1.

3.2.1. Transformation of All the Instances

The implicit condition C1 is directly derived from the definition of polynomial transformation (Subsection "Transformation of Languages").

Considering that L_1 and L_2 are respectively the encodings of two decision problems Π_1 and Π_2, then condition B establishes that there must be a transformation for *all and each one of the strings* of language L_1, i.e., all the instances of problem Π_1. For verifying this assertion, suppose that a transformation $L_1 \propto L_2$ would be defined such that for some string $x' \in L_1$ its image $f(x')$ would not exist, then in this case condition B would not be satisfied, and therefore, such transformation would not be valid.

Comment: This fact is acknowledged by Garey and Johnson (1979) in the following commentary: "The principal technique for demonstrating that two problems are related is that of 'reducing' one to the other, by giving a constructive transformation that maps any instance of the first problem into an equivalent instance of the second" (p. 13). In the last sentence, the words "any instance" mean all the instances.

It is convenient to notice that the definition of problem encoding (Subsection "Encoding of a Decision Problem") implies the division of the set Σ^* of all the strings into two subsets: the subset of yes-strings and the subset of no-strings, such that the subset of yes-strings corresponds to the set of yes-instances of Π, while the subset of no-strings is divided in turn into two subsets: one that corresponds to the no-instances of Π, and the other corresponds to the set of invalid instances of Π.

Finally, from the previous paragraph and the explicit conditions B1 and B2 (Subsection "Explicit Conditions"), it is concluded that the definition of transformation when applied to two problems Π_1 and Π_2, implies that all the yes-instances of problem Π_1 must be transformed to yes-instances of problem Π_2, and all the no-instances and invalid instances of problem Π_1 must be transformed to no-instances and invalid instances of problem Π_2.

3.2.2. Transformation to Equivalent Instances

The rationale behind the implicit condition C2 is not derived from the definitions of the fundamental notions of NP-completeness, but from one of the purposes sought by the transformation among NP-complete problems, which is expressed as follows (Garey & Johnson, 1979):

The principal technique for demonstrating that two problems are related is that of "reducing" one to the other, by giving a constructive transformation that maps any instance of the first problem into an equivalent instance of the second. Such a transformation provides the means for converting any algorithm that solves the second problem into a corresponding algorithm for solving the first problem (p. 13).

The direct approach for converting an algorithm A_2 that solves the second problem to another algorithm A_1 for solving the first problem consists in implementing A_1 with two phases: the first phase converts an instance p_1 of the first problem to an instance p_2 of the second problem, and the second phase uses algorithm A_2 for determining if p_2 is a yes-instance; finally, if the conversion from p_1 to p_2 is a polynomial transformation, then due to the explicit condition B, it can be determined whether p_1 is a yes-instance.

3.2.3. Transformation in Both Ways

The demonstration of the implicit condition C3 is derived from the following definition of NP-completeness (Garey & Johnson, 1979):

Formally, a language L is defined to be NP-complete if $L \in$ NP and, for all other languages $L' \in$ NP, $L' \propto L$.

For the demonstration, consider two NP-complete problems Π_1 and Π_2, whose encodings are L_1 and L_2 respectively; then setting first $L=L_1$ and $L'=L_2$, the definition states that $L_2 \propto L_1$ must be true; next, setting $L=L_2$ and $L'=L_1$, the definition states that $L_1 \propto L_2$ must hold. Therefore, these two results imply that the problems must be transformed in both ways.

This fact is informally acknowledged by Garey and Johnson (1979) when commenting: "The class of NP-complete languages (problems) will form another such equivalence class" (p. 37), in which equivalence is previously defined in the following way: "We can define two languages L_1 and L_2 (two decision problems Π_1 and Π_2) to be polynomially equivalent whenever both $L_1 \propto L_2$ and $L_2 \propto L_1$ (both $\Pi_1 \propto \Pi_2$ and $\Pi_2 \propto \Pi_1$)" (p. 37).

3.3. Anomaly in the Transformation between Partition and Bin Packing

The presumed anomaly consists in the following: it is possible to find a polynomial transformation from Partition to Bin Packing but it is not possible from Bin Packing to Partition, which contradicts the implicit condition C3 (Subsection "Implicit Conditions").

For explaining this anomaly, we will first study the easy transformation: the polynomial transformation from Partition to Bin Packing; next several attempts to find a reverse transformation will be made, which show the difficulties encountered for devising a reverse transformation.

3.3.1. Transformation Algorithm from Partition to Bin Packing

Considering that a transformation algorithm is a sequence of instructions for implementing the function f mentioned in the definition of polynomial transformation, then the algorithm for transforming from Partition to Bin Packing can be defined in the following way (similar to that in Ruiz, 2008):

Algorithm Trans Par-BP

0. Input: an instance (yes, no or invalid) p of the Partition problem.

1. For each element a_i from Partition define an item u_i for Bin Packing such that $s(u_i) = s(a_i)$. (Notes: Thus all the items for Bin Packing are defined, including their sizes in terms of the Partition parameters. The complexity of this step is $O(|A|)$ and, consequently, polynomial.)

2. Set $S = \Sigma_{a \in A} s(a)$ and set $B = S/2$. (Notes: In this way the capacity of the bins for Bin Packing is defined. (Note: the complexity of this step is $O(|A|)$ and, consequently, polynomial.)

3. Set $K = 2$. (Notes: In this way the number of bins for Bin Packing is defined. The complexity of this step is $O(1)$ and, therefore, polynomial.)

3.3.2. Verification of the Correctness of the Trans Par-BP Algorithm

Most of the literature on transformations from one NP-complete problem to another usually omit a detailed proof of the correctness of the proposed transformations (such as Karp, 1972), which might hide possible mistakes, especially those that involve the violation of an implicit condition (Subsection "Implicit Conditions"). For avoiding a possible mistake of this kind, this subsection presents a process that includes the verification of each of the conditions (explicit and implicit) that a transformation must satisfy.

For verifying the validity of the Trans Par-BP algorithm, first the explicit conditions A and B of the definition of polynomial transformation (presented in Subsection "Explicit Conditions") will be considered.

First, since each of the steps of the Trans Par-BP algorithm has polynomial complexity, then the entire algorithm satisfies the explicit condition A.

Second, for the explicit condition B it has to be taken into consideration that L_1 represents the set of strings that encode the yes-instances of Partition, while L_2 is the set of strings that encode the yes-instances of Bin Packing.

First consider any yes-instance p of Partition, then the sum of all its elements sizes ($S = \Sigma_{a \in A} s(a)$) must be even and, consequently, upon applying step 2 of the Trans Par-BP algorithm an integer bin capacity B can be obtained for the Bin Packing instance q that is the image of p. Additionally, since p is a yes-instance, with the elements of instance p it must be possible to form two groups such that the sum of the sizes of the elements in each group is $S/2$ (=B). Finally, this implies that for instance q it must be possible to form two subsets such that each subset contains the items corresponding to a different group of instance p and such that the sum of the item sizes for each subset is B, which in turn implies that q is a yes-instance of Bin Packing, and therefore, the explicit condition B1 is verified.

Now for verifying the explicit condition B2, proof by contradiction will be used; therefore, assume that $x \notin L_1$ implies $f(x) \in L_2$. In this case, since $x \notin L_1$, it implies that x is a no-string of Σ_1^*, which leads to two cases: x is the encoding of an invalid instance of Partition or x is the encoding of a no-instance of Partition. In the following paragraphs the two cases will be dealt with.

- First case: Assume q were a yes-instance of Bin Packing and that it were the image of an invalid instance p of Partition. The

Partition problem does not have many options for the generation of invalid instances. Thus, p being invalid would imply that there would exist at least one element a_i with size $s(a_i) \notin Z^+$; therefore, upon applying step 1 of the Trans Par-BP algorithm to p, an image q of p would be generated, which would have an item u_i with size $s(u_i) = s(a_i) \notin Z^+$. This would imply that q were invalid, which contradicts the initial assumption.

- Second case: Assume that q were a yes-instance of Bin Packing and that it were the image of a no-instance p of Partition. Notice that there exist two subsets of no-instances of Partition: those for which $S = \Sigma_{a \in A} s(a)$ is odd and those for which S is even, which yields two sub-cases:

- Suppose now that S were odd; this would imply that, the application of the Trans Par-BP algorithm to p would cause the bin size being a fractional number in the image q of p, which would imply that q were invalid, which in turn would lead to a contradiction.

- Assume that S were even; then, since p is a no-instance, it should happen that for any possible partition of the elements of Partition (into A' and $A-A'$) it should hold that $\Sigma_{a \in A'} s(a) > S/2$ or $\Sigma_{a \in A-A'} s(a) > S/2$, which would imply that the application of the Trans Par-BP algorithm to p would cause that in the image q of p for each possible partition of the Bin Packing items (into U_1 and U_2) it would also happen that $\Sigma_{u \in U1} s(u) > B$ or $\Sigma_{u \in U2} s(u) > B$, which would imply that q were a no-instance, which in turn would lead to a contradiction.

After verifying that the transformation from Partition to Bin Packing satisfies the explicit conditions, it is necessary to verify that it also satisfies the implicit conditions, presented in Subsection "Implicit Conditions."

Regarding the implicit condition C1, notice that step 0 of the Trans Par-BP algorithm takes any instance (yes, no or invalid) of Partition as input, and steps 1, 2 and 3 of the algorithm permit transforming any instance of Partition, which proves that the transformation satisfies condition C1.

Concerning the implicit condition C2, assume that one had a Partition instance p and an algorithm A_{BP} that could solve any Bin Packing instance (where solving an instance means answering "yes" or "no" for the instance); then, our task is to devise an algorithm A_{Par} based on algorithm A_{BP} that can solve p. To this end consider an algorithm A_{Par} consisting of two phases: the first phase uses the Trans Par-BP algorithm for transforming p to an instance q of Bin Packing, and the second phase uses algorithm A_{BP} for solving instance q. Since it has been shown that the Trans Par-BP algorithm satisfies the explicit condition B, if the answer of A_{BP} is "yes" for instance q, then condition B1' ($f(x) \in L_2$ then $x \in L_1$, where $f(x)=q$ and $x=p$) implies that p must be a yes-instance; otherwise, p must be a no-instance or an invalid instance (because of condition B2'). Therefore, it has been shown that algorithm A_{Par} solves any instance of Partition.

Regarding the implicit condition C3, we will see that it seems unlikely to be satisfied with any reverse transformation (i.e., from Bin Packing to Partition), which constitutes the presumed anomaly, since it should be satisfied according to the theory of NP-completeness, considering that Partition and Bin Packing are considered to be NP-complete.

For detecting the problems that exist in transforming from Bin Packing to Partition, first the logical alternative will be tried: an algorithm that carries out the inverse process of the Trans Par-BP algorithm. From the analysis of the algorithm it is evident that it is possible to invert step 1, but not steps 2 and 3; therefore, the algorithm could be written as follows.

Algorithm Trans BP-Par1

0. Input: an instance (yes, no or invalid) q of the Bin Packing problem.

1. For each item u_i of Bin Packing define an element a_i of Partition such that $s(a_i) = s(u_i)$. (Notes: Thus all the elements for Partition are defined, including their sizes in terms of the Bin Packing parameters. The complexity of this step is $O(|U|)$ and, consequently, polynomial.)

Because of space limitations, a detailed verification of all the explicit and implicit conditions will not be presented, but only the verification of a condition that is violated will be described, which in this case is the explicit condition B1.

For proving that B1 is not satisfied for all strings (or equivalently all instances), it is sufficient to find one case that violates the condition. Then, consider the following yes-instance q of Bin Packing defined as follows: $K=5$, $B=3$, and a set of items $U = \{u_1, u_2, u_3, u_4, u_5, u_6, u_7, u_8, u_9, u_{10}\}$ with their respective sizes $s(u_1)=2$, $s(u_2)=1$, $s(u_3)=2$, $s(u_4)=1$, $s(u_5)=2$, $s(u_6)=1$, $s(u_7)=2$, $s(u_8)=1$, $s(u_9)=2$, $s(u_{10})=1$. Notice that the partition $U_1=\{u_1,u_2\}$, $U_2=\{u_3,u_4\}$, $U_3=\{u_5,u_6\}$, $U_4=\{u_7,u_8\}$, $U_5=\{u_9,u_{10}\}$ satisfies the requirement for q being a yes-instance. Upon applying the Trans BP-Par1 algorithm to instance q, instance p is obtained, which consists of a set of elements $A = \{a_1, a_2, a_3, a_4, a_5, a_6, a_7, a_8, a_9, a_{10}\}$ with their respective sizes $s(a_1)=2$, $s(a_2)=1$, $s(a_3)=2$, $s(a_4)=1$, $s(a_5)=2$, $s(a_6)=1$, $s(a_7)=2$, $s(a_8)=1$, $s(a_9)=2$, $s(a_{10})=1$. It is evident that it is not possible to divide A into two subsets A' and $A-A'$, such that $\sum_{a \in A'} s(a) = \sum_{a \in A-A'} s(a)$, since $\sum_{a \in A'} s(a)$ is odd, which implies that p is a no-instance, and therefore, condition B1 is violated.

For overcoming the difficulty found in the Trans BP-Par1 algorithm, a small modification could be made for fixing the cases in which the summation $\sum_{u \in U} s(u)$ is odd. Then, the algorithm could be rewritten as follows.

Algorithm Trans BP-Par2

0. Input: an instance (yes, no or invalid) q of the Bin Packing problem.
1. For each item u_i of Bin Packing define an element a_i of Partition such that $s(a_i) = s(u_i)$.
2. If $\Sigma_{u \in U} s(u)$ is odd, append to set A of Partition an extra element α with size $s(\alpha)=1$. (Note: the complexity of this step is $O(|U|)$ and, therefore, polynomial.)

Though this algorithm fixes the difficulty of the Trans BP-Par1 algorithm, unfortunately still violates condition B1, because forcing the sum of the item sizes to be even does not guarantee that a Partition instance is a yes-instance, since an even sum is a necessary condition but it is not sufficient, as exemplified by the following case. Consider a yes-instance q of Bin Packing defined as follows: $K=5$, $B=11$, and a set of items $U = \{u_1, u_2, u_3, u_4, u_5, u_6, u_7, u_8, u_9, u_{10}\}$ with their respective sizes $s(u_1)=10$, $s(u_2)=1$, $s(u_3)=10$, $s(u_4)=1$, $s(u_5)=10$, $s(u_6)=1$, $s(u_7)=10$, $s(u_8)=1$, $s(u_9)=10$, $s(u_{10})=1$. Notice that the partition $U_1=\{u_1, u_2\}$, $U_2=\{u_3, u_4\}$, $U_3=\{u_5, u_6\}$, $U_4=\{u_7, u_8\}$, $U_5=\{u_9, u_{10}\}$ satisfies the requirement for q being a yes-instance. Upon applying the Trans BP-Par2 algorithm to instance q, an instance p is obtained, which consists of a set of elements $A = \{a_1, a_2, a_3, a_4, a_5, a_6, a_7, a_8, a_9, a_{10}, a_{11}\}$ (where $a_{11}=\alpha$) with their respective sizes $s(a_1)=10$, $s(a_2)=1$, $s(a_3)=10$, $s(a_4)=1$, $s(a_5)=10$, $s(a_6)=1$, $s(a_7)=10$, $s(a_8)=1$, $s(a_9)=10$, $s(a_{10})=1$, $s(a_{11})=1$. It is evident that it is impossible to divide A into two subsets A' and $A-A'$, such that $\Sigma_{a \in A'} s(a) = \Sigma_{a \in A-A'} s(a)$, which implies that p is a no-instance, thus violating condition B1.

Algorithm Trans BP-Par3

0. Input: an instance (yes, no or invalid) q of the Bin Packing problem.
1. For each item u_i of Bin Packing define an element a_i of Partition such that $s(a_i) = s(u_i)$.

2. In case it is impossible to find two subsets A' and $A-A'$ such that $\Sigma_{a \in A'} s(a) = \Sigma_{a \in A-A'} s(a)$, append to set A of Partition an extra element α with size $s(\alpha)$ such that $\Sigma_{a \in A'} s(a) = \Sigma_{a \in A-A'} s(a) + s(\alpha)$ for some partition of A into A' and $A-A'$.

Though this algorithm guarantees the satisfaction of the explicit condition B1, unfortunately it now violates condition A. Notice that determining that it is impossible to find two subsets A' and $A-A'$ such that $\Sigma_{a \in A'} s(a) = \Sigma_{a \in A-A'} s(a)$ is equivalent to finding out if the Partition instance is a no-instance, which in general is as complex as determining if a Partition instance is a yes-instance; therefore, since there is no known algorithm that can solve a Partition instance in polynomial time, the complexity of step 2 is not polynomial, and consequently, the explicit condition A is violated.

In view of this problem, another algorithm is proposed that fixes the non polynomial complexity of Trans BP-Par3.

Algorithm Trans BP-Par4

0. Input: an instance (yes, no or invalid) q of the Bin Packing problem.
1. For each item u_i of Bin Packing define an element a_i of Partition such that $s(a_i) = s(u_i)$.
2. Append to set A of Partition an extra element α with size $s(\alpha) = \Sigma_{u \in U} s(u)$. (Note: the complexity of this step is $O(|U|)$ and, therefore, polynomial.)
3. If $B \notin Z^+$ or $K \notin Z^+$ set $s(\alpha) = -1$. (Notes: The complexity of this step is $O(2)$. It is necessary to include this step for making sure that the invalid instances of Bin Packing are transformed to invalid instances of Partition.)

Though this algorithm guarantees the satisfaction of conditions A and B1, it now violates the explicit condition B2. For verifying this condition, proof by contradiction will be attempted; therefore, assume that $x \notin L_1$ implies $f(x) \in L_2$. In this case, since $x \notin L_1$, it implies that x is a no-string of Σ_1^*, which leads to two cases: x is the encoding of an invalid instance of Bin Packing or x is the encoding of a no-instance of Bin Packing. The first case leads to contradiction but second case does not. Because of space limitations, the first case will be omitted and only the second case will be presented.

Second case: Assume that p were a yes-instance of Partition and that it were the image of a no-instance q of Bin Packing. In this case, it will be shown that there does exist a case that satisfies this assumption, which would imply that condition B2 is not satisfied. To this end consider a no-instance q of Bin Packing defined as follows: $K=3$, $B=11$, and $U = \{u_1, u_2, u_3, u_4, u_5, u_6\}$ with their respective sizes $s(u_1)=11$, $s(u_2)=1$, $s(u_3)=10$, $s(u_4)=1$, $s(u_5)=10$, $s(u_6)=1$. Notice that, upon applying the Trans BP-Par4 algorithm to q, the Partition instance p obtained is defined as follows: $A = \{a_1, a_2, a_3, a_4, a_5, a_6, \alpha\}$ with their respective sizes $s(a_1)=11$, $s(a_2)=1$, $s(a_3)=10$, $s(a_4)=1$, $s(a_5)=10$, $s(a_6)=1$, $s(\alpha)=34$, which as can be easily seen is a yes-instance of Partition, which in turn implies that condition B2 is not satisfied.

Second case: Assume that p were a yes-instance of Partition and that it were the image of a no-instance q of Bin Packing. In this case, it will be shown that there does exist a case that satisfies this assumption, which would imply that condition B2 is not satisfied. To this end consider a no-instance q of Bin Packing defined as follows: $K=3$, $B=11$, and $U = \{u_1, u_2, u_3, u_4, u_5, u_6\}$ with their respective sizes $s(u_1)=11$, $s(u_2)=1$, $s(u_3)=10$, $s(u_4)=1$, $s(u_5)=10$, $s(u_6)=1$. Notice that, upon applying the Trans BP-Par4 algorithm to q, the Partition instance p obtained is defined as follows: $A = \{a_1, a_2, a_3, a_4, a_5, a_6, \alpha\}$ with their respective sizes $s(a_1)=11$, $s(a_2)=1$, $s(a_3)=10$, $s(a_4)=1$, $s(a_5)=10$, $s(a_6)=1$, $s(\alpha)=34$, which as can be easily seen is a yes-instance of Partition, which in turn implies that condition B2 is not satisfied.

The violation of condition B2 is originated by the application of step 2 of the Trans BP-Par4, since it always appends an element α whose size is the sum of the item sizes of the Bin Packing instance; i.e., appends α to both yes-instances and no-instances. Unfortunately, it is not easy to fix this problem, since if one tried to apply step 2 only to the yes-instances, then it would be necessary to solve first the Bin Packing instance, for which no known algorithm can solve it in polynomial time.

4. CHECKING THE NP-COMPLETENESS OF THE PARTITION PROBLEM

The first hypothesis for explaining the anomaly found in the transformation from the Partition to the Bin Packing problem was that perhaps the Partition problem might not be NP-complete. This hypothesis arose from the fact that most of the transformations documented in the literature usually omit a detailed proof of the correctness of the proposed transformations, which might hide possible mistakes, especially those that involve the violation of an implicit condition.

At this point, it is convenient to remind that the usual process for proving that a problem Π_1 is NP-complete involves constructing a polynomial transformation from a known NP-complete problem Π_2 to problem Π_1 (Subsection "The Class of NP-complete Problems").

In particular, the proof of the NP-completeness of the Partition problem involves a transformation from the 3-Dimensional Matching (3DM) problem to Partition. In turn, the NP-completeness of 3DM involves a transformation from the 3-SATISFIABILITY (3-SAT) to 3DM. Finally, the NP-completeness of 3-SAT involves the transformation from the SATISFIABILITY (SAT) problem to 3-SAT. Therefore, our investigation for trying to explain the anomaly described in the preceding section led us to review the three transformations (3DM $\propto$ Partition, 3-SAT $\propto$ 3DM, and SAT $\propto$

3-SAT) in search for possible mistakes. A summary of our findings is presented in the following subsections.

4.1. Transformation from 3DM to Partition

3-Dimensional Matching problem (3DM): Given three sets $W = \{w_1, w_2, ..., w_q\}$, $X = \{x_1, x_2, ..., x_q\}$, $Y = \{y_1, y_2, ..., y_q\}$ and a ternary relation $M \subseteq W \times X \times Y$ of k triples, the 3-Dimensional Matching problem consists of determining if there exists a subset $M' \subseteq M$ of q triples such that each element (w_i, x_i and y_i) appears just once in the triples of subset M'.

The following algorithm summarizes the process of the transformation 3DM $\propto$ Partition (Garey & Johnson, 1979).

Algorithm Trans 3DM-Par

0. Input: an instance (yes, no or invalid) x of the 3-Dimensional Matching problem.
1. Set the value of p equal to $\lceil \log_2(k+1) \rceil$.
2. For each triple $m_i = (w_{f(i)}, x_{g(i)}, y_{h(i)}) \in M$, define an element $a_i \in A$ of Partition, whose size is given by the following formula:
$$s(a_i) = 2^{p(3q-f(i))} + 2^{p(2q-g(i))} + 2^{p(q-h(i))}$$

where $f(i)$, $g(i)$ and $h(i)$ are the subscripts of each component of the triple m_i.

3. Finally, define two extra elements b_1 and b_2 of Partition, whose sizes are given by the following expressions:

$$s(b_1) = 2\sum_{i=1}^{k} s(a_i) - \sum_{j=0}^{3q-1} 2^{pj}$$

$$s(b_2) = \sum_{i=1}^{k} s(a_i) + \sum_{j=0}^{3q-1} 2^{pj}$$

(Note: since this algorithm is rather involved, the reader is referred to Garey & Johnson, 1979, for an explanation of it.)

A process, similar to the one presented in Subsection "Verification of the Correctness of the Trans Par-BP Algorithm", was carried out for the Trans 3DM-Par algorithm. Due to space limitations, the process for verifying that this algorithm satisfies all the explicit and implicit conditions is not included. As a result from our verification process, it was concluded that the Trans 3DM-Par algorithm satisfies the explicit conditions A, B1 and B2, as well as the implicit conditions C1 and C2. Unfortunately, like the Trans Par-BP Algorithm, it was not possible to prove that there exists a polynomial transformation from Partition to 3DM; incidentally, according to our survey, no such transformation has been reported in the literature on the theory of NP-completeness.

Finally, the conclusion from reviewing the transformation from 3DM to Partition is that it is correct in the sense that it satisfies conditions A, B1, B2, C1 and C2; however, it was not possible to show that it satisfies condition C3 (the existence of the reverse transformation) nor that it does not satisfies it. Incidentally, our survey of the literature on this subject revealed that no reverse transformation has been reported.

4.2. Transformation from 3-SAT to 3DM

3-SATISFIABILITY (3-SAT) problem: Consider a collection $C = \{c_1, c_2, ..., c_m\}$ of boolean clauses, where each clause involves exactly three variables out of the set $U = \{u_1, u_2, ..., u_n\}$, then the problem consists of determining if there exists a value assignment (V or F) for each u_i ($i=1, 2, ..., n$), such that c_j is true for all j ($j=1, 2, ..., m$). (Note: 3-SAT is a special case of the SAT problem, described in Subsection "Transformation from SAT to 3-SAT", where each clause involves only three variables.)

The following algorithm summarizes the process of the transformation 3-SAT $\propto$ 3DM (Garey & Johnson, 1979).

Algorithm Trans 3SAT-3DM

0. Input: an instance (yes, no or invalid) x of the 3-SAT problem.

1. Define the following set of parameters of the 3DM problem: $\{u_{i,j}, \neg u_{i,j}: 1 \leq i \leq n, 1 \leq j \leq m\}$, where n and m represent the number of boolean variables and the number of boolean clauses of the SAT problem. The parameters of this set will constitute the elements of set W of the 3DM problem.

2. Define the following sets of parameters of the 3DM problem: $A = \{a_{i,j}: 1 \leq i \leq n, 1 \leq j \leq m\}$, $S_1 = \{s_{1,j}: 1 \leq j \leq m\}$, $G_1 = \{g_{1,j}: 1 \leq k \leq m(n-1)\}$. The parameters of these sets will constitute the elements of set X of the 3DM problem; i.e.,
    $$X = A \cup S_1 \cup G_1$$

3. Define the following sets of parameters of the 3DM problem: $B = \{b_{i,j}: 1 \leq i \leq n, 1 \leq j \leq m\}$, $S_2 = \{s_{2,j}: 1 \leq j \leq m\}$, $G_2 = \{g_{2,j}: 1 \leq k \leq m(n-1)\}$. The parameters of these sets will constitute the elements of set Y of the 3DM problem; i.e.,
    $$Y = B \cup S_2 \cup G_2$$

4. Construct the *truth-setting and fan-out* set of triples (which is a subset of set M of 3DM) as follows:
    $$T = \left(\bigcup_{i=1}^{n} T_i^t \right) \cup \left(\bigcup_{i=1}^{n} T_i^f \right)$$
    where
    $$T_i^t = \{(\neg u_{i,j}, a_{i,j}, b_{i,j}): 1 \leq j \leq m\}$$
    $$T_i^f = \{(u_{i,j}, a_{i,j+1}, b_{i,j}): 1 \leq j \leq m\}$$

    where the elements of the triples are drawn from the sets W, A and B defined in steps 1, 2 and 3.

5. Construct the *satisfaction testing* set of triples (which is a subset of set M of 3DM) as follows:
    $$C = \bigcup_{j=1}^{m} C_j$$
    where
    $$C_j = \{(u_{i,j}, s_{1,j}, s_{2,j}): u_i \in c_j\}$$
    $$\cup \{(u_{i,j}, s_{1,j}, s_{2,j}): u_i \in \neg c_j\}$$

    where the elements of the triples are drawn from the sets W, S_1 and S_2 defined in steps 1, 2 and 3.

6. Construct the *garbage collection* set of triples (which is a subset of set M of 3DM) as follows:
    $$G = \{(u_{i,j}, g_{1,k}, g_{2,k}), (\neg u_{i,j}, g_{1,k}, g_{2,k}):$$
    $$1 \leq k \leq m(n-1), 1 \leq i \leq n, 1 \leq j \leq m\}$$

    where the elements of the triples are drawn from the sets W, G_1 and G_2 defined in steps 1, 2 and 3.

7. Finally, construct subset M of the 3DM problem as follows: $M = T \cup C \cup G$

(Note: since this algorithm is rather complex, the reader is referred to Garey & Johnson, 1979, for an explanation of it.)

A process for verifying correctness, similar to the one presented in Subsection "Verification of the Correctness of the Trans Par-BP Algorithm", was carried out for the Trans 3SAT-3DM algorithm. As a result from the verification, it was concluded that the Trans 3SAT-3DM algorithm satisfies the explicit conditions A, B1 and B2, as well as the implicit conditions C1 and C2; however, it was not possible to show that it satisfies condition C3 (the existence of the reverse transformation) nor that it does not satisfies it. By the way, our survey showed that no reverse transformation has been reported in the literature.

4.3. Transformation from SAT to 3-SAT

SATISFIABILITY (SAT) problem: Consider a set of boolean variables $U = \{u_1, u_2, \dots, u_n\}$ and a collection $C = \{c_1, c_2, \dots, c_m\}$ of boolean clauses, where $c_i = \{z_1, z_2, \dots, z_{k_i}\}$ for $i=1,..,m$ (note: each z represents a variable u or its negation $\neg u$, and it is called *literal*), then the problem consists of determining if there exists a value assignment (V or F) for each u_i ($i=1, 2, \dots, n$), such that c_j is true for all j ($j=1, 2, \dots, m$). An alternate definition of the SAT problem defines C as a boolean expression in conjunctive normal form (CNF); i.e., $C = (c_1 \wedge c_2 \wedge \dots \wedge c_m)$, where $c_i = z_1 \vee z_2 \vee \dots \vee z_{k_i}$.

The following algorithm summarizes the process of the transformation SAT $\propto$ 3-SAT (Garey & Johnson, 1979).

Algorithm Trans SAT-3SAT

0. Input: an instance (yes, no or invalid) x of the SAT problem.
1. Define the following set of variables for 3-SAT:
    $U' = U \cup U'_1 \cup U'_2 \cup \dots \cup U'_m$
    where U is the set of variables of SAT and for each clause c_j of SAT:
    $U'_j = \{y_{j,1}, y_{j,2}\}$, if $k=1$;
    $U'_j = \{y_{j,1}\}$, if $k=2$;
    $U'_j = \emptyset$, if $k=3$;
    $U'_j = \{y_{j,i} : 1 \le i \le k-3\}$, if $k \ge 4$.
2. Define the following set of clauses for 3-SAT:
    $C' = C'_1 \cup C'_2 \cup \dots \cup C'_m$
    where, for each clause $c_j = \{z_1, z_2, \dots, z_k\}$ of SAT:
    $C'_j = \{(z_1, y_{j,1}, y_{j,2}), (z_1, y_{j,1}, \neg y_{j,2}),$
    $(z_1, \neg y_{j,1}, y_{j,2}), (z_1, \neg y_{j,1}, \neg y_{j,2})\},$
    if $k=1$;
    $C'_j = \{(z_1, z_2, y_{j,1}), (z_1, z_2, \neg y_{j,1})\}$, if $k=2$;
    $C'_j = \{c_j\}$, if $k=3$;
    $C'_j = \{(z_1, z_2, y_{j,1})\}$
    $\cup \{\{(\neg y_{j,i}, z_{i+2}, y_{j,i+1}) : 1 \le i \le k-4\}$
    $\cup \{(\neg y_{j,k-3}, z_{k-1}, z_k)\}$, if $k \ge 4$.

A verification of the correctness of the Trans SAT-3SAT algorithm was carried out. As a result from the verification, it was concluded that the Trans SAT-3SAT algorithm satisfies the explicit conditions A, B1 and B2, as well as the implicit conditions C1 and C2. Regarding the verification of the implicit condition C3 (the existence of a reverse transformation), it is evident that it is satisfied: notice that no reverse transformation (i.e., a transformation from 3-SAT to SAT) is needed since 3-SAT is just a special case of SAT; i.e., each 3-SAT instance is a SAT instance whose clauses involve only three variables.

4.4. Conclusions from the Review of the NP-Completeness of Partition

In order to prove the hypothesis that the Partition problem might not be NP-complete, a detailed verification of the transformations 3DM $\propto$ Partition, 3-SAT $\propto$ 3DM and SAT $\propto$ 3-SAT was carried out. The verification revealed that all the transformations satisfy conditions A, B1, B2, C1 and C2; therefore, the conclusion of this verification is that there is no mistake in the three transformations; and consequently, it can be concluded that the Partition problem is NP-complete.

Unfortunately, except for the last transformation (SAT $\propto$ 3-SAT), it was not possible to prove that the transformations satisfy condition C3. At this point, it is important to mention that not being able to show that condition C3 (the existence of a reverse transformation) is satisfied does not mean that the reverse transformation does not exist; it just might mean that it is very difficult to devise such kind of transformations.

5. THREE-HOP REVERSE TRANSFORMATION FROM PARTITION TO SAT

A possible means for gaining some insight for explaining the presumed anomaly could be obtained from Cook's theorem, which is the foundation of the theory of NP-completeness. Cook's theorem states (Cook, 1971): If L is a language accepted by some nondeterministic Turing machine in polynomial time, then L can be transformed to SAT. In simple words, considering that L is the encoding of a decision problem, then the theorem means that every NP problem Π can be transformed to SAT.

In the previous section we verified the correctness of the forward transformations from SAT to Partition (i.e., SAT $\propto$ 3-SAT, 3-SAT $\propto$ 3DM, 3DM $\propto$ Partition), but we were not able to find the reverse transformations Partition $\propto$ 3DM and 3DM $\propto$ 3-SAT. In this section we will try to find a three-hop reverse transformation from Partition to SAT to find out if it exists as predicted by Cook's theorem, and if it exists, what it looks like. Perhaps by analyzing a transformation from Partition to SAT some knowledge could be derived for devising reverse transformations for other pairs of NP-complete problems.

5.1. Mathematical Formulation of Partition as a Combinatorial Problem

For formulating the Partition problem as a combinatorial problem, consider for each element a_i ($i=1, 2, \ldots, n$) a decision variable x_i such that $x_i = 1$ if a_i is assigned to the set A' and $x_i = 0$ if a_i is assigned to $A-A'$. With this definition of variables, then the Partition problem consists of determining if there exists an assignment of values (0 or 1) to $X = \{x_1, x_2, \ldots, x_n\}$ such that

$$S \overset{?}{=} T \tag{1}$$

where

$$S = \sum_{i=1}^{n} s(a_i) x_i \tag{2}$$

$$T = \sum_{i=1}^{n} s(a_i)(1 - x_i) \tag{3}$$

For illustrating the application of this formulation, consider a yes-instance p of Partition defined as follows: a set of elements $A = \{a_1, a_2, a_3\}$ with their respective sizes $s(a_1)=3$, $s(a_2)=2$, $s(a_3)=5$. In this example, the formulation for instance p is the following:

$$S \overset{?}{=} T \tag{4}$$

where

$$S = 3x_1 + 2x_2 + 5x_3 \tag{5}$$

$$T = 3(1-x_1) + 2(1-x_2) + 5(1-x_3) \tag{6}$$

Notice that if the variables are assigned the following values: $x_1=1$, $x_2=1$, $x_3=0$, then $S = 5$ and $T = 5$; and therefore, $S = T$, which implies that p is a yes-instance of Partition. Notice that other value assignments, such as the following: $x_1=1$, $x_2=0$, $x_3=1$, result in S and T having different values.

5.2. Transformation from Partition to SAT

For carrying out the transformation, it is necessary to formulate Partition as a boolean expression C (in conjunctive normal form) in terms of a set of boolean variables $u_1, u_2, \ldots, u_n$, such that $u_i = T$ if the element a_i of Partition is assigned to set the A' and $u_i = F$ if it is assigned to $A-A'$.

Because of the difficulty for formulating expression C, it will be necessary to define two more sets of boolean variables $V_S = \{v_{S,1}, v_{S,2}, \ldots, v_{S,k}\}$ and $V_T = \{v_{T,1}, v_{T,2}, \ldots, v_{T,k}\}$ (where $k = \lceil \log_2 \Sigma_{a \in A} s(a) \rceil$), where $v_{S,1}$ represents the value of the least significant bit of S (expression (2)) when S is expressed as a binary number, $v_{S,2}$ represents the value of the second least significant bit of S, and so on up to $v_{S,k}$ that represents the most significant bit of S; additionally, the variables of V_T are similarly related to T (expression (3)).

It is convenient to make clear that $v_{S,j}$ and $v_{T,j}$ ($j = 1, 2, \dots, k$) are variables dependent on the basic variables u, and therefore, they can be expressed as boolean expressions in terms of the variables u. Consequently, variables $v_{S,j}$ and $v_{T,j}$ can not adopt arbitrary values, but their values are determined by those of the variables u.

Algorithm Trans Par-Sat1

0. Input: an instance (yes, no or invalid) x of the Partition problem formulated according to expressions (1)-(3).

1. For each element a_i of Partition, define n boolean variables $u_1, u_2, \dots, u_n$. (Notes: Thus all the variables of SAT are defined. The complexity of this step is $O(|A|)$ and, therefore, polynomial.)

2. For each element a_i of Partition, convert the value of $s(a_i)$ to a binary number $s'(a_i)$ with k digits (where $k = \lceil \log_2 \sum_{a \in A} s(a) \rceil$), and set ρ_{i1}=V if the least significant bit of $s'(a_i)$ is 1 and set ρ_{i1}=F otherwise, set ρ_{i2}=V if the second least significant bit of $s'(a_i)$ is 1 and set ρ_{i2}=F otherwise, and so on up to the k-th bit of $s'(a_i)$. (Notes: Thus all the parameters of SAT are defined in terms of the parameters of Partition. The complexity of this step is $O(|A| \log_2 \sum s(a))$ and, therefore, polynomial.)

3. Define k boolean variables $v_{S,1}, v_{S,2}, \dots, v_{S,k}$. The boolean expressions for these variables (in terms of the basic variables u_i and the parameters ρ_{ij}) are generated using the algorithm described below (where $Sum(x, y, z) = (x \lor y \lor z) \land (x \lor \neg y \lor \neg z) \land (\neg x \lor y \lor \neg z) \land (\neg x \lor \neg y \lor z)$ and $Carry(x, y, z) = (x \lor y) \land (x \lor z) \land (y \lor z)$):

```
1 n = number of elements of Partition
2 v_{s,1} = F, v_{s,2} = F, ..., v_{s,k} = F
3 //This cycle adds each summand to S
4 for i=1 to n
5   α_{s,0} = F
6   //This cycle calculates each bit
    of the
7   //sum
8   for j=1 to k
9     if (j<k) then {α_{s,j} =
      Carry(v_{s,j}, ρ_{ij}∧u_i, α_{s,j-1})}
10    v_{s,j} = Sum(v_{s,j}, ρ_{ij}∧u_i, α_{s,j-1})
11  end for
12 end for
```

(Notes: The complexity of this step is $O(|A| \log_2 \sum s(a))$ and, therefore, polyno-mial. Optionally, the expressions for $v_{S,j}$ (for $j = 1, 2, \dots, k$) can be converted to CNF using a truth table (Barland et al., 2011) in order to facilitate obtaining the final expression for C.)

4. Generate k boolean variables $v_{T,1}, v_{T,2}, \dots, v_{T,k}$. The boolean expressions for these variables are generated as follows: $v_{T,j} = f_j(\neg u_1, \neg u_2, \dots, \neg u_n)$, where function f_j is defined by $f_j(u_1, u_2, \dots, u_n) = v_{S,j}$ (for $j = 1, 2, \dots, k$). In simple words, the expression for $v_{T,j}$ is obtained from the expression for $v_{S,j}$ by replacing each basic variable u_i by its complement; i.e., $\neg u_i$. (The complexity of this step is $O(\log_2 \sum s(a))$ and, therefore, polynomial.)

5. Set $C = ((v_{S,1} \land v_{T,1}) \lor (\neg v_{S,1} \land \neg v_{T,1})) \land ((v_{S,2} \land v_{T,2}) \lor (\neg v_{S,2} \land \neg v_{T,2})) \land \dots \land ((v_{S,k} \land v_{T,k}) \lor (\neg v_{S,k} \land \neg v_{T,k}))$, and substitute variables $v_{S,k}$ and $v_{T,k}$ ($k = 1, 2, \dots m$) by the expressions obtained in steps 3 and 4. In simple words, the preceding formula guarantees that C is true if the value of the j-th bit of S (expression (2)) equals the value of the j-th bit of T (expression (3)) for all $j = 1, 2, \dots, k$. (Note: The complexity of this step is $O(\log_2 \sum s(a))$ and, therefore, polynomial.)

6. Convert expression for C obtained in step 5 to CNF. (Notes: This process can be carried out using a truth table (Barland et al., 2011). It cannot be guaranteed that the

complexity of this step is polynomial, as discussed in Subsection "Complexity of the Transformation from Partition to SAT.")

5.3. Example of Transformation from Partition to SAT

For better understanding the operation of the Trans Par-Sat1 algorithm, its use will be illustrated applying it to the Partition instance defined as follows: a set of elements $A = \{a_1, a_2, a_3\}$ with their respective sizes $s(a_1)=3$, $s(a_2)=2$, $s(a_3)=5$.

The application of step 1 of the Trans Par-Sat1 algorithm permits to define the following boolean variables of SAT: u_1, u_2 y u_3; while the application of step 2 generates the following SAT parameters:

$$\rho_{11}=V, \rho_{12}=V, \rho_{13}=F, \rho_{14}=F \text{ (associated to } u_1),$$

$$\rho_{21}=F, \rho_{22}=V, \rho_{23}=F, \rho_{24}=F \text{ (associated to } u_2),$$

$$\rho_{31}=V, \rho_{32}=F, \rho_{33}=V, \rho_{34}=F \text{ (associated to } u_3).$$

The application of step 3 generates the following results:

- Line 2 of the algorithm in step 3 generates the following results: $v_{S,1} = F$, $v_{S,2} = F$, $v_{S,3} = F$, $v_{S,4} = F$.
- The first iteration of the external *for* cycle generates the following results:

$$
\begin{aligned}
\alpha_{s,0} &= F \\
\alpha_{s,1} &= Carry(v_{s,1}, \rho_{11} \wedge u_1, \alpha_{s,0}) \\
&= Carry(F, V \wedge u_1, F) \\
&= Carry(F, u_1, F) \\
&= (F \vee u_1) \wedge (F \vee F) \wedge (u_1 \vee F) \\
&= F \\
v_{s,1} &= Sum(v_{s,1}, \rho_{11} \wedge u_1, \alpha_{s,0}) \\
&= Sum(F, u_1, F) \\
&= (F \vee u_1 \vee F) \wedge (F \vee \neg u_1 \vee \neg F) \\
&\quad \wedge (\neg F \vee u_1 \vee \neg F) \wedge (\neg F \vee \neg u_1 \vee F) \\
&= u_1 \\
\alpha_{s,2} &= Carry(v_{s,2}, \rho_{12} \wedge u_1, \alpha_{s,1})
\end{aligned}
$$

$$
\begin{aligned}
&= Carry(F, V \wedge u_1, F) \\
&= Carry(F, u_1, F) \\
&= F \\
v_{s,2} &= Sum(v_{s,2}, \rho_{12} \wedge u_1, \alpha_{s,1}) \\
&= Sum(F, u_1, F) \\
&= u_1 \\
\alpha_{s,3} &= Carry(v_{s,3}, \rho_{13} \wedge u_1, \alpha_{s,2}) \\
&= Carry(F, F \wedge u_1, F) \\
&= Carry(F, F, F) \\
&= F \\
v_{s,3} &= Sum(v_{s,3}, \rho_{13} \wedge u_1, \alpha_{s,2}) \\
&= Sum(F, F, F) \\
&= (F \vee F \vee F) \wedge (F \vee \neg F \vee \neg F) \\
&\quad \wedge (\neg F \vee F \vee \neg F) \wedge (\neg F \vee \neg F \vee F) \\
&= F \\
v_{s,4} &= Sum(v_{s,4}, \rho_{14} \wedge u_1, \alpha_{s,3}) \\
&= Sum(F, F \wedge u_1, F) \\
&= Sum(F, F, F) \\
&= F
\end{aligned}
$$

- The second iteration of the external *for* cycle generates the following results:

$$
\begin{aligned}
\alpha_{s,0} &= F \\
\alpha_{s,1} &= Carry(v_{s,1}, \rho_{21} \wedge u_2, \alpha_{s,0}) \\
&= Carry(u_1, F \wedge u_2, F) \\
&= Carry(u_1, F, F) \\
&= (u_1 \vee F) \wedge (u_1 \vee F) \wedge (F \vee F) \\
&= F \\
v_{s,1} &= Sum(v_{s,1}, \rho_{21} \wedge u_2, \alpha_{s,0}) \\
&= Sum(u_1, F, F) \\
&= (u_1 \vee F \vee F) \wedge (u_1 \vee \neg F \vee \neg F) \\
&\quad \wedge (\neg u_1 \vee F \vee \neg F) \wedge (\neg u_1 \vee \neg F \vee F) \\
&= u_1 \\
\alpha_{s,2} &= Carry(v_{s,2}, \rho_{22} \wedge u_2, \alpha_{s,1}) \\
&= Carry(u_1, V \wedge u_2, F) \\
&= Carry(u_1, u_2, F) \\
&= (u_1 \vee u_2) \wedge (u_1 \vee F) \wedge (u_2 \vee F) \\
&= u_1 \wedge u_2 \\
v_{s,2} &= Sum(v_{s,2}, \rho_{22} \wedge u_2, \alpha_{s,1}) \\
&= Sum(u_1, u_2, F) \\
&= (u_1 \vee u_2 \vee F) \wedge (u_1 \vee \neg u_2 \vee \neg F) \\
&\quad \wedge (\neg u_1 \vee u_2 \vee \neg F) \wedge (\neg u_1 \vee \neg u_2 \vee F) \\
&= (u_1 \vee u_2) \wedge (\neg u_1 \vee \neg u_2)
\end{aligned}
$$

$\alpha_{s,3}$ = $Carry(v_{s,3}, \rho_{23} \wedge u_2, \alpha_{s,2})$
= $Carry(F, F \wedge u_2, u_1 \wedge u_2)$
= $Carry(F, F, u_1 \wedge u_2)$
= $(F \vee F) \wedge (F \vee (u_1 \wedge u_2))$
  $\wedge (F \vee (u_1 \wedge u_2))$
= F

$v_{s,3}$ = $Sum(v_{s,3}, \rho_{23} \wedge u_2, \alpha_{s,2})$
= $Sum(F, F, u_1 \wedge u_2)$
= $(F \vee F \vee (u_1 \wedge u_2)) \wedge (F \vee \neg F \vee \neg (u_1 \wedge u_2))$
  $\wedge (\neg F \vee F \vee \neg (u_1 \wedge u_2))$
  $\wedge (\neg F \vee \neg F \vee (u_1 \wedge u_2))$
= $u_1 \wedge u_2$

$v_{s,4}$ = $Sum(v_{s,4}, \rho_{24} \wedge u_2, \alpha_{s,3})$
= $Sum(F, F \wedge u_2, F)$
= $Sum(F, F, F)$
= $(F \vee F \vee F) \wedge (F \vee \neg F \vee \neg F)$
  $\wedge (\neg F \vee F \vee \neg F) \wedge (\neg F \vee \neg F \vee F)$
= F

- The third and last iteration of the external *for* cycle generates the results shown below this paragraph. Since the simplification of the expressions for variables $v_{S,j}$ y $\alpha_{S,j}$ becomes increasingly complex, it is necessary to use a method based on the truth table of the expression (Barland et al., 2011). Due to space limitations the simplification will be omitted.

$\alpha_{s,0}$ = F
$\alpha_{s,1}$ = $Carry(v_{s,1}, \rho_{31} \wedge u_3, \alpha_{s,0})$
= $Carry(u_1, V \wedge u_3, F)$
= $Carry(u_1, u_3, F)$
= $(u_1 \vee u_3) \wedge (u_1 \vee F) \wedge (u_3 \vee F)$
= $u_1 \wedge u_3$

$v_{s,1}$ = $Sum(v_{s,1}, \rho_{31} \wedge u_3, \alpha_{s,0})$
= $Sum(u_1, u_3, F)$
= $(u_1 \vee u_3 \vee F) \wedge (u_1 \vee \neg u_3 \vee \neg F)$
  $\wedge (\neg u_1 \vee u_3 \vee \neg F) \wedge (\neg u_1 \vee \neg u_3 \vee F)$
= $(u_1 \vee u_3) \wedge (\neg u_1 \vee \neg u_3)$

$\alpha_{s,2}$ = $Carry(v_{s,2}, \rho_{32} \wedge u_3, \alpha_{s,1})$
= $Carry((u_1 \vee u_2) \wedge (\neg u_1 \vee \neg u_2), F \wedge u_3, u_1 \wedge u_3)$
= $Carry((u_1 \vee u_2) \wedge (\neg u_1 \vee \neg u_2), F,$

$u_1 \wedge u_3)$
= $(((u_1 \vee u_2) \wedge (\neg u_1 \vee \neg u_2)) \vee F)$
  $\wedge (((u_1 \vee u_2) \wedge (\neg u_1 \vee \neg u_2)) \vee (u_1 \wedge u_3))$
  $\wedge (F \vee (u_1 \wedge u_3))$
= $(\neg u_1 \vee \neg u_2) \wedge u_1 \wedge u_3$

$v_{s,2}$ = $Sum(v_{s,2}, \rho_{32} \wedge u_3, \alpha_{s,1})$
= $Sum((u_1 \vee u_2) \wedge (\neg u_1 \vee \neg u_2), F, u_1 \wedge u_3)$
= $(((u_1 \vee u_2) \wedge (\neg u_1 \vee \neg u_2)) \vee F$
      $\vee (u_1 \wedge u_3))$
  $\wedge (((u_1 \vee u_2) \wedge (\neg u_1 \vee \neg u_2)) \vee \neg F$
      $\vee \neg (u_1 \wedge u_3))$
  $\wedge (\neg ((u_1 \vee u_2) \wedge (\neg u_1 \vee \neg u_2)) \vee F$
      $\vee \neg (u_1 \wedge u_3))$
  $\wedge (\neg ((u_1 \vee u_2) \wedge (\neg u_1 \vee \neg u_2)) \vee \neg F$
      $\vee (u_1 \wedge u_3))$
= $(u_1 \vee u_2 \vee u_3) \wedge (u_1 \vee u_2 \vee \neg u_3)$
  $\wedge (\neg u_1 \vee u_2 \vee \neg u_3) \wedge (\neg u_1 \vee \neg u_2 \vee u_3)$

$\alpha_{s,3}$ = $Carry(v_{s,2}, \rho_{32} \wedge u_3, \alpha_{s,1})$
= $Carry(u_1 \wedge u_2, V \wedge u_3, (\neg u_1 \vee \neg u_2) \wedge u_1 \wedge u_3)$
= $Carry(u_1 \wedge u_2, u_3, (\neg u_1 \vee \neg u_2) \wedge u_1 \wedge u_3)$
= $((u_1 \wedge u_2) \vee u_3)$
  $\wedge ((u_1 \wedge u_2) \vee ((\neg u_1 \vee \neg u_2) \wedge u_1 \wedge u_3))$
  $\wedge (u_3 \vee ((\neg u_1 \vee \neg u_2) \wedge u_1 \wedge u_3))$
= $(u_1 \vee u_2 \vee u_3) \wedge (u_1 \vee u_2 \vee \neg u_3)$
  $\wedge (u_1 \vee \neg u_2 \vee u_3) \wedge (u_1 \vee \neg u_2 \vee \neg u_3)$
  $\wedge (\neg u_1 \vee u_2 \vee u_3) \wedge (\neg u_1 \vee \neg u_2 \vee u_3)$

$v_{s,3}$ = $Sum(v_{s,3}, \rho_{33} \wedge u_3, \alpha_{s,2})$
= $Sum(u_1 \wedge u_2, u_3, (\neg u_1 \vee \neg u_2) \wedge u_1 \wedge u_3)$
= $((u_1 \wedge u_2) \vee u_3$
      $\vee ((\neg u_1 \vee \neg u_2) \wedge u_1 \wedge u_3))$
  $\wedge ((u_1 \wedge u_2) \vee \neg u_3$
      $\vee \neg ((\neg u_1 \vee \neg u_2) \wedge u_1 \wedge u_3))$
  $\wedge (\neg (u_1 \wedge u_2) \vee u_3$
      $\vee \neg ((\neg u_1 \vee \neg u_2) \wedge u_1 \wedge u_3))$
  $\wedge (\neg (u_1 \wedge u_2) \vee \neg u_3$
      $\vee ((\neg u_1 \vee \neg u_2) \wedge u_1 \wedge u_3))$
= $(u_1 \vee u_2 \vee u_3) \wedge (u_1 \vee \neg u_2 \vee u_3)$
  $\wedge (\neg u_1 \vee u_2 \vee u_3) \wedge (\neg u_1 \vee u_2 \vee \neg u_3)$
  $\wedge (\neg u_1 \vee \neg u_2 \vee \neg u_3)$

$v_{s,4}$ = $Sum(v_{s,4}, \rho_{34} \wedge u_3, \alpha_{s,3})$
= $Sum(F, F \wedge u_3, \alpha_{s,3})$
= $Sum(F, F, \alpha_{s,3})$
= $(F \vee F \vee \alpha_{s,3}) \wedge (F \vee \neg F \vee \neg \alpha_{s,3})$

$$\land \ (\neg F \lor F \lor \neg \alpha_{s,3}) \ \land \ (\neg F \lor \neg F \lor F \lor \alpha_{s,3})$$
$$= \alpha_{s,3}$$
$$= (u_1 \lor u_2 \lor u_3) \ \land \ (u_1 \lor u_2 \lor \neg u_3)$$
$$\land \ (u_1 \lor \neg u_2 \lor u_3) \ \land \ (u_1 \lor \neg u_2 \lor \neg u_3)$$
$$\land \ (\neg u_1 \lor u_2 \lor u_3) \ \land (\neg u_1 \lor \neg u_2 \lor u_3)$$

The application of step 4 generates the following results:

$$v_{T,1} = (\neg u_1 \lor \neg u_3) \ \land \ (u_1 \lor u_3)$$
$$v_{T,2} = (\neg u_1 \lor \neg u_2 \lor \neg u_3) \ \land \ (\neg u_1 \lor \neg u_2 \lor u_3)$$
$$\land \ (u_1 \lor \neg u_2 \lor u_3) \ \land \ (u_1 \lor u_2 \lor \neg u_3)$$
$$v_{T,3} = (\neg u_1 \lor \neg u_2 \lor \neg u_3) \ \land \ (\neg u_1 \lor u_2 \lor \neg u_3)$$
$$\land \ (u_1 \lor \neg u_2 \lor \neg u_3) \ \land \ (u_1 \lor \neg u_2 \lor u_3)$$
$$\land \ (u_1 \lor u_2 \lor u_3)$$
$$v_{T,4} = (\neg u_1 \lor \neg u_2 \lor \neg u_3) \ \land \ (\neg u_1 \lor \neg u_2 \lor u_3)$$
$$\land \ (\neg u_1 \lor u_2 \lor \neg u_3) \ \land \ (\neg u_1 \lor u_2 \lor u_3)$$
$$\land \ (u_1 \lor \neg u_2 \lor \neg u_3) \ \land \ (u_1 \lor u_2 \lor \neg u_3)$$

The application of step 5 generates the following boolean expression:

$$C = ((v_{S,1} \land v_{T,1}) \ \lor \ (\neg v_{S,1} \land \neg v_{T,1}))$$
$$\land \ ((v_{S,2} \land v_{T,2}) \ \lor \ (\neg v_{S,2} \land \neg v_{T,2}))$$
$$\land \ ((v_{S,3} \land v_{T,3}) \ \lor \ (\neg v_{S,3} \land \neg v_{T,3}))$$
$$\land \ ((v_{S,4} \land v_{T,4}) \ \lor \ (\neg v_{S,4} \land \neg v_{T,4}))$$

Substituting in the preceding expression the expressions for $v_{S,1}$, $v_{S,2}$, $v_{S,3}$, $v_{S,4}$, $v_{T,1}$, $v_{T,2}$, $v_{T,3}$ y $v_{T,4}$ found in steps 3 and 4, and after applying step 6, the following expression is obtained:

$$C = (u_1 \lor u_2 \lor u_3) \ \land \ (u_1 \lor \neg u_2 \lor u_3)$$
$$\land \ (u_1 \lor \neg u_2 \lor \neg u_3) \ \land \ (\neg u_1 \lor u_2 \lor u_3)$$
$$\land \ (\neg u_1 \lor u_2 \lor \neg u_3) \ \land \ (\neg u_1 \lor \neg u_2 \lor \neg u_3)$$
$$\tag{7}$$

Finally, applying De Morgan's laws to (7), a still more simplified expression can be obtained:

$$C = (u_1 \lor u_2 \lor u_3) \ \land \ (u_1 \lor \neg u_2)$$
$$\land \ (\neg u_1 \lor u_2) \ \land \ (\neg u_1 \lor \neg u_2 \lor \neg u_3) \tag{8}$$

The truth table for C (Table 1) shows that expression (8) is the correct transformation of the Partition problem formulated in (4)-(6). Notice that for the following assignment of values: u_1=V, u_2=V, u_3=F, the value of C is true, and the same occurs for the value assignment where u_1=F, u_2=F, u_3=V. Additionally, any other value assignment makes C false.

5.4. Complexity of the Transformation from Partition to SAT

The definition of polynomial transformation between languages (Subsection "Transformation of Languages") establishes two explicit conditions (A and B). Condition A states that the transformation process should be carried out in polynomial time. Therefore, it is necessary to determine if the Trans Par-Sat1 algorithm has polynomial complexity. To this end, some critical steps of the algorithm will be analyzed. First it is necessary to keep in mind that the size of the Partition problem is $|A|$, i.e., the number of elements of set A. In step 3, the internal *for* cycle is executed k times (where

Table 1. True table for expression C of the SAT problem

u_1	u_2	u_3	$C = (u_1 \lor u_2 \lor u_3) \land (u_1 \lor \neg u_2)$ $\land (\neg u_1 \lor u_2) \land (\neg u_1 \lor \neg u_2 \lor u_3)$	Value
F	F	F	(F∨F∨F)∧(F∨V) ∧(V∨V)∧(V∨V∨V)	F
F	F	V	(F∨F∨V)∧(F∨V) ∧(V∨V)∧(V∨V∨V)	V
F	V	F	(F∨V∨F)∧(F∨F) ∧(V∨V)∧(V∨F∨V)	F
F	V	V	(F∨V∨V)∧(F∨F) ∧(V∨V)∧(V∨F∨F)	F
V	F	F	(V∨F∨F)∧(V∨V) ∧(F∨V)∧(F∨V∨V)	F
V	F	V	(V∨F∨V)∧(V∨V) ∧(F∨V)∧(F∨V∨F)	F
V	V	F	(V∨V∨F)∧(V∨F) ∧(F∨V)∧(F∨F∨V)	V
V	V	V	(V∨V∨V)∧(V∨F) ∧(F∨V)∧(F∨F∨F)	F

$k = \lceil \log_2 \Sigma_{a \in A} s(a) \rceil$) and the external *for* cycle is executed $n=|A|$ times; therefore, the complexity of step 3 is polynomial. However, the conversion of the expressions for $v_{S,j}$ (where $j = 1, 2, \ldots, k$) to CNF cannot be guaranteed to be carried out in polynomial time. At this point, it is important to make clear that the conversion is optional and it was performed in the example to facilitate obtaining the expression for C in CNF.

Since SAT requires that the boolean expression is in CNF (Subsection "Trans-formation from SAT to 3-SAT"), then it is necessary to perform the conversion to CNF of the expression for C obtained in step 5 of the Trans Par-Sat1 algorithm. Unfortunately, for the worst case the standard conversion of an arbitrary boolean expression (obtained by the distributive properties of $\wedge$ and $\vee$) results in an exponential increase in the size of the expression (Jackson & Sheridan, 2005); therefore, the complexity of step 6 of the Trans Par-Sat1 algorithm is not polynomial.

However, there exists another type of conversion whose complexity is polynomial; such type of conversion generates an *equisatisfiable* boolean expression. Two boolean expressions ϕ and ϕ' are said to be equisatisfiable if ϕ is satisfiable whenever ϕ' is and vice versa. There exist several algorithms that permit converting in polynomial time from an arbitrary boolean expression ϕ to another expression ϕ' that is equisatisfiable (for example, Tseitin's encoding (Tseitin, 1983). The algorithms for performing this type of conversion from ϕ to ϕ' include in ϕ' additional variables besides those of ϕ. Consequently, in general for two equisatisfiable logic expressions ϕ and ϕ', it happens that the set of value assignments that makes ϕ' true might be different from the set of value assignments that makes ϕ' true; however, what is important for equi-satisfiability is that both (ϕ and ϕ') have such sets or none has them.

A concept related to equisatisfiability is logical *equivalence*. Two expressions ψ and ψ' are said to be equivalent if the set of value assignments that makes ψ true is exactly the same as the set of value assignments that makes ψ' true. Then, according to the definition of equisatisfiability, if two expressions ψ and ψ' are equivalent, they are also equisatisfiable; however, the converse is not true.

An important implication derived from the equivalence and equisatisfiability concepts is the following: if ψ and ψ' are equivalent expressions, a solution for ψ (i.e., a value assignment that makes ψ true) is also a solution for ψ'; however, if ϕ and ϕ' are equisatisfiable expressions, then a solution for ϕ might or might not be a solution for ϕ'. Regarding solutions, equisatisfiablity implies that both have a solution or none has it.

At this time, it is convenient to show the relation that exists between the concept of equisatisfiability and the definition of polynomial transformation (Subsection "Explicit Conditions"), from which only condition B is replicated below:

B. For all $x \in \Sigma_1{}^*$,
1. if $x \in L_1$ then $f(x) \in L_2$ and
2. if $x \notin L_1$ then $f(x) \notin L_2$.

To this end, consider two languages L_1 and L_2 that are the encodings of two logic problems Π_1 (SAT) and Π_2, (which will be called Equi-SAT) such that each string $x \in \Sigma_1{}^*$ and each string $y \in \Sigma_2{}^*$ are respectively encodings of two equisatisfiable instances: p of Π_1 and q of Π_2. In these circumstances, because of the equisatisfiability property, if p is a yes-instance, then q is also a yes-instance, which implies that condition B1 is satisfied; on the other hand, if p is a no-instance, then q is also a no-instance, and therefore, condition B2 is satisfied. In summary, a conversion of instances p of Π_1 (SAT) to equisatisfiable instances q of Π_2 is a polynomial transformation. Additionally, the bi-direction-ality of polynomial transformations implies that there must exist a reverse polynomial transformation $L_2 \propto L_1$ (i.e., from Π_2 to Π_1).

Now, assume L_0 is the encoding of Partition and L_2 is the encoding of the Equi-SAT problem Π_2 defined in the preceding paragraph; if $L_0 \propto$

L_2 (i.e., there exists a polynomial transformation from L_0 to L_2), and considering that $L_2 \propto L_1$ (from the preceding paragraph), then by transitivity it is concluded that $L_0 \propto L_1$; in simple words, this result means that for proving that there exists a polynomial transformation from Partition (L_0) to SAT (L_1) it is only necessary to prove that there exists a polynomial transformation from Partition (L_0) to an Equi-SAT problem (L_2).

Finally, instead of trying to devise an algorithm (like Trans Par-Sat1) that transforms Partition instances to SAT instances that are the logical equivalents of the first ones, it suffices to devise an algorithm that transforms Partition instances to SAT instances that are equisatisfiable. Such an algorithm, which we will call Trans Par-Sat2, is similar to Trans Par-Sat1, except that in step 6 the conversion generates a equisatisfiable expression instead of a logical equivalent expression.

6. FUTURE RESEARCH DIRECTIONS

The argument at the end of the preceding section ("Three-hop Reverse Transformation from Partition to SAT") suggests that there does exist a transformation from Partition to SAT, which is some sort of reverse transformation.

If it really exists a polynomial transformation from Partition to SAT, the generalization of this result would imply that, for every polynomial transformation $\Pi_1 \propto \Pi_2$, there would also exist the reverse transformation $\Pi_1 \propto \Pi_2$. However, as the example of the preceding section suggests, it so happens that there exist two kinds of transformations: *equivalent transformations*, like the one involved in the Trans Par-Sat1 algorithm, and *equisatisfiable transformations*, like the one involved in Trans Par-Sat2. Unfortunately, the concept of equisatisfiability has been defined only for logic expressions, and therefore, it is convenient to extend it to the field of decision problems.

According to the properties of equivalence and equisatisfiability presented in subsection

"Complexity of the Transformation from Partition to SAT", we will loosely define an equivalent transformation from an instance p of Π_1 to an instance q of Π_2 as one in which p and q are "equivalent" in the sense that a solution for p after a (usually simple) conversion becomes a solution for q. On the other hand, we define an equisatisfiable transformation from an instance p of Π_1 to an instance q of Π_2 as one in which p and q are "equisatisfiable" in the sense that if there exists a solution for p then it also exists a solution for q, and if does not exist a solution for p then it does not either for q; however, a solution for p in general cannot be converted to a solution for q.

According to these definitions, the Trans Par-BP algorithm (Subsection "Transformation Algorithm from Partition to Bin Packing") is an example of an equivalent transformation. Incidentally, many of the transformations reported in the literature are equivalent; for example, the Trans 3DM-Par algorithm ("Transformation from 3DM to Partition") and the Trans 3SAT-3DM algorithm ("Transformation from 3-SAT to 3DM"). However, there exist much less equisatisfiable transformations; the Trans Sat-3Sat algorithm is an example of this type of transformations.

A possible explanation for the anomaly in the transformation between NP-complete problems is that, for many pairs of NP-complete problems Π_1 and Π_2 (like Partition and Bin Packing), a transformation from Π_1 to Π_2 is reported in the literature, which is usually an equivalent transformation, but no reverse transformation has been reported, perhaps because there does not exist an equivalent transformation from Π_2 to Π_1. However, according to condition C3 (Subsection "Implicit Conditions") an equisatisfiable transformation should always exist, but this kind of transformations are not easy to devise. From this explanation of the anomaly, the following aspects remain to be studied to fully understand this issue:

- Development of an equisatisfiable transformation from Partition to SAT.

- Development of an equisatisfiable reverse transformation for a pair of problems for which no reverse transformation has been found.
- Development of a transformation from an NP-complete problem (such as Partition) to SAT according to the method implicit in the proof of Cook's theorem (Cook, 1971) for finding out what kind of transformation generates: equivalent or equisatisfiable?
- And the most difficult of all: finding out whether equivalent reverse transformations can be devised for any pair of NP-complete problems.

7. CONCLUSION

This chapter has shown that, though it is very easy to find a polynomial transformation from the Partition problem to the Bin Packing problem, finding the reverse transformation poses many difficulties, which led us to believe that a reverse transformation might not exist.

Our first assumption was that Partition might not be NP-complete, due to a possible mistake in the following transformations: SAT ∝ 3-SAT, 3-SAT ∝ 3DM and 3DM ∝ Partition. From a meticulous review of these transformations, we concluded that they are correct, and consequently, there is no doubt on the NP-completeness of Partition (Sub-section "Conclusions from the Review of the NP-completeness of Partition").

The next assumption for trying to explain the presumed anomaly was that —contrary to the prediction of the theory of NP-completeness— for some pairs of NP-complete problems there might not exist reverse transformations. To this end, a three-hop reverse transformation from Partition to SAT was looked for. This investigation revealed that two kinds of transformations from Partition to SAT can be designed: an equisatisfiable transformation with polynomial complexity

and an equivalent transformation which is not polynomial.

From the preceding results, a preliminary explanation for the presumed anomaly arises: for any pair of NP-complete problems there always exist an equisatisfiable transformation in one direction and also an equisatisfiable reverse transformation, being both polynomial; however, for many pairs of problems, the transformation reported in the literature is of the equivalent type and, it could happen that there might not exist an equivalent reverse transformation with polynomial complexity (although an equisatisfiable reverse transformation must always exist.)

Finally, this explanation has an important practical implication: the adaptation of an algorithm that solves one problem for solving another problem usually exploits the properties of equivalent transformations (the solution for one problem can be converted into a solution for the other), and unfortunately equisatisfiable transformations are usually useless for this purpose. Thus, the bad news is that, although the theory states that for any pair of NP-complete problems there must exist a transformation in both directions, only the equivalent transformations are useful for algorithm adaptation, and since for most problem pairs an equivalent transformation exists only in one direction (let us say, from Π_1 to Π_2), this implies that algorithm adaptation can be applied in one direction; i.e., from problem Π_2 to problem Π_1 but not from Π_1 to Π_2 while no equivalent transformation is devised from Π_2 to Π_1. Consequently, more work needs to be done for finding out equivalent reverse transformations.

REFERENCES

Barland, I., Kolaitis, P., Vardi, M., & Felleisen, M. (2011). Propositional logic: normal forms. *Connexions*. Retrieved January 14, 2011, from http://cnx.org/content/ m12075/1.12/

Cook, S. A. (1971). The complexity of theorem-proving procedures. In *Proceedings of the Third Annual ACM Symposium on Theory of Computing* (pp. 151-158). New York, NY: ACM.

Crainic, T. G., Perboli, G., Rei, W., & Tadei, R. (2011). Efficient lower bounds and heuristics for the variable cost and size bin packing problem. *Computers & Operations Research, 38*(11), 1474–1482. doi:10.1016/j.cor.2011.01.001

Cruz-Reyes, L., Gómez, C. G., Hernández, I. Y., Rangel, N., Álvarez, V. M., & González, J. J. (2008). An architecture for selecting data distribution algorithms. In *Proceeding of the 17th International Multi-conference on Advanced Computer Systems* (pp. 19-25).

Dasgupta, S., Papadimitriou, C. H., & Vazirani, U. V. (2006). *Algorithms*. New York, NY: McGraw-Hill.

Erben, W. (2001). A grouping genetic algorithm for graph colouring and exam timetabling. In E. Burke & W. Erben (Eds.), *Practice and Theory of Automated Timetabling III* (LNCS 2079, pp. 132-156).

Garey, M. R., & Johnson, D. S. (1979). *Computers and intractability: A guide to the theory of NP-completeness*. New York, NY: W. H. Freeman.

González-Barbosa, J. J., Delgado-Orta, J. F., Cruz-Reyes, L., Fraire-Huacuja, H. J., & Ramirez-Saldivar, A. (2010). Comparative analysis of hybrid techniques for an ant colony system algorithm applied to solve a real-world transportation problem . In Melin, P., Kacprzyk, J., & Pedrycz, W. (Eds.), *Soft Computing for Recognition Based on Biometrics, Studies in Computational Intelligence* (*Vol. 312*, pp. 365–385). Berlin, Germany: Springer-Verlag. doi:10.1007/978-3-642-15111-8_23

Jackson, P., & Sheridan, D. (2005). Clause form conversions for boolean circuits. In H. H. Hoos & D. G. Mitchell (Eds.), *Proceedings of the 7th International Conference on Theory and Applications of Satisfiability Testing* (LNCS 3542, pp. 183-198).

Karp, R. M. (1972). Reducibility among combinatorial problems . In Miller, R. E., & Thatcher, J. W. (Eds.), *Complexity of computer computations* (pp. 85–103). New York, NY: Plenum Press.

Kautz, H. A., & Selman, B. (1999). Unifying SAT-based and graph-based planning. In *Proceedings of the Sixteenth International Joint Conference on Artificial Intelligence* (pp. 318-325). San Francisco, CA: Morgan Kaufmann.

Long, D., Fox, M., & Hamdi, M. (2002). Reformulation in planning. In S. Koenig & R. C. Holte (Eds.), *Proceedings of the 5th International Symposium on Abstraction, Reformulation, and Approximation* (LNCS 2371, pp. 18-32).

Mahajan, Y. S., Fu, Z., & Sharad, M. (2005). Zchaff2004: an efficient SAT solver. In H. H. Hoos & D. G. Mitchell (Eds.), *Proceedings of the 7th International Conference on Theory and Applications of Satisfiability Testing* (LNCS 3542, pp. 360-375).

Murty, K. G. (2007). Yard crane pools and optimum layouts for storage yards of container terminals. *Journal of Industrial and Systems Engineering, 1*(3), 190–199.

Natale, M. D., & Bini, E. (2007). Optimizing the FPGA implementation of HRT systems. In *Proceedings of the 13th IEEE Real Time and Embedded Technology and Applications Symposium* (pp. 22-31). Washington, DC: IEEE Computer Society.

Ohrimenko, O., Stuckey, P. J., & Codish, M. (2009). Propagation via lazy clause generation. *Constraints, 14*(3), 357–391. doi:10.1007/s10601-008-9064-x

Piñol, M. (2009). *CSP problems as algorithmic benchmarks measures, methods and models* (Unpublished doctoral dissertation). Universitat de Lleida, Lérida, Spain.

Ruiz, V. J. A. (2008). *Desarrollo de indicadores de casos aplicables a la selección de algoritmos en el problema 2-Partition* (Unpublished doctoral dissertation). Centro Nal. de Investigación y Desarrollo Tecnológico, Cuernavaca, Mexico.

Sathe, M., Schenk, O., & Burkhart, H. (2009). Solving bi-objective many-constraint bin packing problems in automobile sheet metal forming processes. In M. Ehrgott, C. M. Fonseca, X. Gandibleux, J.-K. Hao, & M. Sevaux (Eds.), *Proceedings of the 5th International Conference on Evolutionary MultiCriterion Optimization* (LNCS 5467, pp. 246-260).

Soh, T., Inoue, K., Tamura, N., Banbara, M., & Nabeshima, H. (2010). A SAT-based method for solving the two-dimensional strip packing problem. *Fundamenta Informaticae*, *102*(3-4), 467–487.

Tseitin, G. (1983). On the complexity of proofs in propositional logics . In Siekmann, J., & Wrightson, G. (Eds.), *Automation of reasoning: Classical papers in computational logic* (*Vol. 2*, pp. 1967–1970). Berlin, Germany: Springer-Verlag.

Xing, Z., Chen, Y., & Zhang, W. (2006). Optimal STRIPS planning by maximum satisfiability and accumulative learning. In *Proceedings of the 16th International Conference on Automated Planning and Scheduling* (pp. 442-446). Palo Alto, CA: AAAI.

Chapter 8
Variants of VRP to Optimize Logistics Management Problems

Claudia Gómez Santillán
Instituto Tecnológico de Ciudad Madero, México

Juan Javier González Barbosa
Instituto Tecnológico de Ciudad Madero, México

Laura Cruz Reyes
Instituto Tecnológico de Ciudad Madero, México

Oscar Castillo López
Instituto Tecnológico de Tijuana, México

María Lucila Morales Rodríguez
Instituto Tecnológico de Ciudad Madero, México

Gilberto Rivera Zarate
Instituto Tecnológico de Ciudad Madero, México

Paula Hernández
Instituto Tecnólogico de Ciudad Madero, México

ABSTRACT

The Vehicle Routing Problem (VRP) is a key to the efficient transportation management and supply-chain coordination. VRP research has often been too focused on idealized models with non-realistic assumptions for practical applications. Nowadays the evolution of methodologies allows that the classical problems could be used to solve VRP problems of real life. The evolution of methodologies allows the creation of variants of the VRP which were considered too difficult to handle by their variety of possible restrictions. A VRP problem that includes the addition of restrictions, which represent the variants in the problem, is called Rich VRP. This work presents an algorithm to optimize the transportation management. The authors are including a case of study which solves a real routing problem applied to the distribution of bottled products. The proposed algorithm shows a saving in quantity of vehicles and reduces the operation costs of the company.

INTRODUCTION

The VRP is a generic name given to a whole class of problems. This combinatorial optimization problems considered one of the hardest, defined

over 40 years ago by Dantzig and Ramser in 1959. This problem consists in designing the optimal set of routes for a fleet of vehicles in order to serve a given set of customers. The problem objective is to deliver the known demands to a set of customers, minimizing the vehicles routes costs, starting and finishing at the same depot. The

DOI: 10.4018/978-1-4666-0297-7.ch008

computational experience indicates that VRP is a classic *NP*-hard problem, it is to say, it is difficult to solve optimally. Most real-world vehicle routing problems are solved using heuristic methods (Grer, Golden, & Wasil, 2010).

The VRP has a large number of real-life applications depending of the operation type, for example, picking up and delivering with restrictions like vehicle capacity or multiple depots, among others. Recent researches have shown that an adequate cost minimization in these problems will result in significant savings, approximately from 5% to 20% of the product total cost (Toth & Vigo, 2002).

In our work, we present a case of study which is a real routing problem applied to the distribution of bottled products. The transportation of bottled products is a relevant activity for industrial and commercial processes. The issues related to our research could be divided into three sub-problems: routing, scheduling and loads allocation.

The *routing and scheduling* can be described as a Rich VRP; this is a complex problem where several VRP variants are combined, in order to find a set of paths that allow satisfying the demands. The sub-problem of the *loads allocation* can be viewed as a Bin Packing Problem (BPP) which must determine a minimum set of containers to distribute the products (Rangel N., 2005).

Our research proposes a methodology of solution based on approximated algorithms. The methodology consists on an integrated system that involves the Ant Colony System (ACS) algorithm (Dorigo, 1997) which solves the routing and scheduling tasks.

We solve the *Routing - Scheduling - Loading Problem* (*RoSLoP*) addressing it by a Heuristic-Based System for RoSLoP (*HBS-RoSLoPII*). The *HBS-RoSLoPII* works in two stages: in the first, we created a new algorithm called Ant Colony System for the Routing and Scheduling Problem (*ACS-RoSLoPII*). In the second stage, we designed an algorithm called DiPro that solves the vehicle load problem, modeling it as a Bin Packing Problem

(BPP). In this work we only present and describe the information related to *ACS-RoSLoPII*. In addition, we developed a solution methodology for solving *HBS-RoSLoPII* applied to the distribution of bottled products in a company located in north eastern Mexico.

The proposal of this chapter is to describe the necessary elements to develop this research. First, in the Background section we describe the different concepts related to VRP and *RoSLoP*. In the next sections, we explain how the heuristic algorithm for *RoSLoP* was selected, as well as the solution methodology and the characteristics of real and artificial instances. In addition we describe the strategies used to adapt the classical ACS algorithm in order to solve *RoSLoP*. After that, we describe the experiments that validate the results of the *ACS-RoSLoPII* algorithm. The last section presents the conclusions obtained from the research experimental results, as well as the future work that could be developed to improve the results of solving the *RoSLoP*.

BACKGROUND

The section begins with the origin and description of VRP, we continue with a summary of the variants involved in this work, and with the formal definitions of the BPP and *RoSLoP*. To finish, we describe the basic elements that compose the ACS algorithm that will be used for the solution of the *RoSLoP*.

ORIGIN OF VRP

The *Traveling Salesman Problem* (TSP) is probably the most studied and known combinatorial optimization problem. In this problem a salesman has to visit a defined number of cities. The salesman must perform a tour through all the cities and return to the starting city in the end of the tour. In other words, given an undirected graph $G = (V,E)$

Figure 1. Example that show a solution of TSP a) Original weighted graph G and b) The selected cyclic tour G'

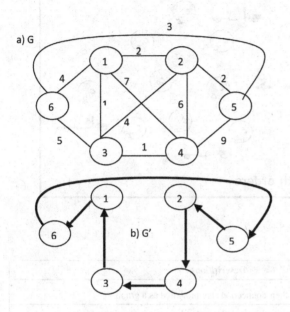

$$\min z = \sum_{i=1}^{n}\sum_{j=1}^{n} c_{ij}x_{ij} \qquad (1)$$

Subject to:

$$\sum_{j=1}^{n} x_{ij} = 1 \qquad (2)$$

$$\sum_{i=1}^{n} x_{ij} = 1 \qquad (3)$$

$$\sum_{i\in S, j\in E} c_{ij}x_{ij} \geq 1 \qquad (4)$$

$$x_{ij} = \{0,1\} \qquad (5)$$

in which each edge $e \in E$ has an associated cost c_e, the goal is to find a cyclic tour, such that each vertex v_i is visited exactly once, minimizing the sum of the edge costs used in the tour (Croes, 1958; Johnson, 1995).

The VRP is a generalization of the TSP, where a salesman has to serve a set of customers using a fleet of homogeneous vehicles kept in a common depot. Each customer has a certain demand for goods which initially are located at the depot. The task is to design vehicle routes that start and finish at the depot such that all customer demands are fulfilled.

Figure 1 shows an example of a TSP instance. In the Figure 1a, the graph G includes all the possible solution paths that the agent should go through the graph. Figure 1b is the G' graph that show the solution path that the agent selected of the G graph. The goal of TSP is to determine the circuit with the associated minimum cost, visiting exactly once each vertex in V.

The formulation of the TSP was proposed in Dantzig (1959), and makes the following mathematical model:

The Equation (1) is the objective function of TSP. The binary variables x_{ij} indicate if the vertex (i,j) is used in the solution. The Equation (2) and (3) are constraints for validate that each city is visited exactly once, for Equation (4) is called the elimination constraint of sub-tours and indicates that each subset of nodes S is visited at least once. There is a generalization of the TSP known as *m*-TSP, in which constraints are incorporated into the model so as to obtain a solution for *m* travel agents. *m*-TSP assumes that since $|E| = O(n^2)$, then in the worst case there are $O(2^n)$ constraints. The objective is to build *m* routes, one for each vehicle so that each customer is visited once by one of the vehicles. The definition of *m*-TSP corresponds to the classical definition of VRP.

THE VEHICLE ROUTING PROBLEM

The scheduling and routing of vehicles has been of great interest to the scientific community over the past fifty years due to the benefits that would bring in order to find an optimal solution, despite the complexity of this task (Thangiah, 2003).

Figure 2. Basic elements of the VRP

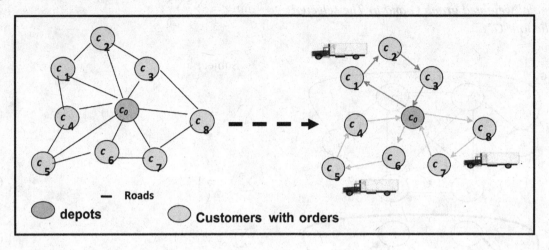

Table 1. m-TSP Elements

Elements	Descriptions
$G=(V,E)$	The set of customers, depot and their connections are modelled as a graph.
$V=\{v_0,v_1,v_2,v_3, ..., v_n\}$	The set of vertex. That represents customers and depot, where v_0 represent the depot.
$Q=\{q_1,q_2,q_3, ..., q_n\}$	The set of demands. Each customer has a demand to be satisfied by the depot.
$E=\{e_1, e_2, e_3, ..., e_m\}$	The set of edges. Each edge has an associated value c_{ij} that represents the transportation cost from v_i to v_j. This set is form by $E = \left\{ (v_i, v_j) \mid v_i, v_j \in V \wedge i \neq j \right\}$.
$C=\{(e_1,c_1),(e_2,c_2), ..., (e_m,c_m)\}$	The set of costs is made up of tuples that include: the starting vertex v_i, and final vertex v_j, which can be a customer or a depot. Also includes the cost assigned c_{ij} to that route segment.
R	The set of routes with a total minimum cost that starts and finalizes in the depot (v_0), where each vertex $v_i \in V - \{v_0\}$ is visited only once and the length of each route must be greater or equal than L.
L	The minimum length for each route.
M	The minimum set of vehicles.
Capacity	Capacity of vehicle load.

The *VRP* defined by Dantzig in Shaw (1998), is a classic problem of combinatorial optimization. The problem consists at visiting a set of customers using a fleet of vehicles, respecting constraints on the vehicles, customers, drivers, and so on. The goal is to minimize the costs of operation, which normally involves reducing a combination of the number of vehicles and the total distance travelled or time taken, as show in Figure 2.

According to Toth (2000), VRP has an unlimited number of vehicles with the same capacity, that is greater than the demand of any customer. The constraint is that the demand sum of customers who are visited at a path must not exceed the vehicle capacity. The goal is to find a set of paths that minimizes the total traveled distance. A mathematical formulation and description of the problem elements corresponds to *m*-TSP is shown in Table 1.

The Equation (6) is the objective function of VRP. The Equation (7) and (8) indicate that at most *M* vehicles were used in the solution and that every vehicle that leaves the shipping center must return. Equations (9) and (10) state that customer must be visited exactly once. Capacity constraints are solved with the Equation (11). All restrictions are applied for each route.

Mathematical Model:

$$\min z = \sum_{i=1}^{n} \sum_{j=1}^{n} c_{ij} x_{ij} \qquad (6)$$

Subject to:

$$\sum_{j \in V} x_{0j} = M \qquad (7)$$

$$\sum_{i \in V} x_{i0} = M \qquad (8)$$

$$\sum_{j=1}^{n} x_{ij} = 1 \qquad j = 1, 2, ..., n \qquad (9)$$

$$\sum_{i=1}^{n} x_{ij} = 1; \qquad i = 1, 2, ..., n \qquad (10)$$

$$x_{ij} = \{0, 1\}$$

$$\sum_{i=1}^{n} \sum_{j=1}^{n} x_{ij} q_i \leq capacity \qquad (11)$$

VARIANTS OF VRP

The original VRP only includes the objective of minimizing the number of vehicles. But in real life there are many other restrictions for this problem caused by a lot of variations that include the original restriction plus some other feature added to the problem. This paper describes the most known variants of VRP, which are shown in Table 2 and Figure 3.

Recent works have approached real situations of transportation with a complexity of until five simultaneous variants of VRP in real applications (Pisinguer & Ropke, 2005; Reimann et al., 2003), and commercial applications have been developed involving until eight variants of VRP ("Vehicle routing software survey," 2006). However until now, it has not been created an efficient method of solution that approaches a considerable number of variants that are related to real-life situations. When VRP includes such variants is called *Rich VRP* that is more complex than classic VRP.

VEHICLE ROUTING PROBLEM WITH TIME WINDOWS

The description given in Courdeau (1999) is similar to the VRP. This variant is called VRPTW, and includes the time windows $[ot_i, ct_i]$ on clients (lapses of time within which caters for vehicles) and shipping center (global service time). If (i, j) is an edge of the solution, t_i and t_j is the time of arrival at customer i and j, the time windows implies that $t_i > ct_i$ and $t_j > ct_j$. On the other hand, if $t_i \leq ot_i$, then the vehicle must wait until the customer opens, then $t_{j=} ot_i + s_i + t_{ij}$.

The VRPTW is classified as multiobjetive problem. The solution technique applied to solve the problem is hierarchical, that means the objectives of the problem are: 1) Minimize the number of vehicles used and 2) Minimize the traveling and waiting times required to provide to all customers.

Table 2. The most known variants for VRP

Name of Variant	Objective	Constraints
Capacitated VRP **(CVRP)** (Blasum, 2002; Shaw, 1998; Ralphs, 2003)	Find a set of routes that minimizes the number of units used.	Capacity of the vehicles.
VRP with Time Windows **(VRPTW)** (Jong,1996; Gambardella, 1999; Shaw, 1998; Dorronsoro, 2005) VRP with Multiple Time Windows **(VRPMTW)** (Jin, 2004; Dorronsoro, 2005)	Find a set the vehicles that satisfy the restrictions in the following order: 1) minimize the number of vehicles used and 2) minimize the total travel time necessary to provide to all customers.	Independent service schedules in the facilities of the customers.
Multiple Depots VRP **(MDVRP)** (Jin, 2004; Mingozzi, 2003)	Minimize the fleet of used vehicles and the amount of travel time, fulfilling the demands of all customers for different shipping center.	Multiple depots to satisfy the demands.
Split Delivery VRP **(SDVRP)** (Archetti, 2001; Dorronsoro, 2005)	Verify if the size of customer orders is greater than or equal to the capacity of the vehicles.	Customers to be satisfied by different vehicles.
site dependent VRP **(sdVRP)** (Thangiah, 2003; Pisinger, 2005)	Verifies that customers can only receive vehicles to a specific size because of the capacity of their platform.	A set of available vehicles to satisfy the orders.
VRP with Multiple Use of Vehicles **(VRPM)** (Taillard, 1996; Dorronsoro, 2005; Fleichsmann, 1990)	Reduce the number of vehicles needed to satisfy the demands and minimizing total costs.	Multiple uses of the vehicles.
Heterogeneous Fleet VRP **(HVRP)** (Taillard, 1999; Gendreau, 1998)	Customers are served by vehicles with different properties, ranging in capacity and cost.	A heterogeneous fleets to deliver the orders.
VRP opened **(OVRP)** (Pisinger, 2005)	Allows the vehicle may or may not return to the depot after visiting customers in the route they are assigned.	Return or not return to the depot.
Customer Capacity VRP **(CCVRP)** (Rangel, 2005)	Both customers and depots may have a limited capacity to attend simultaneously to the supply vehicles.	Constrained capacities of the customers to dock and charge the vehicles.
Dynamic VRP **(DDVRP)** (Bianchi, 2000)	Solutions can't be created a priori, only to identify strategies to specify what actions should be performed based on system status.	The location of customer or demand made initial values can change over the course of a solution.
Road Depended VRP (rdVRP) (Dorronsoro, 2005)	Assign the trucks, but respecting the rules of the secretary of communications and transport, such as size, weight, dimensions, and schedules, among others.	Thresholds of transit of the trucks.

The variables x_{ijk} takes values of 0 or 1, if the edge (i,j) is traversed by the vehicle k. The variables y_{ik} indicate the arrival time at customer i when visited by the vehicle k. The objective function of Equation (12) is the total cost of the routes, the Equation (13) indicates that all customers must be visited; the Equations (14) and (15) determine that each vehicle travels a path from 0 to $n+1$. Equation (16) states that do not exceed the capacity of the vehicle. Let M is large enough, the Equation (17) ensures that if a vehicle k travels

from i to j cannot reach j before that $y_i + s_i + t_{ijk}$ acting as a constraint sub-tours disposal.

RICH VRP

The Rich VRP is defined in Toth and Vigo (2001) as an *Extended Vehicle Routing Problem*. This is an application of VRP for real transportation problems.

Mathematical Model:

Figure 3. The most known variants for VRP

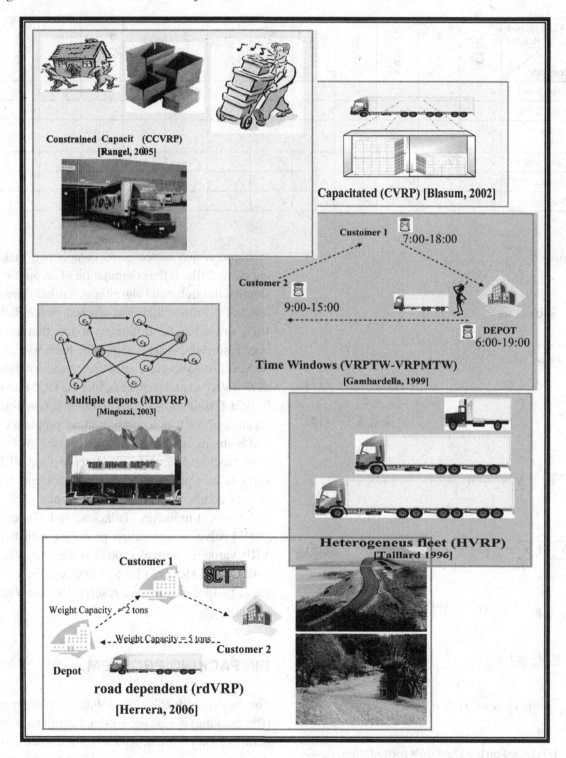

Table 3. State of the art research on rich VRP variants

Variants that Resolve / Research	CVRP	VRPTW	VRPMTW	OVRP	MDVRP	SDVRP	sdVRP	VRPM	HVRP	CCVRP	DVRP	rdVRP
[Goel, 2006]	✓	✓						✓	✓			
[Hasle, 2007]	✓	✓	✓						✓			
[Pisinger, 2005]	✓	✓		✓	✓			✓				
[Cano, 2005]	✓	✓				✓		✓	✓			
[Herrera, 2006]	✓	✓	✓		✓	✓	✓	✓	✓	✓	✓	✓
This work	✓	✓	✓	✓	✓	✓	✓	✓	✓	✓	✓	✓

$$\min z = \sum_{k \in K} \sum_{(i,j) \in E} c_{ijk} x_{ijk} \tag{12}$$

Subject to:

$$\sum_{k \in K} \sum_{j \in V} c_{ijk} x_{ijk} = 1 \qquad i \in C \cup D \tag{13}$$

$$\sum_{j \in C} x_{0jk} = 1 \qquad k \in K \tag{14}$$

$$\sum_{j \in C} x_{ijk} - \sum_{j \in C} x_{ijk} = 0 \qquad k \in K, i \in C \cup D \tag{15}$$

$$\sum_{i \in C \cup D} d_i \sum_{j \in C} x_{ijk} \leq q_k \qquad k \in K \tag{16}$$

$$y_{jk} - y_{ik} \geq s_i + t_{ijk} - M\left(1 - x_{ijk}\right) \tag{17}$$

$$e_i \leq y_{ik} \leq l_i \tag{18}$$

$$x_{ijk} = \left\{0,1\right\} \text{ and } y_{ik} \geq 0$$

It is based on the Dantzig's formulation; however, it requires the addition of restrictions that represent the combination of many variants in a problem; which increases its complexity, making more difficult the computation of an optimal solution through exact algorithms. Table 3 shows some of the researchers that worked on the Rich VRP, as well as the different variants that have been resolved. Figure 4 shows the Rich VRP.

Several works have approached the solution of rich VRP to real problems, like the DOMinant Project (Hasle et al., 2007), which solves four variants of VRP in a transportation problem of goods among industrial facilities located in Norway. Goel and Gruhn (2006) solve four VRP variants in a problem of sending packages for several companies. Pisinger and Ropke (2005) and Cano, Litvinchev, Palacios, and Naranjo (2005) solve transportation problems with five VRP variants. Rangel (2005) solves six VRP variants and Herrera (2006) solves eleven VRP variants. In this work, we resolved twelve VRP variants.

BIN PACKING PROBLEM

The problem of distribution of objects in containers (Bin-packing) is a classic NP-hard combinatorial optimization problem, which is a sequence of n items $L = \{a_1, a_2, ..., n\}$, each object has a given size $s(a_i)$ where $0 < s(a_i)$ whc, and an unlimited number of containers, each of capacity c. The

Figure 4. Universe of rich VRP

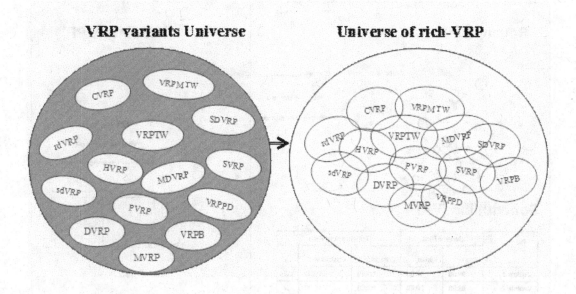

objective is to determine the minimum number of containers m in which all objects can be distributed. This problem is formulated below. Given: n = number of objects to be distributed, c = container capacity, L = sequence of n objects a_i, $s(a_i)$ = size of each object a_i. Find: A partition of L minimum, $L = B_1 \cup B_2 \cup ..., \cup B_m$. Such that each set B_j the sum of the size of each object $s(a_i)$ in B_j does not exceed c, Equation (19).

$$\sum_{a_i \epsilon B_j} s(a_i) \leq c \qquad \forall j,\ 1 \leq j \leq m. \qquad (19)$$

In the one-dimensional discrete version of BPP, the container capacity is an integer c, the number of objects is n, and for simplicity, the size of each object $s(a_i)$ is selected from the set $\{1,2, ...,c\}$ (Coffman, 2002).

THE ROUTING, SCHEDULING AND LOADING PROBLEM

RoSLoP, immersed in the logistic activity of distribution and delivery of products, is a highly complex combinatorial problem as a result of the different variables involved. Because of this, most of the planning and logistics groups focus on finding only a feasible solutions, neglecting the optimization process and the ability to evaluate various alternatives in a reasonable time with the many benefits of this type of approach (Rangel, 2005; Herrera, 2006).

The mathematical model of RoSLoP was formulated with two classical problems: routing and scheduling through VRP and the loading through the Bin Packing Problem (BPP). Figure 5 shows RoSLoP and its relation with BPP. The case of study contains the next elements:

- A set of *ORDERS* to be satisfied for the facilities of the customers, which are formed by boxes of products with different attributes.
- A set of n customers with independent service schedules and a finite capacity of attention of the vehicles.
- A set of depots with independent schedules of service and possibilities to request goods to other depots.

Figure 5. Definition of Routing-Scheduling-Loading Problem (RoSLoP)

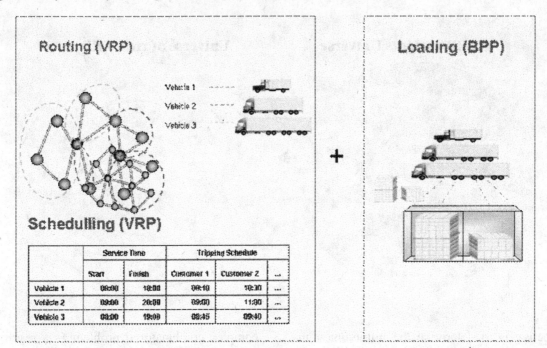

- A fleet of vehicles with heterogeneous capacity to transport goods, with a service time and a time for attention in the facilities of the customers. The attention time depends of the capacity of the vehicle, the available people to dock and the charge of vehicles.
- A set of roads or edges that connect the depots with the facilities of the customers. Each road has an assigned cost C_{ij}, each one with a threshold of supported weight for the vehicles that travel through the roads.

The objective is to get a configuration that allows satisfying the set of *ORDERS* in the set of facilities of the customers, minimizing the number of vehicles used and the travel distance. This scheme of solution includes a modeling of 12 variants of VRP: CVRP, VRPTW, VRP-MTW, MDVRP, SDVRP, sdVRP, VRPM, HVRP, CCVRP, DDVRP, rdVRP and OVRP.

HEURISTIC METHODS

A heuristic is a simple procedure, usually based on common sense that allows an insightful approach of a problem. An important kind of heuristics are the constructive algorithms, that are based on generating solutions from scratch by adding components to each solution step by step. A well-known example is the greedy heuristic, which has a great advantage: they are usually very fast and also often return reasonably good solutions. However, there is no guarantee that these solutions are optimal with respect to small local changes (Michalewicz & Fogel, 2004). Consequently, a typical improvement is to refine the solution obtained by the Greedy Heuristic using local search. Local search algorithms repeatedly try to improve the current solution with movements to neighbor solutions. The simplest case is the *iterative improvement algorithms*.

Unfortunately, the iterative improvement algorithms can get stuck in low-quality solutions. To allow further improvement in the quality of the solutions, the research in this field over the past two decades has focused on the design of general-purpose techniques to guide the construction of solutions using several local search heuristics. These techniques are commonly called metaheuristics and consist of general concepts used to define heuristic methods. In other words, a metaheuristic can be seen as a general framework referred to algorithms that can be applied to various combinatorial optimization problems, with few significant changes. In fact, the metaheuristics are widely recognized as one of the best approaches to address problems of combinatorial optimization (Gómez, 2010).

ANT COLONY SYSTEM

The Ant Colony Algorithm is inspired by the real behavior of ants, which often find the shortest route between the place where they live and their food sources, due to an indirect communication with other members of their colony. This communication is based on the modification of the local environment depositing a chemical substance called pheromone. In search of food, some species use this behavior called "leave-trail" and "follow-trail" to find the shortest route between their nest and the food source (Dorigo, 1997).

Artificial ant colonies are multi-agent systems in the sense that each ant-agent has incomplete information and capabilities for solving the problem because there is no global control system, data is decentralized and computation is asynchronous (Sycara, 1998). In addition, the ant colonies exhibit emergent behavior because they build their results incrementally. Therefore, the ant colonies are complex adaptive systems.

There are several algorithms that model and exploit the above behavior to solve NP-Hard combinatorial optimization problems based on graphs. These algorithms have been widely applied to the Traveling Salesman Problem (Lawler, 1985).

Table 4. ACS Algorithm

Initialize Parameters // Phase 1
For each iteration // Phase 2
For each Ant
Construct a solution with the ant k
Update LOCAL pheromone
Save best route
Update GLOBAL pheromone;// Phase 3
Put ants on the start city
Return best solution found // Phase 4

Ant Colony Optimization is a method based on ant behavior, and includes different types of Ant Systems (Dorigo, 2004). In this section we have chosen to describe the Ant Colony System algorithm (Dorigo, 1997), which is one of the ant algorithms with better performance and most referenced.

In general, the algorithm works as follow: on the first phase, parameters are initialized so they can regulate the behavior of the algorithm, on the second phase, feasible routes are constructed by applying a stochastic greedy rule (the state transition rule), while constructing the routes, ants modify the amount of pheromone on visited edges by applying the local updating rule. When all ants have finished building their tours the third phase starts, where all edges that belong to the best route are updated applying the global updating rule. The end of this iterative process is carried out in phase fourth, which returns the best solution found. Table 4 shows the general ACS algorithm.

Phase 1 is shown in Table 5, here are initialized: the pheromone table τ with τ_0, the value of the total number of cities n, the list of cities not visited by ant k (J_k in lines 01 and 02 of the Table 5) and the list of cities where each ant is positioned on r_k, this allocation may be random (lines 03-06 in Table 5).

Table 6 shows the last phase, where the stop condition is check and the best result is displayed (lines 01 and 02, Table 6). In the case where the

Table 5. Global update phase of the ACS Algorithm

01	**For** each ant
02	Compute the generated distance made by each ant in L_k
03	Compute the tour L_k with the les distance in L_{best}
04	**For** each edge (r,s)
05	$\tau(r_k,s_k) = (1-\alpha)\tau(r_k,s_k) + \alpha(L_{best})^{-1}$ // Update the edges

Table 6. Termination phase of the alg. ACS

01	**If** stopCondition is reached **then**
02	Display shortest route of L_k
03	**Else**
04	Go to Phase 2

stop condition is not reach, the algorithm continues on Phase 2 (lines 03 and 04, Table 6).

Within the algorithm a set of equations is used, through which guides the algorithm to estimate the best possible solution. These equations are analyzed.

RANDOM PROPORTIONAL RULE

The random proportional rule on Equation (20), defines the probability $p_k(r,s)$ which an ant k chooses to move to the city s from r. S is a random variable selected according to the probability p_k.

$$S = f(p_k(r,s)), \ p_k(r,s) =$$

$$\begin{cases} \dfrac{[\tau(r,s)] \cdot [\eta(r,s)]^\beta}{\sum\limits_{u \in J_k(r)} [\tau(r,u)] \cdot [\eta(r,u)]^\beta}, \ \text{si } s \in J_k(r) \\ 0, \hspace{3cm} \text{otherwise}, \end{cases}$$

$$(20)$$

where τ is the pheromone, $\eta = 1/\delta$ is the inverse of the distance from the city r to the city s, $J_k(r)$ is the set of cities visited by the ant k located in the city r, and β is a parameter that determines the relative importance between the pheromone and distance ($\beta > 0$). By increasing the value of β implies giving greater importance at shorter distances than the value stored in the pheromone $\tau(r,u)$. Small values imply greater importance to the pheromone.

STATE TRANSITION RULE

The state transition rule is used when an ant positioned on node r chooses the city s to move. This rule can be expressed as:

$$s = \begin{cases} \arg\max\limits_{u \in J_k(r)} \{[\tau(r,u)] \cdot [\eta(r,u)]^\beta\}, q \le q_0 \ (\text{exploitation}) \\ S, \ \text{otherwise} \hspace{1.5cm} (\text{partial exploration}), \end{cases}$$

$$(21)$$

where q is a random variable that represents a number uniformly distributed between [0,1], q_0 is a parameter (0 le $_0$ is a para$S$ is a random variable selected according to Equation (20). This rule favors transitions toward nodes connected by short edges with large amounts of pheromone. The q_0 parameter determines the relative importance between exploitation and exploration.

GLOBAL UPDATE RULE

The global update rule is performed after all ants have built their tours, only the global best ant (the ant that built the shortest path from the beginning of the process) is the one that its pheromone is deposited. This choice together with the use of Equation (21) is done with the intention to make a guided search. The pheromone level is updated by the following rule:

$$\tau(r,s) \leftarrow (1-\alpha) \cdot \tau(r,s) + \alpha \cdot \Delta\tau(r,s), \hspace{1cm} (22)$$

Where

$$\Delta\tau(r, s) = \begin{cases} (L_{gb})^{-1}, & \text{if } (r, s) \in \text{ best global route} \\ 0, & \text{otherwise.} \end{cases}$$

(23)

Also α ($0 < \alpha < 1$) is the parameter of global evaporation of the pheromone, and LGB is the best overall route length from the beginning of the process. This update is intended to provide a large amount of pheromone to shorter tours. This equation dictates that only those, which edges belong to the best overall route are rewarded.

LOCAL UPDATE RULE

The local update rule is used by the ants for changing the pheromone level applying the Equation 24, where $0 < \rho < 1$ is a parameter that defines the local evaporation rate of pheromone and $\Delta\tau (r, s) = \tau_0$.

$$\tau(r, s) \leftarrow (1 - \rho) \cdot \tau(r, s) + \rho \cdot \Delta\tau(r, s)$$

(24)

ELECTION OF THE ALGORITHM FOR ALLOCATION OF ROUTES AND SCHEDULES

For the choice of the algorithm, four metaheuristic algorithms were evaluated: Greedy, Randomized and Adaptive Search procedure (GRASP), Simulated Annealing (SA), a Genetic Algorithm (GA) and a System Ant Colony (ACS) applied to the VRPTW, VRP variant studied in the scientific field and one that involves greater complexity. From the results obtained from this experiment, the dominant metaheuristic was chosen.

EXPERIMENT CONDITION

The performance of the four algorithms developed was verified with a set widely used to validate models VRPTW, the Solomon's benchmark, consisting of 56 instances of different types (R1, R2, C1, C2, RC1, RC2) with 100 nodes each. The algorithms were coded in Visual C # and tested on a computer with Xeon Processor speed 3.06 GHz, 3.87 GB of RAM, under Windows Server 2003 and carried 30 times for each instance. Figure 6 and 7 describe performance in terms of minimization of vehicle and distance respectively of GRASP, Simulated Annealing, Genetic Algorithm and ACS with each of the six types of instance of Solomon. Table 7 outlines the mean, standard deviation (in terms of optimization of vehicle and distance) and average runtime of each implemented metaheuristic (Duarte et al., 2007).

Tables 8 and 9 compare the number of vehicles and distance traveled of the four metaheuristics implemented respectively, each table provides columns for both the average for each type of instance, and the accumulated count of the total set of instances. The results of both tables are sorted by the accumulated account.

Based on the experiment and its results we conclude that the algorithm more efficient, in terms of minimization of vehicles found, is ACS contrast with GRASP, SA and GA implemented, since ACS reaches the best solution in most managed cases, and the rest ACS was among the best algorithms (Figure 6 and Table 8). The results showed no metaheuristic as relevant in optimizing the distance (Figure 7 and Table 9), therefore ACS had the best performance considering both objectives. In addition, ACS variability is insignificant.

RoSLoP COMPLEXITY

In combinatorial problems the traditional method to find an optimal solution is to perform a comprehensive search of all possible solutions, in other words, generate all feasible configurations, calculate the cost and choose the one that offers better results. This methodology is not efficient due to the exponential growth of computing time depending on several factors including the com-

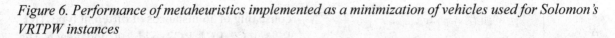

Figure 6. Performance of metaheuristics implemented as a minimization of vehicles used for Solomon's VRTPW instances

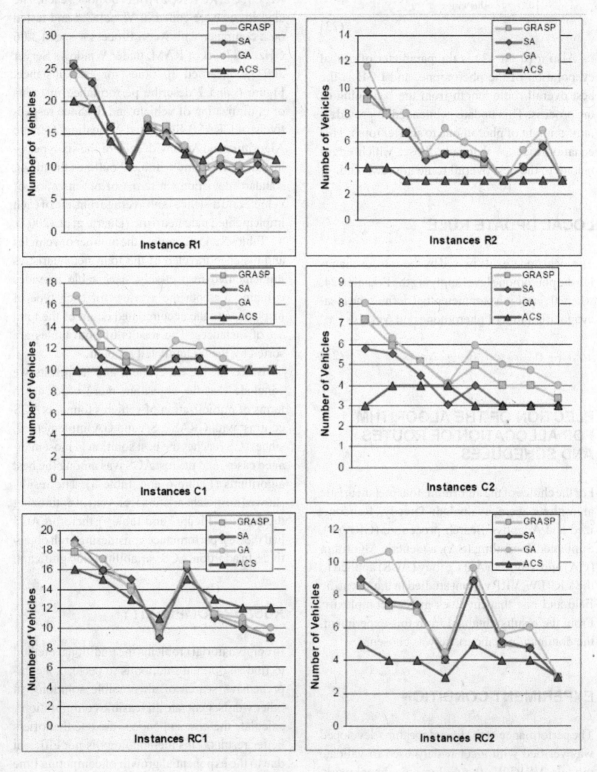

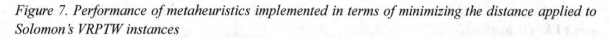

Figure 7. Performance of metaheuristics implemented in terms of minimizing the distance applied to Solomon's VRPTW instances

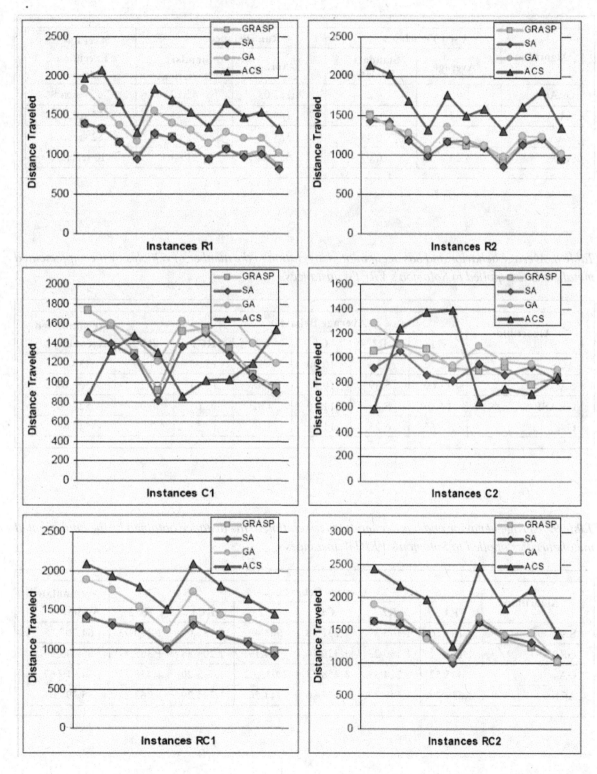

Table 7. Mean, standard deviation and average runtime implemented metaheuristics applied to Solomon's VRPTW instances

Algorithm	Used Vehicles		Run Distance		Average Execution Time
	Average	Standart Deviation	Average	Standart Deviation	
GRASP	9.30	0.28	1,183.03	45.12	17.67 seconds
SA	9.04	0.24	1,155.50	36.49	30.75 seconds
GA	9.78	0.45	1,337.85	48.42	55.82 seconds
ACS	8.14	0.04	1,532.04	21.04	5.10 seconds

Table 8. Average behavior and has accumulated in relation to the number of vehicles by the implemented metaheuristics applied to Solomon's VRPTW instances

Algorithm	Average Behavior						Accumulated Account
	R1	R2	C1	C2	RC1	RC2	
ACS	13.75	3.18	10.00	3.38	13.38	4.00	456.00
SA	13.60	5.39	10.78	3.98	13.11	6.22	506.07
GRASP	14.19	5.33	11.15	4.82	13.07	6.06	521.80
GA	13.65	6.25	11.91	5.40	13.53	7.07	548.60

Table 9. Average behavior and has accumulated in relation to the distance obtained by the implemented metaheuristics applied to Solomon's VRPTW instances

Algorithm	Average Behavior						Accumulated Account
	R1	R2	C1	C2	RC1	RC2	
SA	1,104.16	1,145.37	1,231.88	903.49	1,187.07	1,380.93	64,707.78
GRASP	1,113.71	1,150.23	1,329.71	954.19	1,209.38	1,369.57	66,249.59
GA	1,345.52	1,214.33	1,468.53	1,033.02	1,533.20	1,458.67	74,919.67
ACS	1,619.79	1,648.20	1,177.96	944.56	1,795.29	1,963.24	85,794.01

plexity of the instance of the problem. In 1971 Stephen Cook proposed the basis for what today is known as NP-completeness theory. This conjecture classifies the problems into two classes:

- *Class P*, those for which there are solver algorithms of polynomial time, considering solutions efficiently.
- *Class NP*, those for which there aren't known solver algorithms of polynomial time, considering solutions efficiently.

Stephen Cook proved that there are NP decision problems, which are extremely complicated, called NP-complete. The optimization version of these, because they involve a greater level of difficulty, is named NP-Hard.

COMPLEXITY OF ROUTE ALLOCATION

The task of routing is formed by a Rich VRP, which as explained is a collection of diverse variants of VRP. The classical VRP by definition itself is a NP-Hard optimization problem; this means that the computational effort required for solving it increases exponentially with the input. The VRP difficulty is at the conjunction of two problems:

- VRP is simplified with finding Hamiltonian circuit, which is the definition of TSP where the vehicle's capacity is infinite. On the other hand, if the vehicle capacity is finite, so it is impossible to satisfy all customers in one route, the VRP can be represented as a multiple TSP (m-TSP), an m-TSP instance can be transformed into an equivalent TSP added to the graph k-1 additional copies of the shipping center node and its branches incident (there are no arcs between the k-1 nodes and the shipping center).

- The BPP still described, can be viewed as a VRP, assuming that each path is analogous to a container and each customer order to an object whose weight is the cost of travel to satisfy the demand for it.

From the above we can infer that a feasible solution to the VRP is a TSP path (in an expanded graph) that satisfies the constraints of BPP. VRP can be defined as an intersection between TSP and BPP. Since TSP and BPP are NP-hard (Garey, 1979), it follows that VRP (being even more complex) also belongs to the class NP-hard. If the classical VRP is NP-Hard, it induces that any variant of the VRP is too, well have a Rich VRP complex composed of different versions of the VRP. Therefore, it is conjectured that the task of routing to be defined as a Rich VRP belongs to the class NP-hard.

COMPLEXITY ALLOCATION SCHEDULE

The scheduling task is also a NP-Hard problem because it lays on VRPMTW and VRPTW (Marinakis, 2002). The scheduling is initially solved with the routing problem; however, the solution is obtained by a standard schedule that must be transformed to real time managed by the company, for each client assigned to vehicles available. The generation of the actual times in this work is done in an algorithm process with complexity $O(nm)$, where m is the number of vehicles available to satisfy the demands and n is the number of customers with a demand to satisfy.

COMPLEXITY IN THE ALLOCATION OF LOADS

The load allocation work, where customers order is distributed in the containers from vehicles, is related to the BPP.

Figure 8. Diagram of solution: Heuristic-based methodology for solving problems of allocation comprehensive tour times & loads in distribution process and product delivery

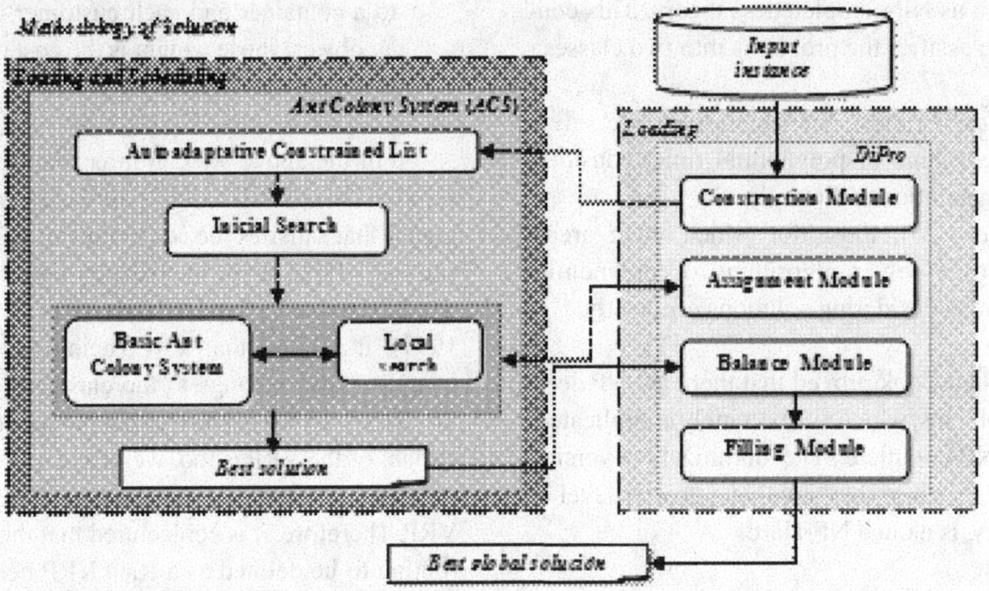

This Problem NP-Hard (Martello, 1990), and the Problem of Planning Process. The distribution of the load also falls within this class, increasing the difficulty of RoSLoP.

HBS-RoSLoPII COMPLEXITY

Because the routing tasks, schedules and load that compose RoSLoP are defined as NP-Hard problems, it is concluded, by simple deduction, that RoSLoP is still more complex.

SOLUTION METHODOLOGY

The designed solution scheme consists of two stages strongly connected and highly cohesive, offering this level of abstraction with a high degree of flexibility and modularity.

The **first stage:** Routing and scheduling, defines the routes to make for each vehicle dealers and their schedules. The engine of this phase is

non-deterministic heuristic ACS, whose solution space is defined by the multiple variants VRP.

The **second step**: Assigning loads, allocates and distributes various products to be transported in each vehicle based on the clients to be visited on the same route, the algorithm that carries out this process is a deterministic heuristic called Dipro.

Figure 8 and 9, shows the proposal and its elements. The ACS stage of routing and scheduling is made up of a core and other three items that extend the capabilities of the algorithm: a shortlist of self-learning, an initial search and local search. For its part, the Dipro algorithm is constituted by three basic modules and one elective that involved at different times: construction module, assignment module, balance module and filling module.

SOLUTION ALGORITHM

In this section, we start describing the changes in the ACS basic scheme for improvements (computation of heuristic information, self-adaptive

Figure 9. Relationship of the problems involved in RoSLoP

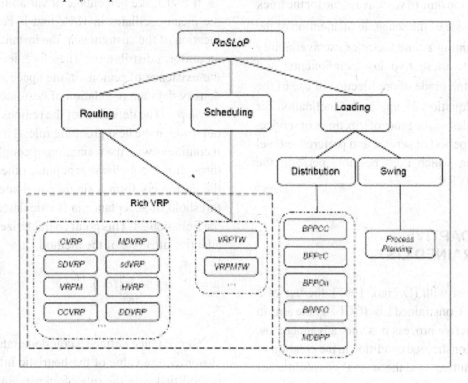

constrained list, initial search and local search). After that, the proposed algorithm is presented.

COMPUTATION OF THE HEURISTIC INFORMATION

The heuristic information is used by the ACS to choose the next node to visit, however, due the existence of the variant HVRP, it is necessary to choose the following more appropriate vehicle to be used. The Equation 25 defines the compute of the heuristic information used in the election of the clients.

$$\eta_{rs} = \left(\Delta t_{rs} \cdot (ws_s + st_s) \cdot tc_{rs} \right)^{-1} \qquad (25)$$

The factor Δt_{rs} is the difference between the current time and the arrival time to node s, ws_s represents the remaining size of the time window

in s, st_s is the time of service in s, and tc_{rs} is the trip cost from node r to node s, solving the variants VRPTW and VRPMTW. This calculation gives preference to those clients where the needed time to arrive to the facilities is smaller. Equation 26 defines the calculus of the heuristic information implied into the selection of the vehicles:

$$\eta_v = \left(nv_v \cdot (\overline{TM_v} + \overline{TR_v}) \cdot \frac{\overline{tr}}{tt_v} \cdot idpref_v \right)^{-1} \qquad (26)$$

Where η_v is the value of the heuristic information for the mobile unit v, nv_v is a bound of the quantity of travels required of the vehicle v to satisfy all the demands of $N_k(r)$. This expression satisfies the variants CVRP, MVRP and rdVRP; $\overline{TM_v}$ is the average of the service time in $N_k(r)$, $\overline{TR_v}$ is the time trip average of the vehicle to

$N_k(r)$, tr_v the time of work available for the truck v, tt_v the size of the schedule of attention of the truck, obtaining a time factor of use/availability by compute these two last components; and $idpref_v$ is the grade of predilection of use of the truck v. Equation 25 implies an inclination for those vehicles whose times of trip, times of service, remaining period of service and preference level are smaller, which does possible perform the variant SDVRP.

SELF-ADAPTIVE CONSTRAINED LIST

In agreement with (Dorigo, 1997), the use of a Candidates Constrained List (CCL) by the ants in the constructive process it is very advantageous, due to the constrained condition in the creation of feasible solutions and the several possibilities of the distribution of the customers and the depots, using CCL can perform the variant DDVRP. The goal of the CCL is to limit the global population into subsets that fulfill certain approaches. The creation of CCL is done in five steps shown next:

Step 1. A Minimum Spanning Tree (MST) is generated including all the customers and the depot of the instance.

Step 2. The mean μ and standard deviation σ are obtained, the minimum and maximum costs associated to the roads included in the MST.

Step 3. The percentage of visibility θ of the associated costs to each road belonging to the MST is computed through the Equation 27.

$$\theta = \frac{\sigma}{2\left(\arg\max\left\{tc_{rs}\right\} - \arg\min\left\{tc_{rs}\right\}\right)}$$

$$(r,s) \in MST$$

$$(27)$$

If $\theta < 0.1$, the percentage of variability around the mean oscillates in 10%, that is because the location of the customers in the instance follows an uniform distribution. Therefore, it is possible the existence of regions in the space with more density than the population of customers.

Step 4. The definition of the regions is carried out through the next grouping rule: if $\theta < 0.1$, then it continues with the formation of conglomerates through a hierarchical grouping, otherwise, all the customers form a single conglomerate. The threshold of acceptance ω is calculated through the Equation 28. This point characterizes the self-adaptive attribute of the method.

$$\omega = 2 \cdot \arg\max_{arc_{rs} \in MST}\left\{tc_{rs}\right\}$$

$$(28)$$

Step 5. Once defined a conglomerate for each customer, the value of the heuristic information is modified with the rule of ownership, only for each customer's c_r and c_s, which belong to different groups: h_i and h_j respect.

If $h_i \neq h_j \mid c_r \in h_i \wedge c_s \in h_j$ **then**

$$\eta_{rs} = \eta_{rs} \cdot \frac{|H|}{|C|}$$

$$(29)$$

$$c_r, c_s \in C; h_i, h_j \in H$$

The Equation 29 allows inhibiting in proportional form the preference of a client with regard to others with base in the ownership to the different conglomerates and their number. The iteration obtains the solution of each sub-set of facilities of the customers to be satisfied for each depot, satisfying the variant MDVRP, this solution is optimized through the initial and local search procedures.

INITIAL SEARCH

Because the exploitative focus is extremely similar to a greedy search, the possibility to use it like an initial search redounds in solutions of good quality over other methods with simpler guideline, like the heuristic of the nearest neighbor. The Equation 30 defines the preference guide in the initial search of the solution method.

$$\eta_{rs} = \left(\Delta t_{rs} \cdot ws_s + st_s\right)^{-1} \quad (30)$$

LOCAL SEARCH

For the incorporation of the Local Search to the ACS, schemes of exchange of axes were chosen: 3-opt (Bock, 1958) and Cross-Exchange (Tallard, 1997), operating respectively on one and two routes, both including implicitly other simpler operators. The first one contains by definition the 2-opt (Croes, 1958), and the second one allows the use of empty segments using movements type 2-opt * (Potvin, 1995), relocation, and exchange (Prosser, 1996), making it extremely versatile.

ANT COLONY SYSTEM FOR ALLOCATION OF ROUTES, SCHEDULES AND LOADS

The ACS routing stage is shown in Figure 10. This algorithm starts in line 4 and ends when the time set as a criterion of failure has expired (line 28). The first line builds the list of candidates based on self-adaptive hierarchical clustering. Then the algorithm create a feasible initial solution using the initial search, this solution is taken as the global best (ψ^{gb}). Line 3 calculates the value of choice of the solution (objective function) when evaluated by adding the number of vehicles used and normalized distance, it aims to minimize that value.

Figure 10. ACS-ROSLOPII algorithm

```
Algorithm Ant Colony System (β, ρ, q0)
1   H ← lcc()
2   ψ^gb ← initialsearch()
3   χ^gb ← #activevehicles(ψ^gb) + (1 − J_ψgb^-1)
4   repeat
5      repeat
6         ψ^ib ← initialsolution
7         χ^ib ← #activevehicles(ψ^ib) + (1 − J_ψib^-1)
8         ∀j : IN_j ← 0
9         for each ant k ∈ K
10  ψ^k ← newsolution(k, #activevehicles(ψ^ib) − 1, IN, H)
11           ∀s ∈ ψ^k : IN_s ← IN_s + 1
12           χ^k ← #activevehicles(ψ^k) + (1 − J_ψk^-1)
13           Local search (ψ^k, 3-opt)
14           Local search (ψ^k, Cross-Exchange)
15           if χ^k < χ^ib then
16              ψ^ib ← ψ^k
17              end repeat
18           end if
19           ∀v ∈ ψ^ib : τ_v ← (1 − ρ)·τ_v + ρ/J_ψib
20           ∀r,s ∈ ψ^ib : τ_rs ← (1 − ρ)·τ_rs + ρ/J_ψib
21        end for each
22        ∀v ∈ ψ^gb : τ_v ← (1 − ρ)·τ_v + ρ/J_ψgb
23        ∀r,s ∈ ψ^gb : τ_rs ← (1 − ρ)·τ_rs + ρ/J_ψgb
24     until
25     if ψ^ib is feasible ∧ χ^ib < χ^gb then
26        ψ^gb ← ψ^ib
27        χ^gb ← #activevehicles(ψ^gb) + (J_ψgb)^-1
       end if
28  until
```

The section between lines 5 and 24 carried out the minimization process of the fitness of the solution, creating a colony of ants for each iteration. In this process seeks to improve the global solution, building a set of ants per colony, and updating (locally and globally) the customer pheromone and vehicles, (lines 19-23). When a local solution has been enhanced line 15, the current settlement is completed line 17, the local solution is compared with the best global solution line 25 and makes the necessary updates, lines 26 and 27 to continue execution algorithm. The stop condition of lines 24 and 28 are set based on the number of iterations and execution time respectively.

Figure 11. Region connection graph representing the company with in the case study

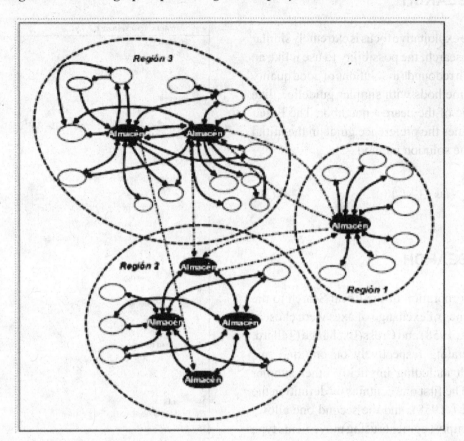

EXPERIMENTATION AND RESULT

To validate the methodology based on heuristics for the solution of problems of allocation of routes, timetables and loads developed from HBS-RoSLoPII, theoretical instances drawn from specialized scientific communities in the area and real instances provided by the company's case study were used.

TEST INSTANCES

ACS-ROSLOPII algorithm was tested with real instances of a case study obtained from a company. The company has three types of regions where each region represents a range consists of a set of clients associated with one or more stores.

Due to the task of implementation of the HBS-RoSLoPII is complex, the company decided to install separately the system on a representative region of each type and then integrate the three regions into one to share resources between them. The graph that connects these regions is shown in Figure 11.

All instances of the same class have the same customer coordinates and vehicle capabilities, but the time window restrictions are different (25%, 50%, 75% density window time). For classes R1, C1 and RC1, the time windows are tight and have a limited capacity in the vehicle (200 units), allowing short courses. Classes R2, C2 and RC2 have broader time windows and a wider transport capacity (100 to 1000 units), which allows services to a greater number of clients (long distances).

Figure 12. Distribution of customer in the geographic area for the instances of Solomon (1987)

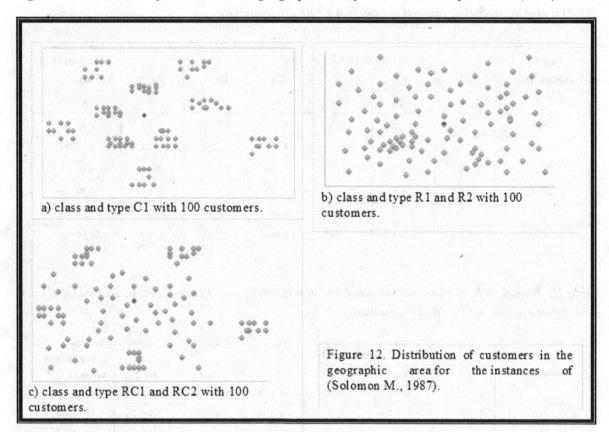

a) class and type C1 with 100 customers.

b) class and type R1 and R2 with 100 customers.

c) class and type RC1 and RC2 with 100 customers.

Figure 12. Distribution of customers in the geographic area for the instances of (Solomon M., 1987).

Finally, travel times and distances are given by the Euclidian distances between the locations of the customers (Solomon, 1987). For the problems posed by Herrera (2006), data sets are similar. It consists of 300 instances divided into 5 groups (G02, G04, G06, G08). Each group has the same structure as the instances of Solomon (1987) described above. However, each group has a higher cardinality and bigger size of customers to serve (200, 400, 600, 800 and 1000 clients).

THEORETICAL EXPERIMENTATION

According to Bräysy (2001) the variant of VRP most studied and with most complex, is the VRPTW, therefore it is used to demonstrate the effectiveness of ACS on the stage of allocation of routes and schedules (called ACS-ROSLOPII). This performance is measured on a test set widely used to validate VRPTW models, Solomon, formed by 56 instances of six different types (C1, C2, R1, R2, RC1, RC2) with 100 nodes each (Solomon, 1987). The features of each instance kind are shown in Figure 12.

The experiments used the following parameter values ACS-ROSLOPII: q_0=0.7, β =11, ρ = 1.0; 15 generations of ants per colony, 10 ants per generation. The algorithm was coded in C # and tested on a computer with Xeon Processor speed 3.06 GHz, 3.87 GB of RAM, under Windows Server 2003 platform.

Tables 10 and 11 detail the behavior of the ACS-ROSLOPII over time, comparing the solution quality against computational effort required, providing a column for each type of analysis,

Table 10. Average behavior and has accumulated in relation to the number of vehicles from the ACS-ROSLOPII-ARH over time applied to Solomon's VRPTW instances

Time (seconds)	Average Behavior						Accumulated Account
	R1	R2	C1	C2	RC1	RC2	
25	13.16	3.14	10.00	3.05	12.90	3.45	437.80
50	13.06	3.10	10.00	3.01	12.80	3.43	435.06
100	12.99	3.09	10.00	3.00	12.68	3.41	434.07
200	12.92	3.08	10.00	3.00	12.57	3.37	430.66
400	12.87	3.08	10.00	3.00	12.45	3.37	429.10
800	12.79	3.05	10.00	3.00	12.37	3.37	427.13
1600	12.73	3.03	10.00	3.00	12.31	3.37	425.70

Table 11. Average behavior and has accumulated in relation to travel time of the ACS-ROSLOPII over time applied to Solomon's VRPTW instances

Time (Seconds)	Average Behavior						Accumulated Account
	R1	R2	C1	C2	RC1	RC2	
25	1,267.76	1,017.67	833.00	613.25	1,431.17	1,218.24	60,006.01
50	1,267.42	1,009.78	832.50	610.34	1,429.01	1,208.78	59,794.43
100	1,265.30	1,001.25	831.92	606.29	1,430.52	1,198.56	59,586.74
200	1,261.65	997.11	831.15	604.01	1,430.46	1,191.35	59,395.22
400	1,259.40	989.96	830.76	601.66	1,431.34	1,182.41	59,202.76
800	1,258.77	987.07	830.17	599.94	1,432.88	1,171.55	59,069.77
1600	1,258.76	984.53	829.70	599.33	1,432.97	1,166.74	58,993.40

Table 12. Mean standard deviation and coefficient of variation in relation to the number of Vehicles and travel time of ACS-ROSLOPII over time applied to Solomon's VRPTW instances

Time (seconds)	Vehicle Quantity			Travel Time		
	Average	Standard Deviation	Coefficient of Variation	Average	Standard Deviation	Coefficient of Variation
25	7.81	0.11	0.70%	1.071.53	18.40	0.85%
50	7.76	0.10	0.64%	1.067.75	17.14	0.80%
100	7.45	0.09	0.60%	1.065.34	16.36	0.76%
200	7.69	0.08	0.52%	1.060.62	15.34	0.72%
400	7.66	0.06	0.39%	1.057.19	13.42	0.63%
800	7.62	0.07	0.45%	1.054.81	14.46	0.68%
1600	7.60	0.05	0.32%	1.053.45	14.71	0.69%

Table 13. Average travel time in the solutions obtained by the ACS-ROSLOPII and the ten best known methods for VRPTW

Algorithm	Average Behavior						Accunt Accumulate
	R1	R2	C1	C2	RC1	RC2	
[Rochat, 1995]	1208.50	961.72	828.38	589.86	1377.39	1119.59	57,231
[Psinger, 2005]	1212.39	957.72	828.38	589.86	1385.78	1123.49	57,332
[Bent, 2001]	1211.09	954.27	838.38	589.86	1384.16	1124.46	57,364
ACS-RoSLoPII	1221.85	954.62	828.66	594.12	1383.40	1128.77	57,471
[Taillard, 1997]	1209.35	980.27	828.38	589.86	1389.22	1117.44	57,523
[Gambardella, 1999]	1217.73	967.75	828.40	589.86	1382.42	1129.19	57,525
[Cordeau, 2001]	1210.14	969.57	828.38	589.86	1389.78	1134.52	57,556
[Bräysy, 2001]	1222.00	975.12	828.40	589.86	1390.00	1128.38	57,710
[Homberger, 1999]	1228.06	969.95	828.38	589.86	1392.57	1144.43	57,876
[Berger, 2001]	1251.40	1056.59	828.50	590.06	1414.86	1258.15	57,925
[Rousseau, 2000]	1210.21	941.08	828.38	589.86	1382.78	1105.22	56,953

and other column for the accumulated score. The results outlined in these tables were calculated on the average of 30 runs of the algorithm on each instance. To complement the above information, Table 12 lists the average statistical results and their variability over time.

Tables 12 shows a comparison of ACS-RO-SLOPII against the ten best methods known so far to VRPTW, which provides a column for the average travel time as appropriate for each type of analysis, the final column in each table shows the accumulated count of the total set of instances.

The Table 13 shows the performance of the most prominent algorithms in the literature.

The methods considered are: a Hybrid Local Search (Bent, 2001), a Hybrid and Parallel Genetic (Berger, 2001), a deterministic heuristic Variable Neighborhood Search (Bräysy, 2001), a Unified Tabu Search (Cordeau, 2001), a system of Multiobjective Ant Colony (Gambardella, 1999), a Genetic Algorithm (Homberger, 1999), a Variable Neighborhood Search (Psinger, 2005), a Tabu Search (Rochat, 1995), a Hybrid Heuristic

(Rousseau, 2000), and Tabu Search (Taillard, 1997). The results of both tables are sorted by the value of your accumulated score.

EXPERIMENTING WITH REAL CASES

As a final validation, the HBS-RoSLoPII was tested with real instances of a case study, subject to this investigation. The company has three types of regions, where each region represents a range consists of a set of clients associated with one or more stores.

HBS-RoSLoPII is currently installed only in region 1. For this reason, there is still no reliable actual data for the operation of the other regions as well as the results of the transportation is done by hand in them. The test cases used to evaluate the HBS-RoSLoPII are from the Region 1 of the company.

Figure 11 shows the connection graph of Region 1. As shown, the Region 1 shows the simplest connection graph and containing seven

Table 14. Comparison of performance of the procedure manual HBS-RoSLoPII and TSHA

Instances	Efficiency Indicators								
	Used Vehicles			Travel Time (minutes)			Run Time (minutes)		
	By Hand	TSHA	HBS-RoSLoPII	By Hand	TSHA	HBS-RoSLoPII	By Hand	TSHA	HBS-RoSLoPII
Case 1	7	7	6	-	3390	2740	180	10	2
Case 2	6	5	5	-	2450	2320	180	10	2
Case 3	6	6	6	-	2780	2680	180	10	2
Case 4	5	5	5	-	2720	2720	180	10	2
Case 5	7	7	6	-	3300	2850	180	10	2

star binding clients and only one available store. However, this level of abstraction does not diminish its complexity, due to the involvement of all the restrictions. Therefore, variants of the VRP and the BPP, it is considered a test case of Region 1 as sufficient to determine the efficiency of HBS-RoSLoPII in complex real world.

Experimental Environment

1. The input to the system configuration is read from a database or a file with defined format, and the output is written to a database.
2. The algorithm execution time should not exceed 10 minutes on a personal computer with Pentium 4 processor and 256 Mb RAM.
3. The programming language is Visual C #. NET.
4. The software is embedded in a warehouse and logistics system as an independent library.

Because of the large amount of information in a real instance we designed a standard input file for specifying all the data. For a more extensive explanation of the case study and the structure of the database, see Rangel (2005).

The HBS-RoSLoPII was tested with five company case studies, comparing against the manual solution and the Transport System based on Heuristic (TSHA) developed in Rangel (2005). Table 13 shows the performance comparison among procedures.

For the five cases shown in Table 14, the three methods satisfy 100% of demand. There was a reduction in the number of vehicles of 9.6% compared to the manual solution and 6.6% compared to TSHA. In relation to travel time, there is no record of the manual operation, so it can only be compared against TSHA, resulting in a 9.1% to minimize the travel times computed. The execution time results in a reduction of 94.4% over the manual process. Finally, it is important to note that as further proof *HBS*-RoSLoPII was executed just 2 minutes away, offering the same quality in their solutions, under this scheme offers an 80% savings in execution time on TSHA and 98.8% on the manual process.

As further proof is necessary to check that TSHA has a behavior similar to HBS-RoSLoPII by limiting the run time.

FUTURE RESEARCH DIRECTIONS

To give continuity to this research, from acquired experience the following areas of opportunity:

- Expand the description of real situations and cargo routing through the use of variants of the companies studied that were not considered in this study, and validate other real applications of RoSLoP.
- Develop methods for solving the test cases presented in the scientific community (a part of VRPTW) to compare the performance of the developed methodology to that reported in other studies.
- Improve the local search process by searching some environment in order to provide greater versatility and variability of solutions.
- Modify the ACS-ROSLOPII with a parallel approach to the construction of solutions by ants, thus increasing the diversity offered by the method.
- Incorporate of a greater number of restrictions, so that the mathematical model can be used in more real problems.
- A detailed study for the generation of a system that is able to obtain a local configuration at runtime, adapting to the changing environment of RoSLoP.

CONCLUSION

In this chapter we describe the different concepts related with VRP and the RoSLoP. In the first sections, we explain how a heuristic algorithm to solve RoSLoP was selected, as well as the design of the solution methodology and the characteristics of real and artificial instances. In addition to algorithm design, ACS-RoSLoPII, we describe the strategies used to modify the ACS algorithm in order to adapt it to solve the RoSLoP. After that, we describe the experiments that validate the results of the algorithm ACS-RoSLoPII. The last section presents the conclusions obtained after having carried out the research and experiments, as well as the future work that could be developed to improve the results of solving the RoSLoP.

This chapter describes the elements related to the feasibility of solving the problem of assigning routes, timetables and Load (RoSLoP) immersed in the process of distribution and delivery of products in a complex real world, this through a solution methodology based on a heuristic optimization approach.

Specifically it considered a specific highly complex RoSLoP case, because of the large number of elements and constraint attached, as the wide range of products being handled. The solution method is basically formed by two stages which are treated each for a specialized algorithm: the allocation of routes and schedules that uses an Ant Colony System (ACS), and the allocation of loads using an ad-hoc, deterministic and approximate algorithm. ACS-RoSLopII simultaneously solves the tasks of defining and assigning of routes, and scheduling of vehicles, treating them as a Vehicle Routing Problem (Rich VRP).

As a result of the proposed methodology was developed an automated tool based on heuristics for allocation of routes, schedule and Loads (ACS-RoSLoPII). Tests with this system demonstrate the feasibility and efficiency on both theoretical and actual instances. The latter belonging to an environment with a high level of complexity in their operations, because a vast number of variants and products in VRP was handle.

We design a framework of solution to real situations of the transportation problem; moreover we integrate the analysis of classical problems found in the scientific community. ACS-RoSLoPII algorithm builds routes and schedules using heuristic information of vehicles and customers with high quality of construction. The results show an average reduction of 9.6% for the number of vehicles used and 9.1% for travel time caused by mobile units.

ACKNOWLEDGMENT

This research was supported in part by CONACYT and DGEST.

REFERENCES

Archetti, C., Mansini, R., & Speranza, M. G. (2001). The vehicle routing problem with capacity 2 and 3, general distances and multiple customer visits. In *Proceedings of the Conference on Operational Research in Land and Resources Management* (p. 102).

Bianchi, L. (2000). *Notes in dynamic vehicle routing* (Tech. Rep. No. IDSIA-05-01). Ticino, Switzerland: Instituto Dalle Molle di Studi Sull'intelligenza Artificiale.

Bianchi, L., Birattari, M., Chiarandini, M., Manfrin, M., Mastrolilli, M., & Schiavinotto, T. (2006). Hybrid metaheuristics for the vehicle routing problem with stochastic demands. *Journal of Mathematical Modelling and Algorithms, 5,* 91–110. doi:10.1007/s10852-005-9033-y

Blasum, U., & Hochstätter, W. (2002). *Application of the branch and cut method to the vehicle routing problem (Tech. Rep.)*. Hagen, Germany: FernUniversität in Hagen.

Bock, W. (1958). An algorithm for solving traveling salesman and related network optimization problems. In *Proceedings of the Fourteenth National Meeting of the Operational Research Society of America*, St. Louis, MO.

Bräysy, O. (2001). *A reactive variable neighborhood search algorithm for the vehicle routing problem with Time Windows (Tech. Rep.)*. Oslo, Norway: SINTEF Applied Mathematics, Department of Optimization.

Cano, I., Litvinchev, I., Palacios, R., & Naranjo, G. (2005). Modeling vehicle routing in a star-case transportation network. In *Proceedings of the 16th Congreso Internacional de Computación* (pp. 373-377).

Coffman, J. E. G., Courboubetis, C., Garey, M. R., Johnson, D. S., Shor, P. W., & Weber, R. R. (2002). Perfect Packing: Theorems and the average case behavior of optimal and online bin packing. *Society for Industrial and Applied Mathematics Review, 44,* 95–108.

Cook, S. A. (1971). The complexity of theorem-proving procedures. In *Proceedings of the Third Annual ACM Symposium on Theory of Computing* (pp. 151-158). New York, NY: ACM Press.

Cordeau, F., Desaulniers, G., Desrosiers, J., Solomon, M., & Soumis, F. (1999). *The VRP with time windows* (Tech. Rep. No. GERAD G-99-13). Montreal, QC, Canada: Ecole des Hautes 'Etudes Commerciales de Montreal.

Cordeau, J., Desaulniers, G., Desrosiers, J., Solomon, M., & Soumis, F. (2002). The VRP with time windows . In Murphy, S. (Ed.), *Monographs on discrete mathematics and applications* (pp. 157–193). Philadelphia, PA: Society for Industrial and Applied Mathematic.

Croes, G. A. (1958). A method for solving traveling salesman problems. *Operations Research, 6*(6), 791–812. doi:10.1287/opre.6.6.791

Dantzig, G. B., & Ramser, R. H. (1959). The truck dispatching problem. *Management Science, 6,* 80–91. doi:10.1287/mnsc.6.1.80

Dorigo, M., & Gambardella, L. (1997). Ant colony system: A cooperative learning approach to the traveling salesman problem. *IEEE Transactions on Evolutionary Computation, 1*(1), 53–66. doi:10.1109/4235.585892

Dorigo, M., & Stützle, T. (2004). *Ant colony optimization*. Cambridge, MA: MIT Press.

Dorronsoro, B. (2005). *The VRP Web*. Retrieved from http://neo.lcc.uma.es/radiaeb/WebVRP/index.html

Duarte, A., Pantrigo, J. J., & Gallego, M. (2007). *Metaheurísticas*. Madrid, Spain: Dykinson.

Fleischmann, B. (1990). *The vehicle routing problem with multiple use of vehicles (Tech. Rep.)*. Hamburg, Germany: Fachbereigh Wirtschaftswissenschaften, University of Hamburg.

Gambardella, L., Taillar, E., & Agazzi, G. (1999). *MACS-VRPTW: A multiple ant colony system for vehicle routing problems with Time Windows* (Technical Report IDSIA-06-99). Ticino, Switzerland: IDSIA.

Gendreau, M., Laporte, G., Musaraganyi, C., & Taillard, E. (1999). A tabu search heuristic for the heterogeneous fleet vehicle routing problem. *PERGAMON Computer & Operations Research, 26,* 1153–1173. doi:10.1016/S0305-0548(98)00100-2

Goel, A., & Grum, V. (2005). Solving a dynamic real life vehicle routing problem. In Haasis, H.-D., Kopfer, H., & Schönberger, J. (Eds.), *Operations research proceedings* (pp. 367–372). New York, NY: Springer. doi:10.1007/3-540-32539-5_58

Gómez, C. G. (2010). *Afinación Estática Global de Redes Complejas y Control Dinámico Local de la Función Tiempo de Vida en el Problema de Direccionamiento de Consultas Semánticas* (Unpublished doctoral dissertation). Instituto Politécnico Nacional, CICATA, UA, México.

Hasle, G., Koster, O., Nilssen, E. J., Riise, A., & Flatberg, T. (2007). Dynamic and stochastic vehicle routing in practice . In Zeimpekis, V., Tarantilis, C. D., Giaglis, G. M., & Minis, I. (Eds.), *Dynamic Fleet Management, Operation Research/Computer Science Interfaces Series* (*Vol. 38*, pp. 45–68). New York, NY: Springer.

Herrera, J. A. (2006). *Desarrollo de una Metodología Basada en Heuristicas para la Solución Integral de Problemas de Asignación de Rutas, Horarios y Cargas en el Proceso de Distribución y Entrega de Productos* (Unpublished master's thesis). Posgrado en Ciencias de la Computación, Instituto Tecnológico de Ciudad Madero, México.

Jin, T., Guo, S., Wang, F., & Lim, A. (2004). One-stage search for multi-depot vehicle routing problem. In *Proceedings of the Conference on Intelligent Systems and Control* (pp. 446-129).

Johnson, D. S., & McGeoch, L. A. (1995). The traveling salesman problem: A case study in local optimization . In Aarts, E. H. L., & Lenstra, J. K. (Eds.), *Local search and combinatorial optimization*. New York, NY: John Wiley & Sons.

Jong, C., Kant, G., & Vliet, A. V. (1996). *On finding minimal route duration in the vehicle routing problem with multiple time windows (Tech. Rep.)*. Utrecht, The Netherlands: Department of Computer Science, Utrecht University.

Lawler, E. (1985). *Combinatorial optimization: Networks and matroids*. New York, NY: Dover.

Lenstra, J. K., & Rinnooy Kan, A. H. G. (1981). Complexity of vehicle routing and scheduling problems. *Networks, 11,* 221–227. doi:10.1002/net.3230110211

Marinakis, Y., & Migdalas, A. (2002). Heuristic solutions of vehicle routing problems in supply chain management . In Pardalos, P. M., & Migdalas, A. (Eds.), *Combinatorial and global optimization* (1st ed.). Singapore: World Scientific. doi:10.1142/9789812778215_0014

Martello, S., & Toth, P. (1990). *Knapsack problems-algorithms and computer implementations*. Chichester, UK: John Wiley & Sons.

Michalewicz, Z., & Fogel, D. B. (2204). *How to solve it: Modern heuristics* (2nd ed.). Berlin, Germany: Springer-Verlag.

Mingozzi, A., & Vallet, A. (2003). An exact algorithm for period and multi-depot vehicle routing problems. In *Proceedings of the 16th Symposium on Mathematical Programming*.

Ombuki, B. M., Runka, A., & Hanshar, F. T. (2007) Waste collection vehicle routing problem with time windows using multi-objetive genetic algorithms. In *Proceedings of the Third IASTED International Conference on Computational Intelligence* (pp. 91-97). New York, NY: ACM.

Pisinger, D., & Ropke, S. (2005). *A general heuristic for vehicle routing problems (Tech. Rep.)*. Copenhagen, Denmark: Department of Computer Science, University of Copenhagen.

Potvin, J. Y., & Rousseau, J. M. (1995). An exchange heuristic for routing problems with time windows. *The Journal of the Operational Research Society, 46*, 1433–1446.

Prosser, P., & Shaw, P. (1996). *Study of greedy search with multiple improvement heuristics for vehicle routing problems (Tech. Rep.)*. Glasgow, UK: University of Strathclyde.

Quiroz, M. (2009). *Caracterización de factores de desempeño de algoritmos de solución de BPP* (Unpublished master's thesis). Posgrado en Ciencias de la Computación, Instituto Tecnológico de Ciudad Madero, Tamaulipas, México.

Ralphs, T., Kopman, L., Pulleyblank, W., & Trotter, L. (2003). On the capacitated vehicle routing problem. *Mathematical Programming, Series B, 94*, 343–359. doi:10.1007/s10107-002-0323-0

Rangel, N. (2005). *Análisis de los Problemas de Asignación de Rutas, Horarios y Cargas en una Distribuidora de Productos* (Unpublished master's thesis). Posgrado en Ciencias de la Computación, Instituto Tecnológico de Ciudad Madero, Tamaulipas, México.

Reimann, M., Doerner, K., & Hartl, R. (2003). Analyzing a unified ant system for the VRP and some of its variants. In *Proceedings of the International Conference on Applications of Evolutionary Computing* (pp. 300-310).

Rizzoli, A. E., Oliverio, F., Montemanni, R., & Gambardella, L. M. (2004). *Ant colony optimisation for vehicle routing problems: from theory to applications*. Ticino, Switzerland: IDSIA.

Secomandi, N. (2000). Comparing neuro-dynamic programming algorithms for the vehicle routing problem with stochastic demands. *Computers & Operations Research, 27*, 1171–1200. doi:10.1016/S0305-0548(99)00146-X

Secomandi, N. (2001). A rollout policy for the vehicle routing problem with stochastic demands. *Operations Research, 49*, 796–802. doi:10.1287/opre.49.5.796.10608

Shaw, P. (1998). Using constraint programming and local search methods to solve vehicle routing problems. In M. Maher & J. F. Puget (Eds.), *Proceedings of the 4th International Conference on Principles and Practice of Constraint Programming* (LNCS 1520, pp. 417-431).

Solomon, M. (1987). Algorithms for the vehicle routing and scheduling problem with time window constraints. *Operations Research, 35*(2), 254–265. doi:10.1287/opre.35.2.254

Sycara, K. (1998). Multiagent systems. *AI Magazine, 19*(2), 79–92.

Taillard, E. (1999). A heuristic column generation method for the heterogeneous fleet VRP. *Operations Research, 33*(1), 1–14. doi:10.1051/ro:1999101

Taillard, E., Badeau, P., Gendreu, M., Guertin, F., & Potvin, J. Y. (1997). A tabu search heuristic for the vehicle routing problem with soft time windows. *Transportation Science, 31*, 170–186. doi:10.1287/trsc.31.2.170

Taillard, E., Laport, G., & Gendreau, M. (1996). Vehicle routing problem with multiple use of vehicles. *The Journal of the Operational Research Society, 47*, 1065–1070.

Thangiah, V. (2003). *A site dependent vehicle routing problem with complex road constraints*. Paper presented at the Colloquium at the Institute of Mathematics, University of Malaya, Kuala Lumpur, Malaysia.

Toth, P., & Vigo, D. (2000). An overview of vehicle routing problems . In Murphy, S. (Ed.), *Monographs on discrete mathematics and applications* (pp. 1–26). Philadelphia, PA: SIAM.

Toth, P., & Vigo, D. (2002). The vehicle routing problem. In *Proceedings of the SIAM Monographs on Discrete Mathematics and Applications*.

Vehicle routing software survey. (2006). *OR/MS Today*. Retrieved from http://www.lionhrtpub.com/orms/surveys/Vehicle_Routing/vrss.html

Yang, W. H., Kamlesh, M., & Ronald, H. B. (2000). Stochastic vehicle routing problem with restocking. *Transportation Science, 34*, 99–112. doi:10.1287/trsc.34.1.99.12278

Chapter 9
Heuristic Algorithms:
An Application to the Truck Loading Problem

Laura Cruz Reyes
Instituto Tecnológico de Cd. Madero, México

Adriana Alvim
Federal University of the State of Rio de Janeiro, Brasil

Claudia Gómez Santillán
Instituto Tecnológico de Cd. Madero, México

Patricia Melin
Instituto Tecnológico de Tijuana, México

Marcela Quiroz
Instituto Tecnológico de Cd. Madero, México

Jorge Ruiz Vanoye
Universidad Autónoma del Estado de Morelos, México

Vanesa Landero Najera
Universidad Politécnica de Nuevo León, México

ABSTRACT

This chapter approaches the Truck Loading Problem, which is formulated as a rich problem with the classic one dimensional Bin Packing Problem (BPP) and five variants. The literature review reveals that related work deals with three variants at the most. Besides, few efforts have been done to combine the Bin Packing Problem with the Vehicle Routing Problem. For the solution of this new Rich BPP a heuristic-deterministic algorithm, named DiPro, is proposed. It works together with a metaheuristic algorithm to plan routes, schedules and loads. The objective of the integrated problem, called RoSLoP, consists of optimizing the delivery process of bottled products in a real application. The experiments show the performance of three version of the Transportation System. The best version achieves a total demand satisfaction, an average saving of three vehicles and a reduction of the computational time from 3 hrs to two minutes regarding their manual solution. For the large scale the authors have develop a competitive genetic algorithm for BPP. As future work, it is intended integrate the approximation algorithm to the transportation system.

DOI: 10.4018/978-1-4666-0297-7.ch009

INTRODUCTION

A relevant and difficult problem in industrial companies is the optimal distribution of its products due to strict requirements from the customers and the increasing demand for better services. Nowadays the transportation cost represents up to 35% of final product prices (Balseiro et al., 2008); besides the dissatisfaction of the customers in not having their products on time. At most of productive and service areas, transportation and pro-duct distribution management represents one of the biggest challengers for logistic.

Products delivery has not been thoroughly studied for practical purposes as a rich problem, which is an emergent concept to denote real world problems involving series of optimization problems to solve; like the Bin Packing Problem, the Vehicle Routing Problem and its variants. The application of appropriated techniques in products delivery may produce savings from 5% to 20% in the distribution process (Toth & Vigo, 2002). The most recent researches (Psinger & Ropke, 2007; Weiss, 2009) approach up to six variants of the well-known Vehicle Routing Problem (VRP). However, they rarely con-template the Truck Loading Problem (TLP) commonly formulated with the Bin Packing Problem (BPP). The integra-tion in real-time of operations like load, resource allocation, dispatching and routing is the goal of future commercial systems to manage the logistics of modern companies (Crainic et al., 2009).

The Bin Packing Problem has the objective to search for the best packing of a set of items into bins. In the literature there are solution al-gorithms with excellent performance, but they do not incorporate relevant constraints derived of companies operation. Some works are focused in the problematic of VRP taking as constraint the vehicle capacity, and only use BPP to determine the number of trucks (Cordeau et al., 2002) re-gardless the arrangement within the container. In (Gendreau et al., 2008), VRP and two-dimensional BPP are approached with few constraints; leav-ing out others variants related with the fragility of items, diversity of trucks, highways with a limited vehicular weight, and trucks with loads from multiple clients.

This chapter shows a methodology based on heuristics for the integral solution of RoSLoP, a rich product transportation problem for routing, scheduling and loading tasks. The description is mainly focused in the Truck Loading Problem formulated as a Bin Packing Problem (TLP-BPP) with five variants, which is solved by means of one deterministic algorithm named DiPro. We also present a competitive genetic algorithm for the one-dimensional BPP; the incorporation of this approximation algorithm to the RoSLoP solution system is still in development. In order to validate the proposal, we use as a case of study, a company dedicated to the transportation of bottled products, mainly soft drinks.

RoSLoP: ROUTING, SCHEDULING AND LOADING PROBLEM

Despite progress in developing solution methods for the transportation logistics, in recent decades most efforts have been aimed at extremely relaxed environments, partially addressing the overall problem. This simplification involves only a small number of the extensive range of constraints, and this partially covering real business situation, this due to the inherent complexity. This section describes RoSLoP, an integral model of a real transportation problem.

The transportation of bottle products formu-lated with RoSLoP was specified by our industrial partner and involves three tasks: routing, schedul-ing and loading. In RoSLoP three optimization objectives must be achieved: satisfy the demands of all clients, minimize the number of used vehicles and reduce the total time of the trip. Scheduling and Routing are modeled using VRP, while loading is formulated with BPP. Figure 1 shows RoSLoP and its relation with VRP and BPP.

Figure 1. Optimization Problems involves in RoSLoP

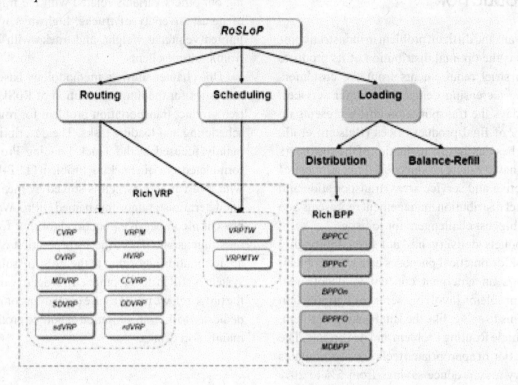

The objective of VRP is to assign routes to vehicles with the minimum total cost. A route is the trip that a truck does to service the customers. It starts and ends in a depot and can just be assigned to one vehicle. The VRP restrictions of RoSLoP are based on twelve variants (CVRP, VRPTW, VRPMTW, OVRP, MDVRP, SDVRP, sdVRP, VRPM, HVRP, CCVRP, DDVRP, rdVRP). The schedules are obtained as part of the solution of VRPTW and VRPMTW.

The Loading involves two tasks: distribution of the goods into the vehicle pallets and balance in weight all sides of the vehicles refilling with products with the highest inventory turnover. In BPP, the distribution of the goods in the vehicles is planned by satisfying a set of five restrictions (BP-POn, BPPMCC, BPPcC, BPPFO, and MDBPP) that depend on the company conditions.

In order to generalize the bottle transportation problem presented in this research, the Routing, Scheduling, and Loading Problem (RoSLoP) is formulated as follows: "Given a set of customers with a demand to be satisfied, a set of depots that are able to supply them and a set of BPP and VRP variants that restrict them, it is needed to design the routes, schedules and loads for vehicles such as: customer demands are completely satisfied; the total cost is minimized; and the constraints are satisfied."

Profitability and productivity of the companies demand a good organization of their logistic processes. In order to gain important savings, heuristic algorithms for BPP and VRP were integrated in a solution methodology. This chapter pays more attention to the design of loading plans of items in bins. In Figure 1 we mark with dark color the BPP variants that are involve in the Loading Truck Problem.

Table 1. Rich BPP variants of RoSLoP

BPP variant	DESCRIPTION
BPPCC	BPP Capacity Constrained. The costs and the sizes of bins satisfy a mono-tonic constraint, in which the ratio cost/size of all bins follows a mono-tonic order relation. Each bin has a specific capacity restricted by this relation (Kang & Park, 2003).
BPPcC	BPP Cardinality Constrained. This variant adds a limit in the number of items that can be placed in a bin (Epstein, 2006).
BPPOn	BPP On-line. The total number of elements to be accommodated is not known at the beginning of the process. Not all previous knowledge is assumed (György et al., 2010).
BPPFO	BPP with Fragile Objects. Each item has a threshold of maximum weight supported so that it does not suffer damage or deterioration (Chan et al., 2007).
MDBPP	Multiple Destinations BPP. The items can be unloaded in multiples destinations. For this reason, the order of their accommodation is important (Verweij, 1996).

BIN PACKING PROBLEM (BPP)

Logistics is an important area for industrial companies. Nowadays, most of the modern companies include exclusive departments dedicated to manage the logistics. One of the challenges of the logistics development is the integration of services in real-time.

In transportation services the loading of vehicles play an important role for this integration. It is well-know that classical BPP has an extensive application in logistics, mainly in loading. An example is the loading of bottle products focused in this work and modeled as BPP.

One-Dimensional BPP Definition

BPP is a classic problem of combinatorial optimization. In one-dimensional Bin Packing there are an unlimited number of bins with capacity c, the number of items is n, the size of each item is s_i ($0 \leq i < n$) and s_i is limited to $0 < s_i \leq c$. The goal is to determine the smallest number of bins m in which the items can be packed; to get a minimal partition of the sequence L of n items, where $L = B_1 \cup B_2 \cup ..., \cup B_m$ such that in each set B_j the sum of the size of each item in B_j does not exceed c (Equation 1).

$$\min z = \sum_{s_i \varepsilon B_j} s_i \leq c \qquad \forall j, \; 1 \leq j \leq m. \tag{1}$$

BPP belongs to the NP-Hard class (Balgoh et al., 2005). This class contains a set of problems considered intractable because they demand many resources for their solution. The quantity required by these is similar to an exponential function or a polynomial of high grade. The demonstration of BPP complexity is based on the partition problem reduction. If the classical BPP is NP-hard, it is induced that any variant of BPP is too. Similar complexity would have a Rich BPP composed of different versions of the BPP. Therefore, it is conjectured that the task of loading trucks is in the NP-hard class.

Rich BPP for RoSLoP: Definition and Related Work

RoSLoP involves additional constraints of Bin Packing integrating a Rich BPP. These related constrains formulate the Truck Loading Problem as a real and complex problem. The five variants of Table 1 were identified as the most relevant to the company case of study (Herrera, 2006).

Table 2 summarizes some related work around Bin Packing Problem with variants. It can be

Table 2. Related Work of Rich BPP and the approached variants

Variants Author	BPPCC	BPPcC	BPPOn	BPPFO	MDBPP
Epstein (Epstein, 2006)	✓	✓	✓		
Chan (Chan et al. 2007)		✓	✓	✓	
Manyem (Manyem, 2002)	✓		✓		
Correia (Correia et al., 2008)	✓				
Balogh (Balgoh et al., 2005)			✓		
Kang (Kang and Park, 2003)	✓				
Verweij (Verweij, 1996)					✓
This Work	✓	✓	✓	✓	✓

observed that other works deal with at the most three dependant variants. In contrast, our work approaches simultaneously five variants of Bin Packing (Cruz et al., 2007).

Functional Model

A detailed analysis of the processes involved in the logistics of the company under study revealed that the transportation of bottled products is subject to the following conditions related with the loading:

a. The existence of diverse depots with multiple schedules.
b. Fleets of vehicles of diverse types and different load possibilities, where the weight should be taken into account for their balance.
c. Clients with a specific demand, a time of service, and certain capacity constraints according to quantity and unit kind.
d. Goods to be distributed, characterized by product boxes with different attributes, such as: weight, size, supported weight and kind.
e. Routes that connect clients and depots with an associate cost of trip.
f. Government constraints that limit the traffic of vehicles that can travel on some roads, or the weight of the goods that can be transported.

In the context of the RoSLoP the general objective of the Rich BPP is to minimize the quantity of necessary vehicles to distribute the total load. Three particular objectives were derived:

a. Maximize the number of assigned products.
b. Maximize the employed space in the vehicle.
c. Balance the weight of the bins in each vehicle.

Table 3 shows five variants of BPP and their interpretation in the RoSLoP context. This operative description is part of the functional model of the RoSLoP.

METHODOLOGY OF RoSLoP SOLUTION

Due to the complexity of RoSLoP, it is at least as difficult as the class NP-Hard; the problem was solved incrementally over five years, resulting in three versions. This section describes the architecture of each solution version: HBTS, HBS-RoSLOP-I and HBS-RoSLOP-II. A brief description of the method related with routing is given: Loading Units Construction, Learning levels, Local Search, Balance and Refilling. The most important methods rela-ted with loading are revised with more detail in the section dedicated to explain the DiPro Algorithm.

Table 3. Operative description of the BPP variants

Variant	Operative Description
BPPCC	Each bin has a specific variable capacity. In the Truck Loading Problem, a bin is called pallet. The pallets in the vehicles can have different height and as consequence different loading capacity that is proportional to its height.
BPPcC	This constrain limits the number of objects to be allocated in a container. The maximum number of pro-ducts that can be stacked in a pallet is delimited by product type, vehicle supported weight and the roads where it travels to.
BPPOn	The total number of element is un-known at the beginning of the loading process. The products to be distributed in a vehicle are not possibly known since the beginning because the assignment depends on the next client to be visited.
BPPFO	Each element has a weight capacity threshold. In the loading problem each product has a quantity of sup-ported weight that should not be overloaded to be able to avoid damage.
MDBPP	Product can be delivered to multiple destinies. Since different discharge points exist in the same route, the product loading should be organized with base in this scheme.

Architecture of HBTS

Figure 2 shows the proposed methodology for solving the transportation problem RoS-LoP (Rangel, 2005). In this diagram are three subproblems: routing, load allocation, and timetabling. The solution method consists of two phases.

In the first phase, the routing is solved by an algorithm of Ant Colony System specifically on an Ant Colony Optimizer (ACO, Ant Colony Optimization). In this phase also is addressed the load allocation through the DiPro algorithm, a deterministic heuristic based on a round-robin strategy to balance the goods distributed in the vehicle.

A solution specifies routes to visit all clients. The process of building solution is done through ACS algorithm. Each time a vehicle visits a customer, ACS invokes the Dipro algorithm, which is responsible for determining the demand that will transport the vehicle. The result achieved in this first step will contain the routes and fleet required to supply customers.

Once the routs and load plans are determined, continues the second step of the methodology: the scheduling. Because the first step also provides indirectly a solution to the scheduling problem, in this second phase is only necessary to transform the obtained hours: from standard to real-time. This is done through a simple conversion.

Architecture of HBS-RoSLoP-I

To build better solutions for RoSLoP, the methodology of solution HBTS was extended in a new one. HBTS-RosSloP-I is based on ACS as shown in Figure 3. The assignment of routes and scheduling is solved by a basic ACS and three more components that extend the skills of this algorithm: Adaptive Clus-tering, Initial Search and Local Search. The DiPro algorithm, which assigns the loads, contains four main modules, one is optional: Loading Unit Construction, Assignment, Balanced and Refill.

The Construction Module creates the units of load used by the algorithm; the Assignment Module is invoked during the process of construction of a route. Each time that a customer is visited this module determines the distribution of the load into the vehicle assigned to the customer. When the search ends, and the best solution is found, this solution is improved through the balanced and refilling modules; they are executed out of line.

This Transportation System HBTS-RosSloP-I uses efficiently the processing time, solving up to five variants of BPP; a detailed review of DiPro is approached.

Figure 2. Architecture of HBTS with DiPro Algorithm

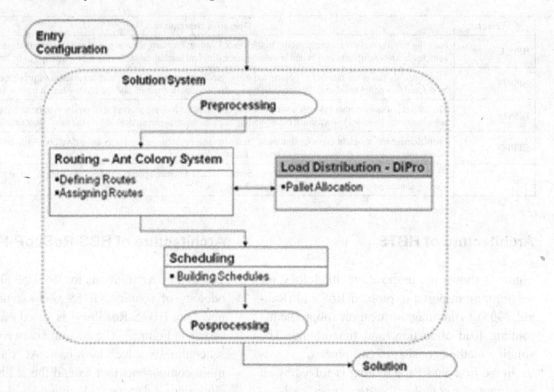

Figure 3. Architecture of HBS-RoSLoP-I with DiPro Algorithm

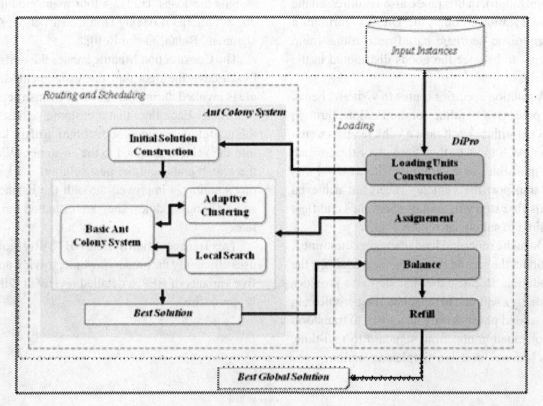

Figure 4. Architecture of HBS-RoSLoP-II with DiPro Algorithm

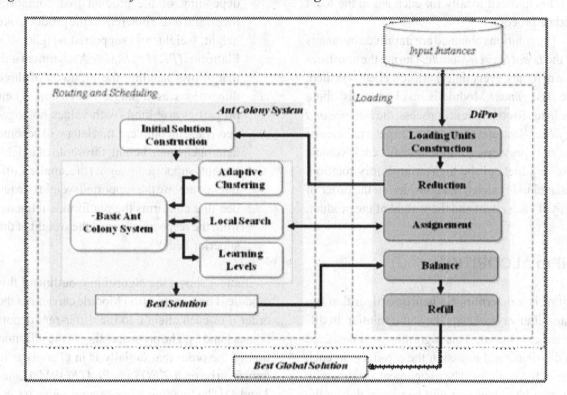

Architecture of HBS-RoSLoP-II

The methodology proposed to solve RoSLoP, shown in Figure 4, includes an Ant Colony System for solving VRP and the algorithm DiPro (Distribution of Products) to solve BPP. Both of them coexist in an integral solution scheme of the tasks of routing, scheduling and loading.

The ACS algorithm is a metaheuristic that uses closeness and pheromone measures to search the solution in an intelligent way, and includes three modules of improvement: Clustering, Local Search and Learning Level (Cruz et al., 2007; González-Barbosa et al., 2010).

The DiPro algorithm is a deterministic heuristic algorithm, and includes five modules: Loading Units Construction, Dimension Reduction, Assignment, Balancing and Refilling (Cruz et al., 2007b).

The general algorithm begins invoking the *Loading Units Construction Module* to trans-form

items of three dimensions to one dimension: bottle products to platforms. Each one-dimensional load unit is transformed into a real number using the *Reduction Module* which uses a rule of thumb, learned of this case study, to diminish the solution space: "bigger objects are the most weightened." The *Clustering Module* determines the grouping level of clients with the purpose to segment the global population into subsets and limit the set of candidate clients to be visited.

Next, a basic *Ant Colony System* builds a solution. The *Learning levels Module* defines two levels of knowledge for the ants: the first level is equal to the values of the original pheromone Table, which only contains the information of the best obtained solution for the ants and it is modified only in the global updating process; while the second level is equal to the copy of the pheromone Table, which contains the local values of the pheromone and it is used for the ants as a guide in the search of better solutions. This level is updated locally for each ant in the local update process.

The solutions obtained are improved by means of the *Local Search Module*. During the construction of routes, every time that a new client is visited, the *Assignment* Module is invoked to distribute the load. To conclude the process, the *Balance and Refilling Modules* are invoked to get a balance of the best previous solution and fill each vehicle with products of the highest inventory rotation. Balancing is carried out considering the order of visit of each client and the weight of the product.

DiPro ALGORITHM

DiPro is a deterministic heuristic algorithm because it always obtains the same solution in different executions. This algorithm was designed to distribute and to assign the pro-ducts in each one of the vehicles. The assignment is made with base in the clients that will be visited during the same route. DiPro is constituted mainly by three modules applied in different times: Construction, Assignment and Balance.

Construction Module

The purpose of the Construction Module is to convert items from three dimensions to one dimension. This process depends of the peculiar characteristics of each product. The construction is described with bottled pro-ducts that are stored in units with special characteristic such as:

a. Boxes (Q): Basic unit of an order from a client. With properties as height and weight; besides the supported weight that is a measure of the quantity of product that can be placed above a box without causing damage.
b. Beds (*BEDS*): Constituted by a set of boxes, ordered in such a way that their length and width is adjusted at the bin of the truck. Some properties are: the number of boxes,

depending of the product that composes them; and those inherent to the product, like height, weight, and supported weight.

c. Platforms (*PLATFORMS*): Assignment unit that allows handing the products of three dimensions as a single dimension. Their properties are: kind (with values homogeneous and incomplete, that later will become heterogeneous), height, threshold of height, weight, supported weight (the smallest difference among the supported weight of each bed that conforms the platform, subtracted from the respective sum of the weight of the superior beds).

Table 4 shows the algorithmic outline of this module. The Construction Module carries out the order d of each client c to the differ-rent depots (Lines 1 and 2). The preprocessing of the information of the order that initially is in Q consists in transform boxes to *BEDS* and *PLATFORMS* (Lines 3 and 4). The function *homogeneus_units()* (Line 3) orders the products by its supported weight and carries out the conversion of boxes to beds and later to platforms, by means of derivative calculations of the product properties; giving place to complete homogeneous plat-forms and remaining homogeneous beds.

Finally, in Line 4 with the function *incomplete_platforms()*, the remaining product boxes of each product are used to form heterogeneous beds with products that have the same category and belong to the same area. Note that a heterogeneous

Table 4. Algorithm of the construction module

Construction Module (*C, ORDERS*)	
1	**for each** $c \in C$
2	**for each** $order_d \in ORDERS_c$
3	*homogeneus_units(order_d)*
4	*incomplete_platforms(order_d)*
5	**end for**
6	**end for**

Figure 5. DiPro: Construction of loading units

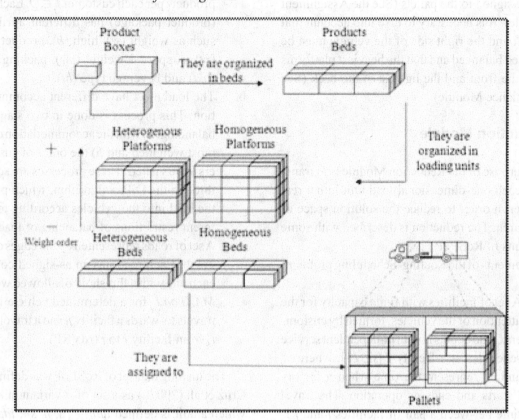

bed contain the same number of boxes that a homogeneous bed due to the compatible products varies only in their weight or supported weight and not in their dimension. The rest of homogeneous and heterogeneous beds that could not form homogeneous platforms in the previous process are combined to form heterogeneous platforms. The heterogeneous plat-forms are created by following the Round Robin mechanism. During this task it is necessary to consider that the beds can be combined to form a heterogeneous platform only if they have the same category.

Figure 5 shows a graphical description of the Construction Module. In order to distribute a customer demand in a vehicle, the products are ordered by its supported weight. After that, the goods are organized in homogeneous beds and homogeneous platforms. Then, the remaining product boxes of each product are used to form

heterogeneous beds with different products that have the same category and belong to the same area. The rest of homogeneous beds that could not form homogeneous platforms in the previous process are combined with heterogeneous beds to form heterogeneous plat-forms by area. As mention above, the heterogeneous platforms are created by following the well-known Round Robin mechanism used in processor scheduling.

A *Round Robin* is an arrangement of choosing all elements in a group equally in some ratio-nal order, usually from the top to the bottom of a list and then starting again at the top of the list and so on. In DiPro, the arrangement is the remaining beds of products that could not be allocated in homogeneous platforms; the order is given by their supported weight.

Once all the platforms have been built, all the created platforms are ordered by weight and then assigned to the pallets (See the Assignment Module). It is necessary to take into account that the left and the right side of the vehicle must be weighed balanced and that the heaviest platforms go in the front and the lightest in the back (See the Balance Module).

Reduction Module

The purpose of the Reduction Module is to transform each one-dimensional load unit into a real number in order to reduce the solution space of the search. The reduction is described with some elements of RoSPoP.

Elements of the Routing-Scheduling problem:

a.   A set of facilities with finite capacity for the attention of the vehicles, formed by customers C and depots D with in-dependent service schedules at a facility j $[st_j, et_j]$, where st_j and et_j represent the time when a facility j starts and ends its operation. The travel time bet-ween a pair of facilities i and j is represented by t_{ij}. An integer variable x_{ijk} is used to assign an arc (i, j) to a route k. Depots have the possibility of request goods to other depots. A set of routes K_d that starts and ends at the depot must be formed. This description is related to VRPTW, VRPMTW, CCVRP, SDVRP, MDVRP and DDVRP.

b.   A fleet of vehicles with heterogeneous capacity V_d, with a service time $stime_v$ and a time for attention tm_{vj}, which depends on the capacity of the vehicle C_{vj} that visit a customer j and the available people for docking and loading the containers $Pallets_v$ of the vehicle v where the goods are transported (HV-RP, CVRP, MVRP, sdVRP). An integer variable y_{vk} is used to assign a vehicle v to a route k.

Elements of the Loading problem:

a.   A set of orders Q to be satisfied at the facilities of the customers, formed by units of products per each customer $I_j \in Q$. Each box (product package) has different attributes such as weight (w), high (h), product type (pt), supported weight (sw), packing type (pkt) and beverage type (bt).

b.   The load must have different accommodation: This process is done in two stages of balancing: *a*) with the accommodation of the most weighted and *b*) the order of customers to be visited. These processes are solved through the DiPro algorithm, which places the load into the vehicles according to different restrictions of balancing of load.

c.   A set of roads represented by the edges of the graph. Each road has an as-signed cost c_{ij}, each one with a threshold of allowed weight $MAXLoad_{vj}$ for a determined vehicle v that travels to-wards a facility j, and a travel time t_{ij} from facility i to j (rdVRP).

The loading dataset of RoSLoP was defined in Cruz et al. (2007b) as a set of n-variant units, in which a unit is defined $unit = (w, h, sw, idp, kp, pkt, bt)$. A preprocessing must be done to reduce the loading dataset into a linear set of object in the domain of multiple variants. The loading dataset is characterized in a linear dataset through a reduction technique, developed through the learned reference of this case study: "bigger objects are the most weighted." The reduction technique is illustrated in Figure 6, in which, an order of a customer j is transformed. It consists of two steps: 1) the construction of loading units and 2) the transformation of these units in a representative set of real numbers.

The construction of loading units is done through the *Construction Module* of DiPro. As a result, two kinds of units are created: homogeneous and heterogeneous platforms. Homogeneous platforms are constituted by products of the same type, while heterogeneous platform are constituted with different types of products with similar characteristics. Both, homogeneous and heterogeneous platforms are defined as a set $ITEMS_j =$

Figure 6. DiPro: Transformation of the orders dataset into a real number

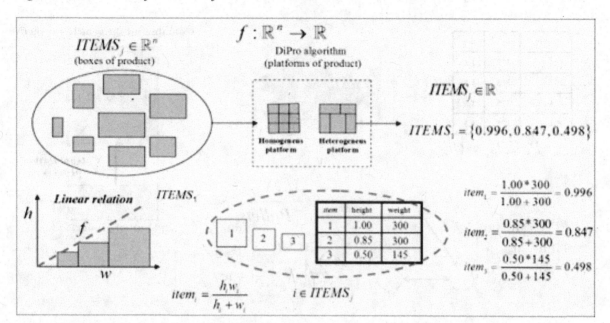

$\{\forall(w_i, h_i)\}$, where w_i and h_i represent the weight and height of each unit. Then, each pair (w_i, h_i) is transformed into a number $item_i$ using the following Equation 2. This equation represents the relationship between the dimensions of the objects. A detailed review of DiPro is presented in Herrera (2006).

$$item_i = \frac{h_i w_i}{h_i + w_i} \qquad i \in ITEMS_j \qquad (2)$$

The capacity C_{vj} of a vehicle v to visit node j is transformed likewise. Each container that belongs to a trailer has two attributes: a high $h_{palletij}$ and weight $w_{palletij}$ of the assigned load to visit customer j. The width of the load is determined by a categorization of products, asked the company to group the products. This is necessary for adjusting the load to the containers. The transformation of the vehicles dimensions is shown in Figure 7.

It is established a uniform distribution of the weight for the load in each container. Equation 3 is used to obtain the capacity of the vehicle. It ensures that the dimensions of the load objects and the vehicles are comparables.

$$C_{vj} = \sum_{i=1}^{Pallets_v} \frac{h_{pallet_{ij}} w_{pallet_{ij}}}{h_{pallet_{ij}} + w_{pallet_{ij}}} \quad j \in C, v \in V_d$$

$$(3)$$

Assignment Module

Their task consists on establishing the pro-duct accommodation inside the pallets of the truck. This is executed while free space exists in the vehicle, the supported weight is not exceeded by this and the demand has not been satisfied in the order from the client to the depot. In each assignment, constraints of BPP are verified (Table 1).

The Assignment Module uses the mechanism of Table 5 called completeness level (variable $completeness_{palletx \in PALLETSv\varsigma, orderd}$) that allows to verify the restrictions imposed by BPPcC, BPPCC and BPPFO.

Figure 7. DiPro: Transformation of the vehicles dimensions into a real number

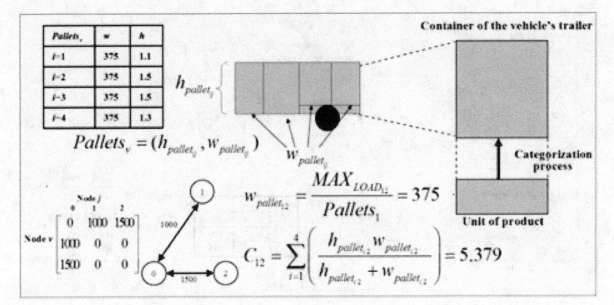

Table 6 shows the Assignment Module Algorithm. This module is executed while the two conditions of Line 1 are satisfied. The first one verifies by means of the completeness level that free space exists in the trip ς of the vehicle v (v_ς), and the supported weight is not exceeded by this. The second one verifies that the demand of the $order_d$ from the client c to the depot d has not been satisfied. In other words, some platforms exist without being assigned. In Line 2 a pallet of the vehicle v_ς is obtained; it is secured that the pallet has space with a completeness level smaller than two. Line 3 allows the assignment of homogeneous and heterogeneous platforms only if: the $order_d$ has not satisfied the demand and that space exists in the $pallet_x$.

Next, Lines 4-9 locate the platforms, which give preference to the homogeneous with the function *assign_homogeneus_platform()* of Line 4. In Line 7, the method *assign_in-complete_platform()* assigns heterogeneous platforms that are formed from the incomplete. Both methods modify the completeness level when some of the constraints are violated.

Table 5. Description of Completeness levels of an ordered in a pallet

Completeness Level	Description
0	Platforms have not been assigned
1	More homogeneous platforms cannot be assigned
2	More heterogeneous platforms cannot be assigned

Figure 8 summarizes the Assignment Module in the different scenarios that can be presented. The Spiral strategy is used to the assignment of homogenous and incomplete platforms. Initially all the elements are organized by descendent order of the supported weight. Then an element that satisfies all the conditions imposed by BPPcC, BPPCC, and BPPFO, is searched, alternating seeks in a descending and ascending way over the elements. This heuristic balances the weight of the goods sent in the different trucks. It is not allowed the programming of vehicles trips with very heavy or very light products.

Figure 9 shows the assignment of incomplete platform using the spiral strategy. As was men-

Table 6. Algorithm of the assignment module

Assignment Module (v_i, c, $order_d \in ORDERS_c$)
1   while $\exists\, pallet_x \in PALLETS_{v_i}$ |$completeness < 2$
$\land\, \exists\, platform_z \in PLATFORMS_{order_d}$ |$isassigned = false$
2   select $pallet_x \in PALLETS_{v_i}$ |$completeness_{pallet_x,order_d} < 2$
3   while
$\exists\, platform_z \in PLATFORMS_{order_d}$ |$isassigned = false \land completeness_{pallet_x,order_d} < 2$
4   if $\exists\, platform_z \in PLATFORMS_{order_d}$ |$kind = homogeneus$
$\land\, completeness_{pallet_x,order_d} = 0$
5   assign_homogeneus_platform($pallet_x, order_d$)
6   else
7   assign_incomplete_platform($pallet_x, order_d$)
8   end if
9   end while
10 end while

Figure 8. Assignment module

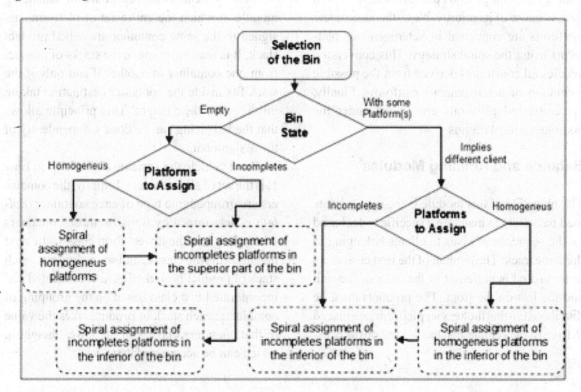

Figure 9. Conversion of incomplete to heterogeneous platforms using spiral assignment

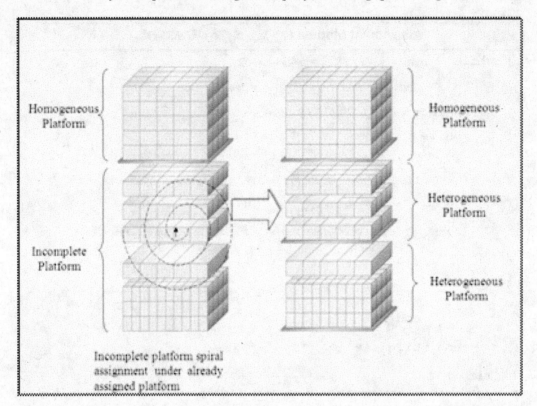

tioned, the homogeneous platforms are assigned first, because of its priority. Next, the incomplete platforms are converted in heterogeneous platforms using the spiral strategy. This conversion verifies all constraints derived from the possible formation of heterogeneous platforms. Finally, the converted platforms are placed under the homogeneous platforms.

Balance and Refilling Modules

The objective of this module is the approximate load balancing to maintain a specific order based on the sequence of visits to clients belonging to the same track. The product of the first customers to be visited is preferred in the back of the unit and the last on the front. The products must be distributed so that the heavier platforms are placed in front of the vehicle, and the lightest on the back.

Table 7 details the procedure of balancing module in which the entire set of platforms assigned to the same container are called product stack. It is feasible to move the stacks of product from one container to another if and only if the stack fits inside the container destination taking into account their height. This principle allows that the balancing can be done independently of the assignment.

For a vehicle the variable $PALLETS_v$ in Line 1, is the set of all containers. Initially, the containers are grouped: the type of each container ($pallet_i$) is determined by the size, those containers whose height is the lowest form class 1, the next height forms the class 2, and so on. Initially, each stack of product is marked as not reallocated and incorporated in a class based on the grouping of containers: each stack of product takes the value of that container class with the lowest height in which can be accommodated.

Table 7. Algorithm of the balance module

Balance Module (v)
1   Assign classes $class_{container_i}$, $\forall container_i \in PALLETS_v$
2   Assign classes $class_\gamma$, $\forall \gamma \in N_\gamma(v)$
3   set $\forall \gamma \in N_\gamma(v)$: not-reassigned
4   set $\forall container_i \in PALLETS_v$: not-used
5   Sort $\gamma \in N_\gamma(v)$ by height/class, visit succession and weight
6   while $N_\gamma(v) \neq \phi$
7   Select not-used $container_i$ the closest to the front
8         $\gamma = \arg\max_{\gamma \in N_\gamma(v)}(N_\gamma(v)) \mid class_\gamma \leq class_{pallet_i}$
9         $pallet_i \leftarrow \gamma$
10   set γ: reassigned
11   set $pallet_x$: used
12 end while

In Line 2, $N_\gamma(v)$ is the set of all products stacks assigned to the vehicle v marked as not-reassigned. In Line 3 and 4, the stacks are marked as non-reassigned and container as non-used, respectively. In Line 5, product stacks are arranged in a vector in ascending order based on their class, then taking the order of access to customers (from first to last visited, if the stack is formed by more than one product customer, the customer order is determined by the owner of the platform top of the stack), and finally by weight of the stack.

While there is a stack of product without being reassigned (Lines 6 to 12), in Line 7 a not-used container is selected (the closest to the front of the vehicle). In this container it is placed the stack of product whose position in the vector system is the largest and whose class is less than or equal to the container class (Lines 8 and 9). Finally, Lines 10 and 11 updates the set $PALLETS_v$ and $N_\gamma(v)$.

GENETIC ALGORITHM FOR BPP: HGGA-BP-I

Over the last twenty years in finding good solutions for BPP, a variety of algorithms have been designed. The most important results have been obtained by using hybrid algorithms and meta-heuristics. Diverse researchers in the computer sciences area have been given to the task of providing practical solutions to implementations related to BPP with promising results. However, given the nature of the problem, the study field still continues open.

Falkenauer proposed to generate a hybrid with a Grouping Genetic Algorithm (named GGA) and a local optimization based on the dominance criterion (Falkenauer, 1996). He established as parameters: 33% of mutation, 50% of crossover, population of 100 individuals and between 1000 to 5000 generations.

Levine and Ducatelle developed a hybrid algorithm of Ant Colony Optimization with a local search algorithm (Ducatelle, 2004). In large

Table 8. General Procedure of HGGA-BP-I

Genetic Algorithm for BPP

```
1   Begin
2     for each generation
3       for each individual
4          new_binsol = creating individual
5          if (random[0-1]>0.9 and fitness(new_binsol)>fitness(binsol))
               or random[0-1]<0.9
6             binsol = new_binsol
7          end if
8       end for
9       Select individuals by means of Tournament
10      Grouping Crossover
11      Grouping Mutation
12      Fitness Computation and search the best solution
13    end for
14  end procedure
```

problems, the hybrid not always finds the best known solution, besides it requires too much computational time, e.g., with 100 individuals demands between 1000 to 5000 generations depending of the size problem.

A hybrid heuristic was proposed by Alvim et al. (2001). The basic structure is composed by reduction techniques, use of limits, a greedy algorithm, redistributions and improvement by means of Tabu Search with 1/n iterations. The algorithm finds the optimal solution in the redistribution phase with more than 95% of the analyzed instances.

HGGA-BP-I (Hybrid Grouping Genetic Algorithm for BPP) is inspired on the grouping encoding scheme proposed by Falkenauer (1996) to represent the genes in the chromosome like groups of items associated to bins and manipulate them with grouping genetic operators. The algorithm includes efficient heuristics to generate the initial population and perform grouping mutation and crossover.

Hybridization of metaheuristic algorithms is a promising approach due to their ability to combine the strategies of different algorithms, taking of them their best features. One type of hybridization is called HC//SC, which is a fusion of methods taken from Hard Computer and Soft Computer areas.

The HGGA-BP-I is a HC//SC hybrid. SC is re-presented with the chromosomal strategy of Falkenauer, where the complete bins are inherited in the *grouping crossover*, and complete bins are eliminated in the *grouping mutation*. HC is constituted by using specific well-know determinist algorithms of BPP (First Fit, Best Fit, and Worst Fit) and limits criterion.

Table 8 describes the general algorithm. After the first generation, the probability to maintain the individual from the previous generation is proportional to its fitness and a random number (Lines 3-8). Posteriori, an evolution process that includes evaluation, selection, crossover and mutation is developed, and the individual with the highest fitness is obtained (Lines 9-12).

Deterministic Heuristics

First Fit (*FF*): Each item is placed in the first bin that has enough available capacity; if none of the bins can store it the item is placed in a new empty

Table 9. Procedure to create individuals using the L_2 criterion limit

Creating Individual with L_2
1 **Begin**
2   Compute L_2
3   Sort items in decreasing way
4   **for** the first L_2 items
5   Put each item in an empty bin
6   **end for**
7   **while** there are items without accommodation
8   Select randomly an item and put it by means of FF
9   **end while**
10 **end procedure**

bin. A variation to this method is established when the items are taken according to the decreasing order of its weights (items are ordered from biggest to smallest weight before being packed), such variation is known as *First Fit Decreasing* (*FFD*) (Johnson, 1974).

Better Fit (*BF*): Each item is packed in the fullest bin that can store it, adding bins when needed. In the same way as *FF*, a variation exists, called *Best Fit Decreasing* (*BFD*), which considers the items in decreasing order of its weights (Johnson, 1974).

Worst Fit (*WF*): Opposite to the previous strategy (*Best Fit, BF*), each considerate item is stored in the emptiest bin with residual capacity enough to contain it, using new bins when required. The variation that takes the items according to the de-creasing order of its weights is named *Worst Fit Decreasing* (*WFD*) (Johnson, 1974).

Lower Bounds

A fundamental part of the GA development is the creation of good individuals. Martello proposed in Martello and Toth (1990) the LBFD method that can be considerate as a HC. In LBFD, the starting point computes the L_2 limit (Line 2). The L_2 biggest items are collocated in independent bins (Lines 4-6), the rest of the items are packed using

the BFD strategy. However, the method has been modified in order to use FF and apply randomness in the accommodation of the items residuals of L_2 (Line 7-9 of Table 9).

Another method incorporated to create individuals takes as base the DB3FD algorithm (Dual Best 3-Fit Decreasing) proposed in Alvim et al. (2003), where given an item into a bin, a pair of free items that fill the bin are searched. This method was modified for the requirements in Table 10, L_2 is computed (Line 2) in order to calculate an initial number of bins near to the optimal. In Lines 4-9, the algorithm tries to fill the first L_2 bins with three items. The rest of the items are accommodated randomize with FF.

The use of L_2 permits from the beginning the use of the Dominance Criterion approach described in Martello and Toth (1990), due that more dominants items are located in empty bins which are translated in a HC and time optimization.

The Equation 4 shows the compute of L_2, for an instance of BPP, where α is an integer, $0 \le \alpha \le {}^c/_2$, $N = \{0,1,...,n\}$, $J_1=\{j \in N: s_j > c-\alpha\}$, $J_2=\{j \in N: c-\alpha \ge s_j > {}^c/_2\}$ and $J_3=\{j \in N: {}^c/_2 \ge s_j > \alpha\}$. The L_2 value represents an inferior limit in order to search an optimal solution. An example of this can be seen in Martello and Toth (1990).

Table 10. Procedure to create individuals using the L_2 and fitting of three items (DB3)

Creating Individuals with DB3 and L_2

```
1   Begin
2     Compute L₂
3     Sort items in decreasing way
4     for the first L₂ bins
5        Select randomly an item and insert it into the bin
6       if there are two free items that fill the bin
7          Insert the items into the bin
8        end if
9     end for
10    while there are items without accommodation
12       Select randomly an item and put it by means of FF
13    end while
14  end procedure
```

$$L(\alpha) = |J_1| + |J_2| + \max\left(0, \left\lceil \frac{\sum_{j \in J_3} s_j - \left(|J_2|c - \sum_{j \in J_2} s_j\right)}{c} \right\rceil\right)$$

$$L_2 = \max\left\{L(\alpha) : 0 \leq \alpha \leq c/2, \ \alpha \text{ int}\right\} \tag{4}$$

HGGA-BP-I: Grouping Crossover Procedure

The two-point grouping crossover was pro-posed in Falkenauer (1996), but in the implementation of this algorithm some opportunity fields were analyzed and a second crossover was developed. Table 11 shows the new procedure, where the first segment of the 1st father is incorporated in a child (Line 2). The fitness in each segment of the 2nd father is evaluated and the best segment is taken and incorporated in the child (Lines 3-9). After that, the rest of the segments of the 1st father are added in the solution (Lines 10-16); however, in the processes of Lines 2-9 and 10-16 some items can already belong to the bins of the child, whereby these bins are discarded and the free items are reallocated with the HC: BFD (Lines 17-19).

HGGA-BP-I: Grouping Mutation Procedure

Taking up the methodology of Falkenauer (1996), which is contrary to normal mutation, the algorithm in Table 12 details the grouping mutation that eliminates a percentage of the bins more empty (Lines 2-5). The free items are distributed with the HC: BFD (Line 6).

An Example of Grouping Operations

Figure 10 exemplifies the grouping operators step by step with an example where: (a) a population is generated and two individuals are selected; (b) two cut points are selected in both fathers; (c) 1st child is generated by injecting in the 1st father the best segment of the 2nd father; (d) bins that duplicate items are eliminated and non duplicated items are saved as free; (e) with BFD the free items are reallocated; (f) the generated solution, has better fitness than its progenitors, however, the mutation could improve it; (g) for this, the emptiest bin is eliminated (4th) and the items are distributed by means of BFD and an optimal solution with three full bins is obtained.

Table 11. Grouping crossover procedure

```
                         Grouping  Crossover
1   Begin
2     Copy in the child the bins of the 1st Segment of the 1st father
3     for each bin of the best segment in the 2nd  father
4       if  items of the actual bin is not in some bin of the child
5         Copy the bin in the child
6       else
7         Save as free_items, those that not belong to the solution
8       end if
9     end for
10    for each bin of the 1st father in the two and three segments
11      if  items of the actual bin is not in some bin of the child
12        Copy the bin in the child
13      else
14        Save as free_items, those that not belong to the solution
15      end if
16    end for
17    if there are free_items
18      Packed free_items with BFD
19    end if
20  end procedure
```

Table 12. Grouping mutation procedure

```
                         Grouping  Mutation
1   Begin
2     for the number of bins to empty
3       Search the bin with the less weight accumulated
        and eliminate it
4       Save as free_items those that belong to the bin
5     end for
6     Packed free_items with BFD
7   end procedure
```

HGGA-BP-I Performance

In order to evaluate the methodology; a population of 50 individuals, 100 generations, 30% crossover and 50% mutation were established. These values are extremely lower than those reported by specialized literature which bears to a faster algorithm. The algorithm was developed in C language; 1370 standard instances divided in five sets were taken from Beasley (1990).

Table 13 shows: the number of cases where the best known solution was found for each set of instances (column 2); the theoretical ratios permit to see a very low error because in the instances where the best known solution is not reached, only one or two additional bins are used (column

Figure 10. Example of Grouping Operations; fitness is the real value

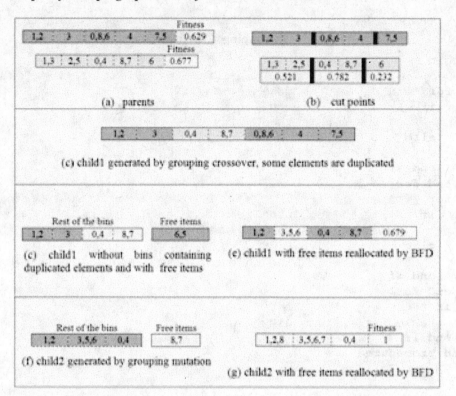

Table 13. Performance of GGA-BP-I

Instances Set	Optimum Instances	Theoretical Ratios	Time	Average Generation
Hard (10)	8	1.0360	1.7407	84.5
NCW (720)	699	1.0002	2.3642	42.3
NWBR (480)	455	1.0008	0.5314	9.84
T (80)	0	1.0235	1.9383	68.3
U (80)	60	1.0011	7.8462	40.7
Total (1370)	1222	1.0123	2.8841	49.1

3); the average time required for each instance (column 4); and the average generation where that solution was reached (column 5).

Many researchers limit the experimentation in the generation of the best solutions with-out

an exhaustive analysis of the algorithm performance which is a preponderant factor in order to evaluate the quality of the solution.

Table 14 shows a sample of instances taken randomly from the total solved cases. The ex-

Table 14. Statistical Analysis of the results of GGA-BP-I

Instance	Better Known Solution Value	Min.	Max.	Avg.	Std. Dev.	Variation Coef.	Time	Avg. Gen.	Theoretical Ratio
Hard2	56	57	57	57	0.000	0.0000	1.893	91	1.017
N1c1w1_a	25	25	25	25	0.000	0.0000	0.180	38	1.000
N4c1w1_m	246	246	246	246	0.000	0.0000	11.480	56	1.000
N2w2b1r6	21	21	21	21	0.000	0.0000	0.327	39	1.000
N3w4b3r1	22	22	22	22	0.000	0.0000	0.756	40	1.000
t60_00	20	21	21	21	0.000	0.0000	0.192	38	1.050
t501_10	167	168	168	168	0.000	0.0000	4.572	60	1.005
u120_10	52	52	52	52	0.000	0.0000	0.470	60	1.000
u1000_16	404	404	405	404	0.258	0.0006	17.402	92	1.000
All Instances	---	---	---	---	0.028	0.0000	4.141	57	1.008

perimentation was repeated 30 times in order to verify the results consistency. As it can be seen in the low values of Standard Deviation, Variation Coefficient, Average Generation as well as the almost null difference among the maximum and minimum number of bins; the proposed algorithm is consistent and robust.

The final results are shown in Table 15, which includes the number of optimal, average time (in seconds) and generations required by the algorithm to find the best solution. The table also shows the number of optimal obtained by the HI-BP algorithm (Alvim et al., 2001), which is currently the second best state of the art algorithm. The results show that HI-BP-I is a competitive algorithm than could help to solve large scale instances of our Transportation System.

EXPERIMENTATION WITH THE TRANSPORTATION SYSTEMS

There is no standard method to compare our proposals because the problem addressed is a new rich BPP with five variants. Then, the evaluation was made in the context of the complete transportation system developed to solve RoSLoP. Mention should be made, that our industrial partner defines an efficient system as the one that can solve a real-world instance in 10 minutes or less, satisfying 100% of the demands and minimizing the number of vehicles used.

General Experimental Conditions

The experimental results contrast the performance of four version of the System. The first version is HBTS, Heuristic-Based Transportation System (Rangel, 2005). The second version is HBS-RoSLoP-I, Heuristic-Based Sys-tem for the Routing-Scheduling-Loading Problem (Herrera, 2006). The third version is HBS-RoSLoP-II (Delgado, 2007). For a better understanding, some names were changes from the original publication.

All the algorithms are implemented in C# and can run on cheap personal computers. This condition was specified by our industrial partner. It is important to say that manual procedure needs 180

Table 15. Comparing GGA-BP-I with HI-BP, an algorithm of the state of the art

Instance Set	Number of Instances	HI-BP (Alvim et al, 2001)	HGGA-BP-I		
			Optimal	Time	Number of Generations
Data Set 1	720	720	699	2.36	42
Data Set 2	480	480	455	0.53	10
Data Set 3	10	10	8	1.74	85
T	80	80	0	1.95	69
U	80	80	60	7.85	42
GAU1	17	12	9	0.57	52
WAE1	100	100	100	0.04	4
WAE2	100	100	98	0.31	25
Hard28	28	5	5	1.48	89
NIRUP	53	3	3	1.05	79
Total	1668	1590	1437	1.78	50
Effectiveness		0.953	0.861		

minutes approximately, but an expert planner is dedicated full time to make adjustments.

The database of the company consists of 212 tables and 312 test cases, of which 12 are frequently used to compare algorithm. The test cases are classified according to the referral orders date, so that each day of operation of the enterprise is a test case.

HBTS Performance

HBTS involve only seven known VRP variants: CVRP, VRPM, HVRP, VRPTW, VRPSD, sdVRP and CCVRP. A new variant was added to re-present that a customer has a limited attention capacity for vehicles. Table 16 shows the description of the cases used in the experiment. The column five is the number of arcs in the connection matrix. Columns six and seven mean the number of vehicles that can be simultaneously loaded or unloaded in a location. The last column is the amount of product boxes demanded by all customers. The HBTS algorithm was executed for 5 seconds and

ten minutes, on a common PC (AMD Athlon XP, 1.3 GHz, 192 Mb in RAM); NNH gets a solution in one second.

In Table 17, the results obtained with HBTS are contrasted with a Nearest Neighborhood Heuristic (NNH) and with the manual solution given by the procedure used in the bottle product transportation company. The performance of HBTS improves the manual procedure in all cases: consumed time, the number of vehicles in 20%. In all cases, HBTS satisfies the demands and does it better than NNH algorithm.

HBS-RoSLoP-I Performance

In HBTS, when no complete platform can be accommodated in the truck, they are segmented to improve the distribution of the load. However, the segmentation represents a bigger effort in the unloading. For this reason the segmentation was eliminated from HBS-RoSLoP-I. In HBTS some trucks could be programmed with a very small load, implying an excessive cost of the

Table 16. Real-world RoSLoP instance description

Instance	Description of the real-world RoSLoP Instances						
	Customers	Vehicle	Depots	Arcs	Customer capacity	Depot Capacity	Customer Demands
Case 01	7	8	1	10	1	2	12681
Case 02	6	8	1	10	1	2	10953
Case 03	7	8	1	10	1	2	15040
Case 04	7	8	1	10	1	2	12624
Case 05	7	8	1	10	1	2	14262

Table 17. Experimental Results with HBTS

Instance	Vehicles used in the solution				Supplied products			
	NNH	HBTS 5 sec.	HBTS 10 min.	Manual	NNH	HBTS 5 sec.	HBTS 10 min.	Manual
Case 01	8	7	7	7	11077	12681	12681	12681
Case 02	8	5	5	6	10953	10953	10953	10953
Case 03	8	7	6	6	8019	15040	15040	15040
Case 04	8	6	5	5	11302	12624	12624	12624
Case 05	8	8	7	7	11283	14262	14262	14262

truck for so little demand. In HBS-RoSLoP-I, the programming of vehicles is verified regarding to a minimum quantity of load; this constraint diminishes costs but reduces the percentage of satisfied demand, requiring a demand threshold from the user to determine the validity of a programming.

The algorithms were executed for two minutes. A sample of the algorithm performance can be observed in Table 18, which shows that HBS-RoSLoP-I obtains a reduction of two trucks on the average regarding to HBTS. Another important discovery reveals that the percentage of satisfied demand is very similar in both algorithms. It is important to mention that in HBTS the assignment unit is the bed and in HBS-RoSLoP-I the unit is the plat-form, which is bigger and therefore more difficulty to distribute.

The number of cancelled tours has little impact on the percentage of unsatisfied demand (2.55%).

In order to increase the satisfaction of the clients a post processing procedure is used to accommodate the remaining products. Table 19 shows the performance results when the constraint of a mini-mum quantity of load is removed. On average, the solution requires less than one additional vehicle, but the demand is completely satisfied.

HBS-RoSLoP-II Performance

HBS-RoSLoP-II incorporates a function used to transform the allocation unit into a real number (see the section where the Reduction Module is explained). Like the previous version of the transportation Systems, HBS-RoSLoP-II consists of two heuristics: ACO and DiPro.

Due to the incorporation of the transformation function, in this version less variants are consid-

Table 18. Comparison between HBTS and HBS-RoSLoP-I, the verification of minimum quantity of load is active

Instances	HBTS		HBS-RoSLoP-I	
	%Demands Satisfied	Used Vehicles	%Demands Satisfied	Used Vehicles
06/12/2005	99.48	5 *	97.66	4 *
09/12/2005	95.93	6 **	100	5
12/12/2005	95.53	3 **	99.06	4 *
01/01/2006	100	5	97.81	4 *
03/01/2006	100	4	100	3
07/02/2006	98.35	7 *	99.21	5 *
13/02/2006	98.43	6 *	99.52	4 *
06/03/2006	100	5	97.63	3 *
09/03/2006	99.30	6 *	98.65	4 *
22/04/2006	98.87	7 **	98.28	5 *
14/06/2006	98.33	7 **	97.83	6 *
04/07/2006	99.70	6 *	100	3 *
Average (All Instances)	98%	6	97.45%	4

* One tour cancelled by the restriction of minimum load of the vehicle
** Two tour cancelled by the restriction of minimum load of the vehicle

Table 19. Comparison between HBTS and HBS-RoSLoP-I, the verification of minimum quantity of load is removed

Instance	n	ORDERS	HBST		HBS-RoSLoP-I	
			Satisfied demand (%)	Used vehicles	Satisfied demand (%)	Used vehicles
06/12/2005	4	6928	100	6	100	4
09/12/2005	5	7600	100	7	100	5
12/12/2005	7	11541	100	5	100	5
01/01/2006	6	9634	100	6	100	4
03/01/2006	4	5454	100	4	100	4
07/02/2006	6	12842	100	8	100	5
13/02/2006	5	9403	100	6	100	4
06/03/2006	6	9687	100	5	100	4
09/03/2006	6	12319	100	7	100	6
18/03/2006	7	11662	100	7	100	5
22/04/2006	8	16903	100	7	100	5
17/05/2006	6	11410	100	7	100	4
Average	6	10873.53	100	6.33	100	4.58

Table 20. Performance of HBS-RoSLoP-II, less variants of BPP are incorporated

Instance	n	ORDERS		SBH-ARHC	
		boxes	Units	Traveled distance	Used vehicles
06/12/2005	4	6928	158	1444	4
09/12/2005	5	7600	171	1580	5
12/12/2005	7	11541	250	2500	6
01/01/2006	6	9634	286	2560	7
03/01/2006	4	5454	116	1340	4
07/02/2006	6	12842	288	2660	7
13/02/2006	5	9403	208	1980	5
06/03/2006	6	9687	224	1960	5
09/03/2006	6	12319	269	2570	6
22/04/2006	8	16903	381	3358	7
14/06/2006	7	10822	245	2350	6
04/07/2006	7	12347	270	2640	6
Average	6	10457	238.8	2245.166	5.666

ered; ACO solves twelve VRP variants (CVRP, VRPM, HVRP, VRPTW, SDVRP, sdVRP, rdVRP, VRPMTW, CCVRP, DDVRP, MDVRP and OVRP) and DiPro solves only three BPP variants (BPPCC, BPPOn, MDBPP). The performance of the system is shown in Table 20. The results reveal that the number of vehicles is bigger than previous version, but the transformation function allow us to build a model of Lineal Integer Programming (González-Barbosa et al., 2010).

CONCLUSION AND FUTURE WORK

In this work the load accommodation into vehicles was approached as a part of a bigger rich problem named RoSLoP because includes routing, scheduling and loading tasks. The deterministic algorithm DiPro is proposed for the construction of load solutions, it interacts with a metaheuristic algorithm developed to plan routes and schedules. The entire Transportation System was evaluated with real instances of a company dedicated to the production and delivery of bottle products;

its performance was compared with the manual procedure.

The Transportation System has evolved over five years with two objectives in mind: solve a complex real problem and contribute with efficient strategies to solve two Rich problems involved in our case study: Rich BPP and Rich VRP. The goal of future commercial systems is to offer the possibility of coordinate operations in real-time, matching: loading, resource allocation, dispatching and routing. This work is an effort in this direction

The best version reduces the time needed to find a solution from 3 hours to two minutes. It also yield an average saving of three vehicles needed to supply the customer and satisfy totally the demand. In general, the solutions can be considered efficient according with the standard given by our industrial partner. All instances were executed in a reasonable time for users that make transportation plans.

The experimental results show the viability of the development of logistic commercial applications based on heuristic methods. This software will allow companies to obtain significant savings for concept of transportation. This in turn, will allow companies to increase their utilities and to offer products with smaller prices.

HGGA-BP-I is a competitive algorithm proposed for solving BPP. As future work, it is intended integrate the HGGA-BP-I algorithm to the transportation system in order to solve large scale instances. Another future contribution can be the application of different neighborhood techniques and the addition of explorative focus to the Adaptive Clustering strategy; right now this method induces mo-re exploration.

ACKNOWLEDGMENT

This research was supported in part by CONACYT and DGEST.

REFERENCES

Alvim, A., Glover, F., Ribeiro, C., & Aloise, D. (2004). A hybrid improvement heuristic for the one-dimensional bin packing problem. *Journal of Heuristics*, *10*(1), 205–229. doi:10.1023/B:HEUR.0000026267.44673.ed

Archetti, C., Mansini, R., & Speranza, M. G. (2001). The vehicle routing problem with capacity 2 and 3, general distances and multiple customer visits. *Operational Research in Land and Resources Management*, *1*(1), 102–112.

Balgoh, J., Békési, J., Galambos, G., & Reinelt, G. (2005). Lower bound for the on-line packing problem with restricted repacking. *SIAM Journal on Computing*, *38*(1), 398–410. doi:10.1137/050647049

Balseiro, S., Loiseau, I., & Ramonet, J. (2008). An ant colony heuristic for the time dependent vehi-cle routing problem with time windows. In *Anales de XIV CLAIO Congreso Latino-Iberoamericano de Investigación Operativa*.

Beasley, J. E. (1990). OR-Library: distributing test problems by electronic mail. *The Journal of the Operational Research Society*, *41*(1), 1069–1072.

Bianchi, L. *Notes on dynamic vehicle routing* (Tech. Rep. No. IDSIA-05-01). Ticino, Switzerland: Istituto Dalle Molle di Studi sull'Intelligenza Artificiale.

Blescha, J., & Goetshalckx, M. *The vehicle routing problem with backhauls: properties and solution algorithms* (Tech. Rep. No. MHRC-TR-88-13). Atlanta, GA: Georgia Institute of Technology.

Cano, I., Litvinchev, I., Palacios, R., & Na-ranjo, G. (2005). Modeling vehicle routing in a star-case transportation network. In *Proceedings of the 14th International Congress of Computation* (pp. 373-377).

Chan, W., Chin, F. Y. L., Ye, D., Zhang, G., & Zhang, Y. (2007). Online bin parking of fragile objects with application in cellular net-works. *Journal of Combinatorial Optimization*, *14*(4), 427–435. doi:10.1007/s10878-007-9043-y

Cordeau, J., Desaulniers, G., Desrosiers, J., Solomon, M., & Soumis, F. (2002). The VRP with time windows . In Toth, P., & Vigo, D. (Eds.), *The vehicle routing problem, monographs on discrete mathematics and applications* (pp. 157–194). Philadelphia, PA: SIAM.

Correia, I., Gouveia, L., & Saldanha, F. (2008). Solving the variable size bin packing problem with discretized formulations. *Computers & Operations Research*, *35*(6), 2103–2113. doi:10.1016/j.cor.2006.10.014

Crainic, T. G., Gendreau, M., & Potvin, J. (2009). Intelligent freight transportation systems: Assessment and the contribution of operations research. *Transportation Research Part C, Emerging Technologies*, *17*(6), 541–557. doi:10.1016/j.trc.2008.07.002

Cruz, L., Delgado, J. F., González, J. J., Torres-Jiménez, J., Fraire, H. J., & Arrañaga, B. A. (2008). An ant colony system to solve routing problems applied to the delivery of bottled products. In A. An, S. Matwin, Z. W. Ras, & D. Slezak (Eds.), *Proceedings of the 17th International Symposium on Foundations of Intelligent Systems* (LNCS 4994, pp. 329-338).

Cruz, L., González, J. J., Romero, D., Fraire, H. J., Rangel, N., Herrera, J. A., et al. (2007). A distributed metaheuristic for solving a real-world scheduling-routing-loading problem. In I. Stojmenovic, R. K. Thulasiram, L. T. Yang, W. Jia, M. Guo, & R. Fernandes (Eds.), *Proceedings of the International Conference on Parallel and Distributed Processing and Applications* (LNCS 4742, pp. 68-77).

Cruz, L., Nieto, D. M., Rangel, N., Herrera, J. A., González-Barbosa, J. J., Castilla-Valdez, G., & Delgado, J. F. (2007). DiPro: an algorithm for the packing in product transportation problems with multiple loading and routing variants. In A. Gelbukh & A. F. Kuri (Eds.), *Proceedings of the International Conference on Advances in Artificial Intelligence* (LNCS 4827, pp. 1078-1088).

Dantzig, G. B., & Ramser, J. H. (1959). The truck dispatching problem. *Management Science, 6*(1), 80–91. doi:10.1287/mnsc.6.1.80

Delgado, J. F. (2007). *Modelado matemático para el análisis y mejoramiento de los métodos aproximados para la solución de los proble-mas de enrutamiento, asignación de horarios y distribución de cargas: una aplicación a la entrega de productos embotellados* (Unpublished master's thesis). Posgrado en Ciencias de la Computación, Instituto Tecnológico de Ciudad Madero, Tamaulipas, México.

Dorronsoro, B. (2007). *The VRP Web. AUREN and Language and Computation Sciences of the University of Malaga.* Retrieved from http://neo.lcc.uma.es/radi-aeb/WebVRP

Epstein, L. (2006). Online bin packing with cardinality constraints. *SIAM Journal on Discrete Mathematics, 20*(4), 1015–1030. doi:10.1137/050639065

Falkenauer, E. (1996). A hybrid grouping genetic algorithm for bin packing. *Journal of Heuristics, 2*(1), 5–30. doi:10.1007/BF00226291

Flatberg, T., Hasle, G., Kloster, O., Nilssen, E. J., & Riise, A. (2007). Dynamic and stochastic vehicle routing in practice . In Zeimpekis, V., Tarantilis, C. D., Giaglis, G. M., & Minis, I. (Eds.), *Dynamic fleet management, operations research/computer science interfaces series* (*Vol. 38*, pp. 41–63). New York, NY: Springer. doi:10.1007/978-0-387-71722-7_3

Fleischmann, B. (1990). *The Vehicle routing problem with multiple use of vehicles.* Hambrug, Germany: Fachbereigh Wirtschaftswissenschaften, Universitt Hamburg.

Gendreau, M., Iori, M., Laporte, G., & Martello, S. (2008). A tabu search heuristic for the vehicle routing problem with two-dimensional loading constraints. *Networks, 51*(1), 4–18. doi:10.1002/net.20192

Goel, A., & Gruhn, V. (2005). Solving a dynamic real-life vehicle routing problem . In Haasis, H., Kopfer, H., & Schönberger, J. (Eds.), *Operations research proceedings* (pp. 367–372). Berlin, Germany: Springer-Verlag. doi:10.1007/3-540-32539-5_58

González, J. J., Delgado, J. F., Cruz, L., Fraire, H. J., & Ramirez, A. (2010). Comparative analysis of hybrid techniques for an ant colony system algorithm applied to solve a real-world transportation problem . In Melin, P., Kacprzyk, J., & Pedrycz, W. (Eds.), *Soft computing for recognition based on biometrics, studies in computational intelligence* (*Vol. 312*, pp. 365–388). Berlin, Germany: Springer-Verlag. doi:10.1007/978-3-642-15111-8_23

György, A., Lugosi, G., & Ottucsàk, G. (2010). On-line sequential bin packing. *Journal of Machine Learning Research*, *11*(1), 89–109.

Herrera, J. (2006). *Development of a methodology based on heuristics for the integral solution of routing, scheduling and loading problems on distribution and delivery processes of products* (Unpublished master's thesis). Posgrado en Ciencias de la Computación, Instituto Tecnológico de Ciudad Madero, Tamaulipas, México.

Johnson, D. S. (1974). Fast algorithms for bin packing. *Journal of Computer and System Sciences*, *8*(3), 272–314. doi:10.1016/S0022-0000(74)80026-7

Kang, J., & Park, S. (2003). Algorithms for the variable sized bin packing problem. *European Journal of Operational Research*, *147*(2), 365–372. doi:10.1016/S0377-2217(02)00247-3

Levine, J., & Ducatelle, F. (2004). Ant colony optimazation for bin packing and cutting stock problems. *The Journal of the Operational Research Society*, *55*(7), 705–716. doi:10.1057/palgrave.jors.2601771

Manyem, P. (2002). Bin packing and covering with longest items at the bottom: online version. *The ANZIAM Journal*, *43*, 186–232.

Martello, S., & Toth, P. (1990). *Knapsack problems: algorithms and computer implementations*. New York, NY: John Wiley & Sons.

Martello, S., & Toth, P. (1990). Lower bounds and reduction procedures for the bin packing problem. *Discrete Applied Mathematics*, *28*(1), 59–70. doi:10.1016/0166-218X(90)90094-S

Mingozzi, A. (2003). An exact algorithm for period and multi-depot vehicle routing problems. In *Proceedings of the Odysseus Second International Workshop on Freight Transportation and Logistics*, Palermo, Italy.

Pisinger, D., & Ropke, S. (2007). A general heuristic for vehicle routing problems. *Computers & Operations Research*, *34*(8), 2403–2435. doi:10.1016/j.cor.2005.09.012

Rangel, N. (2005). *Analysis of the routing, scheduling and loading problems in a Products Distributor* (Unpublished master's thesis). Posgrado en Ciencias de la Computación, Instituto Tecnológico de Ciudad Madero, Tamaulipas, México.

Shaw, P. (1998). Using constraint programming and local search methods to solve vehicle routing problems. In M. Maher & J. Puget (Eds.), *Proceedings of the 4th International Conference on Principles and Practice of Constraint Programming* (LNCS 1520, pp. 417-431).

Taillard, E. D. (1999). A heuristic column generation method for the heterogeneous fleet VRP. *RAIRO - . Operations Research*, *33*, 1–14. doi:10.1051/ro:1999101

Thangiah, S. R. (2003). *A site dependent vehicle routing problem with complex road constraints.* Paper presented at the Colloquium Series, Institute of Mathematics, University of Malaya, Kuala Lumpur, Malaysia.

Toth, P., & Vigo, D. (Eds.). (2002). *The vehicle routing problem. SIAM monographs on discrete mathematics and applications*. Philadelphia, PA: Society for Industrial and Applied Mathematics.

Verweij, B. (1996). *Multiple destination bin packing* (Tech. Rep. No. UU-CS Ext. r. no. 1996-39). Utrecht, Tahe Netherlands: Utrecht University, Information and Computing Sciences.

Weise, T., Podlich, A., & Gorldt, C. (2009). Solving real-world vehicle routing problems with evolutionary algorithms . In Chiong, R., & Dhakal, S. (Eds.), *Natural intelligence for scheduling, planning and packing problems* (*Vol. 250*, pp. 29–53). Berlin, Germany: Springer-Verlag. doi:10.1007/978-3-642-04039-9_2

KEY TERMS AND DEFINITIONS

BPP, the Bin Packing Problem: Has the objective to search for the best packing of a set of items into bins. The classical BPP only considers the capacity constraint of the bins, but in order to approach real problems of transportation logistics new constraints have been incorporated as variants. This formulation is called rich-BPP. The distribution of the goods in the vehicles is planned by satisfying a set of BPP variants that depend on the company conditions.

Heuristics: Are criteria, methods or principles based on intuition for deciding which among several alternative seems to be the best. Many optimization problems are too difficult to be solved exactly within a reasonable quantity of time and heuristics become a practical search alternative to gain computational performance or conceptual simplicity, at the cost of accuracy or precision. The main draw-back of these approaches is that the search often suffers from getting trapped in a local optimum. Greedy heuristics apply some order that is based on greediness or priority. DiPro algorithm uses a weighted round-robin heuristic to balance the products distributed in the vehicle.

Metaheuristic: Is an iterative and intelligent top-level general process that guides and modifies the operations of subordinate heuristics to efficiently produce high-quality solutions, overcoming local optimality, in do-mains where the task is hard. Examples of metaheuristics are Genetic Algorithms, Tabu Search, Simulated Annealing, Ant Colony Sys-tem and their hybrids.

RoSLoP, the Routing-Scheduling-Loading Problem: An integrated problem that models three critical tasks involved in the product transportation using trucks as vehicles. In Ro-SLoP, three optimization objectives must be achieved: satisfy the demands of all clients, minimize the number of used vehicles and reduce the total time of the trip.

TLP, the Truck Loading Problem: One of the critical tasks of RoSLoP. It involves a set of vehicles, each one with m compartments to transport q different products of various sizes from a source (depot) to n different destinations. The optimization problem is how to load the compartments of each vehicle so that the employed space in the container is maximized and, indirectly, the number of used vehicles and the total time of the trip are minimized. The Truck Loading Problem is formulated with the classic one dimensional Bin Packing Problem and several variants.

Chapter 10
Recombination Operators in Permutation–Based Evolutionary Algorithms for the Travelling Salesman Problem

Camelia Chira
Babes-Bolyai University, Romania

Anca Gog
Babes-Bolyai University, Romania

ABSTRACT

The Travelling Salesman Problem (TSP) is one of the most widely studied optimization problems due to its many applications in domains such as logistics, planning, routing, and scheduling. Approximation algorithms to address this NP-hard problem include genetic algorithms, ant colony systems, and simulated annealing. This chapter concentrates on the evolutionary approaches to TSP based on permutation encoded individuals. A comparative analysis of several recombination operators is presented based on computational experiments for TSP instances and a generalized version of TSP. Numerical results emphasize a good performance of two proposed crossover schemes: best-worst recombination and best order recombination which take into account information from the global best and/or worst individuals besides the genetic material from parents.

DOI: 10.4018/978-1-4666-0297-7.ch010

1. INTRODUCTION

The Travelling Salesman Problem (TSP) is a well-known NP-hard problem intensively studied in operations research and computer science and commonly engaged as a standard test bed for combinatorial optimization methods. Given a number of cities and the cost of travelling (or the distance) between any two cities, TSP aims to find a minimum length closed tour that visits each city exactly once. The study of TSP is of significant importance to several application domains in planning, scheduling and logistics. TSP applications include drilling of printed circuit boards, x-ray crystallography, computer wiring, vehicle routing, order-picking problem in warehouses and scheduling problems (Matai, 2010).

Because TSP is NP-hard and exact solutions cannot be found in polynomial time by any algorithm, there is a high interest in developing good approximation methods for solving TSP able to determine a near-optimal (or optimal) solution using reasonable resources. Heuristic approaches to TSP include genetic algorithms (Larranaga, 1999), ant colony systems (Dorigo, 1997) and simulated annealing (Laarhoven, 1987).

This chapter focuses on the traditional evolutionary approach to TSP by which potential solutions are represented as permutation of cities (path representation) and the quality of an individual is assessed based on the corresponding tour cost. An important search operator in genetic algorithms is the recombination of two individuals which should be able to produce new potentially more efficient tours. Main existing recombination operators specific to permutation based encoding are described. Two previously introduced operators (Gog, 2006a, 2006b, 2007) - called adaptive goal guided crossover (AGGX) and best-worst crossover (BWX) - are presented. Furthermore, we introduce the best order crossover (BOX) operator. AGGX, BWX and BOX rely on different schemes for the recombination of genetic material from parents, global best individual, global worst

individual and/or the parent's line best ancestor individual. The comparative performance of all these recombination operators inside a standard genetic algorithm is analyzed for both TSP and a generalized version of TSP. The study is based on extensive numerical experiments for various instances from the TSP library (Reinelt, 1991).

The structure of this chapter is as follows: TSP is described and formalized; genetic algorithms are briefly reviewed with a focus on a simple evolutionary approach to TSP in terms of solution representation and fitness function; existing crossover operators for permutation-based encoding are reviewed; the proposed recombination operators are described in detail; numerical experiments are given for TSP and a generalized version of TSP and comparative results are discussed.

2. THE TRAVELLING SALESMAN PROBLEM

Given a list of cities and a starting point, a travelling salesman has to visit every city exactly once and then return to the starting city. A set of k points in a plane is given, corresponding to the location of k cities. The objective is to find the shortest route for the travelling salesman. The number of possible tours for k cities is (k-1)!/2 which represents a very large search space.

The Travelling Salesman Problem (TSP) can be formalized as follows. A set of k cities

$$C = \{c_1, c_2, ..., c_k\}$$

is given. For each pair

$$(c_i, c_j), i \neq j,$$

Let

$$d(c_i, c_j),$$

be the distance between the city c_i and the city c_j.

The TSP objective of finding the shortest closed path that visits each city exactly once means finding a permutation π' of the cities

$$(c_{\pi'(1)}, ..., c_{\pi'(k)}),$$

such that

$$\sum_{i=1}^{k} d(c_{\pi'(i)}, c_{\pi'(i+1)}) \leq \sum_{i=1}^{k} d(c_{\pi(i)}, c_{\pi(i+1)}), \forall \pi \neq \pi', (k+1 \equiv 1).$$

This problem can be defined as the search for a minimal Hamiltonian cycle in a complete graph.

TSP belongs to the class of NP-complete problems since there is no polynomial time algorithm able to solve it. The large interest in TSP can be explained by several aspects: the simple description of TSP despite the complexity of the problem, the broad application areas including a variety of routing and scheduling problems. Moreover, TSP has become a test bed for new combinatorial optimization methods due to the good amount of information known about TSP (Larranaga, 1999).

3. GENETIC ALGORITHMS FOR TSP

Inspired by the process of natural evolution, genetic algorithms (GAs) (Holland, 1975; Goldberg, 1989) are search heuristics widely used to generate useful solutions to optimization problems. A population of individuals (also called chromosomes) is used to represent the search space of the problem. Each individual encodes a candidate solution to the problem and an evaluation (fitness) function is used to assess its quality. GAs evolve a population of individuals towards better solutions based on mechanisms of selection, recombination and mutation.

The main steps of a standard GA are depicted.

```
Initialize Population;
Evaluate each individual;
Repeat until (TERMINATION CONDITION
is TRUE)
    Select parents;
    Generate new individuals via
crossover and mutation;
    Select individuals for the next
generation;
End.
```

The initial population is usually randomly generated and the quality of each individual is determined based on the fitness function. Every generation (iteration of the algorithm), parents are selected from the population to produce new individuals via crossover (recombination) and mutation operators. A new population is formed based on a selection process influenced by the fitness values of the newly generated chromosomes and the existing individuals. The new population is considered in the next generation of the algorithm. A common termination criterion of the GA is reaching a maximum number of generation (or finding a satisfactory fitness value). The best fitted individual in the final population is returned as the problem solution.

A standard GA is used to address the TSP. The representation of an individual and the fitness function are specified in what follows. A potential solution for the problem (a chromosome) is a string of length k that contains a permutation π of the set

$$\{1, 2, ...k\},$$

and represents the order of visiting the k cities. This is a typical TSP representation commonly referred to as permutation-based encoding or path representation.

Let S denote the search space (the permutation set). Fitness assignment is applied by the criterion function f given by:

$$f : S \rightarrow R^+, f(\pi) = \sum_{i=1}^{k} d(c_{\pi(i)}, c_{\pi(i+1)}), (k+1 \equiv 1).$$

The fitness function is to be minimized. Thus, the fitness of a chromosome is the length of the Hamiltonian path that visits the cities in the order specified by the permutation.

The crossover operator is responsible for generating new permutations of cities based on existing individuals and should facilitate an increase of the average quality of the population.

4. CROSSOVER OPERATORS FOR PERMUTATION BASED ENCODING

A brief review of recombination operators for permutation based encoding is presented in what follows. A detailed review of TSP representations and operators for GAs can be found in Larranaga (1999).

The *Order Crossover (OX)* (Davis, 1985) is based on the idea that the order of alleles and not their positions are relevant. Two cut points are randomly generated for the two selected parents. An offspring is constructed by copying a subtour from one parent and setting the remaining cities in the relative order from the other parent.

In the *Order Based Crossover (OBX)* (Syswerda, 1991) several alleles from one parent are selected and their order in the offspring is imposed by the other parent. The positions from the first parent are selected and random.

The *Edge Recombination Crossover (ERX)* (Whitley, 1989) assumes that only the value of the edges are important. Edges of a tour (and not their direction) are considered as containing the relevant genetic material. It actually considers that the path representation does not contain enough information and therefore, the edges list is added. The edges of a parent are preserved as much as possible in the offspring.

When using the *Partially-Mapped Crossover (PMX)* (Goldberg, 1985), a sequence of one parent is mapped onto a sequence of the other parent and the rest of the alleles are exchanged. This way, offspring inherit ordering and value information from the parent tours.

In *Cycle Crossover (CX)* (Oliver, 1987) the offspring is created by filling each position with the corresponding allele from one of the two parents. CX preserves the absolute position of approximately half of the elements of both parents.

Maximal Preservative Crossover (MPX) (Mühlenbein, 1987) is similar to PMX, but it has the advantage that it destroys a limited number of edges. A random subtour (complying to some specified length restrictions to ensure a meaningful information exchange) is selected from the first parent and copied in the first part of the offspring. The elements of the selected subtour are removed from the second parent. The order of the remaining cities needed in the offspring is given by the second parent.

When using the *Alternating-Position Crossover (APX)* (Larranaga, 1997), the offspring is created by taking one allele from each parent's first position, continuing with the second position and so on, ignoring the alleles already existing.

Position Based Crossover (PBX) (Syswerda, 1991) selects several alleles from one parent and their positions are imposed on the corresponding alleles of the second parent. The set of positions in the parent tours are selected by random.

All the crossover operators reviewed above will be compared via numerical experiments with the recombination operators proposed in the next section for various TSP and generalized TSP instances.

5. PROPOSED RECOMBINATION OPERATORS

The crossover operators presented in the previous section take two parent tours and construct offspring so as to pass information about the absolute position and the relative order of the cities in the parents. From these two types of information, it is expected the order of the cities is more important compared to the absolute position since the cost of a TSP tour does not depend on the starting city (Larranaga, 1999).

In this chapter, it is proposed to construct crossover operators able to consider information from other sources besides the two parent tours. This way, the three crossover schemes proposed in this section use information about the order of cities gathered from the global best individual, the global worst individual and/or the parent's line best ancestor individual (besides the parents) in specific recombination schemes.

The three proposed operators called *Adaptive Goal Guided Recombination (AGGX)*, *Best-Worst Recombination (BWX)* and *Best Order Crossover (BOX)* are detailed in this section.

5.1. Adaptive Goal Guided Recombination

The *Adaptive Goal Guided Recombination (AGGX),* originally introduced in Gog (2006a) and further improved in Gog (2006b), is passing to the offspring not only genetic information from the parents, as a standard crossover, but certain genetic information from the parents best ancestors (*LineBest*) and from the best global (*GlobalBest*) as well.

The concept of relevant genetic material is introduced in this context as representing the chromosomal information that can be retrieved in both *LineBest* and *GlobalBest*. The fact that genetic information from the *GlobalBest* has been preserved in individuals that represent the best ancestors of some chromosomes from the

current population, allows us to consider it as being relevant for the search process. We use this information in order to accelerate the search process by orienting it towards promising regions of the search space.

In order to be able to differentiate between good and bad genetic material, we have to decide what relevant genetic material means when considering permutation based encoding. In TSP for example, it is not important that a certain city has been visited at a certain moment of time, but rather the succession of visited cities, because the edges of a tour can be seen as the carriers of the genetic information, according to Wagner (2004).

Because preserving diversity in the search space, particularly in the first stages of an evolutionary algorithm, represents a condition for avoiding the search to become trapped into a local optimum, the amount of relevant genetic information passed to the offspring is controlled by taking into account the number of the current generation related to the total number of generations.

Let us consider *NoEdges* to be the total number of common genes of *GlobalBest* and *LineBest*, *NoCrt* the number of the current generation and *NoGen* the number of generations after which the algorithm ends if no better solutions are found. The number of (randomly chosen) genes kept in the offspring is given by:

$$NoKept = NoEdges \; e^{-\frac{10*NoGen-NoCrt}{10*NoGen}}.$$

where *m* is a factor that controls the length of the sequences of genes passed to the offspring. Experimental results have shown that *10* is a good value for this parameter.

NoKept is an exponentially increasing function that ensures that the diversity is increased in the first stages of the algorithm and the search becomes more goal-oriented in the final stages by keeping in the configuration of the offspring

Figure 1. Adaptive goal guided recombination operator

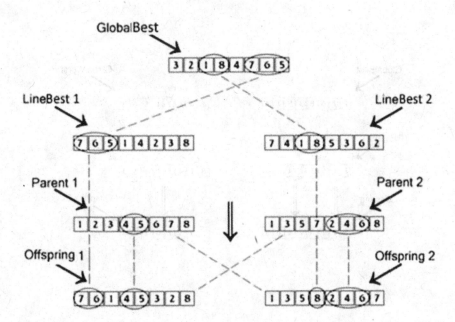

more relevant genetic information from the *Line-Best* and the *GlobalBest*. We also transfer to the offspring a randomly chosen sequence of genes from one parent.

Let us consider the example depicted in Figure 1. The sequence 7-6-5 occurs in both *GlobalBest* and *LineBest1*. *Offspring1* contains only a part of this sequence. The length of this part depends on the number of the current generation, the number of total generations and the number of genes involved in the common sequences, i.e., 3 for our example. Let us suppose that the number of genes kept in the offspring is computed as being 2 for our example. The randomly chosen sequence "7 6" is placed in the first offspring on the same position as in *LineBest1*. A randomly generated sequence from *Parent1* is copied in *Offspring1*: 4-5. The other genes of *Offspring1* are taken from *Parent2*: 1 does not appear in *Offspring1* yet, so it is placed on the 3rd position, 3 is the next gene, 5 already exist in *Offspring1*, the same for 7, 2 does not appear so it is placed on the 7th position, and so on.

5.2. Best-Worst Recombination

The *Best-Worst Recombination (BWX)* scheme, introduced in Gog (2007), is performed in an environment where each individual has extra knowledge about the best individual (*GlobalBest*) obtained so far in the search process and also about the worst individual *GlobalWorst* obtained so far. The goal of *BWX* is twofold: to use the good genetic material contained in the *GlobalBest* while performing recombination and to avoid transmitting to the offspring bad genetic material already contained in the *GlobalWorst* during the search process.

If one of the parents contains genetic material that can be also retrieved in the *GlobalBest*, we consider that these genetic traits should be also passed to the offspring in order to accelerate the search process. This strategy will save time needed to find good characteristics for the offspring, by using the already obtained ones. An exploitation of the search space is achieved by means of this strategy, because we choose good genes that should

Figure 2. Best-worst recombination operator

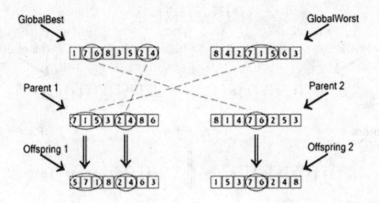

be passed to the offspring and we realize a local search around them.

If one of the parents contains genetic material that can be also retrieved in the *GlobalWorst*, we pass to the offspring a permutation of that succession of edges. This strategy will save search time by avoiding those configurations that prove themselves to represent bad genetic material, as part of the worst individual obtained so far. The exploration of the search space is also performed by the perturbation of these configurations.

However, not all genetic material contained by the *GlobalWorst* can be considered as being not good to the search process: there might be sequences of genes that represent good genetic material, but combined with other sequences of genes lead to the worst configuration obtained so far. In order to avoid the extinction of good genetic material, when performing the permutation of the sequences that belong to both parent and *GlobalWorst*, the probability that we obtain the same sequence is equal to the probability of obtaining any other permutation of those genes.

For the same reason, if there are sequences belonging to both *GlobalBest* and *GlobalWorst*,

these will be considered as good genetic material and passed to the offspring in that exact form.

For each offspring the rest of the genes are taken from the other parent. From the left side to the right side, each gene from the second parent that does not yet appears in the offspring is placed in the offspring beginning with the first available position.

By taking these features into account, the proposed recombination operator called Best-Worst Recombination (BWX) is described in Figure 2.

Let us consider two parents denoted by *Parent1* and *Parent2* selected for BWX recombination (Figure 2). The first offspring contains all the sequences of at least two consecutively genes that occur in both *GlobalBest* and *Parent1*. The position of these sequences is the same as in *Parent1* (2 and 4 for the example given in Figure 2). Also, all the sequences that occur in both *GlobalWorst* and *Parent1* are permuted and kept in *Offspring1* (7-1-5 becomes 5-7-1 in the given example). The rest of the genes in *Offspring1* are taken from *Parent2* in the following way: from the left side to the right side, each gene from *Parent2* that is not contained in *Offspring1* yet is placed in *Off-*

Figure 3. Best order crossover operator

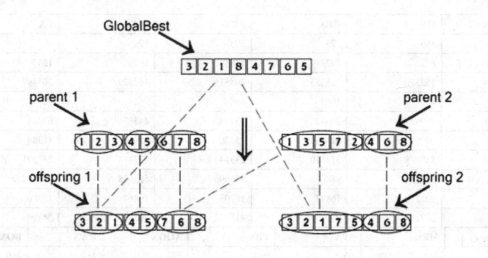

spring1, beginning with the first available position. *Offspring2* is obtained in a similar way only that it contains the sequences that occur in both *GlobalBest* and *Parent2*, the permuted common sequences of *GlobalWorst* and *Parent2* and the rest of the positions in *Offspring2* are filled with genes from *Parent1*.

5.3. Best Order Crossover

The new proposed *Best Order Crossover (BOX)* also exploits the fact that the order of the cities is important, not their positions. The main new feature of the proposed crossover operator is the use of genetic material belonging to the *GlobalBest* individual together with genetic information from the two parents that are subject to recombination.

Several cutting points are randomly chosen. The number of cutting points is randomly selected and can be even zero. Every two consecutive cutting points (including the beginning and the end of the chromosome array) will generate a sequence of alleles; when the number of cutting points is 0, we will only have one sequence containing the whole chromosome.

One of the following values will be assigned to each resulting sequence: -1, -2, -3. These values identify the source used for creating the offspring. A sequence identified by -1 means that the alleles will be taken from the main parent. A sequence identified by -2 means that the alleles will be taken from the other parent and when -3 is assigned to a sequence, the alleles will be taken from *GlobalBest*.

For example, in order to create the first offspring, we consider the first parent as the main parent. When we have a -1 sequence in offspring, we take the corresponding positions in the same order from the main parent. For a -2 sequence, we take the corresponding positions from the main parent but the order is given by the other parent. For a sequence identified by -3, we take the corresponding positions from the main parent but in the order imposed by *GlobalBest*.

In Figure 3, the sequence 4-5 is taken from *Parent 1* is the same order, sequence 1-2-3 from the first parent is copied in *Offspring 1* but the order is given by *GlobalBest* and the sequence 6-7-8 is also taken from the first parent but the order is given by the second parent.

Table 1. Average GA results over 10 runs obtained after 1000 generations with all considered recombination operators for 10 TSP instances

TSP instance	OX	OBX	ERX	PMX	CX
EIL51	486	623	594	520	593
ST70	873	1424	1383	1010	1247
PR76	153359	238253	208515	162829	205497
EIL76	708	1082	1060	751	969
KROA100	36992	70942	73739	44563	62446
LIN105	28907	51956	43120	32064	41386
PR124	149098	314630	233143	173774	239291
TS225	509356	980075	873696	583968	757458
GIL262	9322	16847	16703	10487	13286
PR299	247282	479800	414322	307267	344999

TSP instance	MPX	APX	PBX	AGGX	BWX	BOX
EIL51	841	1067	593	597	464	**460**
ST70	1739	2394	1429	945	792	**741**
PR76	284426	407957	215691	20645	141767	**121591**
EIL76	1265	1826	983	856	652	**605**
KROA100	83980	122240	72991	34876	33652	**27563**
LIN105	55282	88653	52944	25763	23342	**19575**
PR124	317210	498100	311195	135974	129811	**93154**
TS225	811696	1336437	1103359	537425	484764	**383227**
GIL262	14387	22599	19434	12876	9208	**6937**
PR299	357980	626387	513789	354765	226592	**172867**

6. EXPERIMENTAL RESULTS

6.1. Travelling Salesman Problem

Several TSP instances (Reinelt, 1991) are considered in order to provide a comparative analysis of the recombination operators for permutation based encoding.

A standard Genetic Algorithm (GA) is considered for numerical experiments. The population consists of 100 individuals and roulette selection, inverse mutation with 0.05 mutation rate and the various recombination operators are used. Furthermore, elitism ensures that the fitness of the best solution in the population does not deteriorate as the generation advances. For the considered

TSP instances, the GA is applied with the most popular recombination operators for permutation based encoding (Larranaga, 1999) described in Section 4 and the proposed AGGX, BWX and BOX operators presented in Section 5.

Table 1 presents the average results over 10 runs obtained after 1000 generations.

The test results indicate the acceleration of the search process when using the AGGX, BWX and BOX recombination operators (last three columns in Table 1). Moreover, the introduced BOX outperforms all the other operators for all considered problems.

The performance of BWX is clearly better than that of AGGX emphasizing the advantages of considering the information generated by the

276

Figure 4. Difference (in percentages) between obtained solutions and the best known solution for EIL51 TSP instance (426). Best and average GA results over 10 runs obtained after 1000 generations.

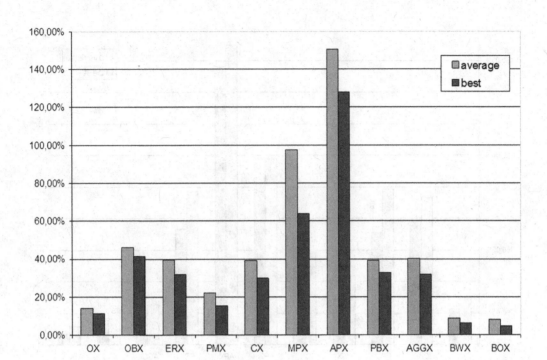

GlobalWorst solution in addition to the genetic material from the parents and the *GlobalBest*. It is interesting to observe that BOX performs better than AGGX and BWX although it relies on a simpler scheme. BOX takes into account positions order from *GlobalBest* only compared to AGGX which also considers *LineBest* or to BWX which also considers *GlobalWorst*.

The difference between obtained solutions with all considered recombination operators and the best known solution for two TSP instances is presented in Figures 4 and 5. It can be noticed that results obtained using BOX are very close to the known solution of the problem. Similar results have been obtained for all the other considered TSP instances.

Figure 6 depicts the improvement in percentages generated by AGGX, BWX and BOX after 1000 generations compared to the best solution reported by all other recombination operators. The analysis of solution improvement confirms BOX as the most efficient operator. AGGX was able to bring an improvement compared to other operators only for a few TSP instances while BWX is able to steadily improve solution quality but a lower rate compared to BOX.

The convergence process for GA using our best proposed recombination operator (BOX) and one of the best existing recombination operators for permutation based encoding (OX) for two TSP instances is depicted in Figures 7 and 8. It can be noticed that better solutions are already obtained within the first generations of the algorithm when using BOX. Similar results have been obtained for all the other considered TSP instances.

Figure 5. Difference (in percentages) between obtained solutions and the best known solution for KROA100 TSP instance (21282). Best and average GA results over 10 runs obtained after 1000 generations.

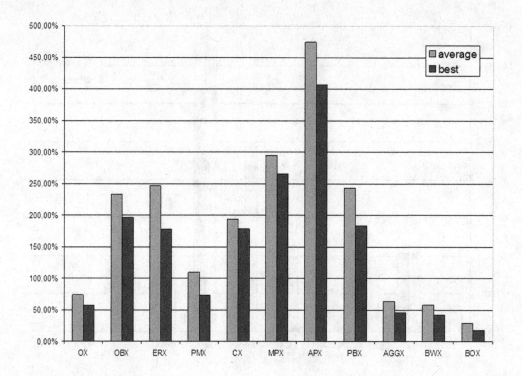

Figure 6. Solution improvement of AGGX, BWX and BOX after 1000 generations for TSP instances

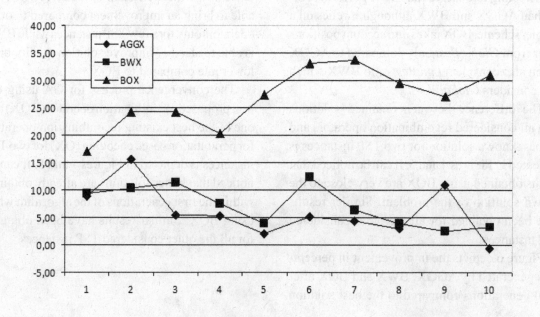

Figure 7. The convergence process for GA using OX and BOX for LIN105 TSP instance. The best solution obtained in each generation for one GA run with OX recombination and one GA run with BOX recombination.

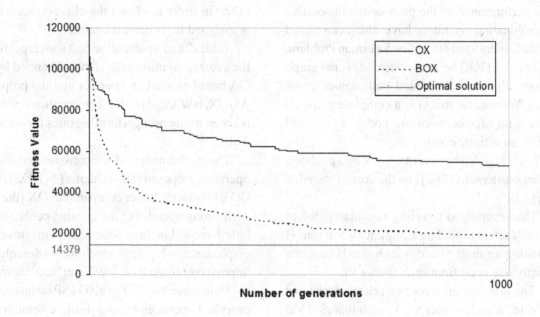

Figure 8. The convergence process for GA using OX and BOX for PR299 TSP instance. The best solution obtained in each generation for one GA run with OX recombination and one GA run with BOX recombination.

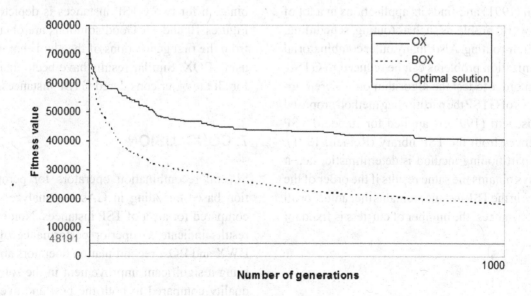

6.2. Generalized Travelling Salesman Problem

The performance of the proposed collaborative recombination operators have also been tested for the Generalized Travelling Salesman Problem.

Let G = (V,E) be an n-node undirected graph whose edges are associated with non-negative costs. We assume that G is a complete graph (if there is no edge between two nodes, we can add it with an infinite cost).

Let V1, ..., Vp be a partition of V into p subsets called clusters. Let c(i, j) be the cost of the edge (i, j) ∈ E.

The generalized traveling salesman problem (GTSP) refers to finding a minimum-cost tour H spanning a subset of nodes such that H contains exactly one node from each cluster Vi, i ∈ {1, ..., p}. The problem involves two related decisions: choosing a node subset S ⊆ V, such that |S ∩ Vk| = 1, for all k = 1, ..., p and finding a minimum cost Hamiltonian in S (the subgraph of G induced by S). Such a cycle is called a Hamiltonian tour. The GTSP is called symmetric if and only if the equality c(i, j) = c(j, i) holds for every i, j ∈ V.

The generalized version of Traveling Salesman Problem has been proposed in Laporte (1983) and Noon (1991) and finds its applications in a lot of real-world problems such as routing, scheduling, location-routing. Also, many other combinatorial optimization problems can be reduced to GTSP.

In order to test the algorithm on different instances of GTSP the partitioning method proposed in Fischetti (1997) is applied for standard TSP instances from the TSP library (Reinelt, 1991). The partitioning method is deterministic, i.e., it always obtains the same results if the order of the nodes in the TSP instance remains the same. For all TSP instances, the number of clusters is fixed to:

$$m = \lceil n / 5 \rceil,$$

where n represents the number of nodes. The m centres of the clusters are determined by considering m nodes as far as possible one from each other. In order to obtain the clusters, each node is assigned to its nearest centre.

Tables 2 and 3 present the best and respectively the average solution over 10 runs obtained by the GA based on the OX operator and the proposed AGGX, BWX and BOX recombination operators (chosen as the best performing ones for standard TSP).

The performance of the new recombination operators proposed in this chapter (AGGX, BWX, BOX) is clearly better compared to OX (the best performing operator of the existing permutation-based recombination schemes). This result is emphasized in Figure 9 which shows the solution improvement of AGGX, BWX and BOX compared to OX in percentages. For all GTSP instances, the proposed operators bring a positive solution improvement. For some instances, the BOX improvement is higher compared to that generated by AGGX or BWX. However, an overall superior performance of BOX over AGGX and BWX for GTSP is not as clear as in the case of TSP.

The convergence process for one GA run using BOX operator and one GA run using OX recombination for two GTSP instances is depicted in Figures 10 and 11. Good solutions are obtained from the first generations of the algorithm when using BOX. Similar results have been obtained for all the other considered GTSP instances.

7. CONCLUSION

Several recombination operators for permutation based encoding in GAs are analyzed and compared for a set of TSP instances. Numerical results indicate a superior performance of the BWX and BOX recombination operators able to bring a significant improvement in the solution quality compared to both the best and average results from the other considered operators. The

Table 2. Best GA results over 10 runs obtained after 200 generations with OX and proposed AGGX, BWX and BOX recombination operators for 17 GTSP instances

GTSP instance	Reported Optimum	OX	AGGX	BWX	BOX
11EIL51	174	201	**174**	175	**174**
14ST70	316	359	**316**	323	318
16EIL76	209	268	**210**	212	212
16PR76	64925	73529	65604	66531	**65274**
20KROA100	9711	14082	**9984**	10678	10112
20KROB100	10328	13661	**10391**	10699	10615
20KROC100	9554	13192	10084	9990	**9835**
20KROD100	9450	14398	**9563**	9935	10099
20KROE100	9523	14863	9961	**9831**	9901
21EIL101	249	375	258	265	**256**
21LIN105	8213	10717	8501	8506	**8349**
22PR107	27898	34894	28302	28205	**28185**
25PR124	36605	46205	**37622**	38254	38027
29PR144	45886	66125	47098	48848	**46322**
30KROA150	11018	19911	**13058**	12868	13280
30KROB150	12196	20215	13818	13845	**13660**
31PR152	51576	76245	**53001**	54748	54163

Table 3. Average GA results over 10 runs obtained after 200 generations with OX and proposed AGGX, BWX and BOX recombination operators for 17 GTSP instances

GTSP instance	Reported Optimum	OX	AGGX	BWX	BOX
11EIL51	174	205,8	179,2	177	**175,8**
14ST70	316	394,6	322,6	328,2	**322,2**
16EIL76	209	289,4	**217**	230,2	221,6
16PR76	64925	80743,6	67101,4	**67077,4**	67990,6
20KROA100	9711	15437,4	10650,6	10806,2	**10473,8**
20KROB100	10328	14933	**10722**	11131,8	11168,2
20KROC100	9554	14188	10685,1	**10145,2**	10177,4
20KROD100	9450	14683,4	10353,6	10892,6	**10338,6**
20KROE100	9523	15820,2	10556,8	**10392,2**	10655,8
21EIL101	249	408,2	286,8	295,6	**284,4**
21LIN105	8213	12322,8	8858,8	**8695,4**	8792,6
22PR107	27898	40152,6	28551,8	28536,2	**28406,8**
25PR124	36605	56487,4	**39016,2**	38698,4	39074,4
29PR144	45886	70545,8	50253	50715,2	**47934,6**
30KROA150	11018	22412,2	14133,4	14353,4	**13930,2**
30KROB150	12196	22073,4	15429,4	**14330,8**	14492
31PR152	51576	83071,2	**54876**	55777,2	55131

Figure 9. Solution improvement of AGGX, BWX and BOX after 500 generations for GTSP instances

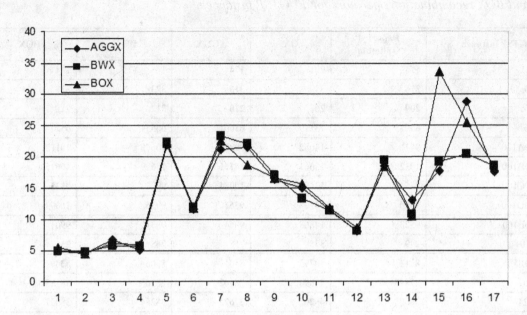

Figure 10. The convergence process for GA using OX and BOX for 29PR144 GTSP instance. The best solution obtained in each generation for one GA run with OX recombination and one GA run with BOX recombination.

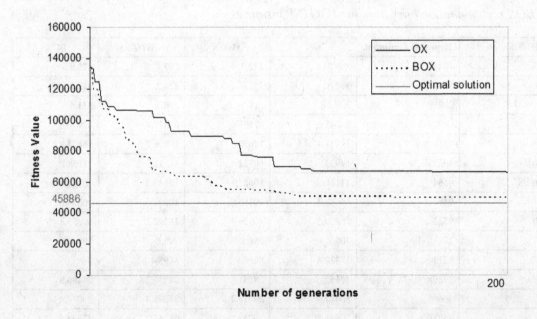

Figure 11. The convergence process for GA using OX and BOX for 30KROA150 GTSP instance. The best solution obtained in each generation for one GA run with OX recombination and one GA run with BOX recombination.

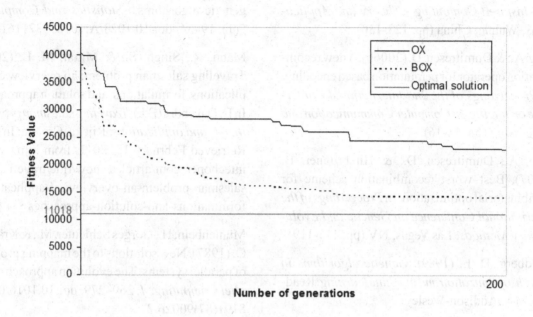

main features which make BWX and BOX more efficient refer to combining genetic material from the selected parents while considering the best (and/or worst) potential solutions obtained up to the current generation in the search process. Comparing BWX to BOX, we notice an interesting behavior as BOX is capable to obtain overall better results based on a more simple recombination scheme compared to BWX. It should be noted that the crossover operators described in this chapter are not limited to usage for TSP or GTSP but they can be engaged for any problems that can be addressed with a permutation-based encoding in a genetic algorithm.

ACKNOWLEDGMENT

This research is supported by Grant PN II TE 320, *Emergence, auto-organization and evolution: New computational models in the study of complex systems*, funded by CNCS Romania.

REFERENCES

Davis, L. (1985). Applying adaptive algorithms to epistatic domains. In *Proceedings of the International Joint Conference on Artificial Intelligence* (pp. 62-164).

Dorigo, M., & Gambardella, L. M. (1997). Ant colony system: A cooperative learning approach to the traveling salesman problem. *IEEE Transactions on Evolutionary Computation, 1*, 53–66. doi:10.1109/4235.585892

Fischetti, M., Gonzales, J. J. S., & Toth, P. (1997). A branch-and-cut algorithm for the symmetric generalized traveling salesman problem. *Operations Research, 45*(3), 378–394. doi:10.1287/opre.45.3.378

Gog, A., & Dumitrescu, D. (2006a). Adaptive search in evolutionary combinatorial optimization. In *Proceedings of the International Conference Bio-Inspired Computing - Theory and Applications*, Wuhan, China (pp. 123-130).

Gog, A., & Dumitrescu, D. (2006b). A new recombination operator for permutation based encoding. In *Proceedings of the 2nd International Conference on Intelligent Computer Communication and Processing* (pp. 11-16).

Gog, A., Dumitrescu, D., & Hirsbrunner, B. (2007). Best–worst recombination scheme for combinatorial optimization. In *Proceedings of the International Conference on Genetic and Evolutionary Methods*, Las Vegas, NV (pp. 115-119).

Goldberg, D. E. (1989). *Genetic algorithms in search, optimization and machine learning.* Reading, MA: Addison-Wesley.

Goldberg, D. E., & Lingle, R., Jr. (1985). Alleles, Loci and the TSP. In *Proceedings of the First International Conference on Genetic Algorithms and their Applications* (pp. 154-159).

Holland, J. (1975). *Adaptation in natural and artificial systems.* Ann Arbor, MI: University of Michigan Press.

Laporte, G., & Nobert, Y. (1983). Generalized traveling salesman problem through n sets of nodes: An integer programming approach. *Infor, 21*(1), 61–75.

Larranaga, P., Kuijpers, C. M. H., Murga, R. H., Inza, I., & Dizdarevic, S. (1999). Genetic algorithms for the traveling salesman problem: A review of representation and operators. *Artificial Intelligence Review, 13*, 129–170. doi:10.1023/A:1006529012972

Larranaga, P., Kuijpers, C. M. H., Poza, M., & Murga, R. H. (1997). Decomposing bayesian networks: Triangulation of the moral graph with genetic algorithms. *Statistics and Computing, 7*(1), 19–34. doi:10.1023/A:1018553211613

Matai, R., Singh, S., & Mittal, M. L. (2010). Traveling salesman problem: an overview of applications, formulations, and solution approaches. In D. Davendra (Ed.), *Traveling salesman problem, theory and applications.* Rijeka, Croatia: InTech. Retrieved February 15, 2011, from http://www.intechopen.com/articles/show/title/traveling-salesman-problem-an-overview-of-applications-formulations-and-solution-approaches

Mühlenbein, H., Gorges Schleuter, M., & Krämer, O. (1987). New solutions to the mapping problem of parallel systems: The evolution approach. *Parallel Computing, 4*, 269–279. doi:10.1016/0167-8191(87)90026-3

Noon, C. E., & Bean, J. C. (1991). A Lagrangian based approach for the asymmetric generalized traveling salesman problem. *Operations Research, 39*, 623–632. doi:10.1287/opre.39.4.623

Oliver, I. M., Smith, D. J., & Holland, J. R. C. (1987). A study of permutation crossover operators on the TSP. In *Proceedings of the Second International Conference Genetic Algorithms and their Applications* (pp. 224-230).

Reinelt, G. (1991). TSPLIB - A traveling salesman problem library. *ORSA Journal of Computing, 3*(4), 376–384. doi:10.1287/ijoc.3.4.376

Syswerda, G. (1991). Schedule optimization using genetic algorithms . In Davis, L. (Ed.), *Handbook of genetic algorithms* (pp. 332–349). New York, NY: Van Nostrand Reinhold.

van Laarhoven, P. J. M., & Aarts, E. H. L. (1987). *Simulated annealing: Theory and applications.* Dordrecht, The Netherlands: Kluwer Academic.

Wagner, S., Affenzeller, M., & Schragl, D. (2004). *Traps and dangers when modelling problems for genetic algorithms* (pp. 79–84). Vienna, Austria: Austrian Society for Cybernetic Studies.

Whitley, D., Starkweather, T., & D'Ann, F. (1989). Scheduling problems and travelling salesman: The genetic edge recombination operator. In *Proceedings of the Third International Conference on Genetic Algorithms* (pp. 133-140).

Section 3
Social Application on Logistic

Chapter 11
Crowdfunding to Improve Environmental Projects' Logistics

Carlos Alberto Ochoa Ortiz Zezzatti
Juarez City University, México

Sandra Bustillos
Juarez City University, Mexico

Yarira Reyes
Juarez City University, Mexico

Alessandra Tagliarducci-Tcherassi
Universitá Della Sapienza, Italy

Rubén Jaramillo
LAPEM/CIATEC, Mexico

ABSTRACT

Evolve computing is the generic name given to the resolution of computational problems, based in models of an evolutionary process. Most evolutionary algorithms propose biological paradigms, and concepts of natural selection, mutation, and reproduction. Nevertheless other paradigms exist which can be adopted in the creation of evolutionary algorithms. Many problems involve environments not structured which can be solved from the perspective of cultural paradigms, which offer plenty of category models where one does not know the possible solutions of a problem, a common situation in real life. This research analyzed the organization of a project using a Crowdfunding Model, supporting to social networking. Sociological research shows that Crowdfunding tends to reveal a bias toward social similarity. Therefore, in order to model this Project supported with Crowdfunding, the authors developed an Agent-Based Model that already manages the social interaction, together with featuring information of issues in different habitats and evolutionary belief spaces. To introduce these theoretical concepts Cultural Algorithms were used in the approach, explaining the process in detail. In recent decades, in all World supporting Environmental Projects evolved from its traditional form of swapping issues with another friend's and stashing those involving too many people from diverse countries all dedicated to conservation of habitats, Natural Reserve or National Parks.

DOI: 10.4018/978-1-4666-0297-7.ch011

"Hide you very well, tries to escape but do not allow that the humans know that you exist, since people never imagined to somebody like you!!! ;) - - Jeanne Raherilalao, discoverer of new bird specie in Madagascar

1. INTRODUCTION

Any specie of plant or animal, when exhibited in a zoo or nature reserve and while it is it pending, leaves its quality of recognizable and usable issue in the scope of a certain culture, to constitute itself in substituted of something different from itself, which this issue, by means of its exhibition, updates or represents a specific environmental habitat. By virtue of this characteristic the task of the coordinator of a zoo or nature reserve takes shape: to offer objects to the perception of the visitors so that these construct something that extends to the issue which they are seeing, but that it is what that issue represents or it means (or what the Zoological specialist tries that represents or means) due to being exhibited.

That is to say, due to being exhibited (and, in this sense, it happens the same if is exhibited it in the habitat of a zoo or the show in a garden of a private collection), happens to be a semiotic object (for example, a specific endemic issue that lives in a detailed habitat in certain community with determine climate, *Siberian Taiga* for example, to cover itself) to acquire the effectiveness of a substituent semiotics, (in the same example, the Zebras or heard of Ñu exhibited in a private collection like representation of a type of endemic habitat, a ecological field, a style of specific zoo, in others, or like identifier of a certain community related with the protection of animals).

On the opposite and as soon as they are originally substituent's semiotics, we excluded from this analysis the issues pertaining to rarely species, threaded or endangered because excessive hunting (Hawaiian Crow, Wyoming Toad, Socorro Dove, Red-tailed Black Shark, Scimitar

Oryx or Catarina Pupfish). To all of them one perceives them, originally, as propose visual destined to give account of something different from themselves, irrespective of whether they are or not in an exhibition situation. When they get to be exhibited, as much in the great collections of Zoos with specific habitats like in the Sultanate Brunei's Zoo or Nouvélle Caledónie Zoo where is possible see new birds discovered in this Century as: Black-capped Woodnymph, Rio Orinoco Spinetail, South Hills Crossbill, Rock Tapaculo, Limestone Leaf Warbler, Socotra Buzzrad, Fenwick's Antipitta, Willard's Sooty Boubou and, Mentocrex beankaensis; they act as a metasemiotic whose problematic it is different from that we are considering here and in that we do not take part, at the moment.

The responsible from a Zoo of an animal exhibition, composed by those semiotic issues that are transformed into substituent's semiotics like effect of their exhibition in a Natural reserve or zoo, will have to consider, anticipating it, an approach to how that issue can be perceived, how its proposal can be interpreted for the visitors according to different habitats. For it will be fundamental that it considers what the visitors know on that issue, to ratify or to modify or to contradict this ecological knowledge.

This exposition of different scenarios with animals in their habitats is the one that allows to affirm, as previous instance to the design and accomplishment of an animal exhibition, the necessity to identify, through public studies, the mental and symbolic processes of the social subjects regarding the type of issues that are going to be, to recover the interpretative modalities, are these zoological, decorative, scientists, aesthetic, or conventionally daily who are applied to them and who circulate in their community at the time of the natural exhibition.

The visitor of the Zoo, Natural Reserve, National Park or Private Animal Collection is with a physical space in which different options with respect to their possibility from perception and interpretation of a determined issue or set of issues (by brevity set out to him, we will in future talk about only "issue", understanding that he also includes himself, if so it is the case, to "set of issues"). It happens through the diverse relations that tie to that issue with the context in which is exhibited and with which are constructed the diverse communicative proposals. The context of an issue in an exhibition will be constituted by each one, and it's unfolding, of the iconic organizations, indicates and symbolic perceptible simultaneous or sequentially with the perception of the own issue.

Between the relational possibilities of an issue with its context we can identify, attempt and exploratory, some that come from the following scopes:

1.   The route and logistics to accede to the issue (trajectory in a Zoo).
2.   The demonstration of the own issue in a specialized habitat (A heard, flock or shoal in their own environment).
3.   The surrounding of ecological elements associated to the demonstration of the own issue. (A descriptive information about the specie including their conservational status.)

It follows a very elementary and merely programmatic development of each of these relational possibilities in a specify location to show ecological environments and their issues.

1.1. The Route to Accede to the Issue

The route designates to the set of the possible routes from access to the place from which the issue can be seen. It implies a sequence thought and planned based on a communicative proposal. The route allows to create in the mind of the visitor ecological references, previous to the perception of the issue in a plethora of different ecological environments as a Zoo, Natural Reserve or a National Park, conducive to suggest certain and not

another interpretation of the exhibited issue and/or its relation of similarity /difference /contradiction with other issues. For this reason, it is important that the responsible of organizing the location of animals will show designs and proposes a route beyond which the visitors accept or ignore it.

The route can consider a partial way (inside a room of exhibition to insect collections), total (in relation to the set of the sample of issues) or be absent (when a route has not been designed or when the exhibited issue is the unique one and immediately shown. In that case, the route is not contributing elements to see something different, but generates an access and visualization space), as in the Figure 1.

The world's largest zoo, in terms of numbers of different species in captivity, is the Toronto Zoo. The 287-ha (710-acre) site currently houses 16,000 animals from 491 different species, ranging from greedy zebra, red panda, Mountain Gorilla, Bactrian Camel, Ethiopian Wolf, Saiga, Takhi, Kakapo, Arakan Forest Turtle, Sumatran Rhinoceros, Javan Rhino, Brazilian Merganser, Axolotl, Leatherback Sea Turtle, Northern White Rhinoceros, Gharial, Vaquita, Philippine Eagle, Brown Spider Monkey, California Condor, Island Fox, Black Rhinoceros, Chinese Alligator, Amazonian Dolphin, Po'ouli, and Douc Langour and receives an average 2.6 million visitors each year.

The largest Zoo in terms of land mass is the Monarto Zoological Park in Australia, with a total of 1450 hectares. The zoo main purpose is the conservation of endangered species, and to educate the public. The Monarto Zoo participates in numerous successful breeding programs.

Vehicle Routing Problem as a Solution to Accede to the Issue in their Natural Habitat

During recent years distribution systems have become increasingly complex. This development is partly due to the high number of company mergers which leave distribution planners with

Figure 1. Map with the different routes at Singapore Zoo in Sentosa Island, this Zoo is considered the better in Environmental Logistics supported by the population via Crowdfunding (73% of Singaporian people support the Zoo)

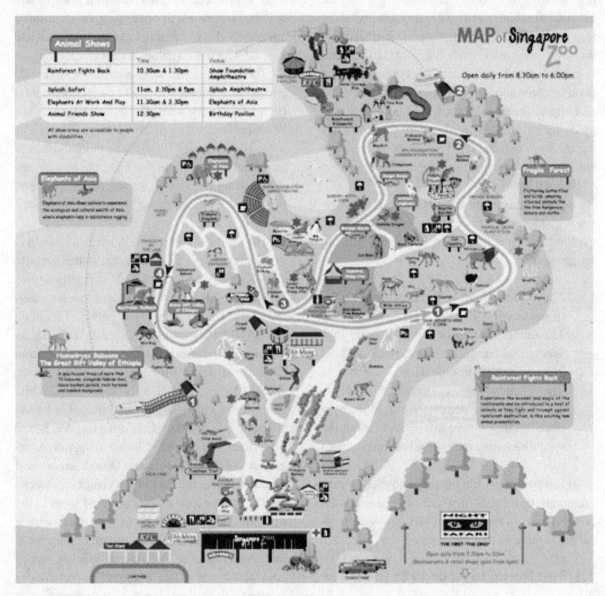

ever bigger and complex problems. Another fact complicating distribution is the increased focus on timeliness in the distribution chains, as intelligent planning offers potential savings in capital bindings in costs related to stock and distribution. In other words time has become an extremely valuable resource. Nowadays most distribution systems must operate under strict temporal restric-

tions. This fact has caused an increasing interest in dynamic transportation models and systems in which data are considered to be time-dependent.

In this research the dynamic counterpart of the conventional vehicle routing problem will be studied. The traditional vehicle routing problem (VRP) consists of constructing minimum cost routes for the vehicles to follow so that the set of customers are visited exactly once. The VRP is an important subproblem in a wide range of distribution systems and a lot of effort has been devoted to research on various aspects of the VRP. However, the vast part of this research has been dealing with static environments, which in this sense means that the problem data are assumed to be static and not subject to change during the planning horizon. The increased focus on just-in-time logistics has together with the rapid development within telecommunications and computer hardware implied that the study of the far more complex dynamic versions of the VRP has received increasing interest from the scientist community as well as from the potential users of these methods.

This research about Logistics begins by introducing the dynamic vehicle routing problem and discusses the differences between static and dynamic, VRPs as well as provides some examples of real-life examples of DVRP. The existing literature dealing with the dynamic vehicle routing problem and related problems is reviewed in order to provide an overview of the richness of problems that have been investigated within this field. The concept of measuring the dynamism within a dynamic vehicle routing problem is investigated and a framework for classifying dynamic routing applications according to their level of dynamism is proposed.

The Dynamic Traveling Repairman Problem (DTRP) proposed by Bertsimas and Van Ryzin is extended to embrace advance request customers as well as immediate request customers. Empirical analysis shows that the performance of the resulting problem has a linear relationship with the level of dynamism of the problem instances in question. Next, the capacitated vehicle routing problem in the presence of time windows (DVRPT) is examined under varying levels of dynamism. The performance of two simple batching strategies is examined in relation to the performance of a pure re-optimization strategy. The A-priori Dynamic Traveling Salesman Problem with Time Windows

(ADTSPTW) is introduced as an extension of the dynamic version of the well-known TSPTW. The extension consists in that a-priori information on future requests is included into the model. Furthermore, a real-life instance of the dynamic vehicle routing problem originating from the pick-ups and deliveries of long-distance courier mail is examined using the algorithm proposed to solve the ADTSPTW.

Finally, this research discusses the present state of various DVRP methodologies used in and a number of different ideas for further research in this area are provided. The thesis concludes that more research on measures for the

Level of dynamism in a dynamic vehicle routing context is needed in order to provide more descriptive measures. Furthermore, the thesis concludes that using a-priori information in order to be able to reposition the vehicles expecting to receive new requests does not seem to offer significant performance improvements with respect to the lateness experienced by the customers.

1.2. The Demonstration of the Own Issue

It alludes to the problematic one of how is the issue, that is to say, to the ways to exhibit it in agreement with which it is decided to privilege of the same. It is possible to be decided to show the issue exclusively and, in such case, to privilege his perception leaving of side his possible relations with other issues or elements. This occurs when the importance of constitutes it to the object in unique object (without necessarily a unique object must be exhibited in its solipsism) or when the force of its implantation in the imaginary group makes preferable leave to the knowledge and imagination of the visitor ruined the construction of its interpretation. However, one of the axioms of the semiotics establishes that the unique sign does not exist. This implies that they are not imaginable nor a system, nor a context of a unique sign. For this reason, still in these cases, the emptiness or

Figure 2. The Georgian Aquarium is considered the biggest in their kind with 147,000 issues; this Aquarium is located in Atlanta, Georgia

the absence of other elements near the unique exhibited object, acts like its context and with the high effectiveness to establish its particularity (Ochoa et al., 2008).

The problematic one of the demonstration concentrates in the characteristics of the proposal of visualization of the object, besides if a route has been designed to arrive until him or if the sample associated with others, for a simultaneous or quasi-simultaneous perception.

It implies an analysis of the support and/or container of the shown object. We speak of "demonstration" in this section to focus attention on the concrete way as it is exposed to the object so that it is seen. It supposes to consider the position and direction (possible formality and laterality) that, by its physical characteristics of form, size and color, they are selected to face the physical visitor, as well as relations that maintain with the elements with which it is in direct bonding and it

includes a study of the illumination that projects envelope; it constitutes its immediate context.

The **Georgia Aquarium** in Atlanta is the largest aquarium in the world, housing more than 100,000 sea creatures. Funded mostly by a \$250 million donation from Home Depot co-founder Bernie Marcus, the aquarium opened in November 2005. The *Georgia Aquarium* is the only institution outside of Asia to house whale sharks as the one shown in Figure 2. The sharks are kept in a gigantic 24 million liter (6.3 million gallon) tank in the Ocean Voyager exhibit. There has been controversy surrounding the decision of the Georgia Aquarium to house whale sharks. Concerns about keeping the whale sharks in captivity were heightened by the *deaths of two of the whale sharks* originally obtained, many people involved in Crowdfunding with this Aquarium has an alternative Virtual Aquarium with many issues from different species organized according to support from benefactors from all World, many

Figure 3. The Virtual Georgian Aquarium conformed by fishes or shoal from different people organized to crowdfunding this Aquarium, each fish has name and is similar to a pet including feed by a crowfunder

of this people contributing with funds in specimen and for this way, many fishes receiving names as pets from them as the shown in Figure 3 where is possible see a part of this Virtual Aquarium.

1.3. The Surroundings of Elements associated to the Demonstration of the Own Issue in an Adequate Habitat

No matter how hard the attention of that perceives something centers which permit show animals in their own context including their habitats, in which it perceives, the vision is registering, simultaneously, the surroundings including in its field of view. What mean or how they are interpreted these associate elements are fundamental for the attribution of certain meaning to the shown issue in your traditional habitat. If it is tried to say that an object always is going to be able to be identified by its individualized features (A Douc Langour always is going to be able to be recognized as a only primate with the capability to sit, or a strange blue bird always is going to be able to be recognized like a Kagu from New Caledonia, although it does not know why it serves), then the zoo becomes

unnecessary; it would be sufficient with a repository of animals. But a Zoo or Nature Reserve is a speech about the animals that it exhibits, as soon as suggests the visitors, like perceptual proposal, the possibility of a certain interpretation of the different origin of them.

In this sense, the surroundings of simultaneous or quasi-simultaneous perception of an issue in a Zoo so confer to issue the specific sense to it according to which the responsible of the Zoo or Nature Reserve proposes that it is interpreted by the visitors. For his analysis and for being three-dimensional organizations, those surroundings of perception are modified as the visitor modifies his point of view, when turning crossing the device of demonstration of the exhibited issue. It is possible that the responsible of the Zoo has privileged perspective determining or that all the sequence of variations concurs to the interpretation task. And in these cases, it returns to be applicable the possibility of using these relations to give to account of aspects regarding the own issue and/or to its relation of similarity/difference/contradiction with other issues, the majority of the presentations is related with bio climates as *Cfb* to Soft Summer and the relational issues of this climate.

Figure 4. The Aviary from London Zoo is characterized by a lot of elements related with the habitat from different species of birds and supported by crowdfunding

These surroundings are fundamental to determine if the issue is proposed to produce a unique interpretation or if, applying the criterion of the dependency of the context for the generation of the meaning, the people in the Zoo will be designed the successive surroundings like variations that they attribute to the meant issue different, for example the use of habitat by continent.

In this case, we consider that is just to say that certain descriptions allow to explain the production of certain meaning, since what is described it is a context and the hypothesis establishes that the context produces the meaning of each one of the elements integrate that it; of some way we tied this operation semiotics, with the premise of the French School of Analysis of the Speech, according to which, "all speech constructs its own biological dictionary".) This empirical practice will also allow being enriching and conferring a greater rigor that it identifies and it verifies the operative effectiveness of the relations that construct the meaning of the issues exhibited in the Zoo or using herds, flocks or shoal to a Nature

Reserve. Also, this practice constitutes a process of validation or falsification of the hypothesis, initially affirmed, about that an issue does not have a unique meaning when this is isolated, but so many as allow constructing their relational possibilities with the different elements from their possible contexts as shown in Figure 4.

2. CROWDFUNDING AS A DIFFERENT WAY TO OBTAIN FUNDS TO AN ENVIRONMENTAL PROJECTS

Crowdfunding, inspired by crowdsourcing, describes the collective cooperation, attention and trust by people who organize a social networking and pool their money together, usually via the Internet, in order to support efforts initiated by other people or organizations as in World Wild Foundation. Crowdfunding occurs for any variety of purposes, from disaster relief to citizen journalism to artists seeking support from fans, to political campaigns, but in recent years many people is interested in protect animal sanctuaries or threatened species in different parts of world as Borneo, Laos, Nouvelle Calédonie or Madagascar.

Crowdfunding, like Crowdsourcing, is very much related to online communities and social networks as World Wild Foundation. The crowd can already exist as a community but they can also suddenly form from disparate groups around the world who all happen to share an interest in funding an environmental activities, person, project, event, campaign in another. The Internet allows for information to flow around the world, increasing awareness. A Crowdfunded social networking can assemble and disassemble at any time. This is the primary difference to traditional co-ops with limited actions to support any specific situation.

Influence of the crowd is another factor, because is important reorganize by temporality the environmental projects. Psychology and sociological crowd sometimes can play part in the success or failure of crowdfunding efforts, because the social cohesion is very important to reach the objectives planned by the people. Likewise, forms of Reciprocity (sociocultural anthropology) are related to the mindset of people who participate in crowdfunding efforts as in the rescue of Iriomote Cat, another successfully situation is related with the reproduction of Giant Panda in Mexico City Zoo which include eight issues born in captivity, all these issues received funds from Crowdfunding in Figure 5 is shown the timeline of this specie.

Crowdfunding can replace the need for specialized grant applications or other formal and traditional fundraising techniques with that of a more casual, yet powerful, approach based on crowd participation. Examples of the basis of Crowdfunding can be seen in Cooperatives (co-ops) around the world. However, the Internet can provide new streamlined approaches to quickly imitating the co-op model for low-level and/or sudden needs (i.e., Rescue habitats with endemic species, disaster relief, travel expenses, legal fees and so on.). It is this reason that a term used to encompass the act of informally generating and distributing funds, usually online, by groups of people for specific social, personal, entertainment, environmental projects or other purposes (Conway, 2004).

3. APPLIED CROWDFUNDING TO AN ENVIRONMENTAL REAL PROJECT

The dynamics of social relationship is a highly complex field to study. Even though it can be found less literature regarding Crowdfunding and its relationship with a Social Networking (Ochoa et al., 2009) and the horizon of time to analyze the social cohesion, we are still far from understanding all the process involved. Social research has shown that people use numerous criteria when they consider the possibility of participate in a same project. But this research considers only two: cultural and sociological attributes of people (society) that determine the emergence and evolution of empathy to support environmental projects. After studying the theory available, we have decided to use "Crowdfunding" in order to model the system to obtain funds and determine the concept of *solidarity*. This principle assesses that the more similar cluster formed by several people are, the stronger their chances of becoming a group of supporters. Thus, we attempt to model the processes in which people of different societies (ethnicity, linguistic, country, religion, thematic community or political vision) turn to be acquaintances, those turn into a social networking (more of 27 participants) try to realize the economic support of an environmental project. Select a social networking to support a project, and thus it is not surprising that crowdfunding tend toward social and cultural homogeneity. People with the same preferences usually associate with other similar persons, in our case the Diorama built represented different societies from different points of view but with similar intentions of protecting the endangered species, the proposed

Figure 5. Issues of Giant Panda born in the Chapultepec Zoo during 10 years from an only couple, which was a gift from Popular China Republic and supported by crowdfunding by this reproduction

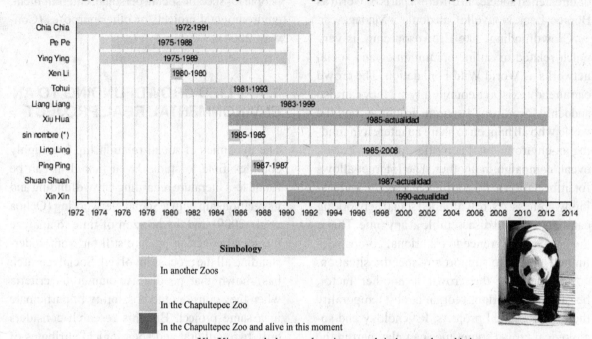

Xin Xin, uno de los pandas gigantes alojados en el zoológico.

- *Pe Pe* (male) and *Ying Ying* (female) were brought in September of 1975 by the Popular Republic of China, *Pe Pe* died in 1988 and *Ying Ying* in 1989.
- *Xen Li* born in August of 1980, but died 9 days after. Was the first issue of Giant Panda in born in captivity out of China.
- *Tohui* (female) born in July 21st of 1981. Was the first female issue of Giant Panda born in captivity out of China and still with life. Died in November 16th of 1993.
- *Liang Liang* (male) born in June 22nd of 1983. His parents were *Ying Ying* and *Pe Pe*. Died in May 23th of 1999.
- *Xiu Hua* (female) born in June 25th of 1985. Her parents were *Ying Ying* and *Pe Pe*. Has a twin male brother which Orly lives two days and the people in the Chapultepec Zoo decide don't put a name.
- *Ling Ling* (male) born in September 5th of 1985 in the Beijing Zoo. Was lead in three opportunities to Chapultepec Zoo: In January 29st of 2001 (Was almost Turing three months), in November 12th of the same year (Was more of five months try to reproduce) and finally in January 27th of 2003 (remained during three months in México). Died in April 30th of 2008 in the Japan Zoo of Ueno, in the great Tokio.
- *Shuan Shuan* (female) born in June 15th of 1987. It is the sister of *Xiu Hua*. In 2010 was translated to Guadalajara Zoo to exhibit and return to Chapultepec Zoo in 2011.
- *Xin Xin* (female) born in July 1st of 1990 and was conceives by artificial insemination. Her mother was *Tohui* and her father was *Chia Chia*. Was the 8th issue of Giant Panda born in Chapultepec Zoo.

model of Crowdfunding was applied to economic support of this project (Figure 6).

4. CURRENT STUDY

The advance in the technology has seated proceeding for the user's needs. Nowadays, they are not satisfied solely to computation programs that solve certain situation to them but they need and they demand integral systems that facilitate

Figure 6. Conceptual diagram of the organization of an environmentalist project

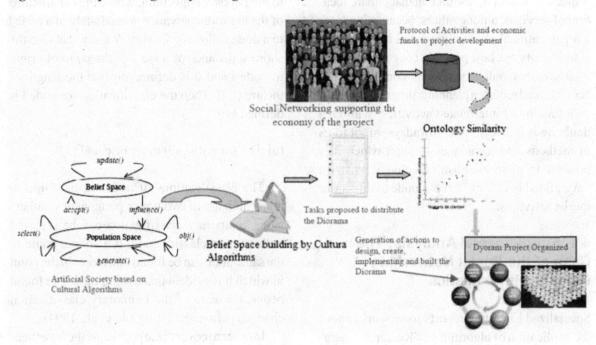

their life, from decisions making by a company, the automatization of processes in convenience stores, solutions to scholastic institutions, global communication of one too many and many to many and, by all means, the optimization of the processes in the real life.

We take for example, the systems of global positioning (GPS), a technology that does about six years we had not listened of it and took an impressive force, thanks perhaps to the exigency of the business users to locate in a global market its merchandises. Now, we transfer that exigency to our "real" world, where the motorists quickly locate certain points in a map and the same system draws up the shortest route to them facilitating its decision making. We are conscious of the problematic one that we are attacking and we create preparations to offer a practical, friendly and reliable solution to any situation.

At present the globalization of the economy demands the improvement of the productive processes and a more efficient quality of services reason why the application of the quantitative models in the Tourist Industry is more important, especially in the efficient allocation of the resources available of a company of tourist services.

The investigation of operations arises like an answer to the functional and geographic segmentation from the administration, natural consequence of the originated industrial growth in the industrial revolution. As of this moment, the necessity to consider the systems like a whole, gives rise to the executive function of the administration; this function requires that all the system like a set is considered, that is to say, to integrate the elements of an organization of efficient way, which generates that the executive function resorts to the participation of advisers with experience in the problems that gradually appear (Ochoa et al., 2007).

Some typical problems of the Investigation of Operations are regarding networks, between which we found the problem of shorter route. This discipline has been used in the businesses, the industry, the militia, governments, hospitals, banks, etc., to solve problems such as planning of project, production, resource management, location of services, among others, because it adopts a organizational point of view and its main goal is to identify the best possible course of action.

The tourist routes contemplate complementary activities and require a planning, programming and coordination of interrelated activities. Without a doubt he is indispensable nowadays, merit to us of methods and techniques through which it is possible to us to establish objectively what we have glided in order to have a guide to direct our tourist activities.

4.1. Supplemental Analysis: The Case of the Social Networking Related with Logistics

Specialized Literature reports some works about the application of algorithms of Research Operations in the solution of problems in the tourist Industry, in addition it exists a variety of studies that are based on the Geographical Information System (GIS), methodology which it is used to store, to manage and to publish and data related to the cartography and the computer technology that allow to conduct operations of information storage relating them to geographic objectives to be consulted when they are required, so is the case of a customized service for recommendations of the tourist route denominated "customized agent technological tourist" which they use besides a network of GIS and a positioning system to recommend routes a the tourists, applying the way of the shortest route based on a Dijkstra Algorithm given the distances of the route.

The Dijkstra Algorithm is designed to determine the shortest routes between the node of the point of origin and each one of the other nodes in the network. We consider connected a network directed in which to each one of the arcs a nonnegative distance is associated dij. The optimization of the route has concentrated in the calculation of minimum way between two nodes. A special procedure of classification was applied

to the Dijkstra Algorithm, where the calculations of the algorithm advance immediately of a node i to a node following j, using. We say that ui is the shortest distance of node 1 of the point of origin to node i and 0 is defined dij like the length of the arc (i, j). Then the classification for node j is defined as:

$$(uj, i) = (ui + dij), dij \text{ more or equal to } 0$$

The classifications of nodes in the Dijkstra Algorithm are of two types: permanent weathers and a temporary classification can be replaced with another classification, if a shorter route to the same node can be found one more. In the point in which it is evident that a route cannot be found better, the state of the temporary classification changes permanent (Bing Liu et al., 1994).

In order to cover these problems, the investigation adopts different algorithms, for example, the method Search Taboo that is a heuristic method that progressively selects each place based on the value that are assigned to him and the value of cost.

4.2. The use of VRP in Environmental Projects

Measuring the performance of a dynamic vehicle routing system is not a trivial assignment. In contrast to a deterministic and static vehicle routing problem the performance of the dynamic counterpart is assumed to be dependent on not only the number of customers and the spatial distribution of these, but also the number of dynamic events and the time when these events actually take place. Therefore, a single measure for describing the system's \dynamism" would be very valuable when one wants to examine the performance of a specific algorithm under varying conditions. As we will see in the following, measures that might seem promising for the use of describing dynamism for one system might turn out to be inadequate for describing the dynamism of other systems. Therefore this research is divided into two

Figure 7. A dynamic vehicle routing scenario with 8 advance and 2 immediate request customers

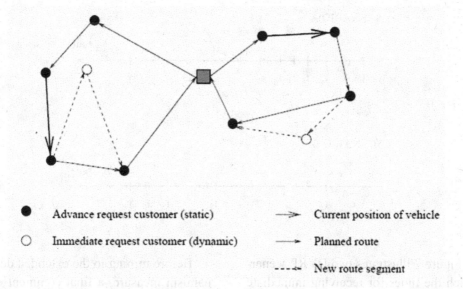

- ● Advance request customer (static)
- ○ Immediate request customer (dynamic)
- ⇢ Current position of vehicle
- → Planned route
- ---→ New route segment

sections where the first section discusses measures for dynamism in systems without time windows while the second section examines systems with the presence of time windows. The intention of this chapter is to examine the existing system measures with respect to describing the dynamism of a vehicle routing system and to introduce new measures for this type of systems. Furthermore, we propose a framework for dynamic vehicle routing systems based on their *degree of dynamism*.

4.3. Dynamism without Time Windows

In this section we examine measures which try to describe the dynamism of a dynamic vehicle routing system without time windows. In a system without time windows only three parameters are relevant: The number of static customers, the number of dynamic customers and the arrival times of the dynamic customers.

The Degree of Dynamism

In many dynamic routing systems information is not always only received while the system is on-line. Often, some level of information is gathered before the day of operation begins. The extent of new information emerging during the operational phase of the system can be used to assess the dynamism of the system in question. The most basic measure is shown in equation 1, for this in a routing context is the number of dynamic requests relative to the total. Following to (Lund et al., 1996), we define this ratio as *the degree of dynamism* of the system considered and denote it *dod* (Figure 7).

$$dod = \frac{Dynamic\ requests}{Total\ requests} \quad (1)$$

In the example shown in this illustration 1, the degree of dynamism is therefore 20% (2 out of 10 customers are dynamic). However, this measure does not take the arrival times of the dynamic requests into account. This means that two systems, one in which the dynamic requests are received at the beginning of the planning horizon and the other in which they occur late during the day, are perceived as equivalent. Naturally, in real world applications these two scenarios are however very

Figure 8. Arrival time of dynamic requests

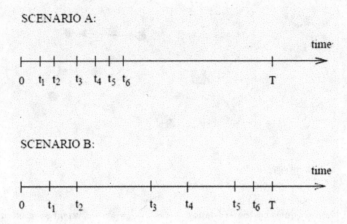

different. Figure 7 illustrates two DVRP scenarios in which the times for receiving immediate requests differ considerably. In Scenario A all six immediate requests are received relatively early during the planning horizon. In Scenario B the requests are distributed almost evenly throughout the planning horizon. We suggest that the planner would prefer the later scenario to the first, since Scenario B gives her time to react to the dynamic requests as opposed to the situation sketched in Scenario A in which she may not have enough time to find a suitable reaction to the dynamic requests received at the very end of the planning horizon.

Furthermore, from a performance point of view it is clear that having the highest number of requests in the pool of waiting requests improves the solution quality with respect to the objective of minimizing the total distance driven. Hence, in the systems illustrated by the two scenarios in Figure 8 the expected length of the route would be shorter in Scenario A than in Scenario B, due to the fact that the planner in the former scenario from time $t6$ has all information on the locations of the requests which means that from that point in time could form an optimal TSP tour through the pool of waiting customers. In the next section we extend the above defined measure to include the times when the immediate requests are received.

Before turning to the extended degree of dynamism measure, a final comment on the scenarios illustrated in Figure 8 should be made. Assuming that a number of advance requests are already in the pool of waiting requests to be served, the system described in Scenario A is likely to be the most difficult to manage, since if the planner is already busy taking care of the advance request customers during the early stages of the planning horizon, they would be likely to prefer to have to deal with the immediate requests later during the day after the advance requests have been serviced. Using this reasoning one might classify Scenario A as the more dynamic of the two systems illustrated. However, we chose to go with the first classification since this seems to be the most intuitively correct with respect to the performance of the system.

Effective Degree of Dynamism - EDOD

Let us now consider a scenario in which the planning horizon starts at time 0 and ends at time T. The advance requests are received *before* the beginning of the planning horizon *or* at time 0 at the latest. The time the i'th immediate request is received is denoted ti, i.e., $0 < ti \_ T$. The number of immediate requests received during the planning horizon is denoted n_{imm} and the number of

Figure 9. The reaction times of two dynamic customers in a DVRP with time windows

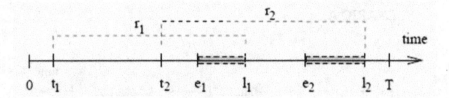

advance requests is denoted n_{adv}. The total number of requests, *ntot* is therefore $n_{adv} + n_{imm}$. We now define using the equation 2, the following measure as the effective degree of dynamism, denoted *edod*:

$$edod = \frac{\sum_{i=1}^{n_{imm}} \left(\frac{t_i}{T} \right)}{n_{tot}} \qquad (2)$$

The effective degree of dynamism then represents an average of how late the requests *are received* compared to the latest possible time the requests *could be received*. It can easily seen that:

$$0 \leq edod \leq 1 \qquad (3)$$

Where *edod* = 0 in a pure dynamic system and *edod* = 1 in a pure static system in which all the requests are received at time 0 and time T respectively. It is also obvious that

$$\lim_{t_i \to T \forall i} edod = 1 \qquad (4)$$

Dynamism and Time Windows

In several vehicle routing applications the service of the customers must commence within a given interval of time - usually referred to as Time Windows (TW). The time the i'th immediate request is received is denoted t_i and the earliest time that service can begin (i.e., the start of the time window) is denoted e_i while the latest possible time that service should begin is denoted l_i.

In applications with time windows the *reaction time* is a very important issue. The reaction time is defined as the temporal distance between the time the request is received and the latest possible time at which the service of the requests should begin. In Figure 9, the reaction time of the i'th immediate request is denoted r_i, i.e., $r_i = l_i - t_i$. In this section the effective degree of dynamism is extended so that the reaction times are included in the measure.

Effective Degree of Dynamism - EDOD-TW

Consider the two scenarios sketched in Figure 10 - in both of these scenarios we have two immediate requests with time windows. In Scenario A the width of the time windows of the immediate requests is relatively wide compared to the width of the time windows in Scenario B. Furthermore, the reaction times in Scenario A are relatively long compared to the reaction times in Scenario B. This means that Scenario A would be preferred by the planner because this situation gives it much more room to insert the dynamic requests into the routes. In general the planner would prefer to have a relatively long reaction time for the immediate requests. The following measure therefore uses the relation between the reaction time and the remaining part of the planning horizon as the key component.

The effective degree of dynamism measure can then be extended to:

Figure 10. Two scenarios with two dynamic requests

SCENARIO A:

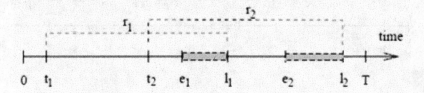

SCENARIO B:

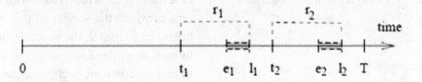

$$edod - tw = \frac{1}{n_{tot}} \sum_{i=1}^{n_{tot}} \left(\frac{T - (l_i - t_i)}{T} \right) \qquad (5)$$

$$= \frac{1}{n_{tot}} \sum_{i=1}^{n_{tot}} \left(1 - \frac{r_i}{T}\right) \qquad (6)$$

Again, it is easy to see that

$$0 \leq edod - tw \leq 1 \qquad (7)$$

because

$$l_i - t_i \leq T, \quad i = 1, 2, ..., n_{tot} \qquad (8)$$

4.4. Framework for Dynamic Systems

In this section we propose a general framework for the dynamic routing systems based on their degree of dynamism. The degree of dynamism measure gives rise to a continuum of dynamic levels. However, we believe it is possible to categorize the vast majority of routing systems found

in practice by using three echelons. Henceforth, we only discern between weakly, moderately, and strongly dynamic systems. We discuss these next.

Weakly Dynamic Systems

Routing environments with a weak degree of dynamism include the distribution of heating oil or liquid gas to private households. In this example, most customers (more than 80%) are known at the time of the construction of the routes. These are "automatic replenishment" customers for whom the company uses their demand profile and "degree days" to schedule deliveries. Requests may also be received during the day from "on call" customers. They get serviced as a function of their level of inventory, the available time, and unused tank capacity. The reaction time is considerably longer in such a problem compared to that in a taxi dispatching system. Other examples include residential utility repair services, such as cable television and telephone. The transportation of elderly and handicapped people - usually referred to as the dynamic dial-a-ride problem – is yet another example of a routing system that can be classified as weakly dynamic.

The traditional approach for solving such problems has been based on adaptation of static procedures. A static vehicle routing problem is solved every time an input update occurs. The relationship between the solution quality of such an approach and the degree of dynamism is examined in detail.

Moderately Dynamic Systems

Practical examples of such systems include long-distance courier mail services and appliance repairs. In the latter setting, for instance, scheduled customers are interspersed with dynamic ones that need immediate attention due to the gravity of their request (e.g., a broken refrigerator will take precedence over an already scheduled partly broken stove top). Compared to weakly dynamic systems, in moderate ones the number of immediate requests account for a substantial part of the total number of customers who have to be serviced. For a wide range of applications, researchers have also included stochastic elements, such as unknown customer demands, and used stochastic programming models. However, these tend to become extremely hard to solve due to their combinatorial nature. Solution strategies have often been based on deferring decisions until the latest possible moment. Ideally, this will improve the quality of the decisions made because the level of uncertainty decreases as time elapses. Yet, the frequent updates of the available information severely limit computation time. As an alternative approach, one could use a model which utilizes the time between input updates to perform improvements of potential routes. This, of course, requires detailed information on future requests.

Strongly Dynamic Systems

Emergency services, such as police, fire and ambulance departments exhibit strong dynamic behavior. Another example is taxi cab services in which only a negligible number of the customers have ordered their ride in advance. The importance of especially the first of these problems has motivated numerous strategic and tactical analyses of their associated costs and quality of service since the early 1970s. In particular, ways to decrease response times have been studied with continued interest. The work of Larson and Odoni (1980) captures many of the key issues. Strongly dynamic systems are characterized by the fast pace of changes in the data and the urgency of almost all requests received. Furthermore, the quality of a-priori information is often relatively poor with regards to data such as the locations of the customers, their demands, etc. If, on the other hand, a-priori information or even expectations are available, it would be evident to try to incorporate them into the algorithms used. For example, this could involve moving an idle vehicle currently situated in a low traffic area to a central location.

Another characteristic of these systems is that queuing begins to occur in relatively heavy traffic. Therefore, handling aspects related to it often plays a central role. This is especially true given the type of systems found in practice and the importance of reaction time. Examples of queueing-based algorithms include those by Bertsimas and Van Ryzin (1991, 1993a, 1993b).

4.5. System Classification

The objective of a dynamic routing system is often closely related to the response time of the service provided. Figure 11 illustrates the relationship between the degree of dynamism and the objectives for different problem classes.

Problems placed in the upper-right corner of the figure are characterized by a strong dynamism and an objective which seeks to minimize the

Figure 11. Illustration of the framework for classifying dynamic routing problems by their degree of dynamism and their objective

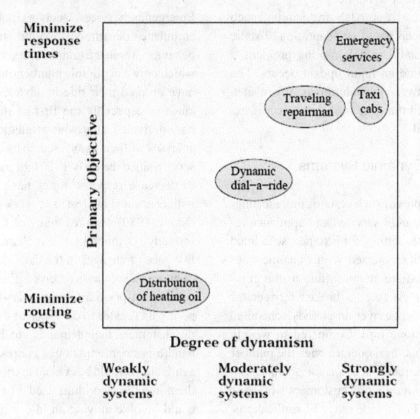

response time of the system. This would be the case in for instance emergency services like police, _re and ambulances services where almost all customers are immediate requests and the time for the emergency service personnel to arrive at the incident is sought to be minimized. Problems placed in the lower-left corner are characterized by few immediate requests and the wish to minimize the routing costs. Of course, using such strict labeling often means that some elements get misplaced and therefore cause misunderstandings. Therefore, the relation scheme illustrated in Figure 11 should be handled with much care and not misused to try to force a problem into a misplaced position in the figure. The dynamic dial-a-ride problem is one example of an application which is found in many different versions. The so-called *tele-bus* version of the dial-a-ride problem (DARP)

is highly likely to be more dynamic than the transportation of the elderly and handicapped people due to the fact that the latter group would usually have planned their trip in advance, while the former group would be more likely to make instant travel decisions.

In this research the degree of dynamism measure was examined for systems both with and without time window constraints. Furthermore, a framework for dynamic vehicle routing systems based on their degree of dynamism was proposed. The framework should prove useful in selecting appropriate models and algorithms according to the dynamic characteristics of the system examined, in this case environmental project where is very important obtain supplies in real time and deliver products and services with alive issues

Figure 12. Generated optimal route by means of Djikstra Algorithm for a route on the visit restrictions in time and specific issues and their habitats

Node	Destinity
1	Lions
2	Macaws
3	Bears
4	Dolphins
5	Horses
6	Elephants
7	Prairie Wolfs

and specialized food or resources which are of vital support in different habitats.

5. EXPERIMENTS

We simulated by means of the developed tool the expectations that propagation of activities to building a Diorama which support an environmental project with all the people described in the literature related at this topic (Ochoa, 2008). One of the observed most interesting characteristics in this experiment were the diversity of the social and cultural patterns established by each community because the selection of different attributes in a potential location according to a specific cluster. The structured scenes associated the agents cannot be reproduced in general, so that the time and space belong to a given moment in. They represent a unique form, needs and innovator of adaptive behavior which solves a followed computational problem of a complex change of relations. Using Cultural Algorithms (Reynolds, 1998) implementing with agents is possible simulate the behavior of many people (Ustaoglu & Yesim, 2009) in the selection of a project and determinate whom people support this social networking. Using Coriolis Vector (Hillier & Lieberman, 1991) (see Equation 9 was possible determine the individuals whom support and move the social networking.

$$q = [M - 2c] \, q'z \, 0 \qquad (9)$$

5.1. Intelligent Logistic Tool Development

The process of work of this tourist technological agent is adopted to a software where the agents apply generally, a class of intelligent learning; this is information in agreement with the tastes and preferences of the tourist, from an algorithm that they can incorporate to the system and the results of the same are indeed the best alternative for the tourist, like the observed thing in arises there (Macy & Willer, 2009).

The construction of the route is an iterative process to select the most attractive way with each step based on the personal interests of the tourist (Figure 12).

Example:

This algorithm allows realizing a planning of the trip determining the shortest route between nodes 1, in this case the node and cage from Lion any other in the network. The shortest route is determined beginning in the wished destination and backing down through the nodes using the information provided by the permanent classifications. For example, if they are desired to visit Praire Wolfs leaving from Lions one, the following sequence determines the shortest route of node 1 to node 7,

Figure 13. Multiagents Systems Environment to organize the different Societies in a Diorama (With people from different societies as Crowfunders) to support an environmental project. Each color represents a different cluster related with: Ethnicity, Use of Technology, Cultural Identity, Commerce, Architecture, Textile Heritage, Language, Environment Protection, Travels to specific habitats and natural collections, Telepathy and Psycho Abilities, The Art of War, Holographic Societies and Living in Class K Climates. Each feature is adjusted according highest interclass similarity and highest intraclass similarity.

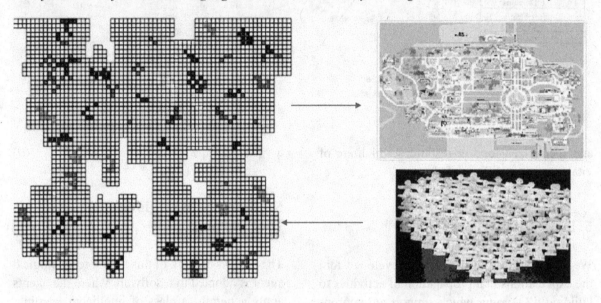

1 - 2 - 4 - 7 with a time of transfer of 26 minutes. That is to say, to leave the section of from Lions one, to visit macaws, to happen to the dolphins and to finish with Prairie Wolfs. The permanent label that it classifies to node 7: [26.4] says to us that the total time of route is of 26 minutes, arriving through node 4. This procedure allows programming the sites to pause a little to watch the animal, as well as the times destined for the recreation and feeding in the visit at Leon Zoo.

Results

The development of oriented computer science applications to the aid in the decision making in problems of routes of vehicles requires of an interface in scale of the situation, frequently based on a motor and GIS, of decision activated with a concrete entrance, the specific time or the "nodes". The results obtained in this last module are summarized and usually outlined in a graphical application. The scope of this study is located in the development of schemes of decision from mathematical models, or algorithms of solution, as it is the case of the Dijkstra algorithm. We undertook the study of classic problems of optimization in the design of routes, for which we propose some methods of solution, which will lead us to the optimal resolution of these problems by means of general techniques. One will be to implement beta versions of the application to collect data that can be to us excellent in another line of research.

6. CONCLUSION

Excellent studies also exist that have been carried out in this field of the investigation of operations, so is the case of Travel Salesman Problem (TSP), Prize collecting Travel Salesman Problem (PCTSP) and Orienteering Tour Problem (OTP). These refer problems that appear like a travelling agent and which they try to as much give to optimal solutions with the application of algorithms using geographic information and attractive data bases of the tourist ones, complementary services, considered distances and times; among others attributes of interest for the tourist.

The problem of the traveler of commerce or Traveling Salesman Problem (TSP) is one of the paradigmatic problems of the Combinatory Optimization, and it is used like reference when it is tried to evaluate a new technique or algorithmic idea for this field. The TSP has a significant influence in the development of algorithms of plane of cuts such as to the algorithms Branch-and-Cut type. The TSP is very easy to define: given a finite number of cities between which a distance associated to the transfer cost is defined, to find the cycle of minimum cost that to begin with visits all the cities returning the point.

First observe that valued crowdfunding (support in the realization of a specific projected with financial funds) always plays a very significant role, which should of course not be surprising. Hidden patterns observed in the agents are related with social, linguistic and cultural distances, and the expectative of selection of a location whit specific relation to another people with similar attributes this permit obtain better funds to reach environmental projects. The nodes with more value in their degree are considered more popular and support the social networking to this proposes. To get some insight, we run 100 regressions on 100 random samples of half the number of observations, and count the number of times each parameter affect the graph built determined the attributes offered by theirs are adequate for others, it permits shown the simulation with multi agents system and finally the Diorama built with these attributes (Figure 13).

7. DISCUSSIONS AND FUTURE RESEARCH

Using Cultural Algorithms, we improved the understanding substantially to obtain the change of "best paradigm", because we appropriately separated the agent communities basing to us on an approach to the relation that keep their attributes, this allowed us to understand the concept of "Crowdfunding" based on the time of époques of interaction. This technique allows including the possibility of generating experimental knowledge created by the community of agents for organized a Diorama to support a specific environmental project. The analysis of the level and degree of cognitive knowledge of each community is an aspect that is desired to evaluate for the future work (Araiza, 2011). Understand the true similarities that have different societies with base in the characteristics that make them contributor of cluster and it as well allows him to keep his own identity, demonstrates that the small variations go beyond physical characteristics and are mainly associate to tastes and similar characteristics developed through the time (Ochoa et al., 2009). A new modeling of Artificial Societies can take care to analyze retail these complexities that each society keeps, without forgetting that still they need to us methods to understand each society and its representation.

REFERENCES

Araiza, C. (2011). Save me: An approach to social isolation through the use of multi-agent systems. In *Proceedings of the 4th Hybrid Intelligent Systems Workshop in conjunction with the 10th Mexican International Conference on Artificial Intelligence.*

Bertsimas, D., & Van Ryzin, G. (1991). A stochastic and dynamic vehicle routing problem in the Euclidean plane. *Operations Research, 39,* 601–615. doi:10.1287/opre.39.4.601

Bertsimas, D., & Van Ryzin, G. (1993a). Stochastic and dynamic vehicle routing problem in the Euclidean plane with multiple capacitated vehicles. *Operations Research*, *41*, 60–76. doi:10.1287/opre.41.1.60

Bertsimas, D., & Van Ryzin, G. (1993b). Stochastic and dynamic vehicle routing with general demand and interarrival time distributions. *Applied Probability*, *25*, 947–978. doi:10.2307/1427801

Conway, J. (2004). Theory of games to improve artificial societies. *International Journal of Intelligent Games & Simulation*.

Hillier, F., & Lieberman, G. (1991). *Introducción a la Investigación de operaciones*. Estado de Mexico, Mexico: McGraw-Hill Interamericana de Mexico S.A. de C.V.

Larson, R. C., & Odoni, A. R. (1980). *Urban operations research*. Upper Saddle River, NJ: Prentice Hall.

Liu, B., Choo, S.-H., Lok, S.-L., Leong, S.-M., Lee, S.-C., Poon, F.-P., & Tan, H.-H. (1994). Finding the shortest route using cases, knowledge, and Djikstra's Algorithm. *IEEE Expert*, *9*(5), 7–11. doi:10.1109/64.331478

Lund, K., Madsen Oli, B. G., & Rygaard, J. M. (1996). *Vehicle routing problems with varying degrees of dynamism (Tech. Rep.)*. Lyngby, Denmark: IMM, The Department of Mathematical Modelling, Technical University of Denmark.

Macy, M. W., & Willer, R. (2002). From factors to actors: Computational sociology and agent-based modeling. *Annual Review of Sociology*, *28*, 143–166. doi:10.1146/annurev.soc.28.110601.141117

Ochoa, A., et al. (2007). Baharastar – Simulador de Algoritmos Culturales para la Minería de Datos Social. In *Proceedings of COMCEV*.

Ochoa, A. (2008). *Data mining in medical and biological research* (Giannopoullou, E. G., Ed.). Vienna, Austria: I-Tech.

Ochoa, A. (2009). *Six degrees of separation in a graph to a social networking*. Zürich, Switzerland: ASNA.

Reynolds, R. G. (1998). An introduction to cultural algorithms. *Cultural Algorithms Repository*. Retrieved from http://www.cs.wayne.edu/~jcc/car.html

Ustaoglu, Y. (2009). *Simulating the behavior of a Kurdish minority in Turkish Society*. Zürich, Switzerland: ASNA.

ADDITIONAL READING

Buresch, T., Eiben, A. E., Nitschke, G., & Schut, M. C. (2005). Effects of evolutionary and lifetime learning on minds and bodies in an artificial society. In *Proceedings of the IEEE Congress on Evolutionary Computation* (pp. 1448-1454).

Kowatsch, T., & Maass, W. (2010). In-store consumer behavior: How mobile recommendation agents influence usage intentions, product purchases, and store preferences. *Computers in Human Behavior*, *26*(4), 697–704. doi:10.1016/j.chb.2010.01.006

Kuramoto, I., Yasuda, A., Minakuchi, M., & Tsujino, Y. (2011). Recommendation system based on interaction with multiple agents for users with vague intention. In *Proceedings of the 14th International Conference on Human-Computer Interaction: Interaction Techniques and Environments - Volume Part II* (pp. 351-357).

Lee, Y. E., & Benbasat, I. (2010). Interaction design for mobile product recommendation agents: Supporting users' decisions in retail stores. *ACM Transactions on Computer-Human Interaction*, *17*(4), 17. doi:10.1145/1879831.1879835

Qiu, L., & Benbasat, I. (2010). A study of demographic embodiments of product recommendation agents in electronic commerce. *International Journal of Human-Computer Studies*, *68*(10), 669–688. doi:10.1016/j.ijhcs.2010.05.005

Wang, H.-C., & Doong, H.-S. (2010). Online customers' cognitive differences and their impact on the success of recommendation agents. *Information & Management, 47*(2), 109–114. doi:10.1016/j.im.2010.01.004

Xavier, J. C., Jr., Signoretti, A., Canuto, A. M. P., Campos, A. M. C., Gonçalves, L. M., & Fialho, S. V. (2011). Introducing affective agents in recommendation systems based on relational data clustering. In *Proceedings of the 22nd International Conference on Database and Expert Systems Applications - Volume Part II* (pp. 303-310).

KEY TERMS AND DEFINITION

Crowdfunding: A grouped effort to realize a task including financial or social activities.

Cultural Algorithms: Popular bioinspired algorithm related with the optimization of problems based on a society its culture and its belief space.

Degree of Dynamism: Level of complexity related with activities to evaluate on a Vehicle Routing Problem and their solutions.

Environmental Project: Activities of a project related with the conservation of the nature and their species.

Multiagent Systems: Artificial intelligence technique which use a combined environment to simulate a variety of optimization problems.

Vehicle Routing Problem: Algorithm related with the solutions to a plethora of logistics problems.

Chapter 12
Improve Card Collection from Memory Alpha using Sociolinguistics and Japanese Puzzles

Carlos Alberto Ochoa Ortiz Zezzatti
Juarez City University, México

José Martínez
Technological Institute of Ciudad Madero, México

Nemesio Castillo
Juarez City University, Mexico

Saúl González
Juarez City University, Mexico

Paula Hernández
Technological Institute of Ciudad Madero, México

ABSTRACT

Research examining the role of species bias in the Memory Alpha card market has been an emerging area of inquiry. However, empirical knowledge on the question: "Does the specie of the personage's role on a series affect the value of the card?" remains inconclusive. This chapter analyzes one of the first studies on this topic. Data were derived for 787 Alpha, Beta. Gamma & Delta species from Memory Alpha which were elected by a vote of the users in this Web Community conformed by fans. Data for each species' society, technology performance registers, design card price, and card availability with a range from common to extremely rare were obtained from secondary sources associated with Memory Alpha. Findings indicate that card availability and, to a lesser extent, technology performance is the most important factor affecting the value of a species' card, while importantly, a society's species is not a significant contributor to card value. Suggestions for future research are outlined.

DOI: 10.4018/978-1-4666-0297-7.ch012

The people say that in the Banean Society, nobody is only born, and that they illuminate everything to his around, but that does not mean that the love of its life, can with "Bioluminescence" saying here I am, Denara Pel you are a very special Viddian Lass for me but what gave so that you were Banean Lass! - Ikaarian Lass and Kelemane Leader, talking about most popular societies in Memory Alpha

INTRODUCTION

In recent decades, Memory Alpha card collecting has evolved from its traditional form of swapping cards with friends and stashing those "prized acquisitions" in dusty shoeboxes under the bed (or using clothespins to attach them to the radios of the bedrooms) into a multibillion economic industry (Fort & Gill, 2000). Perhaps coincidentally, around the same time the hobby of card collecting started to change, scholarly, inquiry into collecting began to appear (McIntosh & Schmeichel, 2004), this passion by collect include Rallies of Knowledge associated with Memory Alpha to obtain clues to resolve Japanese Puzzles is another hobby related with this Community. Scholarly work in this area has quickly explained beyond the hobby associated with collecting cards to other series or books as Star Wars or Andromeda series. So far, this research has found little evidence that species play a role in the value of sports card. For

example in Regoli et al. (2004) found no bias in their study of American traditional sport trading cards. Some researchers have used a relatively unique dependent variable, card placement, based on their symbolic capital status. What explains the contradictory results reported in these different research studies? They are likely the result of different samples and methodologies, but not consider use another kind of Artificial Intelligence techniques to describe this social behavior.

Social scientists recognized that studying the variety of items people collected, and their reasons for collecting could yield insight about human behavior, a collection will increase, according the popularity of items which conformed the collection, in Figure 1 is possible observed as a Collection increases the issues on the time according the value and scarcer of each issue is opinionated by the collector in this case Hasbro has a widely Pet Collection. For example, one reason people collect Memory Alpha cards and other memorabilia is to reconnect with their childhood memories specially science fiction which has a format of series, or to satisfy the simple urge to surround themselves with organized assortments of precious objects or issues. For others, it is a love of history and the great collectors of the past that drive their pursuit. And, of course, others collect Memory Alpha memorabilia because it may be profitable to do so; in fact, sometimes the appreciation for Science Fiction memorabilia is greater than that realized in more conventional investments (i.e.,

Figure 1. Hasbro Corporation has a Pet Collection conformed by 250 issues that increase each year according to the popularity of the items to collect

stocks or bonds) perhaps because of the scarcity of these items (e.g., How many really nice, strong signature related with the personages from series are available on sale?). Regardless of their motives, individual often develop deep personal connections to the object or issues which they collect.

Species Bias and Collection Card Values

Memory Alpha card prices are affected by a variety of factors including the cards' age, condition, scarcity, and the status of the personages or starships pictured on them. Other, not so obvious, factors may also influence the value of series cards, such as the specie or quadrant of the personage who is pictured. The research thus far into "customer specie discrimination" has generated mixed results. So far, this research has found little evidence that specie plays a role in the value of series cards.

Some researchers have used a relatively unique dependent variable, card placement, based on the "Topps Numbering System" (Nardinelli & Curtis, 1990), to assess the possibility of species bias. In these studies (Regoli et al., 2004) found evidence of racial differences in the placement of players' cards with Black baseball players disadvantaged in the early years (1956-1966); however in the letter years (1967-1980), this arrangement is reversed and Black players had more favorable card positions in card sets (compared to White players) than their prior year performances would have indicated. Other research, using card placement as the dependent variable, has reported no evidence of racial differences in the placement of players' cards (Nardinelli & Curtis, 1990; Regoli et al., 2004).

What explains the contradictory results reported in these different research studies? They are likely the result of different samples and methodologies. Further, despite the similar focus of the studies, a variety of independent variables have been utilized. For instance, in some studies composite measures of starships performance

were used, whereas other studies relied on several measures to represent performance (e.g., technology, art, architecture, commerce). Similarly, some studies include card availability measures and others do not. Finally, identifying the specie of a society is not as self-evident as one might think since an issue is not specifically identified on the card on which appears. In an effort to address this limitation, some scholars have constructed a continuous measure of specie for each society (Fort & Grill, 2000); however, most studies have used a more "traditional" method of measuring specie or ethnicity as a discrete variable obtained from photo identification and a specify classification used on Memory Alpha with basis in the quadrant where the society inhabited.

Bioinspired algorithms (BAs) are a class of population based search and optimization techniques that work on a principle inspired by nature: evolution of species (Batenburg, 1997). BAs have proven to be very useful tools in a large number of applications in optimization, control, signal processing, or machine learning (Batenburg & Palenstijn, 2003; Batenburg, 2003) using different BAs to obtain a better resolution. Japanese puzzles, also known as nonograms, are a form of logic drawing: the puzzler gradually makes a drawing on a grid, by means of logical reasoning. This task can be mimicked by using techniques from Artificial Intelligence. The solution is usually unique. Japanese puzzles are very popular in Latin America nowadays and are sold at every newspaper stand. In a Japanese puzzle, the numbers in rows and columns represent how many blocks of cells must be filled in the grid, in the order in which they appear. With two or more numbers, the blocks of cells in the grid must be separated by at least one blank square. In addition, an objective function, which compares the number of 1s and 0s in each line (row or column) of a puzzle solution X with the desired number of 1s and 0s, can be considered. This problem is a constrained combinatorial optimization problem. The puzzler is provided with information about the horizontal and vertical arrangement of the black pixels along every line. Figure 1 shows an image and its corresponding horizontal and vertical description. For each line, the description indicates the sizes of the segments of consecutive black pixels, in the order in which they appear on the line. The problem of solving Japanese puzzles is NP-complete; several complexity results concerning Japanese puzzles, e.g., on uniqueness, were derived in Fort and Gill (2000). In the next section we will give a short description of the evolutionary algorithm applied.

Current Study on Card Collection

The point of departure for the current research is Regoli (1991) analysis, which was one of the first scholarly works related with the topic of evaluate race in Card Collection, and also one of the few with a parsimonious approach to studying racial bias in card market. Specifically, Regoli examined the study "rookie" card of players who had been elected to baseball's HOF by the Baseball Writer's Association of America (BBWAA). He also limited the cases in his study to include only HOF members who had been elected in 1962 or later, which was the year the first non-White player (Jackie Robinson) became eligible and elected into the HOF. After excluding several other players' cards to control for the effects of price outliers, Regoli was left with a very small sample of 29 cases for analysis. Results from his study showed no price difference between the cards of White and non-White HOF members. Since 1990, another 31 players have been elected to baseball's HOF by the BBWAA. This chapter try to determine if with a different and extended repository with 1087 societies (Only 787 participated in Card Collection) described in Memory Alpha (plus) an additional 26 originally excluded for statistical purposes) in an effort to not replicate his research more rigorously, but also to assess whether there have been any changes in the relationship between species and rookie card values since 1990 among

the most important societies which support series, books and movies of the Paramount franchise.

Importantly, this study advances the earlier research by Regoli (1991) in the three ways: (1) the sample size is more than doubled permitting the utilization of more advanced statistical techniques in these research using Bioinspired Algorithms and Data Mining (also see point 3). (2) card prices are log transformed to correct for a positive skew providing not only for an analysis based on data that are normally distributed, but allowing for the inclusion of the 26 societies that were previously excluded because of the extremely high and low values of their cards, and (3) regression analysis is conducted, which improves on the means-difference and Point-Biserial correlation tests utilized in the prior study since the effects of the other potential contributing or intervening factors in the examination of species and card value can be investigated including Sociolinguistics which is the methodology that organize collective information in a society determining collective imaginaries of popularity and writing preferences of collect an issue in particular .

Methods

Data were derived from seven secondary sources related with different topics related with Memory Alpha in several kinds of information related with Card Collection in: (1) Technology, specific in Starships, (2) Species in their societies including landscapes from their planets, (3) Cultural representations including art, music and poetry, (4) Linguistics, specially the differences of the write and speak languages, (5) Commerce, including all forms to realize interchanges of supplies and Ferengi Acquisition Rules, (6) Architecture, including social spaces and habitation models, for example specially environments based on different climates, and (7) Gastronomy, including ways to obtain the ingredients to make food and the plethora to present it . Four variables were used to assess the effort of specie on the value of series cards. The dependent variable is card value (price), and the three independent variables are societies' specie, card availability, and species' symbolic capital.

Dependent Variable

Price. Card value is measured in Euro. Data were obtained from the prices listed on eBay and the Association of Card Collection of Star Trek based on information from Paramount Pictures website (April, 2011) *Price Guide* section, for the different societies including in the series and book related with this Community in the study. The dependent variable, price, was long transformed (base *e*) because of its skewed distribution. The residuals of the regression model described below are approximately normally distributed, indicated that the appropriate transformation was applied.

Independent Variables

Specie. The specie of the society was determined by a visual inspection of each society's photograph as it appears on the series and books related with Memory Alpha in: *The Complete Who is Who of Star Trek*. The societies were divided into non-Alpha Quadrant (*n*=400) and Rest of Quadrants-Beta, Gamma & Delta Quadrants- (*n*=387) groups. While there are drawbacks to this method, a point we return to later, it is the most common method used by card collectors identify a society's specie, and is the approach typically followed in this area of empirical inquiry. As such, this approach also allows us to directly tap into the decisions and consequences of collectors' perceptions and behavior which was established in many times by the symbolic capital related with each society which will be collected.

Availability. A card's value is affected by its relative scarcity which was tagging with four kinds: Uncommon, Rare, Scarce and Legendary to describe the situation of the card in the Market; however, card companies do not publish data about how many cards they produce each year, just as few comic book publishers reveal how many copies of a particular issue of *Legion of the Superheroes*, for example, they printed in this case with 107 members, the popularity is evaluated since 1956 considered the number of apparitions in each issue, for these reasons the top ten members has Caucasian anthropometry but from different planets, the most popular personage without these features is Tasmia Mallor with a dark blue skin and ranking in eleven position). Some researchers have addressed this problem by assuming card value is "driven by demand rather than supply" (Fine, 1987) others, while acknowledging the role of availability in card prices, have included only dummy variables for fewer cards of certain card numbers a company produced, called "short prints," in a set; still others assume uniform availability across individual card sets effectively ignoring the problem altogether (Nardinelli & Curtis, 1990). For this study, we approximated the availability of cards through the population reports published by Memory Alpha and specialized Community websites by constructing a measure based on the number of cards of each that were reported to exist in near-mint condition or higher, divided by the total number of availability is considerably more appropriate than relying on the raw numbers of each card submitted. Because it costs roughly 4-7 Euro or so to have a card graded by one of these services, collectors will be much less likely to submit lower value "common" cards for grading unless they are very confident the cards will be graded highly (otherwise, the card more to grade than its value). On the other hand, unusually sought-after cards are often submitted regardless of their condition, such as a first series, but is important describe that many collectors organize Annual Meetings to compare cards or Dioramas which including different species from diverse Quadrants, for this reason is possible found issues with a different temporality including in specific and innovative

Table 1. Unstandarized regression coefficients and (standard errors) predicting natural log of 2010 card prices

	Model 1	Model 2
(Constant)	5.140**(.252)	7.598 (.327)
Species[a]	.018 (.402)	?.010 (.194)
Availability		?5.742** (0.429)
TSCS (performance)		.012*(.005)
R^2	0	0.779

*p<.05

**p<.001

[a] Alpha Quadrant Species are reference group.

cards inclusive with a 3D aspects as Starships or landscapes.

Performance: Total Symbolic Capital Society (TSCS) which is calculated as an Index: "is an estimate of the number of times, positive or negative, that a society contributed to this quadrant a compared to an average popularity factor" (Thorn et al., 2001). This measure was created with the intent of measuring societies' total performance, thus allowing meaningful comparisons to be made between specific societies across temporality (In another perspective is necessary evaluate the popularity as a Grand Prix Model, because each society arrive in different époque and under different situation in the Mass Media including the number of fans involved in the Community (Thorn et al., 2001).

Results

We begin by exploring a simple, baseline model where we assess the relationship between specie and specific appreciation card prices. As seen in column 1 of Table 1, species has no effect on rookie card prices (*t*=.05, *p*=.96).

Although research examining the role of species bias in the secondary collectible card market has been an emerging area of inquiry, empirical knowledge on the question: "Does the species of a society on a Thematic Community related with

collections card affect the value of the issue card?" remains inconclusive. This chapter revisits one of the first studies on this topic. Data were derived for a sample from different quadrants in Memory Alpha and with acceptable specie's popularity, media and literature performance statics (apparitions in different icons as movies, episodes or books), rookie card price, and card availability were obtained from secondary sources including amateur Diorama Cards with the finality of understand the popularity of a society with respect to others. Findings indicate that card availability and, to a lesser extent, society performance is the most important factor affecting the value of player's card, while importantly, a society's specie is not a significant contributor to card value. Suggestions for future research are outlined, for example the temporality of a society including in the first series but discounted in new movies or series can be represented an important factor to collect this issue.

Next, we estimate a second model (Column Two), where card price is regressed onto the three independent variables: species, availability, and performance. The variance explained in this model is .78. As expected, species' popularity and cultural performance had a significant impact on their card value (*t*=2.34, *p*=.023), indicating that the more a society contributed to his quadrant as compared to an average society, the higher the price of his rookie card. What was unexpected was the relatively small impact of performance when compared to a card's availability, which had nearly six times the influence in determining the value of cards (t=-13.39, p<.001). As expected, less available cards exhibited higher card prices. These findings are not too surprising, however, since all the societies in this study are elected as relevant issues including in Annual Meetings of this Community. They have already been deemed the "best of the best;" therefore, the potential effects of individual-level performance on card values would be logically mitigated as the variance in levels of performance within this group is much smaller than would be the case if non-Alpha Quadrant were included in the analysis. Finally, and perhaps most importantly, a species' society has no significant affect (For example Aenar and Andorian Societies lives on the same planet, but Aenar Cards are more scarcely that Andorian Cards) on the value of his rookie card (t=-.05, p=.96).

To gain a more intuitive grasp of the effects of the coefficients in this model, next we examined a representative or hypothetical card in terms of real economic amounts rather than logged Euro money. Setting performance and availability at their mean levels, 35.3 and .50, respectively, we are able to show the difference between the price of an Alpha Quadrant and non-Alpha Quadrant societies' rookie card. The model predicts that a card of this fictional Alpha Quadrant Specie would be worth $172.53, while the value of the same card for a non-Alpha Quadrant society would be worth $170.81 – a small, but insignificant difference, the majority of these societies arrives with the fans during the last decade and their different appreciation was high accept in the Community but don't exist many issues related with them and for these reason are less popularities with respect to Alpha Quadrant Species which represent the 57% of all societies on Memory Alpha.

However, if we vary the availability (or scarcity), which is the variable with the strongest

influence in the model, while holding species and performance constant in function of continuity on the series, different picture emerges. With average performance levels, the model predicts that if the availability of the card is increased by 10 percentage points above that of the mean (to .6) it reduces the card value of Alpha Quadrant society to $97.16 (from $172.53) and the card value of a non-Alpha Quadrant society is reduced to $96.20 (from $170.81). If we lower the availability levels of this same fictional card to .4 (10 percentage points below the mean) the predicted value increases to $306.37 for an Alpha Quadrant society and to $303.32 for non-Alpha Quadrant society. A further 10 percentage point reduction in availability (less than one standard deviation below the mean) increases the card's predicted value to an impressive $544.03 for a Alpha Quadrant society and $538.61 for a non Alpha Quadrant society.

SUPPLEMENTAL ANALYSIS: THE CASE OF THE "BIG-MARKET" TEAM

Before we conclude our research, it is worthwhile to explore the possible effect or market size of the Quadrant with respect to a society was on and if participate for "big-market" including in Annual Meetings of this Community has an effect on card value. There is very small knowledge base on this issue, largely from the field of economics, which, though inconclusive, suggests that any effects of Quadrants; market sizes on the value of societies' cards tend to even out in the end (Fine, 1987).

We began this supplemental analysis by returning to the Memory Alpha Repository website, which identifies a society "with a roll primary" associated in a specific Quadrant. For the most part, this primary team corresponds to the one with which they demonstrate lives and established connection in a specific Quadrant –Seven societies lives in two different Quadrants-. Next, we classify these Quadrant's societies into big and small – market categories. There are a couple of exceptions to this tendency, but in general we were able to successfully categorize societies fairly well – recognizing that there may be different points of view on what is a big-market associated with series and books but not with movies. In our conception, it deals primary with the value of a Quadrant's worth in Euro. Using this conceptualization, yearly estimates of a Quadrant's worth were obtained from the list of episodes, movies and books, which provides this information across the all merchandise produced relational with each society, for the year 2009. According to these information, the top seven societies, which we defined as "big-market," were: (1) Humans from Earth (9.172 of popularity), (2) Klingon (9.068 of popularity), (3) Vulcan (9.011 of popularity), (4) Bajorian (8.967 of popularity), (5) Cardassian (8.954 of popularity), (6) Ferengi (8.874) and (7) Denobulian (8.747) (*Note;* The average by the species sample was 7.134, the most popular society of one episode was Kelemane with 8.479). Thus, a dichotomous variable was created to reflect big market societies (=1).

Popularity Bias and Collection Card Values

Of the 787 societies in the repository, 122 were from big market associated with the series and books, and 38 of those 122 were including in all series and books, and 11 of those 122 were non-Alpha Quadrant. When we added this variable to the main regression model, it did not change any of the substantive findings regarding the other coefficients in terms of size, direction, or significance, nor did its inclusion exhibit a significant relation to card value ($t=.684$, $p=.497$). We also created an interaction of species and big-market series and books and re-estimated the model. No significant effects were observed here either, though the coefficient for the interaction term (representing non-Alpha Quadrant Species, big-market in series and books) was negative while the other two terms (species and big market without include movies) were positive.

Discussion Associated with Card Collection

The past 25 years has witnessed considerable change in the Community from Memory Alpha card collecting. The hobby saw a rapidly expanding speculative bubble in card prices peak in the early 1990s fueled by double-digit investment returns and the belief that the Science Fiction memorabilia market was "recession-proof" (Robinson, 1987). Just as quickly, also in the early 1990s, that speculative bubble burst and most Memory Alpha card prices, with the exception of highly sought-after-grade cards such as those of first series and book, remained stagnant for about 10 years. Today, the card market is starting to reassert itself with certain cards fetching eye-popping sums at auction for example with innovative societies as Banean, Ikaarian, Kantare, Kelemane, Tzenkheti, Xyrillian or Yaderan Colony considered to expand more, because are very popular to include in the Dyorams built in the Annual Meeting.

Was has not changed the underlying finding that, at least among these "New Kid on the Block" Societies, a Quadrant's society does not play a significant role in determining the value of his rookie card. The analysis presented here suggests that other factors, like a Societies' performance in the time, and specially market factors, like a card's availability, are the primary determinants of a card's value in the secondary market. Does this mean that species plays no role in Science Fiction Collection card values? Not necessarily.

Memory Alpha cards have no value in-and-of themselves, as they are only small slices of cardboard with pictures and words printed on them. What gives a card value is a person's desire to own that card and that is an entirely subjective and social process (Robinson, 1987). There are certainly highly individualistic factors that impact some collectors' choices about the cards they collect. For example, one collector may buy the cards of a specific society because they attended the same social networking related with these society or the actors related with this card signed the fan collector's son or daughter caught at a specific Annual Meeting. However, it is larger forces related to the pictured on it (i.e., availability, condition, and if it is a rookie card) and the society pictured on it (i.e., social performance and status of symbolic capital) that tend to offer the best explanations for the value average card collectors place on Memory Alpha cards.

As noted earlier, some researchers cite species as a significant factor in determining the value of Memory Alpha cards. If species affect the value of Memory Alpha cards, why does it fail to do so in this sample? One reason may be a function of the societies included as well as those whom were excluded. All the societies included for the current analysis were elected to support a specific series or books – an honor reserved for the very best to have ever watched episode or book. It is possible that in the process of building a series or book was built a body of work sufficient for select a specific society with many factors includes in their description; these select few may have transcended the effects of species itself. When the people associated with Star Wars whom are devote fans think in any Jedi, only thinking in the personage but don't in a specific species with all a society developed with Architecture, Starships, Language of Social & Cultural factors detailed as occurs in Memory Alpha. The greatness of these societies is unquestioned and their species becomes, at most, an afterthought. In essence, once a society achieves a certain symbolic capital, their species becomes, at most, an afterthought. In essence, once a society achieves a certain magnitude and intensity associated with popularity, their species no longer matters in the eyes of fans and collectors.

Because this study is not the final word on this issue, several directions for the future research are identified. First, the lack of a species effect for rookie card values does not negate the possibility that there are species differences across societies' cards in subsequent years. One interesting questions is whether the (normal) decrease in the value of a society's rookie card and their 2nd year card is the same across species or whether the two prices are significantly different. There may be something that collectors value about rookie cards regardless of species that they do not value for the same society's 2nd year card. Second, in order to explore the possibility that any personage transcend species, one avenue for the future research is not include societies whom are not considered decisive to support a new series, book or movie as well as those elected to the Annual Meeting' committee. Another area that deserves further investigation deals with the "unpacking" of species and ethnicity from the collectors in many cases in Asian and Arab countries the people with blue skin or with telepathic abilities are considered more popular to be collected. Since there were only four Societies with these two features in the study they were combined with the rest of the Societies to form one category. There may be differences in the value of cards between Alpha, Beta, Gamma and Delta societies that are being masked by their categorization in this study, and this will surely be the case in the future as non humanoid societies become an increasing and dominant presence in Memory Alpha and will be considered more popular. In addition, this is likely to open useful inquires that explore species and ethnicity based on skin tone (Coakley, 2003) with a deep discussion related with "colorism". These and other questions regarding the role of species in Memory Alpha card collecting should offer a rich area for researchers for some time to come.

Memory Alpha card process are affected by a variety of factors including the card's age, condition, scarcity, and the status of the societies pictured on them. Other, not so obvious, factors may also influence the value of a card in these Collectible Community conformed by 87,500 collectors –the double population of Monaco-, such as the species of the society whom is pictured. The research thus far into "customer species discrimination" has generated mixed results. Some scholars have found collector bias in the prices of specific collection cards of for example Black and Latino baseball players; while other researchers have reported minimal or no racial bias or a mix of results in these kinds of collection card values.

Japanese Puzzle, a kind of Collectible Issue in Memory Alpha

Japanese puzzles, also known as nonograms, are a form of logic drawing: the puzzler gradually makes a drawing on a grid, by means of logical reasoning. This task can be mimicked by using techniques from Artificial Intelligence. The solution is usually unique. Japanese puzzles are very popular in Latin America nowadays and are sold at every newspaper stand, in the Community of Memory Alpha are very popular because is necessary resolve using tracks or clues related with the societies in this series and books.

In a Japanese puzzle, the numbers in rows and columns represent how many blocks of cells must be filled in the grid, in the order in which they appear. With two or more numbers, the blocks of cells in the grid must be separated by at least one blank square. In addition, an objective function, which compares the number of 1s and 0s in each line (row or column) of a puzzle solution X with the desired number of 1s and 0s, can be considered. This problem is a constrained combinatorial optimization problem. The puzzler is provided with information about the horizontal and vertical arrangement of the black pixels along every line. Figure 1 shows an image and its corresponding horizontal and vertical description. For each line, the description indicates the sizes of the segments of consecutive black pixels, in the order in which they appear on the line. The problem of solving Japanese puzzles is NP-complete; several complexity results concerning Japanese puzzles, e.g., on uniqueness, were derived in Ueda and Nagao

(1996). In the next section we will give a short description of the evolutionary algorithm applied.

Bioinspired algorithms (BAs) are a class of population-based search and optimization techniques that work on a principle inspired by nature: evolution of species (Batenburg 2004). BAs have proven to be very useful tools in a large number of applications in optimization, control, signal processing, or machine learning (Batenburg & Palenstijn, 2003; Batenburg, 2004) using different BAs to obtain a better resolution.

Algorithm Overview

We have adapted an evolutionary algorithm (Michalewicz, 1996) for solving multiobjective problems when an evaluation function is given. The algorithm optimizes exclusively over the set of all images that satisfy the prescribed projections. At the end of each epoque all candidate solutions have the prescribed horizontal and vertical projections. This requires a suitable crossover operator that is not only capable of mixing features from both solutions, but also of ensuring that the produced solution.

Similar requirements apply to the mutation operator. A Japanese puzzle is an interesting and addictive game, which takes the form of a N * M grid, with numbers situated on the left, top rows, and columns, see Figure 1. In a Japanese puzzle, the numbers in rows and columns represent how many blocks of cells must be filled in the grid, in the order in which they appear. With two or more numbers, the blocks of cells in the grid must be separated by at least one blank square. A Japanese puzzle is a constrained combinatorial optimization problem: consider a Japanese puzzle defined in an N * M grid (N rows, M columns). Since the puzzles are formed by black (filled) and white (blank) squares to be fixed in the grid, the puzzle can be reformulated in terms of finding a N * M binary matrix, with the number of 1s given by the conditions in rows and columns, separated by at least one 0 when more than one condition is present. Our algorithm is based on a Cultural Algorithm (Ochoa et al., 2008) for another view on this approach: after every VIP a stochastic hill climb is performed until the solution has reached a local optimum. In this way, population f beliefs always represent local optima in the search space.

In addition, an objective function, which compares the number of 1s and 0s in each line (row or column) of a puzzle solution X with the desired number of 1s and 0s, can be considered. This desired number of 0s and 1s is a line are given but the conditions of the puzzle rij and cij (where rij, i Q, M, Q Íj, stand for the puzzle conditions in rows and columns, respectively). For example, in Figure 1, r11=2, r12=5, r13=0, and c11=1, c12=1, c42=2. With these simple definitions, the following objective function can be obtained:

$$f(X) = f_1(X) + f_2(X) + f_3(X) + f_4(X) \qquad (1)$$

$$f_1(X) = \sum_{i=1}^{N} \left| \sum_{p=1}^{M} r_{ip} - \sum_{p=1}^{M} x_{ip} \right| \qquad (2)$$

$$f_2(X) = \sum_{k=1}^{M} \left| \sum_{p=1}^{N} c_{kp} - \sum_{p=1}^{N} x_{kp} \right| \qquad (3)$$

$$f_3(X) = \sum_{i=1}^{N} \left| \left(M - \sum_{p=1}^{M} r_{ip} \right) - \left(M - \sum_{p=1}^{M} x_{ip} \right) \right| \qquad (4)$$

$$f_4(X) = \sum_{k=1}^{M} \left| \left(N - \sum_{p=1}^{N} c_{kp} \right) - \left(N - \sum_{p=1}^{N} x_{kp} \right) \right| \qquad (5)$$

Where f1(X), given by (2) takes into account the difference between the desired number of 1s and the actual number of 1s in rows, for a given solution X, and f2(X), given by (3), does the same for columns. On the other hand, the term given in (4) stands for the differences in number of 0 s for rows, and in (5) for columns. The Japanese

puzzle can be redefined then, giving a puzzle grid N*M and a set of puzzle conditions (conditions matrices R with elements rij and C with elements ckj), and finding an N*M binary matrix, which minimizes function f(X). This problem is a constrained combinatorial optimization problem. Let m, n be the image height and width and R, S be vectors that contain the prescribed row and column projections. We denote the class of all images that have these projections by A(R,S). Figure 2 summarizes our algorithm, the belief space function, population size and the number of changes in the beliefs, respectively.

An important operation often used in our algorithm is the computation of an image X = (xij), A(R, S), given R and S: the hard constraints have to be satisfied. We use a network ow approach for computing these matrices. First, we construct a directed graph N. The set V of nodes consists of a source node T1, a sink node T2, one layer V1, Qc, Vm of nodes that correspond to the image rows (row nodes) and one layer W1, Qc, Wn of nodes that correspond to the image columns (column nodes). Figure 3 shows the topology of the graph in case of a simple example. We refer to the top layer of arcs as row arcs and to the bottom layer as column arcs. Every arc in the middle layer corresponds to an entry (cell) of X, so we refer to these arcs as cell arcs. We assign a capacity to each of the arcs: every row arc is assigned the corresponding row projection, every column arc the corresponding column projection and every cell arc is assigned a capacity of 1. It is not difficult to see that a maximum integral ow from T1 to T2 in N corresponds directly to a solution of problem: set xij = 1 if arc (Vi,Wj) carries a ow of 1 and set it to 0 otherwise. Moreover, by assigning an additional set of costs to the cell arcs, and solving a min-cost max-ow problem in N, it is possible to express a preference among the solutions of the max-ow problem. In particular, for a given image M, we can compute in this way the matrix X, A(R, S) which has the same value as M in as many cells as possible. We refer to

Figure 2. The representation of a Japanese Puzzle (Grid M*N)

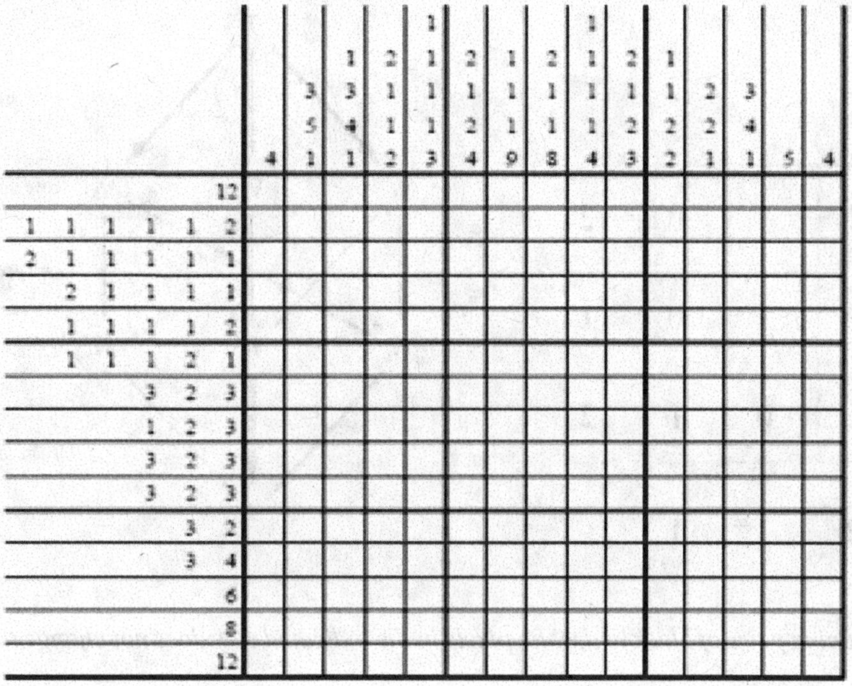

					1				1					
		1	2	1	2	1	2	1	2	1				
	3	3	1	1	1	1	1	1	1	1	2	3		
	5	4	1	1	2	1	1	1	2	2	2	4		
4	1	1	2	3	4	9	8	4	3	2	1	1	5	4

Row clues (left side):

					12
1	1	1	1	1	2
2	1	1	1	1	1
	2	1	1	1	1
	1	1	1	1	2
	1	1	1	2	1
			3	2	3
			1	2	3
			3	2	3
			3	2	3
				3	2
				3	4
					6
					8
					12

Figure 3. Cultural algorithm pseudo code

```
Begin
    t=0;
    Initialize POP (t); /* Initialization of population */
    Initialize BLF (t); /* Initialization of believing space */
    Repeat
        Evaluate POP (t);
        Vote (BLF (t), Accept (POP (t)));
        Adjust (BLF (t));
        Evolve(POP(t), Influence(BLF(t)));
        t = t +1;
        Select POP (t) from POP (t-1);
    Until (Term condition is reached)
End
```

Batenburg and Palenstijn (2003) for the details of this procedure. The crossover operator is one of the main parts of our algorithm. The input of the operator consists of two images, which represent different beliefs. The output is an adapted image, which has certain features from both beliefs. Because all matrices in the population are members of A(R, S) the resulting image should have similar projections.

First, a crossover mask Y = (yij), {0, 1}mxn is computed, which determines for each pixel from which adapted image it is copied. The value 0 means that the image inherits from the first belief, 1 means that the second belief is used. The mask generation procedure is designed so that it assigns around half the pixels to each belief and so that it assigns large connected areas to each belief. In this way, local features in the beliefs images are often inherited as a whole by the adapted image.

From the crossover mask and both parent matrices P =(pij) and Q = (qij), a model image M = (mij) is computed, as follows:

$$m_{ij} = \begin{cases} p_{ij} & \text{if } x_{ij} = 0 \\ q_{ij} & \text{if } x_{ij} = 0 \end{cases}$$

Subsequently, we again use the weighted network ow model to construct an adapted image C,

Figure 4. A 3*3 image instance and its corresponding network ow

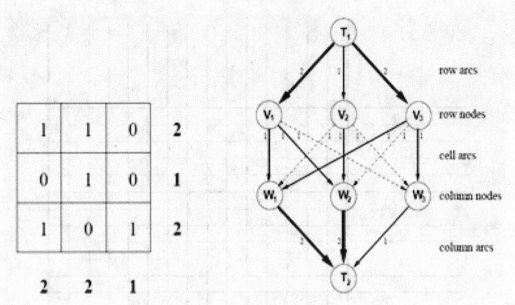

Figure 5. Swapping pairs of black and white pixels in the indicated way does not change the projections

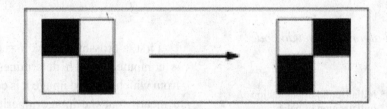

which has the same value as M in as many entries as possible. This will result in a child image that is in A(R, S), resembles the first parent in a certain part and resembles the other parent in the rest of the image (Figure 4).

To ensure that the adapted image has sufficient quality, we apply a local hillclimb operator after the crossover operation. Figure 5 show the basic principle of the hillclimb operator. Pairs of black and white entries are swapped as long as it is possible to improve the evaluation function in this way. The mutation operator uses similar principles. First, a mutation mask is generated which determines a small part of the image that will be distorted. By using the network ow method and subsequent hillclimbing an adapted

image is generated that adheres to the prescribed projections. Over the set of all images that satisfy the prescribed projections over the set of all images that satisfy the prescribed projections. At the end of each époque all candidate solutions have the prescribed horizontal and vertical projections. This requires a suitable crossover operator, which is not only capable of mixing features from both proposed solutions.

Solving Japanese Puzzles

We now turn to the problem of solving Japanese puzzles. As summation of the segment sizes of a line yields the total number of black pixels on that line, Japanese puzzles can be considered to

Figure 6. A line description (top), the corresponding line segmentation (middle), and an actual line that adheres to the description (bottom). The arrows indicate the links between the line and the segmentation.

$$= \begin{cases} 0 & \text{(white)} & \text{if } i \text{ is odd} \\ 1 & \text{(black)} & \text{if } i \text{ is even} \end{cases}$$

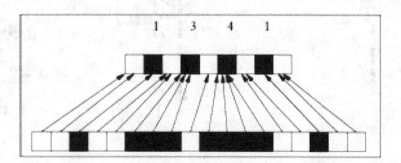

be a special form of the multiobjective problem, in which extra a priori information is available. We will construct an evaluation function which encapsulates all this extra information (Michalewicz, 1996).

The evaluation function should reflect the deviation of a given image from the horizontal and vertical descriptions. We consider this deviation separately for each (horizontal or vertical) line. Then, we can obtain an evaluation function for the whole image by summation of the deviations of all lines. The minimal deviation possible, 0, should of course correspond to a solution of the puzzle.

We refer to the evaluation of a pixel line ¬ which has description s by ds(¬). Ideally, the function ds should make full use of all information available: the value of the pixels on ¬ and the prescribed description s of ¬. Let $(¬1, ¬2,..,¬k)$ be the pixel values of ¬ (where k = n if ¬ is horizontal, k = m if ¬ is vertical). We call the operation of changing the value of one pixel of ¬ a bitflip operation. We now define ds(¬) to be the minimal number of bitflip operations required to make ¬ conform to s.

This definition of ds has several advantages. First, it is a very intuitive way of defining the distance between a given line of pixels and its prescribed description and it uses all available information. If a line ¬ adheres to its description s, we have ds(¬) =0, as desired. Second, ds has the property that performing a single bitflip operation on ¬, yielding a line ¬', can change the value of ds by no more than 1. In a discrete sense, ds can be regarded as a fluent function of ¬. Surprisingly, ds(¬) can be computed quite efficiently by means of dynamic programming. This is of course necessary since the algorithm requires many of these computations. Suppose that the prescribed description s of. This consists of h segments of black pixels, $(s1, Qc, sh)$. Without loss of generality, we may assume that starts and ends with a white pixel: adding white pixels at the beginning or end of a line does not change its description. We define a line segmentation ¬* = $(¬*1, Qc, ¬*2h+1)$, corresponding to the number h of black segments in s: ¬*1

The entries of the line segmentation correspond to the alternating black and white segments in the description (where we consider the white segments to be implicitly present). Figure 6 shows a line description s, its corresponding line segmentation ¬* and a realization of s, which is a line ¬ that adheres to s. The arrows indicate for each pixel of ¬ to which entry of ¬* it corresponds.

Figure 7. Resolution of a Japanese Puzzle using our algorithm

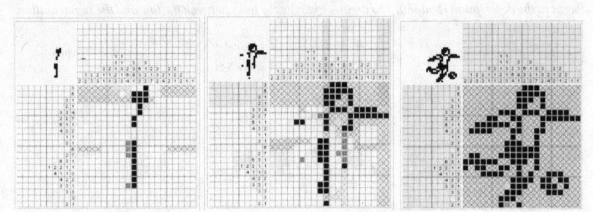

If pixel i corresponds to entry j of ¬*, we say that pixel i is linked to entry j of the line segmentation. We call the corresponding mapping a link mapping. If ¬ does not correspond to s, we can also link every pixel i consecutively to an entry j of ¬*. In that case, however, there are pixels in ¬ that do not match the color of the entries of ¬* to which they are linked. Some bitflip operation will have to be applied to these pixels in order to make ¬ conform to ¬*, with the given links. Valid link mappings must satisfy several requirements: consecutive pixels should be linked either to the same entry of ¬* or to consecutive entries of ¬*. The number of pixels linked to each black entry ¬*j must be sj/2. There must be at least one pixel linked to each white entry of ¬*.

A valid partial link mapping from $(\neg 1, Qc, \neg i)$ to $(\neg*1, Qc, \neg*j)$ satisfies the same requirements as a total valid link mapping. In addition, if pixel i is linked to a black entry ¬*j, the pixels $(\neg i\text{-}sj/2 +1, Qc, \neg i\text{-}1)$ should also be linked to entry j. We now introduce $f\hat{A}(i, j)$ (for 1 to i until k, 1 to j until 2h + 1), the minimal number of bitflip operations, over all valid partial link mappings from $(\neg 1, Qc, \neg i)$ to $(\neg*1, Qc, \neg*j)$, that has to be applied to ¬ in order to make it conform to the partial link mapping (so that all pixels have the same colors as the entries to which they are linked). We remark that $f\hat{A}(k, 2h+1)$ is the minimal number of bitflip

operations that is required to transform ¬ into a line that adheres to s. We can directly use it as the evaluation function for our algorithm. Fortunately, $f\hat{A}(i,j)$ can be computed efficiently by means of dynamic programming. For both the case that j is odd and the case that j is even, it is possible to construct a recurrence relation which computes $f\hat{A}(i,j)$ from other values $Qf\hat{A}(iQe,jQf)$ where always $iQf < i$. By using a nested loop, which iterates over all pairs of (i,j) in the right order, each value $f\hat{A}(i,j)$ can be computed from table values that are already known.

Results

We implemented the evaluation function and performed several test runs. We used a population of agents of 500 for the experiments. Figure 7 shows the test images that we used. The example has size 20*20 which is known by to have a unique solution. We performed one test run for this image. The image was reconstructed perfectly on a Pentium IV at 2.4 GHz in 80 minutes after 27 époques of the algorithm. Note that the reconstruction is quite different from the original image, yet it adheres to nearly all line descriptions. Although the reconstruction process took a long time to complete, this is still a very positive result, since this image is very hard to reconstruct using only logic reasoning. Branching seems inevitable for that type of image. We have adapted an evolutionary algorithm (Ochoa et al., 2007) for solving multiobjective problems when an evaluation function is given. The algorithm optimizes exclusively over the set of all images that satisfy the prescribed projections. At the end of each époque all candidate solutions have the prescribed horizontal and vertical projections. This requires a suitable crossover operator that is not only capable of mixing features from both solutions, but also of ensuring that the produced solution. Similar requirements apply to the mutation operator.

Future research includes a detailed analysis of the performance on puzzles of different difficulty levels and different types (e.g., more than two colors) as is proposed in Ryser (1957). The fact that the evolutionary algorithm from Ochoa et al. (2008b) can also be used to solve Japanese puzzles, which it was not specifically designed for, clearly demonstrates its versatility.

REFERENCES

Batenburg, K. J. (2004). An evolutionary algorithm for discrete tomography. *Discrete Applied Mathematics*, *151*(1-3), 36–54. doi:10.1016/j.dam.2005.02.021

Batenburg, K. J., & Palenstijn, W. J. (2003). A new exam timetabling algorithm. In *Proceedings of the Fifteenth Belgium-Netherlands Artificial Intelligence Conference* (pp. 19-26).

Coakley, J. J. (2003). *Sport in society: Issues and controversies* (8th ed.). New York, NY: McGraw-Hill.

Fine, G. A. (1987). Community and boundary: Personal experience stories of mushroom collectors. *Journal of Folklore Research*, *24*, 223–240.

Fort, R., & Gill, A. (2000). Race and ethnicity assessment in baseball card markets. *Journal of Sports Economics*, *1*, 21–38. doi:10.1177/152700250000100103

McIntosh, W. E., & Schmeichel, B. (2004). Collectors and collecting: A social psychological perspective. *Leisure Sciences*, *26*, 85–97. doi:10.1080/01490400490272639

Michalewicz, Z. (1996). *Genetic programs + data structures = Evolution programs* (3rd ed.). Berlin, Germany: Springer-Verlag.

Nardinelli, C., & Curtis, S. (1990). Customer racial discrimination in the market for memorabilia: The case of baseball. *The Quarterly Journal of Economics*, *105*, 575–595. doi:10.2307/2937891

Ochoa, A., et al. (2007). Baharastar – Simulador de Algoritmos Culturales para la Minería de Datos Social. In *Proceedings of COMCEV*.

Ochoa, A., et al. (2008a). Applying cultural algorithms and data mining to organize elements in a social dyoram. In *Proceedings of the ENC Workshop of Data Mining*.

Ochoa, A., et al. (2008b). Una comparativa de la Inteligencia Grupal desde la perspectiva del Computo Evolutivo. In *Proceedings of the International Congress on Computer Science Research*, Aguascalientes, Mexico.

Regoli, R. M. (1991). Racism in baseball card collecting: Fact or fiction? *Human Relations*, *44*, 255–264. doi:10.1177/001872679104400303

Regoli, R. M., Hewitt, J. D., Muñoz, R. Jr, & Regoli, A. M. (2004). Location, location, location: The transmission of racist ideology in baseball cards. *Negro Educational Review*, *55*, 75–90.

Robinson, R. (1987). *Why this piece? On the choices of collectors in the fine arts*. Paper presented at the Annual Meeting of the American Sociological Association, Chicago, IL

Ryser, H. J. (1957). Combinatorial properties of matrices of zeros and ones. *Canadian Journal of Mathematics*, *9*, 371–377. doi:10.4153/CJM-1957-044-3

Thorn, J., Palmer, P., & Gershman, M. (2001). *Total baseball* (7th ed.). New York, NY: Total Sports.

Ueda, N., & Nagao, T. (1996). *NP-completeness results for nonogram via parsinomius reductions* (Tech. Rep. No. TR96-0008). Tokyo, Japan: Department of Computer Science, Tokyo Institute of Technology.

ADDITIONAL READING

Cruz-Roa, A., Caicedo, J. C., & González, F. A. (2011). Visual pattern mining in histology image collections using bag of features. *Artificial Intelligence in Medicine*, *52*(2), 91–106. doi:10.1016/j.artmed.2011.04.010

de Spindler, A., Leone, S., Nebeling, M., Geel, M., & Norrie, M. C. (2011). Using synchronised tag clouds for browsing data collections. In *Proceedings of the 23rd International Conference on Advanced Information Systems Engineering* (pp. 214-228).

Lagorce, D., Maupetit, J., Baell, J. B., Sperandio, O., Tufféry, P., & Miteva, M. A. (2011). The FAF-Drugs2 server: a multistep engine to prepare electronic chemical compound collections. *Bioinformatics (Oxford, England)*, *27*(14), 2018–2020. doi:10.1093/bioinformatics/btr333

Ovsjanikov, M., Li, W., Guibas, L. J., & Mitra, J., N. J. (2011). Exploration of continuous variability in collections of 3D shapes. *ACM Transactions on Graphics*, *30*(4), 33. doi:10.1145/2010324.1964928

Philippe, N., Salson, M., Lecroq, T., Léonard, M., Commes, T., & Rivals, E. (2011). Querying large read collections in main memory: a versatile data structure. *BMC Bioinformatics*, *2*, 242. doi:10.1186/1471-2105-12-242

Surdeanu, M., Ciaramita, M., & Zaragoza, H. (2011). Learning to rank answers to non-factoid questions from Web collections. *Computational Linguistics*, *37*(2), 351–383. doi:10.1162/COLI_a_00051

KEY TERMS AND DEFINITION

Card Collection: Popular hobby related with the accumulation of thematic objects.

Japanese Puzzle: Strategy puzzle related with the calculation of numbers associated with a grid.

Memorabilia: Issues related with a specific thematic collection increase on the time.

Repository: Set of data in different media presentation related with a specific thematic information.

Sociolinguistics: Language application to analyze the different narrative guide built to describe a particularly event and their implications and consequences by different social actors.

Chapter 13
Mass Media Strategies:
Hybrid Approach using a Bioinspired Algorithm and Social Data Mining

Carlos Alberto Ochoa Ortiz Zezzatti
Juarez City University, México

Darwin Young
COMIMSA Centro Conacyt, Mexico

Camelia Chira
Babeş-Bolyai University, Romania

Daniel Azpeitia
Juarez City University, México

Alán Calvillo
Aguascalientes University, México

ABSTRACT

Evolve computing is a generic name given to the resolution of computational problems with base in models of an evolutionary process. Most of the evolutionary algorithms propose biological paradigms, and concepts of natural selection, mutation, and reproduction. Nevertheless other paradigms exist and can be adopted in the creation of evolutionary algorithms. Many problems involve environments not structured which can be solved from the perspective of cultural paradigms, which offer plenty of category models, where one does which do not know the possible solutions at problem, a common situation in the real life. The intention of this research is analyze the Crowdfunding Model, supporting to a social networking to an Indie Pop Band. Sociological research shows that Crowdfunding tends to reveal a bias toward social similarity. Therefore, in order to model this Project supported with Crowdfunding developing an Agent-Based Model that already manages the social interaction, together with featuring information of MySpace Music evolutionary belief spaces. To introduce these theoretical concepts the authors decided use Cultural Algorithms in our approach, explaining the process in detail.

DOI: 10.4018/978-1-4666-0297-7.ch013

Nul ne peut se sentir seulement dans cette vie, si, dans une autre dimension quelqu'un, te cherche te étrange, te espère, te aspire - Darek Thanderúck, Mass Media Expert in Thanagar

1. INTRODUCTION

The media are linked to the advancement of technology and economic development that can offer a range of products and services to the general public, at ever lower prices, which under the Mass Media can develop enhanced ways to market these goods or services. The impact on society of this form of communication has been very diverse, in part has reduced direct interpersonal communication and has also facilitated the creation of public opinion.

The Mass Media are used in advertising and political propaganda direct or indirect where the progress of marketing are based on the concept of communicating image, design, information and dissemination of any product or service that will be released to an audience. This communication process between the company and its market identifies the requirements, needs and preferences of the market and then the process is used to publicize the product or service with the objective of influencing their purchase or acceptance.

The process of Mass Media has the potential to reach a target audience, which is anonymous but has similar characteristics to the public studied by common processes. The importance of this process, which allows a massive response or immediate feedback on business and social characteristics that can influence the decision of purchasing goods and services, or influence in social situations with ideas, beliefs and opinions; examples:

- Identify characteristics of products or market needs

- Identification of policy initiatives that can be used in political propaganda
- Promote or eliminate behaviors, habits, or points of view

The use of Mass media, easily allows studying the basic elements of any business process or communication:

- Identify needs, losses or deficiencies in the study group.
- Identify the wishes and aspirations of the study group to produce a feature that generates a value for this market segment.
- Identify potential claims and strategies to increase and stimulate the growth of demand according to purchasing power and market interest.
- Allows the development of commodity transactions in various markets, which could not be attacked in the traditional way.
- Allows reaching a strict audience, that is difficult to achieve, identifying their needs and aspirations.
- Development of production to meet potential demand in the market.
- Orient the requirements of a product to the needs and desires that are valued by the market with a relatively short response time.
- Align sales and publicity surrounding the immediate trend of people buying according to the features shown in the marketplace by competitors, defining the characteristics of buyers and niches where the product will be preferred.

The market analysis by Mass Media (Figure 1) generates an ability to identify elements that conventionally requires an endless number of resources to create successful strategies in various market segments. Also allows identifying accelerated trends of technology and constant innovation to existing products and introduction of new

Figure 1. Characteristics of market research analyzed under mass media

Characteristics of Market Research that can be analyzed under Mass Media	Consumer Profile Market Structure Number of competitors Number of brands (national, regional, local) Percentage of products on the market by brand Product Characteristics (prices, materials, design, technology, quality, models, sizes, etc.). Serviceability and maintenance Time Guarantee Pricing strategies and comparisons with competitors Impact on demand Distribution Channels (advantages and disadvantages of channels used) Forecast profit margins and volume of the channels used Identify the impact of marketing strategies and sales promotion

products, which can generate predictions about the obsolescence of products, planning of product lines, and minimal inventories.

One objective of using Mass Media, is seeking new markets and new uses for products that are distributed by a company. Market research should identify unmet needs in the market and determine the parameters:

- Expected volumes of consumption,

- Projected sales and profits.
- Share market expected.

In general, before any market analysis to identify customer needs and marketing appropriate action, you must decide if you are interested in (Figure 2):

Influence the demand for brand competition.

Figure 2. Stages in the process of market research analysis by mass media

Stages in the process of market analysis by Mass Media	**Defining the relevant market**	How you define a market will have a significant impact on the results to be expected in successive steps.
	Diagnosing the purchasing processes or application uses	Once the market has been defined, it must ascertain who will be the buyer: what circumstances motivate and enable them to buy, as they seek information related to purchasing, and choosing between alternatives.
	Define market segments	There are few shopping situations in which all customers have the same motivations, seeking the same information and follow similar processes of selection.
	Describe segments	In any market, it is possible to identify a given number of segments, before making a selection, determine the size of each segment and the best way to achieve it.
	Analize competitors' positions	By identifying the alternatives considered by the buyers, meet the needs of each segment, you can determine who will be the specific competitor for each segment.

Influence the demand for competition in the form of product.

Influence the demand for competition in the class of product, generic products that meet similar needs.

The measurement of the market is of fundamental importance in a great number of decisions that has to know the size and growth rate of the different markets in order to select the marketing strategies, programs and budgets for products and services meet identified market demand and sales forecasts and market potential to represent the upper limit of demand in a given period, i.e., the potential of the maximum sales opportunity can be achieved in the present moment (called the current market potential), or that may occur during some future period of time (future potential of the market).

With the Mass Media studies demand can be analyzed in six different levels of product (product, type of product, product line, company sales, industrial sales, domestic sales), five different levels of space (customer, territory, region, country, world), and three different levels of time (short, medium and long range). Each type of measurement application fills a specific purpose. Thus a company could make a short-range forecast of total demand for a particular product line to provide a basis on which to order raw materials, production planning and scheduling short-term financing. Or, prepare a long-range forecast regional demand for its core product line in order to have a basis to consider expanding market and the life cycle of products by consumer response, which influences fashion, whose stages are: Introduction, Growth, Maturity, Saturation and Neglect.

Analyses by Mass Media identify the minimum distance between the market and the market potential in its two forms: expandable and non-expandable. The expandable market, which enhances the markets for new products, is greatly affected in its full extent by the level of marketing expenditures. The non-expandable market is not affected by the level of marketing expenditures. The firm that sells in a market "non-expandable", will be assumed market size (level of primary demand) and focus your marketing resources to get the desired market share (level of selective demand). In addition to analysis by Mass Media allows market segmentation, identifying homogeneous groups of buyers, i.e., the market is divided into several submarkets or segments according to different purchase desires and requirements of consumers. In studies of Mass Media can make decisions about which market segment to serve, to do so may choose from three methods:

- Undifferentiated marketing: No efforts are channeled towards a single market segment. Considers that the whole market has similar needs, and designs a product and a marketing plan for a large number of buyers, the help of media.
- Differentiated Marketing: This method is characterized by treating each customer as if the only person in the market. The company goes through two or more market segments and design products and marketing programs separately for each of these segments. You get higher sales and are increasing with a diversified line of products that are sold through different channels.
- Marketing concentration: this method is to get a good market position in a few areas.

The instructions to submit a market study by Mass Media after identifying the concepts of market research, continues with the achievement of the following steps:

- Defining the scope of the research: This part means that it is fully informed of problems to solve. It should be noted that there is always more than one alternative solution and each alternative produces a specific result.

- Needs and sources of information: primary sources (surveys Mass Media) and secondary sources (peripheral information).
- Design collection and statistical processing of the data: identify the mechanisms of statistical analysis has been applied to the data.
- Processing and data analysis: After obtaining all the necessary information from any source, proceed with the proper processing and analysis.
- Report: After processing the information properly, generate a report considering the following points:
  1. Product Definition
  2. Demand Analysis
     - Geographical distribution of the consumer market
     - Behavior of demand
     - Projected demand
     - Tabulation of data from primary sources
  3. Analysis of supply
     - Characteristics of competitors (the main producers or service providers)
     - Projection of supply
  4. Imports of the product or service
  5. Price Analysis
     - Determination of the cost
     - Analysis and the expected price
  6. Description of channel marketing and product distribution

Companies must follow specific procedures to build and advertise their competitive advantages and not automatically assume that will be apparent to the market. It should try to avoid falling into one of the three biggest mistakes of positioning:

- Infraposition: occurs when consumers are unaware of what the company offers.
- Overlaps: Buyers may overvalue the company.

- Positioning confused: occurs when different consumers have different ideas about what the company offers.

For the positioning of a product, first, the segmentation should be chosen more desirable and it is interesting to know the size of this segment and its growth, as well as structural interest thereof, which is defined by:

- Threat of competition.
- Threat of new entries.
- Threat of substitute products.
- Threatened by the rising power of buyers.
- Threatened by the power of suppliers and the objectives and resources of the company.

The company needs to develop a strategy of positioning the product to give consumers know how it differs from the company to current and potential competitors. To build a product positioning strategy, there are six alternative bases:

- Positioning on specific product characteristics.
- Product Positioning.
- Positioning for specific occasions of use.
- Positioning for user category.
- Positioning with respect to another product.
- Dissociation products.

2. UNDERSTANDING HYBRID APPROACHES

Market research trying to determine the maximum number of consumers, users or audience who are willing to consume, use any type of product or service or follow a trend, creating a potential market that is so dependent on marketing effort, the economic variables, period of time and diversity of existing products.

Figure 3. Market research strategies through mass media

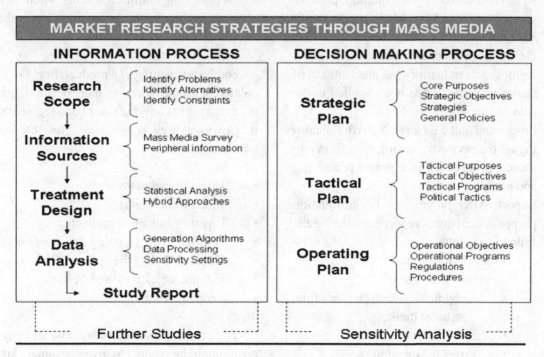

The testing procedure consists of three main stages that develop within a process of information and decision making:

- Status of survey: consumer group location or audience to explore their motivations, attitudes and behaviors.
- Stage of analysis: the use of multivariate techniques to study the data statistically or hybrid approaches.
- Stage Profile: Each segment is profiled in terms of distinguishing attitudes, behaviors, demographic and psychological characteristics, or use and consumption habits. This procedure should be replicated periodically, because the market segments change over time.

Companies must follow specific procedures to build and advertise their competitive advantages and not automatically assume that will be apparent to the market. The use of market research on

Mass Media can develop strategic, tactical and operational plans (Figure 3) to avoid falling into one of the three biggest positioning mistakes:

- Infraposition: Occurs when consumers are unaware of what the company offers.
- Overlaps: Buyers may overvalue the company.
- Positioning confused: occurs when different consumers have different ideas about what the company offers.

To achieve an appropriate level of analysis, advances in computer systems make possible the development of techniques, analysis procedures and algorithms to draw conclusions on the basis of existing information in any niche, also allowing the use of techniques using hybrid combinations different analysis procedures or tools.

Multivariate analysis is a statistical method used to determine the contribution of various factors in a single event or outcome. The study factors are called risk factors, independent variables or explanatory variables. Multivariate analysis using techniques of projection onto latent variables has many advantages over traditional regression methods:

- Using information from multiple input variables, but they are not linearly independent
- Working with matrices and arrays containing more variables than observations
- Working with incomplete matrices, provided that the missing values are randomly distributed and not exceeding 10%
- They are based on the sequential extraction of the factors that extract the greatest possible variability and allow separating information from noise.

It is possible to generate models of multivariate analysis techniques (Figure 4), or optimization algorithms can be used similarly or in combination. These optimization techniques are based on numerical methods to find the response variables by functions that are subject to restrictions, where the input variables can be a scalar or vector of continuous or discrete values. This category has the subcategories shown in Figure 5.

In addition to the mentioned tools or techniques are employable techniques of Data Mining that is non-trivial extraction of information. Data mining encompasses a range of techniques to the extraction of actionable knowledge, implicit in the databases, addressing the solution to problems of prediction, classification and segmentation.

In market analysis, the use of data mining can contribute significantly to the management and marketing applications based on the relationship with customers or users who are more likely to respond positively to a particular offer or promotion by building separate models for each region and/or for each type of customer.

Through the advancement of computational techniques, the use of hybrid approaches or techniques can generate programming structures or analysis that takes advantage of combined techniques for solving problems in order to generate faster and more efficient algorithms (Figure 6). The hybrid procedures as considered a new field techniques and skills in almost all fields of study to search for solutions. As an example of hybrid approach is presented in this work with the ap-

Figure 4. Multivariate techniques

Multivariate Techniques

Principal components analysis
Factor analysis
Discriminant analysis
Canonical Correlation Analysis
Cluster Analysis
Dimensional Scaling Analysis
Correspondence Analysis
Confirmatory factor analysis
Structural Equation Model (SEM), causal analysis.
Conjoint analysis
Optimal Scaling
Multiple Linear Regression
Logit and Probit Regression
Manova Analysis

Figure 5. Optimization algorithms

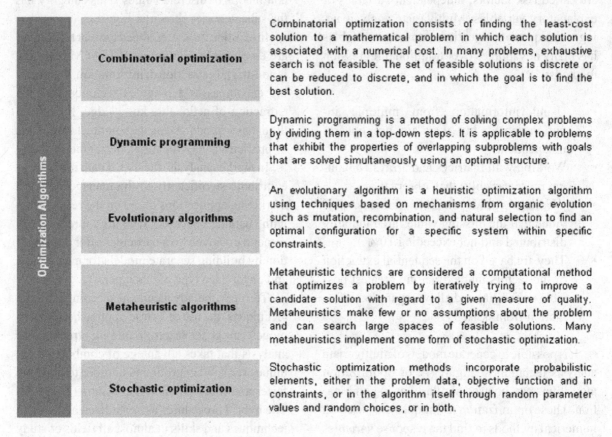

Optimization Algorithms	**Combinatorial optimization**	Combinatorial optimization consists of finding the least-cost solution to a mathematical problem in which each solution is associated with a numerical cost. In many problems, exhaustive search is not feasible. The set of feasible solutions is discrete or can be reduced to discrete, and in which the goal is to find the best solution.
	Dynamic programming	Dynamic programming is a method of solving complex problems by dividing them in a top-down steps. It is applicable to problems that exhibit the properties of overlapping subproblems with goals that are solved simultaneously using an optimal structure.
	Evolutionary algorithms	An evolutionary algorithm is a heuristic optimization algorithm using techniques based on mechanisms from organic evolution such as mutation, recombination, and natural selection to find an optimal configuration for a specific system within specific constraints.
	Metaheuristic algorithms	Metaheuristic technics are considered a computational method that optimizes a problem by iteratively trying to improve a candidate solution with regard to a given measure of quality. Metaheuristics make few or no assumptions about the problem and can search large spaces of feasible solutions. Many metaheuristics implement some form of stochastic optimization.
	Stochastic optimization	Stochastic optimization methods incorporate probabilistic elements, either in the problem data, objective function and in constraints, or in the algorithm itself through random parameter values and random choices, or in both.

plication of Bioinspired Algorithm and Social Data Mining.

3. MARKET ANALYSIS BY MASS MEDIA

Within the market analysis with Mass Media, there are two kinds of easy application: the Analysis of Uses and Attitude and Conjoint Analysis. The first kind of these studies identifies the times, quantities, brands and consumer behaviors to different types of products and services available in the market.

The Analysis of Uses and Attitudes determines the preferences of the product or service and the number of people consuming or using the product or service, identifying consumer profile, indicating the reasons for consumption of the product or ser-

vice or analyzing the current uses of products and knowledge of the attitudes of users or consumers.

Field tests will consist in conducting mass media survey, under the use of networks or groups, whose method of systematic random selection will be according to the segment or place of interest.

The Conjoint Analysis (Figure 7) allows the use of combinations of product attributes that will be presented on a cyclical basis for selecting respondents, in this way detect the slightest interest attributes, and those features which can be exploited commercially in this segment. This analysis helps to measure the importance of various attributes of the marketing mix from the consumer point of view (level of price, performance, type of packaging, brand, in another.). And the way to exchanges the order of attributes to reach a final mixture. Compare both the preference for different product options to total target market level

Figure 6. Common techniques used in data mining

Common techniques used in data mining	Statistical techniques	computer techniques
	Analysis of Variance Regressions Chi-square tests Clustering Analysis Discriminant Analysis Time Series	Genetic algorithms Expert Systems Neural networks

and within predefined segments. The result is the importance of all attributes and the importance of each one of them, just as the potential involvement of the preference of different combinations of product attributes. Conjoint Analysis should always be used with some segmentation analysis and can be used in combination with a "Proof of Concept" or "Product Test". Even in some cases it may be part of a study of Uses and Attitudes. It can be used in parallel with group sessions if there are several products on the same project, with this information is possible make a Tree

Decision which describes the behavior of genre in the use of this kind of Mass Media.

One of the advantages of Conjoint Analysis is to allow a research design considering relevant attributes and levels, executing a routine exclusion for combinations not possible or not feasible, and including in each interview combinations identified as "essential measurement" through an interactive interview format that asks and built a combination preferred by the interviewee, who evaluates similar product combinations and the essential measurement, focusing the client's perspectives and gaining qualifications for as many

Figure 7. Characteristics of conjoint analysis (definition and combination of attributes)

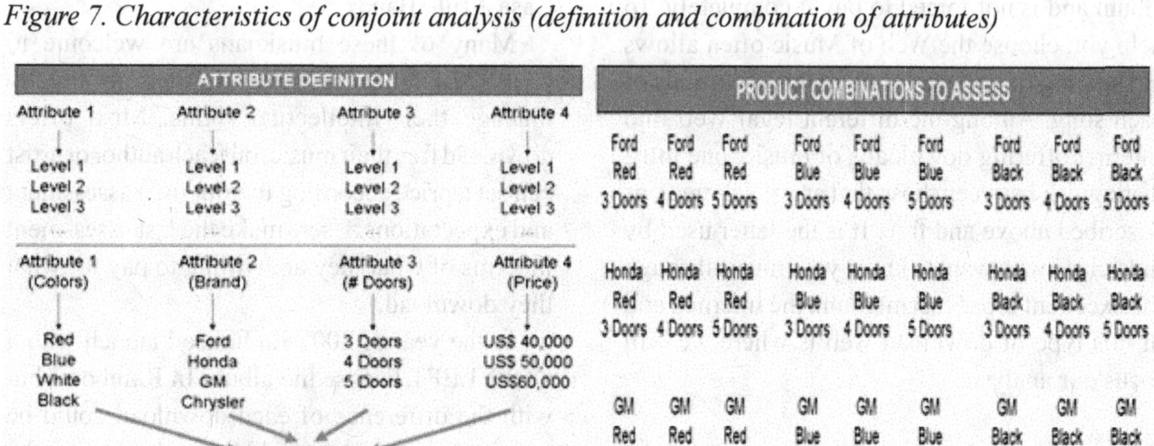

combinations as those labeled as essential. Thus, is possible extending the possibility of obtaining ratings for combinations relevant to the market.

4. CASES OF STUDY

Musical Band Project

There are two ways widespread distribution of music via the Internet: Hearing online (streaming) and downloading to a hard drive (download).

The Internet music listening is done through a technology known as streaming, which involves sending music from a server to your computer that you are requesting. Just listen online but cannot keep on the hard disk is like Radio music online, usually served by hearing or by lists of thematic channels. Downloading music on the Internet is the arrangement that allows, unlike the previous one, save the music on the hard disk, in some cases with limited tenure and other limited to a number of auditions or exports to other external media. Usually used for songs.

This is a major advantage over off-line distribution, which takes place in physical stores with sales of CDs, as in the case of the online sale, the buyer can select the songs you like in an album and is not forced to buy it completely. To help you choose the Web of Music often allows the hearing of a fragment of about 30 seconds of each song. Among the different legal Web find Internet offering downloads of music, one must distinguish between those that are of payment, as described above and free. It is the latter used by musicians who want to know your music through the excellent broadcast medium, the Internet, and in this type of download web is where we will focus our analysis.

Legal Downloads of Music under Payment

When a site wants to offer music downloads from musicians who are associated with any Entity Management of intellectual property rights (Figure 8), there are three licenses must apply and obtain for their legal activities.

Increasingly, Web sites offer space and technology to all musicians who want to upload their work to the Internet so that users can download it free. These musicians generally use this method of distribution for their songs with the aim of reaching the widest possible audience, watching their jobs rewarding when people go to their shows. With ticket sales fund the costs of music production, so the more users know their music, download, sell more tickets and get more profit.

This collective of musicians, which is growing exponentially, want their music to be distributed free over the Internet and any costs that encourages the download, for the users is not welcome, decreasing the chances of discharge to reduce the number of potential users. Therefore, the imposition of a charge on any digital product or service, computer or telematic, reduces the spread of their music damaging their means of financing, the sale of tickets to their concerts, as in the case of "La Casa Azul" Band.

Many of these musicians are welcome to COPYLEFT licenses allowing them to directly manage their intellectual rights. Most offers download free their music, but each author or artist can set a price according to your own assessment and expectations. Users make the last assessment in terms of what they are willing to pay for what they download.

In the year of 2007 Radiohead launch with a COPYLEFT license the album In Rainbows but with the difference of each download could be pay by the user. That could be a mistake, but the band in October of 2008 shows the statistics of sales and the album was number 1 in UK and the USA, first album in sales on iTunes even today

Figure 8. MySpace Music's La Casa Azul Band COPYLEFT and artists offering free downloads of their music.

the band has a 1.75 millions of sales. That shows how even with a COPYLEFT license the musicians could success in the business of music.

COPYLEFT licenses are a clear alternative to control the copyright administration and organizations, allowing desktop publishing and self-management by the musicians of your own work. Thus, there are no conditions or fares charged by a third party not involved in intellectual work, as in the diffusion model and distribution of music through publishers and producers of phonograms in which prices are set solely by the record companies and rights are collected and managed by the Management Entities.

The mass media in journalism is a strong way to publicity educative news and even we can have some interactive patterns in blogs, tweets and videos like YouTube. The most interest thing is the liberty to share information just like the case of wikileaks (Figure 9) in this web site we can found a lot of information about the Afghanistan war, and in this site we can found a diary since 2004 to 2010. The reports, while written by soldiers and intelligence officers, and mainly described lethal military actions involving the United States military, also include intelligence information, reports of meetings with political figures, and related details. This is a perfect example of mass media; publishing information about different things even in the web we can have access to a lot of information.

The use of videogames actually is a big application of mass media, using GUI interfaces to play and act in different scenarios even when the videogames are violent. When the videogames are violent it does appear plausible that the use of video games, at least for some individuals, may provide a mood-management activity that provides them with an ability to tolerate stress (Ferguson & Rueda, 2010).

Figure 9. Wikileaks

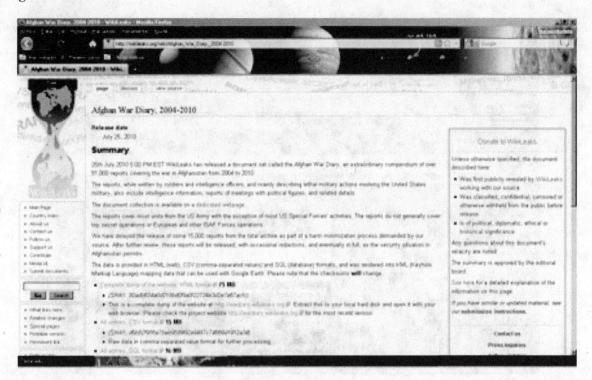

Improve a Karaoke Project

In this research is described an Intelligent Karaoke associated to a Social Networking which uses different songs in a database related with a kind of Music (Eurovision songs) which employs the Dublin Core metadata standard for the documents description, the XML standard for describing user profile, which is based on the user's profile, and on service and data providers to generate musical recommendations to a group of persons. The main contribution of the work is to provide a recommendation mechanism based on the user of this Social Networking reducing the human effort spent on the profile generation. In addition, this paper presents and discusses some experiments that are based on quantitative and qualitative evaluations.

Today, the songs can be electronically accessed as soon as they are published on the Web, and these can be used in a Karaoke, an artifact invented in Japan by Daisuke Inoue in 1969 which displays the lyrics of a song and the musical track. The main advantage of open music is the minimization of the promotion time. In this context, Digital Libraries (DLs) have emerged as the main repositories of digital documents, links and associated metadata. The Recommender System involves personalized information. The personalization is related to the ways in which contents and services can be tailored to match the specific needs of a user or a community (social networking) (Smeaton & Callahan, 2003). The human-centered demand specification is not an easy task. One experiences this difficulty when trying to find a new song in a good indexing and retrieval system such as ESC Radio.

The query formulation is complex and the fine tuning of the user requirements is a time-consuming task. Few users have enough time to spend some hours searching for, eventually new songs. This functionality, the query specification may be reached by the analysis of the user activities, history, information demands, in others. This paper presents a Musical recommendations system of a Karaoke associated to a social networking, the songs recovered are associated with the Karaoke's playlist. The main contribution of this work is to provide a recommendation mechanism based on the user reducing the human effort spent on the profile generation. The paper is organized as follows. We start giving an overview of the background literature and concepts, then the recommender system and detail its architecture and techniques. Finally, we present some quantitative and qualitative experiments to evaluate and validate our system and discuss the results and conclusions of our work.

The semantic Web technologies promote an efficient and intelligent access to the digital documents on the Web. The standards based on metadata to describe information objects have two main advantages: computational efficiency during the information harvesting process and interoperability among DLs. The first is a consequence of the increasing use of Dublin Core (DC) metadata standard (http://dublincore.org); the latter has been obtained as a result of the OAI initiative (Open Archive Initiative) (http://openarchive.org). DC metadata standard was conceived with the objective of defining a minimal metadata set that could be used to describe the available resources of a DL. This standard defines a set of 15 metadata (Dublin Core Metadata Element Set – DCMES).

The main goal of OAI is to create a standard communication way, allowing DLs around the world to interoperate as a federation (Sompel & De Lagoze, 2000). The DL metadata harvesting process is accomplished by the OAI-PMH protocol (Open Archives Initiative Protocol for Metadata Harvesting) (Sompel & De Lagoze, 2005), which define how the metadata transference between two entities, data and service providers, is performed. The data provider acts by searching the metadata in databases and making them available to a service provider, which uses the gathered data to provide specific services.

Considering that a Recommender System concerns with information personalization, it is essential that it copes with user profile. In our work, the user profile is obtained from a social networking similar at used in Laustanou (2003). According to Huang, Chung, Ong, and Chen (2002), there are three different methodologies used in Recommender Systems to perform recommendation: (i) content-based, which recommends items classified accordingly to the user profile and early choices; (ii) collaborative filtering, which deals with similarities among users' interests; and (iii) hybrid approach, which combines the two to take advantage of their benefits. In our work, the content-based approach is used, once the information about the user is taken from Karaoke users.

This recommendation process can be perceived as an information retrieval process, in which user's relevant songs should be retrieved and recommended. Thus, to perform recommendations, we can use the classical information retrieval models such as the Boolean Model, the Vector Space Model (VSM) or the Probabilistic Model (Baeza-Yates & Ribeiro-Neto, 1999; Grossman, 2004; Sompel & De Lagoze, 2000). In this work, the VSM was selected since it provides satisfactory results with a convenient computational effort. In this model, songs and queries are represented by terms vectors. The terms are words or expressions extracted from the documents (lyrics) and from queries that can be used for content identification and representation. Each term has a weight associated to it, to provide distinctions among them according to their importance. According to Salton and Macgill (1983) the weight can vary continuously between 0 and 1. Values near to 1 are more important while values near to 0 are irrelevant.

The VSM uses an n-dimensional space to represent the terms, where n corresponds to the number of distinct terms. For each document or query represented the weights represent the vector's coordinates in the corresponding dimension. The VSM principle is based on the inverse correlation between the distance (angle) among term vectors in the space and the similarity between the songs that they represented. To calculate the similarity score, the cosine (Equation 1) can be used. The resultant value indicates the relevance degree between a query (Q) and a document (song) (D), where w represents the weights of the terms contained in Q and D, and t represents the number of terms (size of the vector). This equation provides ranked retrieval output based on decreasing order of the ranked retrieval similarity values (Salton & Buckley, 1988).

$$similarity(Q, D) = \frac{\sum_{k=1}^{t} w_{qk} - w_{dk}}{\sqrt{\sum_{k=1}^{t} (w_{qk})^2 - \sum_{k=1}^{t} (w_{dk})^2}}$$

(1)

The same equation is widely used to compare the similarity among songs, and similarity, in our case, Q represents the user profile and D the documents descriptors (lyrics) that are harvested in the DL (see Section 3 for details). The term weighting scheme is very important to guarantee an effective retrieval process.

The results depend crucially of the term weighting system chosen, In addition, the query terms selection is fundamental to obtain a recommendation according to the user necessities. Our research is focused in the query terms selection and weighting. Any person of the social networking that required a musical retrieval may evaluate the process complexity and the difficulty to find the adequate songs. The central idea is to develop an automated retrieval and musical recommendation system where the price for the user is limited to the submission of an already existing preferences query similar at the used on Esc Radio.

Intelligent Recommender System

Our system focuses on the recommendation of songs from a Karaoke system and its social net-

working that uses this. The information source to perform recommendations is the database associated with this Karaoke System (Lyrics and Music of each song), while the user profile is obtained from Database Profile Register subset. However, any DL repository providing DC metadata and supporting the OAI-PMH protocol can be used as a source. An alternative to the user profile generation is under development. This alternative approach is composed by an information retrieval system to gather data from another Music sources. A DL repository stores digital songs or its localization (web or physical), and the respective metadata. A DL data provider allows an agent to harvest documents metadata through the OAI-PMH protocol. Our system handles the songs described with XML in DC standard (Johnston, 2002; LPMP-CNPq, 2005).

The Recommendation System Architecture

In this subsection we present the architecture elements of our system and its functionalities (Figure 10). To start the process, the users must supply their preferences in the XML version to the system. Whenever a user makes its registration in the system and sends his preferences list (1), the XML Songs Document module is activated and the information about the user's interests is stored in the local database named User Profile (2). Then the Metadata Harvesting module is activated to update the local database Songs Metadata. This module makes a request to a DL data provider to harvest specific documents metadata. It receives an XML document as response (3) and the XML DC to local DB module is activated (4). This module extracts the relevant metadata to perform the recommendation from the XML document and stores it in the local database named Songs Metadata (5). Once the user profile and the songs metadata are available in the local database, the Recommendation module can be activated (6). The focus is to retrieve lyrics and songs of a DL that the best matches the user profile described through the profile of each user of a social networking related with the Karaoke System.

The Recommendation Model

As stated before, the recommendation is based on the VSM model. The query vector is built with the term parsed from the title, keywords, singer or band, album and date. The parser ignores stopwords (Braschler, Di Nunzio, Ferro, Gonzalo, Peters, & Sanderson, M. 2005) -A list of common or general terms that are not used in the information retrieval process, e.g., prepositions, conjunctions and articles-. The parser considers each term as a single word. On the other hand, the terms are taken integrally, as single expressions.

The query vector terms weights are build up according to the Equation 2. This equation considers the type of term (keyword or title), the language and the year of the first air data. Keyword terms are considered more important than the titles of the songs and have more reading proficiency,

and are more valorized (higher weight), and the terms obtained from the most recent album from an artist or band including cameos and contributions with another singers or bands are assigned a more important weight than the less recent ones.

$$W_t = W_{KeywordOrTitle} * W_{Language} * W_{Year} \qquad (2)$$

The weights $W_{KeywordOrTitle}$, $W_{Language}$, WYear are calculated with Equation 3.

$$Wi = 1 - (i - 1)\left(\frac{1 - w_{min}}{n - 1}\right) \qquad (3)$$

In this equation W_i varies according to the type of weight we want to compute. To illustrate this in the experimental evaluation (Section 4), for $W_{KeywordOrTitles}$ W_{min} was 0.95, and I is 1 if the language-skill. Level is "good", 2 for "reasonable" and 3 for "few". For W_{Years} W_{min} was 0.55 and i vary from 1 to n, where n is the interval of years considered, begin 1 the highest and n the

Figure 10. The recommender system architecture

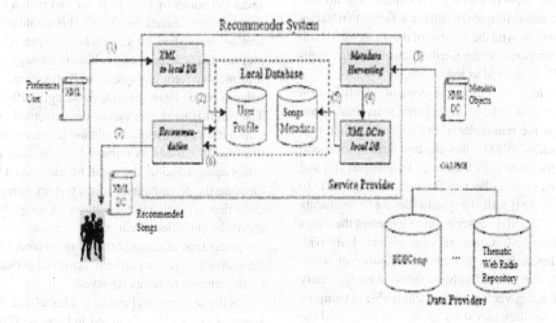

lowest. In the experimental evaluation it was considered the interval of songs between 2008 and 2002. However, if the interval is omitted, it will be considered as between the present year and the less recent year (the smallest between artist:first-album and artist:last-album).

If w$_{min}$ is not informed, the default value will be used (presented in Equation 4). In the situation, Equation 3 is reduced to Equation 5.

$$W_{min\,default} = \frac{1}{n} \qquad (4)$$

$$Wi = \frac{n - i + 1}{n} \qquad (5)$$

Once the query vector is build, the songs vector terms and the respective weights must be defined. The adopted approach was (tf * idf), i.e., the product of the term frequency and the inverse document frequency (Salton & Buckley, 1988). This approach allows automatic term weights assignment for the songs retrieval. The term frequency (tf) corresponds to the number of occurrences of a term in a document. The inverse document frequency (idf) is a factor that varies inversely with the number of the songs n to which a term is assigned in a collection of N songs (typically computed as log (N/n)).

The best terms for content identification are those able to distinguish individuals ones from the remainder of the collection (Salton & Buckley, 1988). Thus, the best terms correspond to the ones with high term frequencies (tf) and low overall collection frequencies (high idf). To compute tf * idf, the system uses the DC metadata dc:title and dc:description to represent the songs content. Moreover, as your system deals with different languages, the total number of songs will vary accordingly. After building the query and songs vectors, the system is able to compute the similarities values among the songs and the query according to Equation 1.

Experimental Evaluation

In order to evaluate the musical recommender system, we have asked for preferences from a social networking entailed to different musical interest terms of different genres as English Pop or Electronic Dance. As response, a group of 47 people send us their list of preferences, whose information was loaded in the Songs Metadata related with the Karaoke System local database. The songs Metadata local database was loaded in the User Profile local database related with the Social Networking. This database stored up to January 2009, totalizing 1007 songs from 267 singers or bands including in 87 albums.

After 20 recommendations were generated by the system for each Karaoke's performance, considering individual's profile of the user and the genres preferences. This information was obtained using the user's data base related with the Social Networking.

Two evaluations were performed. The first was based on the hypothesis that the best songs to describe the profile of a user should be those produced by them. Since we had information about the songs by each user, we can match the items recommended to those. This evaluation was accomplished by the recall and precision metrics that is a standard evaluation strategy for information retrieval systems (Baeza-Yates & Ribeiro-Neto, 1999; Salton, & Macgill, 1983). The recall is used to measure the percentage of relevant songs retrieved in relation to the amount that should have been retrieved. In the case of songs categorization, the recall metric is used to measure the percentage of songs that are correct classified in relation to the number of songs that should be classified. Precision is used to measure the percentage of songs correctly recovered, i.e., the number of songs correctly retrieved divided by the number of songs retrieved.

As the profiles can be seen as classes and the songs as items to be classified in these profiles, we can verify the amount of items from the author that are correctly identified (i.e., classified) by the user profile. As we have many users (i.e., many classes), it is necessary to combine the results. The macroaverage presented in Equation 6 was designed by Lewis (1991) to perform this specific combination ("the unweighted mean of effectiveness across all categories"), and was applied by him in the evaluation of classification algorithms and techniques.

$$macroaverage = \frac{\sum_{i=1} n \cdot X_{i'}}{n} \qquad (6)$$

In this formula, X_i is the recall or the precision, depending on the metric we want to evaluate, of each individual class (user in our case) and n is the number of classes (users). Thus, the macroaverage recall is the arithmetic average of the recalls obtained for each individual, and the macroaverage precision is the arithmetic average of the precisions obtained for each individual.

Given that the users are not interested in its own preferred songs as recommendations, we performed another evaluation that takes in to account only the items from other users. Then, 15 recommendations were presented to each individual ranked on the relative grade of relevance generated by the system. In this rank, the songs with the highest grade of similarity with the user profile were set as 100% relevant and the others were adjusted to a value relative to it. In this case, each author was requested to evaluate the recommendations generated to them assigning one of the following concepts (following the bipolar five-point Lickert scale); "Inadequate", "Bad", "Average", "Good", and "Excellent", and were also asked to comment the results. The following sections present the results obtained.

Analysis of Experiments

The first experiment was designed to evaluate the capability of the system to correctly identify

the user profile (i.e., to represent its preferences), since we believe that the best songs to describe the user profile are those selected by themselves, as stated before. To perform such evaluation, we identified the songs of each user had at Karaoke System. After that, we employed the recall metric to evaluate the number of articles recovered for each author and combined then with the microaverage equation explained before.

We have found a macroaverage recall of 43.25%. It is important to state that each user received 20 recommendations. This is an acceptable value as the query construction was made automatically without human intervention. It happened to be lower than it should be if we have used more songs, maybe access to ESC Radio, but the problem is the limited songs for singer or band. Other important consideration is that the recommendation ranking was generated with a depreciation degree that was dependent on the promotion year and on the user language, as explained in the previous section. As the time-slice considered corresponds to a small part of the full period stored in the database related with the Karaoke System, not all songs are good recommendations since the preferences changes along the time, similar at propose in Ochoa, González, Esquivel, Matozzi, and Maffucci (2009a).

Figure 11 presents the results of the second experiment, which was based on the users' qualitative evaluation of the recommended songs. On this experiment each user received 15 recommendations and evaluated them according to one of the following concepts: "inadequate", "bad", "average", "good", and "excellent". The results were grouped into the categories "first match", "top 5", "top 10", and "top 15", and are presented in Figure 11.

Analyzing three results, it is possible to observe that, if we only consider the first song recommended (the "first match"), the number of items qualified as "excellent" in greater than the others (i.e., 42.86%) and none of them were classified as "inadequate". This strengthens the capability

Figure 11. Users' evaluations of the recommendations

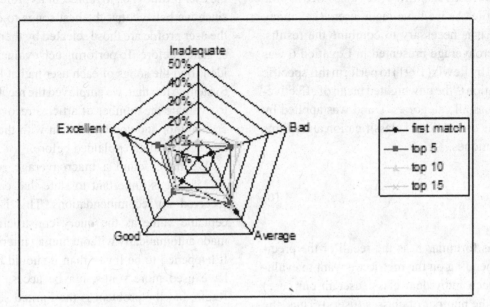

of the system on performing recommendations adjusted to the present user's genre preferences interests. We have also grouped the concepts "good" and "excellent" into a category named "positive recommendation" and the concepts "bad" and "inadequate" into a "negative recommendation" group, so we could obtain a better visualization and comprehension of the results (Figure 12).

We could perceive that the positive recommendations, considering only the "first match", are superior (57.14%) in relation to the negative ones (7.14%). The same behavior can be perceived in the "top 5" and "top 10" categories, the recommendations had a negative evaluation only in the "top 15" category, and that probably happened because as the number of recommendations grows, the number of correct recommendations falls. It is clear that the automated procedure here adopted is adequate for an alert recommender system. Our proposal is to add to the Karaoke System an automated alert system that periodically sends to the user a list of the most relevant songs recently listen on ESC Radio during seven or more weeks.

Further, in our tests the users that have changed their search in the last three months have negatively qualified the recommendations. In the next experiments a variable time threshold and different depreciation values will be employed and the temporal component will be exhaustively analyzed.

This research presented a Musical Recommender System to users of a Karaoke System related with the lyrics of plethora of songs. In current days, in which the recovery of relevant digital information on the Web is a complex task, such systems are of great value to minimize the problems associated to the information overload phenomena, minimizing the time spent to access the right information, with this data is possible applying K-means, by determine the number of clusters in the sample

The main contribution of this research consists on the heavy utilization of automated Music Recommendation and in the use of a Digital Library (DL) metadata to create the recommendations. The system was evaluated with BDBComp, but it is designed to work with the open digital library protocol OAI-PMH, then it may be easily extended to work with any DL that supports this mechanism.

Figure 12. Grouped users' evaluation

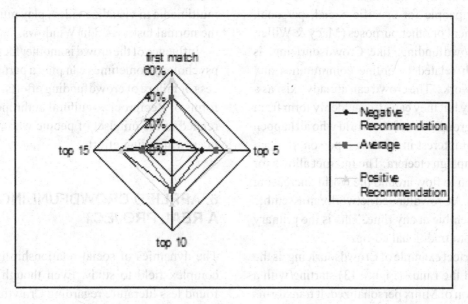

The same occurs with the lyrics format related with the song, but it can be extended to support other formats or to analyze information about the user stored on tools like ESC Radio. Alternatively the operational prototype offers the possibility to the user to load the lyrics via an electronic form.

The developed system will have many applications. One of them is the recommendation of songs to support a Social Networking related with a kind of music to relax activities. Thus, the user could log into a specific distance or electronic Karaoke System environment supported by this system and receive recommendations of songs containing actualized relevant material to complement its current musical selection, for example, to finally describe the different selection of songs by the RAI Internazionale Scholarships and the temporality of them, for try to understand the Italianitá Index in the time.

5. CROWFUNDING AS A DIFFERENT WAY TO OBTAIN FUNDS TO A PROJECT

Crowdfunding, inspired by *crowdsourcing,* describes the collective cooperation, attention and trust by people who network and pool their money together, usually via the Internet, in order to support efforts initiated by other people or organizations. Crowdfunding occurs for any variety of purposes, from disaster relief to citizen journalism to artists seeking support from fans, to political campaigns.

Crowdfunding can replace the need for specialized grant applications or other more formal and traditional fundraising techniques with that of a more casual, yet powerful, approach based on crowd participation. Examples of the basis of Crowdfunding can be seen in *Cooperatives* (co-ops) around the world. However, the Internet can provide new streamlined approaches to quickly imitating the co-op model for low-level and/or sudden needs (i.e., disaster relief, travel expenses, legal fees and so on.). It is this reason that a term be used to encompass the act of informally generating and distributing funds, usually online, by groups of people for specific social, personal, entertainment or other purposes (Macy & Willer, 2002). Crowdfunding, like Crowdsouricing, is very much related to online communities and social networks. The crowd can already exist as a community but they can also suddenly form from disparate groups around the world who all happen to share an interest in funding a person, project, event, campaign etcetera. The Internet allows for information to flow around the world, increasing awareness. A Crowdfunded network can assemble and disassemble at any time. This is the primary difference to traditional co-ops.

The perfect example of Crowdsouricing, is the creation of the Linux (Figure 13) starting with a little version of Minix personalized, it transforms into a big operating system with all kind of tools available like different compilers in java, c, c++, pearl, php, and multiple services to web like apache, tomcat, smtp, samba, in another. All the services available were created by a group of developers and they share knowledge about programming and different versions of code, creating a little version of Minix modified into a big and stable operating system with all the functions necessary to the use in an environment of servers.

The multiple demands for an optimal version of Linux dedicated to final users created the Ubuntu Linux (Figure 14) dedicated to the easy use to simple users, without complicated com-

Figure 13. Tux Linux Icon

mands and a friendly GUI with easy tools for multimedia to visualize video, play music and all the normal tasks used in Windows.

Influence of the crowd is another factor. Crowd psychology sometimes can play a part in the success or failure of crowdfunding efforts. Likewise, forms of Reciprocity (cultural anthropology) are related to the mindset of people who participate in crowdfunding efforts.

6. APPLIED CROWDFUNDING A REAL PROJECT

The dynamics of social relationship is a highly complex field to study. Even though it can be found less literature regarding Crowfunding and its relationship with a Social Networking (Ochoa et al., 2009b), we are still far from understanding all the process involved. Social research has shown that people use numerous criteria when they consider the possibility of participate in a same project. But this research considers only two: cultural and sociological attributes of people (society) that determine the emergence and evolution of friendship. After studying the theory available, we have decided to use "Crowdfunding" in order to model the system to obtain funds and determine the concept of *solidarity*. This principle assesses that the more similar cluster formed by several people are, the stronger their chances of becoming a group of supporters (16,771 friends) with this data is possible make a Model which justifies the behavior associated with Society-Genre. Thus, we attempt to model the processes in which people of different societies turn to be acquaintances, those turn into a social networking (more of 4) try to realize the economic support of a project. Select a social networking to support a project, and thus it is not surprising that crowdfunding tend toward cultural homogeneity. People with the same preferences usually associate with other similar persons, in our case the Diorama built represented different societies from different quadrants, the proposed

Figure 14. Ubuntu Environment

model of Crowfunding was applied to economic support of this project (Figure 15).

7. EXPERIMENTS TO SUPPORT AN INDIE POP BAND

We simulated by means of the developed tool the expectations that propagation of activities to support an Indie Pop Band. One of the observed most interesting characteristics in this experiment, were the diversity of the cultural patterns established by each fan, because the selection of different attributes in a potential supporting specific cluster. The structured scenes associated the agents cannot be reproduced in general, so that the time and space belong to a given moment in. They represent a unique form, needs and innovator of adaptive behavior which solves a followed computational problem of a complex change of

relations. Using Cultural Algorithms (Reynolds, 1998) implementing with agents is possible simulate the behavior of many people (Ochoa, 2007) determination whom people support this social networking. Using Coriolis Vector (Conway, 2004) -See Equation 7- was possible determine the individuals whom support and promote the social networking.

$$q = [M - 2c] \, q'z \, 0 \tag{7}$$

First observe that valued crowfunding (support in the realization of a specific projected with financial funds) always plays a very significant role, which should of course not be surprising. Hidden patterns observed in the agents are related with linguistic and cultural distances, and the expectative of selection of a location with specific relation to another people with similar attributes. The nodes with more value in their

Figure 15. Conceptual diagram of the organization of a musical's project

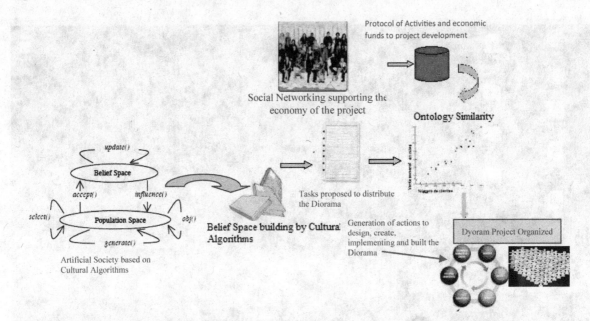

Figure 16. Multiagents Systems Environment to organize fans in Clusters. Each color represents a different intensity and magnitude related with this support

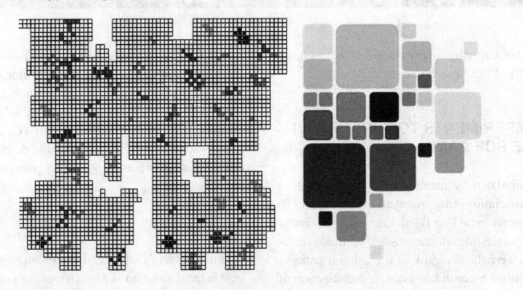

degree are considered more popular and support the social networking. To get some insight, we run 100 regressions on 100 random samples of half the number of observations, and count the number of times each parameter affect the graph built determined the attributes offered by theirs

are adequate for others, it permits shown the simulation with multi agents system and finally the Diorama built with these attributes (Figure 16).

Figure 17 shows the interaction of all the initial patterns taking first a search pattern to create a previous relation between all the information

Figure 17. Architecture of interaction between all the processes in the relationship of the diorama

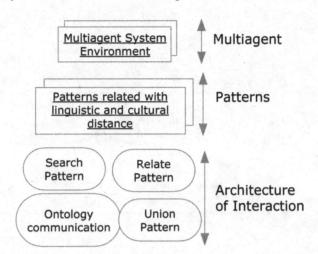

received, then with all the information we create a union with his own pattern and finally we have an ontology communication. This is the first part of the Architecture of interaction, with all this information we have our own patterns with different linguistic and cultural distances. We receive first some information about his linguistic and cultural information, and then all the information is used for the multiagent system to create relations between all the information creating dioramas.

We show in Figure 18 the interaction in the multiagent with the group of information in this case an Indie group band, so the multiagent take the information to process first searching an internal pattern inside the database patterns to continue with the relate pattern creating groups (diorama), then all this groups are created by the union pattern all these process are inside the multiagent, and with an ontology who permits all the communication between the information manipulated in the multiagent environment system.

Figure 19 shows the internal interaction when the group of information are received, the search pattern agent who search directly into the database pattern using a fuzzy string search, then all the

information it's used by the relate pattern agent who interacts directly with the ontology communication, the ontology communication agents are used to get all the relations between the information and validate the correct relations, finally to send to the union pattern agent who creates the correct group of information.

Figure 20 shows the internal work of the ontology communication agent, with the first module who receive all the information sending in form of metadata resources to the ontology search in this step the use of the database pattern are necessary to check all the information in the process of relation between patterns. This is necessary to check the right integration of information between all the internal agents.

8. EXPERIMENTS RELATED WITH A WRESTLING CIRCUIT

We simulated by means of the developed tool -*WREID*- (this software was programming in Java) the expectations of successfully in a circuit of Wrestling and interests of obtain popularity based on their performance associated with specific features. One of the most interesting characteristics

Figure 18. Interaction between the group of information and internal work of the multiagent environment system

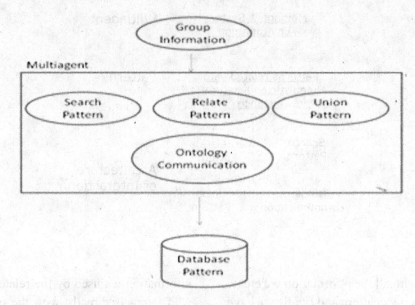

Figure 19. Detailed work in the multiagent environment system

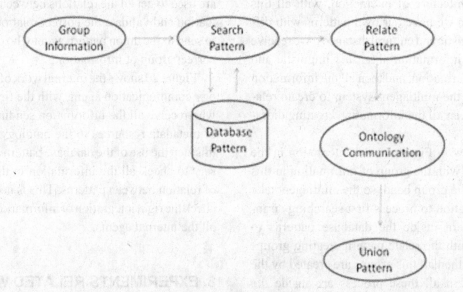

observed in the experimental analysis were the diversity of cultural patterns established by each society because the selection of different attributes in a potential best wrestler: Agility, ability to fight, Emotional Control, Force, Stamina, Speed, Intelligence. The structured scenes associated the agents cannot be reproduced in general, so that

the time and space belong to a given moment in them. They represent a unique form, needs and innovator of adaptive behavior which solves a followed computational problem of a complex change of relations. Using Social Data Mining implementing with agents was possible simulate the behavior of many followers in the selection of a best wrestler and determinate whom people support this professional career. With respect at Node attributes, we summarize the measures required to describe individual nodes of a graph. They allow identifying elements by their topological properties. The *degree* -or *connectivity*- (ki) of a node *vi* is defined as the number of edges of this node. From the adjacency matrix, we easily obtain the degree of a given node as

$$k_i = \sum_{j=1}^{N} a_{ij} \tag{8}$$

$$C_i = \frac{2n}{k_i(k_i - 1)} \tag{9}$$

We first observe that Professional Wrestler Idol (support in features related with age, height and weight are considered) always plays a very significant role, which should of course not be surprising. Hidden patterns observed in the agents are related with size of circuit, match records and cultural distances (ethnicity), and the expectative of selection of a good wrestler with specific attributes, which explain and justify the existence of out layers in the sample. The nodes with more value in their degree are considered more popular and obtain the best contracts. To get some insight, we run 100 regressions on 100 random samples

Figure 20. Internal process of the ontology communication agent

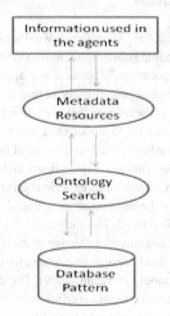

of half the number of observations, and count the number of times each parameter affect the graph built. A Wrestler with the features similar to Scott Steel was selected as the most popular by the majority of societies because the attributes offered by it are adequate for others. In Figure 21 is shown the results of a sample of American Wrestlers.

Figure 21. Individual features of an element and classification of wrestling performance to a sample of 127 wrestlers

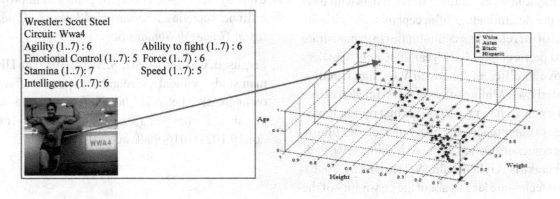

9. CONCLUSION AND FUTURE RESEARCH

Using Cultural Algorithms, we improved the understanding substantially to obtain the change of "best paradigm", because we appropriately separated the agent clusters basing to us on an approach to the relation that keep their attributes, this allowed us to understand the concept of "Crowdfunding" based on the time of époques of interaction. This technique allows including the possibility of generating experimental knowledge created by the community of agents for support an Indie Pop Band. The analysis of the level and degree of cognitive knowledge of each cluster is an aspect that is desired to evaluate for the future work (Ustaoglu & Yesim, 2009). The characteristics that make them contributor of cluster and it as well allows him to keep his own identity, demonstrates that the small variations go beyond associate to tastes and similar characteristics developed through the time (Ochoa et al., 2008). A new modeling of Artificial Societies can take care to analyze retail these complexities that each social networking keeps, without forgetting that still they need to us methods to understand each society and its representation.

Using Social Data Mining in Media Richness we improve the understanding of change for the best paradigm substantially, because we classify the communities of agents appropriately based on their related attributes approach, this allows determine all features associated with an "American Wrestler Idol" which exists with base on the determination of acceptance function by part of the remaining communities to demonstrate best performance. Each year 7000 new wrestlers arrive to different American Wrestling Circuits. Social Data Mining offers a powerful alternative for optimization problems, for that reason it provides a comprehensible panoramic of the cultural phenomenon (Ochoa, Tcherassi, Shingareva, Padméterakiris, Gyllenhaale, & Hernández, 2006). This technique lead us about the possibility of the experimental knowledge generation, created by the community of agents for a given application domain. How much the degree of this knowledge is cognitive for the community of agents is a topic for future work. The answer can be similar to the involved in the hard work of communication between two different societies and their respective perspectives. A new Artificial Intelligence that can be in charge of these systems, continues being distant into the horizon, in the same way that we still lack of methods to understand the original and peculiar things of each society.

The future research is about applied this model in singers of Mexican Society and determine the possible "New Musical Idols or Bands" where only 27% record their second album, this for different genders according theirs profiles, the principal problem is the confidentially of this information and its use for this propose.

REFERENCES

Baeza-Yates, R., & Ribeiro-Neto, B. (1999). *Modern information retrieval*. Workingham, UK: Addison-Wesley.

Braschler, M., Di Nunzio, G., Ferro, N., Gonzalo, J., Peters, C., & Sanderson, M. (2005). *CLEF and multilingual information retrieval*. Neuchâtel, Switzerland: Institut interfacultaire d'informatique, University of Neuchatel. Retrieved from http://www.unine.ch/info/clef/

Conway, J. (2004). Theory of games to improve artificial societies. *International Journal of Intelligent Games & Simulation*.

Ferguson, C. J., & Rueda, S. M. (2010). The Hitman study: Violent video game exposure effects on aggressive behavior, hostile feelings, and depression. *European Psychologist*, *15*(2), 99–108. doi:10.1027/1016-9040/a000010

Grossman, D. A. (2004). *Information retrieval: algorithms and heuristics* (2nd ed.). Dordrecht, The Netherlands: Springer-Verlag.

Huang, Z., Chung, W., Ong, T.-H., & Chen, H. (2002). A graph-based recommender system for digital library. In *Proceedings of the 2nd ACM/IEEE-CS Joint Conference on Digital Libraries* (pp. 65-73).

Johnston, P. (2002). *Schema imports the Dublin Core elements from the DCMI schema for unqualified Dublin Core*. Retrieved from http://www.openarchives.org/OAI/2.0/oai_dc.xsd

Laustanou, K. (2007). *MySpace Music*. Retrieved from http://www.myspace.com/music

Lewis, D. D. (1991). Evaluating text categorization. In *Proceedings of the Speech and Natural Language Workshop on Defense Advanced Research Projects Agency* (pp. 312-318).

LPMP-CNPq. (2005). *Padronização XML: Curriculum Vitae*. Retrieved from http://lmpl.cnpq.br

Macy, M. W., & Willer, R. (2002). From FACTORS TO ACTORS: Computational SOCIOLOGY AND AGENT-BASED MODELING. *Annual Review of Sociology, 28*, 143–166. doi:10.1146/annurev.soc.28.110601.141117

Ochoa, A. (2007). Baharastar – Simulador de Algoritmos Culturales para la Minería de Datos Social. In *Proceedings of COMCEV*.

Ochoa, A. (2008). *Data mining in medical and biological research* (Giannopoullou, E. G., Ed.). Vienna, Austria: I-Tech.

Ochoa, A. (2009). *Six degrees of separation in a graph to a social networking*. Zürich, Switzerland: ASNA.

Ochoa, A., González, S., Esquivel, C., Matozzi, G., & Maffucci, A. (2009). Musical recommendation on thematic Web radio. *Journal of Computers, 4*(8). doi:10.4304/jcp.4.8.742-746

Ochoa, A., Tcherassi, A., Shingareva, I., Padméterakiris, A., Gyllenhaale, J., & Hernández, J. A. (2006). Italianitá: Discovering a Pygmalion effect on Italian communities using data mining. In *Proceedings of the International Conference on Dublin Core and Metadata Application*.

Reynolds, R. G. (1998). An introduction to cultural algorithms. *Cultural Algorithms Repository*. Retrieved from http://www.cs.wayne.edu/~jcc/car.html

Salton, G., & Buckley, C. (1998). Term-weighting approaches in automatic text retrieval. *Information Processing and Management: an International Journal, 24*(5), 513–523. doi:10.1016/0306-4573(88)90021-0

Salton, G., & Macgill, M. J. (1983). *Introduction to modern information retrieval*. New York, NY: McGraw-Hill.

Smeaton, A. F., & Callahan, J. (2003). Personalization and recommender systems in digital libraries. *International Journal on Digital Libraries, 57*(4), 299–308.

Sompel, H. V., & De Lagoze, C. (2000). The Santa Fe convention of the open archives initiative. *D-Lib Magazine, 6*(2).

Sompel, H. V., & De Lagoze, C. (Eds.). (2005). *The open archives initiative protocol for metadata harvesting*. Retrieved from http://www.openarchives.org/OAI/2.0/openarchivesprotocol.htm

Ustaoglu, Y. (2009). *Simulating the behavior of a Kurdish minority in Turkish Society*. Zürich, Switzerland: ASNA.

ADDITIONAL READING

Eigenfeldt, A., & Pasquier, P. (2011). A sonic eco-system of self-organising musical agents. In *Proceedings of the International Conference on Applications of Evolutionary Computation - Volume Part II* (pp. 283-292).

Kaliakatsos-Papakostas, M. A., Epitropakis, M. G., & Vrahatis, M. N. (2011). Weighted Markov chain model for musical composer identification. In *Proceedings of the International Conference on Applications of Evolutionary Computation - Volume Part II* (pp. 334-343).

Özbek, M. E., & Acar Savaci, F. (2011). Correntropy function for fundamental frequency determination of musical instrument samples. *Expert Systems with Applications*, *38*(8), 10025–10030. doi:10.1016/j.eswa.2011.02.015

Özçelik, S., & Hardalaç, N. (2011). The statistical measurements and neural network analysis of the effect of musical education to musical hearing and sensing. *Expert Systems with Applications*, *38*(8), 9517–9521. doi:10.1016/j.eswa.2011.01.149

Romagnoli, M., Fontana, F., & Sarkar, R. (2011). Vibrotactile recognition by Western and Indian population groups of traditional musical scales played with the harmonium. In *Proceedings of the 6th International Conference on Haptic and Audio Interaction Design* (pp. 91-100).

Takai, Y., Ohira, M., & Matsumoto, K.-I. (2011). Effects of a synchronized scoring interface on musical quality. In *Proceedings of the 4th International Conference on Online Communities and Social Computing* (pp. 363-372).

Yamamoto, T. (2011). Synchronization and fluctuation of rhythm in musical cooperative performance. In *Proceedings of the 4th International Conference on Online Communities and Social Computing* (pp. 517-526).

KEY TERMS AND DEFINITIONS

Diorama: Intelligent ambient to represent an Artificial Society which generate several social interactions on the time.

Indie Pop Band: Musical group related with Indie Pop genre and very popular in Asia and Europe.

Mass Media: Group of media activities related with the use of Radio, Television and Web to access to people in different locations.

Multiagent Systems: Artificial intelligence technique which use a combined environment to simulate a variety of optimization problems.

Musical Recommendation: Intelligent process which specifies a playlist to listen according several features and an evaluated analysis of each song is very commonly on Thematic Web Radio or Karaoke systems.

Section 4
Technological Application using Intelligent Optimization

Chapter 14
Optimization of a Hybrid Methodology (CRISP–DM)

José Nava
Centro de Investigación en Ciencias Aplicadas para la Industria, México

Paula Hernández
ITCM, México

ABSTRACT

Data mining is a complex process that involves the interaction of the application of human knowledge and skills and technology. This must be supported by clearly defined processes and procedures. This Chapter describes CRISP-DM (Cross-Industry Standard Process for Data Mining), a fully documented, freely available, robust, and non proprietary data mining model. The chapter analyzes the contents of the official Version 1.0 Document, and it is a guide through all the implementation process. The main purpose of data mining is the extraction of hidden and useful knowledge from large volumes of raw data. Data mining brings together different disciplines like software engineering, computer science, business intelligence, human-computer interaction, and analysis techniques. Phases of these disciplines must be combined for data mining project outcomes. CRISP-DM methodology defines its processes hierarchically at four levels of abstraction allowing a project to be structured modularly, being more maintainable, scalable and the most important, to reduce complexity. CRISP-DM describes the life cycle of a data mining project consisting of six phases: business understanding, data understanding, data preparation, modeling, evaluation, and deployment.

DOI: 10.4018/978-1-4666-0297-7.ch014

1. BRIEF HISTORY

Developed by industry experts and leaders, with input from more than 200 data mining users, data mining tools and service providers from all over the world. In late 1996, CRISP-DM was conceived by three companies, experts in the young and immature data mining market. DaimlerChrysler (then Daimler-Benz) ahead of most industrial and commercial organizations applying data mining techniques in its business. SPSS (then ISL), providing data mining services since 1990 and launched the first commercial data mining workbench – Clementine – in 1994. NCR, with teams of data mining consultants and specialists.

In the 1990's, data mining market was showing an exponential demand in several countries, which was both exciting and terrifying. All data mining users were developing their approaches on demand, and as they went along. Every data mining developer was learning by trial and error. Was that the best approach? Were they doing right? And the most important, how could they demonstrate to the world's prospective customers that data mining was mature enough to be adopted as a key part of their business processes? Then they thought that a standard process model, non-proprietary and freely available, would address those issues for them and for all practitioners.

A year later, they formed a consortium, and come out with the acronym (Cross-Industry Standard Process for Data Mining). They obtained funding from the European Commission and begun to work in their initial ideas. As this methodology was intended to be industry, tool, and application neutral, they knew they had to get input from as wide range as possible of data mining practitioners and others (such data warehouse vendors, and consultancies) with vested interest in this area.

They launched the CRISP-DM Special Interest Group (The SIG, as it became known), by broadcasting an invitation to interested parties to join in Amsterdam for a workshop to share ideas, invite people to present their, and openly discuss how to work together in CRISP-DM project.

This event significantly surpassed expectations: Twice as many people turned up as they had initially expected, there was an overwhelming consensus that the data mining industry needed urgent standardization, and there was a tremendous common ground in how people viewed the general process of data mining.

Once the workshop was ended, they felt confident they could deliver, along with the SIG's input and work, a standard process model to service the data mining community.

They worked hard the next two and a half years developing CRISP-DM, they ran trials in large-scale data mining projects in world-class companies like Mercedes-Benz, and OHRA.

They worked on the integration of CRISP-DM commercial data mining tools. The SIG was invaluable, with a growing to over 200 members and holding workshops in London, New York and Brussels.

As of mid-1999, they produced a draft of the process model. Actual version, CRISP-DM 1.0 is not radically different. In later years, CRISP-DM was strongly tested by DaimlerChrysler in a wide range of applications, having a big success. SPSS' and NCR's Professional Services groups have adopted CRISP-DM and used it successfully on numerous customer engagements covering many industries and business problems. Since this version, interested institutions have been releasing Data Access, Model Generation and Model Representation Standards for data mining, which we will present later in this chapter.

2. CRISP-DM METHODOLOGY

2.1. Description of the Methodology

The most important and core in CRISP-DM methodology is that defines its processes hierarchically, consisting of a set of tasks at four levels

Figure 1. Four level breakdown of the CRISP-DM methodology

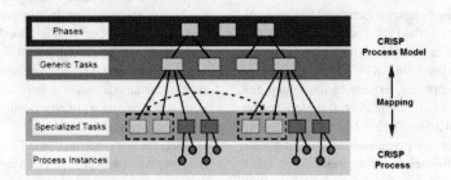

of abstraction, from general to specific, explained (Figure1):

- Using levels of abstraction, at the top level we have the phases, the data mining process is organized into a number of phases, where each phase consists of several second-level generic tasks.
- At the second level we have the generic tasks, which must be general enough to cover all possible data mining situations and must be as complete and stable as possible. Complete means covering all possible applications and the whole process of data mining. Stable means this model and process must be valid for any kind of problems, and for old and new modeling techniques.
- The third level is the specialized task level, which describe how actions in the generic tasks should be carried out in specific situations. Ideally, the phases and tasks must be described as discrete steps and must be performed in a specific order. In practice, many of the tasks can be performed in a different order and it will often be necessary to repeatedly backtrack to previous tasks and repeat certain actions.

- The fourth level is the process instance, a record of the actions, decisions and results of an actual data mining engagement. A process instance is organized according to the tasks defined at the higher levels, but represents what actually happened in a particular engagement, rather than what happens in general.

2.2. Mapping Generic Models to Specialized Models

Data Mining Context

The data mining context drives mapping between the generic and the specialized level in CRISP-DM. There are four different dimensions of data mining contexts:

- The application domain is the specific area in which the data mining project takes place.
- The data mining problem type describes the specific class(es) of objective(s) that the data mining project deals with.
- The technical aspect covers specific issues in data mining that describe different (tech-

nical) challenges that usually occur during data mining.

- The tool and the technique dimension specifies which data mining tool(s) and/or techniques are applied during the data mining project.

Table 1 summarizes these dimensions of data mining contexts and shows specific examples for each dimension.

A specific data mining context is a concrete value for one or more of these dimensions. For example, a data mining project dealing with a classification problem in churn prediction constitutes one specific context. The more values for different context dimensions are fixed, the more concrete is the data mining context (Chapman et al., 2000).

Mappings Whit Contexts

One of the most important concepts on data mining is that exists two different types of mapping between generic and specialized level in CRISP-DM, which are:

Mapping for the present: Which means if we only apply the generic process model to perform a single data mining project and attempt to map generic tasks and their descriptions to the specific project as required, we talk about a single mapping for (probably) only one usage.

Mapping for the future: If we systematically specialize the generic process model according to a pre-defined context (or similarly systematically analyze and consolidate experiences of a single project towards a specialized process model for future usage in comparable contexts), we talk about explicitly writing up a specialized process model in terms of CRISP-DM.

Which type of mapping is more appropriate for a single purpose depends on the specific data mining context and the special needs of the organization.

How to Map

The strategy for mapping the generic process model to the specialized level is the same for both types of mappings:

- Analyze your specific context.
- Remove any details not applicable to your context.
- Add any details specific to your context.
- Specialize (or instantiate) generic contents according to concrete characteristics of your context.
- Possibly rename generic contents to provide more explicit meanings in your context for the sake of clarity.

Table 1. Dimensions of data mining contexts and examples

| Dimension | Data Mining Context | | | |
	Application Domain	Data Mining Problem Type	Technical Aspect	Tool and Technique
Examples	Response Modeling	Description and Summarization	Missing Values	Clementine
	Churn Prediction	Segmentation	Outliers	Mine Set
		Concept Description		Decision tree
		Classification		
		Prediction		
		Dependency Analysis		

Figure 2. Phases of the CRISP-DM reference model

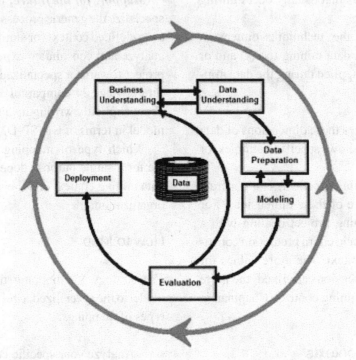

3. THE CRISP-DM REFERENCE MODEL

3.1. The Life Cycle of Data Mining

According to CRISP-DM, the life cycle of a data mining project contains the phases of the project and the respective tasks and relationships between these tasks. At this description level, it is not possible to identify all relationships.

Essentially, relationships could exist between any data mining tasks depending on the goals, the background and interest of the user and most importantly on the data.

A data mining project involves more than modeling. The modeling phase is just one phase in the implementation process of a data mining project. Steps of critical importance proceed and follow model building and have a significant effect on the success of the project (Chorianopoulos & Tsiptsis, 2009).

The CRISP-DM process model contributes to data mining as a process, which is reflected in its origins (McCue, 2007).

The life cycle of a data mining project consists of six phases. Figure 2 shows the phases of a data mining process. The sequence of the phases is not rigid. Moving back and forth between different phases is always required. It depends on the outcome of each phase which phase or which particular task of a phase, has to be performed next. The arrows indicate the most important and frequent dependencies between phases.

The outer circle in Figure 2 symbolizes the cyclical nature of data mining itself. Data mining is not over once a solution is deployed. The lessons learned during the process and from the deployed solution can trigger new, often more focused business questions. Subsequent data mining processes will benefit from the experiences of previous ones.

3.2. The Data Mining Phases

Business Understanding

This initial phase focuses on understanding the project objectives and requirements from a business perspective, then converting this knowledge into a data mining problem definition and a preliminary plan designed to achieve the objectives. This phase includes too assessing the current situation, establishing data mining goals, and developing a project plan (Delen & Olson, 2008).

Data Understanding

The data understanding phase starts with an initial data collection and proceeds with activities in order to get familiar with the data, to identify data quality problems, to discover first insights into the data or to detect interesting subsets to form hypotheses for hidden information.

Data Preparation

The data preparation phase covers all activities to construct the final dataset (data that will be fed into the modeling tool(s)) from the initial raw data. Data preparation tasks are likely to be performed multiple times and not in any prescribed order. Tasks include table, record and attribute selection as well as transformation and cleaning of data for modeling tools.

Modeling

In this phase, various modeling techniques are selected and applied and their parameters are calibrated to optimal values. Typically, there are several techniques for the same data mining problem type. Some techniques have specific requirements on the form of data. Therefore, stepping back to the data preparation phase is often necessary.

Evaluation

Model results should be evaluated in the context of business objectives established in the first phase (Delen & Olson, 2008). At this stage in the project you have built a model (or models) that appears to have high quality from a data analysis perspective. Before proceeding to final deployment of the model, it is important to more thoroughly evaluate the model and review the steps executed to construct the model to be certain it properly achieves the business objectives. A key objective is to determine if there is some important business issue that has not been sufficiently considered. At the end of this phase, a decision on the use of the data mining results should be reached.

Deployment

Creation of the model is generally not the end of the project. Even if the purpose of the model is to increase knowledge of the data, the knowledge gained will need to be organized and presented in a way that the customer can use it. It often involves applying "live" models within an organization's decision making processes, for example in real-time personalization of Web pages or repeated scoring of marketing databases. However, depending on the requirements, the deployment phase can be as simple as generating a report or as complex as implementing a repeatable data mining process across the enterprise. In many cases it is the customer, not the data analyst, who carries out the deployment steps. However, even if the analyst will not carry out the deployment effort it is important for the customer to understand up front what actions need to be carried out in order to actually make use of the created models.

Each phase generates important reports for the project; this part contains detailed descriptions of the purpose, contents and suggested sections of the most important reports.

Figure 3 presents an outline of phases accompanied by generic tasks (bold) and outputs

Figure 3. Generic tasks (bold) and outputs (italic) of the CRISP-DM reference model

Business Understanding	Data Understanding	Data Preparation	Modeling	Evaluation	Deployment
Determine Business Objectives *Background* *Business Objectives* *Business Success Criteria*	**Collect Initial Data** *Initial Data Collection Report*	**Data Set** *Data Set Description*	**Select Modeling Technique** *Modeling Technique* *Modeling Assumptions*	**Evaluate Results** *Assessment of Data Mining Results w.r.t. Business Success Criteria* *Approved Models*	**Plan Deployment** *Deployment Plan*
Assess Situation *Inventory of Resources* *Requirements, Assumptions, and Constraints* *Risks and Contingencies* *Terminology* *Costs and Benefits*	**Describe Data** *Data Description Report* **Explore Data** *Data Exploration Report* **Verify Data Quality** *Data Quality Report*	**Select Data** *Rationale for Inclusion/ Exclusion* **Clean Data** *Data Cleaning Report* **Construct Data** *Derived Attributes* *Generated Records*	**Generate Test Design** *Test Design* **Build Model** *Parameter Settings* *Models* *Model Description*	**Review Process** *Review of Process* **Determine Next Steps** *List of Possible Actions* *Decision*	**Plan Monitoring and Maintenance** *Monitoring and Maintenance Plan* **Produce Final Report** *Final Report* *Final Presentation*
Determine Data Mining Goals *Data Mining Goals* *Data Mining Success Criteria* **Produce Project Plan** *Project Plan* *Initial Assessment of Tools and Techniques*		**Integrate Data** *Merged Data* **Format Data** *Reformatted Data*	**Assess Model** *Model Assessment* *Revised Parameter Settings*		**Review Project** *Experience Documentation*

(italic). In the following sections, we describe each generic task and its outputs in more detail. We focus our attention on task overviews and summaries of outputs (reports that are meant to communicate the results of a phase to people not involved in this phase).

The purpose of the outputs is mostly to document results while performing the project.

3.2.1. Business Understanding

Determine Business Objectives

Task:
Determine business objectives

The first objective of the data analyst is to thoroughly understand, from a business perspective, what the client really wants to accomplish (Figure 4). Often the client has many competing objectives and constraints that must be properly balanced. The analyst's goal is to uncover important factors, at the beginning, that can influence the outcome of the project. A possible consequence of neglecting this step is to expend a great deal of effort producing the right answers to the wrong questions.

Outputs:
Background

Record the information that is known about the organization's business situation at the beginning of the project.

Business objectives

Describe the customer's primary objective, from a business perspective. In addition to the primary business objective, there are typically other related business questions that the customer would like to address. For example, the primary business goal might be to keep current customers by predicting when they are prone to move to a competitor. Examples of related business questions are "How does the primary channel (e.g., ATM, visit branch, internet) a bank customer uses affect whether they stay or go?" or "Will lower ATM fees significantly reduce the number of high-value customers who leave?"

Figure 4. Business understanding

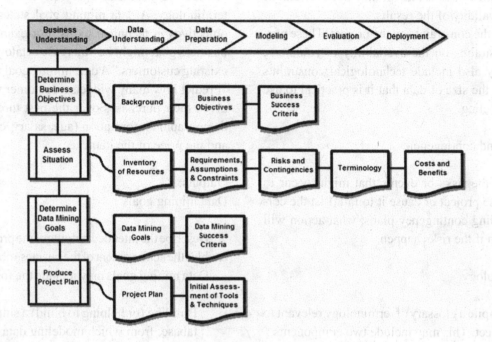

Business success criteria

Describe the criteria for a successful or useful outcome to the project from the business point of view. This might be quite specific and able to be measured objectively, such as reduction of customer churn to a certain level or general and subjective such as "give useful insights into the relationships". In the latter case it should be indicated who makes the subjective judgment.

Assess Situation

Task:
Assess situation

This task involves more detailed fact-finding about all of the resources, constraints, assumptions and other factors that should be considered in determining the data analysis goal and project plan. In the previous task, your objective is to quickly get to the crux of the situation. Here, you want to flesh out the details.

Outputs:
Inventory of resources

List the resources available to the project, including: personnel (business experts, data experts, technical support, data mining personnel), data (fixed extracts, access to live warehoused or operational data), computing resources (hardware platforms) and software (data mining tools, other relevant software).

Requirements, assumptions and constraints

List all requirements of the project including schedule of completion, comprehensibility and quality of results and security as well as legal issues. As part of this output, make sure that you are allowed to use the data.

List the assumptions made by the project. These may be assumptions about the data that can be checked during data mining, but may also include non-checkable assumptions about the business upon which the project rests. It is particularly important to list the latter if they form conditions on the validity of the results.

List the constraints on the project. These may be constraints on the availability of resources, but may also include technological constraints such as the size of data that it is practical to use for modeling.

Risks and contingencies

List the risks or events that might occur to delay the project or cause it to fail. List the corresponding contingency plans; what action will be taken if the risks happen.

Terminology

Compile a glossary of terminology relevant to the project. This may include two components:

1. A glossary of relevant business terminology, which forms part of the business understanding available to the project. Constructing this glossary is a useful "knowledge elicitation" and education exercise.
2. A glossary of data mining terminology, illustrated with examples relevant to the business problem in question.
    Costs and benefits

Construct a cost-benefit analysis for the project, which compares the costs of the project with the potential benefit to the business if it is successful. The comparison should be as specific as possible, for example using monetary measures in a commercial situation.

Determine Data Mining Goals

Task:
Determine data mining goals

A business goal states objectives in business terminology. A data mining goal states project objectives in technical terms. For example, the business goal might be "Increase catalog sales to existing customers." A data mining goal might be "Predict how many widgets a customer will buy, given their purchases over the past three years, demographic information (age, salary, city, etc.) and the price of the item."

Outputs:
Data mining goals

Describe the intended outputs of the project that enables the achievement of the business objectives.
Data mining goals may include the following:

*   Building (or helping to build) a suitable database, from which modeling data sets can be extracted easily.
*   Developing and deploying a model, which generates significant business value.
*   Building a knowledge base of modeling "learnings", which can be leveraged later to do a better job with data mining (easier, faster, cheaper).
    Data mining success criteria

Define the criteria for a successful outcome to the project in technical terms, for example a certain level of predictive accuracy or a propensity to purchase profile with a given degree of "lift". As with business success criteria, it may be necessary to describe these in subjective terms, in which case the person or persons making the subjective judgment should be identified.

Produce Project Plan

Task:
Produce project plan

Describe the intended plan for achieving the data mining goals and thereby achieving the business goals. The plan should specify the anticipated set of steps to be performed during the rest of the project including an initial selection of tools and techniques.

Outputs:
Project plan

List the stages to be executed in the project, together with duration, resources required, inputs, outputs and dependencies. Where possible make explicit the large-scale iterations in the data mining process, for example repetitions of the modeling and evaluation phases.

As part of the project plan, it is also important to analyze dependencies between time schedule and risks. Mark results of these analyses explicitly in the project plan, ideally with actions and recommendations if the risks appear.

Note: the project plan contains detailed plans for each phase. For example, decide at this point which evaluation strategy will be used in the evaluation phase.

The project plan is a dynamic document in the sense that at the end of each phase a review of progress and achievements is necessary and an update of the project plan accordingly is recommended. Specific review points for these reviews are part of the project plan, too.

Initial assessment of tools and techniques

At the end of the first phase, the project also performs an initial assessment of tools and techniques. Here, you select a data mining tool that supports various methods for different stages of the process, for example. It is important to assess tools and techniques early in the process since the selection of tools and techniques possibly influences the entire project.

The activities of this output is to create a list of selection criteria for tools and techniques (or use an existing if available), choose potential tools and techniques, evaluate them, and review according to the evaluation criteria (Figure 5).

3.2.2. Data Understanding

Collect Initial Data

Task:
Collect initial data

Acquire within the project the data (or access to the data) listed in the project resources. This initial collection includes data loading if necessary for data understanding. For example, if you apply a specific tool for data understanding, it makes perfect sense to load your data into this tool. This effort possibly leads to initial data preparation steps.

Note: if you acquire multiple data sources, integration is an additional issue, either here or in the later data preparation phase.

Output:
Initial data collection report

List the dataset (or datasets) acquired, together with their locations within the project, the methods used to acquire them and any problems encountered. Record problems encountered and any solutions achieved to aid with future replication of this project or with the execution of similar future projects.

This phase involves considering the data requirements for properly addressing the defined goal and an investigation of the availability of the required data.

Describe Data

Task:
Describe data

Figure 5. Data understanding

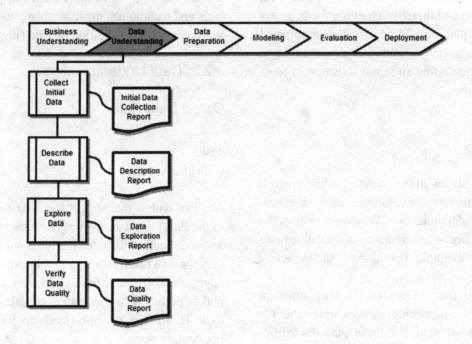

Examine the "gross" or "surface" properties of the acquired data and report on the results.

Output:
Data description report

Describe the data which has been acquired, including: the format of the data, the quantity of data, for example number of records and fields in each table, the identities of the fields and any other surface features of the data which have been discovered: Does the data acquired satisfy the relevant requirements?

Explore Data

Task:
Explore data

This task tackles the data mining questions, which can be addressed using querying, visualization and reporting. These include: distribution of key attributes, for example the target attribute of a prediction task; relations between pairs or small numbers of attributes; results of simple aggregations; properties of significant sub-populations; simple statistical analyses. These analyses may address directly the data mining goals; they may also contribute to or refine the data description and quality reports and feed into the transformation and other data preparation needed for further analysis.

Output:
Data exploration report

Describe results of this task including first findings or initial hypothesis and their impact on the remainder of the project. If appropriate, include graphs and plots, which indicate data characteristics or lead to interesting data subsets for further examination.

Verify Data Quality

Task:
Verify data quality

Figure 6. Data preparation

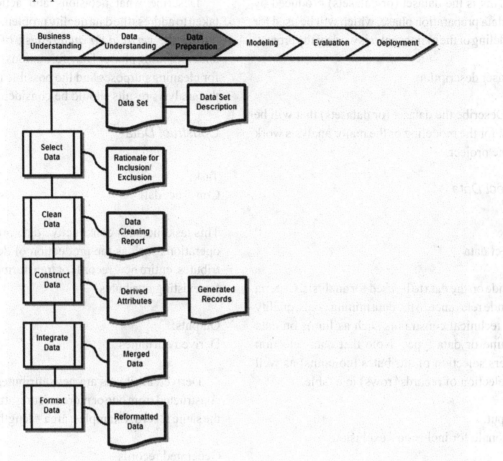

Examine the quality of the data, addressing questions such as: is the data complete (does it cover all the cases required)? Is it correct or does it contain errors and if there are errors how common are they? Are there missing values in the data? If so how are they represented, where do they occur and how common are they?

Output:
Data quality report

The data quality report lists the results of the data quality verification; if quality problems exist, list possible solutions.

Solutions to data quality problems generally depend heavily on both data and business knowledge.

3.2.3. Data Preparation

In data preparation phase (Figure 6), the data to be used should be identified, selected and prepared to inclusion in the data mining model. This phase involves the acquisition, integration, and formatting of the data according to the need of the project (Chorianopoulos & Tsiptsis, 2009).

Outputs:
Dataset

This is the dataset (or datasets) produced by the data preparation phase, which will be used for modeling or the major analysis work of the project.

Dataset description

Describe the dataset (or datasets) that will be used for the modeling or the major analysis work of the project.

Select Data

Task:
Select data

Decide on the data to be used for analysis. Criteria include relevance to the data mining goals, quality and technical constraints such as limits on data volume or data types. Note that data selection covers selection of attributes (columns) as well as selection of records (rows) in a table.

Output:
Rationale for inclusion / exclusion

List the data to be included/excluded and the reasons for these decisions.

Clean Data

Task:
Clean data

Raise the data quality to the level required by the selected analysis techniques. This may involve selection of clean subsets of the data, the insertion of suitable defaults or more ambitious techniques such as the estimation of missing data by modeling.

Output:
Data cleaning report

Describe what decisions and actions were taken to address the data quality problems reported during the *verify data quality* task of the *data understanding* phase. Transformations of the data for cleaning purposes and the possible impact on the analysis results should be considered.

Construct Data

Task:
Construct data

This task includes constructive data preparation operations such as the production of derived attributes, entire new records or transformed values for existing attributes.

Outputs:
Derived attributes

Derived attributes are new attributes that are constructed from one or more existing attributes in the same record. Examples: area = length * width.

Generated records

Describe the creation of completely new records. Example: create records for customers who made no purchase during the past year.

There was no reason to have such records in the raw data, but for modeling purposes it might make sense to explicitly represent the fact that certain customers made zero purchases.

One of the activities of this output is check for available techniques if needed (for example mechanisms to construct prototypes for each segment of segmented data).

Integrate Data

Task:
Integrate data

These are methods whereby information is combined from multiple tables or records to create new records or values.

Output:
Merged data

Merging tables refers to joining together two or more tables that have different information about the same objects. Example: a retail chain has one table with information about each store's general characteristics (e.g., floor space, type of mall), another table with summarized sales data (e.g., profit, percent change in sales from previous year) and another with information about the demographics of the surrounding area. Each of these tables contains one record for each store. These tables can be merged together into a new table with one record for each store, combining fields from the source tables.

Merged data also covers aggregations. Aggregation refers to operations where new values are computed by summarizing together information from multiple records and/or tables. For example, converting a table of customer purchases where there is one record for each purchase into a new table where there is one record for each customer, with fields such as number of purchases, average purchase amount, percent of orders charged to credit card, percent of items under promotion, etc.

Format Data

Task:
Format data

Formatting transformations refer to primarily syntactic modifications made to the data that do not change its meaning, but might be required by the modeling tool.

Output:
Reformatted data

Some tools have requirements on the order of the attributes, such as the first field being a unique identifier for each record or the last field being the outcome field the model is to predict.

It might be important to change the order of the records in the dataset. Perhaps the modeling tool requires that the records be sorted according to the value of the outcome attribute. A common situation is that the records of the dataset are initially ordered in some way but the modeling algorithm needs them to be in a fairly random order. For example, when using neural networks it is generally best for the records to be presented in a random order although some tools handle this automatically without explicit user intervention. Additionally, there are purely syntactic changes made to satisfy the requirements of the specific modeling tool. Examples: removing commas from within text fields in comma-delimited data files, trimming all values to a maximum of 32 characters.

3.2.4. Modeling

Select Modeling Technique

Task:
Select modeling technique

As the first step in modeling (Figure 7), select the actual modeling technique that is to be used. Whereas you possibly already selected a tool in business understanding, this task refers to the specific modeling technique, e.g., decision tree building with C4.5 or neural network generation with back propagation. If multiple techniques are applied, perform this task for each technique separately.

This phase is a mixture of art and science, this part can derive the following activities:

- *Choose modeling algorithms:* How you prepare your data will depend to some degree on what modeling algorithm you

Figure 7. Modeling

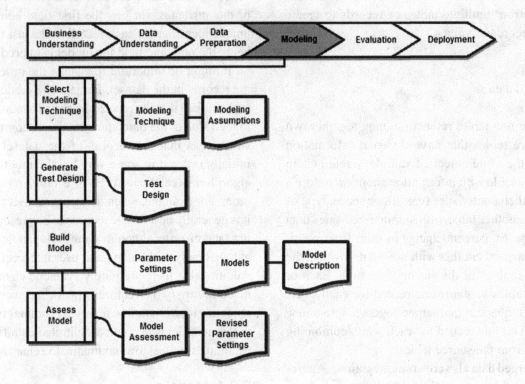

choose. If you choose a parametrical statistical algorithm (such as multiple linear regression), you may have to transform some variables to account for significant nonlinearity.

- *Choose modeling architecture* (single analysis, ensemble, etc): A single, straightforward analysis will include submitting your data to the algorithm and evaluate the models created.
- *Specify modeling assumptions:* Every modeling algorithm makes assumptions. Your challenge is to choose an algorithm whose assumptions fit your data and your modeling goal (Elder et al., 2009).

Outputs:
Modeling technique

Document the actual modeling technique that is to be used.

Modeling assumptions

Many modeling techniques make specific assumptions on the data, e.g., all attributes have uniform distributions, no missing values allowed, class attribute must be symbolic etc. Record any such assumptions made.

Generate Test Design

Task:
Generate test design

Before we actually build a model, we need to generate a procedure or mechanism to test the model's quality and validity. For example, in supervised data mining tasks such as classification, it is common to use error rates as quality measures for data mining models. Therefore, we typically separate the dataset into train and test set, build the model on the train set and estimate its quality on the separate test set.

Output:
Test design

Describe the intended plan for training, testing and evaluating the models. A primary component of the plan is to decide how to divide the available dataset into training data, test data and validation datasets.

Build Model

Task:
Build model

Run the modeling tool on the prepared dataset to create one or more models.

Outputs:
Parameter settings

With any modeling tool, there are often a large number of parameters that can be adjusted. List the parameters and their chosen value, along with the rationale for the choice of parameter settings.

Models

These are the actual models produced by the modeling tool, not a report. This output comes out running the modeling tool on the prepared data set to create one or more models.

Model description

Describe the resultant model. Report on the interpretation of the models and document any difficulties encountered with their meanings.

Assess Model

Task:
Assess model

The data mining engineer interprets the models according to his domain knowledge, the data mining success criteria and the desired test design. This task interferes with the subsequent evaluation phase. Whereas the data mining engineer judges the success of the application of modeling and discovery techniques more technically, he contacts business analysts and domain experts later in order to discuss the data mining results in the business context. Moreover, this task only considers models whereas the evaluation phase also takes into account all other results that were produced in the course of the project.

The data mining engineer tries to rank the models. He assesses the models according to the evaluation criteria. As far as possible he also takes into account business objectives and business success criteria.

Outputs:
Model assessment

Summarize results of this task, list qualities of generated models (e.g., in terms of accuracy) and rank their quality in relation to each other.

Revised parameter settings

According to the model assessment, revise parameter settings and tune them for the next run in the Build Model task. Iterate model building and assessment until you strongly believe that you found the best model(s). Document all, such revisions and assessments.

Table 2 presents some of the widely used data mining modeling techniques together with an indicative listing of the marketing applications they can support (Chorianopoulos & Tsiptsis, 2009).

Table 2. Data mining modeling techniques and their applications

Category of modeling techniques	Modeling Techniques	Applications
Classification (propensity) models	Neural networks, decision trees, logistic regre-sion, etc.	• Voluntary churn predic-tion • Cross/up/deep selling
Clustering models	K-means, two step, Kohonen network/self-organizing map, etc.	• Segmentation
Association and sequence models	Apriori Generalized Rule Induction, Sequence	• Marquet basquet analysis • Web path analysis

3.2.5. Evaluation

The generated models are here formally evaluated (Figure 8) not only in terms of technical measures but also, more importantly, in the context of the business success criteria set out in the business understanding phase.

The project team should decide whether the result of a given model properly address the initial business objectives. If so, this model is approved and prepared for deployment (Chorianopoulos & Tsiptsis, 2009).

Evaluate Results

Task:
Evaluate results

Previous evaluation steps dealt with factors such as the accuracy and generality of the model. This step assesses the degree to which the model meets the business objectives and seeks to determine if there is some business reason why this model is deficient. Another option of evaluation is to test the model(s) on test applications in the real application if time and budget constraints permit.

Moreover, evaluation also assesses other data mining results generated. Data mining results cover models which are necessarily related to the original business objectives and all other findings which are not necessarily related to the original business objectives but might also unveil additional challenges, information or hints for future directions.

Outputs:
Assessment of data mining results with respect to business success criteria

Summarize assessment results in terms of business success criteria including a final statement whether the project already meets the initial business objectives.

Approved models

After model assessment with respect to business success criteria, the generated models that meet the selected criteria become approved models.

Review Process

Figure 8. Evaluation

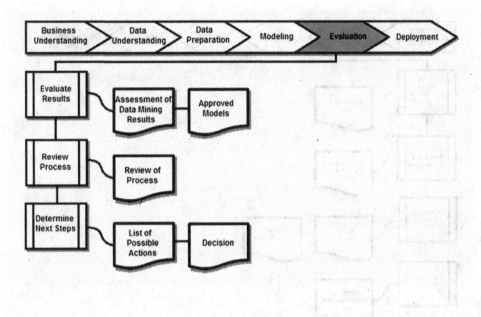

Task:
Review process

At this point the resultant model hopefully appears to be satisfactory and to satisfy business needs. It is now appropriate to do a more thorough review of the data mining engagement in order to determine if there is any important factor or task that has somehow been overlooked. This review also covers quality assurance issues, e.g., did we correctly build the model? Did we only use attributes that we are allowed to use and that are available for future analyses?

Output:
Review of process

Summarize the process review and highlight activities that have been missed and/or should be repeated.

Determine Next Steps

Task:
Determine next steps

According to the assessment results and the process review, the project decides how to proceed at this stage. The project needs to decide whether to finish this project and move on to deployment if appropriate or whether to initiate further iterations or set up new data mining projects. This task includes analyses of remaining resources and budget that influences the decisions.

Outputs:
List of possible actions

List the potential further actions along with the reasons for and against each option.

Decision

Describe the decision as to how to proceed along with the rationale.

In the real world, the models are never as accurate as in the simple exercises presented in books, there are always errors and misclassified records. A comparison of the predicted to the actual values is always the first step in evaluation phase.

Figure 9. Deployment

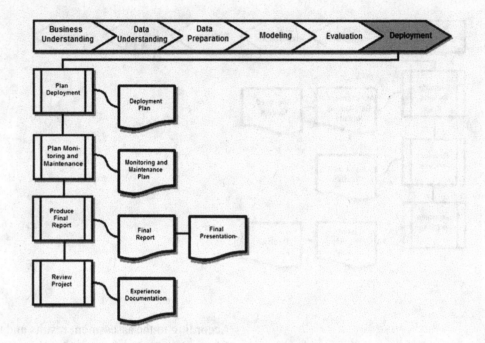

3.2.6. Deployment

Plan Deployment

Task:
Plan deployment

In order to deploy the data mining result(s) into the business (Figure 9), this task takes the evaluation results and concludes a strategy for deployment.

If a general procedure has been identified to create the relevant model(s), this procedure is documented here for later deployment.

Output:
Deployment plan

Summarize deployment strategy including necessary steps and how to perform them.

Plan Monitoring and Maintenance

Task:
Plan monitoring and maintenance

Monitoring and maintenance are important issues if the data mining result becomes part of the day-to-day business and its environment. A careful preparation of a maintenance strategy helps to avoid unnecessarily long periods of incorrect usage of data mining results. In order to monitor the deployment of the data mining result(s), the project needs a detailed plan on the monitoring process. This plan takes into account the specific type of deployment.

Output:
Monitoring and maintenance plan

Summarize monitoring and maintenance strategy including necessary steps and how to perform them.

Produce Final Report

Task:
Produce final report

At the end of the project, the project leader and his team write up a final report. Depending on the deployment plan, this report may be only a summary of the project and its experiences (if they have not already been documented as an ongoing activity) or it may be a final and comprehensive presentation of the data mining result(s).

Outputs:
Final report

This is the final written report of the data mining engagement. It includes all of the previous deliverables and summarizes and organizes the results.

Final presentation

There will also often be a meeting at the conclusion of the project where the results are verbally presented to the customer.

Review Project

Task:
Review project

Assess what went right and what went wrong, what was done well and what needs to be improved.

Output:
Experience documentation

Summarize important experiences made during the project. For example, pitfalls, misleading approaches or hints for selecting the best suited data mining techniques in similar situations could be part of this documentation. In ideal projects, experience documentation covers also any reports that have been written by individual project members during the project phases and their tasks.

4. DATA ACCESS STANDARDS

4.1. XML for Analysis (XMLA)

XMLA is an XML application programming interface (API) based on the Simple Object Access Protocol (SOAP) designed to standardize and facilitate the interaction between clients and data providers across the Web. Traditional data access technologies require the installation of client components that are tightly coupled on the data provider. This coupling creates limitations such as platform – and language – dependence, as well as versioning issues between the client and server components. XMLA is built on the open standards of HTTP, XML and SOAP. Therefore, it is not bound to any specific language or platform.

XML for Analysis is a standard that allows client applications to talk to multi-dimensional or OLAP data sources. The communication of messages back and forth is done using web standards – HTTP, SOAP, and XML. The query language used is MDX, which is the most commonly used multi-dimensional expression language today.

5. MODEL GENERATION STANDARDS

5.1. Java Data Mining (JDM)

Traditionally, data mining algorithms were either home-grown or plugged into applications using raw code, or packaged in an end-user GUI complete with transformations and in some cases scoring code generation. However, the ability to embed data mining end-to-end in applications using commercial data mining products was difficult, if possible at all. Certainly, these APIs were not standards based, making the selection of a particular vendor's solution even more challenging. As such, the ability to leverage data mining functionality easily via a standards-based API greatly reduces the risk of selecting a particular vendor's solution as well as increases accessibility of data mining to application developers. Java™ Data Mining (JDM) addresses this need.

Java technology, specifically as leveraged within the scalable J2EE architecture, facilitates integration with existing applications such as business-to-consumer and business-to-business web sites, customer care centers, campaign management, as well as new applications supporting national security, fraud detection, bioinformatics and life sciences. Java Data Mining allows users to draw on the strengths of multiple data mining vendors for solving business problems, by applying the most appropriate algorithm implementations to a given problem without having to invest resources in learning each vendor's proprietary API. Moreover, vendors and customers can focus on functionality, automation, performance, and price. With JDM's extensible framework for adding new algorithms and functionality, vendors can still differentiate themselves while providing developers with a familiar paradigm.

5.2. SQL Multimedia Application Packages (SQL/MM)

ISO/IEC 13249 SQL/MM is the effort to standardize extensions for multi-media and application-specific packages in SQL. SQL, as defined in ISO99 standard, is extended to manage data like texts, still images, spatial data, or to perform data mining. The standard is grouped into several parts.

Part 1 is the framework for all the subsequent parts and defines the definitional mechanisms and conventions used in the other parts as well the common requirements that an implementation has to adhere to if it wants to support any one of the extensions defined in the standard. Part 2 is the full-text standard, which is concerned about the mechanisms to provide extended text search capabilities, above and beyond the operators provided by SQL, e.g., the LIKE predicate. Part 5 defines the functionality to manage still images, and part 6 is concerned with data mining. The withdrawn part 4 addressed general purpose facilities.

ISO/IEC 13249-3 SQL/MM Part 3: Spatial [ISO02c] is the international standard that defines how to store, retrieve and process spatial data using SQL. It defines how spatial data is to be represented as values, and which functions are available to convert, compare, and process this data in various ways.

5.3. OLEDB for Data Mining (OLEDB DM)

The OLE DB for DM is an OLE DB extension that supports data mining operations over OLE DB data providers. The goal of this specification is to provide an industry standard for data mining so that different data mining algorithms from various data mining ISVs can be easily plugged into user applications. In this documentation, software packages that provide data mining algorithms are called data mining providers and those applications that use data mining features are called data mining consumers. OLE DB for DM specifies the API between data mining consumers and data mining providers.

OLE DB for DM introduces one new virtual object, referred to as the data mining model (DMM), as well as several new commands for manipulating the DMM. In its characteristics and use, the DMM is very similar to a table and is created with a CREATE statement very similar to the SQL CREATE TABLE statement. It is populated using the INSERT INTO statement, just as a table would be populated. The client

Table 3. PMML components of data mining model

PMML Component	Description
Data Dictionary	Data dictionary contains data definitions that do not vary with the model. - Defines the attributes input to models. - Specifies the type and value range for each attribute.
Mining Schema	The mining schema contains information that is specific to a certain model and varies with the model. Each model contains one mining schema that lists the fields used in the model. These fields are a subset of the fields in the Data Dictionary, e.g., the Mining Schema specifies the usage type of an attribute, which may be active (an input of the model), predicted (an output of the model), or supplementary (holding descriptive information and ignored by the model).
Transformation Dictionary	Defines derived fields. Derived fields may be defined by: - Normalization which maps continuous or discrete values to numbers. - Discretization which maps continuous values to discrete values. - Value mapping, which maps discrete values to discrete values. - Aggregation which summarizes or collects groups of values, e.g., by computing averages.
Model Statistics	The Model Statistics component contains basic univariate statistics about the model, such as the minimum, maximum, mean, standard deviation, median, etc. of numerical attributes.
Model Parameters	PMML also specifies the actual parameters defining the statistical and data mining models per se. The different models supported in Version 2.1 are: regression models, clusters models, trees, neural networks, Bayesian models, association rules, sequence models.
Mining Functions	Since different models like neural networks and logistic reasoning can be used for different purposes e.g., some instances implement prediction of numeric values, while others can be used for classification. Therefore, PMML Version 2.1 defines five different mining functions which are association rules, sequences, classifications, regression and clustering.

uses a SELECT statement to make predictions and explore the DMM.

6. MODEL REPRESENTATION STANDARDS

6.1. Predictive Model Markup Language (PMML)

PMML stands for The Predictive Model Markup Language, developed by the Data Mining Group (DMG), is an XML based language which provides a way for applications to define statistical and data mining models and to share models between PMML compliant applications (http://www.dmg.org/).

DMG is a vendor led consortium which currently includes over a dozen vendors including Angoss, IBM, Magnify, MINEit, Microsoft, National Center for Data Mining at the University of Illinois (Chicago), ORACLE, NCR, Salford Systems, SPSS, SASS and Xchange (Kadav, 2008).

PMML allow users to develop models with one vendor's application, and use other vendor's applications to visualize, analyze, evaluate or use the information models. It describes the inputs to data mining models, the transformations used prior to prepare data for data mining, and the parameters which define the models themselves.

PMML components are summarized and described in Table 3.

Since PMML is an XML based standard, the specification comes in the form of an XML Document Type Definition (DTD). A PMML document can contain more than one model. If the application system provides a means of selecting models by name and if the PMML consumer specifies a model name, then that model is used; otherwise the first model is used (stdHB, 2000).

7. CONCLUSION

CRISP-DM was developed in early 1990's where data mining market was showing an exponential demand in several countries. At that time all data mining users were developing their approaches on demand, as they went along, learning by trial and error. Then they thought that developing a standard process model, non proprietary, and freely available, would address those issues for them and for all practitioners.

CRISP-DM was designed to provide guidance to data mining beginners and to provide a generic process model that can be specialized according to the needs of any particular industry or company. The industry's initial use of the methodology confirms that it is a valuable aid to beginners and advanced data miners alike. DaimlerChrysler has adapted CRISP-DM to develop its own specialized customer relationship management (CRM) tool to improve customer marketing.

SPSS's and NCR's Professional Services groups have adopted CRISP-DM and have used it successfully on numerous customer engagements covering many industries and business problems. Service suppliers from outside the consortium have adopted CRISP-DM; repeated references to the methodology by analysts have established it as the de facto standard for the industry; and customers have exhibited a growing awareness of its importance (CRISP-DM is now frequently referenced in invitations to tender and RFP documents).

CRISP-DM was not built in a theoretical, academic manner, working from technical principles; nor did elite committees of gurus create it behind closed doors. CRISP-DM succeeds because it is soundly based on practical, real-world data mining experience. In that respect, the data mining industry is overwhelmingly indebted to the many practitioners who contributed their efforts and their ideas throughout the CRISP-DM project.

The CRISP-DM process model is not meant to be a magical instruction tool that will instantly make the most inexperienced novice succeed in data mining. However, combined with the analysis of very important tools needed for data mining like Data Access, Model Generation and Model Representation standards, as well as assistance from more experienced practitioners, it can be a valuable tool to help less experienced data mining analysts understand the value and the steps involved in the entire data mining process.

REFERENCES

Chapman, P., Clinton, J., Kerber, R., Khabaza, T., Reinartz, T., Shearer, C., & Wirth, R. (2000). *CRISP-DM 1.0: Step by step data mining guide.* Retrieved from http://www.crisp-dm.org

Chorianopoulos, A., & Tsiptsis, K. (2009). *Data mining techniques in CRM: Inside customer segmentation.* Chichester, UK: John Wiley & Sons.

Clifton, C., & Thuraisingham, B. (2001). Emerging standards for data mining. *Computer Standards & Interfaces, 23,* 187–193. doi:10.1016/S0920-5489(01)00072-1

Delen, D., & Olson, D. (2008). *Advanced data mining techniques.* Berlin, Germany: Springer-Verlag.

Elder, J., Mine, G., & Nisbet, R. (2009). *Handbook of statistical analysis and data mining applications.* London, UK: Academic Press.

Grossman, R. L., Hornick, M. F., & Meyer, G. (2002). Data mining standards initiatives. *Communications of the ACM, 45*(8). doi:10.1145/545151.545180

Guazzelli, A., Lin, W., & Tena, T. (2010). *PMML in action: Unleashing the power of open standards for data mining and predictive analytics.* Seattle, WA: CreateSpace.

Hornick, M. (2004). *JSR-73 Expert Group. Java TM Specification Request 73: JavaTM Data Mining.* Retrieved from http://www.jcp.org/en/jsr/detail?id=73

MacLennan, J., Tang, Z., & Crivat, B. (2008). *Data mining with Microsoft SQL.* Mississauga, ON, Canada: John Wiley & Sons.

McCue, C. (2007). *Data mining and predictive analysis: Intelligence gathering and crime analysis.* Oxford, UK: Butterworth-Heinemann.

Melton, J., & Eisenberg, A. (2001). SQL multimedia and application packages (SQL/MM). *SIGMOD Record, 30*(4), 97–102. doi:10.1145/604264.604280

ADDITIONAL READING

Goff, K. S., Mauri, D., Malik, S., & Welch, J. (Eds.). (2009). *Smart business intelligence solutions with Microsoft SQL Server 2008.* Redmond, WA: Microsoft.

Linoff, G. S., & Berry, M. J. (2011). *Data mining techniques.* New York, NY: John Wiley & Sons.

Simoff, S. J., Bohlen, M. H., & Mazeika, A. (Eds.). (2008). *Visual data mining: Theory, techniques and tools for visual analytics (LNCS 4404).* Berlin, Germany: Springer-Verlag.

Witten, I. H., Frank, E., & Hall, M. A. (2011). *Data mining: Practical machine learning tools and techniques.* San Francisco, CA: Morgan Kaufmann.

Zaiane, O. R., Simoff, S. J., & Djeraba, C. (Eds.). (2002). *Mining multimedia and complex data: KDD Workshop MDM/KDD, PAKDD Workshop KDMCD 2002 Revised Papers.* Berlin, Germany: Springer-Verlag.

KEY TERMS AND DEFINITIONS

Business Understanding: the initial phase of the data mining process, this phase focuses on understanding the project objectives and requirements from a business perspective, then converting this knowledge into a data mining problem definition and a preliminary plan designed to achieve the objectives.

Data Access: in data mining takes place with the purpose of accessing to the target information or databases of our data mining process. XML for Analysis (XMLA) is a Standard tool for this purpose.

Knowledge Discovery in Databases (KDD): the process of discovering new patterns from large data sets involving methods from statistics and artificial intelligence but also database management.

Mapping: CRISP-DM Standard, mapping refers to what we can do at the moment of applying the generic process model, depending of the kind of data mining project we are managing. We can predefine contexts and reuse generic process models for specific kind of projects (a very similar analysis and experiences), this is called mapping for the future, or build generic process models for a unique kind of project, for only one usage, this is called mapping for the present.

Modeling: a phase of the data mining process where various modeling techniques are selected and applied and their parameters are calibrated to optimal values. Typically, there are several techniques for the same data mining problem type. Some techniques have specific requirements on the form of data.

Chapter 15
Data Mining Applications in the Electrical Industry

Rubén Jaramillo Vacio
CFE – LAPEM & CIATEC – CONACYT, Mexico

Carlos Alberto Ochoa Ortiz Zezzatti
Juarez City University, México

Armando Rios
Institute Technologic of Celaya, Mexico

ABSTRACT

This chapter describes the experimental study partial discharges (PD) activities with artificial intelligent tools. The results present different patterns using a hybrid system with Self Organizing Maps (SOM) and Hierarchical clustering, this combination constitutes an excellent tool for exploration analysis of massive data such a partial discharge on underground power cables and electrical equipment. The SOM has been used for nonlinear feature extraction and the hierarchical clustering to visualization. The hybrid system is trained with different dataset using univariate phase-resolved distributions. The results show that the clustering method is fast, robust, and visually efficient.

INTRODUCTION

In the field of data analysis two terms are commonly encountered are supervised and unsupervised clustering methodologies. While supervised methods mostly deal with training classifiers for known symptoms, unsupervised clustering provides exploratory techniques for finding hidden patterns in data. What makes a system intelligent is its ability to analyze the data for efficient decision-making based on known or new cluster discovery, this is particularly important given the huge volumes of data being generated from the different systems every day.

Asset management (AM) is a concept used today for planning and operation of the electrical power system. The aim of AM is to handle physical assets in an optimal way in order to fulfill an organizations goal whilst considering risk where:

DOI: 10.4018/978-1-4666-0297-7.ch015

The goal could be maximum asset value, maximum benefit or minimal life cycle cost

The risk could be defined by the probability of failure occurrence and it consequence e.g., unavailability in power supply to customers

The partial discharge (PD) is a common phenomenon which occurs in insulation of high voltage, this definition is given in International Electrotechnical Commission (2000). In general, the partial discharges are in consequence of local stress in the insulation or on the surface of the insulation. This phenomenon has a damaging effect on the equipments, for example transformers, power cables, switchgears, and others. The first approach in a diagnosis is selecting the different features to classify measured PD activities into underlying insulation defects or source that generate PD's. The partial discharge measurement is a typical nondestructive test and it can be used to judge the insulation performance at the beginning of the service time taking into account the reduction of the performance during the service time by ageing, whereby the ageing depends on numerous parameters like electrical stress, thermal stress and mechanical stress. In particular for solid insulation like XLPE on power cables where a complete breakdown seriously damages the test object the partial discharge measurement is a tool for quality assessment (Wills, 1999).

Data Mining allows extraction of new information or knowledge and development of new methods for visualizing and analyzing the data held. Consequently, data mining should be seen as part of a well-considered information and asset management strategy. The database system industry has witnessed an evolutionary path in the development of the following functionalities: data collection and database creation, data management (including data storage and retrieval, and database transaction processing), and advanced data analysis (involving data warehousing and data mining). For instance, the early development of data collection and database creation mechanisms

served as a prerequisite for later development of effective mechanisms for data storage and retrieval, and query and transaction processing. With numerous database systems offering query and transaction processing as common practice, advanced data analysis has naturally become the next target. This chapter outlines some work which has been done to achieve such optimal use of diagnostic data on underground transmission system. Increasing demands to fully exploit the capabilities of existing transmission equipment and systems require the best use from data assets in corporate databases and also require the development of new and comprehensive diagnostics for high voltage equipment.

In Allan, Birtwhistle, Blackburn, Groot, Gulski, and McGrail (2002) two variations of data mining approaches are discussed using examples from different diagnostic measurements and tests. The use of Kohonen mapping applied to existing and new data is illustrated using examples of dissolved gas analysis, tap-changer monitoring and insulator testing. In addition, two other examples are given illustrating the potential for data mining to produce useful information from comprehensive modern diagnostic monitoring of high voltage cables and of circuit breakers. A new task force within SC15 has been established to embark on a coordinated and focused approach to develop guidelines for data mining in practice.

In Strachan, Stephen, and McArthur (2007) proposes a data mining method for the analysis of condition monitoring data, and demonstrates this method in its discovery of useful knowledge from trip coil data captured from a population of in-service distribution circuit breakers and empirical UHF data captured from laboratory experiments simulating partial discharge defects typically found in HV transformers. This discovered knowledge then forms the basis of two separate decision support systems for the condition assessment/defect classification of these respective plant items.

Table 1. Diagnosis in partial discharge using artificial intelligent tools

Authors	Tool and Objective	Constraints
(Mazroua, Salama, & Bartnikas, 1993) (Kravida, 1995)	Tool: Supervised Neural Networks. Objective: Recognition between different sources formed of cylindrical cavities.	Recognition of different sources in the same sample
(Kim *et al.*, 2008)	Tool: Fuzzy-Neural Networks. Objective: Comparison between Back Propagation Neural Network and Fuzzy-Neural Networks	Performance in the case of multiple discharges and including defects and noises.
(Ri-Cheng *et al.*, 2008)	Tool: Particle Swarm Optimization (PSO). Objective: Localization of PD in the power transformer.	On site application should improve performance.
(Chang *et al.*, 2008)	Tool: Self Organizing Map (SOM). Objective: PD pattern recognition and classification.	Quality and optimization structure of SOM.
(Ab Aziz *et al.*, 2007)	Tool: Support Vector Machine (SVM). Objective: Feature Selection and PD classification.	SVM is not reliable for small dataset.
(Hirose *et al.*, 2008)	Tool: Decision Tree Objective: Feature Extraction and PD classification	The allocation rules are sensitive to small perturbations in the dataset (Instability)

Another very important article is Hernández-Mejia, Perkel, Harley, Begovic, Hampton, and Hartlein (2008), this paper discusses the experience of the National Electric Energy Testing Research and Applications Center (NEETRAC) with condition assessment of medium voltage power distribution cable systems using Partial Discharge (PD) measurements. Specifically, the main goal is to address the issue of selection of the appropriate PD diagnostic features. A large number of features for which a physical basis can be described are selected for analysis. The features are investigated using data obtained from field and laboratory tests. The investigation shows that two traditional diagnostic features are not enough to classify samples that are prone to fail in a four-year time window. Subsequently, cluster variable analysis is performed for a considerable number of PD diagnostic features. The analysis enables significant feature elimination and reveals that at least seven different types of PD diagnostic features are needed to achieve an acceptable level of dissimilarity between features.

Table 1 shows a concentration of researchers who worked on the feature extraction, recognition and classification of PD, as well as the different artificial intelligent tools and the constraint with the applied methods.

PARTIAL DISCHARGE: CONCEPTS

Partial discharges occur wherever the electrical field is higher than the breakdown field of an insulating medium:

- Air: 27 kV/cm (1bar)
- SF6: 360 kV/cm (4bar)
- Polymers: 4000 kV/cm

There are two necessary conditions for a partial discharge to occur in a cavity:

- presence of a starting electron to initiate an avalanche
- the electrical field must be higher than the ionization inception field of the insulating medium

They are generally divided into three different groups because of their different origins:

Figure 1. Example of damage in a polymeric power cable from the PD in a cavity to breakdown

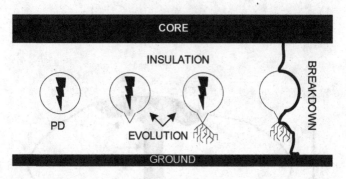

- **Corona Discharges:** Occurs in gases or liquids caused by concentrated electric fields at any sharp points on the electrodes.
- **Internal Discharges:** Occurs inside a cavity that is surrounded completely by insulation material; might be in the form of voids (e.g., dried out regions in oil impregnated paper-cables), delaminations (e.g., in laminated insulation) or cracks (e.g., fatigue stress). Treeing discharges (current pulses within an electrical tree) which may be caused by imperfections in the solid insulation.
- **Surface Discharges:** Occurs on the surface of an electrical insulation where the tangential field is high e.g., end windings of stator windings.

To explain how internal partial discharge is created, we take a Sample of one period of the applied sine wave voltage (60 Hz in México). During the increasing position, the electrons and ions from the gas loosed ions are separated and went to the surface of the "hole" (electrons to one side/ ions to the other side) in the insulation of the material. At one point there is a higher charge on the surface as the insulation gas can keep a breakdown within this hole will happen. That is not a full discharge; it is a partial discharge within the insulation material (Figure 1).

The charge that a PD generates in a cavity (Figure 2) is called the physical charge and the portion of the cavity surface that the PD affects is called the discharge area. Eapplied is the applied electric field and qphysical is the physical charge (Forssén, 2008).

In Figure 3 is showed an equivalent circuit model where C1= capacitor representing the cavity, C2= capacitor representing insulating material around cavity, C3= capacitance of the remaining insulating material and S = spark gap representing discharge of C1, C1 and C2 are generally not measurable.

The canonical discharge source for internal discharges is a void embedded in a dielectric material. The charges liberated by the first discharge are drifted in the applied field to the walls of the void where they are deposited. The field within the void is then the sum of the field from the applied voltage and the field caused by the deposited space (surface-) charges. The consecutive discharges follow the total field within the void and the next discharge occurs when the field again is above the critical field. This process yields that discharges may occur even when the applied voltage is zero because the Poissonian field from deposited charges may be high enough. The Poissonian field component cause a shift of the discharge activity from the peaks of the applied voltage to the rising-parts of the voltage, Figure 4 the discharge process follows the electrical field and not the applied voltage (Edin, 2001).

The shift of the discharge sequences from symmetrical around the peaks to the rising voltage

Figure 2. Schematic picture of a partial discharge in a cavity

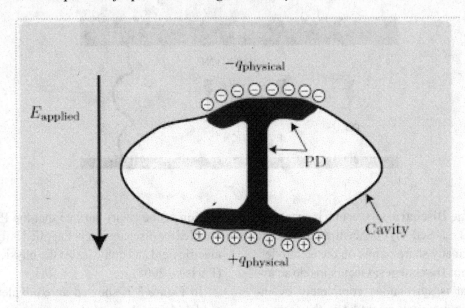

polarity and around the zero-crossings is also observed for other defects than voids, e.g., discharges caused by electrical trees and surface discharges.

The most important parameter of the partial discharge measurements is the apparent charge q, because this value gives a reference for the specified test circuit and test object after calibration. Because of the randomness of the partial discharges, averaging of the measured pulses by

the recording device is necessary to prevent wrong measurement from only a single event. This is in particular important under real measuring conditions where a number of different noise sources influences the partial discharge measurement.

The pulse repetition rate n is given by the number of partial discharge pulses recorded in a selected time interval and the duration of this time interval. The recorded pulses should be above a certain limit, depending on the measuring system

Figure 3. Equivalent circuit for the partial discharge

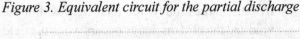

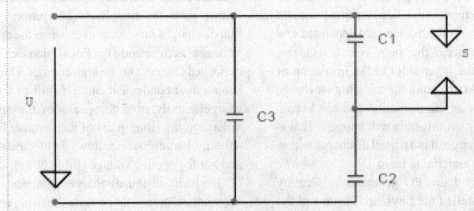

Figure 4. Field in void when no discharge occurs, when discharges occur and the current pulse in the supply leads, arbitrary units. The inception voltage is 50% of applied voltage and equal on both polarities.

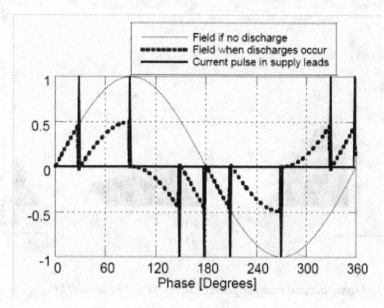

as well as on the noise level during the measurement. The pulse repetition frequency N is the number of partial discharge pulses per second in the case of equidistant pulses. Furthermore, the phase angle φ and the time of occurrence ti are information on the partial discharge pulse in relation to the phase angle or time of the applied voltage with period T.

$$\phi i = 360(ti \, / \, T)$$

In the measurement equipment is recorded the number of the detected partial discharges with a certain combination of phase and charge (Figure 5). This graph shows the behavior of partial discharge in a cavity under high voltage rising.

DIAGNOSIS ON POWER CABLES: OVERVIEW USING DATA MINING TOOLS

Due to the great impact of an insulation failure in the service life of high voltage transmission power cables and their accessories (Figure 5), extensive voltage withstand tests combined with PD detection are applied during the factory acceptance testing. Moreover, after installing the cable system on-site, different types of voltage withstand tests were applied, first attempts using DC voltage, which show good results for XLPE cables, were not successful for AC cable due to different electric stress distribution for AC and DC. In general, the on-site PD detection in HV power cables is performed off-line. For this purpose the power cable to be measured is taken out of service and an external power supply is used to energize the cable circuit and to ignite the discharging defects.

Speaking of diagnostics, typical questions that are raised regard mainly types of properties, effectiveness of a method to prevent failure, location of the defective point.

To carry out diagnostic measurements means first of all to envisage diagnostic quantities, i.e., markers which vary as a function of applied stresses and time in a way that the degradation state of an electrical apparatus can be devised and/

Figure 5. Example of the partial discharge pattern

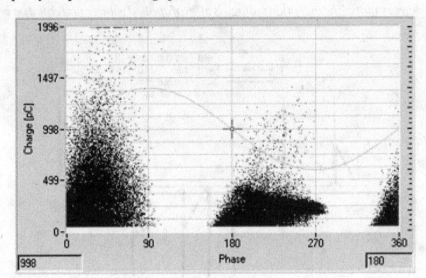

Figure 6. Examples of some accessories for power cables 115, 230 or 400 kV

or predicted. In addition to that, the other most important feature is that the selected quantity (or quantities) is that associated with the fastest degradation mechanism, which is bringing the electrical apparatus to failure in the shortest time.

In the case of organic electrical insulation (which is often the weakest component of an electrical apparatus), PD are in most cases the prevailing and fastest cause of ageing, besides being a diagnostic quantity, and this is the reason why measuring PD is becoming more and more popular in cables and transformers (Figure 6).

Resonance is defined as the condition at which the net inductive reactance cancels the net capacitive reactance. When resonance occurs, the energy absorbed at any instant by one reactive element is exactly equal to that released by another reactive element within the system.

In other words, energy pulsates from one reactive element to the other. Therefore once

Figure 7. Frequency response RLC series circuit

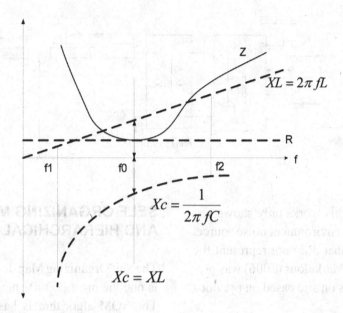

the system has reached a state of resonance, it requires no further reactive power since it is self-sustaining. The total apparent power is then simply equal to the average power dissipated by the resistive elements.

The resonance is adjusted by tuning the frequency converter according to the usual expression for series resonance (Figure 7).

$$f = \frac{1}{2\pi\sqrt{LC}}$$

Where C is the capacitance in μF/km, L is the reactor inductance of the 16 H and f is the resonance frequency.

The tests system (Figure 8) consists of the frequency converter, the exciting transformer, the resonant reactor, the capacitive divider and protection impedance. The three phase source reduces the necessary supply capacity compared to a single phase source. The inverter generates a one phase output with variable voltage and frequency which is applied to the exciter transformer. The exciter transformer excites the series resonant reactor consisting of the reactor inductance of the 16 H and the cable capacitance. This system is an AC Resonant Test Systems for On-Site Testing of High Voltage Cables and accessories up to 260 kV, 83 A, in frequency from 20 Hz to 300 Hz, allowing on-site test cables up and the capacitance range from 1650 nF (equivalent to 6.5 kilometers in length) at 260 kV to 3900 nF (equivalent to 15 kilometers in length) at 128 kV.

In PD diagnosis test, is very important to classify measured PD activities, since PD is a stochastic process, namely, the occurrence of PD very much depends on many factors, such temperature, pressure, applied voltage and test duration, moreover PD signals contain noise and interference. Therefore, the test engineer is responsible for choosing proper methods to diagnosis for the given problem at hand. In order to choose the features are important to know the different source of PD, an alternative is though pattern recognition. This task can be challenging, nevertheless, features selection has been widely used in other field, such as data mining (Lai, Phung, & Blackburn, 2008) and pattern recognition using neural networks (Mazroua, Salama, &

Figure 8. Schematic diagram of resonant test circuit with variable frequency

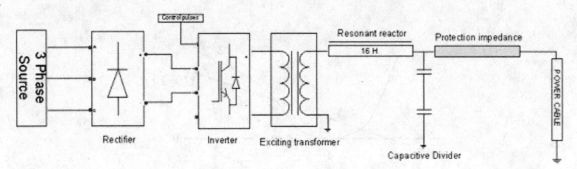

Bartnikas, 1993). In this works only shows test on laboratory without environment noise source, and it is a condition that does not represent the conditions on site, in Markalous (2006) was presented the noise levels on site based on previous experiences.

Raw data that obtained from the PD monitoring contains information about the PD magnitude and the corresponding phase angle. The commonly used phase resolved analysis is performed on the obtained raw data.

The integrated parameters that could be derived from the basic PD quantities (PD magnitude and phase angle) over a period of time are peak discharge magnitude qm, average discharge magnitude qa, etc.

The phase resolved analysis investigates the PD pattern in relation to the variable frequency AC cycle. The voltage phase angle is divided into small equal windows.

The analysis aims to calculate the integrated parameters for each phase window and to plot them against the phase position ϕ.

(n $-\phi$): the total number of PD pulses detected in each phase window plotted against the phase position.

(qa $-\phi$): the average discharge magnitude in each phase window plotted against the phase position ϕ.

(qm $-\phi$): the peak discharge magnitude for each phase window plotted against ϕ.

SELF ORGANIZING MAPS (SOM) AND HIERARCHICAL CLUSTERING

The Self Organizing Map developed by Kohonen, is one the most popular neural network models. The SOM algorithm is based on unsupervised competitive learning, which means that the training in entirely data-driven and that the neurons of the map compete with each other (Kohonen, Oja, Simula, Visa, & Kangas, 1996).

Supervised algorithms, like multi-layered perceptron, required that the target values for each data vector are known, but the SOM does not have this limitation (Mazroua, Salama, & Bartnikas, 1993). The SOM is a neural network model that implements a characteristics non-linear mapping from the high-dimensional space of input signal onto a typically 2-dimensional grid of neurons. The SOM is a two-layer neural network that consists of an input layer in a line and an output layer constructed of neurons in a two-dimensional grid as shown in Figure 9. The task of finding a suitable subset that describe and represent a larger set of data vectors is called vector quantization (VQ) (Kantardzic, 2007). In other words, VQ aims at reducing the number of sample vectors or at substituting them with representative centroids. The SOM performs VQ since the sample vectors are mapped to a (smaller) number of prototype vectors (m).

The neighborhood relation of neuron i, an n-dimensional weight vector w is associated; n is

Figure 9. System structure of SOM

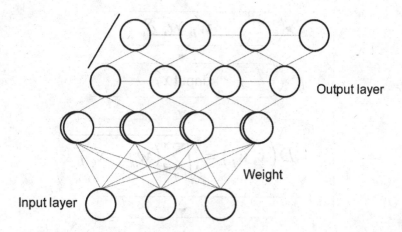

the dimension of input vector. At each training step, an input vector x is randomly selected and the Euclidian distances between x and w are computed.

The image of the input vector and the SOM grid is thus defined as the nearest unit wik (best-matching unit) whose weight vector is closest to the x:

$$D\left(x, w_i\right) = \sqrt{\sum_k \left(w_{ik} - x_k\right)^2}$$

The weight vectors of the best-matching unit and its neighbors on the grid are moved towards the input vector according the following rule:

$$\Delta w_{ij} = \delta\left(c, i\right) \alpha \left(x_j - w_{ij}\right)$$
$$\Delta w_{ij} = \alpha\left(x_j - w_{ij}\right) \quad to \quad i = c$$
$$\Delta w_{ij} = 0 \quad to \quad i \neq 0$$

where c denote the neighborhood kernel around the best-matching unit and α is the learning rated and δ the neighborhood function (Figure 10).

The number of panels in the SOM is according the A x B neurons, the U-matrix representation is

a matrix U ((2A-1) x (2B-1)) dimensional (Rubio-Sánchez, 2004).

Cluster analysis or clustering (Kantardzic, 2007) consists in assigning a set of observations into separate subsets so that observations in the same cluster are similar regarding some attribute. Clustering is a method of unsupervised learning, and a common technique in statistical data analysis which is used in many fields, for example data mining, pattern recognition, image analysis, information retrieval, and bioinformatics. A widely adopted definition of optimal clustering is a partitioning that minimizes distances within and maximizes distances among clusters. However, this leaves much room for variation: within- and between-clusters distances can be defined in several ways; see Table 2. The selection of the distance criterion depends on the application. In this paper, Euclidean distance (Vesanto *et al.*, 2000) is used because it is widely worn with SOM.

It is complicated to measure the quality (Pölzlbauer, 2004) of a SOM. Resolution and topology preservation are generally used to measure SOM quality. There are many ways to measure them. The quantization error (q_e) and topological error (t_e) are calculated to measure the quality of the map. The quantization error q_e is the average distance between each data vector and its BMU,

Figure 10. Flow chart of SOM

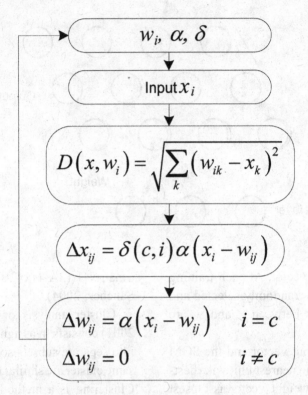

measuring map resolution, in other words, is a measure the quality of a VQ.

$$q_e(m) = \sum_{x \in C_m} \|x - m\|$$

where m is the prototype vector and C_m denote the set of samples that are mapped onto prototype vector. Thus, the quantization error indicates how accurate the data is represented by the codebook vectors. If the SOM is initialized in a linear way, the quantization error usually declines during training.

Another error function measures the quality of the map from a vector projection point of view, or in other words, the structure of the map is considered. It compares the topology of the input and the output space. A simple method investigates the location of all the samples on the map. The topological error t_e is the proportion of all data vectors for which first and second BMUs are adjacent units, otherwise this is regarded as violation of topology and thus penalized by increasing the error value. Formally, this can be written as:

$$t_e = \frac{1}{N} \sum_{k=1}^{N} u(x_k)$$

This is called topological error, with N is the number of rows and

$$u(x) = \begin{cases} 0 & \text{if the BMU of } x \text{ is next to the second BMU of } x \\ 1 & \text{otherwise} \end{cases}$$

Table 2. Within-Clusters distance S(Qk) and Between-clusters distance d(Qk,Ql)

Within-Clusters distance	S(Qk)
Average distance	$S_a = \dfrac{\sum\limits_{i,i'} \left\| x_i - x_{i'} \right\|}{N_k \left(N_k - 1 \right)}$
Nearest neighbor distance	$S_{nn} = \dfrac{\sum\limits_i \min_{i'} \left\{ \left\| x_i - x_{i'} \right\| \right\}}{N_k}$
Centroid distance	$S_c = \dfrac{\sum\limits_i \left\| x_i - c_k \right\|}{N_k}$
Between-clusters distance	**d(Qk,Ql)**
Single linkage	$d_s = \min_{i,j} \left\{ \left\| x_i - x_j \right\| \right\}$
Complete linkage	$d_{co} = \max_{i,j} \left\{ \left\| x_i - x_j \right\| \right\}$
Average linkage	$d_a = \dfrac{\sum\limits_{i,j} \left\| x_i - x_j \right\|}{N_k N_l}$
Centroid linkage	$d_{ce} = \left\| c_k - c_l \right\|$

ANALYSIS OF PD DATA

PD measurements for power cables are generated and recorded through laboratory tests. Corona was produced with a point to hemisphere configuration: needle at high voltage and hemispherical cup at ground. Surface discharge XLPE cable with no stress relief termination applied to the two ends. High voltage was applied to the cable inner conductor and the cable sheath was grounded, this produced discharges along the outer insulation surface at the cable ends. Internal discharge used a power cable with a fault due to electrical treeing. The noise measured is due at switching of power source.

The pattern characteristic of univariate phase-resolved distributions were considered as inputs, the magnitude of PD is the most important input as it shows the level of danger, the input in the SOM is the peak discharge magnitude and phase position, plotted against (qm −ϕ). Figure 11 shows the conceptual diagram training. In the cases analyzed, the original dataset was 1 million of items, it used a U-matrix of 20×20 cells to extract features. The color of a hexagon represents the average distance between the estimated data vector at that position on the map and the neighboring hexagons. White color indicates that the data groups are "close", or more similar, and black means that the data groups are "far", or less similar.

Figure 11. The component interaction between SOM and Hierarchical clustering

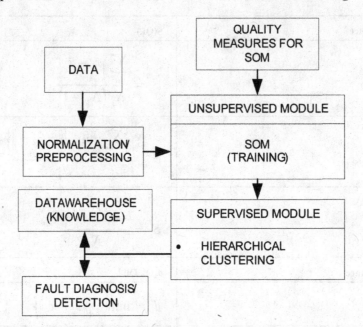

Therefore, we can identify clustering membership by locating white "walls" among data groups. In Figures 12, 15, 18, and 21, is shown the scatter plot of $q_m - \phi$, but it is not possible to extract a pattern characteristic. In Figures 13, 16, 19, and 22, is shown the U-matrix, were the clusters are separates and it is possible to analyze patterns among clusters. The final representation is the hierarchical tree, in which the branch length is proportional to the difference of the average expression patterns of the cluster under the bifurcation of the tree (Figures 14, 17, 20, and 23).

A total amount of 63 dataset were tested for diagnostic test at power cables, we got a very fast data representation with a 95% accuracy level in the discrimination of partial discharge source, this was done considering noise and combined sources.

The dataset were preprocessed with a SOM of 20x20 and validated using quality measures, this validation did not only compared the findings for any given map but also tested the sensitivity of measure changes in map size.

Table 3 shows how q_e declines as the map become larger. Thus, the qe cannot be used to compare maps of different sizes, but it can be visualized as a map lattice, and can be applied to any vector quantization and clustering algorithm. The topological error t_e is the proportion of all data vectors for which first and second BMUs are not adjacent units, a measure of topology preservation.

CONCLUSION AND FUTURE WORKS

PD patterns recognition and classification require an understanding of the traits commonly associated with the relationship between observed partial discharge activity and responsible defect sources. This paper shows how the use of SOM followed by the application of Hierarchical Clustering methods constitutes a fast and reasonably accurate method for exploratory analysis, data mining and diagnosis within a large amount of data like partial discharge on power cables underground. The results reported showed that the proposed method has potential

Figure 12. Surface Discharge: Scatter plot

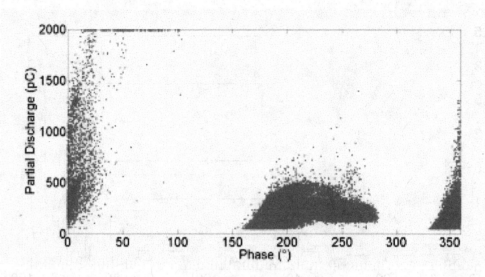

Figure 13. Surface discharge: U-matrix

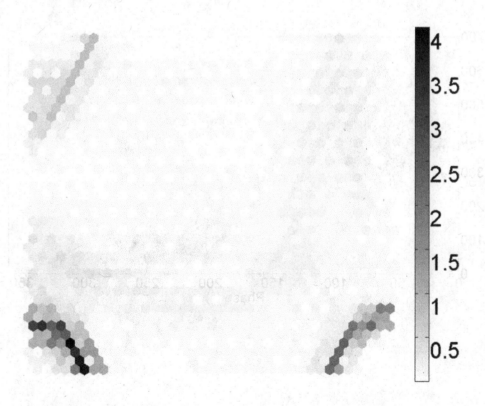

Figure 14. Surface discharge: Dendrogram

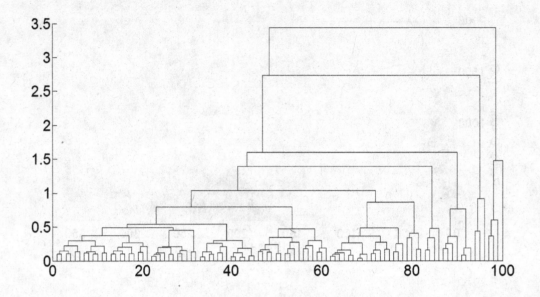

Figure 15. Internal discharge: Scatter plot

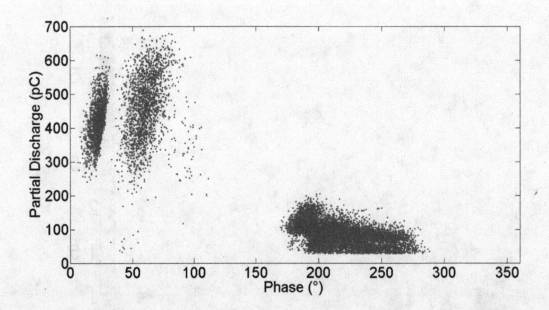

Figure 16. Internal discharge: U-matrix

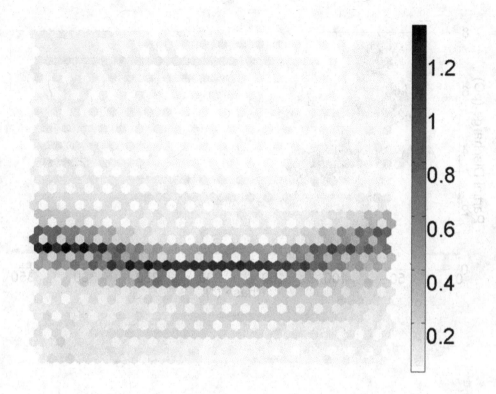

Figure 17. Internal discharge: Dendrogram

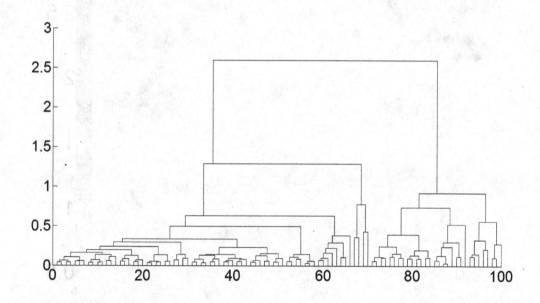

Figure 18. Corona discharge point at ground: Scatter plot

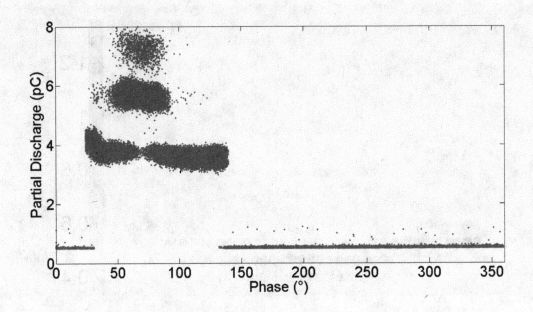

Figure 19. Corona discharge point at ground: U-matrix

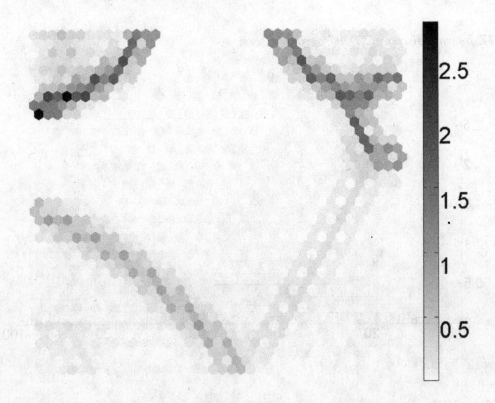

Figure 20. Corona discharge point at ground: Dendrogram

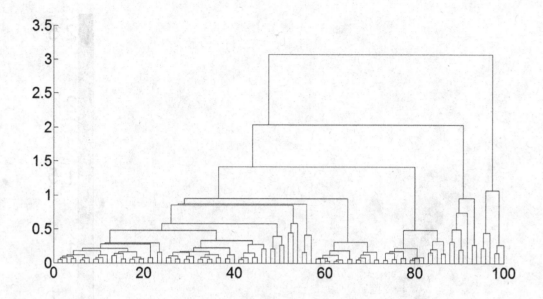

Figure 21. Noise due at switching: Scatter plot

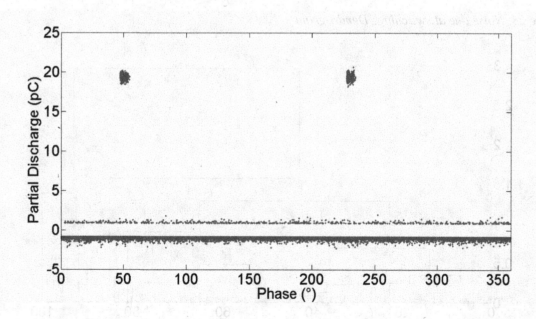

Figure 22. Noise due at switching: U-matrix

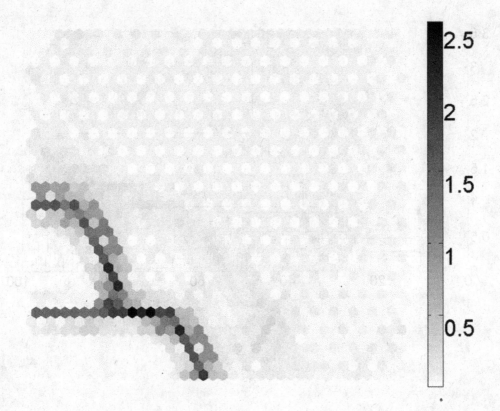

Figure 23. Noise due at switching: Dendrogram

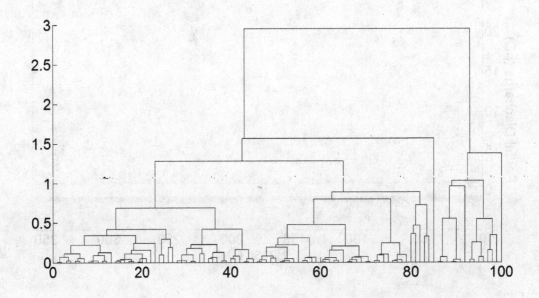

Table 3. Quality measurements for SOM training

Dataset Cells of SOM	Quantization error q_e (%)	Topological error t_e (%)
Surface discharge 5x5	0.378	0.0426
Surface discharge 10x10	0.181	0.0547
Surface discharge 20x20	**0.101**	**0.0561**
Internal discharge 5x5	0.188	0.0865
Internal discharge 10x10	0.097	0.0652
Internal discharge 20x20	**0.038**	**0.0511**
Corona discharge 5x5	0.271	0.0342
Corona discharge 10x10	0.1326	0.0906
Corona discharge 20x20	**0.053**	**0.1342**
Noise 5x5	0.214	0.1818
Noise 10x10	0.0729	0.3065
Noise 20x20	**0.027**	**0.4665**

in investigating and accurate methodologies for condition monitoring and diagnosis.

REFERENCES

Ab Aziz, F., Hao, L., & Lewin, P. L. (2007). Analysis of partial discharge measurement data using a support vector machine. In *Proceedings of the 5th Student Conference on Research and Development* (pp. 1-6).

Allan, D., Birtwhistle, D., Blackburn, T., Groot, E., Gulski, E., & McGrail, A. J. (2002). Data mining techniques to assess the condition of high voltage electrical plant. In *Proceedings of the CIGRE General Session*, Paris, France.

Chang, W., & Yang, H. (2008). Application of self organizing map approach to partial discharge pattern recognition of cast-resin current transformers. *WSEAS Transactions on Computer Research*, 3(3), 142–151.

Cichecki, P., Jongen, R., Gulski, E., Smit, J., Quak, B., Petzold, F., & Vries, F. (2008). Statistical approach in power cables diagnostics data analysis. *IEEE Transactions on Dielectrics and Electrical Insulation, 15*(6), 1559–1569. doi:10.1109/TDEI.2008.4712658

Edin, H. (2001). *Partial discharge studies with variable frequency of the applied voltage* (Unpublished doctoral dissertation). KTH Electrical Engineering, Stockholm, Sweden.

Forssén, C. (2008). *Modelling of cavity partial discharges at variable applied frequency* (Unpublished doctoral dissertation). KTH Electrical Engineering, Stockholm, Sweden.

Hernández-Mejia, J. C., Perkel, J., Harley, R., Begovic, M., Hampton, R. N., & Hartlein, R. (2008). Determining routes for analysis of partial discharge signals derived from field. *IEEE Transactions on Dielectrics and Electrical Insulation, 15*(6), 1517–1525. doi:10.1109/TDEI.2008.4712653

Hirose, H., Hikita, M., Ohtsuka, S., Tsuru, S., & Ichimaru, J. (2008). Diagnosis of electric power apparatus using the decision tree method. *IEEE Transactions on Dielectrics and Electrical Insulation, 15*, 1252–1260. doi:10.1109/TDEI.2008.4656232

International Electrotechnical Commission. (2000). *IEC 60270: High-voltage test techniques - Partial discharge measurements* (2nd ed.). Geneva, Switzerland: Author.

Kantardzic, M. (2007). *Data clustering: Theory, algorithms and methods* (pp. 53–57). Philadelphia, PA: ASA-SIAM.

Kim, J., Choi, W., Oh, S., Park, K., & Grzybowski, S. (2008). Partial discharge pattern recognition using fuzzy-neural networks (FNNs) algorithm. In *Proceedings of the IEEE International Power Modulators and High Voltage Conference* (pp. 272-275).

Kohonen, T., Oja, E., Simula, O., Visa, A., & Kangas, J. (1996). Engineering applications of self organizing map. *Proceedings of the IEEE, 84*.

Krivda, A. (1995). Automated recognition of partial discharge. *IEEE Transactions on Dielectrics and Electrical Insulation, 28*, 796–821. doi:10.1109/94.469976

Lai, K. X., Phung, B. T., & Blackburn, T. R. (2008). Descriptive data mining of partial discharge using decision tree with genetic algorithms. In *Proceedings of the Australasian Universities Conference on Power Engineering* (pp. 1-6).

Markalous, S. (2006). *Detection and location of Partial Discharges in Power Transformers using acoustic and electromagnetic signals* (Unpublished doctoral dissertation). Stuttgart University, Stuttgart, Germany.

Mazroua, A. A., Salama, M. M. A., & Bartnikas, R. (1993). PD pattern recognition with neural networks using the multilayer perception technique. *IEEE Transactions on Electrical Insulation, 28*, 1082–1089. doi:10.1109/14.249382

Pölzlbauer, G. (2004). Survey and comparison of quality measures for self-organizing maps. In *Proceedings of the Fifth Workshop on Data Analysis* (pp. 67-82).

Ri-Cheng, L., Kai, B., Chun, D., Shao-Yu, L., & Gou-Zheng, X. (2008). Study on partial discharge localization by ultrasonic measuring in power transformer based on particle swarm optimization. In *Proceedings of the International Conference on High Voltage Engineering and Application* (pp. 600-603).

Rubio-Sánchez, M. (2004). *Nuevos Métodos para Análisis Visual de Mapas Auto-organizativos* (Unpublished doctoral dissertation). Madrid Politechnic University, Madrid, Spain.

Strachan, S. M., Stephen, B., & McArthur, S. D. J. (2007). Practical applications of data mining in plant monitoring and diagnostics. In *Proceedings of the Power Engineering Society General Meeting* (pp. 1-7).

Vesanto, J., & Alhoniemi, E. (2000). Clustering of the self organizing map. *IEEE Transactions on Neural Networks*, 11(3), 1082–1089. doi:10.1109/72.846731

Wills, L. (1999). *Electrical power cable engineering*. New York, NY: Marcel Dekker.

ADDITIONAL READING

Bramer, M. (2007). *Principles of data mining*. New York, NY: Springer.

Brugger, D., Bogdan, M., & Rosenstiel, W. (•••). (208). Automatic cluster detection in Kohonen's SOM. *IEEE Transactions on Neural Networks*, 19(3), 442–459. doi:10.1109/TNN.2007.909556

Figini, S. (2009). *Applied data mining for business and industry* (2nd ed.). New York, NY: Wiley.

Gan, G., Ma, C., & Wu, J. (2009). *Data clustering: Theory, algorithms and applications*. Philadelphia, PA: SIAM.

Haddad, A., & Warne, D. (Eds.). (2007). *Advances in high voltage engineering* (IEE Power and Energy Series). Hertfordshire, UK: The Institution of Engineering and Technology.

Kohonen, T. (2001). *Self organizing maps*. Berlin, Germany: Springer-Verlag.

Kuffel, E., Zaengl, W. S., & Kuffel, J. (2000). *High voltage engineering: Fundamentals*. Amsterdam, The Netherlands: Newnes.

Moore, G. F. (1997). *Electric cables handbook* (3rd ed.). London, UK: Blackwell Science.

Naidu, M. S., & Kamaraju, V. (1995). *High voltage engineering* (2nd ed.). New York, NY: McGraw-Hill.

Poncelet, P., Teisseire, M., & Masseglia, F. (2008). *Data mining patterns: New methods and applications*. Hershey, PA: Information Science Reference.

Rokach, L. (2010). *Data mining and knowledge discovery handbook* (2nd ed.). New York, NY: Springer.

Ryan, H. M. (2001). *High voltage engineering and testing* (2nd ed.). Los Alamitos, CA: IEEE. doi:10.1049/PBPO032E

Simovici, D., & Djereba, C. (2008). *Mathematical tools for data mining: Set theory, partial orders and combinatorics*. New York, NY: Springer.

Wang, H. (2005). *Classification and clustering for knowledge discovery*. New York, NY: Springer.

Wenyuan, L. (2005). *Risk assessment of power systems: Models, methods and applications*. Indianapolis, IN: IEEE Press/Wiley-Interscience.

Whitaker, J. (2007). *AC power systems handbook* (3rd ed.). Boca Raton, FL: CRC Press.

Xu, R., & Winsch, D. II. (2009). *Clusterings*. Indianapolis, IN: IEEE Press/Wiley-Interscience.

KEY TERMS AND DEFINITIONS

Clustering: Unsupervised classification, lso called cluster analysis, segmentation analysis or taxonomy analysis. Is a method of creating groups of objects, or clusters, in such a way that objects in one cluster are very similar and objects different clusters are quite distinct. Clustering is often confused with classification, in which objects are assigned to predefined classes, in clustering the classes are also to be defined.

Hierarchical Clustering: Allow us to get a family of partitions, each associated with the subsequent levels of grouping among the observations, calculated on the basis of the available data. The different families of partitions can be graphically represented through a tree-like structure called a hierarchical clustering tree or Dendrogram.

Partial Discharge: Are in consequence of local stress in the insulation or on the surface of the insulation and are a significant tool for potential failure diagnosis of the high-voltage equipment.

Self Organizing Map (SOM): A two-layer network with a fan-out input layer of linear nodes, connected to a competitive output layer where the processing units or "neurons" are arranged in a regular lattice structure. Each node in the input layer is connected to every neuron in the competitive layer through weighted connections. During the learning stage the neurons become tuned to different signal patterns so that when a signal is presented to the network only the neurons best representing the signal become active and the response is concentrated in a small neighborhood in the output lattice. During the training process the responses of the neurons become spatially ordered over the lattice, i.e., two similar input signals will activate same or nearby neurons on the SOM lattice. This leads to the distinguishing properties of SOM, namely, 1) topology preservation and 2) density matching. The U-Matrix is the canonical tool for the display of the distance structures of the input data on SOM.

Chapter 16
Decision Making Approaches for Advanced Manufacturing Technology Evaluation and Selection

Aidé Maldonado-Macías
Autonomous University of Ciudad Juárez, Mexico

Jorge Luis García-Alcaraz
Autonomous University of Ciudad Juárez, Mexico

Francisco Javier Marrodan Esparza
University of La Rioja, Mexico

Carlos Alberto Ochoa Ortiz Zezzatti
Juarez City University, México

ABSTRACT

Advanced Manufacturing Technology (AMT) constitutes one of the most important resources of manufacturing companies to achieve success in an extremely competitive world. Decision making processes for the Evaluation and Selection of AMT in these companies must lead to the best alternative available. Industry is looking for a combination of flexibility and high quality by doing significant investments in AMT. The proliferation of this technology has generated a whole field of knowledge related to the design, evaluation and management of AMT systems which includes a broad variety of methodologies and applications. This chapter presents a theoretical review of the term AMT, its diverse classification and a collection of the most effective multi-attribute models and methodologies available to support these processes. Relevant advantages are found in these models since they can manage complex decision making problems which involve large amount of information and attributes. These attributes frequently can be tangible and intangible when vagueness and uncertainty exist. There are several multi-attribute methodologies which are extensively known and used in literature; nevertheless, a new fuzzy multi-attribute axiomatic design approach is explained for an ergonomic compatibility evaluation of AMT.

DOI: 10.4018/978-1-4666-0297-7.ch016

INTRODUCTION

Definition of Technology

The term technology, of Greek origin, is formed by the word tekne ("art, technical or trade") and logos ("group of knowledge") and is used to define the knowledge needed to manufacture objects and modify the environment, with the aim of satisfying human needs.

According to the Spanish Royal Academy, technology is the set of theories and techniques that enable the practical use of scientific knowledge. It should be noted that, in the wrong form, the word technology is used as a synonym for information technology, which is the one that allows the processing of information by artificial means, which includes everything related to computers.

While it is difficult to establish a same schema for the different applications of the technology, one could say that the manufacture of an innovative device begins with the identification of a practical problem to solve. Then, the requirements to be met by the solution are established (materials, costs, etc.) and its operation principles. Finally, the new device is designed, built a prototype and its manufacture. Technology, therefore, covers this process, from the initial idea to its implementation in particular.

By itself, technology is neither good nor bad. Often, references of the positive impacts are the fact of increasing the productivity of human labor and the life's quality of population, with the decline of the efforts entailed. In its negative aspect, the technology can generate unemployment (the man is replaced by machines), social differences (workers are categorized according to their technological knowledge) and contamination of the environment. In society, technology is a result of science and engineering, although many technological advances are subsequent to these two concepts.

Currently, the market and competition in general, demand new technologies continuously in different areas of application (edge technology), assisted often by large global technology transfer (Holmes, 2009; Bubela & Caulfield, 2010).

These areas of application frequently create divisions between different fields, for example, to refer to a farm tractor it is called agricultural technology, to talk about technologies used in the classrooms it is known as educational technologies, etc. In this case, manufacturing applications of modern technology in production systems is identified as Advanced Manufacturing Technology; some further definitions are described.

ADVANCED MANUFACTURING TECHNOLOGY (AMT)

Manufacturing is one of the main activities that support the economy on any industrialized country. For Rao and Deshmukh (1997), manufacturing is the application of mechanical, physical, and chemical processes to modify the geometry, properties and appearance of a given material in the making of new, finished parts or products. In this matter, Advanced Manufacturing Technology is now a complete field of knowledge which implies the design, utilization and management of computer based equipment for manufacturing purposes. AMT can be defined as the family of technologies that include: computer aided design, engineering systems, planning of resources systems, loading systems of automated materials, robots, machines of numerical control, flexible manufacturing systems and manufacturing integrated computer systems (Zammuto & O'Connor, 1992).

Other definitions are more concise, such as the one given by Raafat (2002) that recognizes AMT as the technological auxiliaries that have an effect on production systems, as:

- Automation services of storage.
- Flexible Manufacturing Systems (FMS).
- Improvement of assembly lines.
- Computer Aid Manufacturing (CAM).

- Computer Aid Design (CAD).
- Computer Numerical Control (CNC).

As conclusion of this topic, although AMT has been conceptualized by several authors, Säften et al. (2007) synthetize these concepts into the collective name given to modern technology integrated to manufacturing, as the CAM, CNC, and flexible systems for manufacturing Flexible Manufacturing Systems (FMS).

Classification of AMT

AMTs have been classified according to its functional relationship with any fabrication process. For example, Boyer and Pagell (2000) classify it according to the area of application as for: design, manufacturing and administration. CAD and Computer Aid Engineering, (CAE), are examples of the first one; while CAM, robotics, control systems process in real time, and FMS and the automated systems of materials handling, are examples of the second one. Finally, the uses of electronic media, support systems for decision making, Material Requirements Planning (MRP), are examples of the application for the administration kind.

Another classification frequently used, refers to the degree of integration of AMT in the manufacturing process. Thus there are independent AMT systems, intermediate and integrated systems (Suresh & Meredith, 1985; Small & Yasin, 1997; Su, 2000). Independent AMTs are related mainly to isolated computers that are not directly connected to other computers or computer systems. For example, CAD, when not integrated with the CAM, represents an independent technology. Intermediate AMT represent groups of interconnected and automated machines that are not directly reported to external systems. Finally, integrated AMTs are them connected to at least two different productive functions.

The most diverse AMT taxonomy is presented by Small and Chen (1997), whom have proposed the following classification:

A. Design and engineering technologies
 - Computer Aid Design (CAD)
 - Computer Aid Manufacturing (CAM)
 - Computer Aid Planning Processes (CAPP)
B. Processing / machining and assembly technologies
 - Flexible manufacturing cells and systems (FMC /FMS)
 - Machines Numerically Controlled (NC) and Computer Numerically Controlled (CNC).
 - Laser for Manufacturing (LMM)
 - Pick up and Place Robots (PPR)
 - Other robots (ROB)
 - Computer Integrated Manufacturing (CIM)
 - Technology groups (TG)
C. Automated management of materials technologies
 - Automated Storage and Retrieval Systems (ASRS)
 - Automated Materials Handling Systems (AMHS)
D. Control and test automated equipment
 - Automated inspection and test equipment (AITE)
E. Information technologies
 - Just in time (JIT)
 - Planning of request for materials (PRM)
 - Planning of resources in manufacturing (PRM II)

The Role of AMT in the Industry

Actual manufacturing environments must increase the levels of quality and productivity with applications of modern technologies that make use of the computer, as well as of complex hydraulic, pneumatic, and electromechanical systems. In these environments, the intensified use of automated processes and operations, hazardous work, miniaturization of components, global competition of prices, high requirements of quality and differentiation, as well as the high cost of the direct labor force in some countries; has been exerting strong pressure on enterprises, to continuously improve their performance and renovate their operations. To address this, manufacturing companies have strategically increased their investments on AMT, as a way to stay competitive and increase levels of performance; this contributes to the livelihoods of the economic status of nations (Mital & Pennathur, 2004; Gunasekaran et al., 2001).

These investments in AMT, not only have operational and economic benefits to the interior of production systems, but they also provide many strategic, and competitive advantages which are reflected on the outside (Parkan & Wu, 1999), allowing to produce products in a shorter cycle time with benefits for their customers, a greater consistency and stability of their processes, and therefore increased sales and billing, as well as lower ecological impact. Thus, due to the importance of the AMT in the production processes and competitiveness, AMT decision-making processes investment must be made analytically to enhance benefits, avoiding failures in its transfer and implantation (Abdel-Kader & Dugdale, 1998). Given that the reason for investment in AMT is justified according to its benefits, in the next paragraph presents a further discussion.

Additionally, AMT has created a transcendent change in competitive strategies of manufacturing companies, seeking a combination of flexibility, efficiency, quality and costs (Bayo-Moriones & Merino, 2004; Saraph & Sebastian, 1992). This includes technologies based on the use of the computer as: CNC, automatically guided vehicles systems, machinery and computer-aided design. According to Dean and Snell (1991), the most important feature of AMT stands for its potential to integrate the different stages of the manufacturing process. As a result, it allows the production of both, large volumes of standardized products and small batches with high quality (Gyan-Baffour, 1994). Thus, this type of technology can be defined

as the one that is generally related to the use of the computer and when it is joining a manufacturing operation, has a significant impact on the product, process and the information aspects of the system.

AMT BENEFITS

The benefits offered by the AMT were classified by Kakati (1997); these benefits they can be external or internal and a number of indirect benefits concerning six competitive parameters. A summary of benefits these are illustrated in Table 1.

Some authors have also reported a number of benefits that have been reached in companies because investing in AMT; for example, Yusuff (2004) mentions that the main reason for the implementation of such technology, is the improvement in the manufacturing operations and on the competitiveness of the company.

Similarly, Bessant and Haywood (1989) collected the experience of fifty users of Flexible Manufacturing systems (FMS) in the United Kingdom and reported a significant reduction of process time of a product, reduction of the inventory process and an increased use of the machinery. Ettlie (1997), reported an extensive case of study in several companies about the implementation benefits associated to six types of AMT (Computer Aided Design and its derivatives, Technology Groups, Robots, Flexible Manufacturing Systems, and Computer Integrated Manufacturing Systems) showing similar results.

However, achieving the benefits of AMT mentioned earlier is not always easy and companies face problems with processes of justification, evaluation and selection, during the implementation and operation phases. Some of the most common problems are discussed in this chapter.

Table 1. Benefits of AMT

Competitive Parameter	Internal Benefits	External Benefits	Indirect Benefits
Response time	Inventory rotation Few deviations of forecast Reduction of General Cost Problem identification	Faster product design Meet deadlines	Short-term loans paid Enhancement of Confidence and prestige of the company
Process stability	Operations stability Less inventories Fast performance	Help customers to keep their internal reliability. Satisfied customers. Prevention of claims and guarantees.	Costumers happiness Good relationships outside the company.
Quality	Fewer failures Less rework Least guarantees	Lower maintenance costs Better service Durability	Better corporate image Costumers trust
Flexibility	Less setup time Lower expected cost Lower machine dead time Fewer machines Lower investment on expansion	Better and more variety of products Small lots More focused production	Low prices Increased sales in existing and new products
Cost	Greater savings in production line	Low prices	Business image

Scarce Research in Decision Making about AMT

Modern manufacturing systems are always subject to be optimized, in this matter Decision Makers (DM) in modern manufacturing industries continuously confront the problem of evaluation and selection of equipment among a wide variety of alternatives, also planning and selection processes often involve multiple attributes and conflicting criterion.

AMT selection plays an important role in decision making. Nowadays, this implies a large amount of information and uncertainty. For Kulak (2005), this technology has been broadly used in modern industries around the world and there are accessible evaluation tools and models to handle equipment selection processes, even though the publications on this topic are limited. AMT is relatively new, and sometimes has not reached a sufficient maturity level, about data and information of the market and production systems where they have been implemented, there is always uncertainty when making an investment decision and

this is one of the problems that companies have to solve, especially those in the automotive industry (Beynon, 2005). That's why that companies with an uncertain situation don't take the risk of making technology investments. Once operational, strategic or economic problems have forced a company to take the decision to invest in AMT, they are faced with another type of problems and carried out many question such as:

What is the best AMT which must be selected to solve the technological problem? Who should conduct the evaluation of the AMT? How many people must get involved? What approach and what technique can be used to evaluate the AMT? In the following paragraphs there is a brief description for those questions.

Which is the Best Alternative to Choose?

In relation to the first question that has arisen, to be able to select an AMT, is required of a comparison system of alternatives in evaluation; for example, if the approach that you want to use is entirely economic, then selected one with the lowest cost. Similarly, if the criteria selection is to choose the fastest, then you must buy one faster (Khouja, 1998).

Thus, comparing for example a robot with a single attribute, comparisons are easy to make and therefore decisions are made quickly and generally there is a consensus in relation to them, as stated above. However, looking at various attributes of the alternatives at the same time, problems arise because these may be expressed in different scales, which make search techniques that unify these attributes. In addition, often the achievement of an attribute is in demerit of another; for example, you want to minimize the cost of investment in the robot and maximize its speed, however, faster robots are usually the most expensive (Abdel-Kader & Dugdale, 1998).

Fortunately, when one speaks of robots selection, consistently experts agree that they have several attributes that characterize them. This requires that evaluations are multi-attributes in nature, i.e., that they must consider all those attributes considered important or relevant for the company in particular related to decision-making of investment processes and integrate them into assessment models. However, it is important to note that two companies may be have identical production systems and similar problems, but may be they need to consider different attributes in their evaluation (Chiadamrong & O'Brien 1999).

Consequently, with a multi-attribute approach, it breaks with the traditional approach of the economic analysis on investment of AMT. However, it states that the economic justifications are still the generality of the assessments, even in industrialized countries and this may be due to the broad financial rigor in the companies and the parameters that determine the stability and solvency of these ones (Bozdağ et al., 2000).

Who Must Carry Out the Evaluation of AMT?

In relation to the second question about who should carry out the assessment and justification of the AMT, traditionally this job is a responsibility for finance departments and therefore, its evaluation is made with a wholly economic approach. Thus, through this approach, generally evaluation is performed by a single person. However, it is accepted that requires a multi-criteria approach for the evaluation of AMT, which must integrate a decision group consisting of specialists that dominate different parameters and attributes of technology in assessment, in which each expert provides their own opinion (Choudhury, 2006). Those persons or experts that integrate the group decision come from different departments and can incorporate their points of view in the evaluation of the AMT. Other departments may take part in the investment decision and have members in the group; it all depends on the needs of the company and the problem of investment that is analyzed (Cil, 2004).

What Technique is used to Evaluate the AMT and What Attributes will be Integrated into the Model of Evaluation?

In relation to approaches to assessment, it can be concluded that there are many ways to consider the decision making processes for the investment of AMT. Thus, in response to the attributes that must be integrated into the models, the traditional economic-financial approach is no longer enough, because this techniques include only economical factors, easy to measure. Decision makers need a more complete perspective and usually there is more than one person involved in the decision having a focus conformed by experts.

With regard to the different techniques of assessment of AMT, there are those that integrate quantitative attributes only, but recently those that can include qualitative ones. It is claimed that the integration of these two types of attributes guaranteed the success of the implementation process of the technology. Justification techniques of AMT are a broad topic of discussion, the mainstream that has divided them is discussed in the following paragraphs.

Justification of Investment on AMT

For evaluation techniques of technological projects can be grouped into three main trends which are strategic, economic and analytical, same as described below:

Strategic Techniques

Strategic techniques have less mathematical formality than economic and analytical techniques, and strategic techniques are often used in conjunction. The advantage of this kind of methodologies is its direct relationship with the vision, goals and objectives of the company. A disadvantage is the possibility to overlook the tactical and economic impact of the project, focusing only on the strategic impact (Meredith & Suresh, 1986; Kodali & Sangwan, 2004).

Economic Techniques

In economic techniques there are traditional justification methods that companies use for evaluations of their technologies, which include the period of return, internal return rate, net present value and return on investment. These techniques are used in situations where the uncertainty is not deemed so are little viable (Hart, 2003). In addition, frequently they are strongly criticized given that their models are seen as reductionist and are based on quantitative aspects only (of an economic nature).

Analytical Techniques

Finally, analytical techniques incorporate quantitative and qualitative aspects, because of this, they are more complex than economic techniques and given that they incorporate the intangible attributes; in addition, due to its extensive content, are able to involve more information, including the uncertainties and their effects, so they are more realistic and are appreciated for the analysis of investment decisions of AMT. One of the most important techniques in this group is of multiattribute nature.

MULTI-ATTRIBUTE TECHNIQUES (MAT)

In this part, a few concepts will be presented aiming to enhance the comprehension of the multi-attribute techniques, and their applications.

Attributes

Multi-attributes techniques for AMT evaluation have two types of particular attributes, the first are the objective or quantitative type, that type is easily measurable and established, because represents technical, operative, technologic, and financial characteristics; besides, their value is valid for each one of the evaluators that are participating into the decision making process. A very common example is the cost and the speed that has a robot.

The second kind of attributes has a qualitative or subjective nature, and represents the characteristics that are not easy to evaluate or determine. To be defined, there is necessary the opinions of several experts in the field (some time named decision group), that's the explanation of why the subjective nature. An example of those attributes could be the quality of the robot, flexibility, easiness of programming, operation comfort, or the safety level. All this attributes could be qualified in a different way by different people (Gao et al., 2006).

Also, in the multi-attribute evaluation, frequently the evaluated attributes have a different importance for each one of the evaluators, exampling it, a person who represents the financial department could have preferences by the economic characteristics, like the cost of sale, or the maintenance cost, on the other hand you could have a person who works in the manufacturing department, and in this case the most important characteristics are the technological and operative ones, like the speed, quality, and load capacity that the robot could offer. In this stage, frequently it has to turn to techniques to weight the importance of each attribute in a whole way. There are several methods to give weights to the attributes; there are the analytic hierarchy method, and the consensus analysis of experts (Talluri & Yoon, 2000).

The Matrix Model in the Making Decision Process

Some multi-attribute decision making techniques are based in the representation of a series of alternatives with different attributes, that's why are generally presented in a matrix form. In the next paragraph is presented a briefly explanation of how to generate a multi-attribute matrix. The following procedure is based on the work of Small and Chen (1997).

Suppose that in a generic stage, there are J objective attributes and L subjective attributes that have been identified in relation with the technology selection problem. The J attributes are identified as X1, X2, ... XJ, and the L (subjective attributes) are identified as XJ+1, XJ+2, ... XJ+L . The objective attributes generate an objective values (VO) matrix and are represented in Equation 1.

Equation 1. Objective values

$$VO = \begin{array}{c} A^1 \\ A^2 \\ \cdot \\ \cdot \\ A^k \end{array} \begin{bmatrix} X^1_1 & X^1_2 & \cdot & \cdot & X^1_J \\ X^2_1 & X^2_2 & \cdot & \cdot & X^2_J \\ \cdot & \cdot & \cdot & \cdot & \cdot \\ \cdot & \cdot & \cdot & \cdot & \cdot \\ X^k_1 & X^k_2 & \cdot & \cdot & X^k_J \end{bmatrix}$$

Where X^k_j is the value for the attribute Xj for the alternative Ak for k= 1..... K and j = 1,.., J.

The values of the subjective attributes for the alternative selection are obtained by the experts' judgments. Suppose that P persons are invited to qualify each of the subjective attributes, they form the decision group (DG). It is suggested that the elements of the DG consider the weight of the alternative about the attributes by an entire number between a minimum and a maximum. A subjective matrix (VS) is constructed by each person as is indicated in equation 2 (Goh et al., 1996).

Equation 2. Objective values

$$VS^p = \begin{array}{c} A_1 \\ A_2 \\ \cdot \\ \cdot \\ A_K \end{array} \begin{bmatrix} X^{1P}_{J+1} & X^{1P}_{J+2} & \cdot & \cdot & X^{1P}_{J+L} \\ X^{2P}_{J+1} & X^{2P}_{J+2} & \cdot & \cdot & X^{2P}_{J+L} \\ \cdot & \cdot & \cdot & \cdot & \cdot \\ \cdot & \cdot & \cdot & \cdot & \cdot \\ X^{KP}_{J+1} & X^{KP}_{J+2} & \cdot & \cdot & X^{KP}_{J+L} \end{bmatrix}$$

The P matrices VSp that the members of the DG provide are added up term by term generating a total matrix, in which is divided each one of the elements by the P value, getting the arithmetic mean, that mean represents the average judgment. It is assumed that the P evaluators are rational and logical in their judgment. Thus, the subjective total value matrix, denominated (VST) is determined by equation 3.

Equation 3. Subjective Total values

$$VST = \sum_{P=1}^{P} VS^P / P = \begin{matrix} A_1 \\ A_2 \\ \\ \\ A_K \end{matrix} \begin{vmatrix} \sum_{i=1}^{P} X^1_{J+1}/P & \sum_{i=1}^{P} X^1_{J+2}/P & \cdot & \cdot & \sum_{i=1}^{P} X^1_{J+L}/P \\ \sum_{i=1}^{P} X^2_{J+1}/P & \sum_{i=1}^{P} X^2_{J+2}/P & \cdot & \cdot & \sum_{i=1}^{P} X^1_{J+L}/P \\ \cdot & \cdot & & & \cdot \\ \cdot & \cdot & \cdot & \cdot & \cdot \\ \sum_{i=1}^{P} X^k_{J+1}/P & \sum_{i=1}^{P} X^2_{J+2}/P & \cdot & \cdot & \sum_{i=1}^{P} X^1_{J+L}/P \end{vmatrix}$$

Where $x^k_{J+L} = \dfrac{\sum_{p=1}^{P} x^{kp}_{J+L}}{P}$ for k=1,...K, J=1,...L is the average grade of the P experts for A^k about the subjective attribute X_{J+I} thus. Finally, combining the objective value matrix and the subjective values matrix, a final decision matrix (MDF) is generated for the analyzed decision making problem as is illustrated in equation 4.

Equation 4. Final decision matrix

$$MDF = [VO, VST] = \begin{matrix} A^1 \\ A^2 \\ \\ \\ A^K \end{matrix} \begin{vmatrix} x^1_1 & \cdots & x^1_J & x^1_{J+1} & \cdots & x^1_{J+L} \\ x^2_1 & \cdots & x^2_J & x^2_{J+1} & \cdots & x^2_{J+L} \\ \cdot & & & & & \cdot \\ x^K_1 & \cdots & x^K_J & x^K_{J+1} & \cdots & x^K_{J+L} \end{vmatrix}$$

With the information contained in a matrix form, it can proceed to apply the multi-attribute techniques.

TOPSIS

This technique consider the Ak alternatives and Xi attributes as vectors in the Euclidean space, as is indicated in the equations 5 and 6, considering the assumption that there is an alternative that has to be the best or the worst of the rest; thus, the alternative with the best and worst nominal characteristics in the attributes is called the ideal alternative (A+) and the anti-ideal (A-), respectively, according to the equations 7 and 8 (Yoon, 1980). A+ and A- are alternatives that were generated by the data in the FDM and are not real, are hypothetical.

Equation 5. Alternatives like vectors

$A_k = (x_{1k} ....x_{nk})$ for k = 1,2, ...K

Equation 6. Attributes like vectors

$X_i = (x_{i1} ....x_{ik})$ for n = 1, 2.......N

Equation 7. Ideal alternative

$A_+ = (x_{1+}, x_{2+}, ...x_{n+})$

Equation 8. Anti-ideal alternative

$A- = (x_{1-}, x_{2-}, ...x_{n-})$

Based in the last paragraph, and considering that the alternatives are points in the Euclidean space, it is possible to say that it has to choose the alternative in evaluation that has a small distance to the ideal alternative and at the same time, a long distance from the anti-ideal. TOPSIS is a technique that integrates the both concepts of ideal closeness and anti-ideal distance.

The TOPSIS technique can be resumed in three phases:

1) Normalize each Xi vector of attributes that are restrained to an evaluation as is indicated in the equation 9. The reason of making this normalization process is because frequently the attributes are expressed in a different scale dimension; for example, the initial cost of a tractor is expressed in monetary unites, the diesel litters per hour in litters and so on. Thus, by the normalization process it is generated a non-dimensional vector where the dimension scale is nonexistent.

Equation 9. Attributes normalization

$$TX_i = X_i / \lVert X_i \rVert = (x^1_i / \lVert X_i \rVert, ...x^k_i / \lVert X_i \rVert)$$

Where $\lVert X_n \rVert$ represents the Euclidean norm of the vector (magnitude)

A way to normalize the vectors of the alternatives in a direct way is using the equations 10, 11 and 12. The equation 10 is applied to all the evaluation alternatives and the 11 and the 12 to the ideal and anti-ideal, respectively.

Equation 10. Alternatives normalization

$$TA^k = (t^k,....t_n^k) = (x_1^k / \|X_1\|,........x_n^k / \|X_n\|)$$

Equation 11. Ideal alternative normalization

$$TA^+ = (t^+,....t_n^+) = (x_1^+ / \|X_1\|,........x_n^+ / \|X_n\|)$$

Equation 12. Anti-ideal alternative normalization

$$TA^- = (t^-,....t_n^-) = (x_1^- / \|X_1\|,........x_n^- / \|X_n\|)$$

2) Calculate according to equations 13 and 14, the distances that exist from the points represented by each Ak with the points that represent A+ and A-.

Equation 13. Distance to ideal alternative

$$\rho(A^k, A^+) = \|w * (TA^k - TA^+)\| = \sqrt{\sum_{n=1}^{N} w_1 * (t_n^k - t_n^+)^2}.$$

Equation 14. Distance to anti-ideal alternative

$$\rho(A^k, A^-) = \|w * (TA^k - TA^-)\| = \sqrt{\sum_{n=1}^{N} w * (t_n^k - t_n^-)^2}$$

3) Arrange the k alternatives accord to the proximity and distance that the points that represent them have, with the A+ and A- points. That is given by the rate that is obtained with the equation 15. The selection criteria that is used in

TOPSIS consists in choose an alternative that has the minor value in RC(Ak, A+).

Equation 15. TOPSIS selection index

$$RC(A^k, A^+) = \frac{\rho(A^k, A^+)}{\rho(A^k, A^+) + \rho(A^k, A^-)}$$

Attribute Weight

In the equations 13 and 14, w represents the weight or importance that the elements of the decision group have proportioned to the evaluation attribute. This is an important point to consider, because not all the members off the DG have the same preference about all the attributes and that make sense; for example, suppose that you want to acquire a robot because there's a bottle neck in a process, in that case, the speed of the robot to work is a crucial factor and it will be very important, even above than the cost.

In the same way, the person who works in the financial department could have preference by the financial aspects and give a high level of importance to the economic attributes; but someone who works in the production lines will be worried by the technical aspects, like quality and the working speed.

Several authors recommend to use the direct assignation weight method where it is asked to the DG to give their opinion about the importance that the evaluated attributes have for each one, those opinions are made in a Likert scale, with values between one and nine, where one represents null importance, and the nine an extreme importance (Parkan & Wu, 1999; Goh et al., 1996). The obtained grades of each attribute are averaged as is indicated in the equation 16. The weight (w) assigned to each attribute is the average of that attribute among the total sum of averages, according to the equation 17; thus, the assigned weight sum of the group of attributes is equal to one as is indicated in equation 18.

Equation 16. Arithmetic mean

$$\bar{O}_i = \frac{\sum_{R=1}^{P} O_{iR}}{P} \quad \text{for R} = 1,2,...P$$

Equation 17. Attribute's weight

$$w_i = \frac{\bar{O}i}{\sum_{i=1}^{N} \bar{O}_i} \quad \text{for i} = 1,2...N$$

Equation 18. Attribute's weight sum

$$\sum_{i=1}^{N} w_i = 1$$

Where:

O_{iR} It's the emitted opinion by the expert R for the Attribute i

$\bar{O}_i$ It's the average of the obtained assignments by the attribute i

w_i It's the weight for the attribute i

N It's the total number of attributes

P It's the number of experts that emit their opinion.

Dimensional Analysis (DA)

DA is a mathematical technique that permits to incorporate heterogeneous attributes in a simple rate (Buckingham, 1941), which is very useful when it wants to evaluate multiple attributes simultaneously. The technique has been used in the evaluation of industrial robots and it has been observed consistency in it (Braglia & Gabbrielli, 2000).

DA is based in paired comparisons of each one of the alternatives, A^k, with an standard alternative or ideal(S), which is composed with the best values of the attributes, that alternative

has a similar meaning to A+ (ideal alternative) that is used in other techniques like in TOPSIS (technique for Order Preference by Similarity to an Ideal Solution). The comparisons of each one of the alternatives with the standard alternative are obtained by the equation 19 and that rate is called similarity factor (SF).

Equation 19. Similarity factor

$$FS^k = \sqrt[W]{\prod_{i=1}^{J+L} \left[\frac{X_i^k}{S_i}\right]^{w_i}}$$

Where w represents the weight or importance that the elements of the group decision have proportioned to the evaluate attribute, which has the negative sign if the impact is that for the enterprise and $W = \left|\sum_{i}^{J+L} w_i\right|$. The selection criteria used in DA consists in choose the alternative with the best SF, that theoretically is alike or similar to S.

Linear Additive Model

The Linear additive model is the most simple of the multi-criteria and multi-attribute technique. The technique starts from a Final Decision Matrix (FDM) that consists in objective and subjective values for each one of the alternatives. The technique can be resumed in the following way (Goh et al., 1996).

1. Normalize the evaluation attributes, depending on the case, for those that should be maximized is used the equation 20 and for minimize use the 21.

Equation 20. Normalization for maximizing

$$TX_i = \frac{X_i}{\sum_{i=1}^{K} X_i}$$

Equation 21. Normalization for minimizing

$$TX_i = \frac{1/X_i}{\sum_{i=1}^{K}(1/X_i)}$$

2. Multiply the normalized vectors of each Ak by the weight that has each attributes, obtaining the total contribution of the alternative (TCA), as is indicated in equation 22.

Equation 22. Total contribution

$$TCA^k = \sum_{i=1}^{J+L}(w_i * X_i^k)$$
for $i = 1, 2...J + L$ and $k = 1, 2...K$

The selection criterion is to choose the A^k with the higher rate in the TCA.

INTEGRATIVE EXAMPLE

An automotive enterprise is facing a problem in one of its production lines when it had to attend a special order from its best clients, it couldn't reject it. In the specifications of the automotive piece that is demanded it requires to apply a special thermal treatment, however, this piece is very heavy and must be placed manually with a special accessory in the thermal treatment oven.

The executive managers of the company have declared that the upload and download of the oven in a manually way is very dangerous because of the weight and high temperatures. With the objective of solve this problem, there have been made simulations of the process, in which has been integrated in one of the models a robot to execute this activity. The results indicate that the presence of the robot will diminish to zero the number of errors and falls of the material, as well as eliminate completely the accidents of the operators.

It has been requested to the manufacturing manager to evaluate the robot acquisition with the objective of obtain benefits of it, that's why he consulted six suppliers. The manager organized a reunion with a group of people of different departments, with the objective of integrate a decision group to realize the evaluation, it was integrated by five people, those people were integrated in the execution of the special order that the client had made.

The decision group determined that should be evaluate in all the robots the following characteristics: initial cost, it will be expressed in dollars, and the objective is to minimize it (X1); speed displacement loaded, it will be expressed in meters per second (m/s) and the objective is to minimize it (X2), and finally, the load capacity, is expressed in kilograms (Kgs) and also the objective is to minimize (X3). Related with the qualitative attributes, it was fixed to analyze two of them, the first one is related with how easy is to programming, (X4) and the second with the quality service pre-sale and post-sale that is offered by the supplier (X5). These attributes have to be maximized and are important because this robot only will be used for upload and download of pieces into the thermal treatment oven, and when this special request be completed, it has to be reprogrammed to execute other activities in the process or production lines. To determine the first three attributes it researched with the suppliers and for the last two, it turned to subjective opinions of the decision group, they were emitted in a scale from one to nine. A number one represented the absence of that attribute in the evaluated alternative, and the nine indicated that the robot had that characteristic in the highest possible value.

In the following, the problem will be solved with each one of the explained techniques. It has to be mention that one of the disadvantages of this kind of multi-attribute techniques, because they integrate subjectivity by the evaluators in the qualitative attributes, is possible to offer different solutions to the same selection problem.

TOPSIS Solution

The experts group made a technologic track and determined that six of the robots were evaluated. The subjective attributes of them are illustrated in the Table 2.

In the same way, the experts that integrated the DG gave their opinions related to the presence or absence of the qualitative attributes. The emitted grades are in Table 3 that is on the next and in the final part of it are the means.

Thus, based in Tables 2 and 3, where it appear the values of the objective and subjective attributes, it is generated a MDF, that is illustrated in the Table 4, where also is showed the ideal alternatives and anti-ideal in the last two lines, that are defined by R^+ and R^- respectively.

As it was mentioned before in the problem introduction, attributes are expressed in different units or scales, that's why is required to be non-dimensional units, to be able of make calculations with them, this is achieve by the normalization process. In Table 4 is showed the process of how to obtain the Euclidean norm, and in Tables 5 and 6 are showed the normalized values of the attributes.

With the normalized values is proceed to ask to the five members of the DG their opinion in relation with the importance level that the attributes

Table 2. Subjective values of the attributes

R^i	Attributes		
	X_1	X_2	X_3
R^1	196000	1.6	112
R^2	267000	1.4	90
R^3	217590	1.8	85
R^4	235000	2.2	65
R^5	232545	1.85	115
R^6	248000	1.77	98
S	196000	2.2	115

have. In Table 7 are showed the emitted opinions by the judges, and in the last but one row is showed the average of each one of these. It is clear that the attribute denoted by X_5 is the most important, and X_2 the last.

With the normalized values and the weight, it is proceed to multiply the weight of each one of the attributes by its respective column of the normalized values matrix. The results are showed in Table 8.

Thus, the data in Table 8 is non-dimensional and is weighted; now it proceeds to calculate the distance from the point that represents, to each one of the alternatives, to the ideal and anti-ideal alternatives, which calculations are showed in Tables 9 and 10, respectively. It has been added between square brackets the order of preference that each alternative has, thus, it is clear that ac-

Table 3. Emitted opinions by experts for subjective attributes

R^i	E_1		E_2		E_3		E_4		E_5		Average	
	X_4	X_5	X_4	X_5	X_4	X_5	X_4	X_5	X_4	X_5	X_4	X_5
R^1	8	5	7	6	5	5	5	8	5	8	6	6.4
R^2	6	7	7	8	6	6	8	5	7	7	6.8	6.6
R^3	7	6	8	6	5	5	5	6	5	8	6	6.2
R^4	7	8	5	7	7	6	5	8	6	7	6	7.2
R^5	7	6	5	8	8	7	6	8	8	7	6.8	7.2
R^6	6	6	5	8	5	6	5	6	8	7	5.8	6.6

Table 4. Final decision matrix

R^i	Attributes				
	X_1	X_2	X_3	X_4	X_5
R^1	196000	1.6	112	6	6.4
R^2	267000	1.4	90	6.8	6.6
R^3	217590	1.8	85	6	6.2
R^4	235000	2.2	65	6	7.2
R^5	232545	1.85	115	6.8	7.2
R^6	248000	1.77	98	5.8	6.6
R^+	196000	2.2	115	6.8	7.2
R^-	267000	1.4	65	5.8	6.2

Table 6. Normalized values

R^i	Attributes				
	X_1	X_2	X_3	X_4	X_5
R^1	0.3423	0.3656	0.4779	0.3921	0.3893
R^2	0.4663	0.3199	0.3840	0.4444	0.4015
R^3	0.3800	0.4113	0.3627	0.3921	0.3772
R^4	0.4104	0.5027	0.2774	0.3921	0.4380
R^5	0.4061	0.4227	0.4907	0.4444	0.4380
R^6	0.4331	0.4044	0.4182	0.3791	0.4015
R^+	0.3423	0.5027	0.4907	0.4444	0.4380
R^-	0.4663	0.3199	0.2774	0.3791	0.3772

Table 5. Obtaining the Euclidean norm of the attributes

R^i	Attributes				
	X_1	X_2	X_3	X_4	X_5
R^1	3.84.E+10	2.56	12544	36	40.9
R^2	7.13.E+10	1.96	8100	46.24	43.5
R^3	4.73.E+10	3.24	7225	36	38.4
R^4	5.52.E+10	4.84	4225	36	51.8
R^5	5.41.E+10	3.42	13225	46.24	51.8
R^6	6.15.E+10	3.13	9604	33.64	43.5
Sum	3.28.E+11	19.1	54923	234.1	270.2
Euclidian Norm	572587.6222	4.38	234.3	15.3	16.44

cording to the ideal and anti-ideal distance, it must be chosen the alternative represented by R^5.

With the estimated distances to the ideal and anti-ideal alternatives, it is proceed to calculate the decision rate (DR), is illustrated in Table 11, where it is noted that the alternative represented by R^5 must be select; it is also indicated the order the alternatives have.

$$R^5 \gg R^1 \gg R^6 \gg R^3 \gg R^2 \gg R^4$$

Dimensional Analysis Solution

To estimate the solution for the decision problem with dimensional analysis method, it is use the same FDM that were used in the TOPSIS method, it is illustrated in Table 12, where in the last row was added the standard alternative, that is the same that the ideal alternative used in TOPSIS.

Thus, the best alternative is the one that has a cost of 196,000 Mexican Pesos that has a speed of 2.2 meters per second, that can hold a load of 115 kilograms and that has obtained a grade in client service and flexibility of 6.8 and 7.2, respectively.

Table 7. Judge opinions for weighting the attributes

Expert	Attributes				
	X_1	X_2	X_3	X_4	X_5
E_1	8	2	4	7	8
E_2	8	4	8	9	8
E_3	4	3	7	9	7
E_4	9	4	5	8	9
E_5	6	3	8	4	7
Average	7.0000	3.2000	6.4000	7.4000	7.8000
w	0.2201	0.1006	0.2013	0.2327	0.2453

Table 8. Normalized and weighted values

R^i	Attributes				
	X_1	X_2	X_3	X_4	X_5
R^1	0.0754	0.0368	0.0962	0.0913	0.0955
R^2	0.1026	0.0322	0.0773	0.1034	0.0985
R^3	0.0837	0.0414	0.0730	0.0913	0.0925
R^4	0.0903	0.0506	0.0558	0.0913	0.1074
R^5	0.0894	0.0425	0.0988	0.1034	0.1074
R^6	0.0953	0.0407	0.0842	0.0882	0.0985
R^+	0.0754	0.0506	0.0988	0.1034	0.1074
R^-	0.1026	0.0322	0.0558	0.0882	0.0925

Table 9. Estimate of the distance to A^+

R^i	Attributes					Distance
	X_1	X_2	X_3	X_4	X_5	
R^1	0.0000	0.0002	0.0000	0.0001	0.0001	0.0221[2]
R^2	0.0007	0.0003	0.0005	0.0000	0.0001	0.0403 [5]
R^3	0.0001	0.0001	0.0007	0.0001	0.0002	0.0345 [4]
R^4	0.0002	0.0000	0.0018	0.0001	0.0000	0.0471 [6]
R^5	0.0002	0.0001	0.0000	0.0000	0.0000	0.0162 [1]
R^6	0.0004	0.0001	0.0002	0.0002	0.0001	0.0320 [3]

Table 10. Estimate of the distance to A-

R^i	Attributes					Distance
	X$_1$	X$_2$	X$_3$	X$_4$	X$_5$	
R^1	0.0007	0.0000	0.0016	0.0000	0.0000	0.0491 [2]
R^2	0.0000	0.0000	0.0005	0.0002	0.0000	0.0270 [5]
R^3	0.0004	0.0001	0.0003	0.0000	0.0000	0.0274 [4]
R^4	0.0002	0.0003	0.0000	0.0000	0.0002	0.0269 [6]
R^5	0.0002	0.0001	0.0018	0.0002	0.0002	0.0508 [1]
R^6	0.0001	0.0001	0.0008	0.0000	0.0000	0.0311 [3]

Table 11. Decision rates

R^i	Rate	Order
R^1	0.3101	2
R^2	0.5990	5
R^3	0.5573	4
R^4	0.6367	6
R^5	0.2417	1
R^6	0.5072	3

To estimate the importance levels that each one of the attributes has, it's used the same information that was used in the TOPSIS calculations. The experts' opinions are indicated in Table 13.

In this case, the sum of the absolute values of all the means of the attributes is 31.8 and the only attribute that has a negative impact for the enterprise or that is needed to be minimized is related with the cost of the robot, it's represented by X1 that is why this one has a negative sign. Observe that in this technique it is not necessary to estimate the importance level in a way that the sum of them be 1.

With the last values it proceeds to obtain the similarity rates that each of the alternatives has in evaluation respect the standard alternative. The calculus are indicated in Table 14, where in the last column has been added the similarity rate that each alternative has, and the preference order is in the square bracket. In this case, the alternative represented by R5 must be selected, because literally is the one that is similar in 94.64% to the standard alternative and the order must remain like:

$$R^5 \gg R^1 \gg R^6 \gg R^3 \gg R^4 \gg R^2$$

Table 12. Final decision matrix

R^i	Attributes				
	X$_1$	X$_2$	X$_3$	X$_4$	X$_5$
R^1	196000	1.6	112	6	6.4
R^2	267000	1.4	90	6.8	6.6
R^3	217590	1.8	85	6	6.2
R^4	235000	2.2	65	6	7.2
R^5	232545	1.85	115	6.8	7.2
R^6	248000	1.77	98	5.8	6.6
S	196000	2.2	115	6.8	7.2

Table 13. Importance level of the attributes

Expert	Attributes				
	X_1	X_2	X_3	X_4	X_5
E_1	8	2	4	7	8
E_2	8	4	8	9	8
E_3	4	3	7	9	7
E_4	9	4	5	8	9
E_5	6	3	8	4	7
Average	-7.0000	3.2000	6.4000	7.4000	7.8000

Table 14. Similarity rates

z	Attributes					IS
	X_1	X_2	X_3	X_4	X_5	
R^1	1	0.3609	0.8444	0.3961	0.399	0.9090 [2]
R^2	0.1149	0.2354	0.2083	1	0.5073	0.8318 [6]
R^3	0.4812	0.5262	0.1445	0.3961	0.3115	0.8438 [4]
R^4	0.2807	1	0.026	0.3961	1	0.8320 [5]
R^5	0.3022	0.5744	1	1	1	0.9464 [1]
R^6	0.1926	0.4986	0.3592	0.3082	0.5073	0.8485 [3]

Solution using the additive lineal model

For this technique, it is also used the FDM and the weight that has been used in TOPSIS and DA. The information is showed in Table 15 and Table 16.

With the past information it was proceeded to realize the normalization of the attributes, which is realized depending on the case and if it wants to be minimized or maximized. In this case, the only attribute that wants to be minimized is the cost. The results of this process are shown in Table 17 and the normalized and weighted values, and the contributions of each alternative are shown in Table 18.

Thus, basing on this technique, the robot that must be selected is the one represented by R5, because it gets the maximum contribution of all (CA equal to 0.1811). The preference order that

the alternatives have according to this evaluation technique matches with the one obtained in the DA method and it is showed at next.

$$R^5 \gg R^1 \gg R^6 \gg R^3 \gg R^4 \gg R^2$$

Table 15. Final decision matrix

R^i	Attributes				
	X_1	X_2	X_3	X_4	X_5
R^1	196000	1.6	112	6	6.4
R^2	267000	1.4	90	6.8	6.6
R^3	217590	1.8	85	6	6.2
R^4	235000	2.2	65	6	7.2
R^5	232545	1.85	115	6.8	7.2
R^6	248000	1.77	98	5.8	6.6

Table 16. Experts' opinions to weight the attributes

Expert	Attributes				
	X_1	X_2	X_3	X_4	X_5
E_1	8	2	4	7	8
E_2	8	4	8	9	8
E_3	4	3	7	9	7
E_4	9	4	5	8	9
E_5	6	3	8	4	7
Average	7.0000	3.2000	6.4000	7.4000	7.8000
w	0.2201	0.1006	0.2013	0.2327	0.2453

Table 17. Normalization of the MLA

Ri	Atributos				
	X_1	X_2	X_3	X_4	X_5
R^1	0.196	0.1507	0.1982	0.1604	0.1592
R^2	0.1439	0.1318	0.1593	0.1818	0.1642
R^3	0.1766	0.1695	0.1504	0.1604	0.1542
R^4	0.1635	0.2072	0.115	0.1604	0.1791
R^5	0.1652	0.1742	0.2035	0.1818	0.1791
R^6	0.1549	0.1667	0.1735	0.1551	0.1642

ERGONOMICS AND SAFETY ATTRIBUTES IN THE SELECTION OF AMT: AN ERGONOMIC APPROACH FOR THEIR EVALUATION

According to the argument made in earlier sections, the multiattribute perspective offers several advantages for decision making processes about AMT. However, the selection of this technology involves a vast amount of information and uncertainty and multiple aspects that are difficult to take into account in their totality. Among them are the ergonomic and safety ones. Actual models are found scarce of important ergonomics, human factors and safety attributes required for a more complete decision according to Maldonado (2009, 2010). Usually, decision makers are unaware of these attributes or underestimate them as well. In this section, a new ergonomic approach is presented, for this; a hierarchical fuzzy axiomatic design model was used in an original way. As introduction of this section; the relevance of human intervention in high tech environments is discussed in first place, and then fuzzy logic and axiomatic design in decision making fundamentals are also described. Finally the methodology is deployed with a numerical example.

Human Role in High-tech Environments

For Vicente (1999), the techno-centric approach has historically dominated the integration of the AMT in the industry. In this approach, people interact with AMT systems in a dynamic environment, with inadequate and uncertain information. This may result in unexpected problems and actions which are computer-mediated, generating complex socio-technical systems. In this approach, the systems provide what is technically possible (automation) without the appropriate and adequate attention about the interaction with human beings; and because failures are often unexpected, designers have reduced but not eliminated human intervention (Kesseler & Knapen, 2006).

In this manner, even if such intervention has been reduced or nullify, human beings has been affected in different ways, including the important adaptation of humans to new skills. To this end, the physical abilities are now superseded by the

Table 18. Normalized and weighted values and its contribution

R^i	Attributes					CA
	X1	X2	X3	X4	X5	
R^1	0.0431	0.0152	0.0399	0.0373	0.0391	0.1746 [2]
R^2	0.0317	0.0133	0.0321	0.0423	0.0403	0.1596 [6]
R^3	0.0389	0.0171	0.0303	0.0373	0.0378	0.1614 [4]
R^4	0.036	0.0208	0.0232	0.0373	0.0439	0.1612 [5]
R^5	0.0364	0.0175	0.041	0.0423	0.0439	0.1811 [1]
R^6	0.0341	0.0168	0.0349	0.0361	0.0403	0.1621 [3]

cognitive ones; consequently human capabilities and experience are reduced in the operations which are now automated.

According to Endsley (1993) and Siemieniuch and Sinclair (1995), human skills are still needed, and are even more critical than before, due to a complex man-machine system. Usually these are required for management of heterogeneous equipment, multimedia databases operated in real time, several tasks concerning monitoring, anticipation, judgment, rapid diagnosis, programming, maintenance and adjustment, quality control and fast intervention in difficult situations. Helander (1995) affirms that even though many tasks can be performed by automated systems and through the computer, the very existence of these systems makes the human operator performance and intervention even more critical than before automation. For example, human being must be able to monitor a process using parameters of quality control and perform rapid and pertinent interventions when the parameters of the process are out of limits. Also, in case of an equipment failure, it must carry out corrective actions and become temporarily as a backup for automated processes.

About Advanced Manufacturing Technology (AMT), Corbett (1988) recognizes that concerning its interaction with humans; the first generation including CNC technology, has contributed in some degree to simplify the manual work and improve the quality of life of humans; however there still exist cognitive and manual abilities

that must have built-in. With regard to the second generation of Flexible Manufacturing Systems (FMS), this author points out that considerable complexity of automated systems create jobs that involve low levels of control over the methods and pace of work, as well as high levels of attention and cognitive demand in human operators of the system, therefore high levels of stress and illnesses associated with this conditions prevail. In reference to the third generation of AMT, which includes Computer Integrated Manufacturing Systems (CIM) as well as Computer Aided Design and Computer Aided Manufacturing, CAD and CAM respectively; there is a dominant trend towards the reduction of costs of direct labor among these systems, by which the degree of subordination of man and machine has been increased.

There are important cognitive limitations and skills specifically involved in the interaction with AMT, those related to the processing of data and information; as well as with aspects of the human/ machine interface. AMT systems are highly complex and a considerable amount of cognitive tasks must be performed in every day work. Human beings by nature present limitations thereon; among the most important are: the working memory, the velocity to perform cognitive tasks, the information retrieval, executing numerical operations and space and time orientation. These constraints must be taken into account when selecting AMT, especially in the work that involves monitoring manufacturing process and problems have arisen due to the information processing overload. This may carry a large amount of downtime affecting production times. Furthermore, it has been reported that most of automated equipment does not comply with guidelines for interface design; causing inefficiencies of equipment and human operator (Mital & Pennathur, 2004).

On the other hand, an efficient interface will reduce the workload, will eliminate or minimize human errors, will prevent confusion and will reduce the cost of the time consumed by such inefficiencies. Therefore, even and when human presents limitations, the human being is still the most adaptable and flexible element in the manufacturing system. In addition, because it is unlikely that machines can perform running trials with variable information in real time, at least in the near future; human intervention will be needed and more critical. In this way, these authors affirm that the implementation and successful adoption of AMT depends primarily on the human element. In such a way that this supports the idea of include and objectively assess ergonomic aspects for AMT selection. An ergonomic approach for the evaluation and selection of AMT must take into account human capabilities and limitations in relation with their interaction with technology, as well as the effects of a incompatible ergonomic design of equipment specially about the interface design and the consequences of the error related to the equipment' design.

In this way, even though such a separation between man and machine has been on the increase, businesses and organizations have begun to recognize the Ergonomics Science as a strategic advantage in the selection of manufacturing advanced technology (Erensal & Albayrak, 2004).

A Hierarchical Fuzzy Axiomatic Design Approach for the Ergonomic Compatibility Evaluation of AMT

The new complex computerized and automated manufacturing systems have brought an extraor-

dinary and rapid technological change to industry. Also, they have made modern work environments more complex regarding the human-system interaction. Due to this, and the important role that Ergonomics is having in the performance of these systems, this new approach has been created to identify and integrate the most important ergonomic attributes required for the selection of AMT (Maldonado, 2009a, 2009b). Fuzzy Logic fundamentals and Axiomatic Design principles with a multiattribute structure have been combined in this approach to achieve an ergonomic compatibility evaluation for the selection of AMT. In this manner, main concepts of these topics are described below.

Fuzzy Logic in Decision Making

In all the world and in every day work companies try to achieve their goals of improving their productivity, quality, competitiveness by the use of people, material, money, and the performance of managerial functions such as planning, organizing, directing, and controlling. These functions are usually performed by managers who face the process of making decisions every day. Each decision is a rational option among several alternatives. The manager is therefore a decision maker. However, when a group of managers or individuals must participate in the decision; it is called a group decision making process. For both practices, a wide range of theories, models and methodologies are being created to improve these processes.

Decision making can be defined as the selection process of the best choice from a group of alternatives in order to achieve a goal, and regularly involves uncertainty. Even though decision making is not an easy process; for Decision Makers (DMs) situations containing exact available information are preferable than the ones with inexact information, mainly about the evaluation of alternatives with respect to an attribute. However, according to Kaharaman and Cebi (2008), problems in the real world usually include both; also are complex and involve vagueness and fuzziness. In this way, the creation of the fuzzy set theory (FST) by Zadeh (1965) can deal with this kind of problems by representing and manipulating vague data. For Slowinski (1998), this theory provides a mathematical manner to handle the uncertainties associated with human cognitive process, such as thinking and reasoning.

Fuzzy Logic has proved to be the right methodology to solve a number of problems characterized by unreliable data, imprecise measures, unclear decision rules and vague language. According to Bascetin (2007) and Bascentin et al. (2006), over nearly the past three decades, fuzzy logic has been advanced about handling the implicit imprecision in a wide range of problems, e.g., in industrial control, military operations, economics, engineering, medicine, reliability, pattern recognition and classification. Its incursion can also be found in Ergonomics in manifold studies and research.

In most real world contexts, a Multiple Attribute Decision Making (MADM) problem at tactical and strategic levels often involves fuzziness in its criteria (attributes) and decision makers' judgments. This kind of decision problems is called fuzzy multi-criteria decision making (FMCDM) (Lu et al., 2007).

In relation with the present approach, a FMCDM model will be developed. Also, the Axiomatic Design Theory was combined in this model to generate a new approach for the Ergonomic Compatibility Evaluation of AMT. Some concepts and definitions of this theory will be explained in following sections.

Axiomatic Design in Decision Making

Axiomatic Design (AD) is proposed to establish a scientific basis to improve design activities by providing the designer with a theoretical foundation based on logical and rational thought process and tools (Suh, 1990). According to Suh, (2001)

other purposes of AD are: enhance creativity of human designers, to reduce random searching processes, minimize the iterative trial and error process, to determine the best designs among those proposed, and to provide the computer with some creative power through the creation of a scientific base for the design field. Additionally, the Axiomatic Design theory consists of four domains: (1) Customer Domain, (2) Functional Domain, (3) Physical Domain, and (4) Process Domain. Each domain is characterized by group of information: Customer Attributes (CAs) in the Customer Domain; previous attributes are transformed to Functional Requirements (FRs) and constraints in the Functional Domain; then Design Parameters (DPs) in the Physical Domain are established; and Process Variables (PVs) in the Process Domain are generated. This is achieved by a mapping process between domains.

According to Suh (1990, 2001) and Kulak and Kahraman (2005a) the main significant concept in AD theory is the existence of two design axioms. The first design axiom is known as the Independence Axiom and the second axiom is known as the information axiom. The independence axiom states that the independence of functional requirements (FRs) must always be maintained, where FRs are defined as the minimum set of independent requirements that characterizes the design goals

Fuzzy Axiomatic Design Approach

The approach is based mainly in the extension and adaptation of the Information Axiom (IA). This axiom proposes the selection of the best alternative that has minimum information content. Kahraman and Kulak (2005) affirm that in its conventional form, this axiom cannot be used with incomplete information, since the expression of decision variables by crisp numbers would be poorly defined. For this reason, fuzzy axiomatic design is developed by Kahraman and Kulak (2005) to use Axiomatic Design under fuzzy environment and the method is used for both multi-attribute transportation company selection under determined criteria and the comparison of advanced manufacturing systems among other applications (Kulak & Kahraman, 2005a, 2005b).

About the information axiom, it states that among those designs that satisfy the independence axiom, the design that has the smallest information content is the best design (Suh, 2001).

Information is defined in terms of the information content, I_i, that is related in its simplest form to the probability of satisfying the certain FR_s. Ii determines that the design with the highest probability of success is the best design. Information content Ii for a given FR_i is defined as shown.

Equation 23. Information content

$$I_{i=-log_2} P_i$$

Where P_i is the probability of achieving the functional requirement FRi and log is either the logarithm in base 2 (with the unit of bits). In any design situation, the probability of success is given by what designer or expert wishes to achieve in terms of tolerance (i.e., Design Range, DR) and what the systems capable of delivering (i.e., system range, SR).

In a fuzzy approach data can be linguistic terms, fuzzy sets, or fuzzy numbers. If the fuzzy data are linguistic terms, they are transformed into fuzzy numbers first. Then all the fuzzy numbers (or fuzzy sets) are assigned crisp scores. These numerical approximation systems are proposed to systematically convert linguistic terms to their corresponding fuzzy numbers. The system contains five conversion scales as in Figure 2 and Figure 3.

In this fuzzy case, incomplete information can be used for expression of the SR and DR. Hence, triangular or trapezoidal fuzzy numbers can well define these kinds of expressions. Additionally, there is a membership function of Triangular Fuzzy Number (TFN) instead of probability density. So, the common area is the intersection area

of triangular or trapezoidal fuzzy numbers. Therefore, information content is equal to that shown in equation 24.

Equation 24. Information content in fuzzy case

$$I = \frac{TFN\,area\,of\,System\,Design}{Common\,Area}$$

Ergonomic Compatibility Attributes for the Evaluation and Selection of AMT

From literature, the most important attributes of ergonomic design were determined to become the Ergonomic Compatibility Attributes (ECA) for AMT. Guides and standards of human factors and ergonomics of workspaces and machines, were considered as well. The main attributes were determined in an eclectic manner from the work of Corlett (1995), also the usability attributes proposed by Bruseberg (2006). ECA were classified as tangible and in intangible attributes and they can be benefit attributes or cost attributes from a human-artifact perspective. In benefit attributes maximize its positive influence is recommended and for cost attributes minimize its influence in humans is desirable. Deployment of these attributes is shown in Table 19. Most of ECA were benefit intangible attributes except A125, A141, A142, A143, and A144.

Methodology Description

This new approach enables the evaluation of Ergonomic Compatibility Attributes (ECA) for AMT selection. It evokes the Ergonomic Compatibility Theory proposed by Karwowski (2005, 2006) also the axiomatic approach to ergonomics made by Helander and a new fuzzy multi-attribute axiomatic design methodology created by Kahraman and Kulak (2005). Fuzzy Multiattribute

Table 19. Ergonomic compatibility attributes

(A11) Compatibility w/ Human Skills and Training	(A111) Skill Level Compatibility (A112) Training Compatibility
(A12) Physical Work Space Compatibility	(A121) Access to Machine and Clearances (A122) Horizontal and Vertical Reaches (A123) Adjustability of Design (A124) Postural Comfort of Design (A125) Physical Work of Design
(A13) Usability	(A131) Compatibility with Controls' Design (A132) Controls' Physical Distribution (A133) Visual Work Space Design (A134) Information Load (A135) Error Tolerance of Design (A136) Functional Allocation of Design (A137) Design for Maintainability
(A14) Equipment Emissions Requirements	(A141) Temperature (A142) Vibration (A143) Noise (A144) Residual Materials
(A15) Organizational Requirements	(A151) Compatibility with the Pace of Work (A152) Compatibility with Total Work Content

Axiomatic Design applications are yet very few, so this approach is considered innovative.

This approach includes a procedure of five phases which calculates the Ergonomic Incompatibility Content. This index is based on the extension of the Information Content from the Information Axiom of Axiomatic Design Theory. The procedure is described.

Phase 1:

Step 1: Determine the alternatives to Consider in the evaluation. Where $A_i = (1, 2...N)$ number of alternatives.

Step 2: Determine the attributes to evaluate, establishing the Ergonomic Functional Requirements (EFRs). Where $B_j = (1, 2...M)$ number of attributes.

Step 3: Constitute the group of experts. Where $k = (1, 2...k)$ number of experts.

Table 20. Linguistic scales for evaluation or rating of each sub-attribute using fuzzy triangular numbers

Tangible Attributes	
Linguistic Term	**Triangular Fuzzy Numbers**
Very Low (VL)	(0,0,0.3)
Low (L)	(0,0.25,0.5)
Medium (M)	(0.3.0.5,0.7)
High (H)	(0.5,0.75,1)
Very High (VH)	(0.7,1,1)
Intangible Attributes	
Linguistic Term	**Triangular Fuzzy Numbers**
Poor (P)	(0,0,0.3)
Regular (R)	(0.2,0.35,0.5)
Good (G)	(0.4,0.55,0.7)
Very Good (VG)	(0.6,0.75,0.9)
Excellent (E)	(0.8,1,1)

Figure 1. Membership functions for intangible attributes

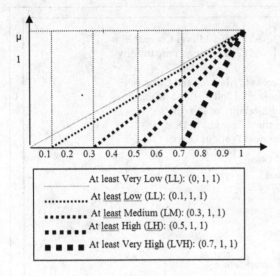

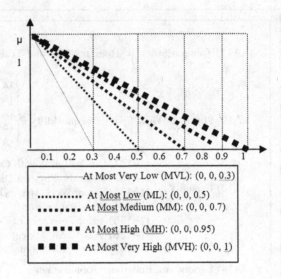

Step 4: Choose appropriate linguistic variables for the evaluation of attributes for each alternative and the linguistic ratings according Table 20.

Phase 2:

Step 1: Convert the linguistic terms of importance and the ratings assigned to each attribute to their numeric value according Chen and Hwang (1992) methodology.

Step 2: Aggregate experts' opinions about the importance to obtain the weight of each attribute from pair wise comparisons of Analytical Hierarchical Process (AHP) methodology using the geometric means.

Step 3: Determine DR for each attribute from experts' opinions and Corollary number 6 of Axiomatic Design Theory. In this way, the widest DR is established among experts' opinions.

Step 4: Aggregate experts' opinions on the assigned rating of each attribute to each alternative obtaining the SR, Eq. 23.

Equation 25. Aggregation procedure for SR

$$m_{ij} = \frac{1}{k}\left[m_{ij1} \oplus m_{ij2} \oplus ..... \oplus m_{ijk}\right].$$

Step 5: Construct decision matrices to the assigned weight importance and SR for each attribute and each alternative.

Phase 3:

In this phase the Definition of the Membership Functions (MF) or *μ(x)* for Ergonomic Design Range (EDR) and System Range takes place. Figure 1 shows MF for Intangible Attributes and Figure 2 shows MF for Tangible attributes. For Ergonomic System Range Membership Functions, Equations 26 and 27 were used.

Equation 26. Membership functions for benefit attributes

$$\mu\left(x\right) = \frac{x_i - \alpha}{\theta - \alpha} \, for \, benefit \, attributes$$

Figure 2. Membership functions for tangible attributes

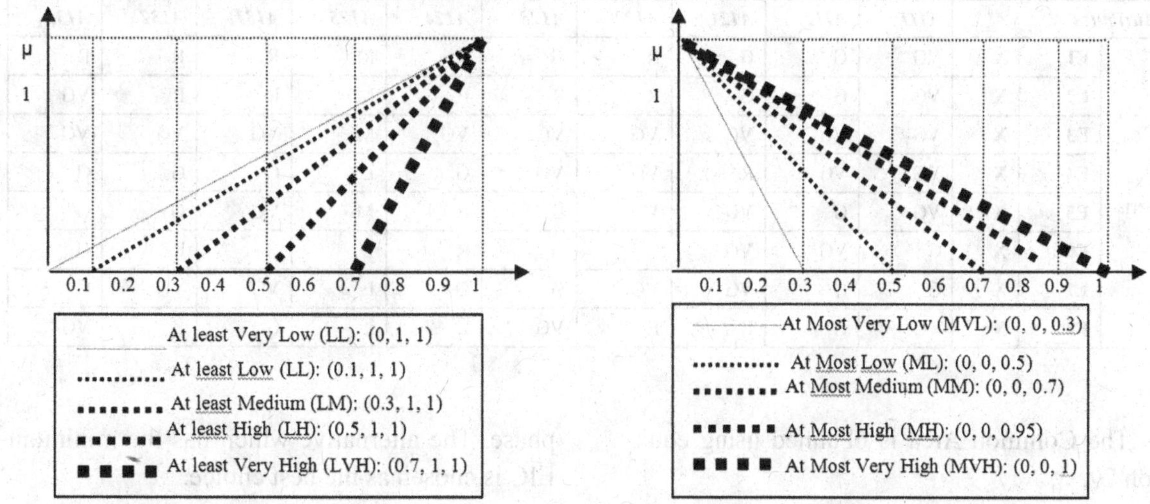

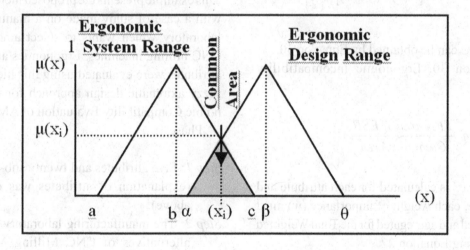

Figure 3. Ergonomic system range ESR, Ergonomic design range EDR and Common Area

Equation 27. Membership functions for cost attributes

$$\mu\left(x\right) = \frac{\alpha - x_i}{\theta - \alpha} \ for \ cost \ attributes$$

Phase 4:

Assess the Ergonomic Incompatibility Content of each attribute for each alternative using the Information Axiom with weight. Figure 3 shows the SR, DR, and the Common Area.

The Ergonomic System Range (ESR) area can be calculated by Equation 28.

Equation 28. Ergonomic system range area

$$ESR\ Area = \left(c - a\right) * \left(\frac{1}{2}\right)$$

Table 21. Evaluation of Alternative X for each Attribute in linguistic terms by experts

Attributes			A111	A112	A121	A122	A123	A124	A125	A131	A132	A133
Ex-perts	E1	X	VG	G	G	R	G	R	M	R	R	R
	E2	X	VG	G	G	R	R	P	M	R	P	VG
	E3	X	VG	VG	VG	VG	VG	VG	M	VG	VG	VG
	E4	X	VG	VG	R	VG	VG	G	L	G	G	G
	E5	X	VG	G	VG	VG	E	E	M	VG	G	G
	E6	X	G	VG	VG	G	G	R	L	G	R	G
	E7	X	G	G	VG	VG	G	G	L	VG	VG	G
	E8	X	VG	G	E	E	VG	E	L	G	E	VG

The Common Area is obtained using equation 29.

Equation 29. Common Area

$$Common\,Area = \left[\mu(x) * (c - \alpha) \right] * \left(\frac{1}{2} \right)$$

The EIC can be obtained by Equation 30.

Equation 30. Ergonomic incompatibility content

$$EIC = log_2 \frac{TFN\,area\,of\,ESR}{Common\,Area}$$

Once EIC is calculated for each attribute and alternative, each weight of importance (w) must me included and aggregated for the Total Weighted EIC by using Equation 27.

Equation 31. Total weighted ergonomic incompatibility content

$$Total\,Weighted\,EIC = \sum_{i=1}^{w} wEIC_i$$

Phase 5:

This phase consists in obtaining the Total Weighted Ergonomic Incompatibility Content for each alternative. Equations 26-29 are used in this phase. The alternative which has the minimum EIC is chosen as the best choice.

Numerical Example

This example presents the proposed methodology with a case of study made on a manufacturing laboratory which wants to select among three CNC milling machines. Ergonomics and Safety attributes were evaluated using this hierarchical fuzzy axiomatic design approach for the Ergonomic Compatibility Evaluation of AMT.

Phase 1:

Step 1: Five attributes and twenty sub-attributes (explanation of attributes was described above).

Step 2: The manufacturing laboratory has three alternatives of CNC Milling Machines. Alternatives X, Y and Z.

Step 3: Eight experts evaluated the alternatives; all experts had vast experience in the manufacturing and academic fields.

Ergonomic Attributes included in the Ergonomic Compatibility Survey were explained individually during a face to face interview.

Step 4: Five linguistic terms were chosen according to Table 20.

Table 22. Evaluation of Alternative X for each Attribute in linguistic terms by experts

Attributes			A111	A112	A121	A122	A123	A124	A125	A131	A132	A133
Ex-perts	E1	X	R	R	G	R	VL	VL	L	M	G	G
	E2	X	VG	VG	G	R	VL	L	M	L	R	G
	E3	X	VG	VG	VG	R	L	L	L	M	VG	G
	E4	X	G	R	R	G	H	M	H	H	R	G
	E5	X	G	G	VG	G	M	M	M	M	G	G
	E6	X	R	G	R	G	L	L	L	L	R	R
	E7	X	VG	VG	G	VG	M	L	M	L	VG	G
	E8	X	G	P	G	G	L	L	M	M	E	E

Table 23. Evaluation of Alternative Y for each Attribute in linguistic terms by experts

Attributes			A111	A112	A121	A122	A123	A124	A125	A131	A132	A133
Ex-perts	E1	Y	VG	G	G	R	G	R	M	R	R	R
	E2	Y	VG	G	G	R	R	P	M	R	P	VG
	E3	Y	VG	VG	VG	VG	VG	VG	M	VG	VG	VG
	E4	Y	VG	VG	R	VG	VG	G	L	G	G	G
	E5	Y	VG	G	VG	VG	E	E	M	VG	G	G
	E6	Y	G	VG	VG	G	G	R	L	G	R	G
	E7	Y	G	G	VG	VG	G	G	L	VG	VG	G
	E8	Y	VG	G	E	E	VG	E	L	G	E	VG
Attributes			A134	A135	A136	A137	A141	A142	A143	A144	A151	A152
Ex-perts	E1	Y	R	R	G	R	VL	VL	L	M	G	G
	E2	Y	VG	VG	G	R	VL	L	M	L	R	G
	E3	Y	VG	VG	VG	R	L	L	L	M	VG	G
	E4	Y	G	R	R	G	H	M	H	H	R	G
	E5	Y	G	G	VG	G	M	M	M	M	G	G
	E6	Y	R	G	R	G	L	L	L	L	R	R
	E7	Y	VG	VG	G	VG	M	L	M	L	VG	G
	E8	Y	G	P	G	G	L	L	M	M	E	E

Step 5: The importance of each attribute was obtained via pairwise comparisons of AHP methodology.

Step 6: Experts subjective evaluations were made using the Ergonomic Compatibility Survey, see Maldonado et al. (2009) for further reading.

Phase 2:

Step 1: Convert the linguistic terms of the ratings assigned to each attribute. This step will be shown only in linguistic terms in Tables 21, 22, 23, and 24, their respective conversion was made according to the scales shown in Table 20.

Table 24. Evaluation of Alternative Z for each Attribute in linguistic terms by experts

	Attributes		A111	A112	A121	A122	A123	A124	A125	A131	A132	A133
Experts	E1	Z	VG	G	G	R	G	R	M	R	R	R
	E2	Z	VG	G	G	R	R	P	M	R	P	VG
	E3	Z	VG	VG	VG	VG	VG	VG	M	VG	VG	VG
	E4	Z	VG	VG	R	VG	VG	G	L	G	G	G
	E5	Z	VG	G	VG	VG	E	E	M	VG	G	G
	E6	Z	G	VG	VG	G	G	R	L	G	R	G
	E7	Z	G	G	VG	VG	G	G	L	VG	VG	G
	E8	Z	VG	G	E	E	VG	E	L	G	E	VG
	Attributes		A134	A135	A136	A137	A141	A142	A143	A144	A151	A152
Experts	E1	Z	R	R	G	R	VL	VL	L	M	G	G
	E2	Z	VG	VG	G	R	VL	L	M	L	R	G
	E3	Z	VG	VG	VG	R	L	L	L	M	VG	G
	E4	Z	G	R	R	G	H	M	H	H	R	G
	E5	Z	G	G	VG	G	M	M	M	M	G	G
	E6	Z	R	G	R	G	L	L	L	L	R	R
	E7	Z	VG	VG	G	VG	M	L	M	L	VG	G
	E8	Z	G	P	G	G	L	L	M	M	E	E

Step 2: AHP was used to obtain the importance of each attribute. The results are shown in Table 25.

Step 3: Determine Design Range for each attribute from experts' opinions and Corollary number 6 of Axiomatic Design Theory. In this case Corollary 6 of Axiomatic Design was used to establish the EFR's, with the widest range among expert opinions which were: EFR_{A111}: At least good, EFR_{A112}: At least good, EFR_{A121}: At least excellent, EFR_{A122}: At least regular, EFR_{A123}: At least good, EFR_{A124}: At least regular, EFR_{A125}: Low, EFR_{A131}: At least good, EFR_{A132}: At least good, EFR_{A133}: At least good, EFR_{A134}: At least good, EFR_{A135}: At least good, EFR_{A136}: At least very good, EFR_{A137}: At least very good, EFR_{A141}: Low, EFR_{A142}: Low, EFR_{A143}: Low, EFR_{A144}: Low, FR_{A151}: At least good, and EFR_{A152}: At least very good.

Step 4: Add the experts' opinions on the assigned rating of each attribute for each alternative obtaining the Ergonomic System Range (ESR). For example, for only one attribute A135 for Alternative X it is calculated as following:

Table 25. Decision Matrix for the Importance Weight of the Attributes by Experts obtained by AHP

	A11	A12	A13	A14	A15	A111	A112	A121	A122	A123	A124	A125	A131
w AHP	0.262	0.178	0.318	0.121	0.120	0.370	0.630	0.280	0.175	0.267	0.17	0.107	0.081
	A132	A133	A134	A135	A136	A137	A141	A142	A143	A144	A151	A152	
w AHP	0.110	0.123	0.246	0.201	0.148	0.090	0.158	0.244	0.332	0.266	0.415	0.585	

$$X_{A135_{11}} = \left(\frac{1}{8}\right)(0.2 + 0.6 + 0.6 + 0.2 + 0.4 + 0.4 + 0.6 + 0) = 0.38$$

$$X_{A135_{11}} = \left(\frac{1}{8}\right)(0.35 + 0.75 + 0.75 + 0.35 + 0.55 + 0.55 + 0.75 + 0) = 0.51$$

$$X_{A135_{11}} = \left(\frac{1}{8}\right)(0.5 + 0.9 + 0.9 + 0.5 + 0.7 + 0.7 + 0.9 + 0.3) = 0.68$$

So, aggregated System Range is:

$$X_{A135} = [0.38, 0.51, 0.68]$$

Complete ratings of alternatives become part of the Decision Matrix which is shown in Table 25.

Step 5: Construct decision matrices to the assigned weight importance, and Ergonomic System Range (ESR) ratings of each attribute for each alternative. The results are shown in Table 26.

Phase 3:

Definition of the Membership Functions for DR and SR using equations. As an example for attribute A135 in Alternative X is shown as an example as following

$$\mu(x) = \frac{0.614 - 0.40}{1 - 0.40} = 0.358$$

Phase 4:

Assess the EIC of each attribute for each alternative using the Information Axiom with weight. In order to obtain the EIC a sample calculation for only one attribute (A135 in Alternative X) is given as an example for attribute A135:

$$Common\ Area\ (CA) = [0.358 * (0.675 - 0.400] * \tfrac{1}{2}] = 0.049$$

$$ESR\ area = [(0.675 - 0.375) * \tfrac{1}{2}] = 0.0.15$$

and

$$EIC_{A135} = \log2(0.15 / 0.049) = 1.609$$

Phase 5:

This phase consists in obtaining the Total Ergonomic Incompatibility Content (TEIC) for each alternative, using Equation 3 at each level of the hierarchy. The alternative which has the minimum EIC is chosen as the best choice. Figure 4 shows the weights (*w*) next to each attribute's name and the Total Ergonomic Incompatibility Content for each attribute and each alternative.

Calculations of EIC using Equation 31 for each level of hierarchy will be shown only as an example for Alternative X:

Second level of hierarchy:

EIC$_{A11-X}$=(0.37 * 0.447 + 0.63 * 0.778) = 0.655

EIC$_{A13-X}$= (0.08 * 4.056 + 0.11 * 1.381 + 0.12 * 0.927 + 0.24 * 4.056 + 0.20 * 1.609 + 0.14 * 0.573 + 0.09 * 0.750) = 2.068

EIC$_{A14-X}$= (0.15 * 2.561 + 0.24 * 3.014 + 0.33 * 1.361 + 0.26 * 1.361) = 1.910

EIC$_{A15-X}$= (0.41 * 1.116 + 0.58 * 0.498) = 0.746

First level of hierarchy:

TEIC$_{X}$ = (0.262 * 0.655 + 0.178 * 0.606 + 0.318 * 2.068 + 0.121 * 1.910 + 0.120 * 0.746) = 1.282

According to previous diagram of Figure 4, with the proposed methodology the minimum EIC value is 1.064 and it belongs to Alternative Z. Hence, this is the best alternative for our goal. The hierarchical structure of the presented

Table 26. Fuzzy Decision Matrix for the Ergonomic System Range and attribute's weight for Alternatives

Alternative	A111	A112	A121	A122	A123
X	(0.55, 0.70, 0.85)	(0.48, 0.63, 0.78)	(0.53, 0.68, 0.81)	(0.5, 0.66, 0.79)	(0.5, 0.66, 0.79)
Y	(0.48, 0.63, 0.78)	(0.23, 0.34, 0.53)	(0.53, 0.68, 0.81)	(0.5, 0.66, 0.79)	(0.4, 0.63, 0.76)
Z	(0.33, 0.46, 0.63)	(0.45, 0.59, 0.74)	(0.55, 0.69, 0.83)	(0.4, 0.56, 0.71)	(0.4, 0.56, 0.71)
w AHP	0.370	0.630	0.280	0.175	0.267

Alternative	A124	A125	A131	A132	A133
X	(0.43, 0.57, 0.7)	(0.15, 0.38, 0.6)	(0.43, 0.58, 0.73)	(0.4, 0.54, 0.69)	(0.45, 0.6, 0.75)
Y	(0.43, 0.57, 0.7)	(0.15, 0.38, 0.6)	(0.40, 0.55, 0.70)	(0.38, 0.51, 0.66)	(0.45, 0.61, 0.74)
Z	(0.37, 0.50, 0.67)	(0.04, 0.28, 0.53)	(0.28, 0.41, 0.56)	(0.43, 0.56, 0.71)	(0.50, 0.64, 0.78)
w AHP	0.170	0.107	0.081	0.110	0.123

Alternative	A134	A135	A136	A137	A141
X	(0.43, 0.58, 0.73)	(0.38, 0.51, 0.68)	(0.40, 0.55, 0.7)	(0.35, 0.5, 0.65)	(0.14, 0.31, 0.56)
Y	(0.35, 0.5, 0.65)	(0.38, 0.51, 0.68)	(0.38, 0.53, 0.68)	(0.38, 0.53, 0.68)	(0.14, 0.31, 0.56)
Z	(0.53, 0.69, 0.8)	(0.53, 0.67, 0.8)	(0.45, 0.6, 0.75)	(0.48, 0.61, 0.78)	(0.11, 0.25, 0.5)
w AHP	*0.246*	*0.201*	*0.148*	*0.090*	*0.158*

Alternative	A142	A143	A144	A151	A152
X	(0.08, 0.28, 0.53)	(0.21, 0.44, 0.66)	(0.21, 0.44, 0.66)	(0.43, 0.58, 0.71)	(0.43, 0.58, 0.71)
Y	(0.11, 0.31, 0.55)	(0.25, 0.47, 0.69)	(0.21, 0.44, 0.66)	(0.43, 0.58, 0.71)	(0.4, 0.56, 0.69)
Z	(0.18, 0.38, 0.61)	(0.19, 0.41, 0.63)	(0.18, 0.38, 0.61)	(0.48, 0.63, 0.76)	(0.53, 0.68, 0.81)
w AHP	*0.244*	*0.332*	*0.266*	*0.415*	*0.585*

Figure 4. Ergonomic incompatibility content diagram

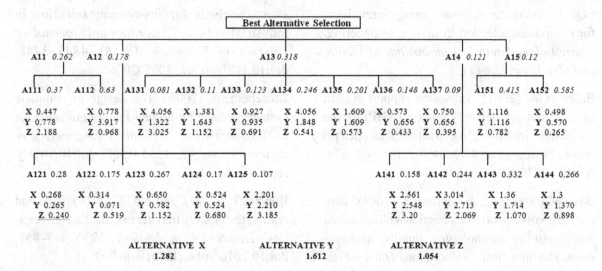

ALTERNATIVE X
1.282

ALTERNATIVE Y
1.612

ALTERNATIVE Z
1.054

problem helps the assessment of the attributes and alternatives.

CONCLUSION

Advanced Manufacturing Technologies are widely used currently in the industry, however, the selection process and its investments justification is a complex problem. Many techniques for evaluation have been proposed, which are differentiated in their focus and the type of attributes being integrated. Currently the most used techniques are those that allow the integration of various AMT´s attributes or characteristics in the evaluation processes and usually are called multiattribute.

In this chapter appears three techniques traditionally used in the processes of AMT selection and always have proposed the same alternative as solution to the problem choice. Also a new approach was described. However, these techniques have been harshly criticized and that is due the subjective assessments of expertise in evaluation process, then it is possible that in the same selection problem, to be evaluated with different techniques, different solutions can be proposed. Additionally, fuzzy techniques are quite imprecise.

As users of multiattribute techniques, all the comments and criticism are well accepted. However, these techniques allow DM to integrate certain attributes in the assessment; some of them have been neglected or obviated in many other methods. This can be the case of the Ergonomics, Human Factors and Safety ones.

Our own conclusion is that in response to the need for investment in advanced manufacturing technology aiming to be competitive in globalized environments, the best thing to do is to make evaluations by several techniques, to integrate all the possible attributes in the analysis and that the decision process of investment must be taken by a group decision, which will allow shared responsibility and commitment to ensure the success of investment.

REFERENCES

Abdel-Kader, M. G., & Dugdale, D. (1998). Investment in advanced manufacturing technology: a study of practice in large U.K. companies. *Management Accounting Research, 9*(3), 261–284. doi:10.1006/mare.1998.0071

Bascetin, A., Öztaª, A., & KanLý, A. (2006). EQS: A computer software using fuzzy logic for equipment selection in mining engineering. *Journal of the South African Institute of Mining and Metallurgy, 106*(1).

Bascetin, A. (2007). A decision support system using analytical hierarchy process (AHP) for the optimal environmental reclamation of an open pit mine. *Environmental Geology, 52*(4), 663–672. doi:10.1007/s00254-006-0495-7

Bayo-Moriones, A., & Merino, J. (2004). Employee involvement: Its interaction with advanced manufacturing technologies, quality, management, and inter-firm collaboration. *Human Factors and Ergonomics in Manufacturing, 14*(2), 117–134. doi:10.1002/hfm.10057

Bessant, J., & Haywood, B. (1989). Islands, archipelagoes and continents: progress along the road to CIM. *Research Policy, 17*, 349–362. doi:10.1016/0048-7333(88)90033-9

Beynon, M. J. (2005). A method of aggregation in DS/AHP for group decision-making with the non-equivalent importance of individuals in the group. *Computers & Operations Research, 32*(7), 1881–1896. doi:10.1016/j.cor.2003.12.004

Boyer, K. K., & Pagell, M. (2000). Measurement issues in empirical research: improving measures of operations strategy and advanced manufacturing technology. *Journal of Operations Management, 18*, 361–374. doi:10.1016/S0272-6963(99)00029-7

Bozdağ, C. E., Kahraman, C., & Ruan, D. (2000). Fuzzy group decision making for selection among computer integrated manufacturing systems. *Computers in Industry, 51*(1), 13–29. doi:10.1016/S0166-3615(03)00029-0

Braglia, M., & Gabbrielli, R. (2000). Dimensional analysis for investment selection in industrial robots. *International Journal of Production Research, 38*(18), 4843–3448. doi:10.1080/00207540050205668

Bruseberg, A. (2006). The design of complete systems: Providing human factors guidance for COTS acquisition. *Reliability Engineering & System Safety, 91*, 1554–1565. doi:10.1016/j.ress.2006.01.016

Bubela, T. M., & Caulfield, T. (2010). Role and reality: technology transfer at Canadian universities. *Trends in Biotechnology, 28*(9), 447–451. doi:10.1016/j.tibtech.2010.06.002

Buckingham, E. (1941). On physically similar systems: illustration of the use of dimensional equations. *The Physician Review, 4*, 345–376. doi:10.1103/PhysRev.4.345

Chen, S. J., & Hwang, C. L. (Eds.). (1999). *Fuzzy multiple attribute decision making methods and applications*. New York, NY: Springer.

Chiadamrong, N., & O'Brien, C. (1999). Decision support tool for justifying alternative manufacturing and production control systems. *International Journal of Production Economics, 60-61*, 177–186. doi:10.1016/S0925-5273(98)00182-0

Choudhury, A. K., Shankar, R., & Tiwari, M. K. (2006). Consensus-based intelligent group decision-making model for the selection of advanced technology. *Decision Support Systems, 42*(3), 1776–1799. doi:10.1016/j.dss.2005.05.001

Cil, I. (2004). Internet-based CDSS for modern manufacturing processes selection and justification. *Robotics and Computer-integrated Manufacturing, 20*(3), 177–190. doi:10.1016/j.rcim.2003.08.004

Corbett, J. M. (1988). Ergonomics in the development of human-centered AMT. *Applied Ergonomics, 19*(1), 35–39. doi:10.1016/0003-6870(88)90196-2

Corlett, E. N., & Clark, T. S. (1995). *The ergonomics of workspaces and machines* (2nd ed.). Boca Raton, FL: Taylor and Francis.

Dean, J., & Snell, S. (1991). Integrated manufacturing and job design: Moderating effects of organisational inertia. *Academy of Management Journal, 34*(4), 776–804. doi:10.2307/256389

Endsley, M. R. (1993). The integration of human and advanced manufacturing systems. *Journal of Design and Manufacturing, 3*, 177–187.

Erensal, Y. C., & Albayrak, E. (2004). Successful adoption of macroergonomics in manufacturing: Using a multicriteria decision- making methodology-analytic hierarchy process. *Human Factors and Ergonomics in Manufacturing, 14*(4), 353–377. doi:10.1002/hfm.20005

Ettlie, J. E. (1997). Integrated design and new product success. *Journal of Operations Management, 5*(1), 33–55. doi:10.1016/S0272-6963(96)00095-2

Gao, J., Gindy, N., & Chen, X. (2006). An automated GD&T inspection system based on non-contact 3D digitization. *International Journal of Production Research, 44*(1), 117–134. doi:10.1080/09638280500219737

Goh, C., Chin, Y., Tung, A., & Chen, C. (1996). A revised weighted sum decision model for robot selection. *Computers & Industrial Engineering, 30*(2), 193–199. doi:10.1016/0360-8352(95)00167-0

Gunasekaran, A., Love, P. E. D., Rahimi, F., & Miele, R. (2001). A model for investment justification in information technology projects. *International Journal of Information Management, 21*, 349–364. doi:10.1016/S0268-4012(01)00024-X

Gyan-Baffour, G. (1994). Advanced manufacturing technology, employee participation and economic performance: An empirical analysis. *Journal of Managerial Issues, 6*(4), 491–505.

Hart, S., Jan, H. E., Tzokas, N., & Commandeur, H. R. (2003). Industrial companies evaluation criteria in new product development gates. *Journal of Product Innovation Management, 20*(1), 22–36. doi:10.1111/1540-5885.201003

Helander, M. (1995). Conceptualizing the use of axiomatic design procedures in ergonomics. In *Proceeding of the IEA World Conference*, Rio de Janeiro, Brazil (pp. 38-41).

Holmes, J. S. Jr. (2009). Societal and economic valuation of technology-transfer deals. *Acta Astronautica, 65*(5), 834–840. doi:10.1016/j.actaastro.2009.01.070

Kahraman, C., & Çebı, S. (2008). A new multi-attribute decision making method: Hierarchical fuzzy axiomatic design. *Expert Systems with Applications, 36*(3).

Kahraman, C., & Kulak, O. (2005). *Fuzzy multi-attribute decision making using an information axiom based approach (fuzzy multi-criteria with recent developments.* New York, NY: Springer.

Kakati, M. (1997). Strategic evaluation of advanced manufacturing technology. *International Journal of Economics, 53*(2), 141–156.

Karwowski, W. (2005). Ergonomics and human factors: the paradigms for science, engineering, design, technology and management of human-compatible systems. *Ergonomics, 48*(5), 436–463. doi:10.1080/00140130400029167

Karwowski, W. (2006). On measure of the human-system compatibility. *Theoretical Issues in Ergonomics Science*, 12.

Kesseler, E., & Knapen, E. G. (2006). Towards human-centre design: Two case studies. *Journal of Systems and Software, 79*(3). doi:10.1016/j.jss.2005.05.012

Khouja, M. (1998). An aggregate production planning framework for the evaluation of volume and flexibility. *Production Planning and Control, 9*(2), 127–137. doi:10.1080/095372898234343

Kodali, R., & Sangwan, K. S. (2004). Multi-attribute decision models for justification of cellular manufacturing systems. *International Journal of Business Performance Management, 6*(3-4), 1–10.

Kulak, O. (2005). Fuzzy multi-attribute equipment section based on information axiom. *Journal of Materials Processing Technology, 169*(3), 337–345. doi:10.1016/j.jmatprotec.2005.03.030

Kulak, O., & Kahraman, C. (2005a). Multi-attribute comparison of advanced manufacturing systems using fuzzy vs. crisp axiomatic design approach. *International Journal of Production Economics, 95*, 415–424. doi:10.1016/j.ijpe.2004.02.009

Kulak, O., & Kahraman, C. (2005b). Fuzzy multi-attribute selection among transportation companies using axiomatic design and analytic hierarchy process. *Information Sciences, 170*, 191–210. doi:10.1016/j.ins.2004.02.021

Lu, J., Zhang, G., & Ruan, D. (2007). *Multi-objective group decision making: Methods software and applications with fuzzy set techniques.* Singapore: Imperial College Press. Retrieved from http://site.ebrary.com/lib/uacj/Doc?id=10188771&ppg=206

Maldonado-Macías, A. (2010). *An ergonomic evaluation model for planning an selection of advanced manufacturing technology* (Unpublished doctoral dissertation). Technological Institute of Juárez, Juárez, Mexico.

Maldonado-Macías, A., Noriega, S., Díaz, J., Sánchez, J., García, J., & De la Riva, J. (2009). Fuzzy axiomatic design approach for the evaluation of ergonomic compatibility of CNC machines: A case of study. In *Proceedings of the 14th Annual International Conference of Industrial Engineering, Theory, Applications and Practice*, Anaheim CA (pp. 182-188).

Maldonado-Macías, A., Sánchez, J., Noriega, S., Díaz, J. J., García, J. L., & Vidal, L. (2009). A hierarchical fuzzy axiomatic design survey for ergonomic compatibility evaluation of advanced manufacturing technology. In *Proceedings of the 21st Annual International Conference of Occupational Safety and Ergonomics, International Society for Occupational Ergonomics and Safety* (pp. 270-277).

Meredith, J. R., & Suresh, N. C. (1986). Justification techniques for advanced manufacturing technologies. *International Journal of Production Research, 24*(5), 1043–1057. doi:10.1080/00207548608919787

Mital, A., & Arunkumar, P. (2004). Advanced technologies and humans in manufacturing workplaces: an interdependent relationship. *International Journal of Industrial Ergonomics, 33*, 295–313. doi:10.1016/j.ergon.2003.10.002

Parkan, C., & Wu, M. L. (1999). Decision-making and performance measurement models with applications to robot selection. *Computers & Industrial Engineering, 36*(3), 503–523. doi:10.1016/S0360-8352(99)00146-1

Raafat, F. (2002). A comprehensive bibliography on justification of advanced manufacturing systems. *International Journal of Production Economics, 79*(3), 197–208. doi:10.1016/S0925-5273(02)00233-5

Rao, K. V. S., & Deshmukh, S. G. (1997). A decision support system for selection and justification of advanced manufacturing technology. *Production Planning and Control, 8*(3), 270–284. doi:10.1080/095372897235325

Säften, K., Winroth, M., & Stahre, J. (2007). The content and process of automation strategies. *International Journal of Production Economics, 110*(1-2), 25–38. doi:10.1016/j.ijpe.2007.02.027

Saraph, J. V., & Sebastian, R. J. (1992). Human resource strategies for effective introduction of advanced manufacturing practices (AMT). *Production and Inventory Management Journal, 33*(1), 64–70.

Siemieniuch, C. E., & Sinclair, M. A. (1995). Information technology and global developments in manufacturing: The implications for human factors input. *International Journal of Industrial Ergonomics, 16*, 245–262. doi:10.1016/0169-8141(95)00011-5

Slowinski, R. (1998). *Fuzzy sets in decision analysis, operation research and statistics.* Boston, MA: Kluwer Academic.

Small, M. H., & Chen, I. J. (1997). Economic and strategic justification of AMT Inferences from industrial practices. *International Journal of Production Economics, 49*(1), 65–75. doi:10.1016/S0925-5273(96)00120-X

Small, M. H., & Yasin, M. (1997). Advanced manufacturing technology: Implementation policy and performance. *Journal of Operations Management, 15*(4), 349–370. doi:10.1016/S0272-6963(97)00013-2

Suh, N. P. (1990). *The principles of design.* New York, NY: Oxford University Press.

Suh, N. P. (2001). *Axiomatic design: Advances and applications.* New York, NY: Oxford University Press.

Suresh, N. C., & Meredith, J. R. (1985). Achieving factory automation through group technology principles. *Journal of Operations Management, 5*(2), 151–167. doi:10.1016/0272-6963(85)90004-X

Talluri, S., & Yoon, K. P. (2000). A cone-ratio DEA approach for AMT justification. *International Journal of Production Economics, 66*(2), 119–129. doi:10.1016/S0925-5273(99)00123-1

Vicente, K. (1999). *Cognitive work analysis, towards safe, productive and healthy computer-based work.* Mahwah, NJ: Lawrence Erlbaum.

Yoon, K. (1980). *Systems selection by multiple attribute decision making* (Unpublished doctoral dissertation). Kansas State University, Manhattan, KS.

Yusuff, R. M. (2004). Manufacturing best practices of the electric and electronic firms in Malaysia. *Benchmarking: An International Journal, 11*(4), 361–369. doi:10.1108/14635770410546764

Zadeh, L. A. (1965). Fuzzy sets. *Information and Control, 8*, 338–353. doi:10.1016/S0019-9958(65)90241-X

Zammuto, R. F., & O'Connor, E. J. (1992). Gaining advanced manufacturing technology's benefits: The roles of organization design and culture. *Academy of Management Review, 17*, 701–728.

ADDITIONAL READING

Balderrama, C., Maldonado-Macías, A., & Pedrozo, J. (2010). Diseño Axiomático como un Modelo para la toma de Decisiones. In *Congreso Internacional de Investigación, Academiajournals*, Juárez, Mexico (pp. 31-37).

Cebi, S., & Kahraman, C. (2010). Extension of axiomatic design principles under fuzzy environment. *Expert Systems with Applications, 37*(3), 2682–2689. doi:10.1016/j.eswa.2009.08.010

Karwowski, W. (205). Ergonomics and human factors: The paradigms of science, engineering, design, technology, and management of human-compatible systems. *Ergonomics*, *48*(5), 436–463. doi:10.1080/00140130400029167

Maldonado-Macías, A., De de la Riva, J., Noriega, S., & Díaz, J. (2008). Aplicaciones del Axioma de Información en procesos de Evaluación y Selección de Equipamiento e Instalaciones. In *Memorias del 1er. Congreso Internacional de Investigación, CIPITECH.*

Maldonado-Macías, A., Sánchez, J., Noriega, S., Díaz, J., De la Riva, J., & Ramírez, M. (2009). Evaluación de la Compatibilidad Ergonómica para la Selección de Tecnología de Manufactura Avanzada Utilizando Diseño Axiomático y Lógica Difusa. In *Memorias del 2°. Congreso Internacional de Investigación, CIPITECH.*

Suh, N. P. (2007). Ergonomics, axiomatic design and complexity theory. *Theoretical Issues in Ergonomics Science*, *8*(2), 101–121. doi:10.1080/14639220601092509

KEY TERMS AND DEFINITIONS

Advanced Manufacturing Technology AMT: Includes usually computer-based technologies such as computer-controlled numerical-control machines (CNC), automatic guided vehicle systems, or computer-aided design (CAD/CAM), also are included robotics, rapid prototyping and environmentally sustainable technologies that have become an integral part of manufacturing.

Axiom: Self-evident truth or fundamental truth for which there are no counterexamples or exceptions.

Axiomatic Design: Theory that provides a scientific basis for design of engineered systems.

Common Range Area: The overlap between the design range and the system range, this is the only region where the Functional Requirement is satisfied. It represents the design´s probability of achieving the specified goal.

Design Range: In Axiomatic Design Theory represents what designers or experts wishes to achieve in terms of tolerance from a product or system.

Ergonomic Compatibility (EC): A construct used in this work that intends to measure in a subjective way, the probability of a design to satisfy ergonomic requirements using the ergonomic incompatibility content.

Ergonomic Incompatibility Content (EIC): An extension and adaptation in a fuzzy environment of the Information Axiom that helps measure the probability of a design to satisfy Ergonomic Functional Requirements.

Functional Requirements: Are a minimum set of independent requirements that completely characterize the functional needs of the product in the Functional Domain.

Multiattribute Decision Making Methods: Are management decision aids used in evaluation competing alternatives defined by multiple attributes.

System Range: In Axiomatic Design Theory represents what the product or system is capable of delivering.

Chapter 17
Optical Application improved with Logistics of Artificial Intelligent and Electronic Systems

Miguel Basurto-Pensado
Research Center for Engineering and Applied Sciences, Mexico

Jesús Escobedo-Alatorre
Research Center for Engineering and Applied Sciences, Mexico

Carlos Alberto Ochoa Ortiz Zezzatti
Juarez City University, Mexico

Jessica Morales-Valladares
Research Center for Engineering and Applied Sciences, Mexico

Rosenberg Romero
Research Center for Engineering and Applied Sciences, Mexico

Arturo García-Arias
Research Center for Engineering and Applied Sciences, Mexico

Margarita Tecpoyotl Torres
UAEM, Mexico

ABSTRACT

Computer science and electronics have a very big incidence in several research areas; optics and photonics are not the exception. The utilization of computers, electronic systems, and devices has allowed the authors to develop several projects to control processes. A description of the computer tool called Laser Micro-Lithography (LML) to characterize materials is realized. The Reasoning Based on Cases (RBC) and its implementation in the software using Java are presented. In order to guarantee the lithography precision, a control system based on a microcontroller was developed and coupled to the mechanical system. An alternative of LML, considering the use of a Personal Digital Assistant (PDA), instead of a Personal Computer (PC) is described. In this case, C language is used for programming. RBC optimizes the materials characterization, recovering information of materials previously characterized. The communication between the PDA and the displacement table is achieved by means of a system based on a micro-controller DSPIC. The developed computers tool permits obtaining lithography with channels

DOI: 10.4018/978-1-4666-0297-7.ch017

narrower than an optical fiber with minimum equipment. The development of irradiance meters based on electronic automation is shown; this section includes the basic theoretical concepts, the experimental device design and the experimental results. Future research trends are presented, and as a consequence of the developed work, perspectives of micro drilling and cutting are also analyzed.

OTHER APPLICATIONS OF ELECTRONICS SYSTEMS: IRRADIANCE METERS

The light detection constitutes a wide field of analysis in optics. As we know, the light can be detected by the eye, but it has several disadvantages, compared with electronic devices designed to this purpose, such as a very slow response, a not adequate sensitivity to low-level signals, and it is not easy connected to electronic receiver for amplification, or other signal processing (Palais, 1984). The selection of the appropriate detector is very important in the irradiance meter design. It must be considered the costs, spectral responsivity, noise levels, and the type of meter where it will be inserted.

On the other hand, the type of meter can be determined in accordance to the objective that could be the determination of the total irradiance or the distribution produced by an illumination source. For the first case it is well known the Ulbrich Sphere, is generally used to determine the lamps performance and the energy emitted in visible, infrared, and ultraviolet radiation. For the second case, different types of meters have been developed in order to provide an empirical base of information for specific characteristics, such as: photometer and portable intensity light meters. The use of electronics and programming tools has been determinant in the development of these devices. For example, some of the portable meters use microprocessors to increase the accuracy and to give them special characteristics. Other ones are equipped with memory or datalogger for the data recording. In both cases, the addition of these characteristics represents a considerable increase in the cost.

Basic Concepts

A high interest in illumination intensity measurement has been shown in several fields, for example in architecture design and public illumination (Westinhouse, 2000), where the selection of the appropriate sources is fundamental and constitutes one of the biggest reasons for the realized studies. Another area of interest is generated by the necessity of manufactures of illumination sources to provide complete information for users, making necessary the characterization of the irradiance profiles. In research activities, the interest in the energy propagation produced by an illumination source has lead to widest studies in the total irradiance and the corresponding distribution.

The power of optic beam is proportional to the light intensity (defined as the square of the electric field). Intensity is proportional to *irradiance*, the power density; its units are watts per square meter.

Semi-Spherical Irradiance Meter

Among the current projects on this area, at first, this group has developed a semi-spherical irradiance meter prototype (Roman et al., 2006), Figures 1 and 2, based on Light Emitting Diodes (LEDs) detectors array, distributed in order to produce an uniform covered area (Figure 3).

The selection of the optical detector was realized in this case considering basically the costs, because its number in the static array is considerably big.

The optic power generated by a LED is linearly proportional to the forward driving current (Palais, 1984). The linear relationship can be understood by the following argument: The current I is the injected charge per second is then $N=i/e$, where e

Figure 1. Complete irradiance meter, based on a detectors array

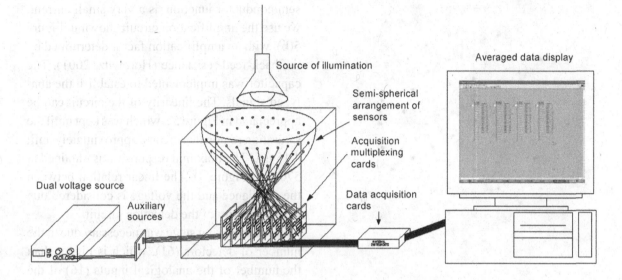

Figure 2. Photograph

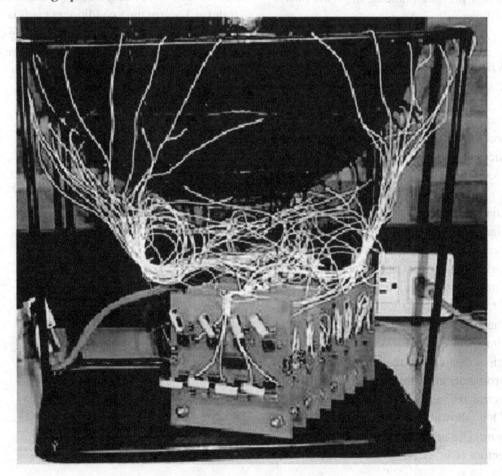

Figure 3. Detectors distribution

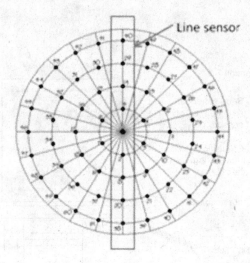

is the magnitude of the charge on each electron. If η is the fraction of these charges that will recombine and produce photons, the optic power output will be:

$$P = \eta N W_g = \frac{\eta W_g}{e} i \qquad (1)$$

For emission, the diode is forward biased, and charges injected into the junction recombine to produce photons. For detection, the process is reversed: the inversed biased and incoming photons generate electron-hole pairs, producing electrical current.

The largest response proving LEDs of different colors, as detectors was given by an amber LED used as detector, so, it was chosen to form part of the semi-spherical arrangement, in order to analyze white illumination sources profiles.

As the LEDs are commonly acquired without a data sheet, it is necessary to characterize them, this action can be realized by means of a monochromator, in this case, the ACTON 300. The spectral responsivity of this detector (E5/AMB-C) is shown in Figure 4, from 350 up to 900 nm. The setup designed to characterize the detectors (LEDs) is shown in Figures 5(a)

and 5(b). As the response to illumination on a semiconductor junction, is a very small current, we use the amplification circuit shown in Figure 5(b), with an amplification factor determined by the back-feed resistance (Horowitz, 2001). The capacitor was implemented to establish the analyzed signals. The linearity of the circuit can be appreciated in Figure 5c, which was kept until the saturation region that means, approximately until 4.15 μA. The maximal response was obtained at 570 nm (Figure 4). The linear relation between the irradiance and the voltage is considered due to the linearity of the detection circuit.

A multiplexing stage was necessary due to the number of detectors (61), which is bigger than the number of the analogical inputs (16) of the used acquisition card (PCI-MIO-16E-1 de National Instruments). The data collection rate was of 1.25/16 MS/s, using a dual (74HC4052) multiplexer. Each of the 8 conditioner cards is formed by the amplification and the multiplexing circuits (Figure 5). The 8 conditioner cards were placed on the meter base (Figures 1 and 2).

Figure 4. Spectral responsivity of LED E5/AMB-C

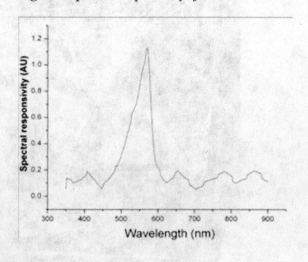

Data Visualization

The flowchart shown in Figures 6 and 7 were used in the development of the collection and average data program. The data collection is realized by the acquisition data card and displayed using a program realized in LABVIEW, the data are storage, and this process is repeated 4 times, completed this cycle all is repeated again. When 100 data are collected in each detector, the corresponding average is calculated, which forms part of the useful data. After, the process is repeated again, and the new averaged data replace to the previous ones, this process continues until the user gives a stop.

The irradiance profiles, generated with this semi-spherical prototype, were presented using bubbles schemes. An X-lamp LED (Figure 8) of warm white light, with an emission diameter of 1.9 cm, was tested. Its irradiance profile and irradiance pattern are shown Figures 9 and 10, respectively. This meter can be used as a quality control device for illumination sources such as lamps and bulbs. In the obtained discrete profiles, the following fact was considered: according to the Pointing vector physics, the irradiance is proportional to the voltage intensity detected in each sensor of the meter. These voltage values permit to obtain the corresponding profile of each source and give the capability to choice of more adequate sources for specifics tasks.

Some disadvantages of this static meter are given by the use of the detectors array produce, which produces a not uniform response also at the same co-latitude angle, as can be appreciated in Figures 6 and 7, especially in the last two external trajectories of detectors. These differences in the spectral response were produced basically for the fabrication processes. As it is known, even in LEDs from the same manufacturing batch, a difference in response exists, although it could be minimal. This fact produces errors in the determination of the irradiance profile from 12% up to 90% in critical cases. The error could be reduced

being more careful with the sensor selection, and replacing them when it is necessary, but always it would be present due to their inherent differences. This fact shows the importance of the individual characterization before the selection final elements of the array. The alignment of the illumination source is another important source of error that can be appreciated in the corresponding data fitting using Zernike polynomials (Sanchez et al., 2003).

The irradiance pattern (Figure 8) generated considering the line sensors shown in Figure 3 has another inconvenient, the appearance of a piece linear graph produced by the small number of sensors (only 9), and the variations in symmetry produced by their differences in the spectral responsivity. In order to reduce these inconvenient, the use of a single detector is suggested, coupled to a mobile mechanical structure. Although the XY table is very expensive, its availability in several optical labs permits to think in them as a very practical solution, after a certain adaptation, and considering its precision. The automation of the movements could be realized, using step motors or servomotors, without an excessive inversion. The use of recyclable convenient surfaces are recommended. In this case, the use of a CD ROM platform is analyzed.

IRRADIANCE METERS FOR CONVERGENT SOURCES: OTHER APPLICATION OF THE XY TABLE AUTOMATION

Manufacturers employ photometric curves for electric lamps, referring them at 1000 lumens, when their emitted fluxes are different of this quantity a normalization is used. These curves are obtained as a section of 3D intensity distribution, for all the solid angles, generally are indicated in polar coordinates, but for specific applications are also provided in Cartesian coordinates, such as in the case of projectors. The attention in this section

Figure 5. Linear response of I-V converter circuit

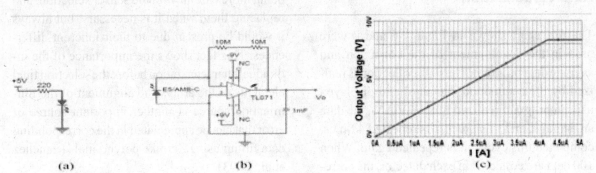

(a)   (b)   (c)

Figure 6. Signal conditioner circuit

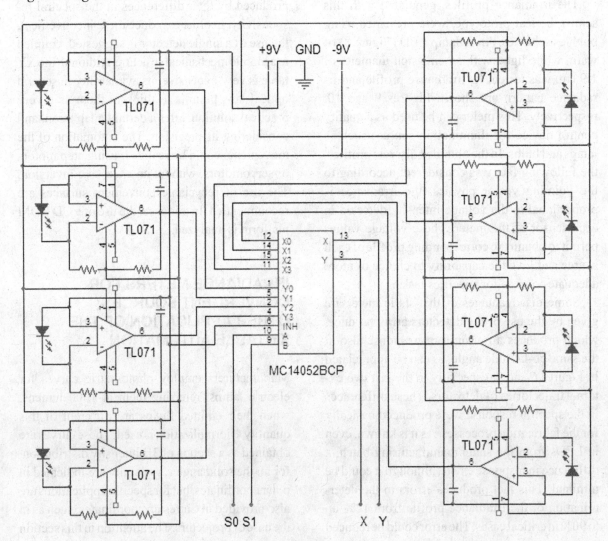

Figure 7. Flowchart of the developed program

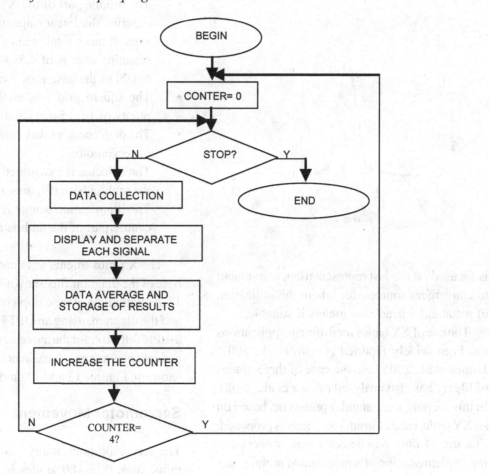

Figure 8. Photograph of X-lamp LED

Figure 9. Irradiance profile of the X-lamp LED

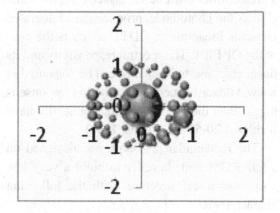

Figure 10. Irradiance pattern of the X-lamp LED

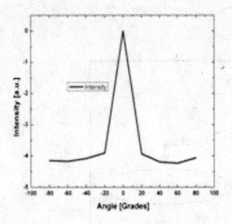

is focused on the last representation, convenient to convergent sources, for whom the utilization of rectangular irradiance meters is suitable.

The use of XY tables for different applications has been widely reported (Gwirc et al., 2007; Jaimes et al., 2005) and the case of three grades of liberty has also analyzed (Yañez et al., 2008). In this section, a rectangular prototype, based on an XY table, used as irradiance meter is proposed. The use of only one detector makes necessary the implementation of a mechanical mobile support. The implemented detector is a photodiode OPT301. The semiconductor photodiodes have some advantages, above the LEDs used as detectors that must be mentioned: they are small, light, sensitive, fasts, and can operate with just few bias volts. In order to increase the response, a preamplifier must be integrated onto the same chip as the photodiode, producing an Integrated Detector Preamplifier (IDT), which is the case of the OPT301. The spectral responsivity and its linear response to irradiance can be consulted in www.Alldatasheet.com. Clearly this response is bigger than the LED one, which generally have widths of 20-50 nm (Palais, 1984).

The rectangular prototype was designed on a CD ROM unit, in order to build a very low cost mechanical structure, with the following characteristics:

- The mobile part of the XY table is used to describe the linear trajectories on X and Y axes. It has a total area of 19x14 cm^2. The scanning area is of 4.5x3.5 cm^2. The total height of the base is of 7 cm.
- The square grid was established for simplicity of 14x15 detection points.
- The displacement was controlled by means of servomotors.
- The detector is assembled at one corner of the mobile base (Figures 11 and 12).
- The illumination source is located over the central part of the mobile area.

The XY movements were programmed on the base of the diagram flux shown in Figures 11 and 12. A photograph of the complete detection circuit and the diagram, using an OPT301M as detector, a dsPIC30F4011 for the movements programming and a display as a graphical interface to the user are shown in Figures 13 and 14, and 15 respectively.

Servomotor Movement

The servomotors normally have a capability to move from 0 to 180 grades in accordance to a signal control (Figure 16). The control program is based on the generation of a very precise rectangular signal, with a period of 200 ms, the width of the pulse is modified depending of the desired position of the rotor, if a position of 90 degrees is required, the sent pulse must be of 1.5 ms. In this application, for the control pulse generation, two timers of 16 bits were implemented, one for the period and the other one for the pulse duration (Figure 17).

They were also implemented interruptions (Figure 18), which permit to each timer "to notify" to the CPU when each temporization finishes. The control signals for the two motors of the system XY are implemented at the pines 3 and 1 of the D port, respectively.

Figure 11. Meter diagram

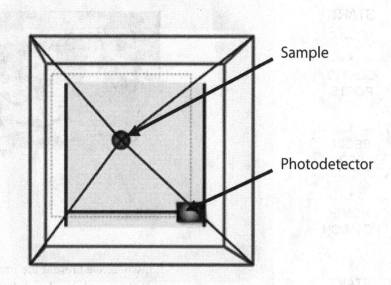

Sample

Photodetector

Communication System between the Mecatronic System and the Computer

The serial port US-232 is used to transfer all data read by the optical sensor in each swept point of the table (x, y coordinate) to the computer. A program developed in C, and compiled in the compiler for C of Microchip for family DSPIC30F was implemented.

The obtained data are storage in a txt file in the PC, and after, the corresponding graphs are generated using suitable software, as ORIGIN.

EXPERIMENTAL RESULTS

The photodetector was biased with 13V, and without a source of illumination, a lecture of 0.606 V was registered. Three luminaries were analyzed with this meter (Figure 19), a dirigible X-lamp LED IL51, a lamp conformed by an array of three LEDs IL1 LED3; and a single ultra bright white LED. The distance between the X-lamp LED and

the photodetector was fixed at 13 cm, and due to the different sizes of the lamp with three LEDs, the distance was reduced at 10 cm. In the case of the single white LED, the distance was of 17 cm.

As can be appreciated in Figures 20, 21, and 22, the illuminated area produced by a dirigible X-lamp is almost regular, showing a deviation of only 0.25 units considering a radius of 4.35 distance units. These deviations can be attributed basically to the differences in the gear teeth

Figure 12. Meter photograph

Figure 13. Flow diagram

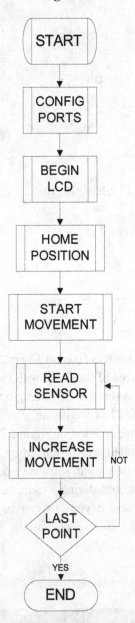

Figure 14. Photograph of the rectangular meter composed by a XY table and the detectoction circuit

25, where we present the irradiance pattern generated by a spherical mobile prototype developed also by our research group, using the same detector and the same detection circuit. In the last case, the beamwidth is easily determined, and complements the information about the source under test.

The use of high brightness LEDs in lamps improves several fields of interest in illumination, such as energy-saving, uniform covering and longer lifetime. The level of directivity of lamps based on LED technology has been modified with the use of special metallic covers, as in the case of the dirigible X-lamp LED IL51. For other applications, such as for decorative exterior in gardens, or for paths illumination, lamps like the IL/1 L3 can be used. Its corresponding radiance profile is given in Figure 26. As can be observed, it provides a wider illumination angle than the dirigible X-lamp, covering almost uniformly to the total scanning area. In Figure 27, the irradiance pattern obtained with the same spherical prototype of Figure 24 is presented. In both cases, the flat surface on the illuminated area is evident.

Finally, a single ultra bright white LED was tested with the prototype. The corresponding irradiance profile is shown in Figure 28. This LED showed problems of stability that means variability in the voltage measurements, and a little

driven by each servomotor. The high directivity of this illumination source permits to suggest its use in architecture and landscape lighting, for visual inspection, among other possible applications. The level of analysis achieved with this prototype permits us to observe very little details, which are very difficult to observe with other devices, as the case shown in Figures 23, 24, and

Figure 15. Schematic of the detection circuit

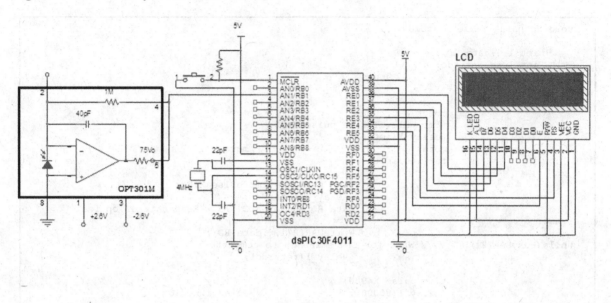

Figure 16. Relationship among the control signal and the movement of the servomotor

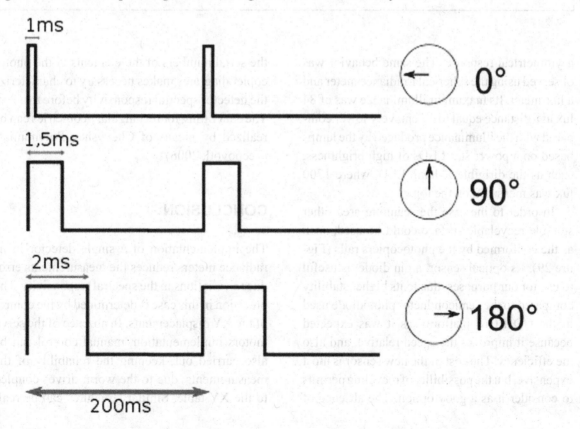

Figure 17. Main program of scanning, reading and sending data to PC

```
void Scanning_table_xy(void)
{
     int i,j,data_RD,;
     int long retardo;
     delay=10000;              //useg
     for(i=0;j<30;j++)
             {
                  motor_X=0;                        //move Y
                  time_pulse_Y=time_pulse_Y+50;
                  _delay_l(retardo);
                  motor_X=1;                        //move X
                  for(i=0;i<26;i++)
                          {
                                 time_pulse_X=time_pulse_X+50;
                                 _delay_l(retardo);
                                 data_RD =Read_ ADC();  //Read data of optical
sensor
                                 WriteUART2(i,j,data_RD);
while(BusyUART2());  //// Wait for transmission to complete
                                 _delay_l(retardo);
                          }                           /
                  time_pulso_X=900;
                  _delay_l(80000);                 //Delay function
             }
}
//Delay function
Void  _delay_l(int long time)
{
     while(time!=0) time--;
}
```

asymmetrical response. The same behavior was observed using the spherical irradiance meter and a lux-meter. Its maximum illuminance was of 84 lux at a distance equal to 27 cm, very lower compared with the illuminance produced by the lamps based on a power star LEDs of high brightness, such as the dirigible X-lamp LED, where 1700 lux was measured on the top.

In order to increase the scanning area other suitable recyclable surface could be used, such as the conformed by the photocopiers rails (Figure 29). Its optical sensor, a pin diode, is useful to use for our purposes, due to its higher stability compared to the semiconductor photodiode used in the CD ROM platform, as it was expected because it improves the speed relative, and also the efficiency. The cost of the new sensor is most expensive, but the possibility of recycling permits to consider it as a good option. The absence of the serial numbers of the elements in the photocopier diagrams makes necessary to characterize the detector spectral responsivity before to use it. The data fitting for rectangular geometries can be realized by means of Chevyshev Polynomials (Tecpoyotl, 2006)

CONCLUSION

The implementation of a single detector in irradiance meters reduces the measurements error due to variations in the spectral responsivity. The precision in this case is determined by the control of the XY displacements. In absence of the servo motors implementation, manual control can be also carried out, keeping the reliability of the measurements, due to the worm drives coupled to the XY table. Similar structures can be real-

Figure 18. Interruptions

```
void __attribute__((__interrupt__,no_auto_psv)) _T1Interrupt(void)
{
    IFS0bits.T1IF = 0; /* clear interrupt flag */
    if ( motor_X == 1)
            {
                PORTDbits.RD3=1;    //motor X
                ini_tmr2(time_pulso_X);
            }
    else
            {
                PORTDbits.RD1=1;    //motor Y
                ini_tmr2(time_pulso_Y);
            }
    return;
}
//interruption to define the period time
void __attribute__((__interrupt__,no_auto_psv)) _T2Interrupt(void)
{
    IFS0bits.T2IF = 0; // clear interrupt flag
    if ( motor_X == 1) PORTDbits.RD3=0;    //motor X
    else PORTDbits.RD1=0;        //motor Y
    return;
}
```

Figure 19. Data sending and configuration function for UART (Universal Asynchronous Receiver-Transmitter)

```
// Send data to PC
WriteUART2(Txdata_x,y);
while(BusyUART2());  //// Wait for complete transmission
Config_uart2 (void)
{
    unsigned int baudvalue;   // Rate value
    unsigned int config1 ;
    unsigned int config2;                    CloseUART2();
    ConfigIntUART2(UART_RX_INT_EN & UART_RX_INT_PR6 &
    UART_TX_INT_DIS & UART_TX_INT_PR5);   //Interrup config
         // config frecuency of transmition
    // Baud = Fosc/(16(UBRG-1)); UBRG=(Fosc/(16*Frec Baud))+1
    baudvalue = 25;          / /for 9600bauds

    // Config1 UART2 for 8 bit transmission with one bit stop
    // Also Enable loopback mode
    config1 =     UART_EN & UART_IDLE_CON &
                    UART_DIS_WAKE & UART_DIS_LOOPBACK &
                    UART_EN_ABAUD & UART_NO_PAR_8BIT &
                    UART_1STOPBIT;
    config2 =     UART_INT_TX_BUF_EMPTY &
                    UART_TX_PIN_NORMAL &
                    UART_TX_ENABLE & UART_INT_RX_CHAR &
    //UART_TX_ENABLE & UART_INT_RX_3_4_FUL
                    UART_ADR_DETECT_DIS &
                    UART_RX_OVERRUN_CLEAR;
    OpenUART2(config1, config2, baudvalue);
}
```

Figure 20. Dirigible X-lamp LED IL51, as a sample and the XY table

ized on the base of the meter presented here, for example, using recycled printer rails or making

mechanical structures of low cost. The bigger inversion would be realized on the detection circuit, which involves the DSPIC programming. A total scanning area, at least at 20x20 cm² is suitable in order to realize measurements of the luminaries of larger sizes. Also it is suggested to be very careful in the selection of all parts of the prototype, because as we mentioned, the little variations for example in the gear teeth can produce deviations in the generated profiles.

The implementation of this meter permits to observe with a great detail the profile produced as a result of the beamwidth of the illumination source under test. The generated information permits us to realize a comparison with other spherical prototype developed by our research

Figure 21. Lamp IL/1 L3 (with a 3 LED array)

Figure 22. Single white LED

Figure 23. Irradiance profile of dirigible X-lamp LED complete

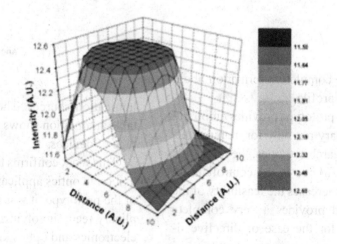

Figure 24. Irradiance profile of dirigible X-lamp LED top view

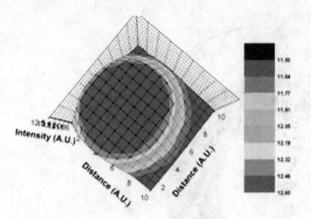

Figure 26. Irradiance profile of lamp with three LEDs (a) complete and (b) a zoom in on the left side

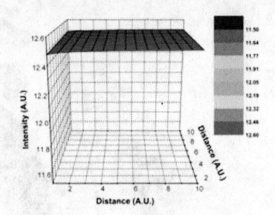

Figure 25. Irradiance pattern of the dirigible X-lamp LED

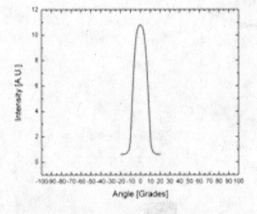

Figure 27. Irradiance pattern of the single ultra bright white LED generated by the spherical prototype

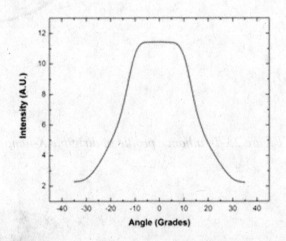

group, and to have complete information about the total irradiance profile.

The rectangular prototype provides empirical information necessary not only for manufacturers, but also for research activities. We found this prototype very useful due to the controllability of position, which increases the feasibility of the measurements, and provides a very complete irradiance pattern for the case of directive il-

lumination sources. The application of the XY table automation shows the high potential of this type of devices.

This work confirms the relevance of the automation in optics applications. For the realization of the prototype, it was required of a multidisciplinary team, involving basically programming, electronics and optics knowledge.

Figure 28. Irradiance profile of the single ultra bright white LED

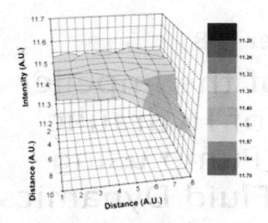

Figure 29. XY table used as irradiance meter

REFERENCES

Alíne, J.-V. E., Basurto-Pensado, M. A., & Escobedo-Alatorre, J. J. (2005). Diseño y programación de una mesa para mili-maquinado. In *Proceedings of Encuentro de Investigación en Ingeniería Eléctrica*, Zacatecas, Mexico.

Gonzalez-Roman, A., Tecpoyotl-Torres, M., Escobedo-Alatorre, J., Pal-Verma, S., & Sánchez-Mondragón, J. (2006). A semi-spherical Irradiance meter used as a quality control device. In *Proceedings of the First Multiconference on Electronics and Photonics* (pp. 253-256).

Gwirc, S., Rigotti, J., Federico, A., & Acquaticci, F. (2007). *6o. Jornada de desarrollo e innovación tecnológica. Imágenes Ultrasónicas con Transductor Piezoeléctrico de Película*. Buenos Aires, Argentina: Instituto Nacional De Tecnología Industrial.

Horowitz, P., & Hill, W. (2001). *The art of electronics* (2nd ed.). Cambridge, UK: Cambridge University Press.

Maida, J. C. (2003). *An illumination modeling system for human factor analyses*. Houston, TX: Space Human Factors Laboratory/Flight Crew Support Division/NASA Johnson Space Center.

Palais, J. C. (1984). *Fiber optic communications* (4th ed.). Upper Saddle River, NJ: Prentice Hall.

Sánchez-Mondragón, J., Tecpoyotl-Torres, M., Andrade-Lucio, J. A., Torres-Cisneros, M., Dávila-Alvarez, A., & Carpio-Valadez, M. (2003). Data fitting on a spherical shell. *Proceedings of the Society for Photo-Instrumentation Engineers*, *5181*, 51–55.

Tecpoyotl-Torres, M., Partida-Rivera, E., Gonzalez-Roman, I. A., Ibarra-Manzano, O., & Sánchez-Mondragón, J. (2006). Reconstruction of atmospheric vertical reflectivity profile images. In *Proceedings of the First Multiconference on Electronics and Photonics* (pp. 262-265).

Westinhouse. (2000). *Manual del alumbrado* (4th ed.). Madrid, Spain: Noriega Editores.

Yañez Valdez, R., Ruiz Torres, M., Morales Sánchez, E., & Castillo Castañeda, E. (2007). Diseño y Construcción de una Mesa de Trabajo XYθ basada en un Mecanismo Paralelo Planar 3RRR. *Tecnólog*, *1*(2), 35–45.

Chapter 18

Optimization of the Impeller and Diffuser of Hydraulic Submersible Pump using Computational Fluid Dynamics and Artificial Neural Networks

Juan Bernardo Sosa Coeto
Universidad Autonoma del Estado de Morelos, Mexico

Gustavo Urquiza Beltrán
Universidad Autonoma del Estado de Morelos, Mexico

Juan Carlos García Castrejon
Universidad Autonoma del Estado de Morelos, Mexico

Laura Lilia Castro Gómez
Universidad Autonoma del Estado de Morelos, Mexico

Marcelo Reggio
Ecole Polythecnique de Montreal, Canada

ABSTRACT

Overall performance of hydraulic submersible pump is strongly linked to its geometry, impeller speed and physical properties of the fluid to be pumped. During the design stage, given a fluid and an impeller speed, the pump blades profiles and the diffuser shape has to be determined in order to achieve maximum power and efficiency. Using Computational Fluid Dynamics (CFD) to calculate pressure and velocity fields, inside the diffuser and impeller of pump, represents a great advantage to find regions where the behavior of fluid dynamics could be adverse to the pump performance. Several trials can be run using CFD with different blade profiles and different shapes and dimensions of diffuser to calculate the effect of them over the pump performance, trying to find an optimum value. However the optimum impeller and diffuser would never be obtained using lonely CFD computations, by this means are necessary the

DOI: 10.4018/978-1-4666-0297-7.ch018

application of Artificial Neural Networks, which was used to find a mathematical relation between these components (diffusers and blades) and the hydraulic head obtained by CFD calculations. In the present chapter artificial neural network algorithms are used in combinations with CFD computations to reach an optimum in the pumps performance.

INTRODUCTION

Several processes on industry are linked directly with liquids' transport, for this reason, the pumping devices are one important part of them. One of the most used devices in the industrial process are hydraulic pumps. For the correct design and operation of a pump is relevant to consider factors such as the working liquid, hydraulic head, vibration, cavitation and efficiency especially. In general, a hydraulic pump is a machine used to move liquids through a piping system and to increase the fluid pressure; this uses the mechanical energy of a impeller to increase the pressure in a liquid. Hydraulic pumps are among the group of machines called turbomachines, all these share similar characteristics between them.

A turbomachine is a rotating engine in which a fluid passes continuously and there are a energy transfer process, the energy exchange process could occur from fluid to rotating engine or vice versa. Turbomachinery differs from other devices because the energy transfer process in continuous, not cyclical or alternating as an internal combustion engine or piston pump, besides they can add or remove power to the working fluid, making pressure, thermal or kinetic energy.

Turbomachinery consists of several parts depending on the type, size, design and application. However, the majority of consists of static and rotating parts, within these two sets may have elements in common, for example all turbomachinery has a rotor and a stator.

The rotor is the central part of the whole turbomachine and is where the exchange of energy occurs. Consists of one or more disks which support the blades, vanes or spoons depending

on the type of the turbomachine. The geometry of the blades is essential for this exchange of energy with the fluid, and directly impacts on the performance of the turbomachine and the rate of energy generated (if the energy is transmitted by exchange pressure or velocity).In the particular case of pumps,the set of blades and support is called impeller.

Stator is the set of all static parts of the turbomachine like housing (volute casing, scroll), stay vanes, bearings, seals, etc. However taking a design lead approach to interaction fluid-machine is considered, the main component of the stator is the diffuser (Lobanoff, 1992).

The pump under study is a submersible hydraulic pump with a power of 1/2 HP, with an impeller diameter of 5.2", closed type and 2 blades, with a discharge diameter of 2", and a hydraulic head of 7.53298 meters to a volumetric flow of 3 Liter/second. The pump is optimized by changing the shape of the blades and the diffusor, the artificial neural network algorithms are used to find the mathematical relation between changes in the shape of the blades and the diffuser and the hydraulic head pump. This mathematical relation is given by a function of two variables, with this mathematical function, local maximum related to the geometrical parameters are found, optimizing this way the hydraulic submersible pump.

As mentioned previously, the shape of the blades and the diffuser affects directly the pump efficiency, equations 1, 2 and 3 shows the variables which are related to efficiency.

$$P = \rho g H \qquad (1)$$

Where P is the power developed by the pump, $\tilde{n}$ is the density of the fluid pumped, g is the acceleration due to gravity and H is the total hydraulic head.

$$\eta = \frac{P}{P_e} \qquad (2)$$

ς is the total efficiency and P_e is the power output of electric motor. Substituting equation 1 into equation 2 gives efficiency in terms of H:

$$\eta = \frac{\rho g H}{P_e} \qquad (3)$$

In the case of the submersible hydraulic pump; $\tilde{n}$, P_e, and g are constant because the same fluid is always pumped with the same engine and the same acceleration due to gravity. Consequently this shows that efficiency has a direct relation with the head of the pump. This work presents the results of CFD computations of the total hydraulic head knowing that an increase in this results in a directly proportional change in efficiency.

Design turbomachinery is a complex task involving many different disciplines, among the contemporary are those concerning the use of computational methods like CAD (Computer Aided Design) and NURBS (Non Uniform Rational B-Splines) (Karassik, 2008). This process is explain in the next section.

We present a description of the computational fluid dynamics. CFD is a branch of fluid dynamics, in recent decades has boomed due to advances in the capabilities of computing in CPU's commercial use, the principle of CFD is to convert the differential equations describing the behavior of the fluid in algebraic equations that can be resolved, this makes flexible the solution of complex problems that exist in fluid engineering.

Artificial neural networks are mathematical models that emulate the form of information processing in neuronal cells in nature, these neural networks are robust in the sense that they are able to find mathematical relations that link input stimuli with responses of output (Arbib, 2003), this allows the application of such networks in complex problems where it is necessary to have mathematical expressions that describe a phenomenon either to find patterns or optimization. We show a description of neural networks in general.

We discuss the process of obtaining the geometry. The first step in optimizing on aerodynamics or hydrodynamics, is to get the shapes of the components that interact directly with the fluid, in the case of turbomachinery, which have complex geometries, such as the blades and the diffuser, due to this complexity a 3D scanning method is used. Once the morphology of the blades and diffuser is obtained, this is defined by parametric equations, the main interest of doing it this way is that the geometry is described by few parameters and is easy to modify in a gradual and orderly way. These modifications in geometry are subject to something like a virtual "wind tunnel" using CFD (Computational Fluid Dynamics).

Finally we show the results of this work.

DESIGN

Turbomachinery design it's a complex task which involves several targets and restrictions, as many disciplines. Generally design begins with the creation of geometry in CAD (Computer Aided Design) software, followed by numerical simulations to predict flow behavior inside the turbomachine, aided with CFD (Computational Fluid Dynamics) software, obtaining with it efficiency, power and other important variables. In addition, using FEA (Finite Element Analysis) mechanic and thermal efforts could be computed (Friedrich, 2010).

In case of hydraulic turbomachinery (as pumps), some disadvantages of classic design are excessive time consumption and resources expended on it, and not guarantee to obtain optimal results, a complete design process requires manufacturing new models and make hydraulic test every time. However, design based in computational tools just requires time to obtain original geometry and computing process. With progress in processing power in CPU's today the time required to obtain results of a new prototype is faster than five years ago. Therefore there are better cost-benefit balances with respect to classical design.

The first step is creation or acquisition of geometry in virtual form, either starting from an initial model (reverse engineering) or calculating dimensions from empirical equations, manipulating or defining the major components that interact directly with the fluid (in geometry). Translate it to computer language is required (using vector graphics) and represent more mathematically precise and can be reproduced accurately any time, for it NURBS (Non Uniform Rational B-Splines) are used. It is worth mentioning that any contemporary commercial CAD software utilize them, however this does not mean that geometrical parameters which define the hydrodynamic profiles of the parts from a turbomachine can be modify easily. These NURBS are parameterized by control points and weights, according to the complexity of the surface are number of control points and the magnitude of the weights, varying both are obtained multiple models that have different effects in performance of the pump.

COMPUTATIONAL FLUID DYNAMICS

For long time the design of engineering equipment, for example, heat exchangers, cooling towers, gas turbines, hydraulic pumps and aerodynamic bodies was strongly supported by empirical knowledge and rules of thumbs (Durbin, 2007). The same applies with a lot of industrial processes like melting, welding, mixing, etc. Typically, empiric

information is showed in form of tables, numerical relations and graphs were someone could be found the relation between the principal variables that affect the phenomenon under consideration. However, this available data is not applied in one wide interval of values or scales. Fortunately there are design tools which can be useful for whatever interval values, like the Computational Fluid Dynamics.

Computational Fluid Dynamics (CFD) applies numerical methods to solve a set of differential equations that govern the fluid dynamics in any region of interest. After a solution for the partial differential equations (PDEs) is reached, one can know the field flow in this region. Nowadays CFD is a powerful tool in research areas or in design stage of practically every device in which fluids are involved. Apply CFD to solve flow field, the region of interest have to be divided in small parts called computations cells, in which the PDEs are solved. Some devices have flow regions with a very complex geometry and it needs a millions of computation cells to solve the PDEs.

Because the complexity of the flow field, CFD in some cases ought to solve more than one PDE in every cell in the computation domain, leading to a large sets of PDEs to be solved. Now can be understated why CFD is at present a popular tool for the researcher or device designers: during the last three decades the software (a variety of numerical methods to solve PDEs and a variety of equations to solve complex flow phenomena) and hardware (computation speed and memory capacity has been improved).

There are three laws that govern the fluid dynamics:

- Law of mass conservation (mass transport)
- Second law of Newton
- Law of energy conservation (energy transport)

CFD have to express the previous laws in the form of PDEs in every computation cell of the domain as follows:

$$\frac{\partial \rho_m}{\partial t} + \frac{\partial (\rho_m u_j)}{\partial u_j} = 0 \tag{4}$$

$$\frac{\partial (\rho_m \omega_k)}{\partial t} + \frac{\partial \left(\rho_m u_j \omega_k\right)}{\partial x_j} = \frac{\partial}{\partial x_j}\left[\rho_m D_{eff} \frac{\partial \omega_k}{\partial x_j}\right] + R_k \tag{5}$$

PDEs for the momentum conservation (Second law of Newton):

$$\frac{\partial (\rho_m u_i)}{\partial t} + \frac{\partial \left(\rho_m u_j \omega_i\right)}{\partial x_j} = \frac{\partial}{\partial x_j}\left[\mu_{eff} \frac{\partial u_i}{\partial x_j}\right] + \frac{\partial p}{\partial x_i} + \rho_m B_i + S_{ui} \tag{6}$$

PDEs for the energy conservation is expressed as:

$$\frac{\partial (\rho_m T)}{\partial t} + \frac{\partial \left(\rho_m u_j T\right)}{\partial x_j} = \frac{\partial}{\partial x_j}\left[\frac{k_{eff}}{C_{pm}} \frac{\partial T}{\partial x_j}\right] + \frac{Q'''}{C_{pm}} \tag{7}$$

The equations are applied for a mix of fluids where the m suffix refers to a particular kind fluid. *eff* refers to the effective values of the mass diffusivity D, viscosity i and k is the thermal conductivity .

The numerical methods, like those used for the CFD, transforms de PDEs into sets of algebraic equations to be solved using algorithms and computers. Among the most popular numerical techniques to solve PDEs are: finite differences method (DFM), finite element method (FEM) and volume finite method (VFM). Generally the VFM is used for the most of the problem resolved using CFD. Sometimes, e.g., for cases in which domain has few computations cells, the FEM is preferred.

Principal stages to apply CFD and to solve the flow field for a given region are listed.

Preprocessing stage. Geometry were fluid flows is defined. Domain of flow, which is bordered by the device walls, is divided in small regions of space, this process is called discretization. These bits of domain are called computations cells from what the DE will be solved. Due to the complexity of the domain's geometry, it is necessary to have a large number of computations cells in order to solve adequately the flow phenomena, such as the boundary layer. Normally this stage expenses more than 50 percent of the time for the whole CFD project. The boundary conditions, turbulence models, interpolation schemes, time step size and level of convergence are defined in this stage.

Processing stage. Once the boundary conditions were established in the previous step, assembled the set of algebraic equations and thus providing the matrix system to solve. There are a large number of mathematical model to solve almost every problem of fluid dynamics. Once the all computation cells are initialized with a numerical value, the iterative solving process runs until the convergence level is reached.

Post processing stage. The analysis of the flow field computed by the CFD is achieved in this stage. The researcher or the designer judges the quality of the results computed by a comparison with some experimental points. Once the numerical results are validated, a completed numerical data base of the flow field is available to be used through several graphics methods (contours, vectors, profiles) for the primary variables (velocity or pressure) or for secondary variables (dimensionless numbers, vorticity, turbulence, etc.) in virtually every point, line or plane in the domain in which the DE were resolved using CFD (this is a big advantage over the experimental results because just a few points, lines or planes could be instrumented to obtain data).

ARTIFICIAL NEURAL NETWORKS

Artificial neural networks (ANN) are an automatic model of learning and processing data based on the animal nervous system. It is a system of interconnected neurons in a network that produce an output stimulus through mathematical models. The goal is get a response similar to those that animal brain could have, which it is characterized by generalization and robustness (Galushkin, 2007).

The simplest neuronal model consist of a propagation function, an activation function and a transferring function. Output response is given by $a=f(wp+b)$, where w is a multiplier (weight), b is an adjustment factor (bias) and f is the transfer function.

In general, the neural model of multiple layers and output neurons is given in Figure 1.

Having thus for each layer at each exit to the equation:

$$a_n = f\left(\sum_{m=1}^{x} p_m w_{m,n} + b_n\right) \tag{8}$$

Where x is number of entries in x layer, n number of neurons and f transfer function. The transfer function is a mathematical model given by a ratio between system response to an input. There are several transfer functions, were used next:

$$tansig(n) = \frac{2}{\left(1 + Exp\left(-2n\right)\right)} - 1$$

$$purelin(n) = n$$

Figure 1. Schematic of a neural model of multiple layers

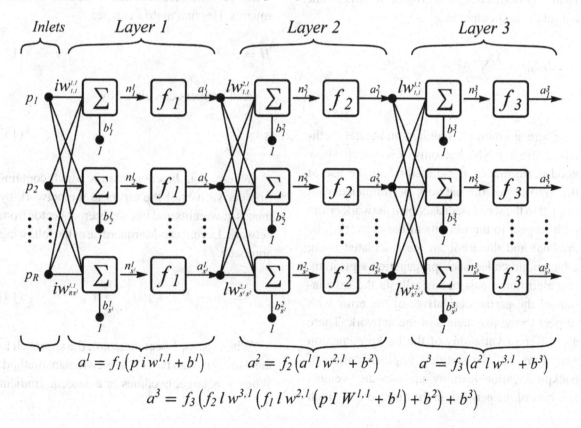

$$a^1 = f_1\left(p\, i\, w^{1,1} + b^1\right) \qquad a^2 = f_2\left(a^1\, l\, w^{2,1} + b^2\right) \qquad a^3 = f_3\left(a^2\, l\, w^{3,1} + b^3\right)$$

$$a^3 = f_3\left(f_2\, l\, w^{3,1}\left(f_1\, l\, w^{2,1}\left(p\, I\, W^{1,1} + b^1\right) + b^2\right) + b^3\right)$$

461

In problems related with patterns recognizing generally are used sigmoid functions (*tansig*) and in problems related with function adjustment lineal transfer function (*purelin*) are used (Livingstone, 2008).

In this particular case, ANN used contains one hidden layer of neurons with sigmoid output, followed by a layer with lineal output. Applying nonlinear transfer functions to neural network allow learning nonlinear relations between input and output vectors. Training a neural network consists in finding the values of the bias and weights in an iterative way. ANN can do it starting from an approximation function (nonlinear regression). In order to initialize the training process a input data set p and output data are required.

Training process of a neural network involves adjusting the values of weights and bias to optimize the performance. The function that optimizes network performance is mean square error (*mse*) which is the mean squared error between network outputs a and output targets t:

$$F = mse = \frac{1}{N}\sum_{i=1}^{N} e_i^2 == \frac{1}{N}\sum_{i=1}^{N}(t_i - a_i)^2$$

(9)

There are multiple standard numerical methods to train ANN, but only few which show good performance, these methods make use of the gradient of the network performance with respect to the weights, or Jacobian network errors with respect to the weights of the network. The gradient and the Jacobian are calculated using a technique called back propagation algorithm, this algorithm consists basically in the calculation of the partial derivatives of the error with respect to the parameters of the network. There are different variations of the backpropagation algorithm, but the simplest implementation of backpropagation learning updates the weights and bias of the network in the direction in which

the performance function decreases most rapidly (negative gradient). One iteration of this algorithm can be written as:

$$x_{k+1} = x_k - \alpha_k g_k$$

(10)

Where x_k is weight vector and bias, g_k is the current gradient and $\acute{a}_k$ are the learning velocity. Backpropagation algorithm used was Levenberg-Marquardt, explained next.

Levenberg-Marquardt Algorithm

This algorithm is based as all the quasi-newtonian in a quadratic model with a matrix H_k:

$$q_k(p) = f(x_k) + \nabla f(x_k)^T p + \frac{1}{2}p^T H_k p$$

(11)

With approaching of a Hessian matrix formed from a function and a gradient of previous steps. When performance function is the sum of mean squares, Hessian matrix can be:

$$H = J^T J$$

(12)

And gradient calculated by:

$$g = J^T e$$

(13)

Where J is Jacobian matrix which contains first derivatives of the errors in the network by means at weights and bias, e is error vector from network. Levenberg-Marquardt uses the following approach:

$$x_{k+1} = x_k - \left(J^T J + \mu\ I\right)^{-1} J^T e$$

(14)

When scalar i becomes zero, the approach to the Hessian matrix, it's a Newtonian method. When i is large, becomes in a descent gradient

Figure 2. Scanning the diffusor

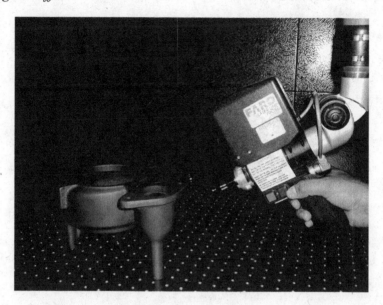

with small timestep. Newtonian methods are faster and precise near of smaller errors.

METHODOLOGY

CFD Computations

To resolve the flow field using CFD, in order to represent certain flow phenomenon, is necessary to know all the physical conditions which are involved. One of the most important conditions is the geometry or region in which the flow occurs, commonly this region is limited by geometric walls. A hydraulic pump has two principal components, which are the diffuser and the impeller, both are geometrically complex and in addition the impeller is rotating at certain speed while the diffuser remains static. The complexity of the geometry makes necessary the use of computational tools to describe it. In this case the flow problem takes place in a model of hydraulic submersible pump and the geometries of the diffuser and the impeller were got using a 3D laser-scanner. The scanned geometries are expressed like a set of 3D coordinates points (x, y, z) which

makes easier to process mathematically those points for creating fitted surfaces. Figures 2, 3, and 4 show the process for obtaining the geometry of hydraulic submersible pump under study. The resulting surfaces were used to define the diffuser and the impeller CAD models and can be mathematically defined using 3D parametric equations.

In the particular case of the pump impeller blades one four-digits-NACA (National Advisory Committee for Aeronautics) equation was used as 3D parametric equation, which has two variables (*surface*): u, v, and m is the digit or variable that determines the camber. The m variable is used to modify the blade profile. Additionally a quadratic relation between the blade leading edge and the components i and j was added. In the case of the volute, a variation of the Archimedes Spiral was used. In order to modify the Archimedes Spiral in terms of u, a parametric equation of one parameter which defines the diffuser's shape, and u a variable of a function that distorts the diffuser's radius.

Figure 3. Resulting surfaces of the 3D scan

Figure 4. CAD model (diffuser and impeller)

The geometrical changes caused to the pump geometry by the mentioned functions are shown in the Figures 5 through 9.

CFD computations were carried out on 2106 different model pumps. These hydraulic pumps were the result of combining 26 impellers (13 pumps with different quadratic blade leading edge and 13 with different linear blade leading edge)

and 81 diffusers were created by means of the variation of the variable h in one intnerval of (-2 to 2) with increments of 0.05. While to modify the blades profile the variable m was used with values of 0.08 to 0.32, using increments of 0.01. Mentioned previously modifications are shown across the Figures 5 through 9. The optimization of the hydraulic pump efficiency is directly pro-

Figure 5. Quadratic blade leading edge

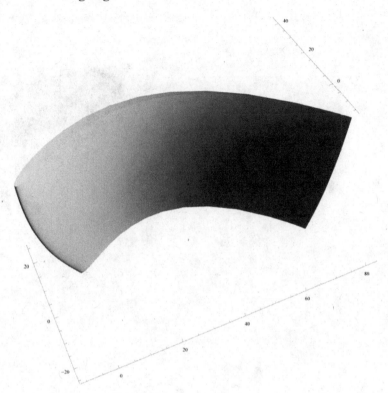

Figure 6. Linear blade leading edge

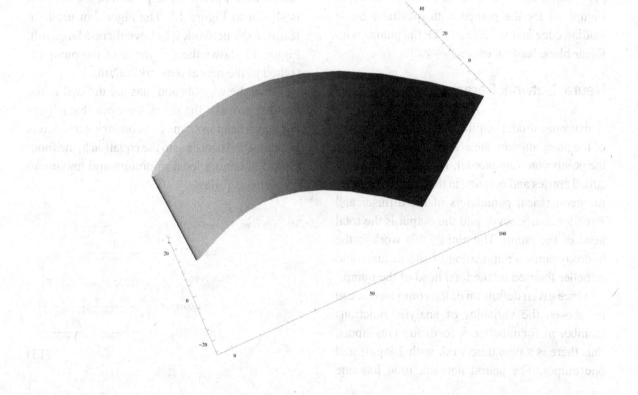

Figure 7. Variation of the variable m

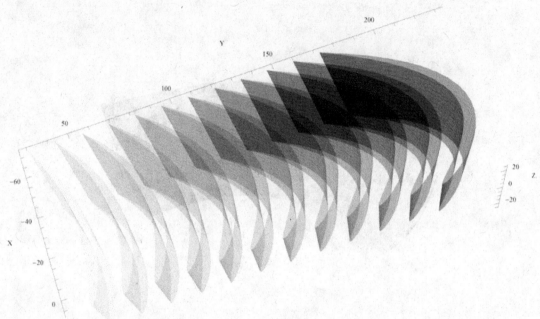

portional to the total head of the pump for a given flow. In this case the flow used was 3 liters per second. The results of the CFD are shown in Figure 10 for the pumps with quadratic blade leading edge and in Figure 11 for the pumps with linear blade leading edge.

Neural Network Parameters

A neuronal model requires statistical modeling of the phenomenon; these statistics should cover the points you want predict. These are commonly called entries and outputs, in this case, entries are the geometrical parameters of the diffuser and impeller components, and the output is the total head of the pump. The aim of this work is the hydrodynamic optimization of the diffuser and impeller focused on the total head of the pump.

Once given definition of the components, can be chosen the variables of analytic functions (camber m for impeller, h for diffuser) as inputs, thus there is a neural network with 2 inputs and one output. The neural network used has one

input layer with transfer function *tansig* and 5 neurons and an output layer transfer function and one neuron *purelin*. The pattern of the network is shown in Figure 12. The algorithm used for learning the network was Levenberg-Marquardt. Figure 13 shows the schematic of the pump attached to the neural network training.

Once the weights and bias are defined in the training process, the neural network that adjusts the pump head in terms of geometric parameters is obtained. According to the equation 8, the function to obtaining local minimum and maximum it's write as follows:

$$
\begin{aligned}
H(m,h) = 9.59329 &- 0.092904207\left(-1+\frac{2}{1+e^{-2(16.077752-63.391691m-0.14176563h)}}\right) \\
&- 0.14860018\left(-1+\frac{2}{1+e^{-2(-5.8694732+50.074154\,m-0.0045181154\,h)}}\right) \\
&- 1.789898\left(-1+\frac{2}{1+e^{-2(13.490717-37.319707\,m-0.004001681\,h)}}\right) \\
&- 0.30992911\left(-1+\frac{2}{1+e^{-2(-2.4749+9.3646778\,m+0.033234879h)}}\right) \\
&+ 0.26608562\left(-1+\frac{2}{1+e^{-2(-5.0826096+13.39774\,m+0.77714286\,h)}}\right)
\end{aligned}
$$

$$(15)$$

Figure 8. Variation of the variable h

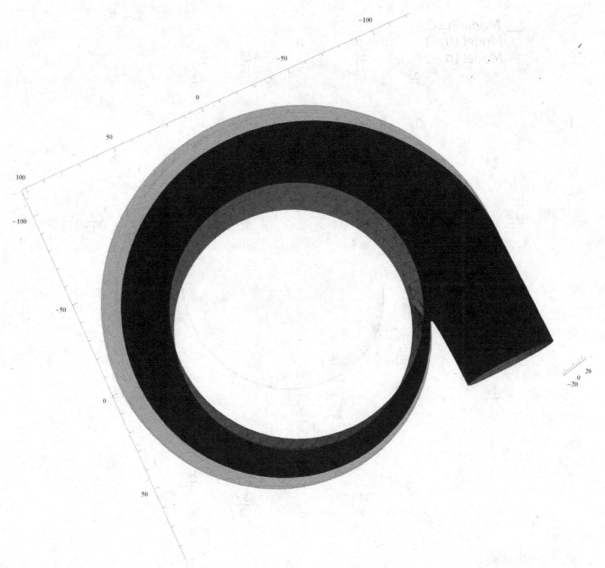

The function 15 correspond to models with linear blade edge and describe the pump head H vs. h and .

Figure 14 shows the graph of the function 15 in lighter gray color, and the values of the head found with CFD computations in darker gray color, percentage error rates of the function with respect to the values obtained with the CFD results is shown in Figure 15, the maximum error is 0.888316%.

With the function $H(m,h)$ which related H to m and h, local maximum are found for $-2 \leq h \leq 2$ and $-0.8 \leq h \leq 0.32$, with the maximum pump head $H = 7.878298466099978$ when $m \to 0.08000000000058634$ and $h \to 1.9999999998459779$.

Similarly the function for pumps models with quadratic blade edge is given:

Figure 9. 2D variation of the variable h

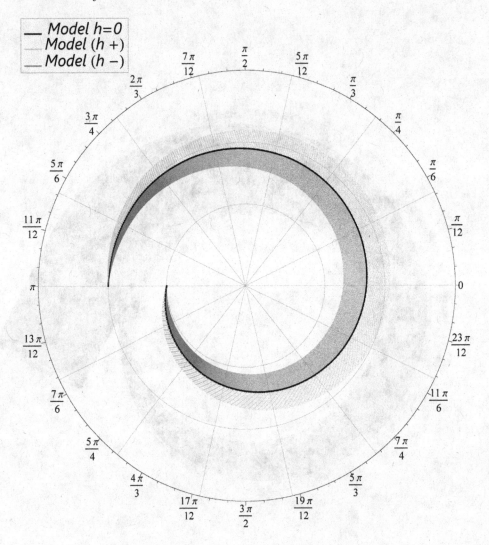

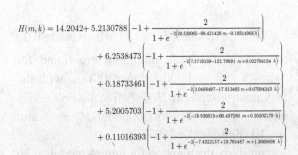

Figure 16 shows the graph of the function 16 and the values of the head found with CFD computations, percentage error rates of the function with respect to the values obtained with the CFD results is shown in Figure 17, the maximum error is 1.3659%.

With the function $H(m, h)$ which related H to m and h, local maximum are found for $-2 \leq h \leq 2$ and $-0.8 \leq h \leq 0.32$, with the maximum pump head $H = 8.10141323144027$ when $m \to 0.28995449104513277$ and $h \to 1.9999958506033366$. Finally with the values of h and m for maximum head H, the components are drawn, the Figures 18 and 19

Figure 10. Pump head, quadratic blade leading edge

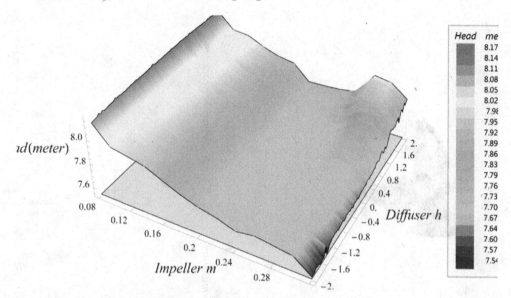

Figure 11. Pump head, linear blade leading edge

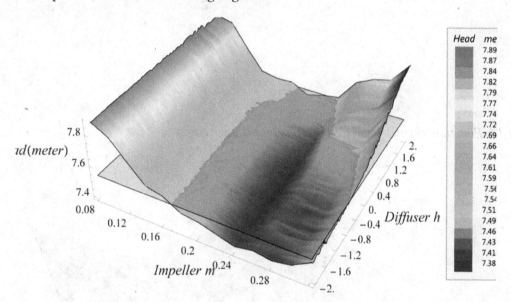

Figure 12. Neural network scheme

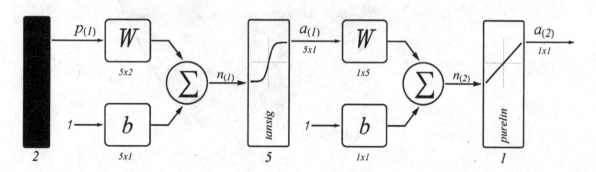

Figure 13. Training neural network scheme

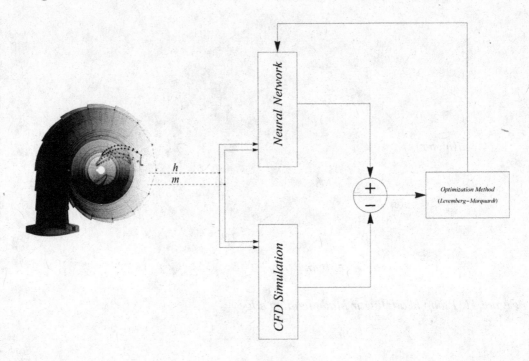

Figure 14. Function $H(m,h)$ *and CFD results plot (linear edge)*

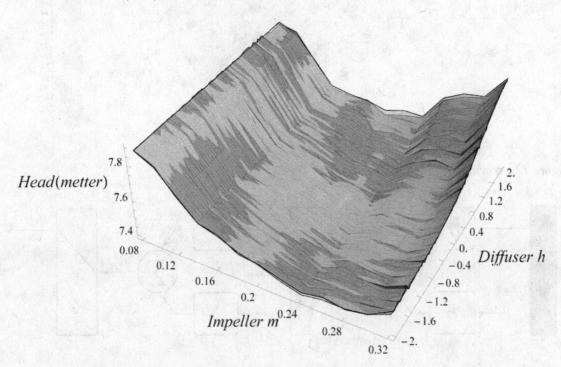

Figure 15. Percentage error (linear edge)

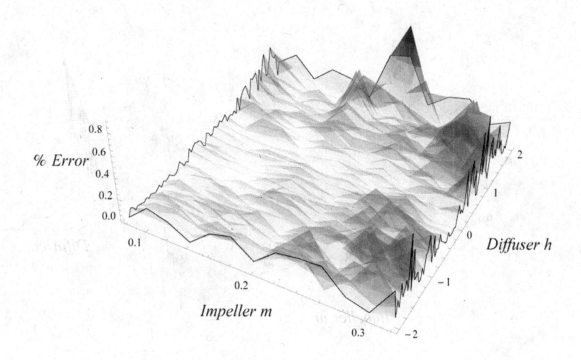

Figure 16. Function $H(m,h)$ and CFD results plot (quadratic edge)

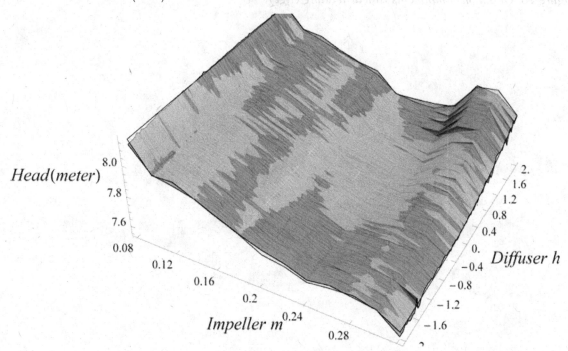

Figure 17. Percentage error (quadratic edge)

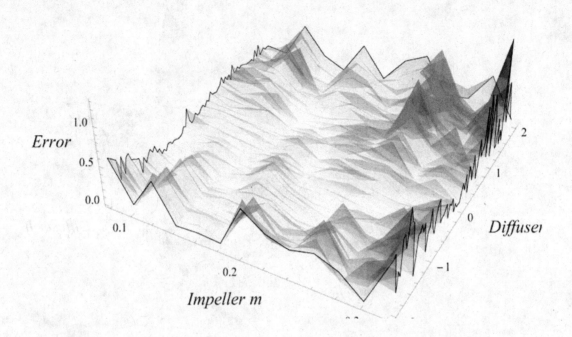

Figure 18. Optimum components (linear leading edge)

Figure 19. Optimum components (quadratic leading edge)

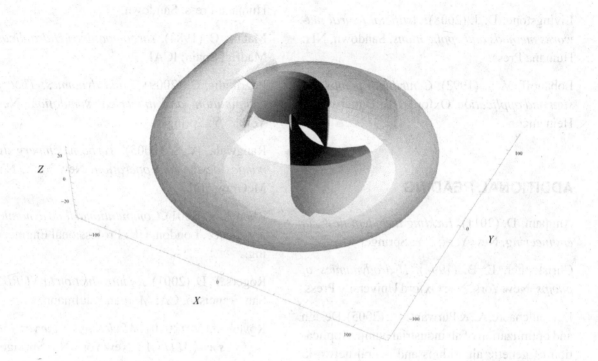

show the impeller and diffuser for these values of m and h.

CONCLUSION

A optimization method both 3D blade and diffuser of centrifugal pump was presented, with parameterized blade and diffuser by means 3D parametric functions, with only one variable for each one, m for impeller and h for diffuser.

ANN technology was used to find a mathematical relation between the geometric parameters and the behavior of the pump, this relation is given by functions of two variables which make easy to find local maximum or minimum. These functions have relatively small error rates compared to the values found with CFD computations; this means that the results are a good approximation.

The method used results in a significant increase in the pump head of 7.532 meter to 8.101

(7.545%) and therefore increasing efficiency. Finally, this combination can be applied to more complex turbomachinery like compressors and gas turbines.

REFERENCES

Arbib, M. A. (2003). *The handbook of brain theory and neural networks* (2nd ed.). Washington, DC: Advisory Board.

Durbin, A. P. (2007). *Fluid dynamics with a computational perspective*. New York, NY: Cambridge University Press. doi:10.1017/CBO9780511619281

Friedrich, G. J. (2010). *Centrifugal pumps*. New York, NY: Springer.

Galushkin, I. (2007). *Neural networks theory*. New York, NY: Springer.

Karassik, J. I. (2008). *Pump handbook* (4th ed.). New York, NY: McGraw-Hill.

Livingstone, D. J. (2008). *Artificial neural networks methods and applications*. Sandown, NH: Humana Press.

Lobanoff, V. S. (1992). *Centrifugal pumps design and application*. Oxford, UK: Butterworth-Heinemann.

ADDITIONAL READING

Anupam, D. (2011). *Tackling turbulent flows in engineering*. New York, NY: Springer.

Christopher, E. B. (1994). *Hydrodynamics of pumps*. New York, NY: Oxford University Press.

Demeulenaere, A., & Purwanto, A. (2005). Design and optimization of an industrial pump: Application of genetic algorithms and neural network. In *Proceedings of the ASME Fluids Engineering Division Summer Meeting*, Houston, TX (Vol. 1).

Dominique, T. (2008). *Optimization and computational fluid dynamics*. Berlin, Germany: Springer-Verlag.

Flores, E., & Bazin, D. (2006). *Design optimization of a Francis runner*. France: Alstom Power Hydro.

Ira, H. A. (1959). *Theory of wing sections*. New York, NY: Dover.

Kleinstreuer, C. (2010). *Modern fluid dynamics*. New York, NY: Springer.

Livingstone, D. J. (2008). *Artificial neural networks methods and applications*. Sandown, NH: Humana Press, Sandown.

Mataix, C. (1984). *Turbomaquinas Hidraulicas*. Madrid, Spain: ICAI.

Pozrikidis, C. (2009). *Fluid dynamics: Theory, computation, and numerical simulation*. New York, NY: Springer.

Rangwala, A. S. (2005). *Turbo-machinery dynamics design and operation*. New York, NY: McGraw-Hill.

Rhodes, N. (2001). *Computational fluid dynamics in practice*. London, UK: Professional Engineering.

Rogers, F. D. (2001). *An introduction to NURBS*. San Francisco, CA: Morgan Kaufmann.

Rovenski, V. (2010). *Modeling of curves and surfaces with MATLAB*. New York, NY: Springer.

Sulzer Pumps Ltd. (2010). *Centrifugal pump handbook* (3rd ed.). Amsterdam, The Netherlands: Elsevier.

Turton, R. K. (2004). *Rotodynamic pump design*. New York, NY: Cambridge University Press.

Wendt, F. J. (2009). *Computational fluid dynamics, an introduction*. New York, NY: Springer. doi:10.1007/978-3-540-85056-4

Xu, J., Wu, Y., Zhang, Y., & Zhang, J. (Eds.). (2009). *Proceedings of the 4th International Symposium on Fluid Machinery and Fluid Mechanics*. New York, NY: Springer.

Compilation of References

Ab Aziz, F., Hao, L., & Lewin, P. L. (2007). Analysis of partial discharge measurement data using a support vector machine. In *Proceedings of the 5th Student Conference on Research and Development* (pp. 1-6).

Abdel-Kader, M. G., & Dugdale, D. (1998). Investment in advanced manufacturing technology: a study of practice in large U.K. companies. *Management Accounting Research, 9*(3), 261–284. doi:10.1006/mare.1998.0071

Alba, C. E., Santana, R., Ochoa, R. A., & Lazo, C. M. (2000). Finding typical testors by using an evolutionary strategy. In *Proceedings of the 5th Iberoamerican Workshop on Pattern Recognition*, Lisbon, Portugal (pp. 267-278).

Alíne, J.-V. E., Basurto-Pensado, M. A., & Escobedo-Alatorre, J. J. (2005). Diseño y programación de una mesa para mili-maquinado. In *Proceedings of Encuentro de Investigación en Ingeniería Eléctrica*, Zacatecas, Mexico.

Allan, D., Birtwhistle, D., Blackburn, T., Groot, E., Gulski, E., & McGrail, A. J. (2002). Data mining techniques to assess the condition of high voltage electrical plant. In *Proceedings of the CIGRE General Session*, Paris, France.

Allgrove, C. C., & Fairhurst, M. C. (1998). Optimisation issues in dynamic and static signature verification. In *Proceedings of the Third European Workshop on Handwriting Analysis and Recognition* (pp. 1-6).

Allgrove, C. C., & Fairhurst, M. C. (2001). Majority voting for improved signature verification. In *Proceedings of the IEEE Colloquium on Visual Biometrics*, London, UK.

Alvim, A., Glover, F., Ribeiro, C., & Aloise, D. (2004). A hybrid improvement heuristic for the one-dimensional bin packing problem. *Journal of Heuristics, 10*(1), 205–229. doi:10.1023/B:HEUR.0000026267.44673.ed

Andersen, A. T. (1995). *Modelling of packet traffic with matrix analytic methods* (Doctoral dissertation). Lyngby, Denmark: IMM, The Technical University of Denmark.

Araiza, C. (2011). Save me: An approach to social isolation through the use of multi-agent systems. In *Proceedings of the 4th Hybrid Intelligent Systems Workshop in conjunction with the 10th Mexican International Conference on Artificial Intelligence*.

Araúzo, A. (2006). *Un Sistema Inteligente para Selección de Características en Clasificación* (Unpublished doctoral dissertation). Universidad de Granada, Granada, Spain.

Arbib, M. A. (2003). *The handbook of brain theory and neural networks* (2nd ed.). Washington, DC: Advisory Board.

Archetti, C., Mansini, R., & Speranza, M. G. (2001). The vehicle routing problem with capacity 2 and 3, general distances and multiple customer visits. In *Proceedings of the Conference on Operational Research in Land and Resources Management* (p. 102).

Archetti, C., Mansini, R., & Speranza, M. G. (2001). The vehicle routing problem with capacity 2 and 3, general distances and multiple customer visits. *Operational Research in Land and Resources Management, 1*(1), 102–112.

Asmar, D. C., Elshamli, A., & Areibi, S. (2005). A comparative assessment of ACO algorithms within a TSP environment. *Dynamics of Continuous Discrete and Impulsive Systems-Series B-Applications & Algorithms, 1*, 462–467.

Azlinah, M., Rohayu, Y., Sofianita, M., & Shulina, A. R. (2009). Online slant signature algorithm analysis. *WEAS Transactions on Computers, 8*(5), 864–873.

Baeza-Yates, R., & Ribeiro-Neto, B. (1999). *Modern information retrieval*. Workingham, UK: Addison-Wesley.

Bai-Ling, Z., Min-Yue, F., & Hong, Y. (1998). Handwritten signature verification based on neural 'gas' based vector quantization. In *Proceedings of the Fourteenth International Conference on Pattern Recognition* (pp. 1862-1864).

Balgoh, J., Békési, J., Galambos, G., & Reinelt, G. (2005). Lower bound for the on-line packing problem with restricted repacking. *SIAM Journal on Computing, 38*(1), 398–410. doi:10.1137/050647049

Balseiro, S., Loiseau, I., & Ramonet, J. (2008). An ant colony heuristic for the time dependent vehi-cle routing problem with time windows. In *Anales de XIV CLAIO Congreso Latino-Ibero-americano de Investigación Operativa*.

Bandyopadhyay, S., Saha, S., Maulik, U., & Deb, K. (2008). A simulated annealing based multi-objective optimization algorithm: AMOSA. *IEEE Transactions on Evolutionary Computation, 12*(3), 269–283. doi:10.1109/TEVC.2007.900837

Barland, I., Kolaitis, P., Vardi, M., & Felleisen, M. (2011). Propositional logic: normal forms. *Connexions*. Retrieved January 14, 2011, from http://cnx.org/content/m12075/1.12/

Baron, R., & Plamondon, R. (1989). Acceleration measurement with an instrumented pen for signature verification and handwriting analysis. *IEEE Transactions on Instrumentation and Measurement, 38*(6), 1132–1138. doi:10.1109/19.46414

Bascetin, A. (2007). A decision support system using analytical hierarchy process (AHP) for the optimal environmental reclamation of an open pit mine. *Environmental Geology, 52*(4), 663–672. doi:10.1007/s00254-006-0495-7

Bascetin, A., Özta³, A., & KanLý, A. (2006). EQS: A computer software using fuzzy logic for equipment selection in mining engineering. *Journal of the South African Institute of Mining and Metallurgy, 106*(1).

Batenburg, K. J., & Palenstijn, W. J. (2003). A new exam timetabling algorithm. In *Proceedings of the Fifteenth Belgium-Netherlands Artificial Intelligence Conference* (pp. 19-26).

Batenburg, K. J. (2004). An evolutionary algorithm for discrete tomography. *Discrete Applied Mathematics, 151*(1-3), 36–54. doi:10.1016/j.dam.2005.02.021

Bayo-Moriones, A., & Merino, J. (2004). Employee involvement: Its interaction with advanced manufacturing technologies, quality, management, and inter-firm collaboration. *Human Factors and Ergonomics in Manufacturing, 14*(2), 117–134. doi:10.1002/hfm.10057

Beasley, J. E. (1990). OR-Library: distributing test problems by electronic mail. *The Journal of the Operational Research Society, 41*(1), 1069–1072.

Berrin, Y., & Alisher, K. (2010). Online signature verification using fourier descriptors. *EURASIP Journal on Advances in Signal Processing*, 1–13.

Bertsimas, D., & Van Ryzin, G. (1993a). Stochastic and dynamic vehicle routing problem in the Euclidean plane with multiple capacitated vehicles. *Operations Research, 41*, 60–76. doi:10.1287/opre.41.1.60

Bertsimas, D., & Van Ryzin, G. (1993b). Stochastic and dynamic vehicle routing with general demand and interarrival time distributions. *Applied Probability, 25*, 947–978. doi:10.2307/1427801

Bessant, J., & Haywood, B. (1989). Islands, archipelagoes and continents: progress along the road to CIM. *Research Policy, 17*, 349–362. doi:10.1016/0048-7333(88)90033-9

Beveridge, G. S. G., & Schechter, R. S. (1970). *Optimization: Theory and practice* (Prime ed.). Auckland, New Zealand: McGraw-Hill.

Beynon, M. J. (2005). A method of aggregation in DS/AHP for group decision-making with the non-equivalent importance of individuals in the group. *Computers & Operations Research, 32*(7), 1881–1896. doi:10.1016/j.cor.2003.12.004

Bianchi, L. (2000). *Notes in dynamic vehicle routing* (Tech. Rep. No. IDSIA-05-01). Ticino, Switzerland: Instituto Dalle Molle di Studi Sull'intelligenza Artificiale.

Bianchi, L. *Notes on dynamic vehicle routing* (Tech. Rep. No. IDSIA-05-01). Ticino, Switzerland: Istituto Dalle Molle di Studi sull'Intelligenza Artificiale.

Bianchi, L., Birattari, M., Chiarandini, M., Manfrin, M., Mastrolilli, M., & Schiavinotto, T. (2006). Hybrid metaheuristics for the vehicle routing problem with stochastic demands. *Journal of Mathematical Modelling and Algorithms, 5*, 91–110. doi:10.1007/s10852-005-9033-y

Blasum, U., & Hochstätter, W. (2002). *Application of the branch and cut method to the vehicle routing problem (Tech. Rep.)*. Hagen, Germany: FernUniversität in Hagen.

Blescha, J., & Goetshalckx, M. *The vehicle routing problem with backhauls: properties and solution algorithms* (Tech. Rep. No. MHRC-TR-88-13). Atlanta, GA: Georgia Institute of Technology.

Blum, A., & Langley, P. (1997). Selection of relevant features and examples in machine learning. *Artificial Intelligence, 97*(1-2), 245–271. doi:10.1016/S0004-3702(97)00063-5

Bobadill, J. L., & Langer, A. (1990). La mortalidad infantil en México: un fenómeno en transición. *Revista Mexicana de Sociologia, 52*(1), 111–131. Retrieved from http://www.jstor.org/stable/3540648 doi:10.2307/3540648

Bock, W. (1958). An algorithm for solving traveling salesman and related network optimization problems. In *Proceedings of the Fourteenth National Meeting of the Operational Research Society of America*, St. Louis, MO.

Boyer, K. K., & Pagell, M. (2000). Measurement issues in empirical research: improving measures of operations strategy and advanced manufacturing technology. *Journal of Operations Management, 18*, 361–374. doi:10.1016/S0272-6963(99)00029-7

Boz, O. (2002). Feature subset selection by using sorted feature relevance. In *Proceedings of the International Conference on Machine Learning and Applications* (pp. 147-153).

Bozdağ, C. E., Kahraman, C., & Ruan, D. (2000). Fuzzy group decision making for selection among computer integrated manufacturing systems. *Computers in Industry, 51*(1), 13–29. doi:10.1016/S0166-3615(03)00029-0

Braglia, M., & Gabbrielli, R. (2000). Dimensional analysis for investment selection in industrial robots. *International Journal of Production Research, 38*(18), 4843–3448. doi:10.1080/00207540050205668

Braschler, M., Di Nunzio, G., Ferro, N., Gonzalo, J., Peters, C., & Sanderson, M. (2005). *CLEF and multilingual information retrieval*. Neuchâtel, Switzerland: Institut interfacultaire d'informatique, University of Neuchatel. Retrieved from http://www.unine.ch/info/clef/

Bräysy, O. (2001). *A reactive variable neighborhood search algorithm for the vehicle routing problem with Time Windows (Tech. Rep.)*. Oslo, Norway: SINTEF Applied Mathematics, Department of Optimization.

Bruseberg, A. (2006). The design of complete systems: Providing human factors guidance for COTS acquisition. *Reliability Engineering & System Safety, 91*, 1554–1565. doi:10.1016/j.ress.2006.01.016

Bubela, T. M., & Caulfield, T. (2010). Role and reality: technology transfer at Canadian universities. *Trends in Biotechnology, 28*(9), 447–451. doi:10.1016/j.tibtech.2010.06.002

Buckingham, E. (1941). On physically similar systems: illustration of the use of dimensional equations. *The Physician Review, 4*, 345–376. doi:10.1103/PhysRev.4.345

Bullnheimer, B., Hartl, R., & Strauss, C. (1997). *A new rank based version of the ant system: a computational study (Tech. Rep.)*. Vienna, Austria: Institute of Management Science, University of Vienna.

Cano, I., Litvinchev, I., Palacios, R., & Na-ranjo, G. (2005). Modeling vehicle routing in a star-case transportation network. In *Proceedings of the 14th International Congress of Computation* (pp. 373-377).

Ceballos, F. J. (2008). *Java 2 Interfaces gráficas y aplicaciones para Internet* (3rd ed.). Benito Juárez, Mexico: Alfaomega Ra-Ma.

Chalkias, C., & Lasaridi, K. (2009). A GIS based model for the optimisation of municipal solid waste collection: the case study of Nikea, Athens, Greece. *WSEAS Transactions on Computers, 5*(10).

Chang, Y., Cheng, W., Liu, X., & Xie, X. (2006). Application of grid technology in multi-objective aircraft optimization system. In *Proceedings of the 10ᵗʰ International Conference on Computer Supported Cooperative Work in Design* (pp. 1-5).

Chang, W., & Yang, H. (2008). Application of self organizing map approach to partial discharge pattern recognition of cast-resin current transformers. *WSEAS Transactions on Computer Research, 3*(3), 142–151.

Chan, W., Chin, F. Y. L., Ye, D., Zhang, G., & Zhang, Y. (2007). Online bin parking of fragile objects with application in cellular net-works. *Journal of Combinatorial Optimization, 14*(4), 427–435. doi:10.1007/s10878-007-9043-y

Chapman, P., Clinton, J., Kerber, R., Khabaza, T., Reinartz, T., Shearer, C., & Wirth, R. (2000). *CRISP-DM 1.0: Step by step data mining guide*. Retrieved from http://www.crisp-dm.org

Chaviano, Q., & López, S. (2000). *Edad materna, riesgo nutricional preconcepcional y peso al nacer*. Matanzas, Cuba: Centro Provincial de Higiene y Epidemiología.

Cheguis, I. A., & Yablonskii, S. V. (1955). About testors for electrical outlines. *Uspieji Matematicheskij Nauk, 4*(66), 182–184.

Cheng-Chung, C., & Smith, S. F. (1995). *A constraint satisfaction approach to makespan scheduling*. Pittsburgh, PA: Carnegie Mellon University.

Cheng-Chung, C., & Smith, S. F. (1997). *Applying constraint satisfaction techniques to job shop scheduling*. Pittsburgh, PA: Carnegie Mellon University.

Chen, S. J., & Hwang, C. L. (Eds.). (1999). *Fuzzy multiple attribute decision making methods and applications*. New York, NY: Springer.

Chiadamrong, N., & O'Brien, C. (1999). Decision support tool for justifying alternative manufacturing and production control systems. *International Journal of Production Economics, 60-61*, 177–186. doi:10.1016/S0925-5273(98)00182-0

Chorianopoulos, A., & Tsiptsis, K. (2009). *Data mining techniques in CRM: Inside customer segmentation*. Chichester, UK: John Wiley & Sons.

Choudhury, A. K., Shankar, R., & Tiwari, M. K. (2006). Consensus-based intelligent group decision-making model for the selection of advanced technology. *Decision Support Systems, 42*(3), 1776–1799. doi:10.1016/j.dss.2005.05.001

Christodoulou, N., Wallace, M., & Kuchenhoff, V. (1994). Constraint logic programming and its application to fleet scheduling. *Information and Decision Technologies, 19*(3), 135–144.

Cichecki, P., Jongen, R., Gulski, E., Smit, J., Quak, B., Petzold, F., & Vries, F. (2008). Statistical approach in power cables diagnostics data analysis. *IEEE Transactions on Dielectrics and Electrical Insulation, 15*(6), 1559–1569. doi:10.1109/TDEI.2008.4712658

Cil, I. (2004). Internet-based CDSS for modern manufacturing processes selection and justification. *Robotics and Computer-integrated Manufacturing, 20*(3), 177–190. doi:10.1016/j.rcim.2003.08.004

Clifton, C., & Thuraisingham, B. (2001). Emerging standards for data mining. *Computer Standards & Interfaces, 23*, 187–193. doi:10.1016/S0920-5489(01)00072-1

Coakley, J. J. (2003). *Sport in society: Issues and controversies* (8th ed.). New York, NY: McGraw-Hill.

Coello, C. A., & López, A. (2009). Multi-objective evolutionary algorithms: A review of the state-of-the-art and some of their applications in chemical engineering . In Pandu, R. G. (Ed.), *Multi-objective optimization techniques and applications in chemical engineering* (pp. 61–90). Singapore: World Scientific.

Coffman, J. E. G., Courboubetis, C., Garey, M. R., Johnson, D. S., Shor, P. W., & Weber, R. R. (2002). Perfect Packing: Theorems and the average case behavior of optimal and online bin packing. *Society for Industrial and Applied Mathematics Review, 44*, 95–108.

Conway, J. (2004). Theory of games to improve artificial societies. *International Journal of Intelligent Games & Simulation*.

Cook, S. A. (1971). The complexity of theorem-proving procedures. In *Proceedings of the Third Annual ACM Symposium on Theory of Computing* (pp. 151-158). New York, NY: ACM Press.

Corbett, J. M. (1988). Ergonomics in the development of human-centered AMT. *Applied Ergonomics, 19*(1), 35–39. doi:10.1016/0003-6870(88)90196-2

Cordeau, F., Desaulniers, G., Desrosiers, J., Solomon, M., & Soumis, F. (1999). *The VRP with time windows* (Tech. Rep. No. GERAD G-99-13). Montreal, QC, Canada: Ecole des Hautes 'Etudes Commerciales de Montreal.

Cordeau, J., Desaulniers, G., Desrosiers, J., Solomon, M., & Soumis, F. (2002). The VRP with time windows . In Murphy, S. (Ed.), *Monographs on discrete mathematics and applications* (pp. 157–193). Philadelphia, PA: SIAM.

Cordeau, J., Desaulniers, G., Desrosiers, J., Solomon, M., & Soumis, F. (2002). The VRP with time windows . In Toth, P., & Vigo, D. (Eds.), *The vehicle routing problem, monographs on discrete mathematics and applications* (pp. 157–194). Philadelphia, PA: SIAM.

Corlett, E. N., & Clark, T. S. (1995). *The ergonomics of workspaces and machines* (2nd ed.). Boca Raton, FL: Taylor and Francis.

Cormen, T. H., Leiserson, C. E., Rivest, R. L., & Stein, C. (2001). *Introduction to algorithms*. Cambridge, MA: MIT Press.

Corporación Universitaria para el Desarrollo de Internet (CUDI). (2011). *A. C. Internet 2, México*. Retrieved July 17, 2011, from http://www.cudi.mx/index.html

Correia, I., Gouveia, L., & Saldanha, F. (2008). Solving the variable size bin packing problem with discretized formulations. *Computers & Operations Research, 35*(6), 2103–2113. doi:10.1016/j.cor.2006.10.014

Crainic, T. G., Gendreau, M., & Potvin, J. (2009). Intelligent freight transportation systems: Assessment and the contribution of operations research. *Transportation Research Part C, Emerging Technologies, 17*(6), 541–557. doi:10.1016/j.trc.2008.07.002

Crainic, T. G., Perboli, G., Rei, W., & Tadei, R. (2011). Efficient lower bounds and heuristics for the variable cost and size bin packing problem. *Computers & Operations Research, 38*(11), 1474–1482. doi:10.1016/j.cor.2011.01.001

Croes, G. A. (1958). A method for solving traveling salesman problems. *Operations Research, 6*(6), 791–812. doi:10.1287/opre.6.6.791

Cruz, L., Delgado, J. F., González, J. J., Torres-Jiménez, J., Fraire, H. J., & Arrañaga, B. A. (2008). An ant colony system to solve routing problems applied to the delivery of bottled products. In A. An, S. Matwin, Z. W. Ras, & D. Slezak (Eds.), *Proceedings of the 17th International Symposium on Foundations of Intelligent Systems* (LNCS 4994, pp. 329-338).

Cruz, L., González, J. J., Romero, D., Fraire, H. J., Rangel, N., Herrera, J. A., et al. (2007). A distributed metaheuristic for solving a real-world scheduling-routing-loading problem. In I. Stojmenovic, R. K. Thulasiram, L. T. Yang, W. Jia, M. Guo, & R. Fernandes (Eds.), *Proceedings of the International Conference on Parallel and Distributed Processing and Applications* (LNCS 4742, pp. 68-77).

Cruz, L., Nieto, D. M., Rangel, N., Herrera, J. A., González-Barbosa, J. J., Castilla-Valdez, G., & Delgado, J. F. (2007). DiPro: an algorithm for the packing in product transportation problems with multiple loading and routing variants. In A. Gelbukh & A. F. Kuri (Eds.), *Proceedings of the International Conference on Advances in Artificial Intelligence* (LNCS 4827, pp. 1078-1088).

Cruz-Chávez, M. A., Díaz-Parra, O., Hernández, J. A., Zavala-Díaz, J. C., & Martínez-Rangel, M. G. (2007, September 25-28). Search algorithm for the constraint satisfaction problem of VRPTW. In *Proceedings of the Electronics, Robotics and Automotive Mechanics Conference*, México (pp 746-751).

Cruz-Chávez, M. A., Martínez-Oropeza, A., & Serna Barquera, S. A. (2010, September 28-October 1). Neighborhood hybrid structure for discrete optimization problems. In *Proceedings of the Electronics, Robotics and Automotive Mechanics Conference*, México (pp. 108-113).

Cruz-Chávez, M. A., & Díaz-Parra, O. (2010). Evolutionary algorithm for the vehicles routing problem with time windows based on a constraint satisfaction technique. *Computación y Sistemas, IPN, 13*(3), 257–272.

Cruz-Chávez, M. A., Rodríguez-León, A., Ávila-Melgar, E. Y., Juárez-Pérez, F., Cruz-Rosales, M. H., & Rivera-López, R. (2010). Gridification of genetic algorithm with reduced communication for the job shop scheduling problem. *International Journal of Grid and Distributed Computing, 3*(3), 13–28.

Cruz-Reyes, L., Gómez, C. G., Hernández, I. Y., Rangel, N., Álvarez, V. M., & González, J. J. (2008). An architecture for selecting data distribution algorithms. In *Proceeding of the 17th International Multi-conference on Advanced Computer Systems* (pp. 19-25).

Dantzig, G. B., & Ramser, J. H. (1959). The truck dispatching problem. *Management Science, 6*(1), 80–91. doi:10.1287/mnsc.6.1.80

Dasgupta, S., Papadimitriou, C. H., & Vazirani, U. V. (2006). *Algorithms*. New York, NY: McGraw-Hill.

Dash, M., & Liu, H. (1997). Feature selection for classification. *Intelligent Data Analysis, 1*, 131–156. doi:10.1016/S1088-467X(97)00008-5

Davis, L. (1985). Applying adaptive algorithms to epistatic domains. In *Proceedings of the International Joint Conference on Artificial Intelligence* (pp. 62-164).

Dawudo, A. H., & Effiong, C. E. (1985). Neonatal mortality: Effects of selective pediatric interventions. *Pediatrics, 75*(1), 51–57.

Dean, J., & Snell, S. (1991). Integrated manufacturing and job design: Moderating effects of organisational inertia. *Academy of Management Journal, 34*(4), 776–804. doi:10.2307/256389

Deb, K. (2001). *Multi-objective optimization using evolutionary algorithms*. Chichester, UK: John Wiley & Sons.

Delen, D., & Olson, D. (2008). *Advanced data mining techniques*. Berlin, Germany: Springer-Verlag.

Delgado, J. F. (2007). *Modelado matemático para el análisis y mejoramiento de los métodos aproximados para la solución de los proble-mas de enrutamiento, asignación de horarios y distribución de cargas: una aplicación a la entrega de productos embotellados* (Unpublished master's thesis). Posgrado en Ciencias de la Computación, Instituto Tecnológico de Ciudad Madero, Tamaulipas, México.

Di Battista, G., Eades, G., Tamassia, R., Ioannis, G., & Tollis, I. (1999). *Graph drawing: Algorithms for the visualization of graphs*. Upper Saddle River, NJ: Prentice Hall.

Dial, R. B. (1995). Autonomous dial a ride transit – Introductory overview. *Transportation Research Part C, Emerging Technologies, 3*, 261–275. doi:10.1016/0968-090X(95)00010-G

Díaz, J., Petit, J., & Serna, M. (2002). A survey of graph layout problems. *ACM Computing Surveys, 34*(3), 313–356. doi:10.1145/568522.568523

Díaz-Parra, O., & Cruz-Chávez, M. A. (2008). Evolutionary algorithm with intelligent mutation operator that solves the vehicle routing problem of clustered classification with Time Windows. *Polish Journal of Environmental Studies, 17*(4), 91–95.

Die Lecce, V., Dimauro, G., Guerreiro, A., Impedovo, S., Pirlo, G., Salzo, A., & Sarcinella, L. (1999). Selection of reference signatures for automatic signature verification. In *Proceedings of the Fifth International Conference on Document Analysis and Recognition* (pp. 597-600).

Dmitriev, A. N., Zhuravlev, Y. I., & Krendeleiev, F. P. (1966). On the mathematical principles of patterns and phenomena classification. *Diskretnyi Analiz, 7*, 3–15.

Dolfing, J. G. A. (1998). *Handwriting recognition and verification. A hidden Markov approach* (Unpublished doctoral dissertation). Eindhoven University of Technology, Centrum, The Netherlands.

Dorigo, M. (1991). *Positive feedback as a search strategy* (Tech. Rep. No. 91-016). Milano, Italy: Politecnico.

Dorigo, M., & Gambardella, L. M. (1996). *Ant colony system: A cooperative learning approach to the traveling salesman problem* (Tech. Rep. No. TR/IRIDIA/1996-5). Brussels, Belgium: IRIDIA, Université Libre de Bruxelles.

Dorigo, M., & Di Caro, G. (1999). Ant algorithms optimization. *Artificial Life*, 5(3), 137–172. doi:10.1162/106454699568728

Dorigo, M., & Gambardella, L. (1997). Ant colony system: A cooperative learning approach to the traveling salesman problem. *IEEE Transactions on Evolutionary Computation*, 1(1), 53–66. doi:10.1109/4235.585892

Dorigo, M., & Gambardella, L. M. (1997a). Ant colonies for the traveling salesman problem. *Biosystem*, 43, 73–81. doi:10.1016/S0303-2647(97)01708-5

Dorigo, M., & Gambardella, L. M. (1997b). Ant colony system: A cooperative learning approach to the traveling salesman problem. *IEEE Transactions on Evolutionary Computation*, 1, 53–66. doi:10.1109/4235.585892

Dorigo, M., & Maniezzo, V. (1996). The ant system: optimization by a colony of cooperating agents. *IEEE Transactions on Systems, Man, and Cybernetics*, 26(1), 1–13.

Dorigo, M., & Stützle, T. (2004). *Ant colony optimization*. Cambridge, MA: MIT Press.

Dorronsoro, B. (2005). *The VRP Web*. Retrieved from http://neo.lcc.uma.es/radiaeb/WebVRP/index.html

Dorronsoro, B. (2007). *The VRP Web. AUREN and Language and Computation Sciences of the University of Malaga*. Retrieved from http://neo.lcc.uma.es/radi-aeb/WebVRP

Duarte, A., Pantrigo, J. J., & Gallego, M. (2007). *Metaheurísticas*. Madrid, Spain: Dykinson.

Du, K.-L., & Swamy, M. N. S. (2010). *Neural networks in a softcomputing framework* (1st ed.). New York, NY: Springer.

Durbin, A. P. (2007). *Fluid dynamics with a computational perspective*. New York, NY: Cambridge University Press. doi:10.1017/CBO9780511619281

Edin, H. (2001). *Partial discharge studies with variable frequency of the applied voltage* (Unpublished doctoral dissertation). KTH Electrical Engineering, Stockholm, Sweden.

Eilon, S., Watson-Gandy, C. D. T., & Christofides, N. (1971). *Distribution management: Mathematical modeling and practical analysis*. UK: Compton Printing.

Elder, J., Miñe, G., & Nisbet, R. (2009). *Handbook of statistical analysis and data mining applications*. London, UK: Academic Press.

Endsley, M. R. (1993). The integration of human and advanced manufacturing systems. *Journal of Design and Manufacturing*, 3, 177–187.

Enríquez, S., Ponce de León, E., & Díaz, E. (2008). Calibración de un Algoritmo Genético para el Problema de la Minimización de Cruces en las Aristas de un Grafo. In *Avances en Computación Evolutiva, Memorias del IV Congreso Mexicano de Computación Evolutiva, Centro de Investigación en Matemáticas* (pp. 61-66).

Enríquez, S., Ponce de León, E., Díaz, E., & Padilla, A. (2010). A hybrid evolutionary algorithm for graph drawing: Edges crossing minimization problem. *Research in Computing Science, 45*.

Enríquez, S. (2009). *Metaheurística Evolutiva Híbrida para la Minimización de Cruces de las Aristas en el Dibujado de Grafos*. Aguascalientes, Mexico: Universidad Autónoma de Aguascalientes, Centro de Ciencias Básicas, Tesis y Disertaciones Académicas.

Epstein, L. (2006). Online bin packing with cardinality constraints. *SIAM Journal on Discrete Mathematics*, 20(4), 1015–1030. doi:10.1137/050639065

Erben, W. (2001). A grouping genetic algorithm for graph colouring and exam timetabling. In E. Burke & W. Erben (Eds.), *Practice and Theory of Automated Timetabling III* (LNCS 2079, pp. 132-156).

Erensal, Y. C., & Albayrak, E. (2004). Successful adoption of macroergonomics in manufacturing: Using a multicriteria decision-making methodology-analytic hierarchy process. *Human Factors and Ergonomics in Manufacturing*, 14(4), 353–377. doi:10.1002/hfm.20005

Ettlie, J. E. (1997). Integrated design and new product success. *Journal of Operations Management*, 5(1), 33–55. doi:10.1016/S0272-6963(96)00095-2

Falkenauer, E. (1996). A hybrid grouping genetic algorithm for bin packing. *Journal of Heuristics*, *2*(1), 5–30. doi:10.1007/BF00226291

Fasquel, J.-B., Stolz, C., & Bruynooghe, M. (2001). Real-time verification of handwritten signatures using a hybrid opto-electronical method. In *Proceedings of the 2nd International Symposium on Image and Signal Processing and Analysis*, Pula, Croatia (pp. 552-557).

Fauziyah, S. M., & Zahariah, M. H. (2009). Signature verification system using support vector machine. *Journal of Basic and Applied Sciences*, *1*(2), 291–294.

Ferguson, C. J., & Rueda, S. M. (2010). The Hitman study: Violent video game exposure effects on aggressive behavior, hostile feelings, and depression. *European Psychologist*, *15*(2), 99–108. doi:10.1027/1016-9040/a000010

Fine, G. A. (1987). Community and boundary: Personal experience stories of mushroom collectors. *Journal of Folklore Research*, *24*, 223–240.

Fischetti, M., Gonzales, J. J. S., & Toth, P. (1997). A branch-and-cut algorithm for the symmetric generalized traveling salesman problem. *Operations Research*, *45*(3), 378–394. doi:10.1287/opre.45.3.378

Flatberg, T., Hasle, G., Kloster, O., Nilssen, E. J., & Riise, A. (2007). Dynamic and stochastic vehicle routing in practice . In Zeimpekis, V., Tarantilis, C. D., Giaglis, G. M., & Minis, I. (Eds.), *Dynamic fleet management, operations research/computer science interfaces series* (Vol. 38, pp. 41–63). New York, NY: Springer. doi:10.1007/978-0-387-71722-7_3

Fleischmann, B. (1990). *The vehicle routing problem with multiple use of vehicles (Tech. Rep.)*. Hamburg, Germany: Fachbereigh Wirtschaftswissenschaften, University of Hamburg.

Fonseca, C. M., & Fleming, P. J. (1993). Genetic algorithms for multiobjective optimization: Formulation, discussion and generalization. In *Proceedings of the Fifth International Conference on Genetic Algorithms* (pp. 416-423).

Forssén, C. (2008). *Modelling of cavity partial discharges at variable applied frequency* (Unpublished doctoral dissertation). KTH Electrical Engineering, Stockholm, Sweden.

Fort, R., & Gill, A. (2000). Race and ethnicity assessment in baseball card markets. *Journal of Sports Economics*, *1*, 21–38. doi:10.1177/152700250000100103

Foster, I., & Kesselman, C. (Eds.). (2004). *The Grid 2, Second Edition: Blueprint for a new computing infrastructure* (The Elsevier Series in Grid Computing). San Francisco, CA: Morgan Kaufmann.

Friedrich, G. J. (2010). *Centrifugal pumps*. New York, NY: Springer.

Fujisawa, K., Kojima, M., Takeda, A., & Yamashita, M. (2004). Solving large scale optimization problems via grid and cluster computing. *Journal of the Operations Research Society of Japan*, *47*(4), 265–274.

Galushkin, I. (2007). *Neural networks theory*. New York, NY: Springer.

Gambardella, L. M., & Dorigo, M. (1995). Ant-Q: A reinforcement learning approach to the traveling salesman problem. In *Proceedings of the Twelfth International Conference on Machine Learning*, Tahoe City, CA (pp. 252-260).

Gambardella, L., Taillar, E., & Agazzi, G. (1999). *MACS-VRPTW: A multiple ant colony system for vehicle routing problems with Time Windows* (Technical Report IDSIA-06-99). Ticino, Switzerland: IDSIA.

Gao, J., Gindy, N., & Chen, X. (2006). An automated GD&T inspection system based on non-contact 3D digitization. *International Journal of Production Research*, *44*(1), 117–134. doi:10.1080/09638280500219737

Garey, M. R., & Johnson, D. S. (1979). *Computer and intractability: a guide to the theory of NP-completeness* (pp. 1-76, 74, 214-226). Paris, France: Bell Telephone Laboratories.

Garey, M. R., & Johnson, D. S. (1979). *Computers and intractability: A guide to the theory of NP-completeness*. New York, NY: W. H. Freeman.

Garey, M. R., & Johnson, D. S. (1983). Crossing number is NP-complete. *SIAM Journal on Algebraic and Discrete Methods*, *4*, 312–316. doi:10.1137/0604033

Garey, M. R., & Jonson, D. S. (1979). *Computers and intractability a guide to the theory of NP- completeness*. New York, NY: W. H. Freeman.

Gehring, H., & Homberger, J. (1999). *A parallel hybrid evolutionary metaheuristic for the vehicle routing problem with Time Windows* (pp. 57-64). Jyvaskyla, Finland: University of Jyvaskyla. Retrieved from http://www.sintef.no/Projectweb/TOP/Problems/VRPTW/Homberger-benchmark/

Gendreau, M., Iori, M., Laporte, G., & Martello, S. (2008). A tabu search heuristic for the vehicle routing problem with two-dimensional loading constraints. *Networks*, *51*(1), 4–18. doi:10.1002/net.20192

Gendreau, M., Laporte, G., Musaraganyi, C., & Taillard, E. (1999). A tabu search heuristic for the heterogeneous fleet vehicle routing problem. *PERGAMON Computer & Operations Research*, *26*, 1153–1173. doi:10.1016/S0305-0548(98)00100-2

Gendreau, M., & Potvin, J.-Y. (1998). Dynamic vehicle routing and dispatching . In Crainic, T. G., & Laporte, G. (Eds.), *Fleet management and logistics* (pp. 115–126). Boston, MA: Kluwer Academic. doi:10.1007/978-1-4615-5755-5_5

Glover, F. (1998). A template for scatter search and path relinking. In J.-K. Hao, E. Lutton, E. M. A. Ronald, M. Schoenauer, & D. Snyers (Eds.), In *Proceedings of Selected Papers from the Third European Conference on Artificial Evolution* (LNCS 1363, pp. 3-54).

Glover, F. (1977). Heuristics for integer programming using surrogate constrains. *Decision Sciences*, *8*, 156–166. doi:10.1111/j.1540-5915.1977.tb01074.x

Glover, F., & Kochenberger, G. (2003). *Handbook of metaheuristics*. Boston, MA: Kluwer Academic.

Goel, A., & Gruhn, V. (2005). Solving a dynamic real-life vehicle routing problem . In Haasis, H., Kopfer, H., & Schönberger, J. (Eds.), *Operations research proceedings* (pp. 367–372). Berlin, Germany: Springer-Verlag. doi:10.1007/3-540-32539-5_58

Goel, A., & Grum, V. (2005). Solving a dynamic real life vehicle routing problem . In Haasis, H.-D., Kopfer, H., & Schönberger, J. (Eds.), *Operations research proceedings* (pp. 367–372). New York, NY: Springer. doi:10.1007/3-540-32539-5_58

Gog, A., & Dumitrescu, D. (2006a). Adaptive search in evolutionary combinatorial optimization. In *Proceedings of the International Conference Bio-Inspired Computing-Theory and Applications*, Wuhan, China (pp. 123-130).

Gog, A., & Dumitrescu, D. (2006b). A new recombination operator for permutation based encoding. In *Proceedings of the 2nd International Conference on Intelligent Computer Communication and Processing* (pp. 11-16).

Gog, A., Dumitrescu, D., & Hirsbrunner, B. (2007). Best–worst recombination scheme for combinatorial optimization. In *Proceedings of the International Conference on Genetic and Evolutionary Methods*, Las Vegas, NV (pp. 115-119).

Goh, C., Chin, Y., Tung, A., & Chen, C. (1996). A revised weighted sum decision model for robot selection. *Computers & Industrial Engineering*, *30*(2), 193–199. doi:10.1016/0360-8352(95)00167-0

Goldberg, D. E., & Lingle, R., Jr. (1985). Alleles, Loci and the TSP. In *Proceedings of the First International Conference on Genetic Algorithms and their Applications* (pp. 154-159).

Goldberg, D. E., & Richardson, J. (1987). Genetic algorithm with sharing for multimodal function optimization. In *Proceedings of the Second International Conference on Genetic Algorithms and their Applications* (pp. 41-49).

Goldberg, D. E. (1989). *Genetic algorithms in search, optimization and machine learning*. Reading, MA: Addison-Wesley.

Gómez, C. G. (2010). *Afinación Estática Global de Redes Complejas y Control Dinámico Local de la Función Tiempo de Vida en el Problema de Direccionamiento de Consultas Semánticas* (Unpublished doctoral dissertation). Instituto Politécnico Nacional, CICATA, UA, México.

González-Barbosa, J. J., Delgado-Orta, J. F., Cruz-Reyes, L., Fraire-Huacuja, H. J., & Ramirez-Saldivar, A. (2010). Comparative analysis of hybrid techniques for an ant colony system algorithm applied to solve a real-world transportation problem . In Melin, P., Kacprzyk, J., & Pedrycz, W. (Eds.), *Soft Computing for Recognition Based on Biometrics, Studies in Computational Intelligence* (*Vol. 312*, pp. 365–385). Berlin, Germany: Springer-Verlag. doi:10.1007/978-3-642-15111-8_23

González, J. J., Delgado, J. F., Cruz, L., Fraire, H. J., & Ramirez, A. (2010). Comparative analysis of hybrid techniques for an ant colony system algorithm applied to solve a real-world transportation problem . In Melin, P., Kacprzyk, J., & Pedrycz, W. (Eds.), *Soft computing for recognition based on biometrics, studies in computational intelligence* (*Vol. 312*, pp. 365–388). Berlin, Germany: Springer-Verlag. doi:10.1007/978-3-642-15111-8_23

Gonzalez-Roman, A., Tecpoyotl-Torres, M., Escobedo-Alatorre, J., Pal-Verma, S., & Sánchez-Mondragón, J. (2006). A semi-spherical Irradiance meter used as a quality control device. In *Proceedings of the First Multiconference on Electronics and Photonics* (pp. 253-256).

Gries, F. D. (2000). *On-line signature verification* (Unpublished master's thesis). Michigan State University, Ann Arbor, MI.

Grossman, D. A. (2004). *Information retrieval: algorithms and heuristics* (2nd ed.). Dordrecht, The Netherlands: Springer-Verlag.

Grossman, R. L., Hornick, M. F., & Meyer, G. (2002). Data mining standards initiatives. *Communications of the ACM, 45*(8). doi:10.1145/545151.545180

Guazzelli, A., Lin, W., & Tena, T. (2010). *PMML in action: Unleashing the power of open standards for data mining and predictive analytics*. Seattle, WA: CreateSpace.

Gunasekaran, A., Love, P. E. D., Rahimi, F., & Miele, R. (2001). A model for investment justification in information technology projects. *International Journal of Information Management, 21*, 349–364. doi:10.1016/S0268-4012(01)00024-X

Guru, D. S., & Prakash, H. N. (2009). Online signature verification and recognition: an approach based on symbolic representation. *IEEE Transactions on Pattern Analysis and Machine Intelligence, 31*(6), 1059–1073. doi:10.1109/TPAMI.2008.302

Gwirc, S., Rigotti, J., Federico, A., & Acquaticci, F. (2007). *6o. Jornada de desarrollo e innovación tecnológica. Imágenes Ultrasónicas con Transductor Piezoeléctrico de Película*. Buenos Aires, Argentina: Instituto Nacional De Tecnología Industrial.

Gyan-Baffour, G. (1994). Advanced manufacturing technology, employee participation and economic performance: An empirical analysis. *Journal of Managerial Issues, 6*(4), 491–505.

György, A., Lugosi, G., & Ottucsàk, G. (2010). On-line sequential bin packing. *Journal of Machine Learning Research, 11*(1), 89–109.

Hangai, S., Yamanaka, S., & Hamamoto, T. (2000). On-line signature verification based on altitude and direction of pen movement. In *Proceedings of the IEEE International Conference on Multimedia and Expo* (pp. 489-492).

Hansen, P., & Mladenovic, N. (2001). Variable neighborhood search: Principles and applications. *European Journal of Operational Research, 130*, 449–467. doi:10.1016/S0377-2217(00)00100-4

Hart, S., Jan, H. E., Tzokas, N., & Commandeur, H. R. (2003). Industrial companies evaluation criteria in new product development gates. *Journal of Product Innovation Management, 20*(1), 22–36. doi:10.1111/1540-5885.201003

Hasle, G., Koster, O., Nilssen, E. J., Riise, A., & Flatberg, T. (2007). Dynamic and stochastic vehicle routing in practice . In Zeimpekis, V., Tarantilis, C. D., Giaglis, G. M., & Minis, I. (Eds.), *Dynamic Fleet Management, Operation Research/Computer Science Interfaces Series* (*Vol. 38*, pp. 45–68). New York, NY: Springer.

Helander, M. (1995). Conceptualizing the use of axiomatic design procedures in ergonomics. In *Proceeding of the IEA World Conference*, Rio de Janeiro, Brazil (pp. 38-41).

Herman, I., Melancon, G., & Marshall, S. (2000). Graph visualization and navigation in information visualization: A survey. *IEEE Transactions on Visualization and Computer Graphics, 6*(1), 24–43. doi:10.1109/2945.841119

Hernández-Mejia, J. C., Perkel, J., Harley, R., Begovic, M., Hampton, R. N., & Hartlein, R. (2008). Determining routes for analysis of partial discharge signals derived from field. *IEEE Transactions on Dielectrics and Electrical Insulation, 15*(6), 1517–1525. doi:10.1109/TDEI.2008.4712653

Herrera, J. (2006). *Development of a methodology based on heuristics for the integral solution of routing, scheduling and loading problems on distribution and delivery processes of products* (Unpublished master's thesis). Posgrado en Ciencias de la Computación, Instituto Tecnológico de Ciudad Madero, Tamaulipas, México.

Herrera, J. A. (2006). *Desarrollo de una Metodología Basada en Heuristicas para la Solución Integral de Problemas de Asignación de Rutas, Horarios y Cargas en el Proceso de Distribución y Entrega de Productos* (Unpublished master's thesis). Posgrado en Ciencias de la Computación, Instituto Tecnológico de Ciudad Madero, México.

Hesketh, G. B. (1997). COUNTERMATCH: a neural network approach to automatic signature verification. In *Proceedings of the IEEE Colloquium on Neural Networks for Industrial Applications*, London, UK (pp. 1-2).

Hillier, F., & Lieberman, G. (1991). *Introducción a la Investigación de operaciones*. Estado de Mexico, Mexico: McGraw-Hill Interamericana de Mexico S.A. de C.V.

Hirose, H., Hikita, M., Ohtsuka, S., Tsuru, S., & Ichimaru, J. (2008). Diagnosis of electric power apparatus using the decision tree method. *IEEE Transactions on Dielectrics and Electrical Insulation, 15*, 1252–1260. doi:10.1109/TDEI.2008.4656232

Ho, K. K., Schroder, H., & Leedharn, G. (2001). Codebooks for signature verification and handwriting recognition. In *Proceedings of the Seventh International Conference on Intelligent Information Systems*.

Hobel, C. J., Hyvarinen, M. A., Okada, D. M., & Oh, W. (1973). Prenatal and intrapartum high-risk screening. I. Prediction of the high-rish neonate. *American Journal of Obstetrics and Gynecology, 117*(1), 1–9.

Holland, J. (1992). *Adaptation in natural and artificial systems*. Ann Arbor, MI: University of Michigan Press.

Holmes, J. S. Jr. (2009). Societal and economic valuation of technology-transfer deals. *Acta Astronautica, 65*(5), 834–840. doi:10.1016/j.actaastro.2009.01.070

Hornick, M. (2004). *JSR-73 Expert Group. Java TM Specification Request 73: JavaTM Data Mining*. Retrieved from http://www.jcp.org/en/jsr/detail?id=73

Horowitz, P., & Hill, W. (2001). *The art of electronics* (2nd ed.). Cambridge, UK: Cambridge University Press.

Horstmann, C. S., & Cornell, G. (2006). *Core Java – Fundamentals* (*Vol. 1*). Santa Clara, CA: Sun Microsystems.

Huang, Z., Chung, W., Ong, T.-H., & Chen, H. (2002). A graph-based recommender system for digital library. In *Proceedings of the 2nd ACM/IEEE-CS Joint Conference on Digital Libraries* (pp. 65-73).

Huang, J. W., Kang, L. S., & Chen, Y. P. (2000). A new graph drawing algorithm for undirected graphs. *Software Journal, 11*(1), 138–142.

International Electrotechnical Commission. (2000). *IEC 60270: High-voltage test techniques - Partial discharge measurements* (2nd ed.). Geneva, Switzerland: Author.

Ismail, Z., & Irhamah. (2008). Solving the vehicle routing problem with stochastic demands via hybrid genetic algorithm-tabu search. *Journal of Mathematics and Statistics, 4*(3), 161–167. doi:10.3844/jmssp.2008.161.167

Ismail, Z., & Loh, S. L. (2009). Ant colony optimization for solving solid waste collection scheduling problems. *Journal of Mathematics and Statistics, 5*(3), 199–205. doi:10.3844/jmssp.2009.199.205

Jackson, P., & Sheridan, D. (2005). Clause form conversions for boolean circuits. In H. H. Hoos & D. G. Mitchell (Eds.), *Proceedings of the 7th International Conference on Theory and Applications of Satisfiability Testing* (LNCS 3542, pp. 183-198).

Jang, J. S., Sun, C. T., & Mizutani, E. (1997). *Neuro-Fuzzy and soft computing: A computational approach to learning and machine intelligence*. Upper Saddle River, NJ: Prentice Hall.

Jansen, B. J. (1998). The graphical user interface: An introduction. *SIGCHI Bulletin, 30*(2), 22–26. doi:10.1145/279044.279051

Jensen, C. N. (1997). *Nonlinear systems with discrete and continuous elements* (Doctoral dissertation). Lyngby, Denmark: IMM, The Technical University of Denmark.

Ji, H. M., Lee, S. G., Cho, S. Y., & Kim, Y.-S. (2009). A hybrid on-line signature verification system supporting multi-confidential levels defined by data mining techniques. *International Journal of Intelligent Systems Technologies and Applications*, *9*(3-4), 262–273.

Jiménez, S., & Gay, J. (1997). *Vigilancia nutricional materno infantil. Guías para la atención primaria de salud*. La Habana, Cuba: Editorial Caguayo.

Jin, T., Guo, S., Wang, F., & Lim, A. (2004). One-stage search for multi-depot vehicle routing problem. In *Proceedings of the Conference on Intelligent Systems and Control* (pp. 446-129).

Johnson, D. S. (1974). Fast algorithms for bin packing. *Journal of Computer and System Sciences*, *8*(3), 272–314. doi:10.1016/S0022-0000(74)80026-7

Johnson, D. S., & McGeoch, L. A. (1995). The traveling salesman problem: A case study in local optimization. In Aarts, E. H. L., & Lenstra, J. K. (Eds.), *Local search and combinatorial optimization*. New York, NY: John Wiley & Sons.

Johnston, P. (2002). *Schema imports the Dublin Core elements from the DCMI schema for unqualified Dublin Core*. Retrieved from http://www.openarchives.org/OAI/2.0/oai_dc.xsd

Jones, T. M. (2005). *AI application programming* (2nd ed.). Hingham, MA: Charles River Media.

Jong, C., Kant, G., & Vliet, A. V. (1996). *On finding minimal route duration in the vehicle routing problem with multiple time windows (Tech. Rep.)*. Utrecht, The Netherlands: Department of Computer Science, Utrecht University.

Jørgensen, M. (1984). *Distribution of everyday necessities- Minimization of the fleet size* (Master's thesis). Lyngby, Denmark: IMM, The Technical University of Denmark.

Kahraman, C., & Kulak, O. (2005). *Fuzzy multi-attribute decision making using an information axiom based approach (fuzzy multi-criteria with recent developments*. New York, NY: Springer.

Kahraman, C., & Çebı, S. (2008). A new multi-attribute decision making method: Hierarchical fuzzy axiomatic design. *Expert Systems with Applications*, *36*(3).

Kakati, M. (1997). Strategic evaluation of advanced manufacturing technology. *International Journal of Economics*, *53*(2), 141–156.

Kang, J., & Park, S. (2003). Algorithms for the variable sized bin packing problem. *European Journal of Operational Research*, *147*(2), 365–372. doi:10.1016/S0377-2217(02)00247-3

Kantardzic, M. (2007). *Data clustering: Theory, algorithms and methods* (pp. 53–57). Philadelphia, PA: ASA-SIAM.

Karadimas, N., Kouzas, G., Anagnostopoulos, I., Loumos, V., & Kayafas, E. (2005). Ant colony route optimization for municipal services. In *Proceedings of the 19th European Conference on Modelling and Simulation*.

Karadimas, N., Doukas, N., Kolokathi, M., & Defteraiou, G. (2008). Routing optimization heuristics algorithms for urban solid waste transportation management. *WSEAS Transactions on Computers*, *7*(12), 2022–2031.

Karassik, J. I. (2008). *Pump handbook* (4th ed.). New York, NY: McGraw-Hill.

Karp, R. M. (1972). Reducibility among combinatorial problems. In Miller, R. E., & Thatcher, J. W. (Eds.), *Complexity of computer computations* (pp. 85–103). New York, NY: Plenum Press.

Karwowski, W. (2005). Ergonomics and human factors: the paradigms for science, engineering, design, technology and management of human-compatible systems. *Ergonomics*, *48*(5), 436–463. doi:10.1080/00140130400029167

Karwowski, W. (2006). On measure of the human-system compatibility. *Theoretical Issues in Ergonomics Science*, 12.

Kasabov, N. K. (1998). *Foundations of neural networks, fuzzy systems, and knowledge engineering*. Cambridge, MA: MIT Press.

Kautz, H. A., & Selman, B. (1999). Unifying SAT-based and graph-based planning. In *Proceedings of the Sixteenth International Joint Conference on Artificial Intelligence* (pp. 318-325). San Francisco, CA: Morgan Kaufmann.

Kesseler, E., & Knapen, E. G. (2006). Towards human-centre design: Two case studies. *Journal of Systems and Software, 79*(3). doi:10.1016/j.jss.2005.05.012

Khouja, M. (1998). An aggregate production planning framework for the evaluation of volume and flexibility. *Production Planning and Control, 9*(2), 127–137. doi:10.1080/095372898234343

Kim, J., Choi, W., Oh, S., Park, K., & Grzybowski, S. (2008). Partial discharge pattern recognition using fuzzy-neural networks (FNNs) algorithm. In *Proceedings of the IEEE International Power Modulators and High Voltage Conference* (pp. 272-275).

Kiran, K. G. (2011). *Online signature verification techniques* (Unpublished master's thesis). National Institute of Technology Rourkela, Orissa, India.

Kodali, R., & Sangwan, K. S. (2004). Multi-attribute decision models for justification of cellular manufacturing systems. *International Journal of Business Performance Management, 6*(3-4), 1–10.

Kohavi, R., & Jhon, G. H. (1997). Wrappers for feature subset selection. *Artificial Intelligence, 97*(1-2), 273–324. doi:10.1016/S0004-3702(97)00043-X

Kohonen, T., Oja, E., Simula, O., Visa, A., & Kangas, J. (1996). Engineering applications of self organizing map. *Proceedings of the IEEE, 84.*

Komiya, Y., & Matsumoto, T. (1999). On-line pen input signature verification PPI (pen-Position/pen-Pressure/pen-Inclination). In *Proceedings of the IEEE International Conference on Systems, Man and Cybernetics.*

Koza, J. R. (1992). *Genetic programming: On the programming of computers by means of natural selection.* Cambridge, MA: MIT Press.

Krivda, A. (1995). Automated recognition of partial discharge. *IEEE Transactions on Dielectrics and Electrical Insulation, 28*, 796–821. doi:10.1109/94.469976

Kröse, B., & Van der Smagt, P. (1996). *An introduction to neural networks* (8th ed.). Amsterdam, The Netherlands: University of Amsterdam. Retrieved from http://www.fwi.uva.nl/research/neuro/

Kulak, O. (2005). Fuzzy multi-attribute equipment section based on information axiom. *Journal of Materials Processing Technology, 169*(3), 337–345. doi:10.1016/j.jmatprotec.2005.03.030

Kulak, O., & Kahraman, C. (2005a). Multi-attribute comparison of advanced manufacturing systems using fuzzy vs. crisp axiomatic design approach. *International Journal of Production Economics, 95*, 415–424. doi:10.1016/j.ijpe.2004.02.009

Kulak, O., & Kahraman, C. (2005b). Fuzzy multi-attribute selection among transportation companies using axiomatic design and analytic hierarchy process. *Information Sciences, 170*, 191–210. doi:10.1016/j.ins.2004.02.021

Kumiko, Y., Daigo, M., Satoshi, S., & Takashi, M. (2010). Visual-based online signature verification using features extracted from video. *Journal of Network and Computer Applications, 33*(3), 333–341. doi:10.1016/j.jnca.2009.12.010

Lai, K. X., Phung, B. T., & Blackburn, T. R. (2008). Descriptive data mining of partial discharge using decision tree with genetic algorithms. In *Proceedings of the Australasian Universities Conference on Power Engineering* (pp. 1-6).

Laporte, G., & Nobert, Y. (1983). Generalized traveling salesman problem through n sets of nodes: An integer programming approach. *Infor, 21*(1), 61–75.

Larrañaga, P., Lozano, J. A., & Mühlenbein, H. (2003). Estimation of distribution algorithms applied to combinatorial optimization problems. *Inteligencia Artificial, Revista Iberoamericana de Inteligencia Artificial,* (19), 149-168.

Larranaga, P., Kuijpers, C. M. H., Murga, R. H., Inza, I., & Dizdarevic, S. (1999). Genetic algorithms for the traveling salesman problem: A review of representation and operators. *Artificial Intelligence Review, 13*, 129–170. doi:10.1023/A:1006529012972

Larranaga, P., Kuijpers, C. M, H., Poza, M., & Murga, R. H. (1997). Decomposing bayesian networks: Triangulation of the moral graph with genetic algorithms. *Statistics and Computing, 7*(1), 19–34. doi:10.1023/A:1018553211613

Larrañaga, P., & Lozano, J. A. (2002). *Estimation of distribution algorithms: a new tool for evolutionary computation.* Boston, MA: Kluwer Academic.

Larsen, A., Madsen Oli, B. G., & Solomon, M. M. (1999). *Partially dynamic vehicle routing - Models and algorithms (Tech. Rep.).* Lyngby, Denmark: The Department of Mathematical Modelling, The Technical University of Denmark.

Larson, R. C., & Odoni, A. R. (1980). *Urban operations research.* Upper Saddle River, NJ: Prentice Hall.

Larson, R. C., & Odoni, A. R. (1980). *Urban operations research.* Upper Saddle River, NJ: Prentice Hall.

Last, M., Kandel, A., & Maimon, O. (2001). Information theoretic algorithm for feature selection. *Pattern Recognition Letters, 22*(6-7), 799–811. doi:10.1016/S0167-8655(01)00019-8

Laustanou, K. (2007). *MySpace Music.* Retrieved from http://www.myspace.com/music

Lawler, E. (1985). *Combinatorial optimization: Networks and matroids.* New York, NY: Dover.

Lazo, C. M. (2003). *Reconocimiento Lógico Combinatorio de Patrones.* Havana, Cuba: Instituto de Cibernética, Matemática y Física.

Lazo, C. M., & Shulcloper, R. J. (1995). Determining the feature relevance for non classically described objects and a new algorithm to compute typical fuzzy testors. *Pattern Recognition Letters, 16*, 1259–1265. doi:10.1016/0167-8655(95)00077-8

Lejtman, D. Z., & George, S. E. (2001). On-line handwritten signature verification using wavelets and back-propagation neural networks. In *Proceedings of the Sixth International Conference on Document Analysis and Recognition,* Seattle, WA.

Lenstra, J. K., & Rinnooy Kan, A. H. G. (1981). Complexity of vehicle routing and scheduling problems. *Networks, 11*, 221–227. doi:10.1002/net.3230110211

Levine, J., & Ducatelle, F. (2004). Ant colony optimazation for bin packing and cutting stock problems. *The Journal of the Operational Research Society, 55*(7), 705–716. doi:10.1057/palgrave.jors.2601771

Lewis, D. D. (1991). Evaluating text categorization. In *Proceedings of the Speech and Natural Language Workshop on Defense Advanced Research Projects Agency* (pp. 312-318).

Lilly, J. H. (2010). *Fuzzy control and identification* (1st ed.). New York, NY: John Wiley & Sons. doi:10.1002/9780470874240

Li, M. (2006). Multiobjective evolutionary algorithms with immunity for SLAM. *Advances in Artificial Intelligence, 26*, 27–36.

Lim, D., Ong, Y.-S., Jin, Y., Sendhoff, B., & Lee, B.-S. (2007). Efficient hierarchical parallel genetic algorithms using grid computing. *Future Generation Computer Systems, 23*(4), 658–670. doi:10.1016/j.future.2006.10.008

Liu, P., Zhu, J., Liu, L., Li, Y., & Zhang, X. (2005, June 13-15). Data mining application in prosecution committee for unsupervised learning. In *Proceedings of the International Conference on Services Systems and Services Management* (Vol. 2, pp 1061-1064).

Liu, B., Choo, S.-H., Lok, S.-L., Leong, S.-M., Lee, S.-C., Poon, F.-P., & Tan, H.-H. (1994). Finding the shortest route using cases, knowledge, and Djikstra's Algorithm. *IEEE Expert, 9*(5), 7–11. doi:10.1109/64.331478

Livingstone, D. J. (2008). *Artificial neural networks methods and applications.* Sandown, NH: Humana Press.

Lobanoff, V. S. (1992). *Centrifugal pumps design and application.* Oxford, UK: Butterworth-Heinemann.

Long, D., Fox, M., & Hamdi, M. (2002). Reformulation in planning. In S. Koenig & R. C. Holte (Eds.), *Proceedings of the 5th International Symposium on Abstraction, Reformulation, and Approximation* (LNCS 2371, pp. 18-32).

LPMP-CNPq. (2005). *Padronização XML: Curriculum Vitae.* Retrieved from http://lmpl.cnpq.br

Lu, J., Zhang, G., & Ruan, D. (2007). *Multi-objective group decision making: Methods software and applications with fuzzy set techniques.* Singapore: Imperial College Press. Retrieved from http://site.ebrary.com/lib/uacj/Doc?id=10188771&ppg=206

Luna, F., Nebro, A., Alba, E., & Durillo, J. (2008). Solving large-scale real-world telecommunication problems using a grid-based genetic algorithm. *Engineering Optimization, 40*(11), 1067–1084. doi:10.1080/03052150802294581

Lund, K., Madsen Oli, B. G., & Rygaard, J. M. (1996). *Vehicle routing problems with varying degrees of dynamism (Tech. Rep.)*. Lyngby, Denmark: IMM, The Department of Mathematical Modelling, The Technical University of Denmark.

MacLennan, J., Tang, Z., & Crivat, B. (2008). *Data mining with Microsoft SQL*. Mississauga, ON, Canada: John Wiley & Sons.

MacQueen, J. B. (1967). Some methods for classification and analysis of multivariate observations. In *Proceedings of the 5th Berkeley Symposium on Mathematical Statistics and Probability*, Berkeley, CA (Vol. 1, pp. 281-297).

Macy, M. W., & Willer, R. (2002). From FACTORS TO ACTORS: Computational SOCIOLOGY AND AGENT-BASED MODELING. *Annual Review of Sociology, 28*, 143–166. doi:10.1146/annurev.soc.28.110601.141117

Mahajan, Y. S., Fu, Z., & Sharad, M. (2005). Zchaff2004: an efficient SAT solver. In H. H. Hoos & D. G. Mitchell (Eds.), *Proceedings of the 7th International Conference on Theory and Applications of Satisfiability Testing* (LNCS 3542, pp. 360-375).

Mahnig, T., & Mühlenbein, H. (2001). Wright's equation and evolutionary computation. In *Proceedings of the Conference on Advances in Fuzzy Systems and Evolutionary Computation*.

Maida, J. C. (2003). *An illumination modeling system for human factor analyses*. Houston, TX: Space Human Factors Laboratory/Flight Crew Support Division/NASA Johnson Space Center.

Malandraki, C. (1989). *Time dependent vehicle routing problems: Formulations, solution algorithms and computational experiments* (Unpublished doctoral dissertation). Northwestern University, New York, NY.

Maldonado-Macías, A. (2010). *An ergonomic evaluation model for planning an selection of advanced manufacturing technology* (Unpublished doctoral dissertation). Technological Institute of Juárez, Juárez, Mexico.

Maldonado-Macías, A., Noriega, S., Díaz, J., Sánchez, J., García, J., & De la Riva, J. (2009). Fuzzy axiomatic design approach for the evaluation of ergonomic compatibility of CNC machines: A case of study. In *Proceedings of the 14th Annual International Conference of Industrial Engineering, Theory, Applications and Practice*, Anaheim CA (pp. 182-188).

Maldonado-Macías, A., Sánchez, J., Noriega, S., Díaz, J. J., García, J. L., & Vidal, L. (2009). A hierarchical fuzzy axiomatic design survey for ergonomic compatibility evaluation of advanced manufacturing technology. In *Proceedings of the 21st Annual International Conference of Occupational Safety and Ergonomics, International Society for Occupational Ergonomics and Safety* (pp. 270-277).

Manyem, P. (2002). Bin packing and covering with longest items at the bottom: online version. *The ANZIAM Journal, 43*, 186–232.

Marinakis, Y., & Migdalas, A. (2002). Heuristic solutions of vehicle routing problems in supply chain management. In Pardalos, P. M., & Migdalas, A. (Eds.), *Combinatorial and global optimization* (1st ed.). Singapore: World Scientific. doi:10.1142/9789812778215_0014

Markalous, S. (2006). *Detection and location of Partial Discharges in Power Transformers using acoustic and electromagnetic signals* (Unpublished doctoral dissertation). Stuttgart University, Stuttgart, Germany.

Martello, S., & Toth, P. (1990). *Knapsack problems: algorithms and computer implementations*. New York, NY: John Wiley & Sons.

Martello, S., & Toth, P. (1990). *Knapsack problems-algorithms and computer implementations*. Chichester, UK: John Wiley & Sons.

Martello, S., & Toth, P. (1990). Lower bounds and reduction procedures for the bin packing problem. *Discrete Applied Mathematics, 28*(1), 59–70. doi:10.1016/0166-218X(90)90094-S

Martens, R., & Claesen, L. (1996). On-line signature verification by dynamic time-warping. In *Proceedings of the 13th International Conference on Pattern Recognition* (pp. 38-42).

Martens, R., & Claesen, L. (1997). Dynamic programming optimisation for on-line signature verification. In *Proceedings of the Fourth International Conference on Document Analysis and Recognition* (pp. 653-656).

Martí, R., & Laguna, M. (2003). Scatter Search: Diseño básico y estrategias avanzadas. Inteligencia Artificial. *Revista Iberoamericana de Inteligencia Artificial, 19*.

Martínez, R. J. C. (2004). *Verificación de Firmas Manuscritas en Línea con Modelado Óptimo de Características y Aproximación Digital Forense* (Unpublished doctoral dissertation). Facultad de Ingeniería, Universidad Nacional Autónoma de México, Ciudad de México, México.

Martínez, R. J. C., & Alcántara, S. R. (2004). Optimal prototype functions of features for on-line signature verification. *International Journal of Pattern Recognition and Artificial Intelligence, 18*(7), 1189–1206. doi:10.1142/S021800140400371X

Maslakowoski, M. (2001), *Aprendiendo MySQL en 21 Días* (pp. 10-65, 78-88, 107-154). Upper Saddle River, NJ: Prentice Hall.

Matai, R., Singh, S., & Mittal, M. L. (2010). Traveling salesman problem: an overview of applications, formulations, and solution approaches. In D. Davendra (Ed.), *Traveling salesman problem, theory and applications.* Rijeka, Croatia: InTech. Retrieved February 15, 2011, from http://www.intechopen.com/articles/show/title/traveling-salesman-problem-an-overview-of-applications-formulations-and-solution-approaches

Mazroua, A. A., Salama, M. M. A., & Bartnikas, R. (1993). PD pattern recognition with neural networks using the multilayer perception technique. *IEEE Transactions on Electrical Insulation, 28*, 1082–1089. doi:10.1109/14.249382

McCue, C. (2007). *Data mining and predictive analysis: Intelligence gathering and crime analysis.* Oxford, UK: Butterworth-Heinemann.

McCulloch, W., & Pitts, W. (1943). A logical calculus of the ideas immanent in neurons activity. *The Bulletin of Mathematical Biophysics, 5*, 115–133. doi:10.1007/BF02478259

McIntosh, W. E., & Schmeichel, B. (2004). Collectors and collecting: A social psychological perspective. *Leisure Sciences, 26*, 85–97. doi:10.1080/01490400490272639

McNeill, D., & Freiberger, P. (1994). *Fuzzy Logic: The revolutionary computer technology that is changing our world.* New York, NY: Simon and Schuster.

Melton, J., & Eisenberg, A. (2002). *SQL y Java, Guía para SQLJ, JDBC y tecnologías relacionadas* (pp. 1-51, 97-325). Benito Juárez, Mexico: Alfaomega RA-MA.

Melton, J., & Eisenberg, A. (2001). SQL multimedia and application packages (SQL/MM). *SIGMOD Record, 30*(4), 97–102. doi:10.1145/604264.604280

Meredith, J. R., & Suresh, N. C. (1986). Justification techniques for advanced manufacturing technologies. *International Journal of Production Research, 24*(5), 1043–1057. doi:10.1080/00207548608919787

Michalewicz, Z., & Fogel, D. B. (2204). *How to solve it: Modern heuristics* (2nd ed.). Berlin, Germany: Springer-Verlag.

Michalewicz, Z. (1996). *Genetic programs + data structures = Evolution programs* (3rd ed.). Berlin, Germany: Springer-Verlag.

Miettinen, K. M. (1999). *Nonlinear multiobjective optimization.* Boston, MA: Kluwer Academic.

Mingming, M., & Wijesoma, W. S. (2000). Automatic on-line signature verification based on Multiple Models. In *Proceedings of the IEEE/IAFE/INFORMS Conference on Computational Intelligence for Financial Engineering* (pp. 30-33).

Mingozzi, A. (2003). An exact algorithm for period and multi-depot vehicle routing problems. In *Proceedings of the Odysseus Second International Workshop on Freight Transportation and Logistics*, Palermo, Italy.

Mingozzi, A., & Vallet, A. (2003). An exact algorithm for period and multi-depot vehicle routing problems. In *Proceedings of the 16th Symposium on Mathematical Programming.*

Mital, A., & Arunkumar, P. (2004). Advanced technologies and humans in manufacturing workplaces: an interdependent relationship. *International Journal of Industrial Ergonomics, 33*, 295–313. doi:10.1016/j.ergon.2003.10.002

Mitchell, M., Holland, J. H., & Forrest, S. (1994). When will a genetic algorithm outperform hill climbing? *Advances in Neural Information Processing Systems, 6*, 51–58.

Mitrovic-Minic, S., & Krishnamurti, R. (2006). The multiple TSP with Time Windows: Vehicle bounds based on precedence graphs. *Operations Research Letters, 34*(1), 111–120. doi:10.1016/j.orl.2005.01.009

Mitsuo, G., & Runwei, C. (2000). *Genetic algorithms & engineering optimization.* New York, NY: John Wiley & Sons.

Moscato, P., & Cotta, C. (2010). A modern introduction to memetic algorithms . In Gendreau, M., & Potvin, J.-Y. (Eds.), *Handbook of metaheuristics, international series in operations research & management science (Vol. 146,* pp. 141–183). New York, NY: Springer.

Muhammad, T. I., Matthew, K. M., Aurangzeb, K., Khurram, S. A., & Ling, G. (2009). On-line signature verification: Directional analysis of a signature using weighted relative angle partitions for exploitation of inter-feature dependencies. In *Proceedings of the 10th International Conference on Document Analysis and Recognition,* Barcelona, Spain (pp. 41-45).

Mühlenbein, H., & Paaß, G. (1996). From recombination of genes to the estimation of distributions I. Binary parameters. In H.-M. Voigt, W. Ebeling, I. Rechenberger, & H.-P. Schwefel (Eds.), *Proceedings of the 4th International Conference on Parallel Problem Solving from Nature* (LNCS 411, pp. 178-187).

Mühlenbein, H., Gorges Schleuter, M., & Krämer, O. (1987). New solutions to the mapping problem of parallel systems: The evolution approach. *Parallel Computing, 4,* 269–279. doi:10.1016/0167-8191(87)90026-3

Mühlenbein, H., Mahnig, T., & Ochoa, A. (1998). Schemata distributions and graphical models in evolutionary optimization. *Journal of Heuristics, 5*(2), 215–247. doi:10.1023/A:1009689913453

Munich, M. E., & Perona, P. (1999). Continuous dynamic time warping for translational-invariant curve alignment with applications to signature verification. In *Proceedings of the Seventh IEEE International Conference on Computer Vision* (pp. 108-115).

Municipality of Athens. (2003). *Estimation, evaluation and planning of actions for municipal solid waste services during Olympic Games 2004.* Athens, Greece: Author.

Murshed, N. A., Bortolozi, F., & Sabourin, R. (1995). Off-line signature verification using fuzzy ARTMAP neural network. In *Proceedings of the Third International Conference on Document Analysis and Recognition* (pp. 2179-2184).

Murty, K. G. (2007). Yard crane pools and optimum layouts for storage yards of container terminals. *Journal of Industrial and Systems Engineering, 1*(3), 190–199.

Nalwa, V. S. (1997). Automatic on-line signature verification. *Proceedings of the IEEE,* 213-239.

Nardinelli, C., & Curtis, S. (1990). Customer racial discrimination in the market for memorabilia: The case of baseball. *The Quarterly Journal of Economics, 105,* 575–595. doi:10.2307/2937891

Natale, M. D., & Bini, E. (2007). Optimizing the FPGA implementation of HRT systems. In *Proceedings of the 13th IEEE Real Time and Embedded Technology and Applications Symposium* (pp. 22-31). Washington, DC: IEEE Computer Society.

Neil, J. (2003). *A mathematical model of fixed-graph estimation of distribution algorithms* (Unpublished doctoral dissertation). Department of Computer Science, University of Birmingham, Birmingham, UK.

Noon, C. E., & Bean, J. C. (1991). A Lagrangian based approach for the asymmetric generalized traveling salesman problem. *Operations Research, 39,* 623–632. doi:10.1287/opre.39.4.623

Nuñez, P. L. (2010). *Brain, mind, and the structure of reality.* Oxford, UK: Oxford University Press. doi:10.1093/acprof:oso/9780195340716.001.0001

Nuortioa, T., Kytöjokib, J., Niskaa, H., & Bräysy, O. (2005). Improved route planning and scheduling of waste collection and transport. *Expert Systems with Applications, 30*(2), 223–232. doi:10.1016/j.eswa.2005.07.009

Ochoa, A. (2007). Baharastar – Simulador de Algoritmos Culturales para la Minería de Datos Social. In *Proceedings of COMCEV.*

Ochoa, A., et al. (2007). Baharastar – Simulador de Algoritmos Culturales para la Minería de Datos Social. In *Proceedings of COMCEV.*

Ochoa, A., et al. (2008a). Applying cultural algorithms and data mining to organize elements in a social dyoram. In *Proceedings of the ENC Workshop of Data Mining*.

Ochoa, A., et al. (2008b). Una comparativa de la Inteligencia Grupal desde la perspectiva del Computo Evolutivo. In *Proceedings of the International Congress on Computer Science Research*, Aguascalientes, Mexico.

Ochoa, A., et al. (2011). Decision support system based on cultural algorithms to organize sportive promotion in a largest city. In *Proceedings of the First Bioinspired Algorithms Workshop*, Morelia, México.

Ochoa, A., Tcherassi, A., Shingareva, I., Padméterakiris, A., Gyllenhaale, J., & Hernández, J. A. (2006). Italianitá: Discovering a Pygmalion effect on Italian communities using data mining. In *Proceedings of the International Conference on Dublin Core and Metadata Application.*

Ochoa, A. (2008). *Data mining in medical and biological research* (Giannopoullou, E. G., Ed.). Vienna, Austria: I-Tech.

Ochoa, A. (2009). *Six degrees of separation in a graph to a social networking*. Zürich, Switzerland: ASNA.

Ochoa, A., González, S., Esquivel, C., Matozzi, G., & Maffucci, A. (2009). Musical recommendation on thematic Web radio. *Journal of Computers*, *4*(8). doi:10.4304/jcp.4.8.742-746

Ochoa, A., Hernández, A., Cruz, L., Ponce, J., Montes, F., Li, L., & Janacek, L. (2010). Artificial societies and social simulation using ant colony, particle swarm optimization and cultural algorithms . In Korosec, P. (Ed.), *New achievements in evolutionary computation*. Rijeka, Croatia: InTech.

Ochoa, A., Hernández, A., González, S., Castro, A., Gelbukh, A., Hernández, A., & Iztebegovič, H. (2008). Social data mining to improve bioinspired intelligent systems . In Giannopoullou, E. G. (Ed.), *Data mining in medical and biological research*. Vienna, Austria: I-Tech.

Ohishi, T., Komiya, Y., Morita, H., & Matsumoto, T. (2001). Pen-input on-line signature verification with position, pressure, inclination trajectories. In *Proceedings of the 15th International Symposium on Parallel and Distributed Processing*, San Francisco, CA (pp. 1757-1763).

Ohrimenko, O., Stuckey, P. J., & Codish, M. (2009). Propagation via lazy clause generation. *Constraints*, *14*(3), 357–391. doi:10.1007/s10601-008-9064-x

Oliver, I. M., Smith, D. J., & Holland, J. R. C. (1987). A study of permutation crossover operators on the TSP. In *Proceedings of the Second International Conference Genetic Algorithms and their Applications* (pp. 224-230).

Ombuki, B. M., Runka, A., & Hanshar, F. T. (2007) Waste collection vehicle routing problem with time windows using multi-objetive genetic algorithms. In *Proceedings of the Third IASTED International Conference on Computational Intelligence* (pp. 91-97). New York, NY: ACM.

Ombuki, B. M., Runka, A., & Hanshar, F. T. (2007). Waste collection vehicle routing problem with time windows using multi-objetive genetic algorithms. In *Proceedings of the Third IASTED International Conference on Computational Intelligence* (pp. 91-97).

Palais, J. C. (1984). *Fiber optic communications* (4th ed.). Upper Saddle River, NJ: Prentice Hall.

Papadimitriou, C. H., & Steiglitz, K. (1982). *Combinatorial optimization: Algorithms and complexity*. Upper Saddle River, NJ: Prentice Hall.

Papastavrou, J. D. (1996). A stochatic and dynamic routing policy using branching processes with state dependent immigration. *European Journal of Operational Research*, *95*(1), 167–177. doi:10.1016/0377-2217(95)00189-1

Pareto, V. (1986). Cours D' []. Lausanne, Switzerland: F. Rouge.]. *Economics and Politics*, *1-2*, •••.

Parkan, C., & Wu, M. L. (1999). Decision-making and performance measurement models with applications to robot selection. *Computers & Industrial Engineering*, *36*(3), 503–523. doi:10.1016/S0360-8352(99)00146-1

Parker, M. (2007). *Planning land information technology research project: Efficient Recycling Collection Routing in Pictou County, 2001*. Retrieved from http://www.cogs.ns.ca/planning/projects/plt20014/images/research.pdf

Peerapong, U., & Monthippa, U. (2010). Online signature verification using angular transformation for e-commerce services. *International Journal of Information and Communication Engineering*, *6*(1), 33–38.

Pelikan, M., Sastry, K., & Cantu-Paz, E. (2006). *Scalable optimization via probabilistic modeling: From algorithms to applications*. New York, NY: Springer.

Pender, D. A. (1991). *Neural networks and handwritten signature verification* (Unpublished doctoral dissertation). Stanford University, Stanford, CA.

Piñol, M. (2009). *CSP problems as algorithmic benchmarks measures, methods and models* (Unpublished doctoral dissertation). Universitat de Lleida, Lérida, Spain.

Pisinger, D., & Ropke, S. (2007). A general heuristic for vehicle routing problems. *Computers & Operations Research, 34*(8), 2403–2435. doi:10.1016/j.cor.2005.09.012

Plamondon, R., & Lorette, G. (1989). On-line signature verification: how many countries are in the race? In *Proceedings of the International Carnahan Conference on Security Technology* (pp. 183-191).

Plamondon, R., & Baron, R. (1989). Acceleration measurement with an instrumented pen for signature verification and handwriting analysis. *IEEE Transactions on Instrumentation and Measurement, 38*(6), 1132–1138. doi:10.1109/19.46414

Plamondon, R., & Parizeau, M. (1990). A comparative analysis of regional correlation, dynamic time warping, and skeletal tree matching for signature verification. *IEEE Transactions on Pattern Analysis and Machine Intelligence, 12*(7), 710–717. doi:10.1109/34.56215

Plamondon, R., & Shihari, S. N. (2000). Online and off-line handwriting recognition: a comprehensive survey. *IEEE Transactions on Pattern Analysis and Machine Intelligence, 22*(1), 63–84. doi:10.1109/34.824821

Pölzlbauer, G. (2004). Survey and comparison of quality measures for self-organizing maps. In *Proceedings of the Fifth Workshop on Data Analysis* (pp. 67-82).

Ponce, J., Hernández, A., Ochoa, A., Padilla, F., Padilla, A., Álvarez, F., & Ponce de León, E. (2009a). Data mining in Web applications . In Ponce, J., & Karahoca, A. (Eds.), *Data mining and knowledge discovery in real life applications*. Rijeka, Croatia: InTech.

Potvin, J. Y., & Rousseau, J. M. (1995). An exchange heuristic for routing problems with time windows. *The Journal of the Operational Research Society, 46*, 1433–1446.

Powell, W. B., Jaillet, P., & Odonim, A. (1995). Stochastic and dynamic networks and routing . In Ball, M. O., Magnanti, T. L., Monma, C. L., & Nemhauser, G. L. (Eds.), *Network routing* (pp. 141–295). Amsterdam, The Netherlands: Elsevier Science. doi:10.1016/S0927-0507(05)80107-0

Prosser, P., & Shaw, P. (1996). *Study of greedy search with multiple improvement heuristics for vehicle routing problems (Tech. Rep.)*. Glasgow, UK: University of Strathclyde.

Quiroz, M. (2009). *Caracterización de factores de desempeño de algoritmos de solución de BPP* (Unpublished master's thesis). Posgrado en Ciencias de la Computación, Instituto Tecnológico de Ciudad Madero, Tamaulipas, México.

Raafat, F. (2002). A comprehensive bibliography on justification of advanced manufacturing systems. *International Journal of Production Economics, 79*(3), 197–208. doi:10.1016/S0925-5273(02)00233-5

Raidl, G. R. (2006). A unified view on hybrid metaheuristics. In F. Almeida, M. J. B. Aguilera, C. Blum, J. M. M. Vega, M. Pérez Pérez, A. Roli, & M. Sampels (Eds.), *Proceedings of the Third International Conference on Hybrid Metaheuristics* (LNCS 4030, pp. 1-12).

Ralphs, T., Kopman, L., Pulleyblank, W., & Trotter, L. (2003). On the capacitated vehicle routing problem. *Mathematical Programming, Series B, 94*, 343–359. doi:10.1007/s10107-002-0323-0

Rangel, N. (2005). *Análisis de los Problemas de Asignación de Rutas, Horarios y Cargas en una Distribuidora de Productos* (Unpublished master's thesis). Posgrado en Ciencias de la Computación, Instituto Tecnológico de Ciudad Madero, Tamaulipas, México.

Rangel, N. (2005). *Analysis of the routing, scheduling and loading problems in a Products Distributor* (Unpublished master's thesis). Posgrado en Ciencias de la Computación, Instituto Tecnológico de Ciudad Madero, Tamaulipas, México.

Rao, K. V. S., & Deshmukh, S. G. (1997). A decision support system for selection and justification of advanced manufacturing technology. *Production Planning and Control, 8*(3), 270–284. doi:10.1080/095372897235325

Regoli, R. M. (1991). Racism in baseball card collecting: Fact or fiction? *Human Relations*, *44*, 255–264. doi:10.1177/001872679104400303

Regoli, R. M., Hewitt, J. D., Muñoz, R. Jr, & Regoli, A. M. (2004). Location, location, location: The transmission of racist ideology in baseball cards. *Negro Educational Review*, *55*, 75–90.

Reimann, M., Doerner, K., & Hartl, R. (2003). Analyzing a unified ant system for the VRP and some of its variants. In *Proceedings of the International Conference on Applications of Evolutionary Computing* (pp. 300-310).

Reinelt, G. (1991). TSPLIB - A traveling salesman problem library. *ORSA Journal of Computing*, *3*(4), 376–384. doi:10.1287/ijoc.3.4.376

Reynolds, R. G. (1998). An introduction to cultural algorithms. *Cultural Algorithms Repository*. Retrieved from http://www.cs.wayne.edu/~jcc/car.html

Reynolds, R. G. (1998). An introduction to cultural algorithms. *Cultural Algorithms Repository*. Retrieved from http://www.cs.wayne.edu/~jcc/car.html

Ri-Cheng, L., Kai, B., Chun, D., Shao-Yu, L., & Gou-Zheng, X. (2008). Study on partial discharge localization by ultrasonic measuring in power transformer based on particle swarm optimization. In *Proceedings of the International Conference on High Voltage Engineering and Application* (pp. 600-603).

Rizzoli, A. E., Oliverio, F., Montemanni, R., & Gambardella, L. M. (2004). *Ant colony optimisation for vehicle routing problems: from theory to applications*. Retrieved from http://www.idsia.ch/idsiareport/IDSIA-15-04.pdf

Rizzoli, A. E., Oliverio, F., Montemanni, R., & Gambardella, L. M. (2004). *Ant colony optimisation for vehicle routing problems: from theory to applications*. Ticino, Switzerland: IDSIA.

Robinson, R. (1987). *Why this piece? On the choices of collectors in the fine arts*. Paper presented at the Annual Meeting of the American Sociological Association, Chicago, IL

Rodriguez-León, A., Cruz-Chávez, M. A., Rivera-López, R., Ávila-Melgar, E. Y., Juárez-Pérez, F., & Díaz-Parra, O. (2010, September 28-October 1). A communication scheme for an experimental grid in the resolution of VRPTW using an evolutionary algorithm. In *Proceedings of the Electronics, Robotics and Automotive Mechanics Conference*, México (pp. 108-113).

Roger, J. S. (1997). *Neuro-fuzzy and soft computing*. Upper Saddle River, NJ: Prentice Hall.

Rosholm, A. (1987). *Statistical methods for segmentation and classification of images* (Doctoral dissertation). Lyngby, Denmark: IMM, The Technical University of Denmark.

Ross, S. M. (1990). *A course in simulation*. New York, NY: Maxwell Macmillan International.

Ross, T. J. (2010). *Fuzzy logic with engineering applications* (3rd ed.). New York, NY: John Wiley & Sons. doi:10.1002/9781119994374

Rubio-Sánchez, M. (2004). *Nuevos Métodos para Análisis Visual de Mapas Auto-organizativos* (Unpublished doctoral dissertation). Madrid Politechnic University, Madrid, Spain.

Rudolph, G. (1996). Convergence of evolutionary algorithms in general search spaces. In *Proceedings of the Third IEEE Conference on Evolutionary Computation*.

Ruiz, V. J. A. (2008). *Desarrollo de indicadores de casos aplicables a la selección de algoritmos en el problema 2-Partition* (Unpublished doctoral dissertation). Centro Nal. de Investigación y Desarrollo Tecnológico, Cuernavaca, Mexico.

Russell, S., & Norving, P. (1995). *Artificial intelligence: A modern approach* (pp. 111–114). Upper Saddle River, NJ: Prentice Hall.

Ryser, H. J. (1957). Combinatorial properties of matrices of zeros and ones. *Canadian Journal of Mathematics*, *9*, 371–377. doi:10.4153/CJM-1957-044-3

Saeys, Y., Inza, I., & Larrañaga, P. (2007). A review of feature selection techniques in bioinformatics. *Bioinformatics (Oxford, England)*, *23*(19), 2507–2517. doi:10.1093/bioinformatics/btm344

Säften, K., Winroth, M., & Stahre, J. (2007). The content and process of automation strategies. *International Journal of Production Economics, 110*(1-2), 25–38. doi:10.1016/j.ijpe.2007.02.027

Sakamoto, D., Morita, H., Ohishi, T., Komiya, Y., & Matsumoto, T. (2001). On-line signature verification algorithm incorporating pen position, pen pressure and pen inclination trajectories. In *Proceedings of the IEEE International Conference on Acoustics, Speech, and Signal Processing*, Salt Lake City, UT (pp. 993-996).

Salton, G., & Buckley, C. (1998). Term-weighting approaches in automatic text retrieval. *Information Processing and Management: an International Journal, 24*(5), 513–523. doi:10.1016/0306-4573(88)90021-0

Salton, G., & Macgill, M. J. (1983). *Introduction to modern information retrieval.* New York, NY: McGraw-Hill.

Sánchez, D. G., & Lazo, C. M. (2008). CT-EXT: An algorithm for computing typical testor set. In L. Rueda, D. Mery, & J. Kittler (Eds.), *Proceedings of the 12th Iberoamericann Congress on Progress in Pattern Recognition, Image Analysis and Applications* (LNCS 4756, pp. 506-514).

Sánchez-Mondragón, J., Tecpoyotl-Torres, M., Andrade-Lucio, J. A., Torres-Cisneros, M., Dávila-Alvarez, A., & Carpio-Valadez, M. (2003). Data fitting on a spherical shell. *Proceedings of the Society for Photo-Instrumentation Engineers, 5181*, 51–55.

Santiesteban, A., & Pons, P. A. (2003). Lex: Un Nuevo Algoritmo para el Cálculo de los Testores Típicos. *Revista Ciencias Matemáticas, 21*(1), 85–95.

Saraph, J. V., & Sebastian, R. J. (1992). Human resource strategies for effective introduction of advanced manufacturing practices (AMT). *Production and Inventory Management Journal, 33*(1), 64–70.

Sathe, M., Schenk, O., & Burkhart, H. (2009). Solving bi-objective many-constraint bin packing problems in automobile sheet metal forming processes. In M. Ehrgott, C. M. Fonseca, X. Gandibleux, J.-K. Hao, & M. Sevaux (Eds.), *Proceedings of the 5th International Conference on Evolutionary MultiCriterion Optimization* (LNCS 5467, pp. 246-260).

Schafer, J. D. (1985). Multiple objective optimization with vector evaluated genetic algorithms. In *Proceedings of the First International Conference on Genetic Algorithms and theirs Applications* (pp. 93-100).

Secomandi, N. (2000). Comparing neuro-dynamic programming algorithms for the vehicle routing problem with stochastic demands. *Computers & Operations Research, 27*, 1171–1200. doi:10.1016/S0305-0548(99)00146-X

Secomandi, N. (2001). A rollout policy for the vehicle routing problem with stochastic demands. *Operations Research, 49*, 796–802. doi:10.1287/opre.49.5.796.10608

Shaw, P. (1998). Using constraint programming and local search methods to solve vehicle routing problems. In M. Maher & J. Puget (Eds.), *Proceedings of the 4th International Conference on Principles and Practice of Constraint Programming* (LNCS 1520, pp. 417-431).

Shulcloper, J. R., Aguila, F. I., & Bravo, M. A. (1985). Algoritmos BT y TB para el cálculo de todos los tests típicos. *Revista Ciencias Matemáticas, 6*(2), 11–18.

Shulcloper, J. R., Alba, C., & Lazo, C. (1995). *Introducción al reconocimiento de Patrones: Enfoque Lógico Combinatorio (Serie Verde No. 51).* México: Cinvestav-IPN.

Siemieniuch, C. E., & Sinclair, M. A. (1995). Information technology and global developments in manufacturing: The implications for human factors input. *International Journal of Industrial Ergonomics, 16*, 245–262. doi:10.1016/0169-8141(95)00011-5

Skalak, D. B. (1994). Prototype and feature selection by sampling and random mutation hill climbing algorithms. In *Proceedings of the Eleventh International Conference on Machine Learning* (pp. 293-301).

Slowinski, R. (1998). *Fuzzy sets in decision analysis, operation research and statistics.* Boston, MA: Kluwer Academic.

Slyter, S. A. (1995). *Forensic signature examination* (1 ed., pp. 1-117). Springfield, IL: Charles C. Thomas.

Small, M. H., & Chen, I. J. (1997). Economic and strategic justification of AMT Inferences from industrial practices. *International Journal of Production Economics, 49*(1), 65–75. doi:10.1016/S0925-5273(96)00120-X

Small, M. H., & Yasin, M. (1997). Advanced manufacturing technology: Implementation policy and performance. *Journal of Operations Management, 15*(4), 349–370. doi:10.1016/S0272-6963(97)00013-2

Smeaton, A. F., & Callahan, J. (2003). Personalization and recommender systems in digital libraries. *International Journal on Digital Libraries, 57*(4), 299–308.

Sodhi, M. S. (2001). Applications and opportunities for operations research in internet-enabled supply chains and electronic marketplaces. *Interfaces, 31*(2), 56–69. doi:10.1287/inte.31.2.56.10633

Soh, T., Inoue, K., Tamura, N., Banbara, M., & Nabeshima, H. (2010). A SAT-based method for solving the two-dimensional strip packing problem. *Fundamenta Informaticae, 102*(3-4), 467–487.

Solis, F., Mardones, G., Castillo, B., & Romer, M. I. (1993). Mortalidad por Inmadurez e hipoxia como causas de atención obstétrica y neonatal. *Revista Chilena de Pediatría.*

Solomon, M. (1987). Algorithms for the vehicle routing and scheduling problem with time window constraints. *Operations Research, 35*(2), 254–265. doi:10.1287/opre.35.2.254

Sommer, H. M. (1997). *Variability in microbiological degradation experiments - Analysis and case study* (Doctoral dissertation). Lyngby, Denmark: IMM, The Technical University of Denmark.

Sompel, H. V., & De Lagoze, C. (Eds.). (2005). *The open archives initiative protocol for metadata harvesting.* Retrieved from http://www.openarchives.org/OAI/2.0/openarchivesprotocol.htm

Sompel, H. V., & De Lagoze, C. (2000). The Santa Fe convention of the open archives initiative. *D-Lib Magazine, 6*(2).

Sporns, O. (2011). *Networks of the brain.* Cambridge, MA: MIT.

Srinvas, N., & Deb, K. (1994). Multiobjective optimization using nondominated sorting in genetic algorithms. *Evolutionary Computation, 2*(3), 221–248. doi:10.1162/evco.1994.2.3.221

Strachan, S. M., Stephen, B., & McArthur, S. D. J. (2007). Practical applications of data mining in plant monitoring and diagnostics. In *Proceedings of the Power Engineering Society General Meeting* (pp. 1-7).

Stützle, T., & Hoos, H. H. (1996). *Improving the ant system: A detailed report on the MAXMIN ant system* (Tech. Rep. No. AIDA-96-12). Darmstadt, Germany: FG Intellektik, FB Informatik, TU Darmstadt.

Sugiyama, K. (2002). Graph drawing and applications for software and knowledge engineers. *Japan Advanced Institute of Science and Technology, 11*, 218.

Suh, N. P. (1990). *The principles of design.* New York, NY: Oxford University Press.

Suh, N. P. (2001). *Axiomatic design: Advances and applications.* New York, NY: Oxford University Press.

Sun Microsystems. (2008a). *JavaTM 2 platform standard edition 5.0 API specification.* Retrieved from http://java.sun.com/j2se/1.5.0/docs/api/

Sun Microsystems. (2008b). *MySQL 6.0 reference manual.* Retrieved from http://dev.mysql.com/doc/refman/6.0/en/news-6-0-x.html

Suresh, N. C., & Meredith, J. R. (1985). Achieving factory automation through group technology principles. *Journal of Operations Management, 5*(2), 151–167. doi:10.1016/0272-6963(85)90004-X

Sycara, K. (1998). Multiagent systems. *AI Magazine, 19*(2), 79–92.

Syswerda, G. (1991). Schedule optimization using genetic algorithms . In Davis, L. (Ed.), *Handbook of genetic algorithms* (pp. 332–349). New York, NY: Van Nostrand Reinhold.

Taillard, E. (1999). A heuristic column generation method for the heterogeneous fleet VRP. *Operations Research, 33*(1), 1–14. doi:10.1051/ro:1999101

Taillard, E. D. (1999). A heuristic column generation method for the heterogeneous fleet VRP. *RAIRO - . Operations Research, 33*, 1–14. doi:10.1051/ro:1999101

Taillard, E., Badeau, P., Gendreu; M., Guertin, F., & Potvin, J. Y. (1997). A tabu search heuristic for the vehicle routing problem with soft time windows. *Transportation Science, 31*, 170–186. doi:10.1287/trsc.31.2.170

Taillard, E., Laport, G., & Gendreau, M. (1996). Vehicle routing problem with multiple use of vehicles. *The Journal of the Operational Research Society, 47*, 1065–1070.

Talluri, S., & Yoon, K. P. (2000). A cone-ratio DEA approach for AMT justification. *International Journal of Production Economics, 66*(2), 119–129. doi:10.1016/S0925-5273(99)00123-1

Tamassia, R., Di Battista, G., & Batini, C. (1988). Automatic graph drawing and readability of diagrams. *IEEE Transactions on Systems, Man, and Cybernetics, 18*(1), 61–79. doi:10.1109/21.87055

Tan, P. N., Steinbach, M., & Kumar, V. (2006). *Introduction to data mining*. Reading, MA: Addison-Wesley.

Tecpoyotl-Torres, M., Partida-Rivera, E., Gonzalez-Roman, I. A., Ibarra-Manzano, O., & Sánchez-Mondragón, J. (2006). Reconstruction of atmospheric vertical reflectivity profile images. In *Proceedings of the First Multiconference on Electronics and Photonics* (pp. 262-265).

Thangiah, S. R. (2003). *A site dependent vehicle routing problem with complex road constraints.* Paper presented at the Colloquium Series, Institute of Mathematics, University of Malaya, Kuala Lumpur, Malaysia.

Thangiah, V. (2003). *A site dependent vehicle routing problem with complex road constraints.* Paper presented at the Colloquium at the Institute of Mathematics, University of Malaya, Kuala Lumpur, Malaysia.

Theodoridis, S., & Koutroumbas, K. (1999). *Pattern recognition* (1st ed.). San Diego, CA: Academic Press.

Thorn, J., Palmer, P., & Gershman, M. (2001). *Total baseball* (7th ed.). New York, NY: Total Sports.

Torres, M. D. (2010). *Metaheurísticas Híbridas en Selección de Subconjuntos de Características para Aprendizaje no Supervisado* (Unpublished doctoral dissertation). Universidad Autónoma de Aguascalientes, Aguascalientes, México.

Torres, M. D., Ponce, L. E., Torres, A., & Díaz, E. (2008). Selección de Características Basada en el Peso Informacional de las Variables en Aprendizaje no Supervisado mediante Algoritmos Genéticos. In *Cuarto Congreso Internacional de Computación Evolutiva, Centro de Investigaciones en Matemáticas*, Guanajuato, México.

Torres, M. D., Ponce, L. E., Torres, A., Ochoa, A., & Díaz, E. (2009). Hybridization of evolutionary mechanisms for feature subset selection in unsupervised learning. In A. H. Aguirre, R. M. Borja, & C. A. R. Garciá (Eds.), *Proceedings of the 8th Mexican International Conference on Advances in Artificial Intelligence* (LNCS 5845, pp. 610-621).

Torres, S. A., Torres, S. M. D., Ponce, L. E., & Díaz, D. E. (2004). Representacion De Los Factores de Riesgo Directos e Indirectos De Los Resultados Del Parto Utilizando Un Modelo Grafico. In *IX Foro Regional De Investigacion En Salud del IMSS.*

Torres, R. A. (1999). *Factores de Riesgo para Morbimortalidad Neonatal*. San Luis Potosí, Mexico: Instituto Mexicano del Seguro Social.

Torres, S. A., Torres, S. M. D., Ponce, L. E., & Torres, R. A. B. (2005). *Modelo Grafico de Los Factores de Riesgo Durante el Embarazo y su Impacto en el Parto*. Revista Cubana De Informática Médica.

Toth, P., & Vigo, D. (2002). The vehicle routing problem. In *Proceedings of the SIAM Monographs on Discrete Mathematics and Applications.*

Toth, P., & Vigo, D. (2000). An overview of vehicle routing problems . In Murphy, S. (Ed.), *Monographs on discrete mathematics and applications* (pp. 1–26). Philadelphia, PA: SIAM.

Toth, P., & Vigo, D. (2001). The vehicle routing problem . In Murphy, S. (Ed.), *Monographs on discrete mathematics and applications*. Philadelphia, PA: SIAM.

Toth, P., & Vigo, D. (Eds.). (2002). *The vehicle routing problem. SIAM monographs on discrete mathematics and applications*. Philadelphia, PA: Society for Industrial and Applied Mathematics.

Tseitin, G. (1983). On the complexity of proofs in propositional logics. In Siekmann, J., & Wrightson, G. (Eds.), *Automation of reasoning: Classical papers in computational logic* (*Vol. 2*, pp. 1967–1970). Berlin, Germany: Springer-Verlag.

Tsoukalas, L. H., & Uhrig, R. E. (1997). *Fuzzy and neural approaches in engineering* (1st ed.). New York, NY: John Wiley & Sons.

Ueda, N., & Nagao, T. (1996). *NP-completeness results for nonogram via parsinomius reductions* (Tech. Rep. No. TR96-0008). Tokyo, Japan: Department of Computer Science, Tokyo Institute of Technology.

Uncu, O., & Türksen, I. B. (2007). A novel feature selection approach: Combining feature wrappers and filters. *Information Sciences*, *177*(2), 449–466. doi:10.1016/j.ins.2006.03.022

Ustaoglu, Y. (2009). *Simulating the behavior of a Kurdish minority in Turkish Society*. Zürich, Switzerland: ASNA.

Vahid, K., Reza, P., & Hamid, R. P. (2009). Offline signature verification using local radon transform and support vector machines. *International Journal of Image Processing*, *3*(6), 184–194.

van Laarhoven, P. J. M., & Aarts, E. H. L. (1987). *Simulated annealing: Theory and applications*. Dordrecht, The Netherlands: Kluwer Academic.

Van VeldHuizen. D. A. (1999). *Multiobjective evolutionary algorithms: Classifications, analyses, and new innovations* (Unpublished doctoral dissertation). Department of Electrical and Computer Engineering, Graduated School of Engineering, Air Force Institute Technology, Wright-Patterson AFB, OH.

Vehicle routing software survey. (2006). *OR/MS Today*. Retrieved from http://www.lionhrtpub.com/orms/surveys/Vehicle_Routing/vrss.html

Verweij, B. (1996). *Multiple destination bin packing* (Tech. Rep. No. UU-CS Ext. r. no. 1996-39). Utrecht, Tahe Netherlands: Utrecht University, Information and Computing Sciences.

Vesanto, J., & Alhoniemi, E. (2000). Clustering of the self organizing map. *IEEE Transactions on Neural Networks*, *11*(3), 1082–1089. doi:10.1109/72.846731

Vicente, K. (1999). *Cognitive work analysis, towards safe, productive and healthy computer-based work*. Mahwah, NJ: Lawrence Erlbaum.

Vrajitoru, D. (2009, April 18-19). Multiobjective genetic algorithm for a graph drawing problem. In *Proceedings of the Midwest Artificial Intelligence and Cognitive Science Conference*, Fort Wayne, IN (pp. 28-43).

VRP. (2007). *The VRP Web*. Retrieved from http://neo.lcc.uma.es/radi-aeb/WebVRP/

Wagner, S., Affenzeller, M., & Schragl, D. (2004). *Traps and dangers when modelling problems for genetic algorithms* (pp. 79–84). Vienna, Austria: Austrian Society for Cybernetic Studies.

Wan-Suck, L., Mohankrishman, N., & Paulik, M. J. (1998). Improved segmentation through dynamic time warping for signature verification using a neural network classifier. In *Proceedings of the IEEE International Conference on Image Processing* (pp. 929-933).

Weise, T., Podlich, A., & Gorldt, C. (2009). Solving real-world vehicle routing problems with evolutionary algorithms. In Chiong, R., & Dhakal, S. (Eds.), *Natural intelligence for scheduling, planning and packing problems* (*Vol. 250*, pp. 29–53). Berlin, Germany: Springer-Verlag. doi:10.1007/978-3-642-04039-9_2

Westinhouse. (2000). *Manual del alumbrado* (4th ed.). Madrid, Spain: Noriega Editores.

Whitley, D., Starkweather, T., & D'Ann, F. (1989). Scheduling problems and travelling salesman: The genetic edge recombination operator. In *Proceedings of the Third International Conference on Genetic Algorithms* (pp. 133-140).

Wijesoma, W. S., Mingming, M., & Sung, E. (2000). Selecting optimal personalized features for on-line signature verification using GA. In *Proceedings of the IEEE International Conference on Systems, Man and Cybernetics* (pp. 2740-2745).

Wills, L. (1999). *Electrical power cable engineering*. New York, NY: Marcel Dekker.

Wirtz, B. (1997). Average prototypes for stroke-based signature verification. In *Proceedings of the Fourth International Conference on Document Analysis and Recognition* (pp. 268-272).

Wolpert, D. (1996). The lack of a priori distinctions between learning algorithms. *Neural Computation*, 1341–1390. doi:10.1162/neco.1996.8.7.1341

Xing, Z., Chen, Y., & Zhang, W. (2006). Optimal STRIPS planning by maximum satisfiability and accumulative learning. In *Proceedings of the 16th International Conference on Automated Planning and Scheduling* (pp. 442-446). Palo Alto, CA: AAAI.

Yañez Valdez, R., Ruiz Torres, M., Morales Sánchez, E., & Castillo Castañeda, E. (2007). Diseño y Construcción de una Mesa de Trabajo XYθ basada en un Mecanismo Paralelo Planar 3RRR. *Tecnólog*, *1*(2), 35–45.

Yang, W. H., Kamlesh, M., & Ronald, H. B. (2000). Stochastic vehicle routing problem with restocking. *Transportation Science*, *34*, 99–112. doi:10.1287/trsc.34.1.99.12278

Yen, J., & Langari, R. (1999). *Fuzzy logic, intelligence, control and information*. Upper Saddle River, NJ: Prentice Hall.

Yoon, K. (1980). *Systems selection by multiple attribute decision making* (Unpublished doctoral dissertation). Kansas State University, Manhattan, KS.

Yusuff, R. M. (2004). Manufacturing best practices of the electric and electronic firms in Malaysia. *Benchmarking: An International Journal*, *11*(4), 361–369. doi:10.1108/14635770410546764

Zadeh, L. A. (1965). Fuzzy sets. *Information and Control*, *8*, 338–353. doi:10.1016/S0019-9958(65)90241-X

Zammuto, R. F., & O'Connor, E. J. (1992). Gaining advanced manufacturing technology's benefits: The roles of organization design and culture. *Academy of Management Review*, *17*, 701–728.

About the Contributors

Carlos Alberto Ochoa Ortiz Zezzatti (B.S. '94, Eng. Master '00, Ph.D. '04, Postdoctoral Researcher,'06, and Industrial Postdoctoral Research '09). He joined the Juarez City University in 2008. He has 1 book, and 7 chapters in books related with AI. He has supervised 17 Ph.D. theses, 27 M.Sc. theses and 29 undergraduate theses. He participated in the organization of COMCEV'07, COMCEV'08, HAIS'07, HAIS'08, HAIS'09, HAIS'10, HAIS'11, HAIS'12, ENC'06, ENC'07, ENC'08 and MICAI'08, MICAI'09, MICAI'10 & MICAI'11. His research interests include evolutionary computation, natural processing language, anthropometrics characterization and Social Data Mining. In his second Postdoctoral Research participated in an internship in ISTC-CNR in Rome, Italy.

Camelia Chira received the B.S. degree in computer science from Babes-Bolyai University, Cluj-Napoca, Romania in 1998. From 2000 to 2005 she was engaged in full-time research at Galway-Mayo Institute of Technology (GMIT), Galway, Ireland focusing in the area of agent-based systems and ontologies for distributed collaborative design environments. She received the M.Sc. and Ph.D. degrees from GMIT Ireland in 2002 and 2005, respectively. Since 2006, Camelia is a researcher at the Centre for the Study of Complexity, Babes-Bolyai University, Romania. Her main research interests include evolutionary computing, swarm intelligence, complex systems and networks, multi-agent systems and bioinformatics.

Arturo Hernández Aguirre is a researcher and professor in the Computer Science Department of the Center for Research in Mathematics (CIMAT). His research interests are Multiobjective Optimization, Evolvable hardware, Evolutionary computation, Evolutionary design of neural network architectures, and Computational Learning Theory using neural networks.

Miguel Basurto was born in Mexico in 1973. He received the B.S. degree in Electronics and Industrial Engineering from Instituto Tecnológico de Veracruz in 1995, a Master of Sciences from Instituto Nacional de Astrofísica, Óptica y Electrónica in 1997, and finally, a Ph.D. in 2001 in the same institution. He is a full professor on CIICAp-UAEM Center; his research includes Lasers Fibers, Optical Fibers Sensors, and Artificial Intelligence applied to Optics.

* * *

Fatima Sayuri Quezada Aguilera received the B.S. degree in computer science engineering from the Universidad Autónoma de Aguascalientes in 2003, and the Ph.D. in computer science from the Universidad Autónoma de Aguascalientes in 2010. He is currently a professor in the Universidad Autónoma de Aguascalientes. His research interests include Evolutionary Computation and Artificial Immune System.

Jorge Luis Garcia Alcaraz was born in Michoacan, México in 1972 and received the B.D. and M.Sc. Degree in Industrial engineering from the Colima Institute of Technology (Mexico) and the Ph.D. from the Ciudad Juarez Institute of Technology (Mexico). He is working for the Department of Industrial Engineering and Manufacturing at the Autonomous University of Ciudad Juarez in Mexico. He is the author of about 70 technical papers in peer-reviewed journals and international conferences. His current research interests include multiple criteria decision analysis, multivariate analysis, and structural equation models applied to advanced manufacturing technologies.

Adriana C. F. Alvim received her M.Sc. degree in Informatics from Pontifícia Universidade Católica do Rio de Janeiro, Brazil, in 1998 and she received the Ph.D. (Informatics) degree from Pontifícia Universidade Católica do Rio de Janeiro, Brazil, in 2003. She is a full time professor at Universidade Federal do Estado do Rio de Janeiro, Brazil. Her research interests include optimization techniques and metaheuristics.

César Eduardo Velázquez Amador is an engineer in Computing Systems (1994) and he has a Master's in Computer Science and Technologies from the Autonomous University of Aguascalientes, Mexico (2002). At the moment he is a full time professor-researcher at Autonomous University of Aguascalientes. His investigation areas are the adoption of information technologies, software engineering and quality in learning objects.

Sergio Enríquez Aranda was born in Aguascalientes, Ags., México, in 1963. He received the B.I. degree in Informatics from the Aguascalientes Institute of Technology (ITA), Aguascalientes, México, in 1989, and the M.C. degree in Artificial Intelligence from the University Autonomous of Aguascalientes (UAA), Aguascalientes, México, in 2008. In 1999, he joined the Department of Information Systems, University Autonomous of Aguascalientes, as a professor. Since August 2006, he has been with the Department of Computer Science, UAA, where he is currently a Professor. His main areas of research interest are multiobjective optimization, evolutionary algorithms, automatic graph drawing, and graph theory.

Daniel Azpeitia is a teacher-researcher within the Industrial Design COORDINATION which belongs to the Department of Design at the Institute of Architecture, Design and Arts (IADA) in Juarez, Mexico.

Juan Javier González Barbosa received his M.Sc. degree in Computer Science from the Leon's Institute of Technology, Mexico, in 2000 and the Ph.D. degree in Computer Science from the National Center of Research and Technological Development, México, in 2006. He is currently professor of Computer Science at Madero Institute of Technology, Mexico. His research interests are optimization techniques and machine learning.

Gustavo Urquiza Beltrán has a Ph.D. obtained in École Polytechnique de Montréal. He is Researcher Level A on Mechanical Technology Department from Center for Research in Engineering and Applied Sciences (CIICAp), State University of Morelos (UAEM), since 2004 to date. He is professor on CIICAp,

Chemical Sciences and Engineering Faculty (FCQeI). Has expertise on: Studies of Efficiency Improvements in hydraulic turbines, steam and gas; Modeling fluid flow and heat transfer using computational fluid dynamics (CFD), Experimental measurement of flow on Hydroelectric turbines using the Pressure-Time Method or Gibson and Winter-Kennedy; Application of Inverse Methods, Genetic Algorithms and Neural Networks in Problems of Engineering; Combined Cycle Thermodynamic Modeling and Process Open Cycles in Electricity Generation Using Computational Tools. He has published on several scientific journals as: *Applied Thermal Engineering* from Elsevier.

Sosa Coeto Juan Bernardo has a Master's in Engineering and Applied Sciences, specializing in analysis and optimization of turbomachinery. In 2008 he graduated in Mechanical Engineering, Faculty of Chemical Sciences and Engineering (FCQeI) of the Autonomous University of Morelos (UAEM) Mexico. In 2011 he concluded his Masters studies at the Center for Research in Engineering and Applied Sciences (CIICAp). He is currently a Ph.D. student CIICAp and professor of Finite Element, Design of Machine Elements and Computer Aided Drawing of the Engineering Mechanics on FCQeI.

Sandra Bustillos holds a Masters in Administration and a Ph.D. in Social Sciences from the Universidad Autonoma Metropolitana in Mexico. She is a professor in the Institute of Social Sciences and Administration at the Universidad Autonoma de Ciudad Juarez. She is also a member of the Academic Committee of the Doctorate Program in Social Sciences and was the Institute of Social Sciences and Administration's Research Coordinator from 2000-2003.

Nemesio Castillo was born in Xalapa, México in 1978. He received the B.S. degree in sociology from Veracruz University, and a Social Sciences Master's and Ph.D. Social Sciences both from Juarez City University. Currently he is full professor at Juarez City University and part of Conacyt Syntems of Researchers Level Candidate. His research includes Social Modelling.

Oscar Castillo holds the Doctor in Science degree in Computer Science from the Polish Academy of Sciences. He is a Professor of Computer Science in the Graduate Division, Tijuana Institute of Technology, Tijuana, Mexico. In addition, he is serving as Research Director of Computer Science and head of the research group on fuzzy logic and genetic algorithms. Currently, he is Vice-President of HAFSA (Hispanic American Fuzzy Systems Association) and President Elect of IFSA (International Fuzzy Systems Association). Prof. Castillo is also Chair of the Mexican Chapter of the Computational Intelligence Society (IEEE).

Laura Cruz R. received his M.S. degree in computer science from the Instituto Tecnológico y de Estudios Superiores de Monterrey, Mexico in 1999 and received the Ph.D. degree in computer science from the Centro Nacional de Investigación y Desarrollo Tecnológico, Mexico in 2004. She is full professor at the Instituto Tecnológico de Cd. Madero, Mexico. Her research interests include optimization techniques, complex networks, autonomous agents, and algorithm performance explanation.

Marco Antonio Cruz-Chávez received his Ph.D. in Computer Sciences from Tec de Monterrey in 2004. He has worked since 2004 as a professor and researcher at the Engineering and Applied Sciences Research Center (CIICAP) at the Autonomous University of Morelos State (UAEM). He is a National

Researcher of Mexico (SNI). He has 19 international publications and 11 national publications. He has been a reviewer of the International Journal of Production Re-search since 2005.

Laura Cruz-Reyes received his M.Sc. degree in Computer Science from the Leon`s Institute of Technology, Mexico, in 2000 and She received the Ph.D. (Computer Science) degree from National Center of Research and Technological Development, Mexico, in 2004. She is a professor at Madero City Institute of Technology, Mexico. Her research interests include optimization techniques, complex networks, autonomous agents and algorithm performance explanation.

Elva Díaz Díaz received Ph.D. degree from Autonomous University of Aguascalientes, Mexico in 2008. She is working as a Professor-researcher in Computer Science Department of Autonomous University of Aguascalientes and ITESM campus Aguascalientes. Her research interests are on Machine Learning, Computational Complexity, and Metaheuristics.

Jesús Escobedo-Alatorre received the Dipl. Electronics Eng. degree from the University of Guadalajara, Mexico, in 1994, the M.Sc. and Ph.D. degrees from National Institute of Astrophysics, Optics and Electronics (INAOE), México, in 1997 and 2005, respectively. Dr. Escobedo works, since 1998, at Research Center of Engineering and Applied Sciences (CIICAp) of the Autonomous University of Morelos (UAEM), Mexico. He collaborated in the design and organization of the undergraduate and graduate programs in CIICAp. His interest research areas are in digital design and systems design based on microcontrollers and microprocessors. He is a member of the Mexican National System of Researchers SNI-I.

Francisco Javier Marrodan Esparza received the Bachelor's Degree in Industrial Engineering from the Technical Higher School of Industrial Engineering of Bilbao, Spain and the Ph.D. from University of La Rioja. He is working for the Technical School of Industrial Engineering at the University of La Rioja, Spain and he is the Chairman of La Rioja Industrial Engineering Association. He is the author of about 35 technical papers in peer-reviewed journals and international conferences. His current research interests include advanced manufacturing technologies like Autocad, MasterCam and CNC technologies.

Héctor J. Fraire H. was born in Piedras Negras, Coahuila, Mexico in 1953. He received the B.S. Math and M.I.S. degrees from the Universidad Autónoma de Nuevo León, Mexico in 1976 and 1988, and the Ph.D. degree in computer science from the Centro Nacional de Investigación y Desarrollo Tecnológico in 1983. Currently he is full professor at the Instituto Tecnológico de Cd. Madero, Mexico. His research interests include heuristic optimization and machine learning.

Julio Cesar Ponce Gallegos received the B.S. degree in computer science engineering from the Universidad Autónoma de Aguascalientes in 2003, received the M.S from the Universidad Autónoma de Aguascalientes in 2007, and the Ph.D. in computer science from the Universidad Autónoma de Aguascalientes in 2010. He is currently a professor in the Universidad Autónoma de Aguascalientes. His research interests include Evolutionary Computation (in especial Ant Colony Optimization) and Data Mining.

Juan Carlos Garcia C. has a Ph.D. in Applied sciences and engineering. He is Associated Researcher Level C, Mechanical Technology Department, Center for Research in Engineering and Applied Sciences (CIICAp), State University of Morelos (UAEM), Since January 20, 2010 to date. Dr. Garcia has expertise in Mechanical Technology applied to turbines. He has been using Numerical simulation of CFD (Fluent) and FEA (ANSYS) applied to diagnosis of turbo machinery failures. He has publications in journals such as: *Engineering Failure Analysis* from Elsevier.

Anca Gog received her M.Sc. in Computer Science in 2002 and Ph.D. in Computer Science in 2007 from Babes-Bolyai University of Cluj-Napoca, Romania. She is lecturer at the Department of Computer Science, Faculty of Mathematics and Computer Science, Babes-Bolyai University. Her current research interests include evolutionary computational techniques, complex networks, cellular automata and data mining. The most recent research contributions include analysis and proposal of new genetic operators able to address complex problems, the development of better performing computational models for analyzing complex networks topology, analysis of dynamic cellular automata with network topology, methods for evolving cellular automata rules that exhibit a high degree of global self-organization for certain tasks, and the use of cellular automata models in the study of complexity. She is the author of more than 40 papers and 2 books.

Laura L. Castro Gomez has a Master's in Engineering and Applied Sciences, specializing in analysis. In 2005 she graduated in Chemical Engineering, Faculty of Chemical Sciences and Engineering (FCQeI) of the Autonomous University of Morelos (UAEM) Mexico. In 2008 she concluded her Masters studies at the Center for Research in Engineering and Applied Sciences (CIICAp). She is currently a Ph.D. student on CIICAp and professor of Thermodynamics and Heat transfer on FCQeI. She has published on Modelling and Simulation in Engineering, from Hindawi publishing.

Claudia Gómez S. received her M.Sc. degree in Computer Science from the Leon`s Institute of Technology, Mexico, in 2000 and the Ph.D. degree in Advanced Technology from National Politechnical Institute, México, in 2010. She is currently professor of Computer Science at Madero Institute of Technology, Mexico. Her research interests are optimization techniques, complex network and autonomous agents.

Saul Gonzalez received the B.S. degree in computer engineering from the Universidad Autonoma de Cd, Juárez in 1990, and the M.S. degree in computer sciences from the University of Texas at El Paso, USA in 2003. He is currently working towards the Ph.D. degree in telematics engineering from the Universidad de Vigo, Spain. He is currently an Associate Professor in the Department of Electrical and Computing Engineering at the Universidad Autónoma de Cd. Juarez, Mexico. His research interests include evolutionary computation, ubiquitous computing and distributed systems.

Paula Hernández Hernández received her M.Sc. degree in Computer Science from the Madero City Institute of Technology, Mexico, in 2011. She is a Ph.D. student of Madero City Institute of Technology. Her research interests are optimization Techniques.

Ruben Jaramillo-Vacio received B.Sc. from ITESI (2002), Master's in Electrical Engineering from San Luis Potosi University (2005), and Master's in Management Engineering from La Salle University (2010). He has joint CIATEC (Conacyt Research Center) in 2010 to carry out his Ph.D. research in the

Industrial Engineering and Manufacturing. Since 2005 he is Test Engineer in CFE-LAPEM in dielectric test, partial discharge diagnosis at power cables. His research interest includes partial discharge diagnosis using intelligence artificial tools.

Cristina Juárez Landin is a Doctor of Communications and Electronics in 2008. Now she is working as professor-researcher at University Autonomous of State of Mexico in Valley of Chalco. Her main research activity is in the area of artificial intelligence and education on-line. She has published works in national and international congresses of signal and image processing, filtering, reconstruction, learning objects, learning of mathematics, and education at distance.

Fredy Juárez-Pérez is currently a doctoral student at the Engineering and Applied Sciences Research Center at the Autonomous University of Morelos State. He received his M.S. degree from the National Center for Research and Technological Development, and has participated in projects involving the installation of intensive computing platforms such as Clusters and Grids. He has developed parallel algorithms in combinatorial optimization with MPI for Grid Multi-Clusters and the European Grid using gLite, further explained at http://gridmorelos.uaem.mx:8080.

Aide Aracely Maldonado-Macías received a B.E. degree in Industrial Engineering in 1995, a M.Sc. degree and Ph.D. degree in Industrial Engineering in Ciudad Juarez Institute of Technology in 2002 and 2010 respectively. In 2002, she joined the Department of Industrial and Manufacturing Engineering as a full time professor in the Autonomous University of Juarez Mexico in the Technology Planning and Ergonomics area and she is a reader in the Ciudad Juarez Institute of Technology. She is a member of the Ergonomics Mexican Society and received a Professional Ergonomics Certification by the Mexican College of Ergonomics. She is the author of about 40 technical papers in peer-reviewed journals and international conferences. Her current research interests include occupational and cognitive ergonomics, multiple criteria decision analysis, fuzzy multi-attribute axiomatic design approach in decision making, and structural equation models applied to advanced manufacturing technologies.

Evelia Martínez-Cano received her Bachelor of Chemistry in 2000, Master of Sciences in Chemistry in 2003, and Ph.D. in Human Genetics in 2006, from the Universidad de Guadalajara, Mexico. From 2000 to date, she is professor at the Universidad Guadalajara, Mexico. Her research interests include human genetics and biochemistry of mitochondrial and neurodegenerative diseases.

José A. Martínez F. was born in Tehuetlán, Mexico in 1969. He received the B.S. degree in computer systems engineering from the Instituto Tecnológico de Cd. Madero (ITCM), Mexico in 1992, and the M.S. and the Ph.D. degrees in computer science from the Centro Nacional de Investigación y Desarrollo Tecnológico, Mexico in 1996 and 2006. Currently he is full professor at ITCM. His research interests include database systems and natural language processing.

Alina Martínez-Oropeza was born in Mexico D.F. on August 10, 1985. She graduated from the Autonomous University of Morelos State (UAEM) with a BA in Informatics. She received her Master's Degree in Engineering and Applied Sciences with a specialty in Combinatorial Optimization from the

Engineering and Applied Sciences Research Center (CIICAp - UAEM). At the present time she is a Ph.D. student at CIICAp-UAEM.

Patricia Melin holds the PC degree in Microcomputer Engineering from the University of California at San Diego, USA in 1991, her Ph.D. degree in Computer Sciences from Kensigton University, USA in 1998 and Doctor in Science degree (Doctor Habilitatus D.Sc.) in Computer Science from the Polish Academy of Sciences, Poland in 2007. She is a Professor of Computer Science in the Graduate Division, Tijuana Institute of Technology, Mexico, since 1998. She has published over 90 journal papers, 5 authored books, 6 edited books, and 200 papers in conference proceedings. She has served as Guest Editor of several Special Issues. Currently she is Chair of the Task Force on Hybrid Intelligent System of the IEEE TNN Committee.

Miguel Mora-González recived his BEng from the Instituto Tecnologico de Aguascalientes, Aguascalientes, Mexico in 1996, and Ph.D. from the Centro de Investigaciones en Optica, Mexico in 2003. From 2003 to 2006, he was with the Universidad Politecnica de Aguascalientes, Aguascalientes, Mexico. Since 2006, he has been with the Universidad de Guadalajara in Lagos de Moreno Jalisco Mexico. His research interests include applied optics, optical metrology, Interferometry, holography, digital image processing, and pattern recognition.

Vanesa Landero Nájera was born in Mexico in 1976. She received the M.Sc. (Administration Engineering Science) degree from Instituto Tecnológico de Ciudad Madero, Mexico, in 2002, also she received the M.Sc. (Computer Science) degree from Instituto Tecnológico de Ciudad Madero, Mexico, in 2004, and She received the Ph.D. (Computer Science) degree from Centro Nacional de Investigación y Desarrollo Tecnológico, Mexico, in 2008. She is a professor at Universidad Politécnica de Apodaca, México. Her research interests include optimization techniques, algorithm performance explanation, and machine learning.

Jose Nava has a M.C. in Systems Engineering. He is registered in RENIECYT (National Register of Scientific and Technological Institutions and Enterprises), from CONACYT. He worked in the Research and Advanced Engineering Development Center (CIDIA), managing projects. Has presented papers for IEEE international congresses, currently he is Program Manager for Tiempo Development, a software development company headquartered in the United States, and he is researching in Artificial Intelligence areas like Data Mining and Collaborative Intelligent Agents.

Ernesto Ong C. was born in México in 1986. He received a B.S. degree in computer systems engineering from the Instituto Tecnológico de Cd. Madero (ITCM), Mexico in 2009. He is currently pursuing an M.S. degree in computer science at ITCM.

Rodolfo A. Pazos R. was born in Tampico, Mexico in 1951. He received the B.S.E.E. and M.S.E.E. degrees from the Instituto Politécnico Nacional, Mexico in 1976 and 1978, and the Ph.D. degree in computer science from U.C.L.A. in 1983. Currently he is full professor at the Instituto Tecnológico de Cd. Madero, Mexico. His research interests include algorithmics and natural language processing.

Miguel Angel Basurto Pensado has a Ph.D. obtained in Instituto Nacional de Astrofísica Optica y Eléctronica in Puebla, México. Currently he is responsible of Fiber Optic Sensor laboratory from Center for Research in Engineering and Applied Sciences (CIICAp), State University of Morelos (UAEM), since 2000 to date. He is professor on CIICAp, Chemical Sciences and Engineering Faculty (FCQeI). Has participated in various developments in optical sensors for the industry. It is part of the National System of Researchers (SNI) of the National Council of Science and Technology (CONACYT) of Mexico.

Jesus del Carmen Peralta-Abarca graduated with her Master's degree in Industrial Engineering from the Faculty of Chemical Sciences and Engineering at UAEM. She has worked in production and quality systems in the manufacturing sector. She currently serves as a full-time research professor of Industrial Engineering. Her research pertains to design, modeling, and simulation processes. She is academic staff in the field Optimization and Software.

Marcelo Reggio has a Ph.D. obtained in École Polytechnique de Montréal. He is Professor in Department of Mechanical Engineering from the École Polytechnique de Montréal, in Quebéc, Canadá. He teaches courses of: Fluid Mechanics, Thermodynamics, Numerical methods in aerodynamics, and Turbomachinery. His research lines are: Fluid Mechanics, Lattice Boltzmann method (LBM), Computational fluid dynamics (CFD), and turbomachinery. He has published in the *International Journal of Computational Fluid Dynamics* from Taylor & Francis.

Armando J. Ríos is a full time professor and researcher in the department of Industrial Engineering at Instituto Tecnológico de Celaya. Dr. Ríos received his B.S. from ITC and obtained his M.S. and Ph.D. from Florida State University. His concentration areas include design of experiments, regression analysis, and simulation.

Rafael Rivera-López received his B.E. degree in computer systems engineering from the Veracruz Institute of Technology in 1989. He finished his M.S. degree in computer science from the Monterrey Technological Institute of Superior Studies, in Morelos in 2000. He is currently working on his Ph.D. in Computer Science at the Monterrey Technological Institute of Superior Studies. He works a Computer Science professor in the Computer and Systems Department at the Veracruz Institute of Technology. His research interests include optimization, artificial intelligence, and robotics.

Abelardo Rodríguez-León received his Bachelor's degree in Computational Systems Engineering from the Veracruz Institute of Technology in 1990 and his Master's in Computer Science with a Software Engineering specialty from the University of Veracruz in 1996. He graduated with his Ph.D. in Computer Science from the Politecnic University in Valencia, Spain in 2007. He is currently a research professor in Systems and Comuptation at the Veracruz Institute of Technology. He works in the fields of grid computation, parallel programming, and optimization.

Francisco Javier Luna Rosas received his B. Eng. degree in Computers Engineering from the Institute of Technology of Aguascalientes, Mexico, in 1991, Master's degree in Computer Science from the Institute of Technology of Tijuana, B.C. México, in 1995, and the Doctor in Engineering degree from the National Autonomous University of México (UNAM), in 2006. He is currently a teacher and researcher at the Institute of Technology of Aguascalientes. His research interests include analysis from load balancing algorithms, on-line and off-line handwritten signature verification, and the related methods of artificial intelligence, such as genetic algorithms, heuristic optimization, neural networks, fuzzy-logic, neuro-fuzzy, and soft computing.

Aida Yarira Reyes was born in México in 1971. She received the Doctor degree in Administration Science from Universidad Nacional Autónoma de Mexico, D.F. México in 2010. From 2008 to now she was engaged in full-time research at Universidad Autónoma de Ciudad Juárez, Ciudad Juárez, Chihuahua, México, focusing in the area of sustainability, organizational studies. She received the M.Sc. from ITCJ in 2005. Since 2008, Aida is a researcher UACJ, leader of organizational studies at the Institute of Social Sciences and Administration (ICSA) of the UACJ, Mexico. Her main research interests include greenways in México, sustainable enterprises, analysis of regional tourism, environmental issues.

J. Valentín López Rivas received the B.S. degree in electronics from the Instituto Politécnico Nacional in 1983, and the M.S. degree in Electrical Engineering in 2002 from the Institute of Technology of Aguascalientes. Since 1989, he has been a teacher in the Department of Electrical and Electronics Engineering at the Institute of Technology of Aguascalientes; he also collaborated as a senior digital design engineer in several companies in México. His research interests include modern control theory, digital signal processing and processors, and field programmable gate arrays (FPGA's).

María Lucila Morales Rodríguez received her M.Sc. degree in Computer Science from the Leon`s Institute of Technology, Mexico, in 2000 and the Ph.D. degree in Artificial Intelligence from Université Paul Sabatier, France, in 2007. She is currently professor of Computer Science at Madero Institute of Technology, Mexico. Her research interests are in machine learning, virtual characters, and emotional interfaces.

Rosenberg J. Romero is full-time researcher and Professor; currently he is responsible of applied thermal engineering laboratory, in Morelos State Autonomous University (UAEM). He has several articles in indexed journals in the areas of engineering and energy and he had participated in national research engineering projects. He is the author of a book and various books' chapters on subjects for renewable energy sources and applications of thermodynamic cycles. Also, he has participated with a great number of talks in national and international congresses. The National Council of Science and Technology (CONACYT) has acknowledged him in the national system of researchers now and until 2013.

Julio César Martínez Romo received the M.S. degree in electronics in 1994 from the Institute of Technology and Higher Studies of Monterrey and the Doctor in Engineering degree from the National Autonomous University of México, in 2004. He is currently a teacher and researcher at the Institute of Technology of Aguascalientes; his research is focused in on-line and off-line handwritten signature verification, and the related methods of artificial intelligence, such as genetic algorithms, as well as its hardware implementation.

Jorge Ruiz-Vanoye received his M.Sc. degree in Management of Information Technologies from Instituto Tecnológico y de Estudios Superiores de Monterrey, Mexico, in 2002 and he received the Ph.D. (Computer Science) degree from Centro Nacional de Investigación y Desarrollo Tecnológico, Mexico, in 2008. He has given courses in diverse Mexican Universities since 1996. He is currently research professor of the UPAEP, Mexico. His research interests include Time Windows, Mathematical Model and Vehicle Routing Problem.

Eunice Esther Ponce de León Sentí received her Ph.D. degree in Mathematics Science from Cybernetic, Mathematics and Physics Institute from Ministry of Science, Technology and Environment, Cuba in 1998. She works as full time professor-researcher at Computer Science Department of Autonomous University of Aguascalientes, Mexico. Her current research interests include, Combinatorial Optimization, Computational Complexity and Metaheuristics.

Aurora Torres Soto received Ph.D. degree from Autonomous University of Aguascalientes, Mexico in 2010. She studied her B.S. degree in Electronic Engineering from the San Luis Potosí Institute of Technology in 1993 and the M.S. degree in Information Technologies from Universidad Autónoma de Aguascalientes in 2001. She is a full time professor at the Autonomous University of Aguascalientes. Her research interests include evolutionary computation and analog circuit synthesis.

María Dolores Torres Soto received Ph.D. degree from Autonomous University of Aguascalientes, Mexico in 2010. She studied her B.S. degree in Computing Sciences from the San Luis Potosí Institute of Technology in 1993 and the M.S. degree in Information Technologies from Universidad Autónoma de Aguascalientes in 2001. She is a full time professor at the Autonomous University of Aguascalientes. Her research interests include evolutionary computation, supervised and unsupervised learning, typical testors and data mining.

Alessandra Tagliarducci-Tcherass has 1 book about Audio Mining, and many papers related with Artificial Intelligence in Videogames. She participated in the Technical Committee of MICAI'10, HAIS'11 and DMIN'11. Her research interests include Hybrid Artificial Intelligent Systems.

Margarita Tecpoyotl Torres received the Mathematician degree from the University of Puebla (UAP), Mexico, in 1991. In this University, she was graduated as Electronic Engineer in 1993. She received the M.Sc. and Ph.D. degrees in Electronics from National Institute of Astrophysics, Optics and Electronics (INAOE), México, in 1997 and 1999, respectively. Dr. Tecpoyotl works, since 1999, at Research Center of Engineering and Applied Sciences (CIICAp) of the Autonomous University of Morelos (UAEM), Mexico, where she is currently a titular professor. She has been visiting research scientist in University of Bristol (2001 and 2003), UK. Her main research interest includes MEMS, Antenna design, and Microwave devices. She has currently two patents under revision. She holds the status of National Researcher (SNI I) in Mexico since 2002.

Wilebaldo l. Martínez Toyes is teacher and researcher at the Universidad Autónoma de Ciudad Juárez since 2002, is Economist from the Universidad Autónoma de Baja California Sur, master in demography from El Colegio de la Frontera Norte, and candidate to Ph.D. in population studies by El Colegio de México. His research lines are internal and international migration, laboral markets, violence and insecurity, and housing. Currently, he coordinates the Center of Social Research at the Universidad Autónoma de Ciudad Juárez.

Jessica Morales Valladares, a Computer Engineer, graduated from National Institute for Astrophysics, Optics and Electronics, at 2005 and 2006, participate at the "Encuentro de Investigación en Ingeniería Eléctrica" at Zacatecas Zac city whit the projects "Herramienta de Computo para Grabado Mediante PDA", and "RBC y PDA como Herramienta de Trabajo" respectively. At 2007, present "Using PDA and CBR for the Control of Motors in a Table Displacement (or milimaquinado) XYZ", at the "XVIII International Conference on Electronics Communications an Computers" at Puebla, Puebla. Since 2008 work's at Cablemas at the NOC (Network Operation Center) and next September 2011 it´s going to start the University Master's Degree Programme in Free Software at the Open University of Catalonia OUC in Spain.

María de Socorro Velazquez Vargas, Professor of the Department of Social Sciences at the Universidad Autónoma de Ciudad Juárez (UACJ) since 1998, she is a sociologist by UACJ, master in demography form El Colegio de la Frontera Norte, and candidate to Ph.D. in population studies by El Colegio de México. Currently, she is responsible for the design and implementation of surveys at the Centre of Social Research of this institution. Her interests on research are youth, quality of employment, violence, and insecurity.

Christian José Correa Villalón received the B.S. degree in computer system engineering from the Instituto Tecnólogico de Aguascalientes in 2003, and the Ph.D. in computer science from the Universidad Autónoma de Aguascalientes in 2010. His research interests include Evolutionary Computation, and worked in the creation of a new optimization algorithm based on transgenic techniques.

Darwin Young is candidate for a doctorate in Industrial and Manufacturing Engineering at COMIMSA-CONACYT in Mexico. He has a M.Sc. in Quality Engineering from CIMAT (Mathematics Research Center) and M.B.A from University of Barcelona in Finances. His research interests centre generally on how to best support decision making in industrial systems management. Currently, He is a Global Continuous Improvement Manager at Grupo Industrial Saltillo in Mexico.

Gilberto Rivera Zárate received his M.Sc. degree in Computer Science from the Madero`s Institute of Technology, Mexico, in 2007. He is currently a candidate for Ph.D. in Computer Science at the Madero's Institute of Technology. His research interests are multicriteria optimization, graph problems, and machine learning.

Index